TALKS
WITH SRI RAMANA MAHARSHI

THREE VOLUMES IN ONE

by
MUNAGALA VENKATARAMIAH

SRI RAMANASRAMAM
TIRUVANNAMALAI
INDIA

TALKS WITH SRI RAMANA MAHARSHI (English):
by Munagala S. Venkataramiah (Swami Ramanananda Saraswati)

© Sri Ramanasramam
   Tiruvannamalai

Reprint   *2010* — *3000 copies*
Reprint   *2013* — *2000 copies*
Reprint   2016
2000 copies

CC No: 1149

ISBN: 978-81-88018-07-9

Price: ₹ 200

Published by:
V.S. Ramanan
President
SRI RAMANASRAMAM
Tiruvannamalai 606 603
Tamil Nadu, INDIA
Email :   ashram@gururamana.org
Web   :   www.sriramanamaharshi.org

Printed by:
Sudarsan Graphics Pvt. Ltd.,
Chennai 600 017, INDIA

FOREWORD[*]

The "Talks", first published in three volumes, is now issued a handy one-volume edition. There is no doubt that the present edition will be received by aspirants all over the world with the same veneration and regard that the earlier edition elicited from them. This is not a book to be lightly read and laid aside; it is bound to prove to be an unfailing guide to increasing numbers of pilgrims to the Light Everlasting.

We cannot be too grateful to Sri Munagala S. Venkataramiah (now Swami Ramanananda Saraswati) for the record that he kept of the "Talks" covering a period of four years from 1935 to 1939. Those devotees who had the good fortune of seeing Bhagavan Ramana will, on reading these "Talks", become naturally reminiscent and recall with delight their own mental record of the words of the Master. Despite the fact that the great Sage of Arunachala taught for the most part through silence, he did instruct through speech also, and that too lucidly without baffling and beclouding the minds of his listeners. One would wish that every word that he uttered had been preserved for posterity. But we have to be thankful for what little of the utterances has been put on record. These "Talks" will be found to throw light on the "Writings" of the Master; and probably it is best to study them along with the "Writings", translations of which are available.

Sri Ramana's teachings were not given in general. In fact, the Sage had no use for "lectures" or "discourses". His words were primarily addressed to the particular aspirant who felt some difficulty in his spiritual path and sought to have it resolved. But, as the same difficulties arise in the quest after the Self and as the method of resolving them is the same, the Maharshi's replies to questions have the quality of universality.

It is not all that can ask the right questions or frame them properly. The "Talks" of the *Guru*, therefore, is not simply to answer to the

---

[*] Originally written for the Second Edition.

point, as in an examination paper. He has often to get behind the words that constitute a question and correct the questioner even in the matter of questioning. And, when irrelevant and futile questions are asked, it is not his business to satisfy the idle curiosity of the questioner or confirm him in his delusions. Sri Ramana does not leave his interlocutor in the place where he was. As one of the devotees put it, "All our questions are from our standpoint, and Sri Bhagavan's replies are from his standpoint. The questions are not only answered, but are also undermined."

Various are the attitudes with which one may approach a saint. Sceptics and agnostics, theists and atheists, seekers of miracles and hunters of psychic phenomena — all used to go to the Maharshi. Each would naturally put questions that came uppermost to his or her mind; and the nature of the questions would depend on the attitude and interests of the person concerned. The glory of the Master lay in removing the attitudes and interests that were base and making the devotee long for realizing the Supreme Truth.

Visitors to the Asramam often used to put questions to Sri Ramana about occult powers and psychic phenomena. Is it not good to acquire occult powers such as telepathy? Is not the power to make one's body invisible a mark of mature wisdom. Can one read others' minds? The Master's reply to all such questions was that the occult and the miraculous are not the spiritual. The supernormal powers are more hindrances than helps in the path to the Supreme Spirit. Some questioners were interested in matters relating to the dead: What happens to the dead? Can one see them? Here again, Sri Ramana taught that these problems were irrelevant and that no seeker after the truth should be concerned with them. An aristocratic and distinguished lady-visitor once enquired: 'Maharajji, can we see the dead?' The Master replied: 'Yes'. The lady asked: 'Can the *yogis* show them to us?' The Master: 'Yes, they may. But do not ask me to show them to you; for I cannot'. The lady: 'Do you see them?' The Master: 'Yes, in dreams.'

Sri Ramana's central teaching is: Self-inquiry. Instead of wanting to know this and that, seek to know the Self. Ask 'Who am I?' instead

iv

of asking about a hundred other things. Self-inquiry ought to be the easiest of all tasks. But it seems to be the most difficult because we have become strangers to our Self. What one has to do is simple — to abide as the Self. This is the ultimate Truth. This is one's eternal, natural, inherent state. On account of ignorance we identify ourselves with the not-I. The most subtle of all these identifications is with the ego. Let us search for the root of the ego. Where from does this pseudo-I arise? At the end of this quest we shall find that the ego disappears letting the eternal Self shine. So the best discipline is the inquiry: 'Who am I?' This is the greatest *japa*. This is the true *pranayama*. The thought 'I am not the body' (*naham*) is exhalation (*rechaka*); the inquiry 'Who am I?' (*koham*) is inhalation (*puraka*); the realization 'I am He' (*soham*) is retention of breath (*kumbhaka*). The fruit of Self-inquiry is the realization that the Self is all, and that there is nothing else. For those who follow this method no other *sadhana* is necessary. But even those who adopt the discipline of devotion (*bhakti*) reach the same goal. If one surrenders one's ego to either the *Guru* or God, one realizes the Self.

Sri Ramana's teachings as found in the "Talks" will bring hope to everyone. No one need think that he is beyond the pale of redemption. An old American visitor once asked the Master, 'Maharshi, do you think we are bad boys'? The Master's characteristic reply was, 'Do not tell me so. But you need not think you are bad boys'. Anything that is bad in us will surely be removed, if only we listen to the Maharshi's wise words that are recorded in the present book.

And, may we read it with a view to preparing ourselves for understanding the Master's higher teaching which was through silence!

University of Madras,
August 11, 1958.

T. M. P. Mahadevan

v

INTRODUCTION*

These 'Talks' cover a period of four years, 1935-1939, and were all recorded by Sri Munagala S. Venkataramiah (now Swami Ramanananda Saraswati), a very old disciple of Sri Ramana Maharshi. Though a Telugu by birth he speaks English and Tamil fluently and is conversant with Sanskrit. These are necessary qualifications for one who wished to record the conversations of Sri Bhagavan with his various disciples and visitors.

The four years that are covered here, were the days when the Asramam reached the summit of its glory. Maharshi's health was on the whole good and the Hall where he sat was open day and night to welcome one and all. Visitors flocked there from every corner of the world, there was hardly a country that was not represented at one time or another. The war naturally interfered with this influx, though the number of Indian visitors steadily increased as time went on. But it was these conversations, many with Westerners, that were especially interesting; the modern tendency towards materialism and irreligion, on which the West often prides itself, met its match here. Sri Bhagavan glowed like the sun, and even those who did not understand him or agree with his words were fascinated and could not help but be elevated by his presence.

Though Sri Venkataramiah was fully qualified for the work, to follow Sri Bhagavan was no easy task when he once started to talk. He had such a command of his subject that he was never at a loss for a word in whichever language he might happen to be speaking; so, few notes could be taken, the listeners being too busy trying not to lose a word of what was being said, added to which it was not always easy to understand. Sri Venkataramiah acted as interpreter for the many English-speaking people who flocked to the Asramam, as Sri Bhagavan was reluctant to say more than a few words in that language, though he knew it sufficiently well to read the English newspapers and magazines. But to act as interpreter was an even more difficult task than just recording; the flow of words was so steady that no

---

* Originally written for the First Edition.

interval was left in which their meaning could be conveyed to the ardent questioner. Often Sri Bhagavan had to be asked to wait while his words were conveyed to the anxious listener. So the difficulties of making this record can easily be imagined; only one who had sat for years at the feet of the Master and had thoroughly absorbed his philosophy and the way he expounded it, was competent for the task. Sri Venkataramiah, the ideal person for this, had luckily been found.

That the language used here is not always elegant is admitted, this was to be expected in the circumstances; doubtless it could have been corrected, but it has been left much as it was, as it was felt that a certain spontaneity that it now possesses would otherwise have been lost. Though the conversations were in various South Indian languages most of it was recorded in English, the rest in Tamil and Telugu, which passages have been translated for the purpose of this book. The completed notes were often shown to the questioners for verification, but the whole had the seal of approval of Sri Bhagavan himself, as the records were always shown to him for his approval or the necessary alteration after they had been entered in the notebook. Thus we may be sure that here we have the exact teaching of the Master, and reading them we once again sit at his feet in the Old Hall, drinking in every word that falls from his lips; enraptured by his smile, the movement of his delicate hands, and his actions; for he was a true artist, often acting the part of the story he was telling, the better to drive home his point.

Some may be inclined to criticise this book as monotonous, but this supposed monotony is deliberate, for some new point is always brought out however similar the talk may seem. Sri Bhagavan always stressed the one essential truth that was necessary for Liberation, that there is only one Self and nothing but the Self. Know that and everything else is known. This cannot be repeated too often.

Doubtless, an intellectual grasp of this fact sets one on the path, but the path once started, mental knowledge must then become actual experience. To know a thing absolutely, not just superficially, one must be that thing, otherwise knowledge is incomplete. As I pointed out, we are always nothing but the Self, but associating ourselves with the ignorance of limitation, with an ego, we forget the Seer and identify ourselves with the seen. But what can we do about it? The habit is so long-standing, birth after birth has been imagined and century after century has been fabricated by the mind. It has thus involved itself more and more in ignorance, that it now finds itself disinclined and, even if willing, almost unable to disentangle itself from the thralls of the play-world it has created.

You are the Self, he tells us, nothing but the Self, anything else is just imagination, so BE the Self here and now. There is no need to run off to a forest or shut oneself in a room; carry on with your essential activities but free yourself from association with the doer of them. Self is the witness, you are That.

Example after example is given in these talks, in language to suit all tastes and mentalities. The reading of the book automatically drives one inward to the source. It is itself a sufficient *sadhana*. Do not delude yourself, you are already That, there is nothing more to be obtained, only false association to be shed, limitation to be recognised as illusory.

His method of doing this is well-known: Self-Enquiry. Always and at all times seek for the source of the ego, the apparent actor, and on the attainment of that goal, he tells us, the ego will drop away of its own accord, and nothing will be left but the all-blissful Self. But this is not the place to go into details of method; for those interested the necessary books can easily be obtained from Sri Ramanasramam.

What more is there to say, but to advise one and all to read this book and try and make it a part of themselves? Not one word to be passed over lightly, or one conversation to be dismissed as superfluous. It is all pure gold. And here again we find the ever-living Sri Ramana Maharshi before us in person, teaching us in his own inimitable words for our benefit and delight.

It was found after preparing this book for the press, that the first part was not in chronological order, but rather than delay publication it was decided not to alter the present arrangement as it makes absolutely no difference to the context. The dates are only included for reference, and as a guarantee of authenticity.

Sri Ramanasramam,   SADHU ARUNACHALA
1st January, 1955.   (Major A. W. Chadwick, O. B. E.)

NOTE BY THE RECORDER

In a very critical and distressing period of his life, an humble devotee sought the Presence of Bhagavan Sri Ramana Maharshi, for his own peace of mind, and lived in the Asramam with the kind permission of the *Sarvadhikari*, Sri Niranjanananda Swami. The seeker took it upon himself to note down, as occasions arose, the sweet, refreshing and enlightening words of the Master. This self-imposed task was undertaken for the purification of his own mind and better understanding of the subtle and profound words of Sri Bhagavan. Shortly after, the *Sarvadhikari* officially took them over to the Asramam. These notes* covering the period 1935-39 are included in the present volumes with the hope that some readers may find them interesting and helpful in their spiritual quest.

Sri Ramanasramam,   RECORDER
1st January, 1955.

---

* A few extracts from these notes have already appeared in the Ashram publication: *Maharshi's Gospel.*

Sri Ramanasramam,
1st January, 1955.

RECORDER

---

xii

Talks with Sri Ramana Maharshi

Volume 1

15th May, 1935

Talk 1.

A wandering monk (*sannyasi*) was trying to clear his doubt: "How to realise that all the world is God?"

Maharshi: If you make your outlook that of wisdom, you will find the world to be God. Without knowing the Supreme Spirit (Brahman), how will you find His all-pervasiveness?

Talk 2.

Someone enquired about the nature of perception.

M.: Whatever state one is in, the perceptions partake of that state. The explanation is that in the waking state (*jagrat*) the gross body perceives gross names and forms; in *swapna* (the dream state) the mental body perceives the mental creations in their manifold forms and names; in the *sushupti* (deep dreamless sleep), the identification with the body being lost, there are no perceptions; similarly in the Transcendental state identity with Brahman places the man in harmony with everything, and there is nothing apart from his Self.

Talk 3.

A question was asked as to the nature of happiness.

M.: If a man thinks that his happiness is due to external causes and his possessions, it is reasonable to conclude that his happiness must increase with the increase of possessions and diminish in proportion to their diminution. Therefore if he is devoid of possessions, his happiness should be nil. What is the real experience of man? Does it conform to this view?

In deep sleep the man is devoid of possessions, including his own body. Instead of being unhappy he is quite happy. Everyone desires to sleep soundly. The conclusion is that happiness is inherent in man and is not due to external causes. One must realise his Self in order to open the store of unalloyed happiness.

Talk 4.

Maharshi was asked by an educated young man: "How do you say that the Heart is on the right, whereas the biologists have found it to be on the left?" The man asked for authority.

M.: Quite so. The physical organ is on the left; that is not denied. But the Heart of which I speak is non-physical and is only on the right side. It is my experience, no authority is required by me. Still you can find confirmation in a Malayalam Ayurvedic book and in *Sita Upanishad*; and he produced the quotation (*mantra*) from the latter and repeated the text (*sloka*) from the former.

Talk 5.

Mr. M. Frydman, an engineer, remarked on the subject of Grace, "A salt doll diving into the sea will not be protected by a waterproof coat".

It was a very happy simile and was applauded as such. Maharshi added, "The body is the waterproof coat".

Talk 6.

A question was asked by a monk (*sannyasi*) about how to prevent the mind from being distracted.

M.: You see the objects on forgetting your own Self. If you keep hold of your Self, you will not see the objective world.

Talk 7.

When asked if occult powers (*siddhis*) can be achieved along with Omnipotence (*Iswaratva*) as mentioned in the last verse of

2

Dakshinamurti Ashtakam, Maharshi said: "Let Omnipotence (*Iswaratva*) be accomplished first and then the other question may be raised."

Talk 8.

"Can anyone get any benefit by repeating sacred syllables (*mantras*) picked up casually?

M.: "No. He must be competent and initiated in such *mantras*." Maharshi illustrated this by the following story: A King visited his Premier in his residence. There he was told that the Premier was engaged in repetition of sacred syllables (*japa*). The King waited for him and, on meeting him, asked what the *japa* was. The Premier said that it was the holiest of all, *Gayatri*. The King desired to be initiated by the Premier. But the Premier confessed his inability to initiate him. Therefore the King learned it from someone else, and meeting the Minister later he repeated the *Gayatri* and wanted to know if it was right. The Minister said that the *mantra* was correct, but it was not proper for him to say it. When pressed for an explanation, the Minister called to a page close by and ordered him to take hold of the King. The order was not obeyed. The order was often repeated, and still not obeyed. The King flew into a rage and ordered the same man to hold the Minister, and it was immediately done. The Minister laughed and said that the incident was the explanation required by the King. "How?" asked the King. The Minister replied, "The order was the same and the executor also, but the authority was different. When I ordered, the effect was nil, whereas, when you ordered, there was immediate effect. Similarly with *mantras*."

Talk 9.

Someone enquired: Why is it said in scriptures that the Sage is like a child?

M.: A child and a Sage (*jnani*) are similar in a way. Incidents interest a child only so long as they last. It ceases to think of them after they have passed away. So then, it is apparent that they do not leave any impression on the child and it is not affected by them mentally. So it is with a Sage.

Talk 10.

A visitor asked how to realise oneself in accordance with Maharshi's instructions, contained in his text of *Truth Revealed*, verse 9, supplement. The difficulty was in controlling the mind.

M.: It is to be done by controlling the breath. If you practise it by yourself without other help, then the mind is controlled. Otherwise the mind comes under control spontaneously in the presence of a superior power. Such is the greatness of association with the wise (*satsanga*).

Talk 11.

"Can destiny (*karma*) ever come to an end?"

M.: The *karmas* carry the seeds of their own destruction in themselves.

Talk 12.

A man asked the Maharshi to say something to him. When asked what he wanted to know, he said that he knew nothing and wanted to hear something from the Maharshi.

M.: You know that you know nothing. Find out that knowledge. That is liberation (*mukti*).

6th January, 1935

Talk 13.

Mrs. M. A. Piggot, an English lady, who had read "Search in Secret India", came to see the Maharshi. The services of a disciple as interpreter were provided. There were many visitors at the time in the hall, including some ladies with their infants. The place resounded with noise. At length silence prevailed. Suddenly Maharshi, who seemed to be looking at infinite space, was heard to say softly, "Monkey"! A little baby was then discovered in the doorway (unobserved by the mother who was seated on the other side of the door) with a large monkey standing on his hind legs, who with both hands was fondling the child not hurting it in the slightest, both being at peace with each other in Maharshi's presence. When Maharshi's

4

voice was heard the monkey jumped away adroitly and disappeared.
The incident greatly impressed the lady.

7th January, 1935

"Is a Master necessary for realisation?" Mrs. Piggot asked first.

M.: The realisation is the result of the Master's grace more than
teachings, lectures, meditation, etc. They are only secondary aids,
whereas the former is the primary and the essential cause.

Devotee: What are the obstacles which hinder realisation of the
Self?

M.: They are habits of mind (*vasanas*).

D.: How to overcome the mental habits (*vasanas*)?

M.: By realising the Self.

D.: That is a vicious circle.

M.: It is the ego which raises such difficulties, creating obstacles
and then suffers from the perplexity of apparent paradoxes. Find out
who makes the enquiries and the Self will be found.

D.: What are the aids for realisation?

M.: The teachings of the Scriptures and of realised souls

D.: Can such teachings be discussions, lectures and meditations?

M.: Yes, all these are only secondary aids, whereas the essential
is the Master's grace.

D.: How long will it take for one to get that?

M.: Why do you desire to know?

D.: To give me hope.

M.: Even such a desire is an obstacle. The Self is ever there, there
is nothing without it. Be the Self and the desires and doubts will
disappear. Such Self is the witness in sleep, dream and waking states
of existence. These states belong to the ego. The Self transcends
even the ego. Did you not exist in sleep? Did you know then that you
were asleep or unaware of the world? It is only in the waking state
that you describe the experience of sleep as being unawareness;
therefore the consciousness when asleep is the same as that when
awake. If you know what this waking consciousness is, you will know
the consciousness which witnesses all the three states. Such

5

consciousness could be found by seeking the consciousness as it was in sleep.

D.: In that case, I fall asleep.

M.: No harm!

D.: It is a blank.

M.: For whom is the blank? Find out. You cannot deny yourself at any time. The Self is ever there and continues in all states.

D.: Should I remain as if in sleep and be watchful at the same time?

M.: Yes. Watchfulness is the waking state. Therefore the state will not be one of sleep, but sleepless sleep. If you go the way of your thoughts you will be carried away by them and you will find yourself in an endless maze.

D.: So, then, I must go back tracing the source of thoughts.

M.: Quite so; in that way the thoughts will disappear and the Self alone will remain. In fact there is no inside or outside for the Self. They are also projections of the ego. The Self is pure and absolute.

D.: It is understood intellectually only. Is not intellect a help for realisation?

M.: Yes, up to a certain stage. Even so, realise that the Self transcends the intellect — the latter must itself vanish to reach the Self.

D.: Does my realisation help others?

M.: Yes, certainly. It is the best help possible. But there are no others to be helped. For a realised being sees the Self, just like a goldsmith estimating the gold in various jewels. When you identify yourself with the body then only the forms and shapes are there. But when you transcend your body the others disappear along with your body-consciousness.

D.: Is it so with plants, trees, etc.?

M.: Do they exist at all apart from the Self? Find it out. You think that you see them. The thought is projected out from your Self. Find out wherefrom it rises. Thoughts will cease to rise and the Self alone will remain.

D.: I understand theoretically. But they are still there.

6

M.: Yes. It is like a cinema-show. There is the light on the screen and the shadows flitting across impress the audience as the enactment of some piece. Similarly also will it be, if in the same play an audience also is shown. The seer, the seen, will then only be the screen. Apply it to yourself. You are the screen, the Self has created the ego, the ego has its accretions of thoughts which are displayed as the world, the trees, plants, etc., of which you are asking. In reality, all these are nothing but the Self. If you see the Self, the same will be found to be all, everywhere and always. Nothing but the Self exists.

D.: Yes, I still understand only theoretically. Yet the answers are simple and beautiful and convincing.

M.: Even the thought, "I do not realise" is a hindrance. In fact, the Self alone is.

8th January, 1935

Talk 14.

An old man came and sat in the hall. Maharshi was reading Sarma's Sanskrit recension of *Arunachala Akshara Manamalai* (the first of *The Five Hymns to Arunachala*). The man asked softly: "It is said that realisation is beyond expression; and expression always fails to describe the realisation. How is it?"

M.: The point has been mentioned in *Arunachala Ashtakam,* Verse three where it is admitted that, although the expression of realisation is impossible, still its existence is indicated.

Soon after there were visible signs of emotion in the man. His breath was deep and hard and he fell on the floor prostrating humbly and got up only after one or two minutes. Remaining calm a brief while, he left the place. Evidently the man had some illumination. He sought confirmation from Maharshi, who responded fittingly. He found confirmation, and humbly and feelingly acknowledged the divine intercession on his behalf.

Talk 15.

A question was asked about the Upanishadic passage, "The Supreme Spirit is subtler than the subtlest and larger than the largest."

7

M.: Even the structure of the atom has been found by the mind. Therefore the mind is subtler than the atom. That which is behind the mind, namely the individual soul, is subtler than the mind. Further, the Tamil saint Manickavachagar has said of the specks dancing in a beam of sunlight, that if each represents a universe, the whole sunlight will represent the Supreme Being.

19th January, 1935

Talk 16.

Mr. Douglas Ainslie (Mr. Grant Duff), an aristocratic English gentleman, 70 years old, nephew of a former Governor of Madras, an author and poet formerly attached to the British Legation in Athens, Paris and The Hague, had come to Madras as a guest of Government House. He came to see Maharshi with a letter of introduction from Paul Brunton. Next day he returned and remained a little less than an hour in the hall. On both days practically no words were exchanged, only gaze meeting gaze. His habits are abstemious; he remains without food of any kind till 1 p.m. and then lunches; he is said to have coffee and biscuits in the evening and retires without any further food. He has been a bachelor all along, walks a few miles a day on an empty stomach, speaks little and is very graceful in his movements. His voice is low and soft and his words appear to come from the heart. He has friends among whom might be counted the late Sir John Woodroffe, Sir Sarvepalli Radhakrishnan and Prof. Thomas, Sanskrit Professor in Oxford University. He expressed a desire to hear the Vedas. On Monday a letter arrived from Riga and the questions therein happened to coincide with the questions the European visitor had asked relating to the existence of departed souls and how best to serve them.

The reply sent to Riga was read out to him. Tamil songs from Maharshi's "Truth Revealed" and the Vedas were repeated in his presence. He considered the recitations magnificent. He came the next afternoon and to the wonder of others, had an experience on the previous night which he repeated to Maharshi. It was that he had seen something like an electric light within himself in the heart centre

8

on the right side. And he added further that he had seen the sun shining within. Maharshi smiled a little and then had a translation of "*Atmavidya*" (Self-Knowledge) read out to him wherein there is the cryptic saying that realisation consists in reaching the *Atman* (Self) which is the expanse of consciousness (*chidvyoman*) as distinguished from the mind, which is the expansion of *chittavyoman*. This explanation appealed to him.

Speaking of him later, Maharshi remarked, "Just think of an old man of 70 not choosing to live peacefully in his own house on the income he had earned! How intense has been his earnestness that he has left his native land, dared a sea-voyage of 6,000 miles, and faced the hardships of long railway journeys in a foreign land, ignorant of the language, undergoing the vicissitudes of a lonely life, submitting to the inclemency of a hot climate, in surroundings uncongenial and unaccustomed to him. He could have been happy in his own house. It is his longing for internal peace that has brought him here." Quite so! The intensity of his earnestness is revealed by his illuminating experiences here within four days of his arrival, people say.

With regard to the question concerning departed souls: so long as a man identifies himself with his gross body the thought materialised as gross manifestations must be real to him. Because his body is imagined to have originated from another physical being, the other exists as truly as his own body. Having existed here once it certainly survives death, because the offspring is still here and feels he has been born of the other. Under these circumstances the other world is true; and the departed souls are benefited by prayers offered for them. On the other hand, considered in a different way, the One Reality is the Self from whom has sprung the ego which contains within itself the seeds of predispositions acquired in previous births. The Self illumines the ego, the predispositions and also the gross senses, whereupon the predispositions appear to the senses to have materialised as the universe, and become perceptible to the ego, the reflection of the Self. The ego identifies itself with the body, and so loses sight of the Self and the result of this inadvertence is dark ignorance and the misery of the present life. The fact of the ego rising

9

from the Self and forgetting it, is birth. So, it may be said that the birth of the individual has killed the mother. The present desire to regain one's mother is in reality the desire to regain the Self, which is the same as realising one-self, or the death of the ego; this is surrender unto the mother, so she may live eternally.

Maharshi then read out from the Tamil version of *Yoga Vasishta* the story of Deerga Tapasi who had two sons, Punya and Papa. After the death of the parents the younger one mourned the loss and the elder brother consoled him as follows: "Why do you mourn the loss of our parents? I shall tell you where they are; they are only within ourselves and are ourselves. For the life-current has passed through innumerable incarnations, births and deaths, pleasures and pains, etc., just as the water current in a river flows over rocks, pits, sands, elevations and depressions on its way, but still the current is unaffected. Again the pleasures and pains, births and deaths, are like undulations on the surface of seeming water in the mirage of the ego. The only reality is the Self from where the ego appears, and runs through thoughts which manifest themselves as the universe and in which the mothers and fathers, friends and relatives appear and disappear. They are nothing but manifestations of the Self so that one's parents are not outside the Self. So there is no reason to mourn. Learn it, realise it and be happy."

24th January, 1935

Talk 17.

Mr. W. Y. Evans-Wentz, an English research scholar of Oxford University, brought a letter of introduction from Mr. Brunton and arrived on a visit.

He was tired after his journey and required rest. He is quite accustomed to Indian ways of living, having visited this country several times. He has learned the Tibetan language and helped in the translation of the "Book of the Dead" and the "Life of Milarepa", the greatest of Tibetan Yogis, and a third book on the "Tibetan Secret Doctrines."

In the afternoon he began to ask a few questions. They related to

Yoga. He wanted to know if it was right to kill animals such as tigers, deer, etc., and use the skin for Yoga posture (*asana*).

M.: The mind is the tiger or the deer.

D.: If everything be illusion, then one can take lives?

M.: To whom is illusion? Find that out! In fact everyone is a "killer of the Self" (*atmahan*) every moment of his life.

D.: Which posture (*asana*) is the best?

M.: Any *asana*, possibly *sukha asana* (easy posture or the half-Buddha position). But that is immaterial for *jnana*, the Path of Knowledge.

D.: Does posture indicate the temperament?

M.: Yes.

D.: What are the properties and effects of the tiger's skin, wool, or deer-skin, etc.?

M.: Some have found them out and related them in Yoga books. They correspond to conductors and non-conductors of magnetism, etc. But it is all immaterial for the Path of Knowledge (*Jnana Marga*). Posture really means location and steadfastness in the Self. It is internal. The others refer to external positions.

D.: Which time is most suitable for meditation?

M.: What is time?

D.: Tell me what it is!

M.: Time is only an idea. There is only the Reality Whatever you think it is, it looks like that. If you call it time, it is time. If you call it existence, it is existence, and so on. After calling it time, you divide it into days and nights, months, years, hours, minutes, etc. Time is immaterial for the Path of Knowledge. But some of these rules and discipline are good for beginners.

D.: What is *Jnana Marga*?

M.: Concentration of the mind is in a way common to both Knowledge and Yoga. Yoga aims at union of the individual with the universal, the Reality. This Reality cannot be new. It must exist even now, and it does exist.

Therefore the Path of Knowledge tries to find out how *viyoga* (separation) came about. The separation is from the Reality only.

11

D.: What is illusion?

M.: To whom is the illusion? Find it out. Then illusion will vanish.

Generally people want to know about illusion and do not examine to whom it is. It is foolish. Illusion is outside and unknown. But the seeker is considered to be known and is inside. Find out what is immediate, intimate, instead of trying to find out what is distant and unknown.

D.: Does Maharshi advise any physical posture for the Europeans?

M.: It may be advisable. However, it must be clearly understood that meditation is not prohibited in the absence of *asanas,* or prescribed times, or any accessories of the kind.

D.: Does Maharshi have any particular method to impart to the Europeans in particular?

M.: It is according to the mental equipment of the individual. There is indeed no hard and fast rule.

Mr. Evans-Wentz began to ask questions, mostly relating to Yoga preliminaries, for all of which Maharshi replied that they are aids to Yoga, which is itself an aid to Self-realisation, the goal of all.

D.: Is work an obstruction to Self-realisation?

M.: No. For a realised being the Self alone is the Reality, and actions are only phenomenal, not affecting the Self. Even when he acts he has no sense of being an agent. His actions are only involuntary and he remains a witness to them without any attachment.

There is no aim for this action. Even one who is still practising the path of Wisdom (*jnana*) can practise while engaged in work. It may be difficult in the earlier stages for a beginner, but after some practice it will soon be effective and the work will not be found a hindrance to meditation.

D.: What is the practice?

M.: Constant search for 'I', the source of the ego. Find out 'Who am I?' The pure 'I' is the reality, the Absolute Existence-Consciousness-Bliss. When That is forgotten, all miseries crop up; when that is held fast, the miseries do not affect the person.

D.: Is not *brahmacharya* (celibacy) necessary for realisation of the Self?

12

M.: Brahmacharya is 'living in Brahman'. It has no connection with celibacy as commonly understood. A real *brahmachari*, that is one who lives in Brahman, finds bliss in the Brahman which is the same as the Self. Why then should you look for other sources of happiness? In fact the emergence from the Self has been the cause of all the misery.

D.: Celibacy is a *sine qua non* for Yoga?

M.: So it is. Celibacy is certainly an aid to realisation among so many other aids.

D.: Is it then not indispensable? Can a married man realise the Self?

M.: Certainly, it is a matter of fitness of mind. Married or unmarried, a man can realise the Self, because that is here and now. If it were not so, but attainable by some efforts at some other time, and if it were new and something to be acquired, it would not be worthy of pursuit. Because what is not natural cannot be permanent either. But what I say is that the Self is here and now and alone.

D.: God being immanent in all, one should not take life of any kind. Is society right in taking the life of a murderer? Can the State do so either? The Christian countries begin to think that it is wrong to do so.

M.: What is it that prompted the murderer to commit the crime? The same power awards him the punishment. Society or the State is only a tool in the hands of the power. You speak of one life taken away; But what about innumerable lives lost in wars?

D.: Quite so. Loss of lives is wrong anyway. Are wars justified?

M.: For a realised man, the one who remains ever in the Self, the loss of one or several or all lives either in this world or in all the three worlds makes no difference. Even if he happens to destroy them all, no sin can touch such a pure soul. Maharshi quoted the Gita, Chapter 18, Verse 17 — "He who is free from the notion of ego, whose intellect is unattached, though he annihilates all the worlds, he slayeth not, nor is he bound by the results of his actions."

D.: Do not one's actions affect the person in after-births?

M.: Are you born now? Why do you think of other births? The fact is that there is neither birth nor death. Let him who is born think of death and palliatives therefore.

D.: How long did it take Maharshi to realise the Self?

M.: This question is asked because the name and form are perceived. These are the perceptions consequent on the identification of the ego with the gross body.

If the ego identifies itself with the subtle mind, as in dream, the perceptions are subtle also. But in sleep there are no perceptions. Was there not the ego still? Unless it was, there cannot be the memory of having slept. Who was it that slept? You did not say in your sleep that you slept. You say it now in your wakeful state. The ego therefore is the same in wakefulness, dream and sleep. Find out the underlying Reality behind these states. That is the Reality underlying these. In that state there is Being alone. There is no you, nor I, nor he; no present, nor past, nor future. It is beyond time and space, beyond expression.

It is ever there.

Just as a plantain tree produces shoots at its roots, before yielding fruits and perishing, and these shoots, being transplanted, do the same again, so also the original primeval Master of antiquity (Dakshinamurti), who cleared the doubts of his rishi disciples in silence, has left shoots which are ever multiplying. The Guru is a shoot of that Dakshinamurti. The question does not arise when the Self is realised.

D.: Does Maharshi enter the *nirvikalpa samadhi*?

M.: If the eyes are closed, it is *nirvikalpa*; if open, it is (though differentiated, still in absolute repose) *savikalpa*. The ever-present state is the natural state *sahaja*.

26th January, 1935

Talk 18.

Mr. Evans-Wentz asked: There are yogis with occult powers. What does Maharshi think of them?

M.: The powers are known by hearsay or by exhibition. Thus they are in the realm of the mind only.

D.: Mr. Brunton mentions a yogi in Madras who is said to hold communion with his master in the Himalayas.

M.: It is not more marvellous than telepathy — so commonly known. Telepathy cannot exist without the hearer and television without the seer. What is the difference between hearing from far and from near? It is only the hearer who matters. Without the hearer there cannot be hearing; without the seer there cannot be vision.

D.: So you want me to consider the subject and not the object.

M.: The subject and object appear only after the mind has arisen. The mind comprises them and also the occult powers.

D.: Can the manifestations of light (*jothis*) be seen on Arunachala Hill?

M.: Yes.

D.: Is there any psychic effect in visiting sacred places like Mt. Kailas, Benares, etc.?

M.: Yes.

D.: Is there any benefit accruing by dying in Benares?

M.: Yes, the meaning will be clear if the real Benares and real dying be understood.

D.: You mean that they are in the Self?

M.: Yes.

D.: There are six centres in the body and there are corresponding centres in the world.

M.: Yes. What is in the world is in the body; and what is in the body is in the world also.

D.: Is the sacredness of Benares a matter of faith, or is it externally also real?

M.: Both.

D.: Some people are attracted to one place of pilgrimage and others to another. Is it according to their temperaments?

M.: Yes. Just consider how all of you born in different places and living in other lands are gathered here today? What is the Force which has attracted you here? If this is understood the other Force is also understood.

15

Talk 19.

Mr. Grant Duff asked: Where are memory and forgetfulness located?

M.: In the mind (*chitta*).

Talk 20.

Mr. Evans-Wentz: Is solitude necessary for a *jnani*?

M.: Solitude is in the mind of man. One might be in the thick of the world and maintain serenity of mind; such a one is in solitude. Another may stay in a forest, but still be unable to control his mind. He cannot be said to be in solitude. Solitude is a function of the mind. A man attached to desire cannot get solitude wherever he may be; a detached man is always in solitude.

D.: So then, one might be engaged in work and be free from desire and keep up solitude. Is it so?

M.: Yes. Work performed with attachment is a shackle, whereas work performed with detachment does not affect the doer. He is, even while working, in solitude.

D.: They say that there are many saints in Tibet who remain in solitude and are still very helpful to the world. How can it be?

M.: It can be so. Realisation of the Self is the greatest help that can be rendered to humanity. Therefore, the saints are said to be helpful, though they remain in forests. But it should not be forgotten that solitude is not in forests only. It can be had even in towns, in the thick of worldly occupations.

D.: It is not necessary that the saints should mix with people and be helpful to them?

M.: The Self alone is the Reality; the world and the rest of it are not. The realised being does not see the world as different from himself.

D.: Thus then, the saint's realisation leads to the uplift of humanity without the latter being aware of it. Is it so?

M.: Yes. The help is imperceptible but is still there. A saint helps the whole of humanity, unknown to the latter.

D.: Would it not be better if he mixed with others?

M.: There are no others to mix with. The Self is the one and only Reality.

D.: If there be a hundred Self-realised men will it not be to the greater benefit of the world?

M.: When you say 'Self' you refer to the unlimited, but when you add 'men' to it, you limit the meaning. There is only one Infinite Self.

D.: Yes, yes, I see! Sri Krishna has said in the Gita that work must be performed without attachment and such work is better than idleness. Is it Karma Yoga?

M.: What is said is given out to suit the temperament of the hearers.

D.: In Europe it is not understood by the people that a man in solitude can be helpful. They imagine that men working in the world can alone be useful. When will this confusion cease? Will the European mind continue wading in the morass or will it realise the truth?

M.: Never mind Europe or America. Where are they except in your mind? Realise your Self and then all is realised.

If you dream and see several men, and then wake up and recall your dream, do you try to ascertain if the persons of your dream creation are also awake?

D.: What does Maharshi think of the theory of universal illusion (*Maya*)?

M.: What is *Maya*? It is only Reality.

D.: Is not *Maya* illusion?

M.: *Maya* is used to signify the manifestations of the Reality. Thus *Maya* is only Reality.

D.: Some say that Sri Sankaracharya was only intellectual and not realised. Is it so?

M.: Why worry about Sankaracharya? Realise your own Self. Others can take care of themselves.

D.: Jesus Christ cured people of their diseases. Is that only an occult power (*siddhi*)?

17

M.: Was Jesus aware at the time that he was curing men of their diseases? He could not have been conscious of his powers. There is a story related as follows: Jesus had once cured a man of his blindness. The man turned wicked, in course of time. Meeting him after some years, Jesus observed his wickedness and asked him why he was so. He replied saying that, when he was blind, he could not commit any sin. But after Jesus had cured him of blindness he grew wicked and Jesus was responsible for his wickedness.

D.: Was not Jesus a Perfected Being possessing occult powers (*siddhi*)?

M.: He could not have been aware of his powers (*siddhis*).

D.: Is it not good to acquire them, such as telepathy, etc.?

M.: Telepathy or radio enables one to see and hear from afar. They are all the same, hearing and seeing. Whether one hears from near or far does not make any difference in hearing. The fundamental factor is the hearer, the subject. Without the hearer or the seer, there can be no hearing or seeing. The latter are the functions of the mind. The occult powers (*siddhis*) are therefore only in the mind. They are not natural to the Self. That which is not natural, but acquired, cannot be permanent, and is not worth striving for.

They denote extended powers. A man is possessed of limited powers and is miserable; he wants to expand his powers so that he may be happy. But consider if it will be so; if with limited perceptions one is miserable, with extended perceptions the misery must increase proportionately. Occult powers will not bring happiness to anyone, but will make him all the more miserable!

Moreover what are these powers for? The would-be occultist (*siddha*) desires to display the *siddhis* so that others may appreciate him. He seeks appreciation, and if it is not forthcoming he will not be happy. There must be others to appreciate him. He may even find another possessor of higher powers. That will cause jealousy and breed unhappiness. The higher occultist (*siddha*) may meet a still higher *siddha* and so on until there will come one who will blow up everything in a trice. Such is the highest adept (*siddha*) and He is God or the Self.

18

Which is the real power? Is it to increase prosperity or bring about peace? That which results in peace is the highest perfection (*siddhi*).

D.: But common people in Europe and America would not appreciate such an attitude and would desire a display of powers and instructions by lectures, etc.

M.: Lectures may entertain individuals for a few hours without improving them. Silence on the other hand is permanent and benefits the whole of humanity.

D.: But silence is not understood.

M.: It does not matter. By silence, eloquence is meant. Oral lectures are not so eloquent as silence. Silence is unceasing eloquence. The Primal Master, Dakshinamurti, is the ideal. He taught his *rishi* disciples by silence.

D.: But then there were disciples for Him. It was all right. Now it is different. They must be sought after and helped.

M.: That is a sign of ignorance. The power which created you has created the world. If it can take care of you, it can similarly take care of the world also.

D.: What does Bhagavan think of the "lost soul" mentioned by Jesus Christ?

M.: Think what there is to be lost. Is there anything to lose? What matters is only that which is natural. Such must be eternal and cannot be experienced. That which is born must die; that which is acquired must be lost. Were you born? You are ever existent. The Self can never be lost.

D.: Buddha advises the eight-fold path as being the best so that none might be lost.

M.: Yes. Such is called Raja Yoga by the Hindus.

D.: Is yoga advised for a spiritual aspirant?

M.: Yoga helps control of mind.

D.: But does it not lead to occult powers (*siddhis*) which are said to be dangerous?

M.: But you qualified your question by the words "a spiritual aspirant". You did not mean a seeker of powers (*siddhis*).

Talk 21.

Mr. Ellappa Chettiar, a member of the Legislative Council of Madras Presidency and an influential Hindu, asked: "Why is it said that the knowledge born of hearing is not firm, whereas that born of contemplation is firm?"

M.: On the other hand it is said that hearsay knowledge (*paroksha*) is not firm, whereas that born of one's own realisation (*aparoksha*) is firm.

It is also said that hearing helps the intellectual understanding of the Truth, that meditation makes the understanding clear, and finally that contemplation brings about realisation of the Truth.

Furthermore, they say also that all such knowledge is not firm and that it is firm only when it is as clear and intimate as a gooseberry in the hollow of one's palm.

There are those who affirm that hearing alone will suffice, because a competent person who had already, perhaps in previous incarnations, qualified himself, realises and abides in peace as soon as he hears the Truth told him only once, whereas the person not so qualified must pass through the stages prescribed above, before falling into *samadhi*.

Talk 22.

Mrs. Piggott returned from Madras for a further visit. She asked questions relating to diet regulation.

D.: What diet is prescribed for a *sadhak* (one who is engaged in spiritual practices)?

M.: Satvic food in limited quantities.

D.: What is *satvic* food?

M.: Bread, fruits, vegetables, milk, etc.

D.: Some people take fish in North India. May it be done?

No answer was made by the Maharshi.

D.: We Europeans are accustomed to a particular diet; change of diet affects health and weakens the mind. Is it not necessary to keep up physical health?

M.: Quite necessary. The weaker the body the stronger the mind grows.

D.: In the absence of our usual diet our health suffers and the mind loses strength.

M.: What do you mean by strength of mind?

D.: The power to eliminate worldly attachment.

M.: The quality of food influences the mind. The mind feeds on the food consumed.

D.: Really! How can the Europeans adjust themselves to *satvic* food only?

M.: (Pointing to Mr. Evans-Wentz) You have been taking our food. Do you feel uncomfortable on that account?

Mr. Evans-Wentz: No. Because I am accustomed to it.

D.: What about those not so accustomed?

M.: Habit is only adjustment to the environment. It is the mind that matters. The fact is that the mind has been trained to think certain foods tasty and good. The food material is to be had both in vegetarian and non-vegetarian diet equally well. But the mind desires such food as it is accustomed to and considers tasty.

D.: Are there restrictions for the realised man in a similar manner?

M.: No. He is steady and not influenced by the food he takes.

D.: Is it not killing life to prepare meat diet?

M.: Ahimsa stands foremost in the code of discipline for the yogis.

D.: Even plants have life.

M.: So too the slabs you sit on!

D.: May we gradually get ourselves accustomed to vegetarian food?

M.: Yes. That is the way.

2nd February, 1935

Talk 23.

Mr. Evans-Wentz continued another day: "May one have more than one spiritual master?"

M.: Who is a Master? He is the Self after all. According to the stages of the development of the mind the Self manifests as the Master

21

externally. The famous ancient saint Avadhuta said that he had more than 24 Masters. The Master is one from whom one learns anything. The Guru may be sometimes inanimate also, as in the case of Avadhuta. God, Guru and the Self are identical.

A spiritual-minded man thinks that God is all-pervading and takes God for his Guru. Later, God brings him in contact with a personal Guru and the man recognises him as all in all. Lastly the same man is made by the grace of the Master to feel that his Self is the Reality and nothing else. Thus he finds that the Self is the Master.

D.: Does Sri Bhagavan initiate his disciples?

Maharshi kept silent.

Thereafter one of the devotees took it upon himself to answer, saying, "Maharshi does not see anyone as outside his Self. So there are no disciples for him. His Grace is all-pervading and He communicates his Grace to any deserving individual in silence."

D.: How does book-lore help in Self-Realisation?

A.: Only so far as to make one spiritually-minded.

D.: How far does intellect help?

A.: Only so far as to make one sink the intellect in the ego, and the ego in the Self.

4th February, 1935

Talk 24.

Mrs. Piggott: Why do you take milk, but not eggs?

M.: The domesticated cows yield more milk than necessary for their calves and they find it a pleasure to be relieved of the milk.

D.: But the hen cannot contain the eggs?

M.: But there are potential lives in them.

D.: Thoughts cease suddenly, then 'I-I' rises up as suddenly and continues. It is only in the feeling and not in the intellect. Can it be right?

M.: It is certainly right. Thoughts must cease and reason disappear for 'I-I' to rise up and be felt. Feeling is the prime factor and not reason.

D.: Moreover it is not in the head but in the right side of the chest.

22

M.: It ought to be so. Because the heart is there.

D.: When I see outside it disappears. What is to be done?

M.: It must be held tight.

D.: If one is active with such remembrance, will the actions be always right?

M.: They ought to be. However, such a person is not concerned with the right or wrong of his actions. Such a person's actions are God's and therefore they must be right.

D.: Why then the restrictions of food given for such?

M.: Your present experience is due to the influence of the atmosphere you are in. Can you have it outside this atmosphere? The experience is spasmodic. Until it becomes permanent practice is necessary. Restrictions of food are aids for such experience to be repeated. After one gets established in truth the restrictions drop away naturally. Moreover, food influences the mind and it must be kept pure.

The lady told a disciple later: "I feel the vibrations from him more intensely and I am able to reach the 'I' centre more readily than before."

Talk 25.

On a former occasion B. V. Narasimha Swami, author of *Self-Realization*, asked: Who am I? How is it to be found?

M.: Ask yourself the question. The body (*annamaya kosa*) and its functions are not 'I'.

Going deeper, the mind (*manomaya kosa*) and its functions are not 'I'.

The next step takes on to the question. "Wherefrom do these thoughts arise?" The thoughts are spontaneous, superficial or analytical. They operate in intellect. Then, who is aware of them? The existence of thoughts, their clear conceptions and their operations become evident to the individual. The analysis leads to the conclusion that the individuality of the person is operative as the perceiver of the existence of thoughts and of their sequence. This individuality is the ego, or as people say 'I'. *Vijnanamaya kosa* (intellect) is only the sheath of 'I' and not the 'I' itself.

23

Enquiring further the questions arise, "Who is this 'I'? Wherefrom does it come?" 'I' was not aware in sleep. Simultaneously with its rise sleep changes to dream or wakefulness. But I am not concerned with dream just now. Who am I now, in the wakeful state? If I originated from sleep, then the 'I' was covered up with ignorance. Such an ignorant 'I' cannot be what the scriptures say or the wise ones affirm. 'I' am beyond even 'Sleep'; 'I' must be now and here and what I was all along in sleep and dreams also, without the qualities of such states. 'I' must therefore be the unqualified substratum underlying these three states (*anandamaya kosa* transcended).

'I' is, in brief, beyond the five sheaths. Next, the residuum left over after discarding all that is not-self is the Self, *Sat-Chit-Ananda*.

D.: How is that Self to be known or realised?

M.: Transcend the present plane of relativity. A separate being (Self) appears to know something apart from itself (non-Self). That is, the subject is aware of the object. The seer is *drik*; the seen is *drisya*.

There must be a unity underlying these two, which arises as 'ego'. This ego is of the nature of *chit* (intelligence); *achit* (insentient object) is only negation of *chit*. Therefore the underlying essence is akin to the subject and not the object. Seeking the *drik*, until all *drisya* disappears, the *drik* will become subtler and subtler until the absolute *drik* alone survives. This process is called *drisya vilaya* (the disappearance of the objective world).

D.: Why should the objects *drisya* be eliminated? Cannot the Truth be realised even keeping the object as it is?

M.: No. Elimination of *drisya* means elimination of separate identities of the subject and object. The object is unreal. All *drisya* (including ego) is the object. Eliminating the unreal, the Reality survives. When a rope is mistaken for a snake, it is enough to remove the erroneous perception of the snake for the truth to be revealed. Without such elimination the truth will not dawn.

D.: When and how is the disappearance of the objective world (*drisya vilaya*) to be effected?

M.: It is complete when the relative subject, namely the mind, is eliminated. The mind is the creator of the subject and the object and

24

is the cause of the dualistic idea. Therefore, it is the cause of the wrong notion of limited self and the misery consequent on such erroneous idea.

D.: What is this mind?

M.: Mind is one form of manifestation of life. A block of wood or a subtle machine is not called mind. The vital force manifests as life-activity and also as the conscious phenomena known as the mind.

D.: What is the relation between mind and object? Is the mind contacting something different from it, *viz.,* the world?

M.: The world is 'sensed' in the waking and the dream states or is the object of perception and thought, both being mental activities. If there were no such activities as waking and dreaming thought, there would be no 'perception' or inference of a 'world'. In sleep there is no such activity and 'objects and world' do not exist for us in sleep. Hence 'reality of the world' may be created by the ego by its act of emergence from sleep; and that reality may be swallowed up or disappear by the soul resuming its nature in sleep. The emergence and disappearance of the world are like the spider producing a gossamer web and then withdrawing it. The spider here underlies all the three states — waking, dreaming, and sleep; such a spider in the person is called *Atman* (Self), whereas the same with reference to the world (which is considered to issue from the sun) is called Brahman (Supreme Spirit). He that is in man is the same as He that is in the sun. (*Sa yaschayam purushe yaschasavaditye sa ekah*).

While Self or Spirit is unmanifest and inactive, there are no relative doubles; *e.g.,* subject and object — *drik* and *drisya*. If the enquiry into the ultimate cause of manifestation of mind itself is pushed on, mind will be found to be only the manifestation of the Real which is otherwise called Atman or Brahman. The mind is termed *sukshma sarira* or 'subtle-body'; and *jiva* is the individual soul. The *jiva* is the essence of the growth of individuality; personality is referred to as *jiva*. Thought or mind is said to be its phase, or one of the ways in which the *jiva* manifests itself — the earlier stage or phase of such manifestation being vegetative life. This mind is always seen as being

25

related to, or acting on, some non-mind or matter, and never by itself. Therefore mind and matter co-exist.

Talk 26.

D.: How shall we discover the nature of the mind *i.e.*, its ultimate cause, or the noumenon of which it is a manifestation?

M.: Arranging thoughts in the order of value, the 'I' thought is the all-important thought. Personality-idea or thought is also the root or the stem of all other thoughts, since each idea or thought arises only as someone's thought and is not known to exist independently of the ego. The ego therefore exhibits thought-activity. The second and the third persons do not appear except to the first person. Therefore they arise only after the first person appears, so all the three persons seem to rise and sink together. Trace, then, the ultimate cause of 'I' or personality. The 'I' idea arises to an embodied ego and should be related to a body or organism. Has it a location in the body or a special relation to any particular spot, as speech which has its centre in the brain or amativeness in the brain? Similarly, has 'I' got any centre in the brain, blood, or viscera? Thought-life is seen to centre round the brain and the spinal-cord which in turn are fed by the blood circulating in them, carrying food and air duly mixed up which are transformed into nerve matter. Thus, vegetative life — including circulation, respiration, alimentation, etc. — or vital force, is said to be (or reside in) the core or essence of the organism. Thus the mind may be regarded as the manifestation of vital force which again may be conceived as residing the Heart.

D.: Now for the art of eliminating the mind and developing intuition in its stead, are they two distinct stages with a possible neutral ground which is neither mind nor intuition? Or does the absence of mental activity necessarily involve Self-Realisation?

M.: To the *abhyasi* (practitioner) there are two distinctive stages. There is a neutral ground of sleep, coma, faint, insanity, etc., in which the mental operations either do not exist or consciousness of Self does not prevail.

D.: Taking the first part first, how is the mind to be eliminated or relative consciousness transcended?

26

M.: The mind is by nature restless. Begin liberating it from its restlessness; give it peace; make it free from distractions; train it to look inward; make this a habit. This is done by ignoring the external world and removing the obstacles to peace of mind.

D.: How is restlessness removed from the mind?

M.: External contacts — contacts with objects other than itself — make the mind restless. Loss of interest in non-Self, (*vairagya*) is the first step. Then the habits of introspection and concentration follow. They are characterised by control of external senses, internal faculties, etc. (*sama, dama,* etc.) ending in *samadhi* (undistracted mind).

Talk 27.

D.: How are they practised?

M.: An examination of the ephemeral nature of external phenomena leads to *vairagya*. Hence enquiry (*vichara*) is the first and foremost step to be taken. When *vichara* continues automatically, it results in a contempt for wealth, fame, ease, pleasure, etc. The 'I' thought becomes clearer for inspection. The source of 'I' is the Heart — the final goal. If, however, the aspirant is not temperamentally suited to *Vichara Marga* (to the introspective analytical method), he must develop *bhakti* (devotion) to an ideal — may be God, Guru, humanity in general, ethical laws, or even the idea of beauty. When one of these takes possession of the individual, other attachments grow weaker, *i.e.*, dispassion (*vairagya*) develops. Attachment for the ideal simultaneously grows and finally holds the field. Thus *ekagrata* (concentration) grows simultaneously and imperceptibly — with or without visions and direct aids.

In the absence of enquiry and devotion, the natural sedative *pranayama* (breath regulation) may be tried. This is known as *Yoga Marga*. If life is imperilled the whole interest centres round the one point, the saving of life. If the breath is held the mind cannot afford to (and does not) jump at its pets — external objects. Thus there is rest for the mind so long as the breath is held. All attention being turned on breath or its regulation, other interests are lost. Again, passions are attended with irregular breathing, whereas calm and happiness

27

are attended with slow and regular breathing. Paroxysm of joy is in fact as painful as one of pain, and both are accompanied by ruffled breaths. Real peace is happiness. Pleasures do not form happiness. The mind improves by practice and becomes finer just as the razor's edge is sharpened by stropping. The mind is then better able to tackle internal or external problems. If an aspirant be unsuited temperamentally for the first two methods and circumstantially (on account of age) for the third method, he must try the Karma *Marga* (doing good deeds, for example, social service). His nobler instincts become more evident and he derives impersonal pleasure. His smaller self is less assertive and has a chance of expanding its good side. The man becomes duly equipped for one of the three aforesaid paths. His intuition may also develop directly by this single method.

D.: Can a line of thought or a series of questions induce Self-hypnotism? Should it not be reduced to a single point analysing the unanalysable, elementary and vaguely perceived and elusive 'I'?

M.: Yes. It is really like gazing into vacancy or a dazzling crystal or light.

D.: Can the mind be fixed to that point? How?

M.: If the mind is distracted, ask the question promptly, "To whom do these distracting thoughts arise?" That takes you back to the 'I' point promptly.

D.: How long can the mind stay or be kept in the Heart?

M.: The period extends by practice.

D.: What happens at the end of the period?

M.: The mind returns to the present normal state. Unity in the Heart is replaced by variety of phenomena perceived. This is called the outgoing mind. The heart-going mind is called the resting mind.

D.: Is all this process merely intellectual or does it exhibit feeling predominantly?

M.: The latter.

D.: How do all thoughts cease when the mind is in the Heart?

M.: By force of will, with strong faith in the truth of the Master's teaching to that effect.

D.: What is the good of this process?

M.: (a) Conquest of the will — development of concentration.

(b) Conquest of passions — development of dispassion.

(c) Increased practice of virtue — (*samatva*) equality to all.

D.: Why should one adopt this self-hypnotism by thinking on the unthinkable point? Why not adopt other methods like gazing into light, holding the breath, hearing music, hearing internal sounds, repetition of the sacred syllable (*Pranava*) or other *mantras*?

M.: Light-gazing stupefies the mind and produces catalepsy of the will for the time being, yet secures no permanent benefit. Breath control benumbs the will for the time being only. Sound-hearing produces similar results — unless the *mantra* is sacred and secures the help of a higher power to purify and raise the thoughts.

Talk 28.

D.: What is the interrelation between regulation of thought and regulation of breath?

M.: Thought (intellectual) and respiration, circulation, etc. (vegetative) activities are both different aspects of the same — the individual life. Both depend upon (or metaphorically 'reside' or 'inhere' in) life. Personality and other ideas spring from it like the vital activity. If respiration or other vital activity is forcibly repressed, thought also is repressed. If thought is forcibly slowed down and pinned to a point, the vital activity of respiration is slowed down, made even and confined to the lowest level compatible with life. In both cases the distracting variety of thought is temporarily at an end. The interaction is noticeable in other ways also. Take the will to live. That is thought-power. That sustains and keeps up life when other vitality is almost exhausted and delays death. In the absence of such will-power death is accelerated. So thought is said to carry life with it in the flesh and from one fleshy body to another.

D.: Are there any aids to (1) concentration and (2) casting off distractions?

M.: Physically the digestive and other organs are kept free from irritation. Therefore food is regulated both in quantity and quality. Non-irritants are eaten, avoiding chillies, excess of salt, onions, wine, opium, etc. Avoid constipation, drowsiness and excitement, and all foods which induce them. Mentally take interest in one thing and fix the mind on it. Let such interest be all-absorbing to the exclusion of everything else. This is dispassion (*vairagya*) and concentration. God or *mantra* may be chosen. The mind gains strength to grasp the subtle and merge into it.

D.: Distractions result from inherited tendencies. Can they be cast off too?

M.: Yes. Many have done so. Believe it! They did so because they believed they could. *Vasanas* (predispositions) can be obliterated. It is done by concentration on that which is free from *vasanas* and yet is their core.

D.: How long is the practice to continue?

M.: Till success is achieved and until yoga-liberation becomes permanent. Success begets success. If one distraction is conquered the next is conquered and so on, until all are finally conquered. The process is like reducing an enemy's fort by slaying its man-power — one by one, as each issues out.

D.: What is the goal of this process?

M.: Realising the Real.

D.: What is the nature of the Reality?

M.: (a) Existence without beginning or end — eternal.

    (b) Existence everywhere, endless, infinite.

    (c) Existence underlying all forms, all changes, all forces, all matter and all spirit.

The many change and pass away (phenomena), whereas the One always endures (noumenon).

(d) The one displacing the triads, *i.e.*, the knower, the knowledge and the known. The triads are only appearances in time and space, whereas the Reality lies beyond and behind them. They are like a mirage over the Reality. They are the result of delusion.

D.: If 'I' also be an illusion, who then casts off the illusion?

M.: The 'I' casts off the illusion of 'I' and yet remains as 'I'. Such is the paradox of Self-Realisation. The realised do not see any contradiction in it. Take the case of *bhakti* — I approach Iswara and

30

pray to be absorbed in Him. I then surrender myself in faith and by concentration. What remains afterwards? In place of the original 'I', perfect self-surrender leaves a residuum of God in which the 'I' is lost. This is the highest form of devotion (*parabhakti*), *prapatti*, surrender or the height of *vairagya*.

You give up this and that of 'my' possessions. If you give up 'I' and 'Mine' instead, all are given up at a stroke. The very seed of possession is lost. Thus the evil is nipped in the bud or crushed in the germ itself. Dispassion (*vairagya*) must be very strong to do this. Eagerness to do it must be equal to that of a man kept under water trying to rise up to the surface for his life.

D.: Cannot this trouble and difficulty be lessened with the aid of a Master or an *Ishta Devata* (God chosen for worship)? Cannot they give the power to see our Self as it is — to change us into themselves — to take us into Self-Realisation?

M.: Ishta Devata and Guru are aids — very powerful aids on this path. But an aid to be effective requires your effort also. Your effort is a *sine qua non*. It is you who should see the sun. Can spectacles and the sun see for you? You yourself have to see your true nature. Not much aid is required for doing it!

D.: What is the relation between my free-will and the overwhelming might of the Omnipotent?

    (a) Is omniscience of God consistent with ego's freewill?

    (b) Is omnipotence of God consistent with ego's freewill?

    (c) Are the natural laws consistent with God's free-will?

M.: Yes. Free-will is the present appearing to a limited faculty of sight and will. The same ego sees its past activity as falling into a course of 'law' or rules — its own free-will being one of the links in that course of law.

Omnipotence and omniscience of God are then seen by the ego to have acted through the appearance of his own free-will. So he comes to the conclusion that the ego must go by appearances. Natural laws are manifestations of God's will and they have been laid down.

D.: Is the study of science, psychology, physiology, philosophy, etc. helpful for:-

(1) this art of yoga-liberation.

(2) the intuitive grasp of the unity of the Real?

M.: Very little. Some knowledge is needed for yoga and it may be found in books. But practical application is the thing needed, and personal example, personal touch and personal instructions are the most helpful aids. As for the other, a person may laboriously convince himself of the truth to be intuited, *i.e.*, its function and nature, but the actual intuition is akin to feeling and requires practice and personal contact. Mere book learning is not of any great use. After realisation all intellectual loads are useless burdens and are thrown overboard as jetsam. Jettisoning the ego is necessary and natural.

D.: How does dream differ from waking?

M.: In dreams one takes on different bodies, and they re-enter this body when one dreams of sense-contacts.

D.: What is happiness? Is it inhering in the Atman or in the object, or in the contact between the subject and the object? But we do not see happiness in our affairs. When does It actually arise?

M.: When there is contact of a desirable sort or memory thereof, and when there is freedom from undesirable contacts or memory thereof, we say there is happiness. Such happiness is relative and is better called pleasure.

But men want absolute and permanent happiness. This does not reside in objects, but in the Absolute. It is Peace free from pain and pleasure — it is a neutral state.

D.: In what sense is happiness our real nature?

M.: Perfect Bliss is Brahman. Perfect Peace is of the Self. That alone exists and is conscious. The same conclusion is arrived at: (a) judged metaphysically, and (b) inferred by *Bhakti Marga* (Path of Devotion).

We pray to God for Bliss and receive it by Grace. The bestower of bliss must be Bliss itself and also Infinite. Therefore, *Iswara* is the Personal God of infinite power and bliss. Brahman is Bliss, impersonal and absolute. The finite egos, deriving their source from Brahman and then *Iswara*, are in their spiritual nature bliss only. Biologically, an organism functions because such functions are attended with happiness.

It is pleasure that helps our growth; food, exercise, rest, and gregarious qualities. The psychology (and metaphysics) of pleasure is perhaps this; Our nature is primarily one, entire, blissful. Take this as a probable hypothesis. Creation is by the entire Godhead breaking into God and Nature (*maya* or *prakriti*). This *maya* is of two parts: (*para*) — the supporting essence and (*apara*) the five elements, mind, intellect, and ego (eight-fold).

Ego's perfection is suddenly broken at a point and a want is felt giving rise to a desire to get something or do something. When that want is cured by the fulfilment of that desire, the ego is happy and the original perfection is restored. Therefore happiness may be said to be our natural condition or nature. Pleasure and pain are relative and refer to our finite state, with progress by satisfaction of want. If relative progress is stopped and the soul merges into Brahman — of the nature of perfect peace — that soul ceases to have relative, temporary pleasure and enjoys perfect peace — Bliss. Hence Self-Realisation is Bliss; it is realizing the Self as the limitless spiritual eye (*jnana dristi*) and not clairvoyance; it is the highest self-surrender. *Samsara* (the world-cycle) is sorrow.

D.: Why then is *samsara* — creation and manifestation as finitised — so full of sorrow and evil?

M.: God's will!

D.: Why does God will it so?

M.: It is inscrutable. No motive can be attributed to that Power — no desire, no end to achieve can be asserted of that one Infinite, All-wise and All-powerful Being. God is untouched by activities, which take place in His presence; compare the sun and the world activities. There is no meaning in attributing responsibility and motive to the One before it becomes many. But God's will for the prescribed course of events is a good solution of the free-will problem (*vexata quaestio*). If the mind is restless on account of a sense of the imperfect and unsatisfactory character of what befalls us or what is committed or omitted by us, then it is wise to drop the sense of responsibility and free-will by regarding ourselves as the ordained instruments of the All-wise and All-powerful, to do and suffer as He pleases. He carries all burdens and gives us peace.

33

Talk 29.

On another occasion, the evening was calm and cloudy. It was drizzling occasionally and somewhat cool in consequence. The windows of the Asramam Hall were closed and Maharshi was seated as usual on the sofa. Facing him sat the devotees. Some visitors had come from Cuddalore. A Sub-Judge, accompanied by two elderly ladies, was among them. The Sub-Judge began the discussion as to the impermanence of all mundane things, by putting the question. "Has the discrimination between Reality and Unreality (*Sat asat vicharana*) the efficacy in itself to lead us to the realisation of the one Imperishable?"

M.: As propounded by all and realised by all true seekers, fixity in the Supreme Spirit (*Brahma nishta*) alone can make us know and realise it. It being of us and in us, any amount of discrimination (*vivechana*) can lead us only one step forward, by making us renouncers, by goading us to discard the seeming (*abhasa*) as transitory and to hold fast to the eternal truth and presence alone.

The conversation turned upon the question as to whether *Iswara Prasad* (Divine Grace) is necessary for the attaining of *samrajya* (universal dominion) or whether a *jiva's* honest and strenuous efforts to attain it cannot of themselves lead him to That from whence is no return to life and death. The Maharshi with an ineffable smile which lit up His Holy Face and which was all-pervasive, shining upon the coterie around him, replied in tones of certainty and with the ring of truth; "Divine Grace is essential for Realisation. It leads one to God-realisation. But such Grace is vouchsafed only to him who is a true devotee or a yogin, who has striven hard and ceaselessly on the path towards freedom."

D.: There are six centres mentioned in the Yoga books; but the *jiva* is said to reside in the Heart. Is it not so?

M.: Yes. The *jiva* is said to remain in the Heart in deep sleep; and in the brain in the waking state. The Heart need not be taken to be the muscular cavity with four chambers which propels blood. There are indeed passages which support the view. There are others who take it to mean a set of ganglia or nerve centres about that region. Whichever

34

view is correct does not matter to us. We are not concerned with anything less than ourselves. That we have certainly within us. There could be no doubts or discussions about that.

The Heart is used in the Vedas and the scriptures to denote the place whence the notion 'I' springs. Does it spring only from the fleshy ball? It springs within us somewhere right in the middle of our being. The 'I' has no location. Everything is the Self. There is nothing but that. So the Heart must be said to be the entire body of ourselves and of the entire universe, conceived as 'I'. But to help the practiser (*abhyasi*) we have to indicate a definite part of the Universe, or of the Body. So this Heart is pointed out as the seat of the Self. But in truth we are everywhere, we are all that is, and there is nothing else.

D.: It is said that Divine Grace is necessary to attain successful undistracted mind (*samadhi*). Is that so?

M.: We are God (*Iswara*). *Iswara Drishti* (*i.e.*, seeing ourselves as God) is itself Divine Grace. So we need Divine Grace to get God's Grace.

Maharshi smiles and all devotees laugh together.

D.: There is also Divine Favour (*Iswara anugraham*) as distinct from Divine Grace (*Iswara prasadam*). Is that so?

M.: The thought of God is Divine Favour! He is by nature Grace (*prasad* or *arul*). It is by God's Grace that you think of God.

D.: Is not the Master's Grace the result of God's Grace?

M.: Why distinguish between the two? The Master is the same as God and not different from him.

D.: When an endeavour is made to lead the right life and to concentrate thought on the Self, there is often a downfall and break. What is to be done?

M.: It will come all right in the end. There is the steady impulse of your determination that sets you on your feet again after every downfall and breakdown. Gradually the obstacles are all overcome and your current becomes stronger. Everything comes right in the end. Steady determination is what is required.

Talk 30.

Mr. N. Natesa Iyer, the leader of the Bar in a South Indian town, an orthodox Brahmin, asked: "Are the gods *Iswara* or *Vishnu* and their sacred regions *Kailasa* or *Vaikuntha* real?

M.: As real as you are in this body.

D.: Do they possess a *vyavahara satya, i.e.,* phenomenal existence, like my body? Or are they fictions like the horn of a hare?

M.: They do exist.

D.: If so, they must be somewhere. Where are they?

M.: Persons who have seen them say that they exist somewhere. So we must accept their statement.

D.: Where do they exist?

M.: In you.

D.: Then it is only idea — that which I can create and control?

M.: Everything is like that.

D.: But I can create pure fictions *e.g.,* hare's horn or only part truths, *e.g.* mirage, while there are also facts irrespective of my imagination. Do the gods *Iswara* or *Vishnu* exist like that?

M.: Yes.

D.: Is He subject to *pralaya* (cosmic dissolution)?

M.: Why? Man becoming aware of the Self transcends cosmic dissolution (*pralaya*) and becomes liberated (*mukta*). Why not God (*Iswara*) who is infinitely wiser and abler?

D.: Do *devas* and *pisachas* (devils) exist similarly?

M.: Yes.

D.: How are we to conceive of Supreme Consciousness (*Chaitanya Brahman*)?

M.: As that which is.

D.: Should it be thought of as Self-Effulgent?

M.: It transcends light and darkness. An individual (*jiva*) sees both. The Self enlightens the individual to see light and darkness.

D.: Should it be realised as "I am not the body, nor the agent, nor the enjoyer, etc."?

M.: Why these thoughts? Do we now think that we are men, etc.? By not thinking so, do we cease to be men?

36

D.: Should one realise it then by the scriptural text such as "There are no differences here".

नेह नानास्ति किंचन

M.: Why even that?

D.: If we think "I am the real," will it do?

M.: All thoughts are inconsistent with realisation. The correct state is to exclude thoughts of ourselves and all other thoughts. Thought is one thing and realisation is quite another.

D.: Is it not necessary or at least advantageous to render the body invisible in one's spiritual progress?

M.: Why do you think of that? Are you the body?

D.: No. But advanced spirituality must effect a change in the body. Is it not so?

M.: What change do you desire in the body, and why?

D.: Is not invisibility evidence of advanced Wisdom (*jnana*)?

M.: In that case, all those who spoke, who wrote and who passed their lives in the sight of others must be considered ignorant (*ajnanis*)!

D.: But the sages Vasistha and Valmiki possessed such powers?

M.: It might have been their fate (*prarabdha*) to develop such powers (*siddhis*) side by side with their wisdom (*jnana*). Why should you aim at that which is not essential but apt to prove a hindrance to wisdom (*jnana*)? Does the Sage (*jnani*) feel oppressed by his body being visible?

D.: No.

M.: A hypnotist can render himself suddenly invisible. Is he therefore a Sage (*jnani*)?

D.: No.

M.: Visibility and invisibility refer to a seer. Who is that seer? Solve that first. Other matters are unimportant.

D.: The Vedas contain conflicting accounts of Cosmogony. Ether is said to be the first creation in one place; vital energy (*prana*) in another place; something else in yet another; water in still another, and so on. How are these to be reconciled? Do not these impair the credibility of the Vedas?

M.: Different seers saw different aspects of truths at different times, each emphasising some one view. Why do you worry about their conflicting statements? The essential aim of the Veda is to teach us the nature of the imperishable Atman and show us that we are That.

D.: I am satisfied with that portion.

M.: Then treat all the rest as *artha vada* (auxiliary arguments) or expositions for the sake of the ignorant who seek to trace the genesis of things and matters.

D.: I am a sinner. I do not perform religious sacrifices (*homas*), etc. Shall I have painful rebirths for that reason? Pray save me!

M.: Why do you say that you are a sinner? Your trust in God is sufficient to save you from rebirths. Cast all burden on Him.

In the *Tiruvachagam* it is said: "Though I am worse than a dog, you have graciously undertaken to protect me. This delusion of birth and death is maintained by you. Moreover, am I the person to sift and judge? Am I the Lord here? Oh Maheswara! It is for you to roll me through bodies (by births and deaths) or to keep me fixed at your own feet." Therefore have faith and that will save you.

D.: Sir, I have faith — and still I encounter difficulties. Weakness and giddiness afflict me after I practise concentration.

M.: Breath-control (*pranayama*) properly performed should increase one's strength.

D.: I have my professional work and yet I want to be in perpetual *dhyana*. Will they conflict with each other?

M.: There will be no conflict. As you practise both and develop your powers you will be able to attend to both. You will begin to look on business as a dream. Says the Bhagavad Gita: "That which is the night of all beings, for the disciplined man is the time of waking; when other beings are waking, then is it night for the sage who seeth." (11.69.)

Talk 31.

A visitor asked: What to do to get liberation (*moksha*)?

M.: Learn what liberation is.

D.: Should I do worship (*upasana*) for it?

M.: Worship is for mind control (*chitta nirodha*) and concentration.

D.: Should I do idol worship? Is there any harm in it?

M.: So long as you think you are the body there is no harm.

D.: How to get over the cycle of births and deaths?

M.: Learn what it means.

D.: Should I not leave my wife and family?

M.: How do they harm you? First find out who you are.

D.: Should not one give up wife, wealth, home?

M.: Learn first what *samsara* is. Is all that *samsara*? Have there not been men living among them and getting realisation?

D.: What are the steps of practical training (*sadhana*) for it?

M.: It depends on the qualifications and the nature of the seeker.

D.: I am doing idol worship.

M.: Go on with it. It leads to concentration of mind. Get one-pointed. All will come out right. People think that freedom (*moksha*) is somewhere yonder and should be sought out. They are wrong. Freedom (*moksha*) is only knowing the Self within yourself. Concentrate and you will get it. Your mind is the cycle of births and deaths (*samsara*).

D.: My mind is very unsteady. What should I do?

M.: Fix your attention on any single thing and try to hold on to it. All will be right.

D.: I find concentration difficult.

M.: Go on practising. Your concentration will be as easy as breathing. That will be the crown of your achievements.

D.: Are not abstinence and pure food helpful?

M.: Yes, all that is good. (Then Maharshi concentrates and silently gazes at vacancy, and thus sets an example to the questioner).

D.: Do I not require Yoga?

M.: What is it but the means to concentration?

D.: To help concentration, is it not good to have some aids?

M.: Breath-regulation, etc., are such helps.

D.: Is it not possible to get a vision of God?

M.: Yes. You see this and that. Why not see God? Only you must know what God is. All are seeing God always. But they do not know it. You find out what God is. People see, yet see not, because they know not God.

D.: Should I not go on with repetition of sacred syllables, (*mantra japa*), e.g., Krishna or Rama's name, when I worship images?

M.: Mental *japa* is very good. That helps meditation. Mind gets identified with the repetition and then you get to know what worship (*puja*) really is — the losing of one's individuality in that which is worshipped.

D.: Is the Universal Soul (*Paramatma*) always different from us?

M.: That is the common belief, but it is wrong. Think of Him as not different from you, and then you achieve identity of Self with God.

D.: Is it not the *Advaita* doctrine to become one with God?

M.: Where is becoming? The thinker is all the while the Real. He ultimately realises the fact. Sometimes we forget our identities, as in sleep and dreams. But God is perpetual consciousness.

D.: Is not the Master's guidance necessary, besides idol worship?

M.: How did you start it without advice?

D.: From sacred books (*puranas*).

M.: Yes. Someone tells you of God, or Bhagavan Himself tells you. In the latter case God Himself is your Master. What matters it who the Master is? We really are one with Master or Bhagavan. The Master is God; one discovers it in the end. There is no difference between human-guru and God-guru.

D.: If we have done virtuous action (*punya*) the achievement will not leave us. I hope.

M.: You will reap your destiny (*prarabdha*) that way.

D.: Will not a Wise Master be a great help in pointing out the way?

M.: Yes. If you go on working with the light available, you will meet your Master, as he himself will be seeking you.

D.: Is there a difference between *prapatti* (self-surrender) and the Path of Yoga of the Seers?

M.: *Jnana Marga* and *Bhakti Marga* (*prapatti*) are one and the same. Self-surrender leads to realisation just as enquiry does. Complete self-surrender means that you have no further thought of 'I'. Then all your predispositions (*samskaras*) are washed off and

40

you are free. You should not continue as a separate entity at the end of either course.

D.: Do not we go to Heaven (*svarga*), etc. as the result of our actions?

M.: That is as true as the present existence. But if we enquire who we are and discover the Self, what need is there to think of heaven, etc.?

D.: Should I not try to escape rebirth?

M.: Yes. Find out who is born and who has the trouble of existence now. When you are asleep do you think of rebirths or even the present existence, etc.? So find out whence the present problem arises and there is the solution also. You will discover that there is no birth, no present trouble or unhappiness, etc. All is That; All is Bliss; we are freed from rebirth in fact. Why fret over the misery of rebirth?

Talk 32.

A visitor: The saints Sri Chaitanya and Sri Ramakrishna wept before God and achieved success. Is that not the path to follow?

M.: Yes. There was a powerful force (*sakti*) drawing them on through all those experiences. Trust in that huge power to take you on to your goal. Tears are often considered a sign of weakness. These great persons were certainly not weak. These manifestations are only passing signs of the great current carrying them on. We must look to the end achieved.

D.: Can this physical body be made to disappear into nothingness?

M.: Why this question? Can you not find out if you are the body?

D.: Can we have disappearance from sight (*antardhana*) like the yogis Vasishta or Viswamitra?

M.: These are only physical matters. Is that the essential object of our interest? Are you not the Self? Why trouble about other matters? Take the essence; reject other learned theories as useless. They who think that physical disappearance counts in freedom are mistaken. No such thing is needed. You are not the body; what does it matter if it disappears in one way or another? There is no great merit in such phenomena. In what does superiority or inferiority consist?

41

Achievement of the Real alone matters. The loss of the 'I' is the main fact, and not the loss of the body. Identity of the Self with the body is the real bondage. Leave off the false notion and perceive intuitively the Real. That alone matters. If you melt a gold ornament before testing it to be gold, what matters it how it is melted, whole or in parts, or of what shape the ornament was? All that you are interested in is if it is gold. The dead man sees not his body. It is the survivor that thinks about the manner in which the body is parted from. The realised have no death with or without the body, the realised man is equally aware and sees no difference. To him the one state is not superior to the other. To an outsider also the fortunes of a liberated one's body need not be of any concern; mind your business. Realise the Self; after realisation there will be time to think of what form of death is preferable to you.

It is the false identity of the Self with the body that causes the idea of preference, etc. Are you the body? Were you aware of it when you were fast asleep last night? No! What is it that exists now and troubles you? It is 'I'. Get rid of it and be happy.

Talk 33.

A visitor: "The Supreme Spirit (Brahman) is Real. The world (*jagat*) is illusion," is the stock phrase of Sri Sankaracharya. Yet others say, "The world is reality". Which is true?

M.: Both statements are true. They refer to different stages of development and are spoken from different points of view. The aspirant (*abhyasi*) starts with the definition, that which is real exists always; then he eliminates the world as unreal because it is changing. It cannot be real; 'not this, not this!' The seeker ultimately reaches the Self and there finds unity as the prevailing note. Then, that which was originally rejected as being unreal is found to be a part of the unity. Being absorbed in the Reality, the world also is Real. There is only being in Self-Realisation, and nothing but being. Again Reality is used in a different sense and is applied loosely by some thinkers to objects. They say that the reflected (*adhyasika*) Reality admits of degrees which are named:

42

(1) *Vyavaharika satya* (everyday life) — this chair is seen by me and is real.

(2) *Pratibhasika satya* (illusory) — Illusion of a serpent in a coiled rope. The appearance is real to the man who thinks so. This phenomenon appears at a point of time and under certain circumstances.

(3) *Paramartika satya* (ultimate) — Reality is that which remains the same always and without change.

If Reality be used in the wider sense the world may be said to have the everyday life and illusory degrees (*vyavaharika* and *pratibhasika satya*). Some, however, deny even the reality of practical life — *vyavaharika satya* and consider it to be only projection of the mind. According to them it is only *pratibhasika satya, i.e.*, an illusion.

Yogi Ramiah's Account Of His Experiences
Talk 34.

Sitting in Maharshi's presence brings peace of mind. I used to sit in *samadhi* for three or four hours together. Then I felt my mind took a form and came out from within. By constant practice and meditation it entered the Heart and was merged into it. I conclude that the Heart is the resting place of mind. The result is peace. When the mind is absorbed in the Heart, the Self is realised. This could be felt even at the stage of concentration (*dharana*).

I asked Maharshi about contemplation. He taught me as follows:-
When a man dies the funeral pyre is prepared and the body is laid flat on the pyre. The pyre is lit. The skin is burnt, then the flesh and then the bones until the whole body falls to ashes. What remains thereafter? The mind. The question arises, 'How many are there in this body — one or two?' If two, why do people say 'I' and not 'we'? There is therefore only one. Whence is it born? What is its nature (*swaroopa*)? Enquiring thus the mind also disappears. Then what remains over is seen to be 'I'. The next question is 'Who am I?' The Self alone. This is contemplation. It is how I did it. By this process attachment to the body (*dehavasana*) is destroyed. The ego vanishes. Self alone shines. One method of getting mind-dissolution (*manolaya*) is association

43

with great ones — the yoga adepts (Yoga *arudhas*). They are perfect adepts in *samadhi*. Self-Realisation has been easy, natural, and perpetual to them. Those moving with them closely and in sympathetic contact gradually absorb the *samadhi* habit from them.

Talk 35.

An educated visitor asked Bhagavan about *dvaita* and *advaita*.

M.: Identification with the body is *dvaita*. Non-identification is *advaita*.

Talk 36.

An aristocratic and distinguished lady visitor from the North accompanied by her Private Secretary arrived at noon, waited a few minutes and asked Maharshi soon after he returned to the hall after lunch:

D.: Maharajji, can we see the dead?

M.: Yes.

D.: Can the yogis show them to us?

M.: Yes. They may. But do not ask me to show them to you. For I cannot.

D.: Do you see them?

M.: Yes, in dreams.

D.: Can we realise the goal through yoga?

M.: Yes.

D.: Have you written on yoga? Are there books on the subject by you?

M.: Yes.

After she left the Master observed: "Did we know our relatives before their birth that we should know them after their death?"

Talk 37.

"What is Karma?" asked someone.

M.: That which has already begun to bear fruit is classified as *prarabdha* Karma (past action). That which is in store and will later bear fruit is classified as *sanchita* Karma (accumulated action). This is multifarious like the grain obtained by villagers as barter for cress

44

(greens). Such bartered grain consists of rice, ragi, barley, etc., some floating on, others sinking in water. Some of it may be good, bad or indifferent. When the most potent of the multifarious accumulated karma begins to bear fruit in the next birth it is called the *prarabdha* of that birth.

Talk 38.

When one of the present attendants came the first time to Bhagavan, he asked: "What is the way for liberation?" Maharshi replied: "The way already taken leads to liberation."

22nd March, 1935

Talk 39.

Conversing with R. Seshagiri Rao, a visitor, Maharshi remarked that a Self-Realised sage (*Atma jnani*) alone can be a good Karma yogi. "After the sense of doership has gone let us see what happens. Sri Sankara advised inaction. But did he not write commentaries and take part in disputation? Do not trouble about doing action or otherwise. Know Thyself. Then let us see whose action it is. Whose is it? Let action complete itself. So long as there is the doer he must reap the fruits of his action. If he does not think himself the doer there is no action for him. He is an ascetic who has renounced worldly life (*sanyasin*)."

D.: How did the ego arise?

M.: It is not necessary to know it. Know the present. Not knowing that, why do you worry about other times?

Maharshi said in reply to a question: "Is the world within you or without you? Does it exist apart from you? Does the world come and tell you 'I exist'?"

Talk 40.

The Brahmin questioner resumed: "How do we know that action is ours or not?"

M.: If the fruits of actions do not affect the person he is free from action.

D.: Is intellectual knowledge enough?

45

M.: Unless intellectually known, how to practice it? Learn it intellectually first, then do not stop with that. Practise it.

Maharshi then made certain remarks: "When you adhere to one philosophical system (*siddhanta*) you are obliged to condemn the others. That is the case with the heads of monasteries (*matadhipatis*)".

All people cannot be expected to do the same kind of action. Each one acts according to his temperament and past lives. Wisdom, Devotion, Action (*jnana, bhakti, karma*) are all interlocked. Meditation on forms is according to one's own mind. It is meant for ridding oneself of other forms and confining oneself to one form. It leads to the goal. It is impossible to fix the mind in the Heart to start with. So these aids are necessary. Krishna says that there is no birth (*janma*) to you, me, etc., and later says he was born before Aditya, etc. Arjuna disputes it. Therefore it is certain that each one thinks of God according to his own degree of advancement.

You say you are the body in wakeful state; not the body in sleep. Bodies being several-fold for an individual, should not there be infinite capacities for God? Whichever method one follows, that method is encouraged by the Sages. For it leads to the goal like any other method.

Talk 41.

D.: Are there heaven (*swarga*) and hell (*naraka*)?

M.: There must be someone to go there. They are like dreams. We see time and space exist in dream also. Which is true, dream or wakefulness?

D.: So we must rid ourselves of lust (*kama*), anger, (*krodha*), etc.

M.: Give up thoughts. You need not give up anything else. You must be there to see anything. It is the Self. Self is ever-conscious.

D.: Are pilgrimages, etc., good?

M.: Yes.

D.: What effort is necessary for reaching the Self?

M.: 'I' should be destroyed. Self is not to be reached. Is there any moment when Self is not? It is not new. Be as you are. What is new cannot be permanent. What is real must always exist.

D.: What is sacrifice through wisdom (*jnana yajna*) or other sacrifices?

M.: Other disciplines exist for it. Practice is for gaining wisdom (*jnana*).

D.: Are *jivanmuktas* (living liberated souls) of different kinds?

M.: What does it matter if they differ externally? There is no difference in their wisdom (*jnana*).

D.: When loyal to one Master can you respect others?

M.: Guru is only one. He is not physical. So long as there is weakness the support of strength is needed.

D.: J. Krishnamurti says, "No Guru is necessary?"

M.: How did he know it? One can say so after realising but not before.

D.: You have gained this state by great effort. What shall we poor souls do?

M.: We are in our Self. We are not in the world.

D.: Heaven and hell — what are they?

M.: You carry heaven and hell with you. Your lust, anger, etc., produce these regions. They are like dreams.

D.: The Gita says that if a man fixes his attention between the eyebrows and holds his breath he reaches the Supreme state. How is that done?

M.: You are always in the Self and there is no reaching it. The eyebrow is only a place where attention is to be fixed (seat of meditation — *upasanasthana*).

D.: You have spoken of the Heart as the seat of meditation?

M.: Yes, it is also that.

D.: What is Heart?

M.: It is the centre of the Self. The Self is the centre of centres. The Heart represents the psychic centre and not the physical centre.

D.: The term '*jnana*' is realised Wisdom. The same term is used for the method also. Why?

M.: '*Jnana*' includes the method also because it ultimately results in realisation.

D.: Is a man to engage in teaching his knowledge however imperfect?

47

M.: If his *prarabdha* be that way.

In the seventh chapter, Arjuna asks if Karma is a method (*sadhana*). Krishna answers that it is so if done without the sense of doership.

So also are Karmas approved by scriptures which deny Karma. The Karma disapproved by them is that which is done with the sense of doership. Do not leave Karma. You cannot do so. Give up the sense of doership. Karma will go on automatically. Or Karma will drop away from you. If Karma be your lot according to *prarabdha*, it will surely be done whether you will it or not; if Karma be not your lot, it will not be done even if you intently engage in it. Janaka, Suka, etc., were also in work without *ahankara*, Karma may be done for fame, or may be done unselfishly and for the public good. Yet even then they want applause. So it is really selfish.

D.: What is that one thing, knowing which all doubts are solved?

M.: Know the doubter. If the doubter be held, the doubts will not arise. *Here the doubter is transcendent.* Again when the doubter ceases to exist, there will be no doubts arising. From where will they arise? All are *jnanis, jivanmuktas*. Only they are not aware of the fact. Doubts must be uprooted. This means that the doubter must be uprooted. Here the doubter is the mind.

D.: What is the method?

M.: 'Who am I?' is the investigation.

D.: May we perform *japa*?

M.: Why should you think I am this? Investigate and the thoughts cease. What is, namely the Self, will be revealed as the inescapable residue.

D.: Is *hatha yoga* necessary?

M.: It is one of the aids — not that it is always necessary. It depends upon the person. *Vichara* surpasses *pranayama*. In *Yoga Vasishta* Chudala advises investigation (*vichara*) to Sikhidvaja for killing the ego.

Reality can be reached by holding on to *prana* or intellect. *Hatha yoga* is the former; *Vichara* is the latter.

D.: Is there any individuality for the *jnani* after Realization?

M.: How can he retain individuality?

Even ordinarily the elders advise *achamana* and *pranayama* before undertaking any work — be it worldly or other-worldly. That means, concentration of mind accomplishes the work.

D.: I meditate *neti-neti* (not this — not this).

M.: No — that is not meditation. Find the source. You must reach the source without fail. The false 'I' will disappear and the real 'I' will be realised. The former cannot exist apart from the latter..

24th March, 1935

Talk 42.

Mr. Duncan Greenlees, Madanapalli, wrote as follows:- One has at times had vivid flashes of a consciousness whose centre is outside the normal self and which seems to be inclusive. Without concerning the mind with philosophical concepts, how would Bhagavan advise us to work towards getting, retaining and extending those flashes? Does *abhyasa* in such experiences involve retirement?

Sri Bhagavan answered: 'Outside' — For whom is inside or outside? They can be only so long as there are the subject and object. For whom are these two again? They both will resolve into the subject only. See who is in the subject. The investigation leads you to pure consciousness beyond the subject.

Normal self is the mind. This mind is with limitations. But pure consciousness is beyond limitations and reached by investigation as above outlined.

Getting — Self is always there. One seeks to destroy the obstacles to the revelation of the Self.

Retaining — Having once gained the Self it will be understood to be Here and Now. It is never lost.

Extending — There is no extending the Self, for it is always without contraction or expansion.

Retirement — Abiding in the Self is solitude. Because there is nothing alien to the Self. Retirement must be from some one place to another. There is neither the one nor the other apart from the Self. All being the Self, retirement is impossible and inconsistent.

Abhyasa is investigation into the Self.

49

28th March, 1935

Talk 43.

Mr. S. Ranganathan, I.C.S., Collector of Vellore, Mr. S. V. Ramamurthi, I.C.S. and Mr. T. Raghaviah, late Diwan of Pudukottah State, visited the Asramam. Mr. Ranganathan asked, "Kindly instruct me as to how the mind may be controlled."

M.: There are two methods. The one is to see what the mind is; then it subsides. The second is to fix your attention on something; then the mind remains quiet.

The questioner repeated the question for further elucidation. The same answer was returned with a little more added. The questioner did not look satisfied.

Mr. Raghaviah: Men of the world that we are, we have some kind of grief or another and do not know how to get over it. We pray to God and still are not satisfied. What can we do?

M.: Trust God.

D.: We surrender; but still there is no help.

M.: Yes. If you have surrendered, you must be able to abide by the will of God and not make a grievance of what may not please you. Things may turn out differently from what they look apparently. Distress often leads men to faith in God.

D.: But we are worldly. There is the wife, there are the children, friends and relatives. We cannot ignore their existence and resign ourselves to Divine Will, without retaining some little of the personality in us.

M.: That means you have not surrendered as professed by you. You must only trust God.

Mr. Ramamurthi: Swamiji, I have read Brunton's book *A Search in Secret India,* and was much impressed by the last chapter, where he says that it is possible to be conscious without thinking. I know that one can think, remaining forgetful of the physical body. Can one think without the mind? Is it possible to gain that consciousness which is beyond thoughts?

M.: Yes. There is only one consciousness, which subsists in the waking, dream and sleep states. In sleep there is no 'I'. The 'I-thought'

50

arises on waking and then the world appears. Where was this 'I' in sleep? Was it there or was it not? It must have been there also, but not in the way that you feel now. The present is only the 'I-thought', whereas the sleeping 'I' is the real 'I'. It subsists all through. It is consciousness. If it is known you will see that it is beyond thoughts.

D.: Can we think without the mind?

M.: Thoughts may be like any other activities, not disturbing to the Supreme consciousness.

D.: Can one read others' minds?

The Master as usual told him to find his Self before worrying about others.

"Where are others apart from one's own Self?" asked the Master.

Mr. Raghaviah: How shall we correlate the higher experience with the lower experience (meaning spiritual experience with mundane affairs)?

M.: There is only one experience. What are the worldly experiences but those built up on the false 'I'? Ask the most successful man of the world if he knows his Self. He will say "No". What can anyone know without knowing the Self? All worldly knowledge is built upon such a flimsy foundation.

Mr. Ramamurthi: How to know the 'Real I' as distinct from the 'false I'.

M.: Is there anyone who is not aware of himself? Each one knows, but yet does not know, the Self. A strange paradox.

The Master added later, "If the enquiry is made whether mind exists, it will be found that mind does not exist. That is control of mind. Otherwise, if the mind is taken to exist and one seeks to control it, it amounts to mind controlling the mind, just like a thief turning out to be a policeman to catch the thief, *i.e.*, himself. Mind persists in that way alone, but eludes itself."

3rd April, 1935

Talk 44.

Mr. Ekanath Rao, an Engineer, asked Sri Bhagavan if solitude is necessary for *vichara*.

M.: There is solitude everywhere. The individual is solitary always. His business is to find it out within, and not seek it without.

D.: The work-a-day world is distracting.

M.: Do not allow yourself to be distracted. Enquire for whom there is distraction. It will not afflict you after a little practice.

D.: Even the attempt is impossible.

M.: Make it and it will be found not so difficult.

D.: But the answer does not come for the search inward.

M.: The enquirer is the answer and no other answer can come. What comes afresh cannot be true. What always is, is true.

6th April, 1935

Talk 45.

A visitor asked: The path of realisation is difficult. Worldly matters are easy of understanding, whereas this is not.

M.: Yes. The mind always seeks external knowledge, leaving aside its own inner knowledge.

D.: A stay of one day with Sri Bhagavan is good; a stay of two days is better; of three days, more so, and so on. If it is a continuous stay here, how shall we get on with our mundane work?

M.: Stay here or elsewhere must be understood to be the same and to have the same effect.

12th April, 1935

Talk 46.

After hearing the Malayalam version of *Upadesa Sara* chanted, Mr. Ramachandra Iyer of Nagercoil asked in a characteristically unsophisticated way about the mind, concentration and control. The Master said that the mind is only identity of the Self with the body. It is a false ego that is created; it creates false phenomena in its turn, and appears to move in them; all these are false. The Self is the only Reality. If the false identity vanishes the persistence of the Reality becomes apparent. It does not mean that Reality is not here and now. It is always there and eternally the same. It is also in everyone's

52

experience. For everyone knows that he is. "Who is he?" Subjectively, "Who am I?" The false ego is associated with objects; this ego itself is its own object. Objectivity is the falsity. Subject is alone the Reality. Do not confound yourself with the object, namely the body. This gives rise to the false ego, consequently of the world and your movements therein with the resulting misery. Do not think yourself to be this, that or anything; to be so and so, or to be such and such. Only leave off the falsity. The Reality will reveal itself. The scriptures say that the Self is *nityasiddha*, ever present, and yet speak of the removal of *ajnana*. If Self is (*nitya*) always and (*siddha*) present, how can there be *ajnana*? For whom is the *ajnana*? These are contradictory. But such statements are for guiding the earnest seeker in the right way. He does not readily understand the only Truth if mentioned in plain words as in *natwam naham neme janadhipah* (not thou, nor I, nor these kings ...). Sri Krishna declared the Truth, but Arjuna could not grasp it. Later Krishna plainly says that people confound Him with the body, whereas in reality He was not born nor will He die. Still Arjuna requires the whole Gita for the Truth to be made clear to him.

Look, the Self is only Be-ing, not being this or that. It is simple Being. Be — and there is an end of the ignorance. Enquire for whom is the ignorance. The ego arises when you wake up from sleep. In deep sleep you do not say that you are sleeping and that you are going to wake up or that you have been sleeping so long. But still you are there. Only when you are awake you say that you have slept. Your wakefulness comprises sleep also in it. Realise your pure Be-ing. Let there be no confusion with the body. The body is the result of thoughts. The thoughts will play as usual, but you will not be affected. You were not concerned with the body when asleep; so you can always remain.

Mr. Ekanatha Rao: How can anyone reconcile such activity with the wage-earning which is a necessity for worldly people?

M.: Actions form no bondage. Bondage is only the false notion. "I am the doer." Leave off such thoughts and let the body and senses play their role, unimpeded by your interference.

20th April, 1935

Talk 47.

A Malayalee visitor expressed his concern for the misery of the world and his opinion that 'Quest for Self' looked selfish in the midst of such suffering environments. His solution appeared to be selfless work.

M.: The sea is not aware of its wave. Similarly the Self is not aware of its ego.

Note: This makes clear what Sri Bhagavan means by quest for the source of ego.

Talk 48.

A visitor asked Sri Bhagavan, "You are Bhagavan. So you would know when I shall get *jnana*. Tell me when I shall be a *jnani*." Sri Bhagavan replied, "If I am Bhagavan there is no one besides the Self — therefore no *jnani* or *ajnani*. If otherwise I am as good as you are and know as much as yourself. Either way I cannot answer your question."

24th April, 1935

Talk 49.

Some men asked the Master questions which ultimately resolved themselves into one, that 'I' is not perceptible however much they might struggle.

The Master's reply was in the usual strain: "Who is it that says that 'I' is not perceptible? Is there an 'I' ignorant, and an 'I' elusive? Are there two 'I's in the same person? Ask yourself these questions. It is the mind which says that 'I' is not perceptible. Where is that mind from? Know the mind. You will find it a myth. King Janaka said, 'I have discovered the thief who had been ruining me so long. I will now deal with him summarily. Then I shall be happy.' Similarly it will be with others."

D.: How to know the 'I'?

M.: The 'I-I' is always there. There is no knowing it. It is not a new knowledge acquired. What is new and not here and now will be

54

evanescent only. The 'I' is always there. There is obstruction to its knowledge and it is called ignorance. Remove the ignorance and knowledge shines forth. In fact this ignorance or even knowledge is not for Atman. They are only overgrowths to be cleared off. That is why Atman is said to be beyond knowledge and ignorance. It remains as it naturally is — that is all.

D.: There is no perceptible progress in spite of our attempts.

M.: Progress can be spoken of in things to be obtained afresh. Whereas here it is the removal of ignorance and not acquisition of knowledge. What kind of progress can be expected in the quest for the Self?

D.: How to remove the ignorance?

M.: While lying in bed in Tiruvannamalai you dream in your sleep that you find yourself in another town. The scene is real to you. Your body remains here on your bed in a room. Can a town enter your room, or could you have left this place and gone elsewhere, leaving the body here? Both are impossible. Therefore your being here and seeing another town are both unreal. They appear real to the mind. The 'I' of the dream soon vanishes, then another 'I' speaks of the dream. This 'I' was not in the dream. Both the 'I's are unreal. There is the substratum of the mind which continues all along, giving rise to so many scenes. An 'I' rises forth with every thought and with its disappearance that 'I' disappears too. Many 'I's are born and die every moment. The subsisting mind is the real trouble. That is the thief according to Janaka. Find him out and you will be happy.

Talk 50.

Sri Bhagavan read out, from the *Prabuddha Bharata,* Kabir's saying that all know that the drop merges into the ocean but few know that the ocean merges into the drop. This is *para bhakti,* said he.

5th June, 1935

Talk 51.

A young Brahmin (25 years of age) came on a visit to the Master. At his sight he became hysterical and shouted *Sivoham, Aham Brahma*

55

Asmi, "You are God", "You are *Para Brahmam*". "You are my father", "Father, save me" and so on. His hysterics waxing, he beat his chest violently alternately with both his hands, shouting *Sivoham, Sivoham*. Then again he shouted hysterically gnashing his teeth, "I will stamp out materialism", as if he was crushing materialism between his teeth. Then he asked. "Either give me power, either give me power — or — or — or — I will..." He began as if to throttle himself.

When gently removed by others he fell prostrate before Sri Bhagavan, saying, "I will take refuge at the feet of my Father. Father! You are Parthasarathi, I am Arjuna. We will stamp out materialism," and so on. He was finally taken away from the presence of Maharshi. He washed himself, took some light refreshment and quietly seated himself in the hall for some hours. He abstained from the midday meal. In the afternoon he had another fit when he shouted, "I will chop off the head of Krishna, if he should come here now. He advised me to give up my job, but does not protect my mother. Or let him chop off my head," and so on.

After some hours of quiet, Sri Bhagavan asked Mr. K. L. Sarma to read out a portion of his commentary on *Anubandha* (Appendix to 40 verses). The gist of it is that people, unable to help themselves, ask for divine powers to be utilised for human welfare. This is similar to the story of a lame man who blustered, saying that he would overpower the enemy if only he were helped on to his legs. The intention is good but there is no sense of proportion. The young man on hearing it suddenly sprang to his feet, saluting Sri Bhagavan and saying "Father! Father! I was mistaken. Pardon me. Teach me. I shall abide by what you say," and so on. Then again in the evening he prostrated himself, saying, "I surrender."

9th June, 1935

Talk 52.

A man from Cocanada asked: "My mind remains clear for two or three days and turns dull for the next two or three days; and so it alternates. What is it due to?"

M.: It is quite natural; it is the play of brightness (*satva*), activity (*rajas*) and darkness (*tamas*) alternating. Do not regret the *tamas*; but when *satva* comes into play, hold on to it fast and make the best of it.

D.: What is the Heart?

M.: It is the seat (if such could be said of it) of the Self.

D.: Is it the physical heart?

M.: No. It is the seat wherefrom 'I-I' arises.

D.: What becomes of the *jiva* after death?

M.: The question is not appropriate for a *jiva* now living. A disembodied *jiva* may ask me, if convenient. In the meantime let the embodied *jiva* solve its present problem and find who he is. There will be an end of such doubts.

D.: What is *dhyana*?

M.: The word *dhyana* usually signifies meditation on some object, whereas *nididhyasana* is used for enquiry into the Self. The triads persist until the Self is realised. *Dhyana* and *nididhyasana* are the same so far as the aspirant is concerned, because they involve trinity and are synonymous with *bhakti*.

D.: How should *dhyana* be practised?

M.: *Dhyana* serves to concentrate the mind. The predominant idea keeps off all others. *Dhyana* varies according to the individual. It may be on an aspect of God, on a *mantra*, or on the Self, etc.

15th June, 1935

Talk 53.

A young man, Mr. Knowles, came for *darsan*. He had read Paul Brunton's two books. He asked: "The Buddhists say that 'I' is unreal, whereas Paul Brunton in the *Secret Path* tells us to get over the 'I-thought' and reach the state of 'I'. Which is true?"

M.: There are supposed to be two 'I's; the one is lower and unreal, of which all are aware; and the other, the higher and the real, which is to be realised.

You are not aware of yourself while asleep, you are aware in wakefulness; waking, you say that you were asleep; you did not know

57

it in the deep sleep state. So then, the idea of diversity has arisen along with the body-consciousness; this body-consciousness arose at some particular moment; it has origin and end. What originates must be something. What is that something? It is the 'I'-consciousness. Who am I? Whence am I? On finding the source, you realise the state of Absolute Consciousness.

D.: Who is this 'I'? It seems to be only a continuum of sense-impression. The Buddhist idea seems to be so too.

M.: The world is not external. The impressions cannot have an outer origin. Because the world can be cognised only by consciousness. The world does not say that it exists. It is your impression. Even so this impression is not consistent and not unbroken. In deep sleep the world is not cognised; and so it exists not for a sleeping man. Therefore the world is the sequence of the ego. Find out the ego. The finding of its source is the final goal.

D.: I believe that we should not inflict suffering on other lives. Should we then endure the mosquito bite and submit to it also?

M.: You do not like to suffer yourself. How can you inflict suffering on others? Just keep off mosquitoes since you suffer by their stings.

D.: Is it right that we kill other lives, *e.g.*, mosquitoes, bugs?

M.: Everyone is a suicide. The eternal, blissful, and natural state has been smothered by this life of ignorance. In this way the present life is due to the killing of the eternal, pristine Being. Is it not a case of suicide? So then, everyone is a suicide. Why worry about murders and killing?

In the course of a later talk the visitor said: "The world sends impressions and I awake!"

M.: Can the world exist without someone to perceive it? Which is prior? The Being-consciousness or the rising-consciousness? The Being-consciousness is always there, eternal and pure. The rising-consciousness rises forth and disappears. It is transient.

D.: Does not the world exist for others even when I am asleep?

M.: Such a world mocks at you also for knowing it without knowing yourself. The world is the result of your mind. Know your

58

mind. Then see the world. You will realise that it is not different from the Self.

D.: Is not Maharshi aware of himself and his surroundings, as clearly as I am?

M.: To whom is the doubt? The doubts are not for the realised. They are only for the ignorant.

16th June, 1935

Talk 54.

An Andhra Pandit — an elderly gentleman — had some doubts regarding Kavyakantha's exposition of Advaita. He has found it in books that Brahman is free from *sajatiya, vijatiya* and *swagata bheda*. Such conditions are satisfied in *vivarta vada* but not in *parinama vada*. In the latter, *swagata bheda* is bound to be. The Master pointed out that Dakshinamurti did not teach anything of the kind. He did not say that Brahman is related to *Sakti* or not related. All that was, was only silence; and the doubts of the *sishyas* (disciples) were cleared. The significance is that there is nothing to be learnt, discussed and concluded. Everyone knows 'I am.' There is the confusion that the 'I' is the body. Because the 'I' arises from the Absolute and gives rise to *buddhi* (Intellect). In *buddhi* the 'I' looks the size and shape of the body, *na medhaya* means that Brahman cannot be apprehended by *buddhi*. Brahman → *aham* ('I-I') → *buddhi* (intellect).

How can such *buddhi* crossing over *aham* discover Brahman? It is impossible. Just get over the false conception of the 'I' being the body. Discover to whom the thoughts arise. If the present 'I'-ness vanishes, the discovery is complete. What remains over is the pure Self. Compare deep sleep and wakefulness. Diversity and body are found only in the latter. In the former the Self remains without the perception of body or of the world. Happiness reigns there.

The *Sruti vakya, 'Aham Brahmasmi'*, relates to the state and not the mode of mind. One cannot become Brahman by continuing to repeat the *mantra*. It means that Brahman is not elsewhere. It is your Self. Find that Self; Brahman is found. Do not attempt to reach Brahman as if it were in some far off place.

The Pandit remarked that thoughts are so persistent that the *aham* cannot be reached.

The Master said: The *Brahma akara vritti* helps to turn the mind away from other thoughts. Either some such practice is necessary or association with sadhus should be made. The sadhu has already overcome the mind and remains in Peace. His proximity helps to bring about such condition in others. Otherwise there is no meaning in seeking a sadhu's company.

Deho aham (I am the body) is limitation and is the root of all mean and selfish actions and desires.

Brahma aham (I am Brahman) is passing beyond limitation and signifies sympathy, charity, love etc., which are divine and virtuous.

D.: How does a *grihasta* (householder) fare in the scheme of *moksha* (liberation)?

M.: Why do you think you are a *grihasta*? If you go out as a *sanyasi*, a similar thought (that you are a *sanyasi*) will haunt you. Whether you continue in the household, or renounce it and go to the forest, your mind haunts you. The ego is the source of thoughts. It creates the body and the world and makes you think you are a *grihasta*. If you renounce the world, it will only substitute the thought *sanyasi* for *grihasta* and the environments of the forest for those of the household. But the mental obstacles are always there. They even increase in new surroundings. There is no help in the change of environment. The obstacle is the mind. It must be got over whether at home or in the forest. If you can do it in the forest, why not in the home? Therefore why change the environment? Your efforts can be made even now, in whatever environment you may be.

The environment never abandons you, according to your desire. Look at me. I left home. Look at yourselves. You have come here leaving the home environment. What do you find here? Is this different from what you left? Even if one is immersed in *nirvikalpa samadhi* for years together, when he emerges from it he will find himself in the environment which he is bound to have. That is the reason for the Acharya emphasising *sahaja samadhi* in preference to *nirvikalpa samadhi* in his excellent work *Viveka Chudamani*.

One should be in spontaneous *samadhi* — that is, in one's pristine state — in the midst of every environment.

Later on Sri Bhagavan said: "Control of breath may be internal or external."

The *antah pranayama* (the internal breath-regulation) is as follows:-

Naham chinta (I-am-not-the-body idea) is *rechaka* (exhalation).

Koham (who am I?) is *puraka* (inhalation).

Soham (I am He) is *kumbhaka* (retention of breath).

Doing thus, the breath becomes automatically controlled.

Bahih pranayama (external control) is for one not endowed with strength to control the mind. There is no way so sure as that; or a *sadhu's* company. The external practice must be resorted to by a wise man if he does not enjoy a *sadhu's* company. If in a *sadhu's* company the *sadhu* provides the needed strength, though unseen by others, *Pranayama* need not be exactly as described in *hatha* Yoga. If engaged in *japa, dhyana, bhakti*, etc., just a little control of breath will suffice to control the mind. The mind is the rider and the breath the horse. *Pranayama* is a check on the horse. By that check the rider is checked.

Pranayama may be done just a little. To watch the breath is one way of doing it. The mind abstracted from other activities is engaged in watching the breath. That controls the breath; and in its turn the mind is controlled.

If unable to do so, *rechaka* and *puraka* need not be practised. Breath may be retained a short while in *japa, dhyana*, etc. Then, too, good results will follow.

18th June, 1935

Talk 55.

D.: Can *advaita* be realised by *japa* of holy names; say Rama, Krishna, etc.?

M.: Yes.

D.: Is it not a means of an inferior order?

M.: Have you been told to make *japa* or to discuss its order in the scheme of things?

Silence.

22nd June, 1935

Talk 56.

A youth of twenty asked how to realise the Self. He sat down in silence and waited more than an hour and then was about to leave. While doing so, he asked:

D.: How to realise Self?

M.: Whose Self? Find out.

D.: Who am I?

M.: Find it yourself.

D.: I do not know.

M.: Think. Who is it that says "I do not know"? What is not known? In that statement, who is the 'I'?

D.: Somebody in me.

M.: Who is the somebody? In whom?

D.: Maybe some power.

M.: Find it.

D.: How to realise Brahman?

M.: Without knowing the Self why do you seek to know Brahman?

D.: The *sastras* say Brahman pervades all and me too.

M.: Find the 'I' in me and then there will be time to think of Brahman.

D.: Why was I born?

M.: Who was born? The answer is the same for all of your questions.

D.: Who am I then?

M.: (Smiling) Have you come to examine me and ask me? You must say who you are.

D.: In deep sleep the soul leaves the body and remains elsewhere. When it re-enters I awake. Is it so?

M.: What is it that leaves the body?

D.: The power, perhaps.

62

M.: Find out the power.

D.: The body is composed of five elements. What are the elements?

M.: Without knowing the Self how do you aim at knowing the elements?

The young man sat awhile and left with permission. The Master remarked later: "All right. It will work."

23rd June, 1935

Talk 57.

Sri Bhagavan said that *sushumna* is the name mostly mentioned in scriptures. Other names also occur; *e.g., para, atma, amrita.* It is also stated that *sushumna* becomes *leena* (merged in *para*). So it may be said that *para* is the terminology of *jnana*, whereas *sushumna* is that of *Yoga.*

24th June, 1935

A DOUBT IN 'SRI RAMANA GITA' ANSWERED

Chapter XIV, Stanza 10 reads: "With yet further progress, invisibility also may result. Such an one, being pure consciousness only, flourishes as a *siddha.*"

Chapter XVIII, Last Stanza reads: "The glory of the *siddhas* is past imagination, they are equal to Siva, yea Siva himself, in being able to grant boons."

The meaning is that, with Self-Realization, real and incessant *tapas* results. With the maturing of such *tapas* some *jnanis* can make their bodies intangible and invisible. They are known as *siddhas.*

Later, "the greatness of the *siddhas* is incomprehensible. They are equal to Siva and can even grant boons." So said Sri Bhagavan.

There is an Upanishad *mantra, atmajnam hyarchayet bhutikamah* (one desirous of liberation or wealth must serve a Self-realised Sage). Here is no mention of *siddha* for granting boons. The *jnani* can do so. The *mantras* again, *swe mahimni pratishtitah* (abiding in his own grandeur), *anantam Brahma* (Brahman is infinite), will seem confounding when read with the *slokas* cited above. *Sarvam*

Khalvidam Brahma (All this is Brahman); *Brahmavid Brahmaiva Bhavati* (the knower of Brahman becomes Brahman Itself), show that a *jnani* is *sarvajna* (all-knower). What then is the distinction between the *jnani* and the *siddha*, and the ability of the latter to grant boons, implying the absence of it in the former?

This was the doubt. The master explained: "The Gita questions were asked in a certain spirit. The answers were according to it. People look to the body only and they want *siddhis* also. With Self-Realisation no powers can extend even into it, and how can they extend beyond? People anxious for *siddhis* are not content with their idea of *jnana* and so want *siddhis* associated with it. They are likely to neglect the supreme happiness of *jnana* and aspire for *siddhis*. For this they are going through the by-lanes instead of the royal path and so will likely lose their way. In order to guide them aright and keep them on the royal road alone the *siddhis* are said to accompany *jnana*. In fact *jnana* comprises all, and a *jnani* will not waste even a thought on them. Let the people get *jnana* and then seek *siddhis* if they so desire.

I have said: *sarira samsrayah siddhayah* (the *siddhis* relate to the body), because their outlook is concerning the body. A *jnani* and *siddha* are not different. In *varan datum* (to bestow boons) the boons include *atmalabha* (the gain of Self) also. The *siddhis* are not merely of an inferior order but of the highest order.

The *sastras* are meant to suit varying conditions. Their spirit remains the same. In *Halasya Mahima* there is a chapter on the eight-fold *siddhis*. There Siva says that His *bhakta* never wastes a thought on them. Again Siva says that He never grants boons. The desires of the devotees are fulfilled according to their *prarabdha* only. When *Iswara* Himself says so, what of others? In order to display *siddhis* there must be others to recognise them. That means there is no *jnana* in the one who displays them. Therefore *siddhis* are not worthy of any thought. *Jnana* alone is to be aimed at and gained.

Sri Ramana Gita Chapter XVII, Verse 4, Translation in Tamil is inaccurate.

Sri Bhagavan pointed out the inaccuracy and corrected it. Vaidharbha's question was: "In practice, the thoughts are found to manifest and subside alternately. Is this *jnana*?" Sri Bhagavan explained the doubt as follows:

Some people think that there are different stages in *jnana*. The Self is *nitya aparoksha, i.e.*, ever-realised, knowingly or unknowingly. *Sravana*, they argue, should therefore be *aparoksha jnana* (directly experienced) and not *paroksha jnana* (indirect knowledge). But *jnana* should result in *duhkha nivriti* (loss of misery) whereas *sravana* alone does not bring it about. Therefore they say, though *aparoksha*, it is not unshaken; the rising of *vasanas* is the cause of its being weak (not unchanging); when the *vasanas* are removed, *jnana* becomes unshaken and bears fruit.

Others say *sravana* is only *paroksha jnana*. By *manana* (reflection) it becomes *aparoksha* spasmodically. The obstruction to its continuity is the *vasanas:* they rise up with reinforced vigour after *manana*. They must be held in check. Such vigilance consists in remembering = "I am not the body" and adhering to the *aparoksha anubhava* (direct experience) which has been had in course of *manana* (reflection). Such practice is called *nididhyasana* and eradicates the *vasanas*. Then dawns the *sahaja* state. That is *jnana*, sure.

The *aparoksha* in *manana* cannot effect *dukha nivritti* (loss of misery) and cannot amount to *moksha, i.e.*, release from bondage because the *vasanas* periodically overpower the *jnana*. Hence it is *adridha* (weak) and becomes firm after the *vasanas* have been eradicated by *nididhyasana* (one-pointedness).

SRI RAMANA GITA AGAIN

Mr. T. K. S. Iyer, a devotee, was speaking of the *chakras* Sri Bhagavan said: Atman (the Self) alone is to be realised. Its realisation holds all else in its compass. *Sakti*, Ganapati; *siddhis*, etc., are included in it. Those who speak of these have not realised the Atman. Atman is in the heart and *is* the Heart itself. The manifestation is in the brain. The passage from the heart to the brain might be considered to be through *sushumna* or a nerve with any other name. The Upanishads say *pare leena* — meaning that *sushumna* or such *nadis* are all comprised in *para, i.e.*, the *atma nadi*. The yogis say that the current rising up to *sahasrara* (brain) ends there. That experience is not complete. For *jnana*, they must come to the Heart. *Hridaya* (Heart) is the alpha and omega.

4th July, 1935

SRIMAD BHAGAVAD GITA

Talk 58.

Mr. Ranganathan, I. C. S: In *Srimad Bhagavad Gita* there is a passage: One's own *dharma* is the best; an alien *dharma* is full of risks. What is the significance of one's own *dharma*?

M.: It is usually interpreted to mean the duties of the orders and of the different castes. The physical environment must also be taken into consideration.

D.: If *varnasrama dharma* be meant, such *dharma* prevails only in India. On the other hand the *Gita* should be universally applicable.

M.: There is *varnasrama* in some form or other in every land. The significance is that one should hold on to the single Atman and not swerve therefrom. That is the whole gist of it.

sva = one's own, *i.e.*, of the Self, of the Atman.

para = the other's, *i.e.*, of the non-self, of the *anatma*.

Atma Dharma is inherence in the Self. There will be no distraction and no fear. Troubles arise only when there is a second to oneself. If the Atman be realised to be only unitary, there is no second and therefore no cause for fear. The man, as he is now, confounds the *anatma* (non-Self) *dharma* with *atma* (the Self) *dharma* and suffers. Let him know the Self and abide in it; there is an end of fear, and there are no doubts.

Even if interpreted as *varnasrama dharma* the significance is only this much. Such *dharma* bears fruit only when done selflessly. That is, one must realise that he is not the doer, but that he is only a tool of some Higher Power. Let the Higher Power do what is inevitable and let me act only according to its dictates. The actions are not mine. Therefore the result of the actions cannot be mine. If one thinks and acts so, where is the trouble? Be it *varnasrama dharma* or *loukika dharma* (worldly activities), it is immaterial. Finally, it amounts to this:

66

sva = *atmanah* (of the Self)

para = *anaatmanah* (of the non-self)

Such doubts are natural. The orthodox interpretation cannot be reconciled with the life of a modern man obliged to work for his livelihood in different capacities.

A man from Pondy interposed: *Sarva dharmaan parityajya maamekam saranam vraja* (leaving all duties surrender to me only).

Sri Bhagavan: (All) *Sarva* is only *anaatmanah* (of the non-self); the emphasis is on *ekam* (only). To the man who has strong hold of the *eka* (one) where are the *dharmas*? It means, "Be sunk in the Self."

D.: The Gita was taught for action.

M.: What does the Gita say? Arjuna refused to fight.

Krishna said, "So long as you refuse to fight, you have the sense of doership. Who are you to refrain or to act? Give up the notion of doership. Until that sense disappears you are bound to act. You are being manipulated by a Higher Power. You are admitting it by your own refusal to submit to it. Instead recognise the Power and submit as a tool. (Or to put it differently), if you refuse you will be forcibly drawn into it. Instead of being an unwilling worker, be a willing one.

"Rather, be fixed in the Self and act according to nature without the thought of doership. Then the results of action will not affect you. That is manliness and heroism."

Thus, 'inherence in the Self' is the sum and substance of *Gita* teaching. Finally, the Master Himself added, "If a man be established in the Self these doubts would not arise. They arise only until he is established there."

D.: Then of what use is such reply to the enquirer?

M.: The words still have force and will surely operate in due course.

Talk 59.

A moulvi asked: How does sleep overtake one?

M.: If the enquirer knows who is awake in the wakeful condition he will also know how sleep comes on. The enquiry arises only to the waking man and not to the sleeper. It must be easier to know the waking Self than the sleeping Self.

D.: I know how I awoke. But I do not know how sleep comes on. I am aware of my wakeful state. For instance if anyone takes away my stick I prevent his doing so, whereas I cannot do so in sleep or in dream. The proof of wakefulness is evident. But what is the proof of sleep?

M.: Your ignorance is the evidence of sleep: your awareness is that of wakefulness.

D.: My wakefulness is known by the opening of my eye. But how does sleep overtake me?

M.: In the same way as sleep overtakes you, wakefulness also overtakes you.

D.: But I do not perceive how sleep comes on in the same way as I know my wakefulness.

M.: Never mind.

D.: Please describe what is sleep, without illustrations. Sleep by itself should be known. I want a real picture of sleep.

M.: Such picture is sleep itself.

D.: Is it better to reach salvation, being married, or being a hermit?

M.: Whatever you think better.

D.: Visvamitra had no fall when in the married state, whereas he had a fall in his hermit life. Does it not apply to others also?

M.: Visvamitra was as pure in the hermit life as when he was married. There was no difference. He was as contaminated when married as when he was a hermit.

D.: Was he a *rishi*?

M.: When contaminated he was not a *rishi*.

D.: Can he become a *rishi* even afterwards?

M.: Yes. By proper *bhakti* he could become a good *rishi*. Repentance and prayer will set him right.

D.: With all your penance for so many years what have you got?

M.: I have got what need be got. I see what need be seen.

D.: Can all see the same?

M.: I see only just what all do. It is immanent in all.

68

D.: Is this the way for seeing It?

M.: Method may be anything. From whatever directions the pilgrims may foregather, they must enter the Kaaba only by one route (passage) or all gather only to enter the Kaaba.

D.: Please tell me two *upadesas* on the way to salvation as known by you.

M.: What *upadesa* do I know? Everything is *upadesa*. Worship of God is the only *upadesa*.

5th July, 1935

ON *MOUNA* (SILENCE)

Talk 60.

Sri Bhagavan: The silence of solitude is forced. Restrained speech in society amounts to silence. For the man then controls his speech. The speaker must come forth before he speaks. If engaged otherwise speech is restrained. Introverted mind is otherwise active and is not anxious to speak.

Mouna as a disciplinary measure is meant for limiting the mental activities due to speech. If the mind is otherwise controlled disciplinary *mouna* is unnecessary. For *mouna* becomes natural.

Vidyaranya has said that twelve years' forced *mouna* brings about absolute *mouna* — that is, makes one unable to speak. It is more like a mute animal than otherwise. That is not *mouna*.

Mouna is constant speech. Inactivity is constant activity.

6th July, 1935

Talk 61.

Mr. Ekanatha Rao: How is *dhyana* practised — with eyes open or closed?

M.: It may be done either way. The point is that the mind must be introverted and kept active in its pursuit. Sometimes it happens that when the eyes are closed the latent thoughts rush forth with great vigour. It may also be difficult to introvert the mind with the eyes open. It requires strength of mind to do so. The mind is contaminated when it takes in objects. Otherwise, it is pure. The main factor in *dhyana* is to keep the mind active in its own pursuit without taking in external impressions or thinking of other matters.

Talk 62.

Mr. Ekanatha Rao: What is *sphurana* (a kind of indescribable but palpable sensation in the heart centre)?

M.: Sphurana is felt on several occasions, such as in fear, excitement, etc. Although it is always and all over, yet it is felt at a particular centre and on particular occasions. It is also associated with antecedent causes and confounded with the body. Whereas, it is all alone and pure; it is the Self. If the mind be fixed on the *sphurana* and one senses it continuously and automatically it is realisation.

Again *sphurana* is the foretaste of Realisation. It is pure. The subject and object proceed from it. If the man mistakes himself for the subject, objects must necessarily appear different from him. They are periodically withdrawn and projected, creating the world and the subject's enjoyment of the same. If, on the other hand, the man feels himself to be the screen on which the subject and object are projected there can be no confusion, and he can remain watching their appearance and disappearance without any perturbation to the Self.

Talk 63.

A high officer asked: If juniors are promoted over oneself the mind is perturbed. Will the enquiry, 'Who am I?' help the man to soothe the mind under such circumstances?

M.: Yes. Quite so. The enquiry 'Who am I?' turns the mind inward and makes it calm.

D.: I have faith in *murti dhyana* (worship of form). Will it not help me to gain *jnana*?

M.: Surely it will. *Upasana* helps concentration of mind. Then the mind is free from other thoughts and is full of the meditated form. The mind becomes it — and thus quite pure. Then think who is the worshipper. The answer is 'I', *i.e.*, the Self. So the Self is gained ultimately.

The present difficulty is that the man thinks that he is the doer. But it is a mistake. It is the Higher Power which does everything and the man is only a tool. If he accepts that position he is free from troubles; otherwise he courts them. Take for instance, the figure in a *gopuram* (temple tower), where it is made to appear to bear the burden of the tower on its shoulders. Its posture and look are a picture of great strain while bearing the very heavy burden of the tower. But think. The tower is built on the earth and it rests on its foundations. The figure (like Atlas bearing the earth) is a part of the tower, but is made to look as if it bore the tower. Is it not funny? So is the man who takes on himself the sense of doing.

Then the Malayalam version of *Ulladu Narpadu* was read out by a devotee for the benefit of the visitor.

After hearing it, he asked: What about the reference to duality in practice and unity at the end?

M.: Some people think that one must begin practice with dualistic idea. It refers to them. They say that there is God; the man must worship and meditate; ultimately the *jiva* merges into God. Others say that the Supreme Being and the *jiva* are always apart and never merge into each other. Howsoever it may be at the end, let us not trouble ourselves about it now. All are agreed that the *jiva* IS. Let the man find out the *jiva, i.e.,* his Self. Then there will be time to find out if the Self should merge in the Supreme, is a part thereof, or remains different from it. Let us not forestall the conclusion. Keep an open mind, dive within and find out the Self. The truth will itself dawn upon you. Why should you determine beforehand if the finality is unity absolute or qualified, or duality? There is no meaning in it. The ascertainment is now made by logic and by intellect. The intellect derives light from the Self (the Higher Power). How can the reflected and partial light of the intellect envisage the whole and the original Light? The intellect cannot reach the Self and how can it ascertain its nature?

Such is the significance of the reference.

D.: One of the stanzas says that the scriptures so scrupulously studied in the earlier stages are ultimately of no use. At what stage do they become useless?

M.: When their essence is realised. The scriptures are useful to indicate the existence of the Higher Power (the Self) and the way to

71

gain it. Their essence is that much only. When that is assimilated the rest is useless. But they are voluminous, adapted to the development of the seeker. As one rising up in the scale finds the regions one has passed to be only steps to the higher stage, and so on, the steps ascended become *purvapaksha* successively until the goal is gained. When the goal is reached it remains alone, and all the rest becomes useless. That is how the *sastras* become useless. We read so much. Do we remember all that we read? But have we forgotten the essentials? The essential soaks in the mind and the rest is forgotten. So it is with the *sastras*.

The fact is that the man considers himself limited and there arises the trouble. The idea is wrong. He can see it for himself. In sleep there was no world, no ego (no limited self), and no trouble. Something wakes up from that happy state and says 'I'. To that ego the world appears. Being a speck in the world he wants more and gets into trouble.

How happy he was before the rising of the ego! Only the rise of the ego is the cause of the present trouble. Let him trace the ego to its source and he will reach that undifferentiated happy state which is sleepless sleep. The Self remains ever the same, here and now. There is nothing more to be gained. Because the limitations have wrongly been assumed there is the need to transcend them. It is like the ten ignorant fools who forded a stream and on reaching the other shore counted themselves to be nine only. They grew anxious and grieved over the loss of the unknown tenth man. A wayfarer, on ascertaining the cause of their grief, counted them all and found them to be ten. But each one of them had counted the others leaving himself out. The wayfarer gave each in succession a blow telling them to count the blows. They counted ten and were satisfied. The moral is that the tenth man was not got anew. He was all along there, but ignorance caused grief to all of them.

Again, a woman wore a necklace round her neck but forgot it. She began to search for it and made enquiries. A friend of hers, finding out what she was looking for, pointed out the necklace round the seeker's neck. She felt it with her hands and was happy. Did she get the necklace anew? Here again ignorance caused grief and knowledge happiness.

Similarly also with the man and the Self. There is nothing to be gained anew. Ignorance of the Self is the cause of the present misery; knowledge of the Self brings about happiness.

Moreover, if anything is to be got anew it implies its previous absence. What remained once absent might vanish again. So there would be no permanency in salvation. Salvation is permanent because the Self is here and now and eternal.

Thus the man's efforts are directed towards the removal of ignorance. Wisdom seems to dawn, though it is natural and ever present.

The visitor, while taking leave, saluted the master, and said, "It is said that the victim in the tiger's mouth is gone for ever."

The reference is to a passage in Who am I? where it is stated that a disciple can never revert to the world after he has once fallen into the field of the Guru's gracious look as surely as the prey in the tiger's jaws cannot escape.

Talk 64.

News of someone's death was brought to Sri Bhagavan. He said, "Good. The dead are indeed happy. They have got rid of the troublesome overgrowth — the body. The dead man does not grieve. The survivors grieve for the man who is dead. Do men fear sleep? On the contrary sleep is courted and on waking up every man says that he slept happily. One prepares the bed for sound sleep. Sleep is temporary death. Death is longer sleep. If the man dies while yet alive he need not grieve over others' death. One's existence is evident with or without the body, as in waking, dream and sleep. Then why should one desire continuance of the bodily shackles? Let the man find out his undying Self and die and be immortal and happy."

13th July, 1935

Talk 65.

A visitor: Is the *jagat* (world) perceived even after Self-Realization?

M.: From whom is this question? Is it from a *jnani* or from an *ajnani*?

73

D.: From an *ajnani*.

M.: Realise to whom the question arises. It can be answered if it arises after knowing the doubter. Can the *jagat* or the body say that it is? Or does the seer say that the *jagat* or the body is? The seer must be there to see the objects. Find out the seer first. Why worry yourself now with what will be in the hereafter?

Sri Bhagavan continued: What does it matter if the *jagat* is perceived or not perceived? Have you lost anything by your perception of *jagat* now? Or do you gain anything where there is no such perception in your deep sleep? It is immaterial whether the world is perceived or not perceived.

The *ajnani* sees the *jnani* active and is confounded. The *jagat* is perceived by both; but their outlooks differ. Take the instance of the cinema. There are pictures moving on the screen. Go and hold them. What do you hold? It is only the screen. Let the pictures disappear. What remains over? The screen again. So also here. Even when the world appears, see to whom it appears. Hold the substratum of the 'I'. After the substratum is held what does it matter if the world appears or disappears?

The *ajnani* takes the world to be real; whereas the *jnani* sees it only as the manifestation of the Self. It is immaterial if the Self manifests itself or ceases to do so.

15th July, 1935

Talk 66.

A letter was received containing some learned questions pertaining to memory, sleep and death. It looked, at first sight, that they were cogent yet baffling to answer. But when the Master was approached on the subject he disentangled the skein very nicely, pointing out that all such confusion was due to the non-differentiation of the real 'I' from the false 'I'. The attributes and modes pertain to the latter and not to the former. One's efforts are directed only to remove one's ignorance. Afterwards they cease, and the real Self is found to be always there. No effort is needed to remain as the Self.

74

21st July, 1935

Talk 67.

A visitor, Mr. K. S. N. Iyer of the South Indian Railway, said, "There is a trifling halting-place in my meditation. When I ask myself, 'Who am I?' my reasoning proceeds as follows; I see my hand. Who sees it? My eye. How to see the eye? In a mirror. Similarly to see me, there must be a mirror. 'Which is to supply the place of the mirror in me?' is my question."

M.: Then why do you enquire, "Who am I?" Why do you say you are troubled and so on? You could as well remain quiet. Why do you rise out of your composure?

D.: Enquiring thus helps me to concentrate. Is concentration the only benefit?

M.: What more do you want? Concentration is the thing. What makes you come out of your quiet?

D.: Because I am drawn out.

M.: Enquiry of "Who am I?" means finding the source of 'I'. When that is found, that which you seek is accomplished.

(The gist of Sri Bhagavan's words seems to be that one should make a concerted effort and not give it up baffled, with a defeatist mentality.)

Talk 68.

Dr. Radhakamal Mukerjee, a well-known Professor, fair man of middle age, with a peaceful look, practising yoga or meditation, has had some occult experiences and desires the mystery to be unravelled by the Master. He has written a book and had it published by Messrs. Longmans Green & Co., London. He finds Self-Realisation hard to attain and requires the Master's help. His question: "The *upanishadic* method of meditation has now disappeared. There was a great sage in Bengal who instructed me in it. After long years of discipline and practice I am having some mystic experiences. I feel sometimes that *Bhuma* (Supreme Consciousness) is infinitude and that I am finite consciousness. Is that correct?"

M.: Bhuma (Perfection) alone is. It is Infinite. There arises from it this finite consciousness taking on an *upadhi* (limiting adjunct).

75

This is *abhasa* or reflection. Merge this individual consciousness into the Supreme One. That is what should be done.

D.: *Bhuma* is an attribute of Supreme Consciousness.

M.: *Bhuma* is the Supreme — *yatra naanyat pasyati yatra naanyat srunoti sa bhuma* (where one does not see any other, hears nothing, it is Perfection). It is indefinable and indescribable. It is as it is.

D.: There is a vastness experienced. Probably it is just below *Bhuma* but close to it. Am I right?

M.: *Bhuma* alone is. Nothing else. It is the mind, which says all this.

D.: Transcending the mind I feel the vastness.

M.: Yes, Yes....

The professor turned to the lady seated just a little further away from him and interpreted in Hindi to her.

She: What is the difference between meditation and distraction?

M.: No difference. When there are thoughts, it is distraction: when there are no thoughts, it is meditation. However, meditation is only practice (as distinguished from the real state of Peace.)

She: How to practice meditation?

M.: Keep off thoughts.

She: How to reconcile work with meditation?

M.: Who is the worker? Let him who works ask the question. You are always the Self. You are not the mind. It is the mind which raises these questions. Work proceeds, always in the presence of the Self only. Work is no hindrance to realisation. It is the mistaken identity of the worker that troubles one. Get rid of the false identity.

The Professor: Is not the state of non-consciousness close to Infinite Consciousness?

M.: Consciousness alone remains and nothing more.

D.: Sri Bhagavan's silence is itself a powerful force. It brings about a certain peace of mind in us.

M.: Silence is never-ending speech. Vocal speech obstructs the other speech of silence. In silence one is in intimate contact with the surroundings. The silence of Dakshinamurti removed the doubts of the four sages. *Mouna vyakhya prakatita tatvam* (Truth expounded by silence.) Silence is said to be exposition. Silence is so potent.

For vocal speech, organs of speech are necessary and they precede speech. But the other speech lies even beyond thought. It is in short transcendent speech or unspoken words, *para vak*.

D.: Is there knowledge in Realisation?

M.: Absence of knowledge is sleep. There is knowledge in Realisation. But this knowledge differs from the ordinary one of the relation of subject and object. It is absolute knowledge. Knowledge has two meanings:

(1) *vachyartha* = *vritti* = Literal meaning.

(2) *lakshyartha* = *Jnana* = *Self* = *Swarupa* = Secondary significance.

D.: With *vritti* one sees knowledge.

M.: Quite so, he also confounds *vritti* with knowledge. *Vritti* is a mode of mind. You are not the mind. You are beyond it.

The Lady: There is sometimes an irresistible desire to remain in *Brahma-akara-vritti*.

M.: It is good. It must be cultivated until it becomes *sahaja* (natural). Then it culminates as *swarupa*, one's own self.

Later Sri Bhagavan explained: *Vritti* is often mistaken for consciousness. It is only a phenomenon and operates in the region of *abhasa* (reflected consciousness). The knowledge lies beyond relative knowledge and ignorance. It is not in the shape of *vritti*. There are no subject and object in it.

Vritti belongs to the *rajasic* (active) mind. The *satvic* mind (mind is repose) is free from it. The *satvic* is the witness of the *rajasic*. It is no doubt true consciousness. Still it is called *satvic* mind because the knowledge of being witness is the function of *abhasa* (reflected consciousness) only. Mind is the *abhasa*. Such knowledge implies mind. But the mind is by itself inoperative. Therefore it is called *satvic* mind.

Such is the *jivanmukta's* state. It is also said that his mind is dead. Is it not a paradox that a *jivanmukta* has a mind and that it is dead? This has to be conceded in argument with ignorant folk.

77

It is also said that Brahman is only the *jivanmukta's* mind. How can one speak of him as *Brahmavid* (knower of Brahman). Brahman can never be an object to be known. This is, however, in accordance with common parlance.

Satvic mind is surmised of the *jivanmukta* and of *Iswara*. "Otherwise," they argue, "how does the *jivanmukta* live and act?" The *satvic* mind has to be admitted as a concession to argument.

The *satvic* mind is in fact the Absolute consciousness. The object to be witnessed and the witness finally merge together and Absolute consciousness alone reigns supreme. It is not a state of *sunya* (blank) or ignorance. It is the *swarupa* (Real Self). Some say that mind arises from consciousness followed by reflection (*abhasa*); others say that the *abhasa* (reflection) arises first followed by the mind. In fact both are simultaneous.

The Professor asked Sri Bhagavan to extend His Grace to him although he would soon be a thousand miles off. Sri Bhagavan said that time and space are only concepts of mind. But *swarupa* (the Real Self) lies beyond mind, time and space. Distance does not count in the Self.

The lady with him was most reluctant to leave the Master and return home. The Master said, "Think that you are always in my presence. That will make you feel right." They left after dusk.

Talk 69.

There were reports of the above said Professor's University lectures in the *Hindu*. The lecturer had emphasised the necessity for birth control and discussed the various possibilities of making the man feel his responsibilities so that birth control might be automatic. The Master, on hearing it, casually remarked. "Let them find out the method of dying." [Here death refers to that of the ego (*ahankar*).]

24th July, 1935

Talk 70.

Sri Raju Sastrigal asked Sri Bhagavan about *nada, bindu* and *kala*.

M.: They are in Vedanta terminology *prana, mana, buddhi* (the life-current, mind and intellect). In the Tantras *nada* is said to be

78

subtle sound with *tejas* — light — in it. This light is said to be the body of Siva. When it develops and sound is submerged, it becomes *bindu*. To be full of light (*tejomaya*) is the aim. *Kala* is a part of the *bindu*.

Talk 71.

CHRONOLOGICAL SEQUENCE OF THE MASTER'S STAY IN DIFFERENT PLACES AT TIRUVANNAMALAI

1896. Arrived at Tiruvannamalai and stayed in the temple premises, beneath the tree, in the interior of the underground cellar, *Pathala Lingam*, sometimes in the *gopurams*, etc.

1897 (early), removed to Gurumurtam. Stayed in the shrine and in the adjoining mango grove (18 months).

1898 (September) in Pavalakunru.

1899 (February) on the hill in caves, the mango tree cave and Virupaksha cave.

1905. Stayed in Pachiamman Koil for six months during the plague ravages. Again on the hill.

1908. January, February and March in Pachiamman Koil. Again on the hill.

1916. Skandasramam.

1922. The Ramanasramam site on the southern slope of the Hill.

25th September, 1935
Talk 72.

Mr. K. S. N. Iyer, a railway officer, asked about *japa*.

M.: The utterance and then remembrance and later meditation are the successive stages finally ending in involuntary and eternal *japa*. The *japakarta* (doer of *japa*) of that kind is the Self. Of all the *japas*, 'Who am I?' is the best.

27th September, 1935
Talk 73.

Mr. Ekanatha Rao, the engineer, asked, "What about the despondency of not obtaining any encouragement from the Master — much less his Grace?"

M.: It is ignorance only. The quest must be made as to who is despondent and so on. It is the phantom of the ego arising after sleep which falls a prey to such thoughts. In deep sleep the person was not afflicted. Who is afflicted now while awake? The sleep state is about the normal one. Let him search and find out.

D.: But there is no incentive for want of encouragement.

M.: Does not one find some kind of peace while in meditation? That is the sign of progress. That peace will be deeper and more prolonged with continued practice. It will also lead to the goal. *Bhagavad Gita* — Chapter XIV — the final verses speak of *gunatita* (one who has transcended the *gunas*). That is the final stage.

The earlier stages are *asuddha satva* (impure being), *misra satva* (mixed being), and *suddha satva* (Pure Being).

Of these, the impure being is when overpowered by *rajas* and *tamas*; the mixed being is that state in which the being — *satva* — asserts itself spasmodically; the *suddha satva* overpowers *rajas* and *tamas*. After these successive stages there comes the state transcending *gunas*.

Talk 74.

Mr. Frydman, the engineer, writes in one of his letters: "Maharshi is with me not only when I think of Him but also when I am not thinking of Him. Otherwise, how do I live?"

Talk 75.

Mr. Grant Duff, formerly in a foreign embassy, writes: ....Pay my respects to Maharshi. He appears to me in my thoughts not only as an *answer* to my questions but also as *Presence*....

29th September, 1935

Talk 76.

Mr. K. S. N. Iyer said that he was not convinced how spiritual life could be reconciled to worldly activities. The Master in answer cited some verses from *Yoga Vasishta*. (The original is said to be millions of verses, of which only 32,000 stanzas are now found in the Sanskrit text. It was condensed to 6,000 and called *Laghu Vasishta*. The latter has been rendered in Tamil in 2,050 stanzas).

D.: Without the mind concentrating on it the work cannot be performed satisfactorily. How is the mind to be spiritually disposed and the work kept going as well?

M.: The mind is only a projection from the Self, appearing in the waking state. In deep sleep, you do not say whose son you are and so on. As soon as you wake up you say you are so and so, and recognise the world and so on. The world is only *lokah, lokah = lokyate iti lokah* (what is perceived is the world). That which is seen is *lokah* or the world. Which is the eye that sees it? That is the ego which rises and sinks periodically. But you exist always. Therefore That which lies beyond the ego is consciousness — the Self.

In deep sleep mind is merged and not destroyed. That which merges reappears. It may happen in meditation also. But the mind which is destroyed cannot reappear. The *yogi*'s aim must be to destroy it and not to sink in *laya*. In the peace of *dhyana, laya* ensues but it is not enough. It must be supplemented by other practices for destroying the mind. Some people have gone into *samadhi* with a trifling thought and after a long time awakened in the trail of the same thought. In the meantime generations have passed away in the world. Such a *yogi* has not destroyed his mind. Its destruction is the non-recognition of it as being apart from the Self. Even now the mind *is not*. Recognise it. How can you do it if not in everyday activities. They go on automatically. Know that the mind promoting them is not real but a phantom proceeding from the Self. That is how the mind is destroyed.

Talk 77.

The Master, while referring to the Bible for "Be still and know that I am God", Psalm 46, found in the Ecclesiastes. "There is one alone and there is no second" and "The wise man's heart is at the right hand and a fool's heart is at the left."

Talk 78.

A man from Masulla asked the Master: "How to realise the Self?"

M.: Everyone has experience of the Self every moment of his life.

D.: But the Self is not realised as one would like.

81

M.: Yes. The present experience is *viparita* — different from real. What is not is confounded with what is.

D.: How to find the Atman?

M.: There is no investigation into the Atman. The investigation can only be into the non-self. Elimination of the non-self is alone possible. The Self being always self evident will shine forth of itself.

The Self is called by different names — Atman, God, *Kundalini, mantra,* etc. Hold any one of them and the Self becomes manifest. God is no other than the Self. *Kundalini* is now showing forth as the mind. When the mind is traced to its source it is *Kundalini. Mantra japa* leads to elimination of other thoughts and to concentration on the *mantra.* The *mantra* finally merges into the Self and shines forth as the Self.

D.: How long is a Guru necessary for Self-Realisation?

M.: Guru is necessary so long as there is the *laghu.* (Pun on Guru = heavy; *laghu* = light). *Laghu* is due to the self-imposed but wrong limitation of the Self. God, on being worshipped, bestows steadiness in devotion which leads to surrender. On the devotee surrendering, God shows His mercy by manifesting as the Guru. The Guru, otherwise God, guides the devotee, saying that God is in you and He is the Self. This leads to introversion of the mind and finally to realisation.

Effort is necessary up to the state of realisation. Even then the Self should spontaneously become evident. Otherwise happiness will not be complete. Up to that state of spontaneity there must be effort in some form or another.

D.: Our work-a-day life is not compatible with such efforts.

M.: Why do you think that you are active? Take the gross example of your arrival here. You left home in a cart, took train, alighted at the Railway Station here, got into a cart there and found yourself in this Asramam. When asked, you say that you travelled here all the way from your town. Is it true? Is it not a fact that you remained as you were and there were movements of conveyances all along the way. Just as those movements are confounded with your own, so also the other activities. They are not your own. They are God's activities.

82

D.: Such idea will lead to blankness of mind and the work will not progress well.

M.: Go up to that blankness and tell me afterwards.

D.: They say that a visit to Sages helps Self-Realisation?

M.: Yes. So it does.

D.: Will not my present visit to you bring it about?

M.: (After a short pause) What is to be brought about? To whom? Consider; investigate. To whom is this doubt. If the source is traced the doubt will disappear.

Talk 79.

An engineer asked: "The animals seem to conform to their own natural laws in spite of their environment and changes. Whereas man flouts social law and is not bound by any definite system. He seems to be degenerating whereas the animals are steady. Is it not so?"

M.: (After a long time). The Upanishads and scriptures say that human beings are only animals unless they are realised beings. Possibly they are worse also.

3rd October, 1935

Talk 80.

A very devoted and simple disciple had lost his only son, a child of three years. The next day he arrived at the Asramam with his family. The Master spoke with reference to them: "Training of mind helps one to bear sorrows and bereavements with courage. But the loss of one's offspring is said to be the worst of all griefs. Grief exists only so long as one considers oneself to be of a definite form. If the form is transcended one will know that the one Self is eternal. There is no death nor birth. That which is born is only the body. The body is the creation of the ego. But the ego is not ordinarily perceived without the body. It is always identified with the body. It is the thought which matters. Let the sensible man consider if he knew his body in deep sleep. Why does he feel it in the waking state? But, although the body was not felt in sleep, did not the Self exist then? How was he in deep sleep? How is he when awake? What is the difference? Ego rises up and that is waking. Simultaneously thoughts arise. Let him find out to whom are the thoughts. Wherefrom do they arise? They must spring up from the conscious Self. Apprehending it even vaguely helps the extinction of the ego. Thereafter the realisation of the one Infinite Existence becomes possible. In that state there are no individuals other than the Eternal Existence. Hence there is no thought of death or wailing.

"If a man considers he is born he cannot avoid the fear of death. Let him find out if he has been born or if the Self has any birth. He will discover that the Self always exists, that the body which is born resolves itself into thought and that the emergence of thought is the root of all mischief. Find wherefrom thoughts emerge. Then you will abide in the ever-present inmost Self and be free from the idea of birth or the fear of death."

A disciple asked how to do it.

M.: The thoughts are only *vasanas* (predispositions), accumulated in innumerable births before. Their annihilation is the aim. The state free from *vasanas* is the primal state and eternal state of purity.

D.: It is not clear yet.

M.: Everyone is aware of the eternal Self. He sees so many dying but still believes himself eternal. Because it is the Truth. Unwillingly the natural Truth asserts itself. The man is deluded by the intermingling of the conscious Self with the insentient body. This delusion must end.

D.: How will it end?

M.: That which is born must end. The delusion is only concomitant with the ego. It rises up and sinks. But the Reality never rises nor sinks. It remains Eternal. The master who has realised says so; the disciple hears, thinks over the words and realises the Self. There are two ways of putting it.

The ever-present Self needs no efforts to be realised, Realisation is already there. Illusion alone is to be removed. Some say the word from the mouth of the Master removes it instantaneously. Others say that meditation, etc., are necessary for realisation. Both are right; only the standpoints differ.

D.: Is *dhyana* necessary?

84

M.: The Upanishads say that even the Earth is in eternal *dhyana.*

D.: How does Karma help it? Will it not add to the already heavy load to be removed?

M.: Karma done unselfishly purifies the mind and helps to fix it in meditation.

D.: What if one meditates incessantly without Karma?

M.: Try and see. The *vasanas* will not let you do it. *Dhyana* comes only step by step with the gradual weakening of the *vasanas* by the Grace of the Master.

15th October, 1935

Talk 81.

Dr. Bernhard Bey, an American Chemist who had interested himself in *Vedanta* for the last twenty years, now in India, came on a visit to the Master. He asked: "How is *abhyasa* to be made? I am trying to find the Light." (He himself explained *abhyasa* as concentration = one-pointedness of mind.)

The Master asked, what was his *abhyasa* till now.

The visitor said he concentrated on the nasal base, but his mind wandered.

M.: Is there a mind?

Another devotee gently put in: The mind is only a collection of thoughts.

M.: To whom are the thoughts? If you try to locate the mind, the mind vanishes and the Self alone remains. Being alone, there can be no one-pointedness or otherwise.

D.: It is so difficult to understand this. If something concrete is said, it can be readily grasped. *Japa, dhyana*, etc., are more concrete.

M.: 'Who am I?' is the best *japa.*

What could be more concrete than the Self? It is within each one's experience every moment. Why should he try to catch anything outside, leaving out the Self? Let each one try to find out the known Self instead of searching for the unknown something beyond.

D.: Where shall I meditate on the Atman? I mean in which part of the body?

M.: The Self should manifest itself. That is all that is wanted.

A devotee gently added: On the right of the chest, there is the Heart, the seat of the Atman.

Another devotee: The illumination is in that centre when the Self is realised.

M.: Quite so.

D.: How to turn the mind away from the world?

M.: Is there the world? I mean apart from the Self? Does the world say that it exists? It is you who say that there is a world. Find out the Self who says it.

16th October, 1935

Talk 82.

A question was raised about the differences in the various *samadhis*.

M.: When the senses are merged in darkness it is deep sleep; when merged in light it is *samadhi*. Just as a passenger when asleep in a carriage is unaware of the motion, the halting or the unharnessing of the horses, so also a *jnani* in *sahaja samadhi* is unaware of the happenings, waking, dream and deep sleep. Here sleep corresponds to the unharnessing of the horses. And *samadhi* corresponds to the halting of the horses, because the senses are ready to act just as the horses are ready to move after halting.

In *samadhi* the head does not bend down because the senses are there though inactive; whereas the head bends down in sleep because the senses are merged in darkness. In *kevala samadhi*, the activities (vital and mental), waking, dream and sleep, are only merged, ready to emerge after regaining the state other than *samadhi*. In *sahaja samadhi* the activities, vital and mental, and the three states are destroyed, never to reappear. However, others notice the *jnani* active e.g., eating, talking, moving etc. He is not himself aware of these activities, whereas others are aware of his activities. They pertain to his body and not to his Real Self, *swarupa*. For himself, he is like the sleeping passenger — or like a child interrupted from sound sleep and fed, being unaware of it. The child says the next day that he did

86

not take milk at all and that he went to sleep without it. Even when reminded he cannot be convinced. So also in *sahaja samadhi*.

Sushumna pare leena. Here *sushumna* refers to *tapo marge* whereas the *para nadi* refers to *jnana marga.*

Talk 83.

The Master relating some stories of the *bhaktas* told how Sri Krishna served Eknath for twelve years, how Panduranga relieved Sakku Bai from her home prison and enabled her to visit Pandharpur.

Then he recollected the appearance of a mysterious Moulvi on his way from Madura to Tiruvannamalai in 1896, how he appeared, spoke and disappeared suddenly.

Talk 84.

Mr. Grant Duff asked the Master if any mongoose had had anything to do with him. The Master said, "Yes. It was the occasion of Ardra and Jayanti, I was living up the hill in Skandasramam. Streams of visitors were climbing up the hill from the town A mongoose, larger than the ordinary size, of golden hue (not grey as a mongoose is), with no black spot on its tail as is usual with the wild mongoose, passed these crowds fearlessly. People took it to be a tame one belonging to someone in the crowd. The animal went straight to Palaniswami, who was having a bath in the spring by the Virupaksha Cave. He stroked the creature and patted it. It followed him into the cave, inspected every nook and corner and left the place and joined the crowd to pass up to Skandasramam. I noticed it. Everyone was struck by its attractive appearance and its fearless movements. It came up to me, got on my lap and rested there some time. Then it raised itself up, looked about and moved down; it went round the whole place and I followed it lest it should be harmed by the unwary visitors or by the peacocks. Two peacocks of the place looked at it inquisitively, whereas the mongoose moved nonchalantly from place to place and finally disappeared into the rocks on the south-east of the Asramam."

87

Talk 85.

The same gentleman asked the Master about the material relation between memory and will and their relation to the mind.

M.: They are functions of the mind The mind is the outcome of the ego and the ego is from the Self.

6th November, 1935
Talk 86.

The Master gave the true significance of the Christian faith thus:
Christ is the ego.

The Cross is the body.

When the ego is crucified, and it perishes, what survives is the Absolute Being (God), (*cf.* "I and my Father are one") and this glorious survival is called Resurrection.

Talk 87.

Major A. W. Chadwick, an ardent English devotee, asked, "Why did Jesus call out 'My God! My God!' while being crucified?"

M.: It might have been an intercession on behalf of the two thieves who were crucified with Him. Again a *jnani* has attained liberation even while alive, here and now. It is immaterial as to how, where and when he leaves his body. Some *jnanis* may appear to suffer, others may be in *samadhi*, still others may disappear from sight before death. But that makes no difference to their *jnana*. Such suffering is apparent only to the onlooker and not to the *jnani*, for he has already transcended the mistaken identity of the Self with the body.

Talk 88.

The same gentleman asked: What is the significance of Christ in the illumination of St. Paul?

M.: Illumination is absolute, not associated with forms. After St. Paul became Self-conscious he identified the illumination with Christ-consciousness.

D.: But Paul was not a lover of Christ then?

M.: Love or hatred is immaterial. The thought of Christ was there. It is similar to Ravana's case. Christ-consciousness and Self-Realisation are all the same.

Talk 89.

M.: Karpura arati is symbolic of the burning away of the mind by the light of illumination, *vibhuti* (sacred ashes) is Siva (Absolute Being) and *kunkuma* (vermilion powder) is Sakti (consciousness).

Vibhuti is of two kinds: *Para vibhuti* and *apara vibhuti*. The sacred ashes are of the latter class. The *para* is what remains over after all the dross has been burnt away by the Fire of Realisation. It is Absolute Being.

Talk 90.

Again, the Trinity was explained:

God the Father represents Isvara

God the Holy Spirit represents Atman

God the Son represents Guru

Isvaro gururatmeti murti bheda vibhagine vyomavad vyapta dehaya dakshinamurtaye namah:

Meaning that God appears to his devotee in the form of a Guru (son of God) and points out to him the immanence of the Holy Spirit. That is to say that God is spirit, that this spirit is immanent everywhere and that the Self must be realised, which is the same as realising God.

Talk 91.

A Bengali visitor asked: How is the mind controlled?

M.: What do you call 'the mind'?

D.: When I sit down to think of God, thoughts wander away to other objects. I want to control those thoughts.

M.: In the *Bhagavad Gita* it is said that it is the nature of the mind to wander. One must bring one's thoughts to bear on God. By long practice the mind is controlled and made steady.

The wavering of the mind is a weakness arising from the dissipation of its energy in the shape of thoughts. When one makes the mind stick to one thought the energy is conserved, and the mind becomes stronger.

D.: What is the meaning of the strength of the mind?

M.: Its ability to concentrate on one thought without being distracted.

D.: How is that achieved?

M.: By practice. A devotee concentrates on God; a seeker, follower of the *jnana-marga*, seeks the Self. The practice is equally difficult for both.

D.: Even if the mind is brought to bear on the search for the Self, after a long struggle the mind begins to elude him and the man is not aware of the mischief until after some time.

M.: So it would be. In the earlier stages the mind reverts to the search at long intervals; with continued practice it reverts at shorter intervals until finally it does not wander at all. It is then that the dormant *sakti* manifests. The *satvic* mind is free from thoughts whereas the *rajasic* mind is full of them. The *sattvic* mind resolves itself into the Life-current.

D.: Can one keep the mind away from entering into the phase of thoughts before one experiences the current?

M.: Yes; the current is pre-existent.

7th November, 1935

Talk 92.

A visitor said: Some say that one should practise meditation on gross objects only: it may be disastrous if one constantly seeks to kill the mind.

M.: For whom is it disastrous? Can there be disaster apart from the Self?

Unbroken 'I-I' is the ocean infinite, the ego, 'I' thought, remains only a bubble on it and is called *jiva, i.e.,* individual soul. The bubble too is water; when it bursts it only mixes in the ocean. When it remains a bubble it is still a part of the ocean. Ignorant of this simple truth, innumerable methods under different denominations, such as yoga, *bhakti*, karma....... each again with many modifications, are being taught with great skill and in intricate detail only to entice the seekers and confuse their minds. So also are the religions and sects and dogmas. What are they all for? Only for knowing the Self. They are aids and practices required for knowing the Self.

Objects perceived by the senses are spoken of as immediate knowledge (*pratyaksha*). Can anything be as direct as the Self — always experienced without the aid of the senses? Sense-perceptions can only be indirect knowledge, and not direct knowledge. Only one's own awareness is direct knowledge, as is the common experience of one and all. No aids are needed to know one's own Self, *i.e.*, to be aware.

The one Infinite Unbroken Whole (plenum) becomes aware of itself as 'I'. This is its original name. All other names, *e.g.*, OM, are later growths. Liberation is only to remain aware of the Self. The *mahavakya* "I am *Brahman*" is its authority. Though the 'I' is always experienced, yet one's attention has to be drawn to it. Only then does knowledge dawn. Thus the need for the instruction of the Upanishads and of wise sages.

9th November, 1935

Talk 93.

All are aware of their own Self only. Wonder of wonders! They take what is not as what is, or they see the phenomena apart from the Self. Only so long as there is the knower is there knowledge of all kinds (direct, inferential, intellectual etc.); should the knower vanish they all vanish together with him; their validity is of the same degree as his.

Talk 94.

A man prayed to the Master to pardon his sins. He was told that it would be enough if he took care to see that his mind did not trouble him.

13th November, 1935

Talk 95.

A question was raised as follows by Maj. A. W. Chadwick:-

Mr. Edward Carpenter, a certain mystic, has written in a book that he had Self-Realisation on some occasions and that its effects lasted sometimes afterwards, only to be gradually lost. Whereas *Sri Ramana Gita* says, "*Granthi* (knot = bondage), snapped once, is snapped for ever." In the case of this mystic, the bondage seems to have persisted even after Self-Realisation. How can it be so?

The Master cited *Kaivalya* as follows:-

The disciple, after realising the all-shining, unitary, unbroken state of Being-Knowledge-Bliss, surrendered himself to the master and humbly prayed to know how he could repay the master's Grace. The Master said:

"My reward consists in your permanent unbroken Bliss. Do not slip away from it."

D.: Having once experienced the Supreme Bliss, how can one stray away from it?

M.: Oh yes! It happens. The predisposition adhering to him from time immemorial will draw him out and so ignorance overtakes him.

D.: What are the obstacles to remaining steady in unbroken Bliss? How can they be overcome?

M.: The obstacles are:

(1) Ignorance which is forgetfulness of one's pure being.

(2) Doubt which consists in wondering if even the experience was of the Real or of the unreal.

(3) Error which consists in the "I-am-the-body" idea, and thinking that the world is real. These are overcome by hearing the truth, reflection on it and concentration.

The Master continued: Experience is said to be temporary or permanent. The first experience is temporary and by concentration it can become permanent. In the former the bondage is not completely destroyed; it remains subtle and reasserts itself in due course. But in the latter it is destroyed root and branch, never to appear again. The expression *yogabhrashta* (those who have fallen down from yoga) in *Srimad Bhagavad Gita* refers to the former class of men.

D.: Is then hearing the Truth meant only for a limited few?

M.: It is of two kinds. The ordinary one is to hear it enunciated and explained by a master. However, the right one is to raise the question for oneself and seek and find the answer in oneself as the unbroken 'I-I'.

To be reflecting on this experience is the second stage. To remain one-pointed in it is the third stage.

D.: Can the temporary experience be called *samadhi*?

M.: No. It forms part of the third stage.

D.: It looks then as if even hearing the Truth is limited to a very few.

M.: The seekers fall into two classes; *kritopasaka* and *akritopasaka.* The former having already overcome his predisposition by steady devotion, his mind thus made pure, has had some kind of experience but does not comprehend it; as soon as instructed by a competent master, permanent experience results.

The other class of seeker needs great effort to achieve this end. How will the hearing of the Truth, reflection and concentration help him?

They comprise *upasana* (the nearest approach to Truth) and will end in his Self-Realization.

The fourth stage is the final one of liberation. Even there some distinction is made according to the degree, as
    (1) the knower of the Brahman (*Brahmavid*)
    (2) *Brahmavid-vara*
    (3) *Brahmavid-varya*
    (4) *Brahmavid-varishta*
But all of them are in fact liberated even while alive.

Talk 96.

Maj. A. W. Chadwick: Of what nature is the realisation of Westerners who relate that they have had flashes of cosmic consciousness?

M.: It came as a flash and disappeared as such. That which has a beginning must also end. Only when the ever-present consciousness is realised will it be permanent. Consciousness is indeed always with us. Everyone knows 'I am!' No one can deny his own being. The man in deep slumber is not aware; while awake he seems to be aware. But it is the same person. There is no change in the one who slept and the one who is now awake. In deep sleep he was not aware of his body; there was no body-consciousness. In the wakeful state he is aware of his body; there is body-consciousness. Therefore the difference lies in the emergence of body-consciousness and not in any change in the Real Consciousness. The body and

93

body-consciousness arise together and sink together. All this amounts to saying that there are no limitations in deep sleep, whereas there are limitations in the waking state. These limitations are the bondage; the feeling 'The body is I' is the error. This false sense of 'I' must go. The real 'I' is always there. It is *here and now*. It never appears anew and disappears again. That which is must also persist for ever. That which appears anew will also be lost. Compare deep sleep and waking. The body appears in one state but not in the other. Therefore the body will be lost. The consciousness was pre-existent and will survive the body. In fact, there is no one who does not say 'I am'. The wrong knowledge of 'I am the body' is the cause of all the mischief. This wrong knowledge must go. That is Realisation. Realisation is not acquisition of anything new nor it is a new faculty. It is only removal of all camouflage.

Maj. Chadwick: I try to shake off the body.

M.: A man shakes off his clothes and remains alone and free. The Self is unlimited and is not confined to the body. How can the body be shaken off? Where will he leave it? Wherever it is, it is his still.

Maj. Chadwick: (Laughter.)

M.: The ultimate Truth is so simple. It is nothing more than being in the pristine state. This is all that need be said.

Still, it is a wonder that to teach this simple Truth there should come into being so many religions, creeds, methods and disputes among them and so on! Oh the pity! Oh the pity!

Maj. Chadwick: But people will not be content with simplicity; they want complexity.

M.: Quite so. Because they want something elaborate and attractive and puzzling, so many religions have come into existence and each of them is so complex and each creed in each religion has its own adherents and antagonists.

For example, an ordinary Christian will not be satisfied unless he is told that God is somewhere in the far-off Heavens not to be reached by us unaided. Christ alone knew Him and Christ alone can guide us. Worship Christ and be saved. If told the simple truth — "The Kingdom of Heaven is within you" — he is not satisfied and will read complex

94

and far-fetched meanings in such statements. Mature minds alone can grasp the simple Truth in all its nakedness.

Maj. Chadwick later expressed a certain involuntary fear while meditating. He feels the spirit separated from the gross body and the sensation creates a fright.

M.: To whom is the fright? It is all due to the habit of identifying the body with the Self. Repeated experience of separation will make one familiar and the fright will cease.

19th November, 1935

Talk 97.

One Mr. Ramachandar, a gentleman from Ambala, asked where the Heart is and what Realisation is.

M.: The Heart is not physical; it is spiritual. *Hridayam = hrit + ayam* — This is the centre. It is that from which thoughts arise, on which they subsist and where they are resolved. The thoughts are the content of the mind and, they shape the universe. The Heart is the centre of all. *Yatova imani bhutani jayante* (that from which these beings come into existence) etc. is said to be Brahman in the Upanishads. That is the Heart. Brahman is the Heart.

D.: How to realise the Heart?

M.: There is no one who even for a trice fails to experience the Self. For no one admits that he ever stands apart from the Self. He is the Self. The Self is the Heart.

D.: It is not clear.

M.: In deep sleep you exist; awake, you remain. The same Self is in both states. The difference is only in the awareness and the non-awareness of the world. The world rises with the mind and sets with the mind. That which rises and sets is not the Self. The Self is different, giving rise to the mind, sustaining it and resolving it. So the Self is the underlying principle.

When asked who you are, you place your hand on the right side of the breast and say 'I am'. There you involuntarily point out the Self. The Self is thus known. But the individual is miserable because he confounds the mind and the body with the Self. This confusion is due to wrong knowledge. Elimination of wrong knowledge is alone needed. Such elimination results in Realisation.

D.: How to control the mind?

M.: What is mind? Whose is the mind?

D.: Mind always wanders. I cannot control it.

M.: It is the nature of the mind to wander. You are not the mind. The mind springs up and sinks down. It is impermanent, transitory, whereas you are eternal. There is nothing but the Self. To inhere in the Self is the thing. Never mind the mind. If its source is sought, it will vanish leaving the Self unaffected.

D.: So one need not seek to control the mind?

M.: There is no mind to control if you realise the Self. The mind vanishing, the Self shines forth. In the realised man the mind may be active or inactive, the Self alone remains for him. For the mind, the body and the world are not separate from the Self. They rise from and sink into the Self. They do not remain apart from the Self. Can they be different from the Self? Only be aware of the Self. Why worry about these shadows? How do they affect the Self?

Talk 98.

Bhagavan further explained: The Self is the Heart. The Heart is self-luminous. Light arises from the Heart and reaches the brain, which is the seat of the mind. The world is seen with the mind, that is, by the reflected light of the Self. It is perceived with the aid of the mind. When the mind is illumined it is aware of the world. When it is not itself so illumined, it is not aware of the world. If the mind is turned in towards the source of light, objective knowledge ceases and Self alone shines forth as the Heart.

The moon shines by the reflected light of the sun. When the sun has set, the moon is useful for revealing objects. When the sun has risen, no one needs the moon, although the pale disc of the moon is visible in the sky.

So it is with the mind and the Heart. The mind is useful because of its reflected light. It is used for seeing objects. When it is turned inwards, the source of illumination shines forth by itself, and the mind remains dim and useless like the moon in day-time.

Talk 99.

A sannyasi asked: It is said that the Self is beyond the mind and yet the realisation is with the mind. *Mano na manute, Manasa na matam*, and *Manasaivedamaptavyam* (The mind cannot think it. It cannot be thought of by the mind and the mind alone can realise it). How are these contradictions to be reconciled?

M.: Atman is realised with *mruta manas* (dead mind), *i.e.*, mind devoid of thoughts and turned inward. Then the mind sees its own source and becomes That. It is not as the subject perceiving an object.

When the room is dark a lamp is necessary to illumine and eyes to cognise objects. But when the sun is risen there is no need of a lamp, and the objects are seen; and to see the sun no lamp is necessary, it is enough that you turn your eyes towards the self-luminous sun.

Similarly with the mind. To see the objects the reflected light of the mind is necessary. To see the Heart it is enough that the mind is turned towards it. Then the mind loses itself and the Heart shines forth.

Talk 100.

Later Sri Bhagavan quoted from *Kaivalya* some verses and explained:

A

The Supreme

(Knowledge Absolute; witness; the Self-shining core;
the Heart; the Self).

↓

the individual
[the *jiva*, the knower consisting of *vritti* (the mode
of mind-stuff) and reflected light, in the latent form.]

↓

the internal intellect and the outgoing mind
[*buddin* and *manas* consisting of *vritti* and reflected light
as a sprout; this is the *antahkarana* (the inner organ)]

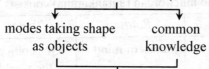

together form the world as we perceive it

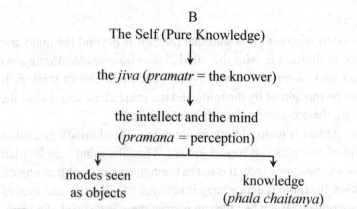

B
The Self (Pure Knowledge)
↓
the *jiva* (*pramatr* = the knower)
↓
the intellect and the mind
(*pramana* = perception)
↓

| modes seen as objects | knowledge (*phala chaitanya*) |

The modes of mind take shape as external objects and the light reflected on the modes illumines the objects. Now neglecting the modes of mind, look for the light illumining them. The mind becomes still and the light remains self-shining. The undulating mind (*i.e.*, the mind associated with *rajas* = activity and *tamas* = darkness) is commonly known as the mind. Devoid of *rajas* and *tamas*, it is pure and self-shining. This is Self-Realisation. Therefore the mind is said to be the means for it.

C
Pure Consciousness
(said to be the Eternal or the Ever-present Witness)
↓
(*antahkarana*)
Inner organ + the reflected light (*jiva : pramtr*)
↓
modes together with the lig ht are said to be *prameya* =
the known; of these, the objects are gross and the
light is called *phala chaitanya.*

D
In the *jiva* the inner organ (antahkarana) consists of -

Satva	Rajas	Tamas
knowledge light	modes of mind intellect, mind	gross objects the world

Similarly for the cosmos-

The Cosmic mind (the Eternal Being)

Satva	Rajas	Tamas
Isvara the Lord of the universe	the individual *jiva*	the universe

E

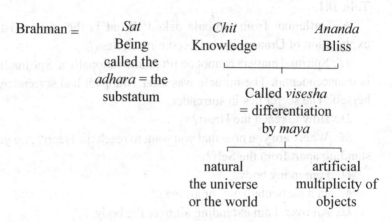

Brahman = *Sat* Being called the *adhara* = the substatum   *Chit* Knowledge   *Ananda* Bliss

Called *visesha* = differentiation by *maya*

natural the universe or the world   artificial multiplicity of objects

Maya cannot obscure *Sat*, but it does obscure *Chit* and *Ananda*, making them appear as particulars.

F

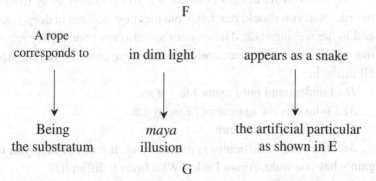

A rope corresponds to   in dim light   appears as a snake

Being the substratum   *maya* illusion   the artificial particular as shown in E

G

Sat = Being = the substratum (*adhara*). From this proceeds the particular, namely the *jiva* who veiled by ignorance identifies himself with the gross body. Here ignorance stands for not investigating the

99

Self. *Jiva* is in fact knowledge only; yet owing to ignorance the wrong identity with the gross body results.

H

Again, the Master illustrated it with the red-hot iron ball (*tapta-ayah-pindavat*).

A ball of iron + fire together form red-hot iron ball. The World + *Chit* = (Pure Knowledge) together form the *jiva* = the individual.

Talk 101.

A gentleman from Ambala asked: What is the rationalistic explanation of Draupadi's sari becoming endless?

M.: Spiritual matters cannot be fitted into rationalism. Spirituality is transcendental. The miracle was after Draupadi had surrendered herself. The secret lies in surrender.

D.: How to reach the Heart?

M.: Where are you now that you want to reach the Heart? Are you standing apart from the Self?

D.: I am in my body.

M.: In a particular spot, or all over?

D.: All over. I am extending all over the body.

M.: Wherefrom do you extend?

D.: I do not know.

M.: Yes. You are always in the Heart. You are never away from it in order that you should reach it. Consider how you are in deep sleep and in the waking state. These states are also not yours. They are of the ego. The consciousness remains the same and undifferentiated all through.

D.: I understand but I cannot feel it so.

M.: Whose is the ignorance? Find it out.

D.: All this is so difficult.

M.: The idea of difficulty is itself wrong. It will not help you to gain what you want. Again I ask: "Who finds it difficult?"

D.: I see that I am coming round to 'I'.

M.: Because you are always that and never away from that. There is nothing so simple as being the Self. It requires no effort, no aid.

One has to leave off the wrong identity and be in his eternal, natural, inherent state.

Talk 102.

He returned with a request next day. He said, "It is said that one should receive instruction from a Guru. Mere reading of books is not helpful. I have read many books; but there is no practical help derived from such learning. Please tell me what I should do, how I should do it, at what times, in which places, and so on."

The Master remained silent. His silence seemed to say, "Here and now, be at peace and tranquil. That is all". But the questioner could not interpret it that way; he wanted something concrete.

Talk 103.

The next day Sri Bhagavan said: These people want some *japa, dhyana*, or yoga or something similar. Without their saying what they have been doing so far what more can be said to them? Again, why *japa*, its *phalasruti*, etc.? Who is it that makes the *japa*? Who gets the fruits thereof? Can they not look to the Self? Or again, even if instructed by others to do *japa* or *dhyana*, they do it for some time, but are always looking to some results, *e.g.*, visions, dreams, or thaumaturgic powers. If they do not find them they say they are not progressing or the *tapas* is not effective. Visions, etc., are no signs of progress. Mere performance of *tapas* is its progress also. Steadiness is what is required. Moreover they must entrust themselves to their *mantra* or their God and wait for its Grace. They don't do so. *Japa* even once uttered has its own good effect, whether the individual is aware or not.

28th November, 1935

Talk 104.

Mr. Kishorilal, an officer of the Railway Board, Government of India, hails from Delhi. He looks simple, gentle and dignified in behaviour. He has gastric ulcer and has arranged for his board and lodging in the town.

101

Five years ago he took up the study of devotional literature. He is a *bhakta* of Sri Krishna. He could feel Krishna in all that he saw. Krishna often appeared to him and made him happy. His work was going on without any effort on his part. Everything seemed to be done for him by Krishna himself.

Later he came in contact with a Mahatma who advised him to study Vedanta and take to *nirakara upasana, i.e.*, devotion to formless Being. He has since read about seven hundred books of philosophy and Vedanta, including the Upanishads, *Ashtavakra, Avadhuta* and *Srimad Bhagavad Gita*. He has also studied Sri Bhagavan's works in English and is much impressed by them.

Once when he was in the jaws of death, no other thought haunted him but that he had not yet visited Sri Bhagavan in his life. So he has come here on a short visit. He prays only for Sri Bhagavan's touch and His Grace.

The Master said to him: *atmaivaham gudakesa, i.e.*, I am Atman; Atman is the Guru; and Atman is Grace also. No one remains without the Atman. He is always in contact. No external touch is necessary.

D.: I understand. I do not mean external touch.

M.: Nothing is more intimate than the Atman.

D.: Again Sri Krishna appeared to me three months back and said, "Why do you ask me for *nirakara upasana*? It is only *sarva bhutesu cha atmanam sarva bhutani cha atmani.* (The Self in all and all in the Self.)

M.: That contains the whole truth. Even this is *oupacharika* (indirect). There is in fact nothing but the Atman. The world is only a projection of the mind. The mind originates from the Atman. So Atman alone is the One Being.

D.: Yet it is difficult to realise.

M.: There is nothing to realise. It is *nitya suddha buddha mukta* (the Eternal, pure, aware and liberated) state. It is natural and eternal. There is nothing new to gain. On the other hand a man must loose his ignorance. That is all.

This ignorance must be traced to its origin. To whom is this ignorance? Of what is one ignorant? There are the subject and the

102

object. Such duality is characteristic of the mind. The mind is from the Atman.

D.: Yes. Ignorance itself cannot exist. (He finally surrendered saying, "Just as a doctor learns what is wrong with the patient and treats him accordingly, so may Sri Bhagavan do with me". He also said that he had lost all inclination to study books and learn from them.)

Talk 105.

M.: Yena asrutam srutam bhavati (*Chandogya Upanishad*). (By knowing which, all the unknown becomes known.)

Madhavaswami, Bhagavan's attendant: Are there nine methods of teaching the *Mahavakya 'Tattvamasi'* in the *Chandogya Upanishad*?

M.: No. Not so. The method is only one. Uddalaka started teaching *Sat eva Somya* ... (There is only Being ...) illustrating it with Svetaketu's fast.

(1) *Sat*, the Being in the individual, is made obvious by the fast.

(2) This (*sat*) Being is similar in all, as honey gathered from different flowers.

(3) There is no difference in the *sat* of individuals as illustrated by the state of deep sleep. The question arises — if so, why does not each know it in sleep?

(4) Because the individuality is lost. There is only *sat* left. Illustration: rivers lost in the ocean. If lost, is there *sat*?

(5) Surely — as when a tree is pruned it grows again. That is a sure sign of its life. But is it there even in that dormant condition?

(6) Yes, take the instance of salt and water. The presence of the salt in water is subtle. Though invisible to the eye it is recognised by other senses. How is one to know it? What is the other means?

(7) By enquiry, as the man left in the Gandhara forest regained his home.

(8) In evolution and involution, in manifestation and resolution, *sat* alone exists. *Tejah parasyam, devatayam* (the light merges in the Supreme).

(9) An insincere man is hurt by the touch of fire test. His insincerity is brought out by fire. Sincerity is Self-evident. A true man or a Self realised man remains happy, without being affected by the false appearances (namely the world, birth and death, etc.), whereas the false or ignorant man is miserable.

29th November, 1935

Talk 106.

Swami Yogananda with four others arrived at 8.45 a.m. He looks big, but gentle and well-groomed. He has dark flowing hair, hanging over his shoulders. The group had lunch in the Asramam.

Mr. C. R. Wright, his secretary, asked: How shall I realise God?

M.: God is an unknown entity. Moreover He is external. Whereas, the Self is always with you and it is you. Why do you leave out what is intimate and go in for what is external?

D.: What is this Self again?

M.: The Self is known to everyone but not clearly. You always exist. The Be-ing is the Self. 'I am' is the name of God. Of all the definitions of God, none is indeed so well put as the Biblical statement "*I AM THAT I AM*" in EXODUS (Chap. 3). There are other statements, such as *Brahmaivaham, Aham Brahmasmi* and *Soham*. But none is so direct as the name *JEHOVAH = I AM*. The Absolute Being is *what* is — It is the Self. It is God. Knowing the Self, God is known. In fact God is none other than the Self.

D.: Why are there good and evil?

M.: They are relative terms. There must be a subject to know the good and evil. That subject is the ego. Trace the source of the ego. It ends in the Self. The source of the ego is God. This definition of God is probably more concrete and better understood by you.

D.: So it is. How to get Bliss?

M.: Bliss is not something to be got. On the other hand you are always Bliss. This desire is born of the sense of incompleteness. To whom is this sense of incompleteness? Enquire. In deep sleep you were blissful: Now you are not so. What has interposed between that Bliss and this non-bliss? It is the ego. Seek its source and find you are Bliss.

There is nothing new to get. You have, on the other hand, to get rid of your ignorance which makes you think that you are other than Bliss. For whom is this ignorance? It is to the ego. Trace the source of the ego. Then the ego is lost and Bliss remains over. It is eternal. You are That, here and now.... That is the master key for solving all doubts. The doubts arise in the mind. The mind is born of the ego. The ego rises from the Self. Search the source of the ego and the Self is revealed. That alone remains. The universe is only expanded Self. It is not different from the Self.

D.: What is the best way of living?

M.: It differs according as one is a *jnani* or *ajnani*. A *jnani* does not find anything different or separate from the Self. All are in the Self. It is wrong to imagine that there is the world, that there is a body in it and that you dwell in the body. If the Truth is known, the universe and what is beyond it will be found to be only in the Self. The outlook differs according to the sight of the person. The sight is from the eye. The eye must be located somewhere. If you are seeing with the gross eyes you find others gross. If with subtle eyes (*i.e.*, the mind) others appear subtle. If the eye becomes the Self, the Self being infinite, the eye is infinite. There is nothing else to see different from the Self.

He thanked Maharshi. He was told that the best way of thanking is to remain always as the Self.

Talk 107.

Later the Yogi asked: How is the spiritual uplift of the people to be effected? What are the instructions to be given them?

M.: They differ according to the temperaments of the individuals and according to the spiritual ripeness of their minds. There cannot be any instruction *en masse*.

D.: Why does God permit suffering in the world? Should He not with His omnipotence do away with it at one stroke and ordain the universal realisation of God?

M.: Suffering is the way for Realisation of God.

D.: Should He not ordain differently?

M.: It is the way.

D.: Are Yoga, religion, etc., antidotes to suffering?

M.: They help you to overcome suffering.

D.: Why should there be suffering?

M.: Who suffers? What is suffering?

No answer! Finally the Yogi rose up, prayed for Sri Bhagavan's blessings for his own work and expressed great regret for his hasty return. He looked very sincere and devoted and even emotional.

Talk 108.

In continuation of dialogue 105: Uddalaka explained that all proceeds from *sat* (as illustrated by deep sleep).

The body takes food. Food requires water. Water requires heat to digest the food. (*Tejo mulamanvichcha*) It is *sat parasyam devatayam* (merged in the Be-ing). If we are *sat sampannah* (merged in the Be-ing), how is it that we do not realise it?

M.: Just as the honey gathered from different flowers forms the bulk in a honeycomb, and each drop does not indicate wherefrom it has been collected, so also *sat sampannah* in deep sleep, death, etc., people do not recognise their individualities. They slip into that state unawares. But when they wake up they regain their original individual characteristics.

D.: Honey, though collected from different flowers, becomes the bulk and does not possess individual characteristics. But the individual parts do not also exist in the drops and they do not return to their sources. Whereas the individuals after going to deep sleep wake up individuals as formerly. How is it?

M.: Just as the rivers discharged into the ocean lose their individualities, still the waters evaporate and return as rain on the hills and through rivers to the ocean, so also the individuals going to sleep lose their individualities and yet return as individuals according to their previous *vasanas* unawares. Thus, even in death, *sat* is not lost.

D.: How can that be?

M.: See how a tree, whose branches are cut, grows again. So long as the life-source is not affected it will grow. Similarly the *samskaras* (anamneses) sink into the heart in death: they do not perish. They will in right time sprout forth from the heart. That is how the *jivas* are reborn.

D.: How does the wide universe sprout forth from such subtle *samskaras* remaining sunk in the heart?

M.: Just as a big banyan tree sprouts from a tiny seed, so the wide universe with names and forms sprouts forth from the heart.

D.: If the origin is *sat* why is it not felt?

M.: The salt in the lump is visible; it is invisible in solution. Still its existence is known by taste. Similarly *sat*, though not recognised by the intellect, can still be realised in a different way, *i.e.*, transcendentally.

D.: How?

M.: Just as a man blindfolded and left by robbers in a jungle enquires his way home and returns there, so also the ignorant one (blinded by ignorance) enquires of those not so blinded and seeks his own source and returns to it.

Then, *Gurupadesa* — "*Vang manasi sampadyate, manah prane, pranastejasi, tejah parasyam devatayam iti.*"

D.: If so, a *jnani* or an *ajnani* dies in the same manner. Why is an *ajnani* reborn, whereas a *jnani* is not?

M.: Just as an innocent man *satyabhisandha* is not affected by the test of touching red hot iron but a thief is affected, so also the *sadbrahma satyabhisandha*, *i.e.*, a *jnani*, enters into *sat* consciously and merges, whereas the other enters unaware and is thrown out unawares also.

13th December, 1935

Talk 109.

Two gentlemen from Ambala (the Punjab) had been here for a few weeks. Just before taking leave of Sri Bhagavan one of them asked how he should remove the spiritual drowsiness of his friends or of other people in general.

M.: Have you removed your own 'spiritual drowsiness?' The force which is set up to remove your own 'drowsiness' will also operate in other centres. There is the will-power with which you can act on others. But it is on a lower plane and not desirable. Take care of yourself first.

D.: How to remove my own 'drowsiness'?

M.: Whose 'drowsiness' is it? Enquire. Turn within. Turn all your enquiries towards search for Self. The force set up within you will operate on others also.

14th December, 1935

Talk 110.

An American lady asked Bhagavan what his experiences of *samadhi* were. When suggested that she should relate her experiences and ask if they were right, she replied that Sri Bhagavan's experiences ought to be correct and should be known, whereas her own were unimportant. She thus wanted to know if Sri Bhagavan felt his body hot or cold in *samadhi*, if he spent the first three and a half years of his stay at Tiruvannamalai in prayers and so on.

M.: Samadhi transcends mind and speech and cannot be described. For example, the state of deep slumber cannot be described; *samadhi* state can still less be explained.

D.: But I know that I am unconscious in deep sleep.

M.: Consciousness and unconsciousness are only modes of the mind. *Samadhi* transcends the mind.

D.: Still you can say what it is like.

M.: You will know only when you are in *samadhi*.

16th December, 1935

Talk 111.

A Telugu gentleman asked about *Brahma bhavana*.

M.: Not to think "I am Brahman" or "All is Brahman" is itself *jivanmukti*.

He asked about inspired action.

M.: Let activities go on. They do not affect the pure Self.

17th December, 1935

Talk 112.

Mr. P. Brunton, while reading *Upadesa Manjari*, came across the statement that the ego, the world and God are all unreal. He desired to use a different word for God or at least a qualifying adjective, *e.g.*, the Creative Force or personal God.

Sri Bhagavan explained that God means *SAMASHTI* — *i.e.*, all that is, *plus* the Be-ing — in the same way as 'I' means the individual *plus* the Be-ing, and the world means the variety plus Be-ing. The Be-ing is in all cases real. The all, the variety and the individual is in each case unreal. So also in the union of the real and the unreal, the mixing up or the false identification is wrong. It amounts to saying *sad-asadvilakshana*, *i.e.*, transcending the real and the unreal — *sat* and *asat*. Reality is that which transcends all concepts, including that of God. Inasmuch as the name of God is used, it cannot be true. The Hebrew word *Jehovah* = (I am) expresses God correctly. Absolute Be-ing is beyond expression.

The word cannot be replaced nor need it be replaced. The Englishman casually said that in prehistoric ages there was spirituality but not high intellect, whereas intellect has now developed. Sri Bhagavan pointed out that *intellect* raises the question "whose intellect?" The answer is, of the *Self*. So intellect is a tool of the Self. The Self uses intellect for measuring variety. Intellect is not the Self nor apart from the Self. The Self alone is eternal. Intellect is only a phenomenon. People speak of the development of variety as being the development of intellect. Intellect was always there. *Dhata yatha parvam akalpayat* (The Creator created just as before). Consider your own state, day by day. There is no intellect in dreamless deep sleep. But it is there now. There is no intellect in a child. It develops with age. How could there be manifestation of intellect without its seed in the sleep state and in the child? Why go to history to teach this fundamental fact? The level of truth of history is only the level of truth of the individual.

Talk 113.

A Telugu gentleman asked about Karma Yoga. Sri Bhagavan said that the man should act as an actor on the stage. In all actions there is the *sat* as the underlying principle. "Remember it and act." He asked about the purity of mind — *chitta suddhi*. Sri Bhagavan said that *chitta suddhi* is to engage in one thought only to the exclusion of all others. It is otherwise called one-pointedness of the mind. The practice of meditation purifies the mind.

23rd December, 1935

Talk 114.

Baron Von Veltheim — Ostran, an East German Baron, asked, There should be harmony between knowledge of the Self and knowledge of the world. They must develop side by side. Is it right? Does Maharshi agree?

M.: Yes.

D.: Beyond the intellect and before wisdom dawns there will be pictures of the world passing before one's consciousness. Is it so?

Sri Bhagavan pointed out the parallel passage in *Dakshinamurti stotram* to signify that the pictures are like reflections in a mirror; again from the Upanishad — as in the mirror, so in the world of *manes*, as in the water, so in the world of Gandharvas; as shadow and sunlight in Brahma Loka.

D.: There is spiritual awakening since 1930 all the world over? Does Maharshi agree?

Maharshi said: "The development is according to *your* sight."

The Baron again asked if Maharshi would induce a spiritual trance and give him a message — which is unspoken but still understandable.

No answer was made.

25th December, 1935

Talk 115.

Mr. M. Frydman: Even without any initial desires there are some strange experiences for us. Wherefrom do they arise?

M.: The desire may not be there now. Enough if it was there before. Though forgotten by you now it is bearing fruit in due course. That is how the *jnani* is said to have *prarabdha* left for him. Of course it is only according to others' point of view.

Talk 116.

D.: Jiva is said to be bound by karma. Is it so?

M.: Let karma enjoy its fruits. As long as you are the doer so long are you the enjoyer.

D.: How to get released from karma.

M.: See whose karma it is. You will find you are not the doer. Then you will be free. This requires grace of God for which you should pray to Him, worship Him and meditate on Him.

The karma which takes place without effort, *i.e.,* involuntary action, is not binding.

Even a *jnani* is acting as seen by his bodily movements. There can be no karma without effort or without intentions (*sankalpas*). Therefore there are *sankalpas* for all. They are of two kinds (1) one, binding — *bandha-hetu* and the other (2) *mukti-hetu* — not binding. The former must be given up and the latter must be cultivated. There is no fruit without previous karma; no karma without previous *sankalpa*. Even *mukti* must be the result of effort so long as the sense of doership persists.

Talk 117.

A Ceylonese: What is the first step for Realisation of Self? Please help me towards it. There is no use reading books.

Another: This one man's request is that of us all.

M.: Quite so. If the Self be found in books it would have been already realised. What wonder can be greater than that we seek the Self in books? Can it be found there?

Of course books have given readers the sense to ask this question and to seek the Self.

D.: Books are utterly useless. They may all be burnt. The spoken word alone is useful. Grace alone is useful.

Others spoke according to their own light, until finally they returned to the original question, but Sri Bhagavan remained silent.

Talk 118.

Mr. Rangachari, a Telugu Pandit in Voorhees' College at Vellore, asked about *nishkama karma*. There was no reply. After a time Sri Bhagavan went up the hill and a few followed him, including the pandit. There was a thorny stick lying on the way which Sri Bhagavan picked up; he sat down and began leisurely to work at it. The thorns were cut off, the knots were made smooth, the whole stick was polished with a rough leaf. The whole operation took about six hours. Everyone was wondering at the fine appearance of the stick made of a spiky material. A shepherd boy put in his appearance on the way as the group moved off. He had lost his stick and was at a loss. Sri Bhagavan immediately gave the new one in his hand to the boy and passed on.

The pandit said that this was the matter-of-fact answer to his question.

Talk 119.

Again at the same time there were four dogs in the Asramam. Sri Bhagavan said that those dogs would not accept any food not partaken by Himself. The pandit put the matter to the test. He spread some food before them; they would not touch it; then Sri Bhagavan, after a time, put a small morsel of it into His mouth. Immediately they fell to and devoured the food.

Talk 120.

Later a man brought two peacocks with their eyes screened. When let loose in Maharshi's presence they flew away to a distance. They were brought back but still they flew away. Sri Bhagavan then said, "It is no use trying to keep them here. They are not ripe in their minds as these dogs." However much they tried to keep the peacocks they would not remain there even a minute.

Talk 121.

Talks between the Master and two Moslems on a previous occasion.

D.: Has God a form?

M.: Who says so?

D.: Well, if God has no form is it proper to worship idols?

112

M.: Leave God alone because He is unknown. What about you? Have you a form?

D.: Yes. I am this and so and so.

M.: So then, you are a man with limbs, about three and a half cubits high, with beard, etc. Is it so?

D.: Certainly.

M.: Then do you find yourself so in deep sleep?

D.: After waking I perceive that I was asleep. Therefore by inference I remained thus in deep sleep also.

M.: If you are the body why do they bury the corpse after death? The body must refuse to be buried.

D.: No, I am the subtle *jiva* within the gross body.

M.: So you see that you are really formless; but you are at present identifying yourself with the body. So long as you are formful why should you not worship the formless God as being formful?

The questioner was baffled and perplexed.

1st January, 1936

Talk 122.

A crowd had gathered here during Christmas.

D.: How to attain Unity Consciousness?

M.: Being Unity Consciousness how to attain it? Your question is its own answer.

D.: What is *Atman* (Self), *anatman* (non-self) and *paramatman* (Supreme Self)?

M.: *Atman* is *jivatman* (the individual Self) and the rest are plain. The Self is ever-present (*nityasiddha*). Each one wants to know the Self. What kind of help does one require to know oneself? People want to see the Self as something new. But it is eternal and remains the same all along. They desire to see it as a blazing light, etc. How can it be so? It is not light, not darkness (*na tejo, na tamah*). It is only as it is. It cannot be defined. The best definition is 'I am that I AM.' The *Srutis* speak of the Self as being the size of one's thumb, the tip of the hair, an electric spark, vast, subtler than the subtlest, etc. They

113

have no foundation in fact. It is only Being, but different from the real and the unreal; it is Knowledge, but different from knowledge and ignorance. How can it be defined at all? It is simply Being.

Again Sri Bhagavan said that in the whole Thayumanavar literature, he preferred one stanza which says: "Ego disappearing another 'I-I' spontaneously manifests in full glory," etc. Again he cites *Skandar Anubhuti*: "Not real, nor unreal; not darkness nor light, it is."

One man said, that a *siddha* of Kumbakonam claimed to overcome the defects in Sri Sankara's system which deals only with transcendentalism and not the work-a-day life. One must be able to exercise super-human powers in ordinary life, that is to say, one must be a *siddha* in order to be perfect.

Sri Bhagavan pointed out a stanza in Thayumanavar which condemns all *siddhis*. Further he said that Thayumanavar mentions *mouna* (silence) in numerous places but defines it in only one verse. *Mouna* is said to be that state which spontaneously manifests after the annihilation of the ego. That state is beyond light and darkness, but still it is called light since no other proper word could be found for it.

3rd January, 1936

Talk 123.

Dr. Mohammed Hafiz Syed, a Muslim Professor of Persian and Urdu in the University of Allahabad, asked: " What is the purpose of this external manifestation?"

M.: This manifestation had induced your question.

D.: True. I am covered by *maya*. How to be free from it?

M.: Who is covered by *maya*? Who wants to be free?

D.: Master, being asked 'Who?', I know that it is ignorant me, composed of the senses, mind and body. I tried this enquiry 'Who?' after reading Paul Brunton's book. Three or four times I was feeling elated and the elation lasted sometime and faded away. How to be established in 'I'? Please give me the clue and help me.

M.: That which appears anew must also disappear in due course.

114

D.: Please tell me the method of reaching the eternal Truth.

M.: You are *That*. Can you ever remain apart from the Self? To be yourself requires no effort since you are always That.

Talk 124.

Another impatient questioner elaborated long premises and finished asking why some children die a premature death. He required the answer not to satisfy the grown-up ones who look on, but the babies who are the victims.

M.: Let the victims ask. Why do you ask and desire the answer from the standpoint of the child?

Talk 125.

The Muslim Professor asked: When I am here my mind is *satvic*; as soon as I turn my back on this, my mind hankers after so many objects.

M.: Are the objects different from you? There can be no objects without the subject.

D.: And how shall I know it?

M.: Being That, what do you want to know? Are there two selves for the one to know the other?

D.: Again, I repeat, sir, how to know the truth of all this and experience the same?

M.: There is no gaining of anything new. All that is required is to rid the Self of ignorance. This ignorance is the identification of the Self with the non-Self.

D.: Yes. Still I do not understand. I must have your help. Everyone here is waiting on you for your Grace. You yourself must have sought originally the help of a Guru or of God. Extend that Grace to others now and save me.

Before I came here I desired to see you very much. But somehow I could not find an opportunity to do so. In Bangalore I made up my mind to return to my place. I met Mr. Frydman and others who sent me here. You have dragged me here. My case is like Paul Brunton's in Bombay, when he was dragged here having cancelled his passage home.

I hesitated at first on arrival. I wondered if I would be permitted to approach you and converse with you. My doubts were soon set at rest. I find that all are equal here. You have established an equality among all. I dined with you and others. If I should say so to my people in U.P., they would not believe it. The Brahmins would not drink water with me, nor chew *pan* with me. But here you have taken me and others like me in your fold. Though Gandhi is striving hard he cannot bring about such a state of affairs in the country. I am very happy in your presence.

I regard you as God. I consider Sri Krishna to be true God because He has said, "Whomsoever one may worship, the worshipper worships me only and I save him." Whereas all others have said, "Salvation is through me (meaning himself) only," Krishna alone is so broad-minded and has spoken like God. You observe the same kind of equality.

4th January, 1936

Talk 126.

Dr. Syed again asked: "Should anyone desirous of spiritual progress take to action or renunciation (*pravritti-marga* or *nivritti-marga*)?"

M.: Do you go out of the Self? What is meant by giving up?

An American Engineer asked about *sat-sanga* (association with sages).

M.: Sat is within us.

D.: In the book "*Who am I?*" you have said the Heart is the seat of the mind. Is it so?

M.: The mind is Atman.

D.: Is it Atman itself or its projection?

M.: The same.

D.: The Westerners look on the mind as the highest principle, whereas the Easterners think the contrary — why?

M.: Where psychology ends, there philosophy begins. This is experience; the mind is born; we see it; even without the mind we exist. There is everyone's experience to prove it.

D.: In deep sleep I do not seem to exist.

116

M.: You say so when awake. It is the mind which speaks now. You exist in deep sleep beyond mind.

D.: Western philosophy admits the Higher Self as influencing the mind.

Talk 127.

The American Engineer asked: "Does distance have any effect upon Grace?"

M.: Time and space are within us. You are always in your Self. How do time and space affect it?

D.: In radio those who are nearer hear sooner. You are Hindu, we are American. Does it make any difference?

M.: No.

D.: Even thoughts are read by others.

M.: That shows that all are one.

5th January, 1936

Talk 128.

There were some French ladies and gentlemen and American as visitors to the Asramam. They asked Sri Bhagavan several questions. Among them, one was: "What is the message of the East to the West?"

M.: All go to the same goal.

To another question Sri Bhagavan said: "How do you say 'I am'? Do you take a light to find yourself? Or did you come to know it on reading books? How?"

The questioner said: "By experience."

M.: Yes. Experience is the word. Knowledge implies subject and object. But experience is non- terminal, eternal.

6th January, 1936

Talk 129.

An elderly gentleman, formerly a co-worker with B. V. Narasimha Swami and author of some *Visishtadvaita* work, visited the place for the first time. He asked about rebirths, if it is possible for the *linga sarira* (subtle body) to get dissolved and be reborn in two years after death.

M.: Yes. Surely. Not only can one be reborn, one may be twenty or forty or even seventy years old in the new body though only two years after death. Sri Bhagavan cited Lila's story from *Yoga Vasishta*.

Sreyo hi jnanam abhyasat jnanat dhyanam,
dhyanat karmaphala tyagah.

Here *jnana* stands for knowledge without practice; *abhyasa* stands for practice without knowledge; *dhyana* stands for practice with knowledge.

"Knowledge without practice accompanying it is superior to practice without knowledge. Practice with knowledge is superior to knowledge without practice accompanying it. *Karmaphala tyagah Nishkama karma* as of a *jnani* — action without desire — is superior to knowledge with practice."

D.: What is the difference between *yoga* and surrender?

M.: Surrender is *Bhakti Yoga*. To reach the source of the 'I-thought' is the destruction of the ego, is the attainment of the goal, is *prapatti* (surrender), *jnana*, etc.

Talk 130.

Lakshman Brahmachari from Sri Ramakrishna Mission asked: Enquiry of 'Who am I?' or of the 'I-thought' being itself a thought, how can it be destroyed in the process?

M.: When Sita was asked who was her husband among the *rishis* (Rama himself being present there as a *rishi*) in the forest by the wives of the *rishis*, she denied each one as he was pointed out to her, but simply hung down her head when Rama was pointed out. Her silence was eloquent.

Similarly, the Vedas also are eloquent in '*neti*' — '*neti*' (not this — not this) and then remain silent. Their silence is the Real State. This is the meaning of exposition by silence. When the source of the 'I-thought' is reached it vanishes and what remains over is the Self.

D.: Patanjali Yoga Sutras speak of identification.

M.: Identification with the Supreme is only the other name for the destruction of the ego.

Talk 131.

Mr. Subba Rao asked: What is *mukhya prana* (the chief *prana*)?

M.: It is that from which the ego and the *prana* rise. It is sometimes called *Kundalini*. Consciousness is not born at any time, it remains eternal. But ego is born; so also the other thoughts. Associated with the absolute consciousness they shine forth; not otherwise.

D.: What is *moksha* (liberation)?

M.: Moksha is to know that you were not born. "*Be still and know that I am God.*"

To be still is not to think. Know, and not *think*, is the word.

D.: There are said to be six organs of different colours in the chest, of which the heart is said to be two finger-breadths to the right of the middle line. But the Heart is also formless. Should we then imagine it to have a shape and meditate on it?

M.: No. Only the quest "Who am I?" is necessary. What remains all through deep sleep and waking is the same. But in waking there is unhappiness and the effort to remove it. Asked who wakes up from sleep you say 'I'. Now you are told to hold fast to this 'I'. If it is done the eternal Being will reveal Itself. Investigation of 'I' is the point and not meditation on the heart-centre. There is nothing like within or without. Both mean either the same thing or nothing.

Of course there is also the practice of meditation on the heart-centre. It is only a practice and not investigation. Only the one who meditates on the heart can remain aware when the mind ceases to be active and remains still; whereas those who meditate on other centres cannot be so aware but infer that the mind was still only after it becomes again active.

Talk 132.

An educated man asked: Is there an Absolute Being? What is its relation to the relative existence?

M.: Are they different from each other? All the questions arise only in the mind. The mind arises with waking and subsides in deep sleep. As long as there is a mind, so long will there be such questions and doubts.

119

D.: There must be stage after stage of progress for gaining the Absolute. Are there grades of Reality?

M.: There are no grades of Reality. There are grades of experience for the *jiva* and not of Reality. If anything can be gained anew, it could also be lost, whereas the Absolute is central — here and now.

D.: If so, how do I remain ignorant of it (*avarana*)?

M.: For whom is this ignorance (veiling)? Does the Absolute tell you that it is veiled? It is the *jiva* who says that something veils the Absolute. Find out for whom this ignorance is.

D.: Why is there imperfection in Perfection? That is, how did the Absolute become relative?

M.: For whom is this relativity? For whom is this imperfection? The Absolute is not imperfect and cannot ask. The insentient cannot ask the question. Between the two something has risen up which raises these questions and which feels this doubt. Who is it? Is it the one who has now arisen? Or is it the one who is eternal?

Being perfect, why do you feel yourself imperfect? Such is the teaching of all the religions. Whatever may be the experiences, the experiencer is one and the same.

'I' is *purna* — perfection. There is no diversity in sleep. That indicates perfection.

D.: Being perfect, why do I not feel it?

M.: Nor is imperfection felt in deep sleep. The 'I' in sleep being perfect, why does the waking 'I' feel imperfect? Because the one who feels imperfect is a spurious offshoot, a differentiation from the Infinite — a segregation from God.

D.: I am the same in all the three states. Did this ego submerge me or did I entangle myself into it?

M.: Did anything come up without you?

D.: I am always the same.

M.: Because you see it, this appears to have come up. Did you feel this difficulty in deep sleep? What is new now?

D.: The senses and the mind.

120

M.: Who says this? Is it the sleeper? If so he should have raised the question in deep sleep also. The sleeper has been lost hold of, some spurious offshoot has differentiated himself and speaks now.

Can anything new appear without that which is eternal and perfect? This kind of dispute is itself eternal. Do not engage in it. Turn inward and put an end to all this. There will be no finality in disputations.

D.: Show me that Grace which puts an end to all this trouble. I have not come here to argue. I want only to learn.

M.: Learn first what you are. This requires no *sastras*, no scholarship. This is simple experience. The state of *being* is now and here all along. You have lost hold of yourself and are asking others for guidance. The purpose of philosophy is to turn you inward. "If you know your Self, no evil can come to you. Since you asked me I have taught you."

The ego comes up only holding you (the Self). Hold yourself and the ego will vanish. Until then the sage will be saying, "There is." — The ignorant will be asking "Where?"

D.: The crux of the problem lies in "Know Thyself."

M.: Yes. Quite so.

Talk 133.

There are two schools in *Advaita*: (1) *Drishti srishti* (simultaneous creation) and (2) *Srishti drishti* (gradual creation).

There is the *Tantric Advaita* which admits three fundamentals *jagat, jiva, Isvara* — world, soul, God. These three are also real. But the reality does not end with them. It extends beyond. That is the *Tantric Advaita*. The Reality is limitless. The three fundamentals do not exist apart from the Absolute Reality. All agree that Reality is all-pervading; thus *Isvara* pervades the *jiva*; therefore the *jiva* has eternal being. His knowledge is not limited. Limited knowledge is only imagined by him. In truth, his is infinite knowledge. Its limit is Silence. This truth was revealed by *Dakshinamurti*. For those who still perceive these three fundamentals they are said to be realities. They are concomitant with the ego.

True, the images of gods are described in great detail. Such description points only to the final Reality. Otherwise why is the

121

special significance of each detail also given? Think. The image is only a symbol. Only that which lies beyond name and form is Reality. *Saiva Siddhanta* and *Vedanta* have the common aim of the same Truth. Otherwise how could Sri Sankaracharya, the greatest exponent of *Advaita*, sing praises of gods? Obviously he did so knowingly.

The questioner earnestly explained that his faith in *Saiva Siddhanta, Vedanta*, etc., was shaken after reading Bahaic literature. "Please save me," he said.

M.: Know the Self which is here and now; you will be steady and not waver.

D.: The Bahaists read others' minds.

M.: Yes. That is possible. Your thoughts were read by another. There must be one to know your mind. That is the Truth always present which is to be realised. Truth does not waver.

D.: Show me Grace.

M.: Grace always *is*, and is *not given*. Why do you consider the pros and cons of Bahaullah or others being incarnations or otherwise? Know Thyself. Regard everything as Truth. Regard him also as the Truth. Can he exist besides Truth? Your beliefs may change but not Truth.

D.: Show me the truth of *Siddhanta*, etc.

M.: Follow their instructions and then if you have doubts you may ask. Adherence to those instructions will take you only to *mouna*. Differences are perceived in external objects only. If you follow their instructions all differences will be lost. No one but the son of a king can be called a prince; so also only That which is perfect is called Perfection.

One should not be content with mere discipleship, initiation, ceremony of surrender, etc.; these are external phenomena. Never forget the Truth underlying all phenomena.

D.: What is the significance of the Silence of *Dakshinamurti*?

M.: Many are the explanations given by scholars and sages. Have it any way you please.

14th January, 1936

Talk 134.

A question about the Heart was raised.

Sri Bhagavan said that one should seek the Self and realise it. The Heart will play its part automatically. The seat of realisation is the Heart. It cannot be said to be either in or out.

D.: Did Bhagavan feel the Heart as the point of Realisation in his first or early experience?

M.: I began to use the word after seeing literature on the subject. I correlated it with my experience.

15th January, 1936

Talk 135.

Three European ladies from the Theosophical Conference came here and asked: "Is the whole scheme, the Plan, really good? Or is it in the nature of an error, a mistake of which we have to make the best?"

M.: The Plan is indeed good. The error is on our part. When we correct it in ourselves the whole scheme becomes all right.

D.: Have you any formula to teach us how to bring it about through a remembrance of what we do during sleep?

M.: No formula is needed. Everyone has the experience that he slept happily and knew nothing then. Nothing else was experienced.

D.: The answer does not satisfy me. We wander in the astral plane in our sleep but we do not remember it.

M.: The astral plane is concerned with dreams, not with deep sleep.

D.: What do you consider to be the cause of world suffering? And how can we help to change it, (*a*) as individuals? or (*b*) collectively?

M.: Realise the Real Self. It is all that is necessary.

D.: Can we hasten our illumination for greater service? and how?

M.: As we are not able to help ourselves, so we have to surrender ourselves to the Supreme completely. Then He will take care of us as well as the world.

D.: What do you consider the goal?

M.: Self-Realisation.

D.: Is there any way to meet the appointed Guru for each?

M.: Intense meditation brings it about.

Talk 136.

Dr. G. H. Mees, a young Dutchman, was here for a few days. He asked Sri Bhagavan: "I have an impression that in deep sleep I have something akin to *samadhi*. Is it so?"

M.: It is the waking 'I' that asks the questions — not the 'I' in sleep. If you attain the state of wakeful sleep which is the same as *samadhi*, while still awake, doubts will not arise.

Samadhi is one's natural state. It is the under-current in all the three states. This — that is, 'I' — is not in those states, but these states are in It. If we get *samadhi* in our waking state that will persist in deep sleep also. The distinction between consciousness and unconsciousness belongs to the realm of mind, which is transcended by the state of the Real Self.

D.: Is the Buddhist view, that there is no continuous entity answering to the ideas of the individual soul, correct or not? Is this consistent with the Hindu notion of a reincarnating ego? Is the soul a continuous entity which reincarnates again and again, according to the Hindu doctrine, or is it a mere mass of mental tendencies — *samskaras*?

M.: The Real Self is continuous and unaffected. The reincarnating ego belongs to the lower plane, namely, thought. It is transcended by Self-Realisation.

Reincarnations are due to a spurious offshoot. Therefore it is denied by the Buddhists. The present state is due to a mixing up of the *chit* (sentient) with *jada* (insentient).

Talk 137.

Lakshman Brahmachari of Sri Ramakrishna Mission asked: "Can one imagine oneself as witness of the thoughts?"

M.: It is not the natural state. It is only an idea (*bhavana*) — an aid to stilling the mind. The Self is ever the witness, whether so imagined or not. There is no need to so imagine except for that purpose. But it is best to remain as one's Self.

Talk 138.

The Financial Secretary of Mysore asked: "Is Paul Brunton's *Secret Path* useful for Indians as well?"

M.: Yes — for all.

D.: The body, the senses, etc. are not 'I'. This is common amongst us. But how to practise it?

M.: By the threefold method mentioned therein.

D.: Is breath-control necessary for enquiry?

M.: Not quite.

D.: "There is a blankness intervening," it is said in the book.

M.: Yes. Do not stop there. See for whom the blankness appears.

D.: For devotees there is no blankness, it is said.

M.: Even there, there is the latent state, *laya*; the mind wakes up after some time.

D.: What is the experience of *samadhi*?

M.: It is as it is. For onlookers it may seem to be a swoon. Even to the practiser it may appear so in the early experiences. After a few repeated experiences it will be all right.

D.: Do they soothe *nadis* or do they excite them by such experiences?

M.: They are excited at first. By continued experience it becomes common and the man is no longer excited.

D.: Proceeding on safe lines there should be no unpleasantness. Excitement is uncongenial to smooth being and working.

M.: A wandering mind is on the wrong way; only a devotional mind is on the right way.

19th January, 1936

Talk 139.

Mr. Ellappa Chettiar, a Member of the Legislative Council, from Salem, asked: "Is it enough to introvert the mind or should we meditate on 'I am Brahman'?"

M.: To introvert the mind is the prime thing. The Buddhists consider the flow of 'I' thought to be Liberation; whereas we say that such flow proceeds from its underlying substratum — the only — Reality.

Why should one be meditating 'I am Brahman'? Only the annihilation of 'I' is Liberation. But it can be gained only by keeping the 'I-I' always in view. So the need for the investigation of the 'I' thought. If the 'I' is not let go, no blank can result to the seeker. Otherwise meditation will end in sleep.

There is only one 'I' all along, but what arises up from time to time is the mistaken 'I-thought'; whereas the intuitive 'I' always remains Self-shining, *i.e.*, even before it becomes manifest.

The birth of the gross body does not amount to one's own birth, on the other hand, the birth of the ego is one's own birth.

For liberation, nothing new remains to be gained. It is the original state and continues unchanged too.

Talk 140.

D.: What is reality?

M.: Reality must be always real. It is not with forms and names. That which underlies these is the Reality. It underlies limitations, being itself limitless. It is not bound. It underlies unrealities, itself being real. Reality is that which is. It is as it is. It transcends speech, beyond the expressions, *e.g.*, existence, non-existence, etc.

Talk 141.

The same gentleman later, after quoting a verse from *Kaivalya*, asked: "Can *jnana* be lost after being once attained?"

M.: Jnana, once revealed, takes time to steady itself. The Self is certainly within the direct experience of everyone, but not as one imagines it to be. It is only as it is. This Experience is *samadhi*. Just as fire remains without scorching against incantations or other devices but scorches otherwise, so also the Self remains veiled by *vasanas* and reveals itself when there are no *vasanas*. Owing to the fluctuation of the *vasanas, jnana* takes time to steady itself. Unsteady *jnana* is not enough to check rebirths. *Jnana* cannot remain unshaken side by side with *vasanas*. True, that in the proximity of a great master, the *vasanas* will cease to be active, the mind becomes still and *samadhi* results, similar to fire not scorching because of other devices. Thus the disciple gains true knowledge and right experience in the presence of the master. To remain unshaken in it further efforts are necessary. He will know it to be his real Being and thus be liberated even while alive. *Samadhi* with closed eyes is certainly good, but one must go further until it is realised that actionlessness and action are not hostile to each other. Fear of loss of *samadhi* while one is active is the sign of ignorance. *Samadhi* must be the natural life of everyone.

There is a state beyond our efforts or effortlessness. Until it is realised effort is necessary. After tasting such Bliss, even once one will repeatedly try to regain it. Having once experienced the Bliss of Peace no one would like to be out of it or engaged himself otherwise. It is as difficult for a *jnani* to engage in thoughts as it is for an *ajnani* to be free from thought.

The common man says that he does not know himself; he thinks many thoughts and cannot remain without thinking.

Any kind of activity does not affect a *jnani*; his mind remains ever in eternal Peace.

20th January, 1936

Talk 142.

Mr. Prakasa Rao from Bezwada: Does not illusion become inoperative even before identity with Brahman results (*Brahmakaravritti*)? Or does it persist even afterwards?

M.: Illusion will not persist after *vasanas* are annihilated. In the interval between the knowledge of the identity and annihilation of *vasanas*, there will be illusion.

D.: How can the world influence a man even after identity with Brahman?

M.: First do it and see. You can then raise this question, if necessary.

D.: Can we know it in the same way as we know our identity?

M.: Are you different from the mind? How do you expect it to be known?

D.: Can the full scope of the *Chitta* (*Chittavilasa*) be known?

M.: Oh! Is this the identity of Brahman?

Ignorance vanishing, the residue reveals itself. It is experience, not in the category of knowledge.

23rd January, 1936

Talk 143.

Mr. P. Brunton asked Sri Bhagavan if the Hill here is hollow.

M.: The *puranas* say so. When it is said that the Heart is a cavity, penetration into it proves it to be an expanse of light. Similarly the Hill is one of light. The caves, etc., are covered up by the Light.

D.: Are there caves inside?

M.: In visions I have seen caves, cities with streets, etc., and a whole world in it.

D.: Are there *Siddhas* too in it?

M.: All the *Siddhas* are reputed to be there.

D.: Are there only *Siddhas* or others also?

M.: Just like this world.

D.: *Siddhas* are said to be in the Himalayas.

M.: Kailas is on the Himalayas: it is the abode of Siva. Whereas this Hill is Siva Himself. All the paraphernalia of His abode must also be where He Himself is.

D.: Does Bhagavan believe that the Hill is hollow, etc.?

M.: Everything depends on the viewpoint of the individual. You yourself have seen hermitages, etc., on this Hill in a vision. You have described such in your book.

D.: Yes. It was on the surface of the Hill. The vision was within me.

M.: That is exactly so. Everything is within one's Self. To see the world, there must be a spectator. There could be no world without the Self. The Self is all-comprising. In fact Self is all. There is nothing besides the Self.

D.: What is the mystery of this Hill?

M.: Just as you have said in *Secret Egypt*, "The mystery of the pyramid is the mystery of the Self," so also the mystery of this Hill is the mystery of the Self.

128

Maj. Chadwick: I do not know if the Self is different from the ego.

M.: How were you in your deep sleep?

D.: I do not know.

M.: Who does not know? Is it not the waking Self? Do you deny your existence in your deep sleep?

D.: I was and I am; but I do not know who was in deep sleep.

M.: Exactly. The man awake says that he did not know anything in the state of sleep. Now he sees the objects and knows that he is there; whereas in deep sleep there were no objects, no spectator, etc. The same one who is now speaking was in deep sleep also. What is the difference between these two states? There are objects and play of senses now which were not in sleep. A new entity, the ego, has risen up in the meantime, it plays through the senses, sees the objects, confounds itself with the body and says that the Self is the ego. In reality, what was in deep sleep continues to exist now too. The Self is changeless. It is the ego that has come between. That which rises and sets is the ego; that which remains changeless is the Self.

Talk 144.

Mr. Prakasa Rao: What is the root-cause of *maya*?

M.: What is *maya*?

D.: *Maya* is wrong knowledge, illusion.

M.: For whom is the illusion? There must be one to be deluded. Illusion is ignorance. The ignorant Self sees the objects according to you. When the objects are not themselves present how can *maya* exist? *Maya is ya ma* (*maya is what is not*). What remains over is the true Self. If you say that you see the objects, or if you say that you do not know the Real Unity, then are there two selves, one the knower and the other the knowable object. No one will admit of two selves in himself. The awakened man says that he himself was in deep slumber but not aware. He does not say that the sleeper was different from the present one. There is only one Self. That Self is always aware. It is changeless. There is nothing but the Self.

D.: What is the astral body?

129

M.: Do you not have a body in your dream? Is it not different from the recumbent body on the bed?

D.: Do we survive after death? Does the astral body outlive physical death?

M.: Just as in dreams you wake up after several novel experiences, so also after physical death another body is found and so on.

D.: They say that the astral body lives for forty years after death.

M.: In the present body you say the dream body is astral. Did you say so in the dream body? What is astral now would appear real then, the present body itself is astral according to that view-point. What is the difference between one astral body and another? There is no difference between the two.

Mr. P. Brunton: There are degrees of reality.

M.: To say the dream body is unreal now, and to say that this body was unreal in the dream, does not denote degrees of reality. In deep sleep there is no experience of the body at all. There is always only one and that is the Self.

Talk 145.

Mr. P. Brunton: Why do religions speak of Gods, heaven, hell, etc.?

M.: Only to make the people realise that they are on a par with this world and that the Self alone is real. The religions are according to the view-point of the seeker. Take the *Bhagavad Gita* for instance: When Arjuna said that he would not fight against his own relatives, his elders, etc., in order to kill them and gain the kingdom, Sri Krishna said, "Not that these, you or I, were not before, are not now, nor will not be hereafter. Nothing was born, nothing was dead, nor will it not be so hereafter" and so on. Later as he developed the theme and declared that He had given the same instruction to the Sun, through him to Ikshvaku, etc. Arjuna raised the doubt, "How could it be? You were born a few years ago. They lived ages ago." Then Sri Krishna understanding Arjuna's standpoint, said: "Yes. There have been so many incarnations of myself and yourself, I know them all but you do not know."

Such statements appear contradictory, but still they are correct according to the viewpoint of the questioner. The Christ also declared that He was even before Abraham.

D.: What is the purpose of such descriptions in religions?

M.: Only to establish the Reality of the Self.

D.: Bhagavan always speaks from the highest standpoint.

Sri Bhagavan (with a smile): People would not understand the simple and bare truth — the truth of their every day, ever-present and eternal experience. That Truth is that of the Self. Is there anyone not aware of the Self? They would not even like to hear it (the Self), whereas they are eager to know what lies beyond — heaven, hell, reincarnation. Because they love mystery and not the bare truth, religions pamper them — only to bring them round to the Self. Wandering hither and thither you must return to the Self only. Then, why not abide in the Self even here and now?

The other worlds require the Self as a spectator or speculator. Their reality is only of the same degrees as that of the spectator or thinker. They cannot exist without the spectator, etc. Therefore they are not different from the Self. Even the ignorant man sees only the Self when he sees objects. But he is confused and identifies the Self with the object, *i.e.,* the body and with the senses and plays in the world. Subject and object — all merge in the Self. There is no seer nor objects seen. The seer and the seen are the Self. There are not many selves either. All are only one Self.

26th January, 1936

Talk 146.

In reply to Miss Leena Sarabhai, a cultured Indian lady of high rank, Sri Bhagavan said: The state of equanimity is the state of bliss. The declaration in the Vedas 'I am This or That', is only an aid to gain equanimity of mind.

D.: So, it is wrong to begin with a goal: is it?

M.: If there be a goal to be reached it cannot be permanent. The goal must already be there. We seek to reach the goal with the ego, but the goal exists before the ego. What is in the goal is even prior to our birth, *i.e.*, to the birth of the ego. Because we exist the ego appears to exist too.

If we look on the Self as the ego then we become the ego, if as the mind we become the mind, if as the body we become the body. It is the thought which builds up sheaths in so many ways. The shadow on the water is found to be shaking. Can anyone stop the shaking of the shadow? If it should cease to shake you would not notice the water but only the light. Similarly to take no notice of the ego and its activities, but see only the light behind. The ego is the I-thought. The true 'I' is the Self.

D.: It is one step to realisation.

M.: Realisation is already there. The state free from thoughts is the only real state. There is no such action as Realisation. Is there anyone who is not realising the Self? Does anyone deny his own existence? Speaking of realisation, it implies two selves — the one to realise, the other to be realised. What is not already realised, is sought to be realised. Once we admit our existence, how is it that we do not know our Self?

D.: Because of the thoughts — the mind.

M.: Quite so. It is the mind that stands between and veils our happiness. How do we know that we exist? If you say because of the world around us, then how do you know that you existed in deep sleep?

D.: How to get rid of the mind?

M.: Is it the mind that wants to kill itself? The mind cannot kill itself. So your business is to find the real nature of the mind. Then you will know that there is no mind. When the Self is sought, the mind is nowhere. Abiding in the Self, one need not worry about the mind.

D.: How to get rid of fear?

M.: What is fear? It is only a thought. If there is anything besides the Self there is reason to fear. Who sees the second (anything external)? First the ego arises and sees objects as external. If the ego does not rise, the Self alone exists and there is no second (nothing external). For anything external to oneself implies the seer within.

132

Seeking it there will arise no doubt, no fear — not only fear, all other thoughts centred round the ego will disappear along with it.

D.: This method seems to be quicker than the usual one of cultivating qualities alleged necessary for salvation (*sadhana chatushtaya*)?

M.: Yes. All bad qualities centre round the ego. When the ego is gone Realisation results by itself. There are neither good nor bad qualities in the Self. The Self is free from all qualities. Qualities pertain to the mind only. It is beyond quality. If there is unity, there will also be duality. The numeral one gives rise to other numbers. The truth is neither one nor two. IT is as it is.

D.: The difficulty is to be in the thought-free state.

M.: Leave the thought-free state to itself. Do not think of it as pertaining to you. Just as when you walk, you involuntarily take steps, so too in your actions; but the thought-free state is not affected by your actions.

D.: What is it that is discriminative in action?

M.: Discrimination will be automatic, intuitive.

D.: So Intuition alone matters; Intuition develops also.

M.: Those who have discovered great Truths have done so in the still depths of the Self.

The ego is like one's shadow thrown on the ground. If one attempts to bury it, it will be foolish. The Self is only one. If limited it is the ego. If unlimited it is Infinite and is the Reality.

The bubbles are different from one another and numerous, but the ocean is only one. Similarly the egos are many, whereas the Self is one and only one.

When told that you are not the ego, realise the Reality. Why do you still identify yourself with the ego? It is like saying, "Don't think of the monkey while taking medicine" — it is impossible. Similarly it happens with common folk. When the Reality is mentioned why do you continue to meditate *Sivoham* or *Aham Brahmasmi*? The significance must be traced and understood. It is not enough to repeat the bare words or think of them.

Reality is simply the loss of the ego. Destroy the ego by seeking its identity. Because the ego is no entity it will automatically vanish and Reality will shine forth by itself. This is the direct method. Whereas all other methods are done, only retaining the ego. In those paths there arise so many doubts and the eternal question remains to be tackled finally. But in this method the final question is the only one and it is raised from the very beginning. No *sadhanas* are necessary for engaging in this quest.

There is no greater mystery than this — *viz.*, ourselves being the Reality we seek to gain reality. We think that there is something hiding our Reality and that it must be destroyed before the Reality is gained. It is ridiculous. A day will dawn when you will yourself laugh at your past efforts. That which will be on the day you laugh is also here and now.

D.: So it is a great game of pretending?

M.: Yes.

In *Yoga Vasishtha* it is said, "What is Real is hidden from us, but what is false, is revealed as true." We are actually experiencing the Reality only; still, we do not know it. Is it not a wonder of wonders?

The quest "Who am I?" is the axe with which to cut off the ego.

Talk 147.

In answer to a Canarese Sanyasi, Sri Bhagavan said: There are different grades of mind. Realisation is of Perfection. It cannot be comprehended by the mind. *Sarvajnatva* (the state of all-knowing) is to be *sarvam* (the all); 'the all' pertains only to the mind. The known and unknown together form 'the all'. After transcending the mind you remain as the Self. The present knowledge is only of limitation. That Knowledge is unlimited. Being so it cannot be comprehended by this knowledge. Cease to be a knower, then there is perfection.

27th January, 1936

Talk 148.

A Gujerati gentleman said that he was concentrating on sound — *nada* — and desired to know if the method was right.

134

M.: Meditation on *nada* is one of the several approved methods. The adherents claim a very special virtue for the method. According to them it is the easiest and the most direct method. Just as a child is lulled to sleep by lullabies, so *nada* soothes one to the state of *samadhi*; again just as a king sends his state musicians to welcome his son on his return from a long journey, so also *nada* takes the devotee into the Lord's Abode in a pleasing manner. *Nada* helps concentration. After it is felt the practice should not be made an end in itself. *Nada* is not the objective; the subject should firmly be held; otherwise a blank will result. Though the subject is there even in the blank he would not be aware of the cessation of *nada* of different kinds. In order to be aware even in that blank one must remember his own self. *Nada upasana* (meditation on sound) is good; it is better if associated with investigation (*vichara*). In that case the *nada* is made up of *chinmaya* and also *tanmaya* (of Knowledge and of Self). *Nada* helps concentration.

28th January, 1936

Talk 149.

In reply to a *sadhu* who asked if *bhakti* consisted in forgetting the body, etc. Sri Bhagavan said:

"What do you care for the body? Practise *bhakti* and don't worry about what happens to the body."

Talk 150.

Mrs. and Mr. Kelly, an elderly couple from America, and others of their company desired to know what they should do to gain concentration in face of discomforts of sitting and the sting of mosquitoes, etc.

M.: The discomforts will not worry you if your concentration is right. Do not mind the discomforts. Keep your mind steady in meditation. If you have not the strength and endurance to bear mosquito stings how do you hope to gain realisation of the Self? Realisation must be amidst all the turmoils of life. If you make yourself comfortable and go to bed you fall asleep. Face the troubles but keep yourself steady in meditation.

Talk 151.

The American gentleman is a little hard of hearing. Being accustomed to be self-reliant from his youth he naturally feels worried on account of his hearing becoming defective.

M.: You were not self-reliant; you were ego-reliant. It is good that ego-reliance is banished and that you become truly Self-reliant.

Again Bhagavan said:

"There is no cause for worry. Subjugation of senses is a necessary preliminary for Self-Realisation. One sense is subdued for you by God Himself. So much the better."

The questioner said that he appreciated the humour, but that still his self-respect suffered.

M.: The Self is only one. Do you feel hurt if you blame yourself or scorn yourself for your errors? If you hold the Self there is no second person to scorn you. When you see the world you have lost hold of the Self. On the contrary, hold the Self and the world will not appear.

1st February, 1936

Talk 152.

Mrs. Kelly desired to know how she should best learn to meditate.

Sri Bhagavan asked if she had made *japa* (rolling beads as Roman Catholics do). She said: "No".

M.: Have you thought of God, His qualities, etc.?

D.: I have read, talked, etc. about such themes.

M.: Well, if the same be revolved in the mind without open expression through the senses it is meditation.

D.: I mean meditation as signified in *The Secret Path* and *Who am I?*

M.: Long for it intensely so that the mind melts in devotion. After the camphor burns away no residue is left. The mind is the camphor; when it has resolved itself into the Self without leaving even the slightest trace behind, it is Realisation of the Self.

Talk 153.

Some Peshawaris, among them a Judicial Commissioner and a young man well-read and earnest, with a strong belief in the existence of *Paramatman* (Supreme Self) as different from the *Jivatman* (individual self), raised some questions.

Sri Bhagavan clinched his various doubts by this one statement: Remove the *upadhis* (adjuncts), *jiva* and *parama*, from the Atman and say if you still find the difference. If later these doubts still persist ask yourself, "Who is the doubter? Who is the thinker?" Find him. These doubts will vanish.

Talk 154.

The next day he asked about *pranayama*.

M.: Pranayama according to *jnana* is:

"*Na aham*"	I am not this	= out-breathing
"*Koham*"	Who am I?	= in-breathing
"*Soham*"	I am He	= Retention of breath

This is *vichara*. This *vichara* brings about the desired result.

For one not so advanced as to engage in it, some meditation brings about suspension of breath and the mind ceases to be restless. Control of mind spontaneously effects control of breath; rather *kevala kumbhaka* (spontaneous retention of breath, without attention to inhalation or exhalation) results.

For one unable to do this also, regulation of breath is prescribed for making the mind quiescent. Quiescence lasts only so long as the breath is controlled. So it is transient. The goal is clearly not *pranayama*. It extends on to *pratyahara, dharana, dhyana* and *samadhi*. Those stages deal with the control of mind. Such control becomes easier for the man who had earlier practised *pranayama*. *Pranayama* leads him to the higher stages involving control of mind. Therefore control of mind is the aim of yoga also.

A more advanced man will naturally go direct to control of mind without wasting his time in practising control of breath. A simple development of *pranayama* alone may confer *siddhis* which so many hanker for.

When asked if there are any food restrictions, Sri Bhagavan said: "*Mita hita bhuk*" — agreeable food in moderate quantity. When asked about the efficacy of *bhakti*, Sri Bhagavan said: So long as there is *vibhakti*, there must be *bhakti*. So long as there is *viyoga*, there must be *yoga*. So long as there is duality, there must be God and devotee. Similarly also in *vichara*. So long as there is *vichara*, there is duality too. But merging into the Source there is unity only. So it is with *bhakti* too. Realising the God of devotion, there will be unity only. God too is thought of in and by the Self. So God is identical with the Self. If one is told to have *bhakti* for God and he does so straightaway, it is all right. But there is another kind of man who turns round and says: "There are two, I and God. Before knowing the far-off God, let me know the more immediate and intimate 'I'." For him the *vichara-marga* has to be taught. There is in fact no difference between *bhakti* and *vichara*.

Talk 155.

The same man again asked about the nature of *samadhi* and the means to get *samadhi*.

M.: When the one who asks the nature of *samadhi* and the method of getting into it vanishes, *samadhi* will result.

Maj. Chadwick: It is said that one look of a Mahatma is enough; that idols, pilgrimages, etc. are not so effective. I have been here for three months, but I do not know how I have been benefited by the look of Maharshi.

M.: The look has a purifying effect. Purification cannot be visualised. Just as a piece of coal takes long to be ignited, a piece of charcoal takes a short time, and a mass of gunpowder is instantaneously ignited, so it is with grades of men coming in contact with Mahatmas.

Mr. Cohen: I get into meditation and reach a point which may be called peace and a contemplative mood. What should be the next step?

M.: Peace is Self-Realisation. Peace need not be disturbed. One should aim at Peace only.

D.: But I do not have the satisfaction.

M.: Because your peace is temporary. If made permanent it is called Realisation.

9th February, 1936

Talk 156.

D.: Is solitude helpful for practice?

M.: What do you mean by solitude?

D.: To keep away from others.

M.: Why should it be done? It is actuated only by fear. Even in solitude there is the fear of intrusion by others and of solitude being spoilt. Moreover, how are thoughts to be erased in solitude? Should it not be done in the present environment?

D.: But the mind is distracted now.

M.: Why do you let go the mind? Solitude amounts to making the mind still. This can be done in a crowd too. Solitude cannot efface one's thoughts. Practice does it. The same practice can be made here too.

Talk 157.

D.: In the quest of I, the seeker is at a certain stage directed to keep the mind in a negative attitude for Grace to enter. How can a negative yield positive result?

M.: The Self is always there — not to be newly got.

D.: I mean to ask, what has been done in the negative attitude to deserve the Grace?

M.: Are you asking this question without Grace? Grace is in the beginning, middle and end. Grace is the Self. Because of the false identification of the Self with the body the Guru is considered to be with body. But from the Guru's outlook the Guru is only the Self. The Self is one only. He tells that the Self alone is. Is not then the Self your Guru? Where else will Grace come from? It is from the Self alone. Manifestation of the Self is a manifestation of Grace and

139

vice versa. All these doubts arise because of the wrong outlook and consequent expectation of things external to oneself. Nothing is external to the Self.

D.: All our questions are from our standpoint and Sri Bhagavan's replies are from his standpoint. The questions are not only answered, but are also undermined.

11th February, 1936

Talk 158.

Mr. Frydman: Janaka was a *jnani* and still he ruled his dominions. Does not action require activity of the mind? What is the rationale of the working of a *jnani's* mind?

M.: You say, "Janaka was a *jnani* and yet active, etc." Does Janaka ask the question? The question is in your mind only. The *jnani* is not aware of anything besides the Self. He has no doubts of the kind.

D.: Probably it is like a dream. Just as we speak of our dreams, so they think of their actions.

M.: Even the dream, etc. is in your mind. This explanation too is in your mind only.

D.: Yes. I see. All is *Ramana-Maya* — made up of the Self.

M.: If so, there will be no duality and no talk.

D.: A man, on realising the Self, can help the world more effectively. Is it not so?

M.: If the world be apart from the Self.

12th February, 1936

Talk 159.

Mr. Cohen desired to know if trance is a *sine qua non* for Self-Realisation.

M.: You are always in the Self — now, in trance, in deep sleep, in Realisation. If you lose hold of the Self and identify yourself with the body or the mind, these states appear to overtake you, and it also looks like a blank in trance, etc.; whereas you are the Self and ever-present.

D.: Sri Aurobindo says that the Light which resides in the head must be brought down to the heart below.

M.: Is not the Self already in the Heart? How can the all-pervading Self be taken from one place to another?

D.: Is a karma yogi or a *bhakta* too subject to trance?

M.: When you concentrate on one point you merge in it, and this merging is called trance. The other features disappear and the Self alone remains over. The *karmi* or *bhakta* also must experience the same.

Talk 160.

D.: What is the *hridaya* and what the *sphurana* therein? How do they appear?

M.: The *hridaya* and the *sphurana* are the same as the Self. The *sphurana* requires a basis for its manifestation. This is explained in the book *Vichara Sangraham* (*Self-Enquiry*).

D.: How does the *sphurana* appear — as light, movement, or what?

M.: How can it be described in words? It includes all these — It is the Self. Fix your attention on it and do not let go the idea of its ultimate character.

13th February, 1936

Talk 161.

An elderly man from Ananthapur, after hearing the *Vedas* recited in the hall, stood up and asked:

"It is said that the non-Brahmins should not hear the recital of the Vedas."

M.: Mind your business. Take care of what you came here for. Why do you waste your time in these matters? "I heard the recital," you say. "Who is that 'I'? Without knowing the 'I' you are using the word. If its significance be known there will be no doubt. Find the 'I' first and you may afterwards speak of other matters."

Continuing, Sri Bhagavan said:

"The *smritis* say something. They are not appropriate now. I will reform the world, rewrite the *smritis*." Saying so, people are cutting capers in the world from time immemorial. Such reformers have come and gone; but the ancient *smritis* still stand. Why waste time over such matters? Let each one mind his business. All will be well.

23rd February, 1936

Talk 162.

A Maharashtra lady of middle-age, who had studied *Jnaneswari*, *Bhagavata* and *Vichara Sagara*, and was practising concentration between the eyebrows, had felt shivering and fear, and did not progress. She required guidance.

Maharshi told her not to forget the seer. The sight is fixed between the eyebrows, but the seer is not kept in view. If the seer be always remembered it will be all right.

24th February, 1936

Talk 163.

Dr. Henry Hand, an American of about seventy, asked "What is ego?"

M.: Ego being internal and not external to you it must be clear to yourself.

D.: What is its definition?

M.: The definition also must proceed from the ego. The ego must define itself.

D.: What is soul?

M.: Find the ego, the soul is found.

D.: Are they then the same?

M.: Soul can be without the ego; but the ego cannot be without the soul. They are like bubble and the ocean.

D.: That clarifies the matter. What is *Atman*?

M.: Atman and soul are the same.

Talk 164.

Another American asked about thought-forms.

M.: Trace the source of thoughts, they will disappear.

D.: Thoughts materialise.

M.: If there be thoughts they will materialise. If they disappear there is nothing to materialise. Moreover if you are physical the world is physical and so on. Find out if you are physical.

D.: How shall I be useful to God's world?

M.: Find out if 'I' is different from the divine part of the world. Not being able to help yourself yet you are seeking the divine part of it to help you to help the world. The divinity is directing and controlling you. Where do you go in deep sleep? Wherefrom do you come out?

D.: I have been influenced by deeds and thoughts.

M.: Thoughts and deeds are the same.

D.: Is there any way of sensing super-physical phenomena, *e.g.*, guardian angels?

M.: The state of the object is according to the state of the seer.

D.: A group of seers see the same.

M.: Because there is only one seer behind all, and there is diversity of phenomena. Do you perceive diversity in deep sleep?

D.: We see Abraham Lincoln who died long ago.

M.: Is there the object without the seer? The experiences may be real. The objects are only according to the seer.

D.: An assistant of mine was killed in the war. A photo was taken of another group nine years after his death. His picture appears in the photo. How is it?

M.: Possibly thoughts have materialised . . . . Go to the root of it.

D.: How?

M.: If the way is external, directions are possible, but it lies within. Seek within. The Self is always realised. Something not already realised might be sought afresh. But the Self is within your experience.

D.: Yes. I realise myself.

M.: Myself. Are there two — *my* and *self*?

D.: I do not mean it.

M.: Who is it that has or has not realised?

D.: There is only one Self.

M.: The question can arise only if there be two. Abandon the wrong identification of the Self with the non-self.

D.: I mean the higher stage of consciousness.

M.: There are no stages.

D.: Why does not a man get illumination instantly.

143

M.: The man is illumination itself. He is illumining

D.: Is your teaching different from that of others?

M.: The path is one and the realisation is only one.

D.: But people speak of so many methods.

M.: Depending on their own state of mentality.

D.: What is yoga?

M.: Yoga (union) is for one in viyoga (separation). But there is only one. If you realise the Self there will be no difference.

D.: Is there efficacy in bathing in the Ganges?

M.: The Ganges is within you. This Ganges does not make you feel cold or shiver. Bathe in it.

D.: Should we read Gita once in a while?

M.: Always.

D.: May we read the Bible?

M.: The Bible and the Gita are the same.

D.: The Bible teaches that Man is born in sin.

M.: The Man is sin. There was no man-sense in deep sleep. The body-thought brings out the idea of sin. The birth of thought is itself sin.

To another question the Master said: Everyone sees only the Self. The divine forms are only like bubbles in the ocean of Reality, or like pictures moving on a screen.

D.: The Bible says that the human soul may be lost.

M.: The 'I-thought' is the ego and that is lost. The real 'I' is "I am That I Am."

D.: There is conflict in the teachings of Aurobindo and of the Mother.

M.: First surrender the Self and then harmonise the conflicts.

D.: What is Renunciation?

M.: Giving up of the ego.

D.: Is it not giving up possessions?

M.: The possessor too.

D.: The world will change if the people will give up their possessions for the benefit of others.

M.: First give yourself up and then think of the rest.

In answer to another question Sri Bhagavan said:

144

The methods appear easy according to the nature of the individual. It depends on what he has practised before.

D.: Can we not get realisation instantaneously?

M.: Realisation is nothing new. It is eternal. There is no question of instantaneous or gradual realisation.

D.: Is there reincarnation?

M.: Reincarnation can be if you are incarnate now. Even now you are not born.

To another question:

M.: The ego is the root of all diseases. Give it up. There will be no disease.

D.: If all renounce will there be a practical world? Who will plough? Who will harvest?

M.: Realise first and then see. The help through Realisation transcends all the help through words, thoughts and deeds, etc. If you understand your own reality then that of the *rishis* and masters will be clear to you. There is only one master and that is the Self.

D.: Why do masters insist on silence and receptivity?

M.: What is silence? It is eternal eloquence.

D.: What is receptive attitude of mind?

M.: Not to be distracted in mind.

D.: Is there use in bringing America and India closer by bringing the intelligentsia of the two countries together, say, by exchange of professors, etc.?

M.: Such events will take place automatically. There is a Power guiding the destinies of nations. These questions arise only when you have lost touch with Reality. Is America apart from you, or India apart? Get hold of it and see.

D.: Sri Ramakrishna prepared Vivekananda. What is the power behind?

M.: The power is only one in all.

D.: What is the nature of that force?

M.: Just like iron filings drawn towards a magnet, the force is inside and not outside. Ramakrishna was in Vivekananda. If you think Vivekananda to be a body, Ramakrishna also is a body. But they are

145

not bodies. Vivekananda could not go into Samadhi had not Ramakrishna been within him.

D.: Why should one suffer when stung by a scorpion?

M.: What is the cause of the appearance of the body and of the world?

D.: It is part of the cosmic mind.

M.: Let the cosmic mind worry about such happenings. If the individual wants to know let him discover his Self.

D.: About yogic mysteries of drinking nitric acid, swallowing poisons, walking on fire, etc., are these due to a state of vibration?

M.: Let the physical body question it. You are not physical. Why worry about what you are not. If the Self had any form it might be affected by objects. But the Self has no form, therefore it is immune from contact with things.

D.: What is the significance of the sea of Love?

M.: Spirit, Holy Ghost, Realisation, Love, etc., are all synonymous.

D.: Very, very illuminating conversation.

Mr. N. Subba Rao: What is *visishtadvaita*?

M.: The same as this.

D.: They do not admit *maya*?

M.: *Sarvam* is Brahman, we say. They repeat Brahman remains qualified (*visishta*) in all.

D.: They say that the world is a reality.

M.: We say so too. Acharya has only said, "Find out the reality behind the world." What is called illusion by one is called changefulness by another. The end is the same in both.

Dr. Hand: Maharshi! Do not think we are bad boys.

M.: Do not tell me so. But you need not think you are bad boys.

All laughed and dispersed at 5 p.m.

Sri Bhagavan a minute later: If they remain a day longer they will become silent.

Talk 165.

Mr. Subba Rao: Do not men go into *samadhi*?

M.: Is there no *samadhi* now?

146

D.: Is it eternal?

M.: If not, how can it be real?

D.: Then?

M.: There is no *then*, no *now*.

D.: It appears so.

M.: To whom?

D.: To the mind.

M.: What is mind? Who am I?

D.: (Silence).

Talk 166.

A man asked if it was possible to ward off old age and disease by the intake of divine force.

M.: You can ward off the body itself.

D.: How to take in the divine force?

M.: It is already there. No need to take it in. It can be done only if it is out of you. But it is only you. There is no taking in or giving out.

D.: Is there any necessity to obey physical laws, *i.e.*, dieting?

M.: These are in imagination only.

Talk 167.

A man was worried because he could not succeed in concentrating the mind.

M.: Is it not only One even now? It always remains One only. Diversity lies in your imagination only. Unitary Being need not be acquired.

Talk 168.

It was mentioned to Sri Bhagavan that a Self-realised being needs no food, etc.

M.: You understand according to your state only.

Talk 169.

D.: How to control the mind?

M.: Catch hold of the mind.

D.: How?

147

M.: What is mind? Find it out. It is only an aggregate of thoughts.

D.: How to root out sexual impulse?

M.: By rooting out the false idea of the body being Self. There is no sex in the Self.

D.: How to realise it?

M.: Because you think you are the body, you see another as the body. Difference in sex arises. But you are not the body. Be the real Self. Then there is no sex.

Talk 170.

D.: Can a yogi know his past lives?

M.: Do you know the present life so well that you wish to know the past. Find out the present life, then the rest will follow. Even with our present limited knowledge we suffer so much. Why do you wish to burden yourself with more knowledge and suffer more?

D.: Can fasting help realisation?

M.: But it is temporary. Mental fast is the real aid. Fasting is not an end in itself. There must be spiritual development side by side. Absolute fasting makes the mind weak too. You cannot derive sufficient strength for the spiritual quest. Therefore take moderate food and go on practising.

D.: They say that after breaking a month's fast, ten days afterwards the mind becomes pure and steady and remains so forever.

M.: Yes, if the spiritual quest has been kept up right through the fast also.

Talk 171.

To another question Master said: The best is heart to heart speech and heart to heart hearing. That is the best *upadesa*.

D.: Is not guidance from Guru necessary?

M.: Are you apart from Guru?

D.: Is proximity helpful?

M.: Do you mean physical proximity? What is the good of it? The mind alone matters. The mind must be contacted.

28th February, 1936

Talk 172.

A visitor: What is the difference between meditation (*dhyana*) and investigation (*vichara*)?

M.: Both amount to the same. Those unfit for investigation must practise meditation. In this practice the aspirant forgetting himself meditates 'I am Brahman' or 'I am Siva'; thus he continues to hold to Brahman or Siva; this will ultimately end on the residual Being as Brahman or Siva which he will realise to be Pure Being, *i.e.* the Self.

He who engages in investigation starts holding on to himself, asks 'Who am I?' and the Self becomes clear to him.

D.: Will the knowledge gained by direct experience be lost afterwards?

M.: Kaivalya Navanita says it may be lost. Experience gained without rooting out all the *vasanas* cannot remain steady. Efforts must be made to eradicate the *vasanas*. Otherwise rebirth after death takes place. Some say direct experience results from hearing from one's master; others say it is from reflection; yet others say from one-pointedness and also from *samadhi*. Though they look different on the surface, ultimately they mean the same.

Knowledge can remain unshaken only after all the *vasanas* are rooted out.

29th February, 1936

Talk 173.

D.: Lord, how can the grip of the ego be slackened?

M.: By not adding new *vasanas* to it.

D.: Any amount of *japa* has not slackened the grip!

M.: How so! It will duly slacken and vanish.

2nd March, 1936

Talk 174.

Dr. Hand, the American gentleman, asked: Are there two methods for finding the source of the ego?

149

M.: There are no two sources and no two methods. There is only one source and only one method.

D.: What is the difference between meditation and enquiry into the Self?

M.: Meditation is possible only if the ego be kept up. There is the ego and the object meditated upon. The method is indirect. Whereas the Self is only one. Seeking the ego, *i.e.*, its source, ego disappears. What is left over is the Self. This method is the direct one.

D.: Then what am I to do?

M.: To hold on to the Self.

D.: How?

M.: Even now you are the Self. But you are confounding this consciousness (or ego) with the absolute consciousness. This false identification is due to ignorance. Ignorance disappears along with the ego. Killing the ego is the only thing to accomplish. Realisation is already there. No attempt is needed to attain realisation. For it is nothing external, nothing new. It is always and everywhere here and now too.

3rd March, 1936

Talk 175.

Mr. N. Subba Rao asked: The *Visishtadvatins* say that *Atma Sakshatkara* (Self-Realisation) is preliminary to *Paramatma Sakshatkara* (God-Realisation). The difficulty seems to be considerable.

M.: What is *Atma Sakshatkara*? Are there two Atmas that one realises the other? There are not two selves. First get *Atma Sakshatkara* and then judge what follows.

D.: The Bhagavad Gita says there is God whose body is made up of all the souls.

M.: All are agreed on the annihilation of the ego. Let us get to business on the agreed point. *Nanajivatva* (different individualities) are mentioned by some *Advaitins* also. All that is immaterial to one's spiritual uplift. First realise the Self and then see what lies further.

Talk 176.

Dr. Hand intends leaving the Asramam tomorrow, visit the Himalayas (Hardwar), return here, go to Bombay and embark for Egypt, Palestine, Europe and finally to his native land, America

He wants to go to the peak of the hill and desires Sri Bhagavan to accompany him. Sri Bhagavan might go up as high as is convenient for him and then wait for him to finish the climb — and catch him at an appointed spot on the hill. Sri Bhagavan smiled and asked him if he had heard of the experience of Dr. Beasly.

Dr. Hand: He is my friend. He has told me everything — wonderful! I am older than you, Maharshi. But do not give me up as a back number. I can climb up the hill as a boy would. When did you go to the peak last?

M.: About eleven years before. What did Dr. Beasly say?

D.: It is in strict confidence. I shall tell you everything if you are left alone with me.

Maharshi simply smiled.

D.: Maharshi! Are you conscious of a brotherhood of invisible *rishis*?

M.: If invisible, how to see them?

D.: In consciousness.

M.: There is nothing external in consciousness.

D.: Is there not the individuality? I fear to lose my individual being. Is there not in consciousness the consciousness of being human?

M.: Why fear to lose individuality? What is your state in dreamless sleep? Are you conscious of your individuality then?

D.: It is possible.

M.: But what is your experience? If individuality be there, would it be deep sleep?

D.: That depends on the interpretation. What does Maharshi say?

M.: Maharshi cannot speak for *your experience*. He does not force anything down your throat.

D.: I know. That is why I like Him and His teachings so much.

M.: Do you not really prepare your bed and are you not anxious to lose your individuality in deep sleep? Why fear it?

D.: What is the *nirvana* of Buddha?

M.: Loss of individuality.

D.: I dread that loss. Can there not be human consciousness in *nirvana*?

M.: Are there two selves in that case? Consider your present experience of sleep and say.

D.: I should think it possible to retain individual consciousness in *nirvana*. I fear the loss of individuality.

Later, the questioner went up and round the hill and wandered about fifteen miles between twelve noon and eight p.m. He returned tired and gave a very lucid speech on agriculture, social conditions, caste system, spiritual quality of the Indians, etc.

10th March, 1936

Talk 177.

D.: What is *mahat*?

M.: The projected light from Absolute Consciousness. Just as a seed swells up before sprouting and then sprouts and grows, so also the Absolute Consciousness projects light, manifests as the ego and grows up as the body and the universe.

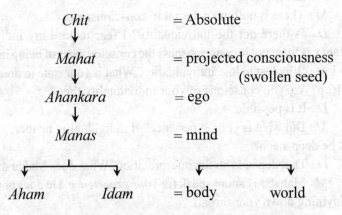

Chit ↓	= Absolute
Mahat ↓	= projected consciousness (swollen seed)
Ahankara ↓	= ego
Manas	= mind
Aham *Idam*	= body world

Maj. Chadwick: Is it the same as cosmic consciousness?

152

M.: Yes, it is so before the birth of the ego and the universe. It comprises them all. Just as all the pictures thrown on the screen are visible by the light projected from a spot, so also the body and the other objects are all visible in that reflected consciousness. It is, therefore, also cosmic consciousness.

Again, (in the microcosm) the body and all other objects are all contained in the brain. The light is projected on the brain. The impressions in the brain become manifest as the body and the worlds. Because the ego identifies itself with limitations, the body is considered separate and the world separate.

Lying down on your bed in a closed room with eyes closed you dream of London, the crowds there and you among them. A certain body is identified as yourself in the dream. London and the rest could not have entered into the room and into your brain; however, such wide space and duration of time were all perceptible to you. They must have been projected from the brain. Although the world is so big and the brain so small, is it not a matter of wonder that such a big creation is contained in such small compass as one's brain? Though the screen is limited, still all the pictures of the cinema pass on it and are visible there. You do not wonder how such a long procession of events could be manifest on such a small screen. Similarly with the objects and the brain.

D.: Then cosmic consciousness is not the same as realisation?

M.: Cosmic consciousness is behind the ego. It may be called *Isvara*, and the ego is *jiva*. *Isvara* may also be said to be the Absolute. There is no difference there.

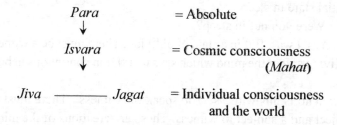

The consciousness which pervades even *Isvara* is the Absolute one.

Talk 178.

D.: What is the flame mentioned in *Vichara Sangraha*. It is said to be *Atma Jyoti* and one is directed to find the reality behind it.

M.: The Vedas mention the flame, *Tasyas sikhaya madhye paramatma vyavasthitah*. That flame is to be identified with the ego-consciousness.

11th March, 1936

Talk 179.

Mr. Frydman had asked Swami Ramdas something, to which he replied that there would be no more births for himself. The engineer had pointed out there should be no anxiety regarding rebirth. There will be the same Rama, the same Ramdas, the same search for Rama and the same bliss of realisation. What objection could be there for the repetition of this Rama-Lila? Ramdas had admitted that there could be no objection, that it would be an enjoyment and a game. The engineer further said that Ramdas added that Ramdas had found Rama merged in Him and happy in that union. They are the same, still there was Ramdas, there was Rama, there was the union, there was the Bliss. That is eternal. Saying it, he asked what Sri Bhagavan would say to it.

M.: It is all as true as the present events.

Talk 180.

Later, the same gentleman said that sleep was a state of oblivion and the wakeful state was the mind's activity. The mind was in a potential state in sleep.

M.: Were you not in sleep?

D.: Yes, I was. But in a state of oblivion. There must be a witness of oblivion and of the mind which says that 'I' am continuous in both states.

M.: Who is this witness? You speak of 'witness'. There must be an object and a subject to witness. These are creations of the mind. The idea of witness is in the mind. If there was the witness of oblivion did he say, 'I witness oblivion'? You, with your mind, said just now that there must be a witness. Who was the witness? You must reply 'I'. Who is that 'I' again? You are identifying yourself with the ego and say 'I'. Is this ego 'I', the witness? It is the mind that speaks. It cannot be witness of itself. With self-imposed limitations you think that there is a witness of mind and of oblivion. You also say, "I am the witness". That one who witnesses the oblivion must say, "I witness oblivion". The present mind cannot arrogate to itself that position.

The whole position becomes thus untenable. Consciousness is unlimited. On becoming limited it simply arrogates to itself the position. There is really nothing to witness. IT is. simple BEING.

Talk 181.

D.: Yad gatva na nivartante tad dhama paramam mama. Which is that *dhama*? Is it not the Absolute state beyond cosmic consciousness?

M.: Yes.

D.: '*Na Nivartante*' would mean not covered by ignorance again.

M.: Yes.

D.: Does it follow by inference that those who reach Cosmic Consciousness have not escaped from the clutches of ignorance?

M.: That is what is meant by saying that all lokas, even the Brahma loka, do not release one from rebirth. *Vide.* the *Bhagavad Gita:* "Reaching ME, there is no rebirth .... All others are in bondage." Moreover, so long as you think that there is *gati* (movement) — as implied in the word *gatva* (having gone to) — there is *punaravritti* (return) also. Again *gati* implies your *Purvagamanam* (birth). What is birth? It is birth of ego.

Once born you reach something; if you reach it you return also. Therefore leave off all this verbiage! *Be as you are.* See who you are and remain as the Self, free from birth, going, coming and returning.

D.: True. However often this truth is heard, still it eludes us and we forget it.

M.: Quite so. Reminders are often necessary.

Talk 182.

In the course of the day an interesting photo was missing. Sri Bhagavan appeared concerned about it. Mr. Frydman asked how

Sri Bhagavan viewed all these matters. Sri Bhagavan said: "Suppose you dream that you are taking me to Poland. You wake up and ask me. 'I dreamt so and so. Did you dream so or know it? Or how do you view it'?"

D.: But you are not aware of the happenings in front of you?

M.: These are all workings of the mind and the questions also.

Then again Sri Bhagavan related an episode in Sri Rama's search for Sita. Parvati asked Siva why Rama, the Perfect Being, was grieving at the loss of Sita. Siva said that Rama was still Perfect. If the Perfection need be tested and made clear, Parvati might appear as Sita before Rama and see what happened. So she did. Rama ignored her appearance and was still crying out, "Ha! Sita! Ha! Sita!" and moved on like a blind man, without taking any notice of Parvati — (*Cf.* Dialogue 218.)

13th March, 1936

Talk 183.

A gentleman from Bombay said: "I asked Mother in Sri Aurobindo Ashram the following question: 'I keep my mind blank without thoughts arising so that God might show Himself in His true Being. But I do not perceive anything.

"*The reply was to this effect:* 'The attitude is right. The Power will come down from above. It is a direct experience'."

So he asked what further he should do.

M.: Be what you are. There is nothing to come down or become manifest. All that is needful is to lose the ego, That what is, is always there. Even now you are That. You are not apart from it. The blank is seen by you. You are there to see the blank. What do you wait for? The thought "I have not seen," the expectation to see and the desire of getting something, are all the working of the ego. You have fallen into the snares of the ego. The ego says all these and not *you. Be yourself* and nothing more!

Talk 184.

M.: To imagine *Muladhara* at the bottom, the Heart at the centre,

156

or the head at the top or over all these, is all wrong. In one word, *to think is not your real nature.*

Talk 185.

M.: In the sacred literature the following are seen:-
"Said without uttering"
"Showed remaining still as ever," etc.

Which is this unspoken word? It is only Silence, *Pranava* or the *Mahavakya.** These are also called *the Word.*

Talk 186.

M.: We read a newspaper and all the articles therein, but do not care to know anything about the paper itself. We take the chaff but not the substance. The substratum on which all this is printed is the paper and if we know the substratum all else will be known (like wall and paintings).

D.: You said the only ONE which exists is the REAL. What is that only ONE?

M.: The ONE only is the *Sat*, the existence, that appears as the world, the things that we see and we ourselves.

D.: What is Atman? Is there a finality for the ATMAN?

M.: First learn what is Atman. If we know this then we can query as to whether it has a finality or not. Which do you call ATMAN?

D.: Jiva is ATMAN.

M.: Learn what *jiva* is. What is the difference between *jiva* and Atman? Is *jiva* itself Atman or is there any separate thing as Atman? There is an end for what you observe; that which is created has a destruction or end. That which is not created has no end. That which exists cannot be observed. It is unobservable. We must find out what it is that appears; the destruction of that which appears is the end. *That which exists, exists for ever; that which newly appears is later lost.*

D.: What happens after birth in human form, what happens to the *jiva?*

---

* Mahavakyas are four: (1) "That art Thou." (2) "I am Brahman." (3) "This Self is Brahman." (4) "*Prajnana* (Absolute Knowledge) is Brahman."

M.: Let us know first what we are. We do not understand what we are, and until we know what we are there is no room for such a question. (Bhagavan obviously here refers to the confusion of body as Atman — *dehatma buddhi* — which is the cause for this confusion of ideas of death and birth, for Atman has no birth or death, it is untainted by the elements of Earth, Fire, Air and Water, etc.) (*Gita* II, 11) — *Asochyam anvosochas tvam, projnavadamscha bhashase*, etc. — What is it that had birth? Whom do you call a man? If, instead of seeking explanation for birth, death and after-death matters, the question is raised as to who and how you are now, these questions will not arise. You are the same while asleep (deep sleep), in dream and in waking state. Is the 'I' thought *jiva*, or the body *jiva*? Is this thought or nature? Or is the experience that we live, etc., our nature? (Quotes the sloka from the *Gita: Yada te . . .* II, 52.)

D.: Why is *Atma vichara* necessary?

M.: If you do not make *Atma vichara*, then *loka vichara* creeps in. That which is not, is sought for, but not that which is obvious. When once you have found what you seek, *vichara* (enquiry) also ceases and you rest in it. As long as one is confusing the body with the Atman, Atman is said to be lost and one is said to seek for it, but the ATMAN itself is never lost. It always exists. A body is said to be Atman, an *indriya* is said to be Atman, then there is the *Jivatman* and *Paramatman* and what not. There are a thousand and one things called Atman. The search for Atman is to know that which is really Atman.

SAMADHI: KEVALA AND SAHAJA

Talk 187.

D.: I maintain that the physical body of the man sunk in *samadhi* as a result of unbroken contemplation of the Self becomes motionless for that reason. It may be active or inactive. The mind fixed in such contemplation will not be affected by the body or the senses being restless. A disturbance of the mind is not always the forerunner of physical activity. Another man asserts that physical unrest certainly prevents *nirvikalpa samadhi* or unbroken contemplation. What is your opinion? You are the standing proof of my statement.

M.: Both of you are right, you refer to *sahaja nirvikalpa* and the other refers to *kevala nirvikalpa*. In the one case the mind lies immersed in the Light of the Self (whereas the same lies in the darkness of ignorance in deep sleep). The subject discriminates one from the other — *samadhi*, stirring up from *samadhi*, and activity thereafter, unrest of the body, of the sight of the vital force and of the mind, the cognizance of objects and activity, are all obstructions for him.

In *sahaja*, however, the mind has resolved itself into the Self and has been lost. Differences and obstructions mentioned above do not therefore exist here. The activities of such a being are like the feeding of a somnolent boy, perceptible to the onlooker (but not to the subject). The driver sleeping on his moving cart is not aware of the motion of the cart, because his mind is sunk in darkness. Similarly the *sahaja jnani* remains unaware of his bodily activities because his mind is dead — having been resolved in the ecstasy of *Chit Ananda* (Self).

The two words contemplation and *samadhi* have been used loosely in the question.

Contemplation is a forced mental process, whereas *samadhi* lies beyond effort.

Sleep	Kevala	Sahaja
(1) Mind alive; (2) sunk in Oblivion.	(1) mind alive; (2) sunk in light; (3) like a bucket With the rope left lying in the water in a well; (4) to be drawn out by the other end of the rope.	(1) mind dead; (2) resolved into the Self; (3) like a river discharged into the ocean and its identity lost; (4) a river cannot be redirected from the ocean.

Talk 188.

The essence of mind is only awareness or consciousness. When the ego, however, dominates it, it functions as the reasoning, thinking

159

or sensing faculty. The cosmic mind being not limited by the ego, has nothing separate from itself and is therefore only aware. This is what the Bible means by "I am that I AM".

The ego-ridden mind has its strength sapped and is too weak to resist the torturing thoughts. The egoless mind is happy in deep, dreamless sleep. Clearly therefore Bliss and misery are only modes of mind; but the weak mode is not easily interchangeable with the strong mode. Activity is weakness and consequently miserable; passivity is strength and therefore blissful. The dormant strength is not apparent and therefore not availed of.

The cosmic mind, manifesting in some rare being, is able to effect the linkage in others of the individual (weak) mind with the universal (strong) mind of the inner recess. Such a rare being is called the GURU or *God in manifestation*.

19th May, 1936

Talk 189.

Mr. M. Oliver Lacombe, a middle-aged Frenchman who was on a visit to India being delegated by the Institute of Indian Civilisation of the University of Paris, came here from French India. Among others he had desired to meet Maharshi; he came and stayed here about three hours. He had read, in the Sanskrit original, the Bhagavad Gita, the Upanishads and the Sutras with commentaries by Sri Sankara and Ramanuja.

He asked: Is Maharshi's teaching the same as Sankara's?

M.: Maharshi's teaching is only an expression of his own experience and realisation. Others find that it tallies with Sri Sankara's.

D.: Quite so. Can it be put in other ways to express the same realisation?

M.: A realised person will use his own language. Sri Bhagavan added: SILENCE is the best language.

D.: What does Maharshi say about *hatha yoga* or *Tantric* practices?

M.: Maharshi does not criticise any of the existing methods. All are good for the purification of the mind. Because the purified mind alone is capable of grasping his method and sticking to its practice.

D.: Which is the best of the different yogas, *Karma, Jnana, Bhakti* or *Hatha?*

M.: See stanza 10 of *Upadesa Sara.* To remain in the Self amounts to all these in their highest sense.

Maharshi added: In dreamless sleep there is no world, no ego and no unhappiness. But the Self remains. In the waking state there are all these; yet there is the Self. One has only to remove the transitory happenings in order to realise the ever-present beatitude of the Self. Your nature is Bliss. Find that on which all the rest are superimposed and you then remain as the pure Self.

D.: Yes. It amounts to the removal of alien limitations for discovering the ever-present Self. That is what Sankara says. There is no attainment or loss.

M.: Quite so. (Aside) He understands.

D.: How is work to be done ordinarily for an aspirant?

M.: Without self-identification with the actor. For instance, did you intend visiting this place while in Paris?

D.: No!

M.: You see how you are acting without your intention to do so? The Gita says that a man cannot remain without acting. The purpose of one's birth will be fulfilled whether you will it or not. Let the purpose fulfil itself.

D.: Why are there so many methods mentioned? For instance Sri Ramakrishna says that *bhakti* is the best means for salvation.

M.: It is according to the standpoint of the aspirant. You have studied the Gita. Sri Krishna said: "There was never a time when I, and you, and these kings were not; nor will they not be in future. That which is unreal never exists. But that which is real never disappears. All that ever was even now is and will ever be." Again, "I taught this Truth to Aditya; he taught it to Manu; etc." Arjuna asked: "How can it be? You were born some years back and only recently. How could you have taught Aditya?" Sri Krishna answered; "Yes. We have had several births in the past. I know mine; whereas you do not know yours. I tell you what happened in those past births."

161

Look! That Krishna who began saying there was not I, nor were you, nor these kings, says now that he had several births before. Krishna does not contradict Himself, though it looks like it. He conforms to the outlook of Arjuna and speaks to him from his level.

There is a parallel passage in the Bible where Jesus says, "Before Abraham was, I am". The teachings of the Sages are suited to the time, place, people and other surroundings.

The visitor said he was leaving with regret. ...

Maharshi smilingly interrupted, "There is no leaving or returning." The Frenchman at once said, "He has transcended time and space." He returned to Pondicherry.

30th May, 1936

Talk 190.

There is a pet squirrel in the hall which usually retires into its cage before nightfall. Just as Maharshi was telling it to retire for the night a visitor who had announced that he had attained the transcendent consciousness suggested that water might be offered to it, since it was likely to be thirsty on this hot evening. His presumption to understand animals evoked no response. He repeated it. After a few minutes' silence Maharshi said, "You are probably thirsty after your long meditation in the hot Sun on the hotter rocks and you would like to drink a jug of water."

D.: Quite so. I have taken water.

M.: The squirrel is not so thirsty. Because you were practising austerities in the heat of the Sun you should feel thirsty. Why prescribe it for the squirrel?

Maharshi added: I noticed him standing on the hot rocks facing the Sun with eyes closed. I stood there for a while but did not want to disturb him and came away. These people do as they please.

D.: What I did, I did not intend beforehand. It was spontaneous.

M.: Oh! I see! Whatever we others do, we do with intention! You seem to have transcended all!

D.: This is not the first time I did so. You yourself inspire me and make me do all these things. Yet you ask me why I did it. How is it?

162

M.: I see. You are doing actions being controlled by me. Then the fruits also should be considered similarly to be mine and not yours.

D.: So they are undoubtedly. I act not of my free will but inspired by you. I have no will of my own.

M.: Enough of this rubbish! So did Duryodhana of old (in the *Mahabharata*) say:

> *janami dharmam nacha me pravrittih,*
> *janamyadharmam nacha me nivrittih.*
> *kenapi devana hridi sthitena*
> *yatha niyuktosmitatha karomi.*

What is the difference between you two?

D.: I see no difference. But I have no will and act without it.

M.: You have risen high above the common run. We others are acting with personal will.

D.: How, Sir? You have said in one of your works that action can be automatic.

M.: Enough! Enough! You and another visitor behave as transcendental beings! You are both fully learned. You need not learn more. I would not have said all this had you not been coming here frequently. Do as you please. But these eccentricities of the beginner's stage will become known in their true light after some time.

D.: But I have been in this state for such a long time.

M.: Enough!

Talk 191.

Mr. Cohen, a resident disciple, was speaking of yoga method.

Maharshi remarked: Patanjali's first sutra is applicable to all systems of yoga. The aim is the cessation of mental activities. The methods differ. So long as there is effort made towards that goal it is called yoga. The effort is the yoga.

The cessation can be brought about in so many ways.

(1) By examining the mind itself. When the mind is examined, its activities cease automatically. This is the method of *jnana*. The pure mind is the Self.

(2) Looking for the source of the mind is another method. The source may be said to be God or Self or consciousness.

(3) Concentrating upon one thought make all other thoughts disappear. Finally that thought also disappears; and

(4) *Hatha Yoga.*

All methods are one and the same inasmuch as they all tend to the same goal.

It is necessary to be aware while controlling thoughts. Otherwise it will lead to sleep. That awareness, the chief factor, is indicated by the fact of Patanjali emphasising *pratyahara, dharana, dhyana, samadhi* even after *pranayama. Pranayama* makes the mind steady and suppresses thoughts. Then why develop further? Because awareness then is the one necessary factor. Such states can be imitated by taking morphia, chloroform, etc. They do not lead to *Moksha* because they lack awareness.

3rd June, 1936

Talk 192.

Maharshi explained in the course of conversation:

Whoever desires liberation? Everyone wants only happiness — happiness too as found in the enjoyment of the senses. This question was asked of a Guru, and the latter answered: "Quite so. That happiness which is the result of enjoyment by the senses is the same as that of liberation. That desire of such liberation is one of the four qualifications for attainment. This is common to all. So all are eligible for this knowledge — Self-knowledge."

In fact there may not be found any individual in the world who possesses all the qualities in perfection necessary for an aspirant as mentioned in Yoga Sutras, etc. Still pursuit of Self-knowledge should not be abandoned.

Everyone is the Self by his own experience. Still he is not aware, he identifies the Self with the body and feels miserable. This is the greatest of all mysteries. One is the Self. Why not abide as the Self and be done with miseries?

In the beginning one has to be told that he is not the body, because he thinks that he is the body only. Whereas he is the body and all else. The body is only a part. Let him know it finally. He must first discern consciousness from insentience and be the consciousness only. Later let him realise that insentience is not apart from consciousness.

This is discrimination (*viveka*). The initial discrimination must persist to the end. Its fruit is liberation.

Talk 193.

Maharshi observed: Free-will and destiny are ever-existent. Destiny is the result of past action; it concerns the body. Let the body act as may suit it. Why are you concerned with it? Why do you pay attention to it? Free-will and Destiny last as long as the body lasts. But wisdom (*jnana*) transcends both. The Self is beyond knowledge and ignorance. Should anything happen, it happens as the result of one's past actions, of divine will and of other factors.

Talk 194.

Mr. Subba Rao, a visitor from Amalapuram, asked: How to control the mind?

M.: Get hold of the mind.

D.: How?

M.: Mind is intangible. In fact, it does not exist. The surest way of control is to seek it. Then its activities cease.

6th June, 1936

Talk 195.

Mr. Jharka, a gentleman from the University of Benares, holding the M.A. and the M.Sc. degrees, said that he was stricken with grief due to bereavement of wife and children. He sought peace of mind and asked how to get it.

M.: It is in the mind that birth and death, pleasure and pain, in short the world and ego exist. If the mind is destroyed all these are destroyed too. Note that it should be annihilated, not just made latent. For the mind is dormant in sleep. It does not know anything. Still, on waking up, you are as you were before. There is no end of grief. But

165

if the mind be destroyed the grief will have no background and will disappear along with the mind.

D.: How to destroy the mind?

M.: Seek the mind. On being sought, it will disappear.

D.: I do not understand.

M.: The mind is only a bundle of thoughts. The thoughts arise because there is the thinker. The thinker is the ego. The ego, if sought, will vanish automatically. The ego and the mind are the same. The ego is the root-thought from which all other thoughts arise.

D.: How to seek the mind?

M.: Dive within. You are now aware that the mind rises up from within. So sink within and seek.

D.: I do not yet understand how it is to be done.

M.: You are practising breath-control. Mechanical breath-control will not lead one to the goal. It is only an aid. While doing it mechanically take care to be alert in mind and remember the 'I' thought and seek its source. Then you will find that where breath sinks, there 'I-thought' arises. They sink and rise together. The 'I-thought' also will sink along with breath. Simultaneously, another luminous and infinite 'I-I' will become manifest, which will be continuous and unbroken. That is the goal. It goes by different names — God, Self, *Kundalini Sakti, Consciousness, Yoga, Bhakti, Jnana*, etc.

D.: Not clear yet.

M.: When the attempt is made, it will of itself take you to the goal.

9th June, 1936

Talk 196.

A visitor asked about the three methods mentioned in *Ramana Gita* — Chapter II.

Maharshi pointed out that breath-retention is an aid to control of mind, *i.e.*, suppression or annihilation of thoughts. One person may practise breath-control, inhalation, exhalation and retention or retention only. Still another type of practising meditator, on controlling the mind, controls the breath and its retention automatically results. Watching the inhalation and exhalation is also breath-control. These

166

methods are only apparently three-fold. They are in fact really one, because they lead to the same goal. They are however differently adopted according to the stage of the aspirant and his antecedent predisposition or tendencies. Really there are only two methods: enquiry and devotion. One leads to the other.

D.: Seeking the 'I' there is nothing to be seen.

M.: Because you are accustomed to identify yourself with the body and sight with the eyes, therefore, you say you do not see anything. What is there to be seen? Who is to see? How to see? There is only one consciousness which, manifesting as 'I-thought', identifies itself with the body, projects itself through the eyes and sees the objects around. The individual is limited in the waking state and expects to see something different. The evidence of his senses will be the seal of authority. But he will not admit that the seer, the seen and the sight are all manifestations of the same consciousness — namely, 'I-I'. Contemplation helps one to overcome the illusion that the Self must be visual. In truth, there is nothing visual. How do you feel the 'I' now? Do you hold a mirror before you to know your own being? The awareness is the 'I'. Realise it and that is the truth.

D.: On enquiry into the origin of thoughts there is a perception of 'I'. But it does not satisfy me.

M.: Quite right. The perception of 'I' is associated with a form, maybe the body. There should be nothing associated with the pure Self. The Self is the unassociated, pure Reality, in whose light, the body, the ego, etc. shine. On stilling all thoughts the pure consciousness remains over.

Just on waking from sleep and before becoming aware of the world there is that pure 'I-I'. Hold to it without sleeping or without allowing thoughts to possess you. If that is held firm it does not matter even though the world is seen. The seer remains unaffected by the phenomena.

Talk 197.

Gul and Shirin Byramjee, two Parsi ladies of Ahmedabad, arrived this day. They spoke at night to Maharshi: "Bhagavan! We have been

167

spiritually inclined from our childhood. We have read several books on philosophy, and are attracted by Vedanta. So we read the Upanishads, *Yoga Vasishtha*, Bhagavad Gita, etc. We try to meditate, but there is no progress in our meditation. We do not understand how to realise. Can you kindly help us towards realisation?"

M.: How do you meditate?

D.: I begin to ask myself "Who am I?", eliminate body as not 'I', the breath as not 'I', the mind as not 'I' and I am not able to proceed further.

M.: Well, that is so far as the intellect goes. Your process is only intellectual. Indeed, all the scriptures mention the process only to guide the seeker to know the Truth. The Truth cannot be directly pointed out. Hence this intellectual process.

You see, the one who eliminates all the *not I* cannot eliminate the 'I'. To say 'I am not this' or 'I am that' there must be the 'I'. This 'I' is only the ego or the 'I-thought'. After the rising up of this 'I-thought', all other thoughts arise. The 'I-thought' is therefore the root-thought. If the root is pulled out all others are at the same time uprooted. Therefore seek the root 'I', question yourself "Who am I?"; find out its source. Then all these will vanish and the pure Self will remain ever.

D.: How to do it?

M.: The 'I' is always there — in deep sleep, in dream and in wakefulness. The one in sleep is the same as that who now speaks. There is always the feeling of 'I'. Otherwise do you deny your existence? You do not. You say 'I am'. Find out who is.

D.: Even so, I do not understand. 'I', you say, is the wrong 'I' now. How to eliminate this wrong 'I'?

M.: You need not eliminate the wrong 'I'. How can 'I' eliminate itself? All that you need do is to find out its origin and abide there. Your efforts can extend only thus far. Then the Beyond will take care of itself. You are helpless there. No effort can reach it.

D.: If 'I' am always — here and now, why do I not feel so?

M.: That is it. Who says it is not felt? Does the real 'I' say it or the false 'I'? Examine it. You will find it is the wrong 'I'. The wrong 'I' is the obstruction. It has to be removed in order that the true 'I' may

168

not be hidden. The feeling that I have not realised is the obstruction to realisation. In fact it is already realised; there is nothing more to be realised. Otherwise, the realisation will be new; it has not existed so far, it must take place hereafter. What is born will also die. If realisation be not eternal it is not worth having. Therefore what we seek is not that which must happen afresh. It is only that which is eternal but not now known due to obstructions; it is that we seek. All that we need do is to remove the obstruction. That which is eternal is not known to be so because of ignorance. Ignorance is the obstruction. Get over this ignorance and all will be well.

The ignorance is identical with the 'I-thought'. Find its source and it will vanish.

The 'I-thought' is like a spirit which, although not palpable, rises up simultaneously with the body, flourishes and disappears with it. The body-consciousness is the wrong 'I'. Give up this body-consciousness. It is done by seeking the source 'I'. The body does not say 'I am'. It is you who say, 'I am the body!' Find out who this 'I' is. Seeking its source it will vanish.

D.: Then, will there be bliss?

M.: Bliss is coeval with Being-Consciousness. All the arguments relating to the eternal Being of that Bliss apply to Bliss also. Your nature is Bliss. Ignorance is now hiding that Bliss. Remove the ignorance for Bliss to be freed.

D.: Should we not find out the ultimate reality of the world, individual and God?

M.: These are all conceptions of the 'I'. They arise only after the advent of the 'I-thought'. Did you think of them in your deep sleep? You existed in deep sleep and the same you are now speaking. If they be real should they not be in your sleep also? They are only dependent upon the 'I-thought'. Again does the world tell you 'I am the world'? Does the body say 'I am body'? You say, "This is the world", "this is body" and so on. So these are only your conceptions. Find out who you are and there will be an end of all your doubts.

D.: What becomes of the body after realisation? Does it exist or not? We see realised beings acting like others.

M.: This question need not arise now. Let it be asked after realisation, if need be. As for the realised beings let them take care of themselves. Why do you worry about them?

In fact, after realisation the body and all else will not appear different from the Self.

D.: Being always Being-Consciousness-Bliss, why does God place us in difficulties? Why did He create us?

M.: Does God come and tell you that He has placed you in difficulties? It is you who say so. It is again the wrong 'I'. If that disappears there will be no one to say that God created this or that.

That which is does not even say 'I am'. For, does any doubt rise that 'I am not'? Only in such a case should one be reminding oneself 'I am a man'. One does not. On the other hand, if a doubt arises whether he is a cow or a buffalo he has to remind himself that he is not a cow, etc., but 'I am a man.' This would never happen. Similarly with one's own existence and realisation.

10th June, 1936

Talk 198.

Some ladies asked if there is rebirth of man as a lower animal.

M.: Yes. It is possible, as illustrated by Jada Bharata — the scriptural anecdote of a royal sage, having been reborn as a deer.

D.: Is the individual capable of spiritual progress in the animal body?

M.: Not unlikely, though it is exceedingly rare

D.: What is Guru's Grace? How does it work?

M.: Guru is the Self.

D.: How does it lead to realisation?

M.: Isvaro gururatmeti ... (God is the same as Guru and Self ...). A person begins with dissatisfaction. Not content with the world he seeks satisfaction of desires by prayers to God; his mind is purified; he longs to know God more than to satisfy his carnal desires. Then God's Grace begins to manifest. God takes the form of a Guru and appears to the devotee; teaches him the Truth; purifies the mind by his teachings and contact; the mind gains strength, is able to turn inward; with meditation it is purified yet further, and eventually remains still without the least ripple. That stillness is the Self. The Guru is both exterior and interior. From the exterior he gives a push to the mind to turn inward; from the interior he pulls the mind towards the Self and helps the mind to achieve quietness. That is Grace.

Hence there is no difference between God, Guru and Self.

Talk 199.

The ladies later asked several questions relating to their present inability to realise the already realised, eternal Self. The sign of Realisation would be Bliss, which was absent.

Maharshi said: There is only one consciousness. But we speak of several kinds of consciousness, as body-consciousness, Self-consciousness. They are only relative states of the same Absolute consciousness. Without consciousness, time and space do not exist. They appear in consciousness. It is like a screen on which these are cast as pictures and move as in a cinema show. The Absolute consciousness is our real nature.

D.: From where do these objects arise?

M.: Just from where you rise. Know the subject first and then question about the object.

D.: It is only one aspect of the question.

M.: The subject comprehends the object also. That one aspect is an all-comprehensive aspect. See yourself first and then see the objects. What is not in you cannot appear outside.

D.: I am not satisfied.

M.: Satisfaction can be only when you reach the source. Otherwise restlessness exists.

D.: Is the Supreme Being with or without attributes?

M.: Know first if you are with or without attributes.

D.: What is samadhi?

M.: One's own true nature.

D.: Why then is effort necessary to attain it?

M.: Whose is the effort?

D.: Maharshi knows that I am ignorant.

M.: Do you know that you are ignorant? Knowledge of ignorance is no ignorance.

All scriptures are only for the purpose of investigating if there are two consciousnesses. Everyone's experience proves the existence of only one consciousness. Can that one divide itself into two? Is any division felt in the Self? Awaking from sleep one finds oneself the same in the wakeful as well as in the sleep states. That is the experience of each one. The difference lies in seeking, in the outlook. Because you imagine that you are the seer separate from the experience, this difference arises. Experience shows that your being is the same all through.

D.: From where did ignorance come?

M.: There is no such thing as ignorance. It never arises. Everyone is Knowledge itself. Only Knowledge does not shine easily. The dispelling of ignorance is Wisdom which always exists — *e.g.*, the necklace remaining round the neck though supposed to have been lost; or each of the ten fools failing to count himself and counting only the others. To whom is knowledge or ignorance?

D.: Can we not proceed from external to internal?

M.: Is there any difference like that? Do you feel the difference — external and internal — in your sleep? This difference is only with reference to the body and arises with body-consciousness ('I-thought'). The so-called waking state is itself an illusion.

Turn your vision inward and then the whole world will be full of Supreme Spirit. The world is said to be illusion. Illusion is really Truth. Even the material sciences trace the origin of the universe to some one primordial matter — subtle, exceedingly subtle.

God is the same both to those who say the world is real and to their opponents. Their outlook is different. You need not entangle yourself in such disputations. The goal is one and the same for all. Look to it.

14th June, 1936

Talk 200.

Mr. Cohen desired an explanation of the term "blazing light" used by Paul Brunton in the last chapter of *A Search in Secret India*.

172

Maharshi: Since the experience is through the mind only it appears first as a blaze of light. The mental predispositions are not yet destroyed. The mind is however functioning in its infinite capacity in this experience.

As for *nirvikalpa samadhi* i.e., *samadhi*, of non-differentiation (undifferentiated, supreme, beatific repose), it consists of pure consciousness, which is capable of illumining knowledge or ignorance; it is also beyond light or darkness. That it is not darkness is certain; can it be however said to be not light? At present objects are perceived only in light. Is it wrong to say that realisation of one's Self requires a light? Here *light* would mean the consciousness which reveals as the Self only.

The yogis are said to see photisms of colours and lights preliminary to Self-Realisation by the practice of yoga.

Once before Goddess Parvati practised austerities for realising the Supreme. She saw some kinds of light. She rejected them because they emanated from the Self, leaving the Self as it was ever before. She determined that they were not supreme. She continued Her austerities and experienced a limitless light. She determined that this also was only a phenomenon and not the Supreme Reality. Still she continued Her austerities until she gained transcendental peace. She realised that it was Supreme, that the Self was the sole Reality.

The *Taittiriya Upanishad* says, "Seek Brahman through penance". Later on, "Penance is Brahman". Another Upanishad says, "Itself is penance which is again made up of wisdom alone". "There the sun shines not, nor the moon, nor the stars, nor fire; all these shine forth by Its light".

Talk 201.

The Parsi ladies asked for an illustration to explain why the Self, though ever-present and most intimate, is not being realised.

Maharshi cited the stories of (1) *Svakanthabharanam katha* — the story of the necklace, on the neck itself, not being detected; (2) *Dasama* — of the ten fools who counted only nine, each of them omitting to count himself; (3) the lion's cub, brought up in a herd of goats; (4) Karna not knowing his real parentage and (5) the king's son brought up in a low-class family.

They further asked for Maharshi's opinion of Sri Aurobindo's Yoga, and his claim to have probed beyond the experiences of the Vedic *rishis* and the Mother's opinion of the fitness of her disciples to begin with the realisation of the Upanishadic *rishis*.

M.: Aurobindo advises complete surrender. Let us do that first and await results, and discuss further, if need be afterwards and not now. There is no use discussing transcendental experiences by those whose limitations are not divested. Learn what surrender is. It is to merge in the source of the ego. The ego is surrendered to the Self. Everything is dear to us because of love of the Self. The Self is that to which we surrender our ego and let the Supreme Power, *i.e.*, the Self, do what it pleases. The ego is already the Self's. We have no rights over the ego, even as it is. However, supposing we had, we must surrender them.

D.: What about bringing down divine consciousness from above?

M.: As if the same is not already in the Heart? "O Arjuna, I am in the expanse of the Heart," says Sri Krishna "He who is in the sun, is also in this man", says a *mantra* in the Upanishads. "The Kingdom of God is within", says the Bible. All are thus agreed that God is within. What is to be brought down? From where? Who is to bring what, and why?

Realisation is only the removal of obstacles to the recognition of the eternal, immanent Reality. Reality is. It need not be taken from place to place.

D.: What about Aurobindo's claim to start from Self-Realisation and develop further?

M.: Let us first realise and then see.

Then Maharshi began to speak of similar theories: The *Visishtadvaitins* say that the Self is first realised and the realised individual soul is surrendered to the universal soul. Only then is it complete. The part is given up to the whole. That is liberation and *sayujya* union. Simple Self-Realisation stops at isolating the pure Self, says *Visishtadvaita*.

174

The *siddhas* say that the one who leaves his body behind as a corpse cannot attain *mukti*. They are reborn. Only those whose bodies dissolve in space, in light or away from sight, attain liberation. The *Advaitins* of Sankara's school stop short at Self-Realisation and this is not the end, the *siddhas* say.

There are also others who extol their own pet theories as the best, *e.g.*, late Venkaswami Rao of Kumbakonam, Brahmananda Yogi of Cuddappah, etc.

The fact is: There is Reality. It is not affected by any discussions. Let us abide as Reality and not engage in futile discussions as to its nature, etc.

15th June, 1936

Talk 202.

A sad-looking Punjabi gentleman announced himself to Maharshi as having been directed to him by Sri Sankaracharya of Kamakotipeetam, from Jalesvar near Puri, Jagannath. He is a world tourist. He has practised *Hatha Yoga* and some contemplation along the lines of "I am Brahman". In a few moments a blank prevails, his brain gets heated and he gets afraid of death. He wants guidance from Maharshi.

M.: Who sees the blank?

D.: I know that I see it.

M.: The consciousness overlooking the blank is the Self.

D.: That does not satisfy me. I cannot realise it.

M.: The fear of death is only after the 'I-thought' arises. Whose death do you fear? For whom is the fear? There is the identification of the Self with the body. So long as there is this, there will be fear.

D.: But I am not aware of my body.

M.: Who says that he is not aware?

D.: I do not understand.

He was then asked to say what exactly was his method of meditation. He said: "*Aham Brahmasmi*" ("I am Brahman").

M.: "I am Brahman" is only a thought. Who says it? Brahman itself does not say so. What need is there for it to say it? Nor can the real 'I' say so. For 'I' always abides as Brahman. To be saying it is only a thought. Whose thought is it? All thoughts are from the unreal 'I'. *i.e.,* the 'I'- thought. Remain without thinking. So long as there is thought there will be fear.

D.: As I go on thinking of it there is forgetfulness, the brain becomes heated and I am afraid.

M.: Yes, the mind is concentrated in the brain and hence you get a hot sensation there. It is because of the 'I-thought'. So long as there is thought there will be forgetfulness. There is the thought "I am Brahman"; forgetfulness supervenes; then the 'I-thought' arises and simultaneously the fear of death also. Forgetfulness and thought are for 'I-thought' only. Hold it; it will disappear as a phantom. What remains over is the real 'I'. That is the Self. 'I am Brahman' is an aid to concentration. It keeps off other thoughts. That one thought alone persists. See whose is that thought. It will be found to be from 'I'. Wherefrom is the 'I' thought? Probe into it. The 'I-thought' will vanish. The Supreme Self will shine forth of itself. No further effort is needed.

When the one Real 'I' remains alone, it will not be saying; "I am Brahman". Does a man go on repeating "I am a man"? Unless he is challenged, why should he declare himself a man? Does anyone mistake oneself for a brute, that he should say "No. I am not a brute; I am a man"? Similarly, Brahman or 'I' being alone, there is no one there to challenge it and so there is no need to be repeating "I am Brahman".

17th June, 1936

Talk 203.

Mr. Varma, Financial Secretary of the Posts and Telegraphs Department, Delhi: He has read Paul Brunton's *Search in Secret India* and *The Secret Path*. He lost his wife with whom he had led a happy life for eleven or twelve years. In his grief he seeks solace. He does not find solace in reading books: wants to tear them up. He does not intend to ask questions. He simply wants to sit here and derive what solace he can in the presence of Maharshi.

176

Maharshi, as if in a train of thoughts, spoke now and then to the following effect:

It is said, "The wife is one-half of the body". So her death is very painful. This pain is however due to one's outlook being physical; it disappears if the outlook is that of the Self. The *Brahadaranyaka Upanishad* says, "The wife is dear because of the love of the Self". If the wife and others are identified with the Self, how then will pain arise? Nevertheless such disasters shake the mind of philosophers also.

We are happy in deep sleep. We remain then as the pure Self. The same we are just now too. In such sleep there was neither the wife nor others nor even 'I'. Now they become apparent and give rise to pleasure or pain. Why should not the Self, which was blissful in deep sleep, continue its blissful nature even now? The sole obstruction to such continuity is the wrong identification of the Self with the body.

The Bhagavad Gita says: "The unreal hath no being; the real never ceaseth to be; the truth about both hath been perceived by the seers of the essence of things." "The real is ever real, the unreal is ever unreal." Again: "He is not born, nor doth he die; nor, having been, ceaseth he anymore to be; unborn, perpetual, eternal ancient, he is not slain when the body is slaughtered." Accordingly, there is neither birth nor death. Waking is birth and sleep is death.

Was the wife with you when you went out to the office, or in your deep sleep? She was away from you. You were satisfied because of your thought that she was somewhere. Whereas now you think that she is not. The difference lies in the different thoughts. That is the cause of pain. The pain is because of the thought of the wife's non-being. All this is the mischief of the mind. The fellow (*i.e.* the mind) creates pain for himself even when there is pleasure. But pleasure and pain are mental creations.

Again, why mourn the dead? They are free from bondage. Mourning is the chain forged by the mind to bind itself to the dead.

"What if anyone is dead? What if anyone is ruined? Be dead yourself — be ruined yourself". In that sense there is no pain after one's death. What is meant by this sort of death? Annihilation of the ego, though the body is alive. If the ego persists the man is afraid of

177

death. The man mourns another's death. He need not do so if he predeceases them (by waking up from the ego-dream, which amounts to killing the ego-sense). The experience of deep sleep clearly teaches that happiness consists in being without the body. The wise also confirm it, speaking of liberation after the body is given up. Thus the sage is awaiting the casting off of the body. Just as a labourer carrying a load on his head for the sake of wages bears the burden with no pleasure, carries it to the destination, and finally unburdens himself with relief and joy; so also the sage bears this body, awaiting the right and destined time to discard it. If now you are relieved of one half of the burden, i.e., the wife, should you not be thankful and be happy for it?

Nevertheless you cannot be so because of your physical outlook.

Even men who ought to know better and who have known the teaching about liberation after death etc., glorify liberation along with the body and call it some mysterious power of keeping the body eternally alive!

There will be no pain if the physical outlook is given up and if the person exists as the Self. Mourning is not the index of true love. It betrays love of the object, of its shape only. That is not love. True love is shown by the certainty that the object of love is in the Self and that it can never become non-existent. (Maharshi cited the story of Ahalya and Indra from *Yoga Vasishta* in this connection.)

Still it is true, pain on such occasions can only be assuaged by association with the wise.

18th June, 1936

Talk 204.

Maharshi on Self-Illumination: The 'I' concept is the ego. I-illumination is the Realisation of the Real Self. It is ever shining forth as 'I-I' in the intellectual sheath. It is pure Knowledge; relative knowledge is only a concept. The bliss of the blissful sheath is also but a concept. Unless there is the experience, however subtle it is, one cannot say "I slept happily". From his intellect he speaks of his blissful sheath. The bliss of sleep is but a concept to the person, the same as intellect. However, the concept of experience is exceedingly subtle in sleep. Experience is not possible without simultaneous knowledge of it (*i.e.* relative knowledge).

The inherent nature of the Self is Bliss. Some kind of knowledge has to be admitted, even in the realisation of Supreme Bliss. It may be said to be subtler than the subtlest.

The word *vijnana* (clear knowledge) is used both to denote the Realisation of the Self and knowing the objects. The Self is wisdom. It functions in two ways. When associated with the ego the knowledge is objective (*vijnana*). When divested of the ego and the Universal Self is realised, it is also called *vijnana*. The word raises a mental concept. Therefore we say that the Self-Realised Sage knows by his mind, but his mind is pure. Again we say that the vibrating mind is impure and the placid mind is pure. The pure mind is itself Brahman; therefore it follows that Brahman is not other than the mind of the sage.

The *Mundaka Upanishad* says: "The knower of Brahman becomes the Self of Brahman." Is it not ludicrous? To know Him and become Him? They are mere words. The sage is Brahman — that is all. Mental functioning is necessary to communicate his experience. He is said to be contemplating the unbroken expanse. The Creator, Suka and others are also said never to swerve from such contemplation.

निमिषार्धं न तिष्ठन्ति वृत्तिं ब्रह्ममयीं विना ।
यथा तिष्ठन्ति ब्रह्मबाः सनकाबाः शुकादयः ॥

- Tejo Bindu Upanishad. 1 — 47

Such 'contemplation' is again a mere word. How is that to be contemplated unless it is divided (into the contemplator and the contemplated). When undivided, how is contemplation possible? What function can Infinity have? Do we say that a river after its discharge into the ocean has become an ocean-like river? Why should we then speak of contemplation which has become unbroken, as being that of unbroken Infinity? The statement must be understood in the spirit in which it is made. It signifies the merging into the Infinite.

179

Self-Illumination or Self-Realisation is similar to it. The Self is ever shining. What does this 'I-illumination' mean then? The expression is an implied admission of mind function.

The gods and the sages experience the Infinite continuously and eternally, without their vision being obscured at any moment. Their minds are surmised by the spectators to function; but in fact they do not. Such surmise is due to the sense of individuality in those who draw inferences. There is no mental function in the absence of individuality. Individuality and mind functions are co-existent. The one cannot remain without the other.

The light of the Self can be experienced only in the intellectual sheath. Therefore *vijnana* of whatever kind (of object or of the Self) depends on the Self being Pure Knowledge.

Talk 205.

Mr. Cohen had been cogitating on the nature of the Heart, if the 'spiritual heart' beats; if so, how; or if it does not beat, then how is it to be felt?

M.: This heart is different from the physical heart; beating is the function of the latter. The former is the seat of spiritual experience. That is all that can be said of it.

Just as a dynamo supplies motive power to whole systems of lights, fans, etc., so the original Primal Force supplies energy to the beating of the heart, respiration, etc.

D.: How is the 'I-I' consciousness felt?

M.: As an unbroken awareness of 'I'. It is simply consciousness.

D.: Can we know it when it dawns?

M.: Yes, as consciousness. You are that even now. There will be no mistaking it when it is pure.

D.: Why do we have such a place as the 'Heart' for meditation?

M.: Because you seek consciousness. Where can you find it? Can you reach it externally? You have to find it internally. Therefore you are directed inward. Again the 'Heart' is only the seat of consciousness or the consciousness itself.

D.: On what should we meditate?

180

M.: Who is the meditator? Ask the question first. Remain as the meditator. There is no need to meditate.

Talk 206.

Mr. B. C. Das, a Lecturer in Physics of Allahabad University, asked: "Does not intellect rise and fall with the man?"

M.: Whose is the intellect? It is man's. Intellect is only an instrument.

D.: Yes. Does it survive man's death?

M.: Why think of death? See what happens in your sleep. What is your experience there?

D.: But sleep is transient whereas death is not.

M.: Sleep is intermediate between two waking states, so also death is between two successive births. Both are transient.

D.: I mean when the spirit is disembodied, does it carry the intellect with it?

M.: Spirit is not disembodied. The bodies differ. It may not be a gross body. It will then be a subtle body, as in sleep, dream or day-dream. Intellect does not alter; the bodies may differ according to circumstances.

D.: The spirit-body is the astral body then?

M.: The intellect is the astral body now.

D.: How can it be?

M.: Why not? You seem to think that the intellect cannot be limited like a body. It is only an aggregate of certain factors. What else is the astral body?

D.: But intellect is a sheath?

M.: Yes. Without intellect, no sheath is cognised. Who says that there are five sheaths? Is it not the intellect that declares thus?

Talk 207.

Deep sleep is only the state of non-duality. Can the difference between the individual and Universal souls persist there? Sleep implies forgetfulness of all differences: This alone constitutes happiness. See how carefully people prepare their beds to gain that happiness. Soft cushions, pillows and all the rest are meant to induce sound sleep, that is to say to end wakefulness. And yet the soft bed, etc., are of no use in the state of deep sleep itself. The implication is that all efforts are meant only to end ignorance. They have no use after realisation.

Talk 208.

It is enough that one surrenders oneself. Surrender is to give oneself up to the original cause of one's being. Do not delude yourself by imagining such source to be some God outside you. One's source is within yourself. Give yourself up to it. That means that you should seek the source and merge in it. Because you imagine yourself to be out of it, you raise the question "Where is the source?" Some contend that the sugar cannot taste its own sweetness and that a taster must taste and enjoy it. Similarly, an individual cannot be the Supreme and enjoy the Bliss of that state; therefore the individuality must be maintained on the one hand and God-head on the other so that enjoyment may result! Is God insentient like sugar? How can one surrender oneself and yet retain one's individuality for supreme enjoyment? Furthermore they say also that the soul, reaching the divine region and remaining there, serves the Supreme Being. Can the sound of the word "service" deceive the Lord? Does He not know? Is He waiting for these people's service? Would not He — the Pure Consciousness — ask in turn: "Who are you apart from Me that presume to serve Me?"

Still more, they assume that the individual soul becomes pure by being divested of the ego and fit for being the body of the Lord. Thus the Lord is the Spirit and the purified souls constitute His body and limbs! Can there be a soul for the souls? How many souls are there? The answer must be, "There are many individual souls and One Supreme Soul." What is soul in that case? It cannot be the body, etc. What remains over after all these are eliminated must be said to be the soul. Thus even after realising the soul as that which cannot be discarded, the Supreme Soul must be known to exist. In that case, how was the soul realised to be the ultimate reality after discarding all that was alien to it? Should this be right, the soul which was described as that inalienable reality is not the true soul. All such confusion is due to the word 'soul' (atma). The same word atma is used to signify the body, the senses, the mind, the vital principle, the individual soul and the Supreme Being. This wide application of the word has given rise to the idea that the individual soul (*jivatma*), goes to constitute the body of the Supreme (*Paramatma*). "I, O Arjuna! am the *Self*, seated in the heart of all beings; ..." (Bhagavad Gita, X-20). The stanza shows that the Lord is the Atma (Self) of all beings. Does it say, "the Self of the selves"? If, on the other hand, you merge in the Self there will be no individuality left. You will become the Source itself. In that case what is surrender? Who is to surrender what and to whom? This constitutes devotion, wisdom, and investigation.

Among the Vaishnavites too, Saint Nammalvar says, "I was in a maze, sticking to 'I' and 'mine'; I wandered without knowing my Self. On realising my Self I understand that I myself am You and that 'mine' (*i.e.*, my possessions) is only You."

Thus — you see — Devotion is nothing more than knowing oneself. The school of Qualified Monism also admits it. Still, adhering to their traditional doctrine, they persist in affirming that the individuals are part of the Supreme — his limbs as it were. Their traditional doctrine says also that the individual soul should be made pure and then surrendered to the Supreme; then the ego is lost and one goes to the regions of Vishnu after one's death; then finally there is the enjoyment of the Supreme (or the Infinite)!

To say that one is apart from the Primal Source is itself a pretension; to add that one divested of the ego becomes pure and yet retains individuality only to enjoy or serve the Supreme, is a deceitful stratagem. What duplicity is this — first to appropriate what is really His, and then pretend to experience or serve Him! Is not all this already known to Him?

19th June, 1936

Talk 209.

Mr. B.C. Das, the Physics Lecturer, asked about freewill and destiny.

M.: Whose will is it? 'It is mine', you may say. You are beyond will and fate. Abide as that and you transcend them both. That is the meaning of conquering destiny by will. Fate can be conquered. Fate is the result of past actions. By association with the wise the bad tendencies are conquered. One's experiences are then viewed to their proper perspective.

I exist now. I am the enjoyer. I enjoy fruits of action. I was in the past and shall be in the future. Who is this 'I'? Finding this 'I' to be pure Consciousness beyond action and enjoyment, freedom and happiness are gained. There is then no effort, for the Self is perfect and there remains nothing more to gain.

So long as there is individuality, one is the enjoyer and doer. But if it is lost, the divine Will prevails and guides the course of events. The individual is perceptible to others who cannot perceive divine force. Restrictions and discipline are for other individuals and not for the liberated.

Free-will is implied in the scriptural injunctions to be good. It implies overcoming fate. It is done by wisdom. The fire of wisdom consumes all actions. Wisdom is acquired by association with the wise, or rather, its mental atmosphere.

Talk 210.

Man owes his movements to another Power, whereas he thinks that he does everything himself — just like a lame man bluffing that, were he helped to stand up, he would fight and chase away the enemy. Action is impelled by desire; desire arises only after the rise of the ego; and this ego owes its origin to a Higher Power on which its existence depends. It cannot remain apart. Why then prattle, "I do, I act, or I function"?

A Self-realised being cannot help benefiting the world. His very existence is the highest good.

Talk 211.

Mr. B. C. Das, the Physics Lecturer, asked: "Yoga means union. I wonder union of which with which."

M.: Exactly. Yoga implies prior division and it means later union of one with another. Who is to be united with whom? You are the seeker, seeking union with something. That something is apart from you. Your Self is intimate to you. You are aware of the Self. Seek it and be it. That will expand as the Infinite. Then there will be no question of yoga, etc. Whose is the separation (*viyoga*)? Find it.

D.: Are the stones, etc. destined to be always so?

M.: Who sees stones? They are perceived by your senses, which are in turn actuated by your mind. So they are in your mind. Whose mind is it? The questioner must find it himself. If the Self be found this question will not arise.

The Self is more intimate than the objects. Find the subject, and the objects will take care of themselves. The objects are seen by different persons according to their outlook and these theories are evolved. But who is the seer, the cogniser of these theories? It is you. Find your Self. Then there is an end of these vagaries of the mind.

D.: What is this mind?

M.: A bundle of thoughts.

D.: Wherefrom has it its origin?

M.: Consciousness of the Self.

D.: Then thoughts are not real.

M.: They are not: the only reality is the Self.

Talk 212.

Maharshi observed: Pradakshina (the Hindu rite of going round the object of worship) is "All is within me." The true significance of the act of going round Arunachala is said to be as effective as circuit round the world. That means that the whole world is condensed into this Hill. The circuit round the temple of Arunachala is equally good; and self-circuit (*i.e.*, turning round and round) is as good as the last. So all are contained in the Self. Says the Ribhu Gita: "I remain fixed, whereas innumerable universes becoming concepts within my mind, rotate within me. This meditation is the highest circuit (*pradakshina*)."

20th June, 1936

Talk 213.

Mr. B. C. Das asked why the mind cannot be turned inward in spite of repeated attempts.

M.: It is done by practice and dispassion and that succeeds only gradually. The mind, having been so long a cow accustomed to graze stealthily on others' estates, is not easily confined to her stall. However much her keeper tempts her with luscious grass and fine fodder, she refuses the first time; then she takes a bit; but her innate tendency to stray away asserts itself; and she slips away; on being repeatedly tempted by the owner, she accustoms herself to the stall; finally even if let loose she would not stray away. Similarly with the mind. If once it finds its inner happiness it will not wander outward.

Talk 214.

Mr. Eknatha Rao, a frequent visitor, asked: Are there not modulations in contemplation according to circumstances?

M.: Yes. There are; at times there is illumination and then contemplation is easy; at other times contemplation is impossible even with repeated attempts. This is due to the working of the three Gunas (qualities in nature).

D.: Is it influenced by one's activities and circumstances?

M.: Those cannot influence it. It is the sense of doership — *kartrutva buddhi* — that forms the impediment.

22nd June, 1936

Talk 215.

Maharshi was reading G. U. Pope's translation of *Tiruvachakam* and came across the stanzas describing the intense feeling of *bhakti* as thrilling the whole frame, melting the flesh and bones, etc. He remarked: "Manickavachakar is one of those whose body finally resolved itself in a blazing light, without leaving a corpse behind."

Another devotee asked how it could be.

Maharshi said the gross body is only the concrete form of the subtle stuff — the mind. When the mind melts away and blazes forth

186

as light, the body is consumed in that process. Nandanar is another whose body disappeared in blazing light.

Maj. Chadwick pointed out that Elisha disappeared in the same way. He desired to know if the disappearance of Christ's body from the tomb was like that.

M.: No. Christ's body was left as a corpse which was at first entombed, whereas the others did not leave corpses behind.

In the course of conversation, Maharshi said that the subtle body is composed of light and sound and the gross body is a concrete form of the same.

The Lecturer in Physics asked if the same light and sound were cognisable by senses.

M.: No. They are super-sensual. It is like this:

	Isvara (Universal)	*Jiva* (Individual)
Gross	Universe	Body
Subtle	Sound and Light - *Nada, Bindu*	Mind and *Prana*
Primal	*Atma* (Self) *Param* (transcendental)	*Atma* (Self) *Param* (transcendental)

They are ultimately the same.

The subtle body of the Creator is the mystic sound *Pranava*, which is sound and light. The universe resolves into sound and light and then into transcendence — *Param*.

Talk 216.

Maharshi gave the meaning of Arunachala:

Aruna = Red, bright like fire.

The fire is not ordinary fire which is only hot.

This is *Jnanagni* (Fire of Wisdom) which is neither hot nor cool.

Achala = a hill.

So it means Hill of Wisdom.

29th June, 1936

Talk 217.

Mr. A. Bose, an engineer from Bombay, asked: Does Bhagavan feel for us and show grace?

M.: You are neck-deep in water and yet cry for water. It is as good as saying that one neck-deep in water feels thirsty, or a fish in water feels thirsty, or that water feels thirsty.

D.: How may one destroy the mind?

M.: Is there a mind in the first place? What you call mind is an illusion. It starts from the 'I-thought'. Without the gross or subtle senses you cannot be aware of the body or the mind. Still it is possible for you to be without these senses. In such a state you are either asleep or aware of the Self only. Awareness of Self is ever there. Remain what you truly are and this question will not arise.

D.: Is the body consciousness an impediment to realization?

M.: We are always beyond the body or the mind. If however you feel the body as the Self, then it is of course an impediment.

D.: Is the body or the mind of any use for the Self?

M.: Yes, inasmuch as it helps Self-realisation.

30th June, 1936

Talk 218.

Maharshi has been looking into the *Siva Purana* this day. He says:
Siva has the transcendental and immanent aspects as represented by His invisible, transcendental being and the *linga* aspect respectively. The *linga* originally manifested as Arunachala stands even to this day. This manifestation was when the moon was in the constellation of Orion (*Ardra*) in December. However it was first worshipped on Sivaratri day which is held sacred even now.

In the sphere of speech *Pranava* (the mystic sound AUM) represents the transcendental (*nirguna*) and the *Panchakshari* (the five-syllabled mantra) represents the immanent aspect (*saguna*).

Again Sri Bhagavan recounts the anecdote of Parvati testing Rama. The story is as follows:

188

Rama and Lakshmana were wandering in the forest in search of Sita. Rama was grief-stricken. Just then Siva and Parvati happened to pass close by. Siva saluted Rama and passed on. Parvati was surprised and asked Siva to explain why He, the Lord of the Universe, being worshipped by all, should stop to salute Rama, an ordinary human who having missed his consort was grief-stricken and moving in anguish in the wilderness and looking helpless. Siva then said: "Rama is simply acting as a human being would under the circumstances. He is nevertheless the incarnation of Vishnu, and deserves to be saluted. You may test him if you choose."

Parvati considered the matter, took the shape of Sita and appeared in front of Rama, as he was crying out the name of Sita in great anguish. He looked at Parvati appearing as Sita, smiled and asked, "Why, Parvati, are you here? Where is Sambhu? Why have you taken the shape of Sita?" Parvati felt abashed and explained how she went there to test him and sought an explanation for Siva saluting him.

Rama replied: "We are all only aspects of Siva, worshipping Him at sight and remembering Him out of sight."

Talk 219.

Ramakrishna Swami, a long-resident disciple, asked Maharshi the meaning of *Twaiyarunachala Sarvam*, a stanza in *The Five Hymns*.

Maharshi explained it in detail, saying that the universe is like a painting on a screen — the screen being the Red Hill, Arunachala. That which rises and sinks is made up of what it rises from. The finality of the universe is the God Arunachala. Meditating on Him or on the seer, the Self, there is a mental vibration 'I' to which all are reduced. Tracing the source of 'I', the primal 'I-I' alone remains over, and it is inexpressible. The seat of Realisation is within and the seeker cannot find it as an object outside him. That seat is bliss and is the core of all beings. Hence it is called the Heart. The only useful purpose of the present birth is to turn within and realise it. There is nothing else to do.

D.: How is annihilation of predispositions to be accomplished?

M.: You are in that condition in realisation.

D.: Does it mean that, holding on to the Self, the tendencies should be scorched as they begin to emerge?

M.: They will themselves be scorched if only you remain as you truly are.

1st July, 1936

Talk 220.

Mr. B. C. Das, the Physics Lecturer, asked: Contemplation is possible only with control of mind and control can be accomplished only by contemplation. Is it not a vicious circle?

M.: Yes, they are interdependent. They must go on side by side. Practice and dispassion bring about the result gradually. Dispassion is practised to check the mind from being projected outward; practice is to keep it turned inward. There is a struggle between control and contemplation. It is going on constantly within. Contemplation will in due course be successful.

D.: How to begin? Your Grace is needed for it.

M.: Grace is always there. "Dispassion cannot be acquired, nor realization of the Truth, nor inherence in the Self, in the absence of Guru's Grace," the Master quoted.

Practice is necessary. It is like training a roguish bull confined to his stall by tempting him with luscious grass and preventing him from straying.

Then the Master read out a stanza from *Tiruvachakam*, which is an address to the mind, saying: "O humming bee (namely, mind)! Why do you take the pains of collecting tiny specks of honey from innumerable flowers? There is one from whom you can have the whole storehouse of honey by simply thinking or seeing or speaking of Him. Get within and hum to Him (*hrimkara*)."

D.: Should one have a form in one's mind, supplemented with reading or chanting God's name in one's meditation?

M.: What is mental conception except it be meditation?

D.: Should the form be supplemented by repetition of *mantras* or dwelling on divine attributes?

190

M.: When *japa* is the predominating tendency, vocal *japa* becomes eventually mental, which is the same as meditation.

Talk 221.

Mr. Bose: A form means duality. Is that good?

M.: One who questions like that had better adopt the path of enquiry. Form is not for him.

D.: In my meditation a blank interposes; I see no figure.

M.: Of course not.

D.: What about the blank?

M.: Who sees the blank? You must be there. There is consciousness witnessing the blank.

D.: Does it mean that I must go deeper and deeper?

M.: Yes. There is no moment when you are not.

2nd July, 1936

Talk 222.

Dr. Popatlal Lohara, a visitor, has studied several books including *Upadesa Sara* and visited several saints, *sadhus* and yogis, probably 1,500 as he puts their number. A *sadhu* in Trimbak has told him that he has still debts to pay which, if done, will enable him to have realisation. His only debt, as he conceived it, was the marriage of his son. It has since been performed and he now feels himself free from *karmic* indebtedness. He therefore seeks Sri Bhagavan's guidance for freedom from 'mental unhappiness' which persists in spite of his not being indebted.

M.: Which text of "Upadesa Sara" did you read?

D.: The Sanskrit text.

M.: It contains the answer to your question.

D.: My mind cannot be made steady by any amount of effort. I have been trying it since 1918.

The Master quoted from "Upadesa Sara": "Merging the mind into the Heart certainly comprises meritorious duty (*karma*), devotion (*bhakti*), yoga and supreme wisdom (*jnana*)." That is the whole truth in a nutshell.

D.: That does not satisfy my search for happiness. I am unable to keep my mind steady.

The Master quoted again from the same book: "Continuous search for what the mind is results in its disappearance. That is the straight path."

D.: How to search for the mind then?

M.: The mind is only a bundle of thoughts. The thoughts have their root in the 'I-thought'. He quoted; "Whoever investigates the origin of the 'I-thought', for him the ego perishes. This is the true investigation." The true "I" is then found shining by itself.

D.: This 'I-thought' rises from me. But I do not know the Self.

M.: All these are only mental concepts. You are now identifying yourself with a wrong 'I', which is the 'I-thought'. This 'I-thought' rises and sinks, whereas the true significance of 'I' is beyond both. There cannot be a break in your being. You, who slept, are also now awake. There was not unhappiness in your deep sleep. Whereas it exists now. What is it that has happened now so that this difference is experienced? There was no 'I-thought' in your sleep, whereas it is present now. The true 'I' is not apparent and the false 'I' is parading itself. This false 'I' is the obstacle to your right knowledge. Find out wherefrom this false 'I' arises. Then it will disappear. You will be only what you are — *i.e.,* absolute Being.

D.: How to do it? I have not succeeded so far.

M.: Search for the source of the 'I-thought'. That is all that one has to do. The universe exists on account of the 'I-thought'. If that ends there is an end of misery also. The false 'I' will end only when its source is sought.

Dr. Lohara asked for the meaning of one stanza in "Upadesa Sara".

M.: The one then in sleep is also now awake. There was happiness in sleep; but misery in wakefulness. There was no 'I'- thought in sleep; but it is now, while awake. The state of happiness and of no 'I-thought' in sleep is without effort. The aim should be to bring about that state even now. That requires effort.

192

Sleep	Wakefulness	Bring about sleep even in the waking state and that is realisation. Effort is directed to extinguishing the 'I-thought' and not for ushering the true 'I'. For the latter is eternal and requires no effort on your part.
Effortless Happiness No 'I-thought'	No happiness 'I-thought'	

Talk 223.

Dr. Lohara: Why does the mind not sink into the Heart even while meditating?

M.: A floating body does not readily sink unless some means are adopted for making it do so. Breath-control makes the mind quiescent. The mind must be alert and meditation pursued unremittingly even when it is at peace. Then it sinks into the heart. Or the floating body might be loaded with weights and made to sink. So also association with the wise will make the mind sink into the Heart.

Such association is both mental and physical. The extremely visible being (of the Guru) pushes the mind inward. He is also in the heart of the seeker and so he draws the latter's inward-bent mind into the Heart.

This question is asked only when the man begins to meditate and finds it difficult. Let him practise breath-control just a little and the mind will be purified. It does not now sink into the heart because the latent tendencies stand as obstacles. They are removed by breath-control or association with the wise. In fact the mind is always in the Heart. But it is restive and moves about on account of latent tendencies. When the tendencies are made ineffective it will be restful and at peace.

By breath-control the mind will be only temporarily quiescent, because the tendencies are still there. If the mind is transformed into the Self it will no longer give trouble. That is done by meditation.

Talk 224.

A disciple asked how he could recognise his own natural primal condition.

193

M.: Absolute freedom from thoughts is the state conducive to such recognition.

(From the attendant's notes)

Talk 225.

When Sri Bhagavan and Rangaswami, an attendant, were on the rocks, Bhagavan noticed someone in the Asramam rocking in a rocking chair, and remarked to the attendant:

"Siva made over all His own possessions to Vishnu and wandered away in the forests and wilderness and cemeteries and lived on food begged by Him. In His view non-possession is higher in the scale of happiness than possession of things."

D.: What is that higher happiness?

M.: To be free from anxieties. Possessions create anxieties such as their safeguarding, their utilisation, etc. Non-possession does not bring any anxieties in its train. Therefore Siva resigned everything in favour of Vishnu and He himself went away happy.

Divestment of possessions is the highest happiness.

3rd July, 1936

Talk 226.

A visitor from Tirukoilur asked if the study of the sacred books will reveal the truth.

M.: That will not suffice.

D.: Why not?

M.: Samadhi alone can reveal it. Thoughts cast a veil over Reality and so it cannot be clear in states other than *Samadhi*.

D.: Is there thought in Samadhi? Or is there not?

M.: There will only be the feeling '*I am*' and no other thoughts.

D.: Is not '*I am*' a thought?

M.: The egoless '*I am*' is not thought. It is realisation. The meaning or significance of 'I' is God. The experience of '*I am*' is to *Be Still*.

4th July, 1936

Talk 227.

The Master observed: "Being of the nature of Bliss why does one continue to crave for happiness? To be rid of that craving is

194

itself salvation. The Scriptures say, 'You are That'. The imparting of that knowledge is their purpose. The realisation must be by your finding out who you are and abiding as That, *i.e.* your Self. To be repeating, 'I am that' or 'not this' is only a waste of time. For the worthy disciple, the work lies within himself and not without."

As Bhagavan was descending the Hill, one of the workers, just outside the Asramam stopped work and was about to prostrate before the Master.

Then the Master said: "To engage in your duty is the true prostration."

The Master's attendant asked: "How?"

M.: To perform one's duty carefully is the greatest service to God. (Then, smiling, he entered the hall.)

Talk 228.

At lunch a visitor from Nellore asked the Master for a tiny bit of food (*prasad*) from His dish.

M.: Eat without thinking of the ego. Then what you eat becomes Bhagavan's *prasad*.

After lunch the Master continued humorously: "If I had given you one morsel from my plate, each one would ask for a morsel too. What will be left for me if I distribute the whole plate to others? So you see that it is not devotion. There is no significance in eating a morsel from my plate. Be a true devotee."

8th July, 1936

Talk 229.

At 8 a.m. the pet squirrel was watching for an opportunity to run out. The Master remarked. "All wish to rush out. There is no limit to going out. Happiness lies within and not without."

20th July, 1936

Talk 230.

A visitor: Can one realise the Truth by learning the scriptures and study of books?

195

M.: No. So long as predispositions remain latent in the mind, realisation cannot be achieved. Sastra learning is itself a *vasana*. Realisation is only in *samadhi*.

Talk 231.

A visitor asked: 'What is *mouna* (silence)?'

M.: Mouna is not closing the mouth. It is eternal speech.

D.: I do not understand.

M.: That state which transcends speech and thought is *mouna*.

D.: How to achieve it?

M.: Hold some concept firmly and trace it back. By such concentration silence results. When practice becomes natural it will end in silence. Meditation without mental activity is silence. Subjugation of the mind is meditation. Deep meditation is eternal speech.

D.: How will worldly transaction go on if one observes silence?

M.: When women walk with water pots on their heads and chat with their companions they remain very careful, their thoughts concentrated on the loads on their heads. Similarly when a sage engages in activities, these do not disturb him because his mind abides in Brahman.

Talk 232.

The Master said on another occasion: "Only the sage is a true devotee."

Talk 233.

D.: What is the result of "Rama Japa" (repetition of God Rama's name)?

M.: 'Ra' is Reality, 'Ma' is the mind; their union is the fruit of "Rama Japa". Utterance of words is not enough. The elimination of thoughts is wisdom. It is the Absolute Existence.

Talk 234.

A Muslim visitor asked about *asana* (physical posture).

M.: Abidance in God is the only true posture.

Talk 235.

Mr. T. K. S. Iyer, a disciple, was excited because someone in the town had spoken disparagingly of the Master. He did not retort and came away excited. So he asked Master what penalty should be paid for his failure to defend him.

M.: Patience, more patience; tolerance, more tolerance!

Talk 236.

On the death of King George V two devotees were discussing the matter in the hall. They were very upset. The Master said to them. "Whoever dies or is lost, what is that to you? Die yourself and lose yourself, becoming one with love."

Talk 237.

A man brought with him a silver idol of Subrahmanya and copper idols of Valli and Devayanai. He said to Sri Bhagavan: "I have been worshipping them for the last ten years but have been rewarded only with calamities. What shall I do with them?

When I asked others, they attribute my worries to some fault in the make-up of the idols — for instance, the difference in the metals of their make. Is it so?"

M.: Did they say that it was wrong to worship?

Talk 238.

In answer to some question Maharshi said: "There is a state when words cease and silence prevails."

D.: How to communicate thought to each other?

M.: That is only when there is the notion of two.

D.: How to get peace?

M.: That is the natural state. The mind obstructs the innate peace. Our investigation is only in the mind. Investigate the mind; it will disappear.

There is no entity by name mind. Because of the emergence of thoughts we surmise something from which they start. That we term mind. When we probe to see what it is, there is nothing like it. After it has vanished, Peace will be found to remain eternal.

D.: What is *buddhi* (intellect)?

M.: The thinking or discriminating faculty. These are mere names. Be it the ego, the mind or the intellect, it is all the same. Whose mind? Whose intellect? The ego's. Is the ego real? No. We confound the ego and call it intellect or mind.

D.: Emerson says, "Soul answers soul by itself — not by description or words."

M.: Quite so. However much you learn, there will be no bounds to knowledge. You ignore the doubter but try to solve the doubts. On the other hand, hold on to the doubter and the doubts will disappear.

D.: Then the question resolves itself to knowing the Self.

M.: Quite so.

D.: How to know the Self?

M.: See what the Self is. What you consider to be the Self, is really either the mind or the intellect or the 'I-thought'. The other thoughts arise only after the 'I-thought'. So hold on to it. The others will vanish leaving the Self as the residuum.

D.: The difficulty lies in reaching it.

M.: There is no reaching it at all because it is eternal, here and now. If the Self were to be gained anew, it would not be permanent.

D.: How to obtain equanimity or peace or equilibrium of mind? What is the best way?

M.: I have already answered it. Investigate the mind. It is eliminated and you remain over. Let your standpoint become that of wisdom then the world will be found to be God.

dristin jnanamayim kritva pasyet Brahmamayam jagat.

So the question is one of outlook. You pervade all. See yourself and all are understood. But you have now lost hold of your Self and go about doubting other things.

D.: How to know the Self?

M.: Are there two 'I's? How do you know your own existence? Do you see yourself with these eyes? Question yourself. How does this question arise? Do I remain to ask it or not? Can I find my Self as in a mirror?

Because your outlook has been outward bent, it has lost sight of the Self and your vision is external. The Self is not found in external objects. Turn your look within and plunge down; you will be the Self.

D.: Is discovery of the Self dependent on the observance of caste rules? Or should we flout them?

M.: Not in the beginning. Observe them to start with. Caste-rules serve as a check on the vagaries of the mind. It is thus purified.

D.: The unknowable can be attained only by the grace of the unknowable.

M.: He helps the attainment. That is the Grace.

D.: How to check the mind?

M.: Will a thief betray himself? Will the mind find itself? The mind cannot seek the mind. You have ignored what is real and are holding on to the mind which is unreal and also trying to find what it is. Was there mind in your sleep? It was not. It is now here. It is therefore impermanent. Can the mind be found by you? The mind is not you. You think you are the mind and therefore ask me how it is checked. If it is there it can be checked. But it is not. Understand this truth by search. Search for unreality is fruitless. Therefore seek the reality, *i.e.*, the Self. That is the way to rule over the mind. There is only one thing Real!

D.: What is the one Real thing?

M.: That is what is: the others are only appearances. Diversity is not its nature. We are reading the printed characters on paper but ignore the paper which is the background. Similarly you are taken up by the manifestations of the mind and let go the background. Whose fault is it?

D.: Is there a limit to the Self?

M.: What is the Self?

D.: The Individual soul is the Self.

M.: What is the individual soul? Is there any difference between the two or are they identical?

Any new appearances are bound to disappear. Anything created will certainly be destroyed. The eternal is not born nor does it die. We are now confounding appearances with reality. Appearance carries its end in itself. What is it that appears newly? If you cannot find it, surrender to the substratum of appearances unreservedly; then, the reality will be left over as the residue.

D.: What happens to the man after death?

M.: Engage yourself in the living present. The future will take care of itself. Do not worry about the future. The state before creation and the process of creation are dealt with in the scriptures in order that you may know the present. Because you say you are born, therefore they say, yes, and add that God created you.

But do you see God or anything else in your sleep? If God be real why does He not shine forth in your sleep also? *You are always —* now the same as you were in sleep. You are not different from that one in sleep. But why should there be difference in the feelings or experiences of the two states?

Did you ask, while asleep, the question regarding your birth? or where do I go after death? Why think of all these now in the wakeful state? Let what is born think of its birth and the remedy, its cause and ultimate results.

What is birth? Is it of the 'I-thought' or of the body? Is 'I' separate from the body or identical with it? How did this 'I-thought' arise? Is the 'I-thought' your nature or is anything else of your nature?

D.: Who is to ask these questions?

M.: Exactly — that is it. There is no end to it all.

D.: Are we then to keep quiet?

M.: Doubts cease to afflict when the confusion (*moha*) is surpassed.

D.: Your statements amount to cessation of *vichara* — investigation.

M.: If *atma-vichara* (self-investigation), ceases, *loka vichara* (world-investigation) takes its place. (Laughter in the hall).

Engage in Self-investigation, then the non-self will disappear. The Self will be left over. This is self-investigation of the Self. The one word Self is equivalent to the mind, body, man, individual. the Supreme and all else.

Talk 239.

Mr. M. Frydman: One imagines things and enjoys them by strength of imagination. Such creations are possible to Brahma the Creator. Can the same statement apply to His creature, man?

M.: This is also your thought.

D.: Krishnamurti says that man should find out the 'I'. Then 'I' dissolves away, being only a bundle of circumstances. There is nothing behind the 'I'. His teaching seems to be very much like Buddha's.

M.: Yes — yes, beyond expression.

Talks with Sri Ramana Maharshi

Volume II

23rd August, 1936

Talk 240.

D.: The world is materialistic. What is the remedy for it?

M.: Materialistic or spiritual, it is according to your outlook. *Drishtim jnanamayim kritva, Brahma mayam pasyet jagat* Make your outlook right. The Creator knows how to take care of His Creation.

D.: What is the best thing to do for ensuring the future?

M.: Take care of the present, the future will take care of itself.

D.: The future is the result of the present. So, what should I do to make it good? Or should I keep still?

M.: Whose is the doubt? Who is it that wants a course of action? Find the doubter. If you hold the doubter the doubts will disappear. Having lost hold of the Self the thoughts afflict you; the world is seen, doubts arise, also anxiety for the future.

Hold fast to the Self, these will disappear.

D.: How to do it?

M.: This question is relevant to matters of non-self, but not to the Self. Do you doubt the existence of your own Self?

D.: No. But still, I want to know how the Self could be realised. Is there any method leading to it?

M.: Make effort. Just as water is got by boring a well, so also you realise the Self by investigation.

D.: Yes. But some find water readily and others with difficulty.

M.: But you already see the moisture on the surface. You are hazily aware of the Self. Pursue it. When the effort ceases the Self shines forth.

D.: How to train the mind to look within?

M.: By practice. The mind is the intelligent phase leading to its own destruction, for Self to manifest.

D.: How to destroy the mind?

M.: Water cannot be made dry water. Seek the Self; the mind will be destroyed.

29th August, 1936

Talk 241.

D.: How to avoid misery?

M.: Has misery a shape? Misery is only unwanted thought. The mind is not strong enough to resist it.

D.: How to gain such strength of mind?

M.: By worship of God.

D.: Meditation of the God of Immanence is hard to understand.

M.: Leave God alone. Hold your Self.

D.: How to do *japa* (repetition of *mantras*)?

M.: It is of two kinds — gross and subtle. The latter is meditation on it, and it gives strength to the mind.

D.: But the mind does not get steady for meditation.

M.: It is due to lack of strength.

D.: Sandhya is usually done mechanically. Similarly other religious duties. Is it useful? Is it not better to do *japa*, etc., knowing their meanings?

M.: Um! Um!

Talk 242.

A Gujarati gentleman asked Sri Bhagavan: They say that choice is offered to us to enjoy merits or demerits after our death. Their succession will be according to our choice. Is it so?

M.: Why raise these questions relating to events after death? Why ask "Was I born? Am I reaping fruits of my past karma," and so on? They will not be raised some time hence when you fall asleep. Why? Are you now different from the one in sleep? You are not. Why do these questions arise now and not in sleep? Find out.

Talk 243.

A middle-aged, weak-looking man came with a walking stick in his hand, placed it before Bhagavan, bowed low and sat near Maharshi. He got up and with great humility offered the stick to Bhagavan, saying that it was sandal-wood. Sri Bhagavan told him to keep it for himself. Because nothing of Bhagavan's can be safeguarded. Being common property but coveted by some, it will be taken away by any visitor with or without Bhagavan's permission. Then the donor may be displeased.

But the man still humbly insisted. Sri Bhagavan could not resist his supplications, and said, "Keep it yourself as *prasad* from Bhagavan." The man then requested that the stick might first be taken and then given to him by Sri Bhagavan with blessings. Sri Bhagavan received it, smelled it, said it was fine, nodded, and handed it back to the man, saying, "Keep it. It will make you always remember me."

Talk 244.

A Maharani Saheba spoke in a gentle and low voice, but quite audibly:

D.: "Maharajji, I have the good fortune to see you. My eyes have had the pleasure of seeing you, my ears the pleasure of hearing your voice.

"I am blessed with everything that a human being would like to have." Her Highness's voice choked. With great strength of mind she rallied and proceeded slowly, "I have all that I want, a human being would want …. But … But … I … I … do not have peace of mind … Something prevents it. Probably my destiny…."

There was silence for a few minutes. Then Maharshi in his usual sweet manner spoke:

M.: "All right. What need be said has been said. Well. What is destiny? There is no destiny. Surrender, and all will be well. Throw all the responsibility on God. Do not bear the burden yourself. What can destiny do to you then?"

D.: Surrender is impossible.

M.: Yes. Complete surrender is impossible in the beginning. Partial surrender is certainly possible for all. In course of time that will lead to complete surrender. Well, if surrender is impossible, what can be done? There is no peace of mind. You are helpless to bring it about. It can be done only by surrender.

204

D.: Partial surrender — well — can it undo destiny?

M.: Oh, yes! It can.

D.: Is not destiny due to past karma?

M.: If one is surrendered to God, God will look to it.

D.: This being God's dispensation, how does God undo it?

M.: All are in Him only.

D.: How is God to be seen?

M.: Within. If the mind is turned inward *God* manifests as inner consciousness.

D.: God is in all — in all the objects we see around us. They say we should see God in all of them.

M.: God is in all and in the seer. Where else can God be seen? He cannot be found outside. He *should* be felt within. To see the objects, mind is necessary. To conceive God in them is a mental operation. But that is not real. The consciousness within, purged of the mind, is felt as God.

D.: There are, say, beautiful colours. It is a pleasure to watch them. We can see God in them.

M.: They are all mental conceptions.

D.: There are more than colours. I *mentioned* colours only as an example.

M.: They are also similarly mental.

D.: There is the body also — the senses and the mind. The soul makes use of all these for knowing things.

M.: The objects or feelings or thoughts are all mental conceptions. The mind rises after the rise of the I-thought or the ego. Wherefrom does the ego rise? From the abstract consciousness or Pure intelligence.

D.: Is it the soul?

M.: Soul, mind or ego are mere words. There are no entities of the kind. Consciousness is the only truth.

D.: Then that consciousness cannot give any pleasure.

M.: Its nature is Bliss. Bliss alone is. There is no enjoyer to enjoy pleasure.

Enjoyer and joy — both merge in it.

D.: There are pleasure and pain in ordinary life. Should we not remain with only pleasure?

M.: Pleasure consists in turning and keeping the mind within; pain in sending it outward. There is only pleasure. Absence of pleasure is called pain. One's nature is pleasure — Bliss (*Ananda*)

D.: Is it the soul?

M.: Soul and God are only mental conceptions.

D.: Is God only a mental conception?

M.: Yes. Do you think of God in sleep?

D.: But sleep is a state of dullness.

M.: If God be real He must remain always. You remain in sleep and in wakefulness — just the same. If God be as true as your Self, God must be in sleep as well as the Self. This thought of God arises only in the wakeful state. Who thinks now?

D.: I think.

M.: Who is this 'I'? Who says it? Is it the body?

D.: The body speaks.

M.: The body does not speak. If so, did it speak in sleep? Who is this I?

D.: I within the body.

M.: Are you within the body or without?

D.: I am certainly within the body.

M.: Do you know it to be so in your sleep?

D.: I remain in my body in sleep also.

M.: Are you aware of being within the body in sleep?

D.: Sleep is a state of dullness.

M.: The fact is, you are neither within nor without. Sleep is the natural state of being.

D.: Then sleep must be a better state than this.

M.: There is no superior or inferior state. In sleep, in dream and in the wakeful state you are just the same. Sleep is a state of happiness; there is no misery. The sense of want, of pain, etc., arises only in the wakeful state. What is the change that has taken place? You are the same in both, but there is difference in happiness. Why? Because the mind has risen now. This mind rises after the 'I-thought'. The thought arises from consciousness. If one abides in it, one is always happy.

D.: The sleep state is the state when the mind is quiet. I consider it a worse state.

206

M.: If that were so, why do all desire sleep?

D.: It is the body when tired that goes to sleep.

M.: Does the body sleep?

D.: Yes. It is the condition in which the wear and tear of the body is repaired.

M.: Let it be so. But does the body itself sleep or wake up? You yourself said shortly before that the mind is quiet in sleep. The three states are of the mind.

D.: Are they not states of the soul functioning through the senses, etc.?

M.: They are not of the soul or of the body. The soul remains always uncontaminated. It is the substratum running through all these three states. Wakefulness passes off, I am; the dream state passes off, I am; the sleep state passes off, I am. They repeat themselves, and yet I am. They are like pictures moving on the screen in a cinema show. They do not affect the screen. Similarly also, I remain unaffected although these states pass off. If it is of the body, are you aware of the body in sleep?

D.: No.

M.: Without knowing the body to be there how can the body be said to be in sleep?

D.: Because it is still found after waking up.

M.: The sense of body is a thought; the thought is of the mind, the mind rises after the 'I-thought', the 'I-thought' is the root thought. If that is held, the other thoughts will disappear. There will then be no body, no mind, not even the ego.

D.: What will remain then?

M.: The Self in its purity.

D.: How can the mind be made to vanish?

M.: No attempt is made to destroy it. To think or wish it is itself a thought. If the thinker is sought, the thoughts will disappear.

D.: Will they disappear of themselves? It looks so difficult.

M.: They will disappear because they are unreal. The idea of difficulty is itself an obstacle to realisation. It must be overcome. To remain as the Self is not difficult.

D.: It looks easy to think of God in the external world, whereas it looks difficult to remain without thoughts.

M.: That is absurd; to look at other things is easy and to look within is difficult! It must be contrariwise.

D.: But I do not understand. It is difficult.

M.: This thought of difficulty is the chief obstacle. A little practice will make you think differently.

D.: What is the practice?

M.: To find out the source of 'I'.

D.: That was the state before one's birth.

M.: Why should one think of birth and death? Are you really born? The rising of the mind is called birth. After mind the body-thought arises and the body is seen; then the thought of birth, the state before birth, death, the state after death — all these are only of the mind. Whose is the birth?

D.: Am I not now born?

M.: So long as the body is considered, birth is real. But the body is not 'I'. The Self is not born nor does it die. There is nothing new. The Sages see everything in and of the Self. There is no diversity in it. Therefore there is neither birth nor death.

D.: If sleep be such a good state, why does not one like to be always in it?

M.: One is always only in sleep. The present waking state is no more than a dream. Dream can take place only in sleep. Sleep is underlying these three states. Manifestation of these three states is again a dream, which is in its turn another sleep. In this way these states of dream and sleep are endless.

Similar to these states, birth and death also are dreams in a sleep. Really speaking, there are no birth and death.

8th September, 1936

Talk 245.

Misses Gulbai and Shirinbai Byramjee, two Parsi ladies, were asking questions round one central point. All their questions amounted to one.

"I understand that the Self is beyond the ego. My knowledge is theoretical and not practical. How shall I gain practical realisation of the Self?"

M.: Realisation is nothing to be got afresh. It is already there. All that is necessary is to be rid of the thought: "I have not realised."

D.: Then one need not attempt it.

M.: No. Stillness of mind or peace is realisation. There is no moment when the Self is not.

So long as there is doubt or the feeling of non-realisation, attempt must be made to rid oneself of these thoughts.

The thoughts are due to identification of the Self with the non-self. When the non-self disappears the Self alone remains. To make room anywhere it is enough that things are removed from there. Room is not brought in afresh. Nay, more — room is there even in cramping.

Absence of thoughts does not mean a blank. There must be one to know the blank. Knowledge and ignorance are of the mind. They are born of duality. But the Self is beyond knowledge and ignorance. It is light itself. There is no necessity to see the Self with another Self. There are no two selves. What is not Self is non-self. The non-self cannot see the Self. The Self has no sight or hearing. It lies beyond these — *all alone,* as pure consciousness.

A woman, with her necklace round her neck, imagines that it has been lost and goes about searching for it, until she is reminded of it by a friend; she has created her own sense of loss, her own anxiety of search and then her own pleasure of recovery. Similarly the Self is all along there, whether you search for it or not. Again just as the woman feels as if the lost necklace has been regained, so also the removal of ignorance and the cessation of false identification reveal the Self which is always present — here and now. This is called realisation. It is not new. It amounts to elimination of ignorance and nothing more.

Blankness is the evil result of searching the mind. The mind must be cut off, root and branch. See who the thinker is, who the seeker is. Abide as the thinker, the seeker. All thoughts will disappear.

209

D.: Then there will be the ego — the thinker.

M.: That ego is pure Ego purged of thoughts. It is the same as the Self. So long as false identification persists doubts will persist, questions will arise, there will be no end of them. Doubts will cease only when the non-self is put an end to. That will result in realisation of the Self. There will remain no other there to doubt or ask. All these doubts should be solved within oneself. No amount of words will satisfy. Hold the thinker. Only when the thinker is not held do objects appear outside or doubts arise in the mind.

Talk 246.

Language is only a medium for communicating one's thoughts to another. It is called in only after thoughts arise; other thoughts arise after the 'I-thought' rises; the 'I-thought' is the root of all conversation. When one remains without thinking one understands another by means of the universal language of silence.

Silence is ever-speaking; it is a perennial flow of language; it is interrupted by speaking. These words obstruct that mute language. There is electricity flowing in a wire. With resistance to its passage, it glows as a lamp or revolves as a fan. In the wire it remains as electric energy. Similarly also, silence is the eternal flow of language, obstructed by words.

What one fails to know by conversation extending to several years can be known in a trice in Silence, or in front of Silence — *e.g.,* Dakshinamurti, and his four disciples.

That is the highest and most effective language.

Talk 247.

There arose a doubt if 'I-I' consciousness be the same as *nirvikalpa samadhi* or anything anterior to it.

Sri Bhagavan said that the tiny hole in the Heart remains always closed, but it is opened by *vichara* with the result that 'I-I' consciousness shines forth. It is the same as *samadhi*.

D.: What is the difference between fainting and sleep?

M.: Sleep is sudden and overpowers the person forcibly. A faint is slower and there is a tingle of resistance kept up. Realisation is possible in a faint and impossible in sleep.

D.: What is the state just before death?

M.: When a person gasps for breath it indicates that the person is unconscious of this body; another body has been held and the person swings to and fro. While gasping there is a more violent gasp at intervals and that indicates the oscillation between the two bodies due to the present attachment not having been completely snapped. I noticed it in the case of my mother and of Palaniswami.

D.: Does the new body involved in that state represent the next re-incarnation of the person?

M.: Yes. While gasping the person is in something like a dream, not aware of the present environment.

(It must be remembered that Sri Bhagavan had been with His mother from 8 a.m. to 8 p.m. until she passed away. He was all along holding her head with one hand, the other hand placed on her bosom. What does it signify? He Himself said later that there was a struggle between Himself and His mother until her spirit reached the Heart.

Evidently the soul passes through a series of subtle experiences, and Sri Bhagavan's touch generates a current which turns the soul back from its wandering into the Heart.

The *samskaras*, however, persist and a struggle is kept up between the spiritual force set up by His touch and the innate *samskaras*, until the latter are entirely destroyed and the soul is led into the Heart to rest in eternal Peace, which is the same as Liberation.

Its entry into the Heart is signified by a peculiar sensation perceptible to the Mahatma — similar to the tinkling of a bell.

When Maharshi attended on Palaniswami on his death-bed, He took away His hand after the above signal. But Palaniswami's eyes opened immediately, signifying that the spirit had escaped through them, thereby indicating a higher rebirth, but not Liberation. Having once noticed it with Palaniswami, Maharshi continued touching His mother for a few minutes longer — even after the signal of the soul passing into the Heart — and thus ensured her Liberation. This was confirmed by the look of perfect peace and composure on her features).

15th September, 1936

Talk 248.

Sri Bhagavan said: The *jnani* says, "I am the body"; The *ajnani* says, "I am the body"; what is the difference? 'I am' is the truth. The body is the limitation. The *ajnani* limits the 'I' to the body. 'I' remains independent of the body in sleep. The same 'I' is now in the wakeful state. Though imagined to be within the body, 'I' is without the body. The wrong notion is not 'I am the body.' 'I' says so. The body is insentient and cannot say so. The mistake lies in thinking that 'I' is what 'I' is not. 'I' is not insentient. 'I' cannot be the inert body. The body's movements are confounded with 'I' and misery is the result. Whether the body works or not, 'I' remains free and happy. The *ajnani's* 'I' is the body only. That is the whole error. The *jnani's* 'I' includes the body and everything else. Clearly some intermediate entity arises and gives rise to the confusion.

Mr. Vaidyanatha Iyer, a lawyer, asked: If the *jnani* says "I am the body," what happens to him in death?

M.: He does not identify himself with the body even now.

D.: But you said just before that the *jnani* says "I am the body."

M.: Yes. His 'I' includes the body. For there cannot be anything apart from 'I' for him. If the body falls away there is no loss for the 'I'. 'I' remains the same. If the body feels dead let it raise the question. Being inert it cannot. 'I' never dies and does not ask the question. Who then dies? Who asks questions?

D.: For whom are all the *sastras* then? They cannot be for the real 'I'. They must be for the unreal 'I'. The real one does not require them. It is strange that the unreal should have so many *sastras* for him.

M.: Yes. Quite so. Death is only a thought and nothing more. He who thinks raises troubles. Let the thinker tell us what happens to him in death. The real 'I' is silent. One should not think 'I am this — I am not that'. To say 'this or that' is wrong. They are also limitations. Only 'I am' is the truth. Silence is 'I'. If one thinks 'I am this', another thinks 'I am this' and so on, there is a clash of thoughts and so many

212

religions are the result. The truth remains as it is, not affected by any statements, conflicting or otherwise.

D.: What is death? Is it not the falling away of the body?

M.: Do you not desire it in sleep? What goes wrong then?

D.: But I know I shall wake up.

M.: Yes — thought again. There is the preceding thought 'I shall wake up'. Thoughts rule the life. Freedom from thoughts is one's true nature — Bliss.

24th September, 1936

Talk 249.

M.: Ignorance — *ajnana* — is of two kinds:

(1) Forgetfulness of the Self.

(2) Obstruction to the knowledge of the Self.

Aids are meant for eradicating thoughts; these thoughts are the re-manifestations of predispositions remaining in seed-form; they give rise to diversity from which all troubles arise. These aids are: hearing the truth from the master (*sravana*), etc.

· The effects of *sravana* may be immediate and the disciple realises the truth all at once. This can happen only for the well-advanced disciple.

Otherwise, the disciple feels that he is unable to realise the truth, even after repeatedly hearing it. What is it due to? Impurities in his mind: ignorance, doubt and wrong identity are the obstacles to be removed.

(a) To remove ignorance completely, he has to hear the truth repeatedly, until his knowledge of the subject-matter becomes perfect;

(b) to remove doubts, he must reflect on what he has heard; ultimately his knowledge will be free from doubts of any kind;

(c) to remove the wrong identity of the Self with the non-self (such as the body, the senses, the mind or the intellect) his mind must become one-pointed.

All these things accomplished, the obstacles are at an end and *samadhi* results, that is, Peace reigns.

Some say that one should never cease to engage in hearing, reflection and one-pointedness. These are not fulfilled by reading books, but only by continued practice to keep the mind withdrawn.

The aspirant may be *kritopasaka* or *akritopasaka*. The former is fit to realise the Self, even with the slightest stimulus: only some little doubt stands in his way, it is easily removed if he hears the truth once from the Master. Immediately he gains the *samadhi* state. It is presumed that he had already completed *sravana*, reflection, etc. in previous births, they are no more necessary for him.

For the other all these aids are necessary; for him doubts crop up even after repeated hearing; therefore he must not give up aids until he gains the *samadhi* state.

Sravana removes the illusion of the Self being one with the body, etc. Reflection makes it clear that Knowledge is Self. One-pointedness reveals the Self as being Infinite and Blissful.

27th September, 1936

Talk 250.

A certain devotee asked Maharshi about some disagreeable statements made by a certain man well-known to Maharshi.

He said, "I permit him to do so. I have permitted him already. Let him do so even more. Let others follow suit. Only let them leave me alone. If because of these reports no one comes to me, I shall consider it a great service done to me. Moreover, if he cares to publish books containing scandals of me, and if he makes money by their sale, it is really good. Such books will sell even more quickly and in larger numbers than others. Look at Miss Mayo's book. Why should he not also do it? He is doing me a very good turn." Saying so, He laughed.

29th September, 1936

There was again a reference to the same subject when Maharshi was alone. The villifier seems to be getting into hot waters on account of his inconsiderate action. When it was mentioned, Maharshi seemed to be concerned for the man's safety, and He said with obvious sympathy: "Even if allowed to have his own way for earning money, the man gets into trouble. If he availed himself of our indulgence and acted sensibly, he could have got on well. But what can we do?"

Talk 251.

An aristocratic lady looking very intelligent, though pensive, asked: "We had heard of you, Maharajji, as the kindest and noblest soul. We had long desired to have your *darsan*. I came here once before, on the 14th of last month, but could not remain in your holy presence as long as I wished. Being a woman and also young, I could not stand the people around, and so broke away hurriedly after asking one or two simple questions. There are no holy men like you in our part of the country. I am happy as I have every thing I want. But I do not have that peace of mind which brings happiness. I now come here seeking your blessing so that I may gain it."

M.: Bhakti fulfils your desire.

D.: I want to know how I can gain that peace of mind. Kindly be pleased to advise me.

M.: Yes — devotion and surrender.

D.: Am I worthy of being a devotee?

M.: Everyone can be a devotee. Spiritual fare is common to all and never denied to anyone — be the person old or young, male or female.

D.: That is exactly what I am anxious to know. I am young and a *grihini* (housewife). There are duties of *grihastha dharma* (the household). Is devotion consistent with such a position?

M.: Certainly. What are you? You are not the body. You are Pure Consciousness. *Grihastha dharma* and the world are only phenomena appearing on that Pure Consciousness. It remains unaffected. What prevents you from being your own Self?

D.: Yes I am already aware of the line of teaching of Maharshi. It is the quest for the Self. But my doubt persists if such quest is compatible with *grihastha* life.

M.: The Self is always there. It is you. There is nothing but you. Nothing can be apart from you. The question of compatibility or otherwise does not arise.

215

D.: I shall be more definite. Though a stranger, I am obliged to confess the cause of my anxiety. I am blessed with children. A boy — a good *brahmachari* — passed away in February. I was grief-stricken. I was disgusted with this life. I want to devote myself to spiritual life. But my duties as a *grihini* do not permit me to lead a retired life. Hence my doubt.

M.: Retirement means abidance in the Self. Nothing more. It is not leaving one set of surroundings and getting entangled in another set, nor even leaving the concrete world and becoming involved in a mental world.

The birth of the son, his death, etc., are seen in the Self only.

Recall the state of sleep. Were you aware of anything happening? If the son or the world be real, should they not be present with you in sleep? You cannot deny your existence in sleep. Nor can you deny you were happy then. You are the same person now speaking and raising doubts. You are not happy, according to you. But you were happy in sleep. What has transpired in the meantime that happiness of sleep has broken down? It is the rise of ego. That is the new arrival in the *jagrat* state. There was no ego in sleep. The birth of the ego is called the birth of the person. There is no other kind of birth. Whatever is born is bound to die. Kill the ego: there is no fear of recurring death for what is once dead. The Self remains even after the death of the ego. That is Bliss — that is Immortality.

D.: How is that to be done?

M.: See for whom these doubts exist. Who is the doubter? Who is the thinker? That is the ego. Hold it. The other thoughts will die away. The ego is left pure; see where from the ego arises. That is pure consciousness.

D.: It seems difficult. May we proceed by *bhakti marga*?

M.: It is according to individual temperament and equipment. *Bhakti* is the same as *vichara*.

D.: I mean meditation, etc.

M.: Yes. Meditation is on a form. That will drive away other thoughts. The one thought of God will dominate others. That is concentration. The object of meditation is thus the same as that of *vichara*.

216

D.: Do we not see God in concrete form?

M.: Yes. God is seen in the mind. The concrete form may be seen. Still it is only in the devotee's mind. The form and appearance of God-manifestation are determined by the mind of the devotee. But it is not the finality. There is the sense of duality.

It is like a dream-vision. After God is perceived, *vichara* commences. That ends in Realisation of the Self. *Vichara* is the ultimate route.

Of course, a few find *vichara* practicable. Others find *bhakti* easier.

D.: Did not Mr. Brunton find you in London? Was it only a dream?

M.: Yes. He had the vision. He saw me in his mind.

D.: Did he not see this concrete form?

M.: Yes, still in his mind.

D.: How shall I reach the Self?

M.: There is no reaching the Self. If the Self were to be reached, it would mean that the Self is not now and here, but that it should be got anew. What is got afresh, will also be lost. So it will be impermanent. What is not permanent is not worth striving for. So I say, the Self is not reached. You are the Self. You are already That. The fact is that you are ignorant of your blissful state. Ignorance supervenes and draws a veil over the pure Bliss. Attempts are directed only to remove this ignorance. This ignorance consists in wrong knowledge. The wrong knowledge consists in the false identification of the Self with the body, the mind, etc. This false identity must go and there remains the Self.

D.: How is that to happen?

M.: By enquiry into the Self.

D.: It is difficult. Can I realise the Self, Maharaj? Kindly tell me. It looks so difficult.

M.: You are already the Self. Therefore realisation is common to everyone. Realisation knows no difference in the aspirants. This very doubt, "Can I realise?" or the feeling, "I have not realised" are the obstacles. Be free from these also.

D.: But there should be the experience. Unless I have the experience how can I be free from these afflicting thoughts?

M.: These are also in the mind. They are there because you have identified yourself with the body. If this false identity drops away, ignorance vanishes and Truth is revealed.

D.: Yes, I feel it difficult. There are disciples of Bhagavan who have had His Grace and realised without any considerable difficulty. I too wish to have that Grace. Being a woman and living at a long distance I cannot avail myself of Maharshi's holy company as much as I would wish and as often as I would. Possibly I may not be able to return. I request Bhagavan's Grace. When I am back in my place, I want to remember Bhagavan. May Bhagavan be pleased to grant my prayer!

M.: Where are you going? You are not going anywhere. Even supposing you are the body, has your body come from Lucknow to Tiruvannamalai? You had simply sat in the car and one conveyance or another had moved; and finally you say that you have come here. The fact is that you are not the body. The Self does not move. The world moves in it. You are only what you are. There is no change in you. So then even after what looks like departure from here, you are here and there and everywhere. These scenes shift.

As for Grace — Grace is within you. If it is external it is useless. Grace is the Self. You are never out of its operation. Grace is always there.

D.: I mean that when I remember your form, my mind should be strengthened and that response should come from your side too. I should not be left to my individual efforts which are after all only weak.

M.: Grace is the Self. I have already said, "If you remember Bhagavan, you are prompted to do so by the Self." Is not Grace already there? Is there a moment when Grace is not operating in you? Your remembrance is the forerunner of Grace. That is the response, that is the stimulus, that is the Self and that is Grace.

There is no cause for anxiety.

D.: Can I engage in spiritual practice, even remaining in *samsara*?

M.: Yes, certainly. One ought to do so.

D.: Is not *samsara* a hindrance? Do not all the holy books advocate renunciation?

218

M.: Samsara is only in your mind. The world does not speak out, saying 'I am the world'. Otherwise, it must be ever there — not excluding your sleep. Since it is not in sleep it is impermanent. Being impermanent it has no stamina. Having no stamina it is easily subdued by the Self. The Self alone is permanent. Renunciation is non-identification of the Self with the non-self. On the disappearance of ignorance the non-self ceases to exist. That is true renunciation.

D.: Why did you then leave your home in your youth?

M.: That is my *prarabdha* (fate). One's course of conduct in this life is determined by one's *prarabdha*. My *prarabdha* is this way. Your *prarabdha* is that way.

D.: Should I not also renounce?

M.: If that had been your *prarabdha*, the question would not have arisen.

D.: I should therefore remain in the world and engage in spiritual practice. Well, can I get realisation in this life?

M.: This has been already answered. You are always the Self. Earnest efforts never fail. Success is bound to result.

D.: Will Maharshi be pleased to extend Grace to me also! Maharshi smiled and said "Um! Um!" With blessings and salutation, the interview came to a close and the party departed directly.

30th September, 1936

Talk 252.

D.: Sri Ramakrishna touched Vivekananda and the latter realised Bliss. Is it possible?

M.: Sri Ramakrishna did not touch all for that purpose. He did not create Atma. He did not create Realisation. Vivekananda was ripe. He was anxious to realise. He must have completed the preliminary course in his past births. Such is possible for ripe persons only.

D.: Can the same miracle be worked for all?

M.: If they are fit. Fitness is the point. A strong man controls the weaker man. A strong mind controls the weaker mind. That was what happened in the case cited. The effect was only temporary. Why did

219

Vivekananda not sit quiet? Why did he wander about after such a miracle? Because the effect was only temporary.

D.: How is the mind to dive into the Heart?

M.: The mind now sees itself diversified as the universe. If the diversity is not manifest it remains in its own essence, that is the Heart. Entering the Heart means remaining without distractions.

. The Heart is the only Reality. The mind is only a transient phase. To remain as one's Self is to enter the Heart.

Because a man identifies himself with the body he sees the world separate from him. This wrong identification arises because he has lost his moorings and has swerved from his original state. He is now advised to give up all these false ideas, to trace back his source and remain as the Self. In that state, there are no differences. No questions will arise.

All the *sastras* are meant only to make the man retrace his steps to the original source. He need not gain anything new. He must only give up his false ideas and useless accretions. Instead of doing it he tries to catch hold of something strange and mysterious because he believes that his happiness lies elsewhere. That is the mistake.

If one remains as the Self there is bliss. Probably he thinks that being quiet does not bring about the state of bliss. That is due to his ignorance. The only practice is to find out "to whom these questions arise."

D.: How to control lust, anger, etc.?

M.: Whose are these passions? Find out. If you remain as the Self, there will be found to be nothing apart from the Self. Then there will be no need to control, etc.

D.: If a person whom we love dies, grief results. Shall we avoid such grief by either loving all alike or by not loving at all?

M.: If one dies, it results in grief for the other who lives. The way to get rid of grief *is not to live*. Kill the one who grieves. Who will remain then to suffer? The ego must die. That is the only way.

The two alternatives amount to the same state. When all have become the one Self, who is there to be loved or hated?

D.: What is the Sun *marga*? What is the Moon *marga*? Which of them is easier?

M.: Ravi marga (Sun marga) is *jnana*. Moon *marga* is Yoga. They think that after purifying the 72,000 *nadis* in the body, *sushumna* is entered and the mind passes up to the *sahasrara* and there is nectar trickling.

These are all mental concepts. The man is already overwhelmed by world concepts. Other concepts are now added in the shape of this Yoga. The object of all these is to rid the man of concepts and to make him inhere as the pure Self — *i.e.*, absolute consciousness, bereft of thoughts! Why not go straight to it? Why add new encumbrances to the already existing ones?

1st October, 1936

Talk 253.

Mr. F. G. Pearce, Principal, Scindia School, Gwalior: Bhagavan has stated [in *Sad Vidya Anubandham* (Supplement) sloka 36]: "The illiterates are certainly better off than the literates whose egos are not destroyed by the quest of the self." This being so, could Bhagavan advise a school master (who feels this to be true) how to carry on education in such a way that the desire for literacy and intellectual knowledge may not obscure the more important search for the Self? Are the two incompatible? If they are not, then from what age, and by what means, can young people best be stimulated towards the search for the Real Truth within?

M.: Pride of learning and desire for appreciation are condemned and not learning itself. Learning leading to search for Truth and humility is good.

[A request from the same seeker: The above questioner has spent two very precious days in physical proximity to Bhagavan Maharshi (whom he has not seen since — 17 years ago — he visited Him for a few minutes on the hillside). His duties now compel him to take his body far away again to the north, and it may be years before he can return. He humbly requests Bhagavan to make a strong link with him, and to continue to help him with His grace, in the quest of the Self.

Maharshi had a gentle smile for this.]

221

Talk 254.

Mr. Duncan Greenlees quoted a few verses from *Srimad Bhagavatam* to the following effect:

"See the Self in yourself like the pure ether in all beings, in and out."

"Unashamed, fall prostrate before even an outcast, a cow or an ass."

"So long as 'I' am not perceived in all, worship all with body and mind."

"With right knowledge see all as Brahma. This once clear, all doubts are at an end and you will remain withdrawn in the Self."

He then raised the following questions:

D.: Is this a True Path to the realisation of the, One Self? Is it not easier for some thus to practise seeing Bhagavan in whatever meets the mind than to seek the Super-Mental through the mental inquiry "Who am I?"

M.: Yes. When you see God in all, do you think of God or do you not? You should certainly keep God in your mind for seeing God all round you. Keeping God in your mind becomes *dhyana. Dhyana* is the stage before realisation. Realisation is in the Self only. *Dhyana* must precede it. Whether you make *dhyana* of God or of Self, it is immaterial. The goal is the same.

But you cannot escape the Self. You want to see God in all, but not in yourself? If all are God, are you not included in that all? Yourself being God, is it a wonder that all are God? There must be a seer and thinker for even the practice. Who is he?

D.: Through poetry, music, *japa, bhajan*, beautiful landscapes, reading the lives of spiritual heroes, etc., one sometimes experiences a true sense of all-unity. Is that feeling of deep blissful quiet (wherein the personal self has no place) the "entering into the heart" whereof Bhagavan speaks? Will practice of that lead to a deeper *samadhi*, and so ultimately to a full vision of the Real?

M.: Again, there is happiness at agreeable sights, etc. It is the happiness inherent in the Self. That happiness is not alien and after. You are diving into the Pure Self on occasions which you consider pleasurable. That diving reveals the Self-existent Bliss. But the

222

association of ideas is responsible for foisting this bliss on to other things or happenings. In fact, it is within you. On these occasions you are plunging into the Self, though unconsciously. If you do so consciously you call it Realisation. I want you to dive consciously into the Self, *i.e.*, into the Heart.

Talk 255.

D.: If the Self be always realised we should only keep still. Is that so?

M.: If you can keep still without engaging in any other pursuits, it is very good. If that cannot be done, where is the use of being quiet so far as realisation is concerned? So long as one is obliged to be active, let him not give up the attempt to realise the Self.

Talk 256.

A question was asked regarding the position of one whose *jnana* is weak in the scheme of things. The doubt was if that *manda jnani* had stopped short of *kevala nirvikalpa*.

M.: Kevala nirvikalpa happens even in the *tanumanasi* stage (of attenuated mind).

D.: The middling and superior *jnanis* are said to be *jivanmuktas*. *Kevala nirvikalpa* is in *tanumanasa*. Where does one whose *jnana* is weak fit in?

M.: He comes in *sattvapatti* (realisation) — whereas the middling and the superior ones come in *asamsakti* and *padarthabhavini* respectively. This division as dull, middling, and superior is according to the momentum of *prarabdha*. If it is strong he is weak; if it is middling he is middling too; if *prarabdha* is weak he is superior; if it is very weak he is in *turyaga*.

There is no difference in the *samadhi* state or the *jnana* of the *jnanis*. The classification is only from the standpoint of the observer.

D.: Is *tanumanasi* the same as *mumukshutva*?

M.: No. The six qualities, discrimination, dispassion and *mumukshutva*, etc., precede *subhechcha*. The first stage follows *mumukshutva*, then comes *vicharana* (search), then the tenuous mind. Direct perception is in *sattvapatti* (realisation).

There is no need to discuss similar points. *Jivanmukti* and *Videhamukti* are differently described by different authorities; *Videhamukti* is sometimes said to occur even when the man is seen with a body. The fact is that *mukti* is another name for *Aham* ('I').

The Seven *Jnana bhumikas* (stages of knowledge) are: (1) *Subhechcha* (desire for enlightenment); (2) *Vicharana* (hearing and reflection); (3) *Tanumanasi* (tenuous mind); (4) *Sattvapatti* (Self-Realisation); (5) *Asamsakti* (non-attachment); (6) *Padarthabhavani* (absolute non-perception of objects); (7) *Turyaga* (beyond words).

Those who have attained the last four *Bhumikas* are respectively called *Brahmavit, Brahmavidvara, Brahmavidvarya* and *Brahmavidvarishtha*.

Talk 257.

D.: A certain young man from Dindigul spoke to Sri Bhagavan, saying that he had learnt by his stay for a few days; that all that he need do was to enquire, "Who am I?" He wanted to know if any discipline was to be observed and started with the question: "Where should I do the enquiry?" meaning if he should do it in Guru sannidhi (the presence of the Master).

M.: The enquiry should be from where the 'I' is.

D.: People labour for gaining the *summum bonum* of life. I think that they are not on the right track. Sri Bhagavan has made considerable *tapas* and achieved the goal. Sri Bhagavan is also desirous that all should reach the goal and willing to help them to that end. His vicarious *tapas* must enable others to reach the goal rather easily. They need not undergo all the hardships which Sri Bhagavan has already undergone. Their way has been made easy for them by Sri Bhagavan. Am I not right?

Maharshi smiled and said: If that were so everyone would easily reach the goal, but each one must work for himself.

Talk 258.

D.: A young man from Mysore gave a written slip to Sri Bhagavan and waited for an answer. He had asked Sri Bhagavan to say where other Mahatmas could be found whom he might approach for

224

guidance. He confessed that he had left his home without informing his elders in order that he might seek God through Mahatmas. True, he knew nothing of God or of search for Him. Therefore he desired to see Mahatmas.

Sri Bhagavan simply returned the note saying: I must answer any and every question. Unless I do so I am not great.

The boy tore away the slip and wrote another, which said, "You are kind to squirrels and hares. You fondle them when they struggle to run away from you. Yet you are indifferent to human beings. For instance, I have left my home and am waiting here for a fortnight. I have had no food some days. I am struggling. Still you do not care for me."

M.: Look here. I am not endowed with television. God has not bestowed that gift on me. What shall I do? How can I answer your questions? People call me Maharshi and treat me like this. But I do not see myself as a Maharshi. On the other hand everyone is a Maharshi to me. It is good that you in this early age are attempting to seek God. Concentrate on Him. Do your work without desiring the fruits thereof. That is all that you should do.

Talk 259.

Nada, Bindu and *Kala* correspond to prana, mind and intellect.

Isvara is beyond *nada* (sound).

Nada, jyoti (light), etc., are mentioned in Yoga literature. But God is beyond these.

The circulation of blood, respiration of air, and other functions of the body are bound to produce sound. That sound is involuntary and continuous. That is *nada*.

Talk 260.

An extract from "A Hermit in the Himalayas" was found in the *Sunday Times*. It related to recapitulation of past incarnations. In it Paul Brunton has mentioned the Buddhist methods of gaining that faculty. Sri Bhagavan said, "There is a class of people who want to know all about their future or their past. They ignore the present. The load from the past forms the present misery. The attempt to recall the past is mere waste of time."

Talk 261.

There was a reference to reincarnation. Reincarnation of Shanti Devi tallies with the human standards of time. Whereas the latest case reported of a boy of seven is different. The boy is seven years now. He recalls his past births. Enquiries go to show that the previous body was given up 10 months ago.

The question arises how the matter stood for six years and two months previous to the death of the former body. Did the soul occupy two bodies at the same time?

Sri Bhagavan pointed out that the seven years is according to the boy; ten months is according to the observer. The difference is due to these two different *upadhis*. The boy's experience extending to seven years has been calculated by the observer to cover only 10 months of his own time.

Sri Bhagavan again referred to Lila's story in *Yoga Vasishta*.

Talk 262.

Dr. Syed, a Muslim Professor, is now here. A sceptic friend of his had confronted him with the question: "What miracle does your Maharshi work?" He had replied that the ordinary people being no better than animals are made men and that we being only His children are endowed with strength by Maharshi. He desired to know if he was right in replying to him. "Refreshing Peace within is the highest miracle. Maharshi possesses it."

"What is that to us?" the other man asked. I replied "The same Peace is bestowed on all visitors to be shared by them. Mr. Paul Brunton has mentioned it in his book. Everyone feels it every day in Maharshi's presence."

The whole conversation was mentioned to Sri Bhagavan with the following addition:

Parasurama has said that he felt some refreshing peace within when he met Samvritta on the way. So he made him out to be a great saint. Is not such peace the sole criterion of a Mahatma's Presence? Is there anything else?

Sri Bhagavan said: A Madhva saint Tatvaroyar had composed a *bharani* on his master Swarupanand. Pandits objected to the

226

composition, saying that it was reserved to such as have killed more than a thousand elephants in battle, whereas Swarupanand was an idle man sitting somewhere unknown to people and he did not deserve that panegyric. Tatvaroyar asked them all to assemble before his master so that they might see for themselves if he could slay one thousand elephants at a time. They did so. As soon as they appeared they were struck dumb and remained in beatific peace for a few days without the least movement. When they regained their senses, they saluted both the master and the disciple, saying that they were more than satisfied. Swarupanand excelled the warriors in that he could subdue the egos, which is a much more formidable task than slaying a thousand elephants.

Maharshi said that the moral was clear. Peace is the sole criterion of a Mahatma's Presence.

20th October, 1936

Talk 263.

Dr. Syed: Sri Bhagavan says that the Heart is the Self. Psychology has it that malice, envy, jealousy and all passions have their seat in the heart. How are these two statements to be reconciled?

M.: The whole cosmos is contained in one pinhole in the Heart. These passions are part of the cosmos. They are *avidya* (ignorance).

D.: How did *avidya* arise?

M.: Avidya is like Maya [she who is not is *maya* (illusion)]. Similarly that which is not is ignorance. Therefore the question does not arise. Nevertheless, the question is asked. Then ask, "Whose is the *avidya*? *Avidya* is ignorance. It implies subject and object. Become the subject and there will be no object.

D.: What is *avidya*?

M.: Ignorance of Self. Who is ignorant of the Self? The self must be ignorant of Self. Are there two selves?

Talk 264.

D.: Does Bhagavan see the world as part and parcel of Himself? How does He see the world?

227

M.: The Self alone *is* and nothing else. However, it is differentiated owing to ignorance. Differentiation is threefold: (1) of the same kind: (2) of a different kind, and (3) as parts in itself. The world is not another self similar to the self. It is not different from the self; nor is it part of the self.

D.: Is not the world reflected on the Self?

M.: For reflection there must be an object and an image. But the Self does not admit of these differences.

D.: Does not then Bhagavan see the world?

M.: Whom do you mean by Bhagavan?

D.: A *jiva* advanced more than I.

M.: If you understand your *jiva* the other *jiva* is also understood.

D.: I do not want to discuss. I want to learn. Please instruct me.

M.: Because you desire to learn, discussion is unavoidable. Leave all this aside. Consider your sleep. Are you then aware of bondage or do you seek means for release? Are you then aware of the body itself? The sense of bondage is associated with the body. Otherwise there is no bondage, no material to bind with and no one to be bound. These appear, however, in your wakeful state. Consider to whom they appear.

D.: To the mind.

M.: Watch the mind. You must stand aloof from it. You are not the mind. And the Self will remain ever.

D.: Does Sri Bhagavan believe in evolution?

M.: Evolution must be from one state to another. When no differences are admitted, how can evolution arise?

D.: Why does Sri Krishna say, "After several rebirths the seeker gains knowledge and thus knows Me." There must be evolution from stage to stage.

M.: How does Bhagavad Gita begin?" Neither I was not nor you nor these chiefs, etc." "Neither it is born, nor does it die, etc." So there is no birth, no death, no present as you look at it. Reality was, is, and will be. It is changeless. Later Arjuna asked Sri Krishna how he could have lived before *Aditya*. Then Krishna, seeing Arjuna was confounding Him with the gross body, spoke to him accordingly. The instruction is for the one who sees diversity. In reality there is no bondage nor *mukti* for himself or for others from the *jnani's* standpoint.

D.: Are all in liberation?

M.: Where is all? There is no liberation either. It could be only if there was bondage. There was really no bondage and so, it follows, there is no liberation.

D.: But to evolve through births, there must be practice, years of *abhyasa*.

M.: *Abhyasa* is only to prevent any disturbance to the inherent peace. There is no question of years. Prevent this thought at this moment. You are only in your natural state whether you make *abhyasa* or not.

Another man asked: Why do not all realise the Self in that case?

M.: It is the same question in another guise. Why do you raise this question? Inasmuch as you raise this question of *abhyasa* it shows you require *abhyasa*. Make it.

But to remain without questions or doubts is the natural state.

God created man; and man created God. They both are the originators of forms and names only. In fact, neither God nor man was created.

21st October, 1936

Talk 265.

The aristocratic lady again came after a few days, went straight to Bhagavan, saluted him and said:

"I came last time with my husband and children. I was thinking of their food and time was pressing. So I could not stay here as long as I would have wished. But I was later worried over the hurried nature of the visit. I have returned now to sit quiet and imbibe Sri Bhagavan's Grace. May He give me strength of mind!"

The hall was already kept clear of people. She sat on a crude carpet in front of Sri Bhagavan. Sri Bhagavan said smiling: "Yes. Silence is perpetual speaking. Ordinary speech hinders that heart-to-heart talk."

She agreed and sat quiet. Sri Bhagavan was sitting reclining on the sofa. His eyes were fixed in her direction with a gracious smile on His lips. Both remained silent and motionless for about an hour.

229

Prasad was distributed. The lady said: "Now I want to return. The river between Bangalore and this place is in floods. On my way here a bus was overturned in the floods. My car came later, and I saw the sad accident. Still I was not afraid to ford the river. My car came out safe. I would like to return in daytime.

"This time I shall not say 'is the last time I shall come' as I said on former occasions. I do not know, but it may be so. Yet Maharshi should give me strength of mind.

"I long for *bhakti*. I want more of this longing. Even realisation does not matter for me. Let me be strong in my longing."

M.: If the longing is there, Realisation will be forced on you even if you do not want it. *Subhechcha* is the doorway for realisation.

D.: Let it be so. But I am content with longing. Even when I am away from this place I must not relax in my devotion. May Sri Bhagavan give me the necessary strength. Such longing could only be through His Grace. I am personally too weak.

Again, when I was here on a previous occasion I asked several questions. But I could not follow Sri Bhagavan's answers. I thought I would not ask any more questions but only sit quiet in His Presence imbibing Grace which might be extended to me. So I do not pursue Maharshi with more questions this time. Only let me have His Grace.

M.: Your repeated visits to this place indicate the extension of Grace.

She was surprised and said: "I was going to ask Maharshi if He called me. For all of a sudden my husband told me this morning: 'There are two days free. If you want you may visit Maharshi and return.'

"I was very agreeably surprised and pleased. I took it to be a call from Maharshi."

She also expressed a desire to reside near Maharshi and asked for His blessings.

Maharshi said: A Higher Power is leading you. Be led by the same.

D.: But I am not aware of it. Please make me aware of it.

M.: The Higher Power knows what to do and how to do it. Trust it.

230

Talk 266.

The Muslim Professor asked: It is said that one should give up desire. But there are the needs of the body which are irrepressible. What is to be done?

M.: An aspirant must be equipped with three requisites: (1) *Ichcha*; (2) *Bhakti*; and (3) *Sraddha. Ichcha* means satisfaction of bodily wants without attachment to the body (such as hunger and thirst and evacuation). Unless it is done meditation cannot progress. *Bhakti* and *Sraddha* are already known.

D.: There are two kinds of desires — the baser and the nobler. Is it our duty to transmute the baser one to the nobler?

M.: Yes.

D.: Well, Bhagavan, you said there are three requisites of which *ichcha* is the satisfaction of natural wants without attachment to the body, etc. I take food three or four times a day and attend to bodily wants so much so that I am oppressed by the body. Is there a state when I shall be disembodied so that I might be free from the scourge of bodily wants?

M.: It is the attachments (*raga, dwesha*) which are injurious. The action is not bad in itself. There is no harm in eating three or four times. But only do not say, "I want this kind of food and not that kind" and so on.

Moreover you take those meals in twelve hours of wakeful state whereas you are not eating in the hours of sleep. Does sleep lead you to *mukti*? It is wrong to suppose that simple inactivity leads one to *mukti*.

D.: There are said to be *sadeha mukta* (liberated in body) and *videha mukta* (liberated without body).

M.: There is no liberation, and where are *muktas*?

D.: Do not Hindu *sastras* speak of *mukti*?

M.: Mukti is synonymous with the Self. *Jivan mukti* (liberation while alive) and *videha mukti* (liberation after the body falls) are all for the ignorant. The *jnani* is not conscious of *mukti* or *bandha* (bondage). Bondage, liberation and orders of *mukti* are all said for an *ajnani* in order that ignorance might be shaken off. There is only *mukti* and nothing else.

231

D.: It is all right from the standpoint of Bhagavan. But what about us?

M.: The difference 'He' and 'I' are the obstacles to *jnana*.

D.: But it cannot be denied that Bhagavan is of a high order whereas we are limited. Will Bhagavan make me one with Him?

M.: Were you aware of limitations in your sleep?

D.: I cannot bring down the state of my sleep in the present state and speak of it.

M.: You need not. These three states alternate before the unchanging Self. You can remember your state of sleep. That is your real state. There were no limitations then. After the rise of the 'I-thought' the limitations arose.

D.: How to attain the Self?

M.: Self is not to be attained because you are the Self.

D.: Yes. There is an unchanging Self and a changing one in me. There are two selves.

M.: The changefulness is mere thought. All thoughts arise after the arising of the 'I-thought'. See to whom the thoughts arise. Then you transcend them and they subside. This is to say, tracing the source of the 'I-thought', you realise the perfect 'I-I'. 'I' is the name of the Self.

D.: Shall I meditate on "I am Brahman" (*Aham Brahmasmi*)?

M.: The text is not meant for thinking "I am *Brahman*". *Aham* ('I') is known to everyone. *Brahman* abides as *Aham* in everyone. Find out the 'I'. The 'I' is already Brahman. You need not think so. Simply find out the 'I'.

D.: Is not discarding of the sheaths mentioned in the *sastras*?

M.: After the rise of the 'I-thought' there is the false identification of the 'I' with the body, the senses, the mind, etc. 'I' is wrongly associated with them and the true 'I' is lost sight of. In order to shift the pure 'I' from the contaminated 'I' this discarding is mentioned. But it does not mean exactly discarding of the non-self, but it means the finding of the real Self.

The real Self is the Infinite 'I-I', *i.e.*, 'I' is perfection. It is eternal. It has no origin and no end. The other 'I' is born and also dies. It is impermanent. See to whom are the changing thoughts. They will be found to arise after the 'I-thought'. Hold the 'I-thought'. They subside. Trace back the source of the 'I-thought'. The Self alone will remain.

D.: It is difficult to follow. I understand the theory. But what is the practice?

M.: The other methods are meant for those who cannot take to the investigation of the Self. Even to repeat *Aham Brahmasmi* or think of it, a doer is necessary. Who is it? It is 'I'. Be that 'I'. It is the direct method. The other methods also will ultimately lead everyone to this method of the investigation of the Self.

D.: I am aware of the 'I'. Yet my troubles are not ended.

M.: This 'I-thought' is not pure. It is contaminated with the association of the body and senses. See to whom the trouble is. It is to the 'I-thought'. Hold it. Then the other thoughts vanish.

D.: Yes. How to do it? That is the whole trouble.

M.: Think 'I' 'I' 'I' and hold to that one thought to the exclusion of all others.

23rd October, 1936

Talk 267.

While speaking of the animal companions in the hall Sri Bhagavan quoted a Tamil stanza by Avvai.

When the old lady was going along she heard on one occasion some one praising Kambar. She replied with a stanza which means:

"Each is great in its own way. What is Kambar's greatness when compared with a bird which builds its nest so fine, the worms which give lac, the honey-bee which builds the comb, the ants which build cities, and the spider its web?"

Bhagavan then began to describe their activities.

While living on the hill He had seen a hut built of stones and mud and roofed with thatch. There was constant trouble with white ants. The roof was pulled down and the walls demolished to get rid of the mud which harboured the ants. Sri Bhagavan saw that the hollows protected by stones were made into towns. These were skirted by walls plastered black, and there were roads to neighbouring cities which were also similarly skirted with black plastered walls. The roads were indicated by these walls. The interior of the town contained holes in which ants used to live. The whole wall was thus tenanted by white ants which ravaged the roofing materials above.

Sri Bhagavan had also watched a spider making its web and described it. It is seen in one place, then in another place, again in a third place. The fibre is fixed at all these points. The spider moves along it, descends, ascends and goes round and round and the web is finished. It is geometrical. The net is spread out in the morning and rolled up in the evening.

Similarly the wasps build their nests of lac (crude), and so on.

So then, each animal has got some remarkable instinct. Kambar's learning is not to be wondered at because it is God's will, as it is in the other cases.

Talk 268.

Dr. Syed: What is salvation? What did Christ mean by it?

M.: Salvation for whom? and from what?

D.: Salvation for the individual and from the sorrows and sufferings of the world.

M.: Whose are the sorrows, etc.?

D.: Of the mind.

M.: Are you the mind?

D.: I shall now explain how this question arose. I was meditating. I began to reflect on the Grace shown by Christ to some devotees who got salvation. I consider that Sri Bhagavan is similar. Is not salvation the result of similar Grace? That is what I mean by my questions.

M.: Yes. Right.

D.: The booklet *Who am I?* speaks of *swarupa drishti* (seeing the essence). Then there must be a seer and the seen. How can this be reconciled with the Ultimate Unity?

M.: Why do you ask for salvation, release from sorrow, etc.? He who asks for them sees them also. The fact is this. *Drishti* (sight) is consciousness. It forms the subject and object. Can there be *drishti* apart from the Self? The Self is all — *drishti*, etc.

234

D.: How to discern the ego from the Perfect 'I-I'?

M.: That which rises and falls is the transient 'I'. That which has neither origin nor end is the permanent 'I-I' consciousness.

D.: Will continuous thought on the Self make the mind more and more refined so that it will not think of anything but the highest?

M.: There is the peaceful mind which is the supreme. When the same becomes restless, it is afflicted by thoughts. Mind is only the dynamic power (*sakti*) of the Self.

D.: Are the sheaths material and different from the Self?

M.: There is no difference between matter and spirit. Modern science admits that all matter is energy. Energy is power or force (*sakti*). Therefore all are resolved in Siva and *Sakti i.e.*, the Self and the Mind.

The *kosas* are mere appearances. There is no reality in them as such.

D.: How many hours a day should one devote to meditation?

M.: Your very nature is meditation.

D.: It will be so when ripe, but not now.

M.: You become conscious of it later. That does not mean that your nature is now different from meditation.

D.: What about practice?

M.: Meditation must always be practised.

D.: A Persian mystic says: "There is nothing but God." The Quran says: "God is immanent in all."

M.: There is no 'all', apart from God, for Him to pervade. He alone is.

D.: Is it morally right for a man to renounce his household duties when he once realises that his highest duty is *Atma-chintana* (continuous thought on the Self)?

M.: This desire to renounce things is the obstacle. The Self is simple renunciation. The Self has renounced all.

D.: It is true from Bhagavan's standpoint. But for us .... my work demands the best part of my time and energy; often I am too tired to devote myself to *Atma-chintana*.

M.: The feeling "I work" is the hindrance. Enquire, "Who works?" Remember, "Who am I?" The work will not bind you. It will go on

235

automatically. Make no effort either to work or to renounce work. Your effort is the bondage. What is bound to happen will happen.

If you are destined to cease working, work cannot be had even if you hunt for it. If you are destined to work you cannot leave it; you will be forced to engage in it. So leave it to the Higher Power. You cannot renounce or hold as you choose.

Talk 269.

D.: How is all-immanent God said to reside in *daharakasa* (Ether of the Heart).

M.: Do we not reside in one place? Do you not say that you are in your body? Similarly, God is said to reside in *Hritpundarika* (the heart-lotus). The heart-lotus is not a place. Some name is mentioned as the place of God because we think we are in the body. This kind of instruction is meant for those who can appreciate only relative knowledge.

Being immanent everywhere there is no particular place for God. Because we think we are in the body we also believe that we are born. However we do not think of the body, of God, or of method of realisation in our deep slumber. Yet in our waking state we hold on to the body and think we are in it.

The Supreme Being is that from which the body is born, in which it lives and into which it resolves. We however think that we reside within the body. Hence such instruction is given. The instruction means: "Look within."

Talk 270.

Mr. G. V. Subbaramiah, a lecturer in English in Nellore, asked: *Brahman* is the one by whom all this is pervaded (*yena sarvamidam thatham*). But then how does Sri Krishna specify the *vibhutis* in Chapter X of *Bhagavad Gita*?

M.: The specifications are in reply to a definite question by Arjuna who required to know the Lord's *vibhutis* for convenience of worship (*upasana soukaryam*). The fact is that God is all. There is nothing apart from Him.

236

D.: The individual is said to give up decayed bodies (*jirnani sarirani*) and to take up new ones (*navani*). Would the statement apply to infant deaths also?

M.: You do not know, in the first place, what is *jirnani* and what is *navani*. Secondly, *jirna* and *nava* are relative terms. What is old to a king may be new to a beggar. The truth is that the individuality signifies the state of embodiment till the time of liberation!

Talk 271.

Dr. Syed: How is Grace to be obtained?

M.: Similar to obtaining the Self.

D.: Practically, how is it to be for us?

M.: By self-surrender.

D.: Grace was said to be the Self. Should I then surrender to my own Self?

M.: Yes. To the one from whom Grace is sought. God, Guru and Self are only different forms of the same.

D.: Please explain, so that I may understand.

M.: So long as you think you are the individual you believe in God. On worshipping God, God appears to you as Guru. On serving Guru He manifests as the Self. This is the rationale.

Talk 272.

D.: There are widespread disasters spreading havoc in the world e.g., famine and pestilence. What is the cause of this state of affairs?

M.: To whom does all this appear?

D.: That won't do. I see misery around.

M.: You were not aware of the world and its sufferings in your sleep; you are conscious of them in your wakeful state. Continue in that state in which you were not afflicted by these. That is to say, when you are not aware of the world, its sufferings do not affect you. When you remain as the Self, as in sleep, the world and its sufferings will not affect you. Therefore look within. See the Self! There will be an end of the world and its miseries.

D.: But that is selfishness.

M.: The world is not external. Because you identify yourself wrongly with the body you see the world outside, and its pain becomes

237

apparent to you. But they are not real. Seek the reality and get rid of this unreal feeling.

D.: There are great men, public workers, who cannot solve the problem of the misery of the world.

M.: They are ego-centred and therefore their inability. If they remained in the Self they would be different.

D.: Why do not Mahatmas help?

M.: How do you know that they do not help? Public speeches, physical activity and material help are all outweighed by the silence of Mahatmas. They accomplish more than others.

D.: What is to be done by us for ameliorating the condition of the world?

M.: If *you* remain free from pain, there will be no pain anywhere. The trouble now is due to your seeing the world externally and also thinking that there is pain there. But both the world and the pain are within you. If you look within there will be no pain.

D.: God is perfect. Why did He create the world imperfect? The work shares the nature of the author. But here it is not so.

M.: Who is it that raises the question?

D.: I — the individual.

M.: Are you apart from God that you ask this question?
So long as you consider yourself the body you see the world as external. The imperfections appear to you. God is perfection. His work also is perfection. But you see it as imperfection because of your wrong identification.

D.: Why did the Self manifest as this miserable world?

M.: In order that you might seek it. Your eyes cannot see themselves. Place a mirror before them and they see themselves. Similarly with the creation.

"See yourself first and then see the whole world as the Self."

D.: So it amounts to this — that I should always look within.

M.: Yes.

D.: Should I not see the world at all?

M.: You are not instructed to shut your eyes from the world. You are only to "see yourself first and then see the whole world as the

238

Self". If you consider yourself as the body the world appears to be external. If you are the Self the world appears as Brahman.

Talk 273.

Dr. Syed asked: I have been reading the *Five Hymns*. I find that the hymns are addressed to Arunachala by you. You are an Advaitin. How do you then address God as a separate Being?

M.: The devotee, God and the Hymns are all the Self.

D.: But you are addressing God. You are specifying this Arunachala Hill as God.

M.: You can identify the Self with the body. Should not the devotee identify the Self with Arunachala?

D.: If Arunachala be the Self why should it be specially picked out among so many other hills? God is everywhere. Why do you specify Him as Arunachala?

M.: What has attracted you from Allahabad to this place? What has attracted all these people around?

D.: Sri Bhagavan.

M.: How was I attracted here? By Arunachala. The Power cannot be denied. Again Arunachala is within and not without. The Self is Arunachala.

D.: Several terms are used in the holy books — *Atman, Paramatman, Para*, etc. What is the gradation in them?

M.: They mean the same to the user of the words. But they are understood differently by persons according to their development.

D.: But why do they use so many words to mean the same thing?

M.: It is according to circumstances. They all mean the Self. *Para* means 'not relative' or 'beyond the relative', that is to say, the Absolute.

D.: Should I meditate on the right chest in order to meditate on the Heart?

M.: The Heart is not physical. Meditation should not be on the right or the left. Meditation should be on the Self. Everyone knows 'I am'. Who is the 'I'? It will be neither within nor without, neither on the right nor on the left. 'I am' — that is all.

239

The Heart is the centre from which everything springs. Because you see the world, the body and so on, it is said that there is a centre for these, which is called the Heart. When you are in the Heart, the Heart is known to be neither the centre nor the circumference. There is nothing else. Whose centre could it be?

D.: May I take it that the Self and the non-Self are like substance and its shadow?

M.: Substance and shadow are for the one who sees only the shadow and mistakes it for the substance and sees its shadow also. But there is neither substance nor shadow for the one who is aware only of the Reality.

D.: Buddha, when asked if there is the ego, was silent; when asked if there is no ego, he was silent; asked if there is God, he was silent; asked if there is no God, he was silent. Silence was his answer for all these. *Mahayana* and *Hinayana* schools have both misinterpreted his silence because they say that he was an atheist.
If he was an atheist, why should he have spoken of *nirvana*, of births and deaths, of *karma*, reincarnations and *dharma*? His interpreters are wrong. Is it not so?

M.: You are right.

27th October, 1936

Talk 274.

The Muslim Professor asked how *Vaishnavism* can be reconciled to *Advaitism*.

M.: The *Vaishnavites* call themselves *Visishtadvaitins*. This is also *Advaita*. Just as the individual body comprises the soul, the ego and the gross body, so also God comprises *Paramatma*, the world and the individuals.

D.: Does not *bhakti* imply duality?

M.: Swa swarupanusandhanam bhaktirityabhidheeyate (Reflection on one's own Self is called *bhakti*). *Bhakti* and Self-Enquiry are one and the same. The Self of the *Advaitins* is the God of the *bhaktas*.

D.: Is there a spiritual hierarchy of all the original propounders of religions watching the spiritual welfare of the humans?

M.: Let them be or let them not be. It is only a surmise at the best. Atma is *pratyaksha* (self-evident). Know it and be done with speculation. One may admit such a hierarchy; another may not. But no one can gainsay the Atma.

D.: What does Sri Bhagavan think of *Pravritti* and *nivritti margas*?

M.: Yes. Both are mentioned. What of that?

D.: Which is the better of the two?

M.: If you see the Self — pure and simple — it is *nivritti*; if you see the Self with the world, it is *pravritti*. In other words, inward-turned mind (*antarmukhi manas*) is *nivritti*; outward-going mind (*bahirmukhi manas*) is *pravritti*. Anyway, there is nothing apart from the Self. Both are the same.

Similarly also, with the spiritual hierarchy; they cannot exist apart from the Self. They are only in the Self and remain as the Self. Realisation of the Self is the one Goal of all.

5th November, 1936

Talk 275.

In the course of conversation, someone referred to the fact that when Mr. Brunton and a lady were walking home in the night, they saw a bright glow on half the hill moving slowly and gently from North to South.

Sri Bhagavan said: This hill is said to be wisdom in visible shape.

D.: How is it visible to the physical eye?

M.: Sambandar had sung "The One who fascinated my heart or the captivator of my heart, I sing of Him in my mind". The Heart is captivated: consequently the mind must have sunk into the Heart; and yet there is the remembrance which enables the saint to sing of God later.

Then the experience of a young disciple was mentioned. The young man, educated and in good circumstances, in good health and sober mind, was once facing Sri Bhagavan's picture in his home and meditating on the figure. The figure suddenly appeared animated with

241

life, which threw the young man into a spasm of fear. He called out for his mother. His mother came and asked him what the matter was. He was surrounded by his relatives who were perplexed by his appearance. He was aware of their presence, but was still overpowered by a mysterious force which he tried to resist. He became unconscious for a short time. Fear seized him as he regained consciousness. The people became anxious and tried to bring him round with medicines.

When later he came to Tiruvannamalai he had some foreboding of similar experience. The proximity of Sri Bhagavan prevented any untoward happening. But whenever he wandered away from the hall he found the force almost irresistible and himself in the grip of fear.

Sri Bhagavan said: "Is it so? No one told me this before."

A devotee asked, if it was not *saktipata* (descent of divine power)?

M.: Yes it is. A madman clings to *samskaras*, whereas a *jnani* does not. That is the only difference between the two. *Jnana* is madness of a kind.

D.: But *saktipata* is said to occur in *karmasamya*, *i.e.*, when merit and demerit are equal.

M.: Yes. *Malaparipaka, karmasamya* and *saktipata* mean the same, A man is running the course of his *samskaras*; when taught he is the Self, the teaching affects his mind and imagination runs riot. He feels helpless before the onrushing power. His experiences are only according to his imagination of the state "I am the Self", whatever he may conceive it to be. *Saktipata* alone confers the true and right experience.

When the man is ripe for receiving the instruction and his mind is about to sink into the Heart, the instruction imparted works in a flash and he realises the Self all right. Otherwise, there is always the struggle.

Mano-nasa, jnana, and *chittaikagrata* (annihilation of the mind, knowledge and one-pointedness) means the same.

Talk 276.

The U. P. lady arrived with her brother, a woman companion and a burly bodyguard.

When she came into the hall she saluted Maharshi with great respect and feeling, and sat down on a wool blanket in front of Sri

Bhagavan. Sri Bhagavan was then reading *Trilinga* in Telugu on the reincarnation of a boy. The boy is now thirteen years old and reading in the Government High School in a village near Lucknow. When he was three years he used to dig here and there; when asked, he would say that he was trying to recover something which he had hidden in the earth. When he was four years old, a marriage function was celebrated in his home. When leaving, the guests humorously remarked that they would return for this boy's marriage. But he turned round and said: "I am already married. I have two wives." When asked to point them out, he requested to be taken to a certain village, and there he pointed to two women as his wives. It is now learnt that a period of ten months elapsed between the death of their husband and the birth of this boy.

When this was mentioned to the lady, she asked if it was possible to know the after-death state of an individual.

Sri Bhagavan said, "some are born immediately after, others after some lapse of time, a few are not reborn on this earth but eventually get salvation in some higher region, and a very few get absolved here and now."

She: I do not mean that. Is it possible to know the condition of an individual after his death?

M.: It is possible. But why try to know it? All facts are only as true as the seeker.

She: The birth of a person, his being and death are real to us.

M.: Because you have wrongly identified your own self with the body, you think of the other one in terms of the body. Neither you are nor the other is the body.

She: But from my own level of understanding I consider myself and my son to be real.

M.: The birth of the 'I-thought' is one's own birth, its death is the person's death. After the 'I-thought' has arisen the wrong identity with the body arises. Thinking yourself the body, you give false values to others and identify them with bodies. Just as your body has been born, grows and will perish, so also you think the other was born, grew up and died. Did you think of your son before his birth? The

243

thought came after his birth and persists even after his death. Inasmuch as you are thinking of him he is your son. Where has he gone? He has gone to the source from which he sprang. He is one with you. So long as you are, he is there too. If you cease to identify yourself with the body, but see the real Self, this confusion will vanish. You are eternal. The others also will similarly be found to be eternal. Until this truth is realised there will always be this grief due to false values arising from wrong knowledge and wrong identity.

She: Let me have true knowledge by Sri Bhagavan's Grace.

M.: Get rid of the 'I-thought'. So long as 'I' is alive, there is grief. When 'I' ceases to exist, there is no grief. Consider the state of sleep!

She: Yes. But when I take to the 'I-thought', other thoughts arise and disturb me.

M.: See whose thoughts they are. They will vanish. They have their root in the single 'I-thought'. Hold to it and they will disappear. Again the Master pointed to the story of *Punya* and *Papa* in *Yoga Vasishta*, V. Ch. 20, where *Punya* consoles *Papa* on the death of their parents and turns him to realising the Self. Further, creation is to be considered in its two aspects, *Isvara srishti* (God's creation) and *jiva srishti* (individual's creation). Of these two, the universe is the former, and its relation to the individual is the latter. It is the latter which gives rise to pain and pleasure, irrespective of the former. A story was mentioned from *Panchadasi*. There were two young men in a village in South India. They went on a pilgrimage to North India. One of them died. The survivor, who was earning something, decided to return only after some months. In the meantime he came across a wandering pilgrim whom he asked to convey the information regarding himself and his dead companion to the village in South India. The wandering pilgrim did so, but by mistake changed the names. The result was that the dead man's parents rejoiced in his safety and the living one's parents were in grief. Thus, you see, pain or pleasure has no reference to facts but to mental conceptions. *Jiva Srishti* is responsible for it. Kill the *jiva* and there is no pain or pleasure but the mental bliss persists forever. Killing the *jiva* is to abide in the Self.

344

She: I hear all this. It is beyond my grasp. I pray Sri Bhagavan to help me to understand it all.

"I had been to a waterfall in Mysore. The cascade was a fascinating sight. The waters streamed out in the shapes of fingers trying to grasp the rocks but were rushed on by the current to the depths below. I imagined this to be the state of the individuals clinging to their present surroundings. But I cannot help clinging.

"I cannot imagine that we are no better than seasonal flowers, fruits and leaves on trees. I love flowers but still this idea has no hold on me."

After a few minutes, she pointed out that she had intended to ask Maharshi about death and matters relating to it but did not however do it. Yet Maharshi was reading the related matter in the newspaper and the same topic came up for enlightenment. She left after seeing the cow Lakshmi.

9th November, 1936

Talk 277.

Mr. Cohen: What is will? I mean — where does it fit in, in the five *kosas*?

M.: The 'I-thought' arises first and then all other thoughts. They comprise the mind. The mind is the object and the 'I' is the subject. Can there be will without the 'I'? It is comprised in the 'I'. The 'I-thought' is the *vijnanamaya kosa* (intellectual sheath). Will is included in it.

Sri Bhagavan said further: *Annamaya kosa* is the gross body sheath. The senses with the *prana* and the *karmendriyas* form the *pranamayakosa* (sense-sheath). The senses with the mind form the *manomaya kosa* (mind-sheath). They are the *jnanendryas*. The mind is formed of thoughts only *Idam* (this) is the object and *aham* ('I') is the subject; the two together form the *vijnanamayakosa* (intellect-sheath).

10th November, 1936

Talk 278.

Miss W. Umadevi, a Polish lady, convert to Hinduism, had travelled in Kashmir and brought views from Kashmir at which we were looking. Sri Bhagavan humorously, remarked, "We have seen those places without the trouble of travel."

D.: I wish to go to Kailas.

M.: One can see these places only if destined. Not otherwise. After seeing all, there will still remain more — if not in this hemisphere, maybe in the other. Knowledge implies ignorance of what lies beyond what is known. Knowledge is always limited.

After some time Sri Bhagavan continued: Appar was decrepit and old and yet began to travel to Kailas. Another old man appeared on the way and tried to dissuade him from the attempt, saying that it was so difficult to reach there. Appar was however obdurate and said that he would risk his life in the attempt. The stranger asked him to dip himself in a tank close by. Appar did so and found Kailas then and there. Where did all this happen? In Tiruvayyar, nine miles from Tanjore. Where is Kailas then? Is it within the mind or outside it? If Tiruvayyar be truly Kailas, it must appear to others as well. But Appar alone found it so.

Similarly it is said of other places of pilgrimage in the South, that they are the abodes of Siva, and devotees found them so. This was true from their standpoint. Everything is within. There is nothing without.

Talk 279.

D.: How long does it take a man to be reborn after death? Is it immediately after death or some time after?

M.: You do not know what you were before birth, yet you want to know what you will be after death. Do you know what you are now? Birth and rebirth pertain to the body. You are identifying the Self with the body. It is a wrong identification. You believe that the body has been born and will die, and confound the phenomena relating to the one with the other. Know your real being and these questions will not arise.

Birth and rebirth are mentioned only to make you investigate the question and find out that there are neither births nor rebirths. They relate to the body and not to the Self. Know the Self and be not perturbed by doubts.

Talk 280.

D.: Can you help me to get rid of *Maya*?

M.: What is *Maya*?

D.: Attachment to the world.

M.: Was the world in your deep sleep? Was there attachment to it?

D.: There was not.

M.: Were you there or not?

D.: Maybe.

M.: Then do you deny having existed in sleep?

D.: I do not.

M.: You are therefore now "the same one as there was in sleep."

D.: Yes.

Sleep	Wakefulness
No world	World
No attachment	Attachment
The Self	The Self

M.: What is it then that raises the question of *Maya* just now?

D.: The mind was not in sleep. The world and the attachment to it are of the mind.

M.: That is it. The world and the attachment to it are of the mind, not of the Self.

D.: I was ignorant in sleep.

M.: Who says that he was ignorant? Is he not ignorant now? Is he a *jnani*?

Ignorance is now mentioned by the contaminated Self here.

D.: Was the Self pure then in sleep?

M.: It did not raise any doubts. It did not feel imperfect or impure.

D.: Such Self is common to all, even in a dead body.

M.: But the man in sleep or in dead body does not raise questions. Consider who raises questions. It is you. Were you not in sleep? Why was there no imperfection? The pure Self is simple Being. It does not associate itself with objects and become conscious as in the wakeful state. What you now call consciousness in the present state is

247

associated consciousness requiring brain, mind, body, etc., to depend upon. But in sleep consciousness persisted without these.

D.: But I do not know the consciousness in sleep.

M.: Who is not aware of it? You admit "I am". You admit "I was" in sleep. The state of *being* is your self.

D.: Do you mean to say that sleep is Self-Realisation?

M.: It is the Self. Why do you talk of Realisation? Is there a moment when the Self is not realised? If there be such a moment, the other moment might be said to be one of Realisation. There is no moment when the Self is not nor when the Self is not realised. Why pick out sleep for it? Even now you are Self-realised.

D.: But I do not understand.

M.: Because you are identifying the Self with the body. Give up the wrong identity and the Self is revealed.

D.: But this does not answer my question to help me to get rid of *Maya, i.e.,* attachment.

M.: This attachment is not found in sleep. It is perceived and felt now. It is not your real nature. On whom is this accretion? If the Real Nature is known these exist not. If you realise the Self the possessions are not perceived. That is getting rid of *Maya. Maya* is not objective, that it could be got rid of in any other way.

15th November, 1936
SPARKS FROM THE ANVIL — I

Talk 281.

A certain man, who claims to have been Sri Maharshi's quondam disciple, has filed a suit in the court praying for a declaration that he is the legitimate Sarvadhikari of the Asramam.

Sri Maharshi was examined on Commission. There was a crowd but the proceedings went on smoothly in the room on the North East.

The following are a few tit-bits therefrom: Sri Bhagavan's answers were quite spontaneous and smooth.

Q.: To which asramam does Sri Bhagavan belong?

M.: Atiasramam (beyond the four stages).

Q.: What is it?

248

M.: It is beyond the four commonly known *asramas*.

Q.: Is it *sastraic*?

M.: Yes. It is mentioned in the *sastras*.

Q.: Are there others of the same type besides yourself?

M.: There may be.

Q.: Have there been any?

M.: Suka, Rishabha, Jada Bharata and others.

Q.: You left home at an early age because you had no attachment for home and property. But here, there is property in the Asramam. How is it?

M.: I do not seek it. Property is thrust on me. I neither love nor hate it.

Q.: Are they given to you?

M.: They are given to the Swami, whoever he may be. But the body is considered the Swami in the world. That body is this. It reduces itself to myself.

Q.: In that case the attachment to property is now renewed. Is it so?

M.: I do not hate it — that is all I said.

Q.: In practical life it amounts to what I say.

M.: Just as we live and move in practical matters.

Q.: Do you give *upadesh*? Have you ever done it?

M.: Visitors ask questions. I answer them as well as I know. It is for them to treat my words as they please.

Q.: Is it *upadesh*?

M.: How shall I say how others take it?

Q.: Have you disciples?

M.: I do not give *upadesh* in the ceremonial manner. For instance, keeping a *kumbha*, making *puja* to it and whispering to the person. The person may call himself my disciple or devotee. I do not consider anyone to be my disciple. I have never sought *upadesh* from anyone nor do I give ceremonial *upadesh*. If the people call themselves my disciples I do not approve or disapprove. In my view all are alike. They consider themselves fit for being called disciples. What can I say to them? I do not call myself a disciple or a Guru.

Q.: How did you approve the building of Skandasramam on the Hill which was temple-land, without previously obtaining permission from the authorities?

M.: Guided by the same Power which made me come here and reside on the Hill.

Q.: When you threw away your cash, etc., within an hour after your arrival in this place, you did so because you did not desire possessions. You never touch money. There were no possessions for several years after your arrival here. How is it that donations are now accepted by the Asramam?

M.: This practice grew up at a later stage because a few associates began to use my name to collect funds. I did not approve of their action nor check them. So it is going on. One man leaves, another steps in, but the process goes on. I do not desire that contributions should be accepted. But people do not heed that advice. I do not desire to give ineffective advice. I do not therefore check them. Since money comes in property grows spontaneously.

Q.: Why do you not sign your name?

M.: The author of *Self-Realisation* has furnished his answer for this question. Moreover, by what name am I to be known? I myself do not know. People have given me several names from time to time since my arrival here. If I should sign by one name, all would not understand it. So I used to say to the people seeking autographs that, even if they should show my signature, people in general would not believe it to be true.

Q.: You do not touch money nor other offerings, I trust.

M.: People sometimes place fruits in my hands. I touch them.

Q.: If you receive one kind of offering, why should you not receive money also?

M.: I cannot eat money. What shall I do with it? Why should I take that with which I do not know what to do?

Q.: Why do visitors stop at the Asramam?

M.: They must know why.

Q.: You have no objection to anyone coming and staying here, I suppose.

M.: No.

Q.: You have similarly no objection to any length of their stay.

M.: No. If I do not find it agreeable I will go away. That is all.

A lawyer devotee asked Sri Bhagavan if the previous day's examination by Commission caused much strain.

M.: I did not use my mind and so there was no strain. Let them examine me for a thousand days. I don't mind.

16th November, 1936

Talk 282.

D.: Does the *Tantrik sadhana* bring about Self-Realisation?

M.: Yes.

D.: Which worship in *Tantra* is the best?

M.: It depends on temperament.

D.: What part does *Kundalini* play in bringing about Self-Realisation?

M.: Kundalini rises from any *lakshya* that you have. *Kundalini* is *prana-sakti* (life-current).

D.: Different deities are said to reside in different *chakras.* Does one see them in course of *sadhana*?

M.: They can be seen if desired.

D.: Does the path to Self-Realisation go through *samadhi*?

M.: They are synonymous.

D.: It is said that the Guru can make his disciple realise the Self by transmitting some of his own power to him? Is it true?

M.: Yes. The Guru does not bring about Self-Realisation. He simply removes the obstacles to it. The Self is always realised.

D.: Is there absolute necessity of a Guru for Self-Realisation?

M.: So long as you seek Self-Realisation the Guru is necessary. Guru is the Self. Take Guru to be the Real Self and your self as the individual self. The disappearance of this sense of duality is removal of ignorance. So long as duality persists in you the Guru is necessary. Because you identify yourself with the body you think the Guru, too, to be some body. You are not the body, nor is the Guru. You are the Self and so is the Guru. This knowledge is gained by what you call Self-Realisation.

251

D.: How can one know whether a particular individual is competent to be a Guru?

M.: By the peace of mind found in his presence and by the sense of respect you feel for him.

D.: If the Guru happens to turn out incompetent, what will be the fate of the disciple who has implicit faith in him?

M.: Each one according to his merits.

D.: What are your opinions about social reform?

M.: Self-reform automatically brings about social reform. Confine yourself to self-reform. Social reform will take care of itself.

D.: What is your opinion about Gandhiji's Harijan movement?

M.: Ask him.

D.: Is it necessary to take bath if we touch dead bodies?

M.: The body is a corpse. So long as one is in contact with it one must bathe in the waters of the Self.

D.: If the *advaita* is final, why did Madhvacharya teach *dvaita*?

M.: Is your Self *dvaita* or *advaita*? All systems agree on Self-surrender. Attain it first, then there will be time to judge whose view is right or otherwise.

D.: Why do you not preach to the people to set them on the right path?

M.: You have already decided by yourself that I do not preach. Do you know who I am and what preaching is?

D.: Is the shaving of widows among Brahmins not cruel?

M.: This may be asked of *Dharma Sastris* or reformers. Reform yourself first and let us then see about the rest.

17th November, 1936

Talk 283.

D.: How can one become *jitasangadoshah* (free from the stain of association)?

M.: By *satsanga* (association with the wise). "*Satsangatve nissangatvam, nissangatve nirmohatvam, nirmohatve nischalatatvam, nischalatatve jivanmuktih.*"

Satsanga means *sanga* (association) with *sat*. *Sat* is only the Self. Since the Self is not now understood to be *Sat*, the company of the

252

sage who has thus understood it is sought. That is *Sat-sanga*. Introversion results. Then *Sat* is revealed. For whom is association? For whom is *dosha*?

D.: To the Self.

M.: No. The Self is pure and unaffected. The impurities affect only the ego.

D.: Can the soul remain without the body?

M.: It will be so a short time hence — in deep slumber. The Self is bodiless. Even now it is so.

D.: Can a *sanyasi* remain in the midst of *samsara*?

M.: So long as one thinks that he is a *sanyasi,* he is not one, so long as one does not think of *samsara*, he is not a *samsari*; on the other hand he is a *sanyasi.*

18th November. 1936

Talk 284.

D.: It is said in Srimad Bhagavad Gita: "Realise the Self with pure intellect and also by service to Guru and by enquiry." How are they to be reconciled?

M.: Iswaro Gururatmeti — Iswara, Guru and Self are identical. So long as the sense of duality persists in you, you seek a Guru considering that he stands apart. He however teaches you the truth and you gain the insight.

D.: Kindly explain:

ahameko name kaschit nahamanyasya kasyachit naham pasyami yasyaham tam na pasyami yo mama (I am alone; none is mine; of none else am I, I see none whose I am, none who is mine).

M.: This sloka occurs in different scriptures, holy books, *e.g.,* *Bhagavata, Maha Bharata,* etc. It also forms the motto of Chapter XI in *Self-Realisation.*

Aham — 'I', is only one. Egos are different. They are in the One Self. The Self is not affected by the egos. 'I' is one only. 'I' is the Truth. All that follows is meant to refute the sense of duality.

253

Talk 285.

D.: If the Self be itself aware, why am I not aware of the same, even now?

M.: There is no duality. Your present knowledge is due to the ego and only relating. Relative knowledge requires a subject and an object. Whereas the awareness of the Self is absolute and requires no object. Remembrance also is similarly relative, requiring an object to be remembered and a subject to remember. When there is no duality, who is to remember whom?

D.: What happens to the created ego when the body dies?

M.: Ego is 'I-thought'. In its subtle form it remains a thought, whereas in its gross aspect it embraces the mind, the senses and the body. They disappear in deep slumber along with the ego. Still the Self is there; similarly it will be in death.

Ego is not an entity independent of the Self in order that it must be created or destroyed by itself. It functions as an instrument of the Self and periodically ceases to function. That is to say, it appears and disappears; this might be considered to be birth and death.

Relative knowledge pertains to the mind and not to the Self. It is therefore illusory and not permanent. Take a scientist for instance. He formulates a theory that the Earth is round and goes on to prove it and establish it on an incontrovertible basis. When he falls asleep the whole idea vanishes; his mind is left a blank; what does it matter if the world remains round or flat when he is asleep? So you see the futility of all such relative knowledge.
One should go beyond such relative knowledge and abide in the Self. Real knowledge is such experience and not apprehension by the mind.

D.: Why does not Sri Bhagavan go about and preach the Truth to the people at large?

M.: How do you know that I am not doing it? Does preaching consist in mounting a platform and haranguing to the people around? Preaching is simple communication of knowledge. It may be done in Silence too.

What do you think of a man listening to a harangue for an hour and going away without being impressed by it so as to change his life? Compare him with another who sits in a holy presence and leaves after some time with his outlook on life totally changed. Which is better: To preach loudly without effect or to sit silently sending forth intuitive forces to play on others?

Again how does speech arise? There is abstract knowledge (unmanifest). From it there rises the ego which gives rise to thoughts and words successively. So then:

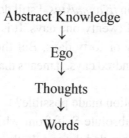

Abstract Knowledge
↓
Ego
↓
Thoughts
↓
Words

Words are therefore the great grandson of the original source. If words can produce an effect, how much more powerful should the preaching through silence be? Judge for yourself.

Talk 286.

D.: Why can we not remain in *sushupti* as long as we like and be also voluntarily in it just as we are in the waking state?

M.: *Sushupti* continues in this state also. We are ever in *sushupti*. That should be consciously gone into and realised in this very state. There is no real going into or coming from it. Becoming aware of that is *samadhi*. An ignorant man cannot remain long in *sushupti* because he is forced by nature to emerge from it. His ego is not dead and it will rise up again. But the wise man attempts to crush it in its source. It rises up again and again for him too impelled by nature, *i.e.*, *prarabdha*. That is, both in *jnani* and *ajnani*, ego is sprouting forth, but with this difference, namely the *ajnani's* ego when it rises up is quite ignorant of its source, or he is not aware of his *sushupti* in the dream and *jagrat* states; whereas a *jnani* when his ego rises up enjoys his transcendental experience with this ego keeping his *lakshya* (aim) always on its source. This ego is not dangerous: it is like the skeleton of a burnt rope: in this form it is ineffective. By constantly

255

keeping our aim on our source, our ego is dissolved in its source. like a doll of salt in the ocean.

D.: Sri Ramakrishna says that *nirvikalpa samadhi* cannot last longer than twenty-one days. If persisted in, the person dies. Is it so?

M.: When the *prarabdha* is exhausted the ego is completely dissolved without leaving any trace behind. This is final liberation. Unless *prarabdha* is completely exhausted the ego will be rising up in its *pure* form even in *jivanmuktas*. I still doubt the statement of the maximum duration of twenty-one days. It is said that people cannot live if they fast thirty or forty days. But there are those who have fasted longer, say a hundred days. It means that there is still *prarabdha* for them.

D.: How is realisation made possible?

M.: There is the absolute Self from which a spark proceeds as from fire. The spark is called the ego. In the case of an ignorant man it identifies itself with an object simultaneously with its rise. It cannot remain independent of such association with objects. This association is *ajnana* or ignorance, whose destruction is the objective of our efforts. If its objectifying tendency is killed it remains pure, and also merges into the source. The wrong identification with the body is *dehatmabuddhi* ('I-am-the-body' idea). This must go before good results follow.

D.: How to eradicate it?

M.: We exist in *sushupti* without being associated with the body and mind. But in the other two states we are associated with them. If one with the body, how can we exist without the body in *sushupti*? We can separate ourselves from that which is external to us and not from that which is one with us. Hence the ego is not one with the body. This must be realised in the waking state. *Avasthatraya* (the three states of waking, dream and deep sleep) should be studied only for gaining this outlook.

The ego in its purity is experienced in intervals between two states or two thoughts. Ego is like that caterpillar which leaves its hold only after catching another. Its true nature can be found when it is out of contact with objects or thoughts. Realise this interval with the conviction gained by the study of *avasthatraya* (the three states of consciousness).

D.: How do we go to sleep and how do we wake up?

M.: Just at nightfall the hen clucks and the chicks go and hide themselves under her wings. The hen then goes to roost in the nest with the chicks in her protection. At dawn the chicks come out and so does the hen. The mother-hen stands for the ego which collects all the thoughts and goes to sleep. At sunrise the rays emerge forth and are collected again at sunset. Similarly, when the ego displays itself, it does so with all its paraphernalia. When it sinks, everything disappears with it.

D.: What does *sushupti* look like?

M.: In a cloudy dark night no individual identification of objects is possible and there is only dense darkness, although the seer has his eyes wide open; similarly in *sushupti* the seer is aware of simple nescience.

Sri Bhagavan is said to have remarked to an inquisitive person: "What is the meaning of this talk of truth and falsehood in the world which is itself false?"

27th November, 1936

Talk 287.

A Punjabi gentleman, a doctor by profession, came here with his wife to visit Sri Bhagavan. He was in the hall when Sri Bhagavan came in after lunch; then he asked: "How should I meditate? I do not have peace of mind."

M.: Peace is our real nature. It need not be attained. Our thoughts must be obliterated.

D.: I have been trying to obliterate them but I am not successful.

M.: The Gita method is the only one for it. Whenever mind strays away bring it back to bear on meditation.

D.: I cannot bring my mind to meditate.

Another devotee: An elephant when free puts its trunk here and there and feels restless. If a length of chain is given to it, the trunk holds it and is no longer restless. Similarly, mind without an aim is restless, with an aim it remains at peace.

D.: No, no, it is all theory. I have read many books. But no use. It is practically impossible to make the mind concentrate.

M.: Concentration is impossible so long as there are predispositions. They obstruct *bhakti* also.

The interpreter advised the questioner to study *Who am I?* The doctor was ready with his protestations: "I have read it also. I cannot still make my mind concentrate."

M.: By practice and dispassion — *abhyasa vairagyabhyam*.

D.: *Vairagya* is necessary ....

M.: *Abhyasa* and *vairagya* are necessary. *Vairagya* is the absence of diffused thoughts; *abhyasa* is concentration on one thought only. The one is the positive and the other the negative aspect of meditation.

D.: I am not able to do so by myself. I am in search of a force to help me.

M.: Yes, what is called Grace. Individually we are incapable because the mind is weak. Grace is necessary. *Sadhu seva* is meant only for it. There is however nothing new to get. Just as a weak man comes under the control of a stronger one, the weak mind of a man comes under control easily in the presence of the strong-minded *sadhus*. That which is — is only Grace; there is nothing else.

The questioner said, "I request your blessings for the good of myself".

Bhagavan said: "Yes — yes."

He left with his wife.

29th November, 1936

Talk 288.

Explaining *Maya* of *Vedanta* and *swatantra* of *Pratyabhijna* (independence of recognition), Sri Bhagavan said:

The Vedantins say that *Maya* is the *sakti* of illusion premised in Siva. *Maya* has no independent existence. Having brought out the illusion of the world as real, she continues to play upon the ignorance of the victims. When the reality of her *not being* is found, she disappears. 'Recognition' says that *Sakti* (power) is coeval with Siva. The one does not exist without the other. Siva is unmanifest, whereas *Sakti* is manifest on account of Her independent will *swatantra*. Her manifestation is the display of the cosmos on pure consciousness, like images in a mirror. The images cannot remain in the absence of a mirror. So also the world cannot have an independent existence. *Swatantra* becomes eventually an attribute of the Supreme. Sri Sankara says that the Absolute is without attributes and that *Maya* is *not* and has *no* real being. What is the difference between the two? Both agree that the display is not real. The images of the mirror cannot in any way be real. The world does not exist in reality (*vastutah*). Both schools mean the same thing. Their ultimate aim is to realise the Absolute Consciousness. The unreality of the cosmos is implied in Recognition (*Pratyabhijna*), whereas it is explicit in *Vedanta*. If the world be taken as *chit* (consciousness), it is always real. *Vedanta* says that there is no *nana* (diversity), meaning that it is all the same Reality. There is agreement on all points except in words and the method of expression.

30th November, 1936

Talk 289.

While discussing *Karma*, Sri Bhagavan said: "*Karma* has its fruit (*phala*). They are like cause and effect. The interrelation of a cause and its effect is due to a *Sakti* whom we call God. God is *phala data* (dispenser of fruit).

A visitor had been speaking of the Self having forgotten its true nature. Sri Bhagavan after some time said: "People speak of memory and oblivion of the Fullness of the Self. Oblivion and memory are only thought-forms. They will alternate so long as there are thoughts. But Reality lies beyond these. Memory or oblivion must be dependent on something. That something must be foreign too; otherwise there cannot be oblivion. It is called 'I' by everyone. When one looks for it, it is not found because it is not real. Hence 'I' is synonymous with illusion or ignorance (*maya, avidya* or *ajnana*). To know that there never was ignorance is the goal of all the spiritual teachings. Ignorance must be of one who is aware. Awareness is *jnana*. *Jnana* is eternal and natural. *Ajnana* is unnatural and unreal.

D.: Having heard this truth, why does not one remain content?

259

M.: Because *samskaras* have not been destroyed. Unless the *samskaras* cease to exist, there will always be doubt and confusion (*sandeha, viparita*). All efforts are directed to destroying doubt and confusion. To do so their roots must be cut. Their roots are the *samskaras*. These are rendered ineffective by practice as prescribed by the Guru. The Guru leaves it to the seeker to do this much so that he might himself find out that there is no ignorance. This truth mentioned is in the stage of the hearing of the Truth (*sravana*). That is not *drdha* (firm). For making it unshaken, one has to practise reflection (*manana*) and one-pointedness (*nididhyasana*). These two processes scorch the seeds of *vasanas* so that they are rendered ineffective.

Some extraordinary persons get *drdha jnana* (unshaken knowledge) even on hearing the Truth only once (*sakrchhravana matrena*). Because they are *krthopasakah* (advanced seekers), whereas the *akrthopaṣakah* (raw seekers) take longer to gain *drdha jnana* (unshaken knowledge). People ask: "How did ignorance (*avidya*) arise at all?" We have to say to them: "Ignorance never arose. It has no real being. That which is, is only *vidya* (knowledge)."

D.: Why then do I not realise it?

M.: Because of the *samskaras*. However, find out who does not realise and what he does not realise. Then it will be clear that there is no *avidya* (ignorance).

Talk 290.

Mr. Sagarmull, a Marwari gentleman, a cotton merchant from Bombay, seems learned in Srimad Bhagavad Gita. He asked:

Srimad Bhagavad Gita says: *mattah parataram nanyat kinchit* and later on *sutre manigana iva* — "there is nothing different from Me" and later on "like beads strung on a thread." If there is nothing but Sri Krishna, how can the world be said to be like "beads on a string?"

M.: It means that the *sutra* (string) and the *mani* (jewel beads) are not apart from ME. There are no *maniganah* (row of beads) apart from the string (*sutra*) and no string apart from Me. The *sloka* emphasises unity and not multiplicity which is only on the surface.

D.: Unity can only be after merging into Bhagavan. True — but till then there must be diversity. That is *samsara.*

M.: Where are we now? Are we apart from Bhagavan? The *samsara* and we are all in Bhagavan.

D.: But that is the experience of the *jnanis.* Differentiation persists until *jnana* dawns. So there is *samsara* for me.

M.: Samskara (predisposition) is *samsara* (cycle of births and deaths).

D.: Right. "All this is Vasudeva" — this truth has been forgotten by us. So we cannot identify ourselves with God.

M.: Where is forgetfulness?

D.: Like *svapna.*

M.: Whose *svapna?*

D.: Jiva's.

M.: Who is *jiva?*

D.: It is *Paramatma's.*

M.: Let *Paramatma* ask then.

D.: I shall make my doubt clear by means of an illustration.

M.: Whoever wants the doubt to be illustrated and made clear? Direct experience — *pratyaksha* — does not require examples for elucidation.

D.: There is *pratyaksha* and also forgetfulness.

M.: What is forgotten and by whom?

D.: Listen. One dreams; the dream-world disappears on waking.

M.: Wake up similarly from the present dream.

D.: Prakrti (nature) is too powerful.

M.: See the *Purusha* (lord) also. What can *prakrti* do then?

D.: There is a *granthi* (knot) between them.

M.: Whose is that knot? Is it of the Lord or of Nature? or of both?

D.: Due to Brahman.

M.: Then Brahman must ask or must be asked. To whom is *svapna?* or the knot? You are always saying "I ask." Who is that 'I'?

D.: I do not perceive.

M.: 'I' is eternal. It would vanish if it were anything particular. It is Perfection. So it is not found as an object.

D.: But I am imperfect.

261

M.: Why bring in imperfection? Why are you not perfect? Did you feel imperfection in your sleep? Why do you not remain so even now? Bring sleep into the waking state (*jagrat sushupti*) and you will be all right. *Ya nisa sarva bhootanam ... pasyato muneh ...* (That which is night for the ignorant is day for the wise).

D.: Yes, if he is a *muni* (sage).

M.: Who is a *muni*? Is he not a man?

D.: Do you not feel a slap if given to you? Is there no differentiation? Is it *jnana*?

M.: A man under chloroform or under the influence of drink does not feel it. Is he a *jnani*? Is *jnana* inconsistent with that feeling?

D.: There is seer, seen and sight. They are not characteristic of *jnana*.

M.: In sleep, in trance, in absent-mindedness, there is no differentiation. Do you call it *jnana*? What has happened in these states? Is that which then was, absent now? That which is exists for ever. The difference is due to the mind. The mind is sometimes present at other times absent. There is no change in the Reality. Reality is always Bliss — *Ananda*.

D.: Bliss is the outcome of practice. What is that practice?

M.: *Sadhana* is the enquiry to find out to whom all these doubts arise.

D.: It is for the ego (*ahamkara*).

M.: Wherefrom does *ahamkara* arise?

D.: Guidance is necessary to show me the way.

M.: Go within and find the route. You cannot find it from without; nor should you seek it externally.

D.: I am unable to find the ego by search. I stop there.

M.: How can you get it? It is not apart from you. Leave alone not finding it. Where are you now? Do you mean to say "I am not"?

D.: What or how am I?

M.: Do not trouble yourself about it. Let it be as it is. Why do you care? Did you care for the whole or part (*samashti, vyashti*) in your sleep? The same person is present now too. You are the same in sleep and in waking.

D.: Sleep and waking are different states having different effects ....

M.: How does it matter to you? The Self is the same, all through.

D.: The mind is not steady in meditation.

M.: Whenever it wanders, turn it inward again and again.

D.: When *duhka* (misery) overpowers me, enquiry is impossible.

M.: Because the mind is too weak. Make it strong.

D.: By what means?

M.: Sat-sanga, Isvara Aradhana, Pranayama — (association with the wise, worship of God, breath control).

D.: What happens?

M.: Misery is removed; our aim is removal of misery. You do not acquire happiness. Your very nature is happiness. Bliss is not newly earned. All that is done is to remove unhappiness. These methods do it.

D.: Association with the wise may strengthen the mind. There must also be practice. What practice should be made?

M.: Yes. Practice is necessary too. Practice means removal of predispositions. Practice is not for any fresh gain; it is to kill the predispositions.

D.: *Abhyasa* (practice) should give me that power.

M.: Practice is power. If thoughts are reduced to a single thought the mind is said to have grown strong. When practice remains unshaken it becomes *sahaja* (natural).

D.: What is such practice?

M.: Enquiring into the Self. That is all. *Atmanyeva vasam nayet* .....

Fix the mind on the SELF.

D.: What is the aim to be kept in view? Practice requires an aim.

M.: *Atman* is the aim. What else can there be? All other aims are for those who are incapable of *atmalakshya* (having the Self for the aim). They lead you ultimately to *atma-vichara* (enquiry into the Self). One-pointedness is the fruit of all kinds of practice. One may get it quickly; another after a long time. Everything depends on the practice.

D.: Peace is extolled more than anything else. How shall we gain it?

M.: It is your very nature. Forgetfulness never overtakes the Self. The Self is now confounded with non-self and that makes you speak of forgetfulness of the Self, Peace, etc. Oblivion will never rear up its head if this confusion is put an end to.

D.: How is that done?

M.: Enquiry into the Self. One-pointedness means cessation of mental activities. Forgetfulness must be for the self — well, of what? Of the Self? Are there then two selves? Practice removes the *samskaras*.

D.: But *samskaras* are infinite and eternal — from beginningless time.

M.: This itself is a *samskara*. Give up that idea and all *samskaras* will disappear at once. That is *visranti* (repose), *santi* (peace). Peace is ever present. But you hold it down and rise over it and thus disturb it. Then you say, "I want Peace".

D.: Will Peace be gradual?

M.: Yes. Make the mind gradually still (*Sanaissanaih uparamet*) says the Bhagavad Gita.

After some time, the visitor asked if one Mr. G. had been here on or about the 20th instant. He himself had heard of Maharshi from him. Mr. G. was full of joy after his visit here.

M.: How can I know the names of all the visitors? He might have been here. All are full of joy. There is no name, no form .... Name is however needed for *vyavahara* (empirical life).

5th December, 1936
SPARKS FROM THE ANVIL — II

Talk 291.

Question: You spoke of *atyasrama* (beyond the *asramas* — beyond the orders of life) the other day. Is there any authority for it? Is it mentioned anywhere?

Maharshi: Yes, in the Upanishads, the *Suta Samhita* (*Skanda Purana*), *Bhagavata*, *Bharata* and other works.*

---

* For *atyasrama*, refer to *Narada Parivrajaka Upanishad*, v. 1-15; *Svetasvatara Up.* VI. 21; *Tejobindu Up.* I. 47-48; *Suta Samhita-Mukti Khanda* Ch. V. v. 9, 14-43; *Sivamahatmya Khanda* Ch. V. 32, 37fi 55.

Q.: Are there any restrictions or discipline for that state?

M.: There are characteristics of it mentioned.

Q.: There are Gurus for each *asrama*. Is there a Guru for *atyasrama*?

M.: Yes.

Q.: But you do not admit a Guru.

M.: There is a Guru for everyone. I admit a Guru for me also.

Q.: Who is your Guru.

M.: The Self.

Q.: For whom?

M.: For myself. The Guru may be internal or external. He may reveal Himself internally or communicate externally.

Q.: Can the *atyasramis* own property?

M.: There is no restriction for them. They may do what they please. *Suka* is said to have married and begotten children also.

Q.: The *atyasrami* is like a householder in that case.

M.: I have already said that he is above the four recognised *asramas*.

Q.: If they can marry, own property, etc., they are only *grihasthas*.

M.: That may be your view.

Q.: Can they own property and convey the same to others?

M.: They may or may not. All depends on their *prarabdha*.

Q.: Is there any *Karma* for them?

M.: Their conduct is not regulated according to any rules or codes.

Q.: When visitors want to stay here, say two or three days, do they take your permission?

M.: The permission from the management is permission from me. The visitors come here for me, the management is for me. Wherever there is mutual agreement, I do not interfere. When visitors come here and I admit them, will others dare go against my wishes? My consent is implied in the actions which take place with mutual goodwill.

Sri Bhagavan was shown a stanza in His own handwriting in praise of Himself as Subrahmanya.

Sri Bhagavan said that the handwriting was His own whereas the ideas were Perumalswami's.

Q.: But do you not agree with the statement made in it?

M.: In the same way as an idol is praised as Subrahmanya.

265

13th December 1936

Talk 292.

In reply to a question if *tanmatras* are the operating factors in dreams, Sri Bhagavan said: No. *Tanmatras* are *sukshma* — subtler than that. Although the dream-creations are subtle as compared with the gross world of the wakeful state, yet the dream-creations are gross compared to *tanmatras*. *Tanmatras* after *panchikarana* give rise to the form of the *antahkarnas* (inner organ, mind). There too, by the different sets of operating causes. Influenced by *satva* the predominance of ether (*akasa*) it gives rise to *jnana* (knowledge) whose seat is the brain.

vayu (air) gives rise to *manas* (mind)
tejas (light) gives rise to *buddhi* (intellect)
jala (water) gives rise to *chitta* (memory etc.)
prthvi (earth) gives rise to *ahankara* (ego).

They are *samashti* (collective) for the reason that they can operate collectively or individually with any or all of the senses or organs. By *rajoguna* they are changed to *jnanendriyas* in the *vyashti* (individual); by *tamoguna* to *karmendriyas* in the *vyashti* (the individual). The relation between the external world and the individual now becomes easy because the *tanmatras* are common to them.

The *tanmatras* proceed from *Prakriti*. The statements on creation differ considerably. There is mentioned *yugapatsrshti* (simultaneous creation) and *kramasrshti* (gradual creation). The significance is not emphasis on creation but on the original source.

Talk 293.

Mr. K. K. V. Iyer: There is no way found to go inward by means of meditation.

M.: Where else are we now? Our very being is that.

D.: Being so, we are ignorant of it.

M.: Ignorant of what, and whose is the ignorance? If ignorant of the Self, are there two selves?

D.: There are no two selves. The feeling of limitation cannot be denied. Due to limitations....

266

M.: Limitation is only in the mind. Did you feel it in deep sleep? You exist in sleep. You do not deny your existence then. The same Self is now and here, in the wakeful state. You are now saying that there are limitations. What has now happened is that there are these differences between the two states. The differences are due to the mind. There was no mind in sleep. whereas it is now active. The Self exists in the absence of the mind also.

D.: Although it is understood, it is not realised.

M.: It will be by and by, with meditation.

D.: Meditation is with mind and how can it kill the mind in order to reveal the Self?

M.: Meditation is sticking to one thought. That single thought keeps away other thoughts; distraction of mind is a sign of its weakness. By constant meditation it gains strength, *i.e.*, to say, its weakness of fugitive thought gives place to the enduring background free from thoughts. This expanse devoid of thought is the Self. Mind in purity is the Self. Sri Bhagavan continued in reply to the former questioner: Everyone says "I am the body". It is the experience of the sage as also of the ignorant. The ignorant man believes that the Self is confined to the body only, whereas the wise man believes that the body cannot remain apart from the Self. The Self is infinite for him and includes the body also.

Mr. Bose said that he felt peace in His presence which lasts some time after. He added: "Why is it not enduring?"

M.: That Peace is the Real nature. Contrary ideas are only superimpositions. This is true *bhakti*, true yoga, true *jnana*. You may say that this peace is acquired by practice. The wrong notions are given up by practice. This is all. Your true nature always persists. These flashes are only signs of the ensuing revelation of the Self.

In reply to the first questioner Bhagavan said: The Heart is the Self. It is not within or without. The mind is Its *sakti*. After the emergence of the mind, the universe appears and the body is seen to be contained in it. Whereas all these are contained in the Self and they cannot exist apart from the Self.

14th December 1936

Talk 294.

Mr. Parkhi: How is meditation to be practised?

M.: Meditation is, truly speaking, *Atmanishtha* (to be fixed as the Self). But when thoughts cross the mind and an effort is made to eliminate them the effort is usually termed meditation. *Atmanishtha* is your real nature. Remain as you are. That is the aim.

D.: But thoughts come up. Is our effort meant to eliminate thoughts only?

M.: Yes. Meditation being on a single thought, the other thoughts are kept away. Meditation is only negative in effect inasmuch as thoughts are kept away.

D.: It is said *Atma samstham manah krtva* (fixing the mind in the Self). But the Self is unthinkable.

M.: Why do you wish to meditate at all? Because you wish to do so you are told *Atma samstham manah krtva* (fixing the mind in the Self); why do you not remain as you are without meditating? What is that *manah* (mind)? When all thoughts are eliminated it becomes *Atma samstha* (fixed in the Self).

D.: If a form is given I can meditate on it and other thoughts are eliminated. But the Self is formless.

M.: Meditation on forms or concrete objects is said to be *dhyana*, whereas the enquiry into the Self is *vichara* (enquiry) or *nididhyasana*. Explaining *adhyaropapavadabhyam* (superimposition and its elimination), Sri Bhagavan pointed out that the first turns you inward to the Self; and then according to the second, you know that the world is not apart from the Self.

16th December, 1936

Talk 295.

Mr. Natverlal Parekh, a Gujerati gentleman who had attended the International Religious Conference as a delegate from Baroda, came here on a visit. He is a young man, well-groomed, alert, and quite conscious of his well-earned merit. He presented a note containing some questions to Sri Bhagavan.

D.: Pray help me realise *Atma — Paramatma — Satchidananda.*

M.: Atma — Paramatma — Satchidananda mean one and the same thing, *i.e.,* the Self. The Self is eternally realised. Otherwise there will be no pleasure in it. If it is not eternal it must have a beginning; what begins will also end; so that it is only transient. There is no use seeking for a temporary state of affairs. The fact is that it is the state of effortless, ever alert Peace. Effortlessness while remaining aware is the state of Bliss, and that is Realisation.

D.: I do not want intellectual answers. I want them to be practical.

M.: Yes. Direct knowledge does not require intellectual discourses. Since the Self is directly experienced by everyone, they are not at all necessary. Everyone says "I am". Is there anything more to realise?

D.: It is not clear to me.

M.: You exist. You say 'I am'. That means existence.

D.: But I am not sure of it, *i.e.,* my existence.

M.: Oh! Who then is speaking now?

D.: I, surely. But whether I exist or not, I am not sure. Moreover, admitting my existence leads me nowhere.

M.: There must be one even to deny the existence. If you do not exist, there is no questioner, and no question can arise.

D.: Let us take it that I exist.

M.: How do you know that you exist?

D.: Because I think, I feel, I see, etc.

M.: So you mean that your existence is inferred from these. Furthermore, there is no feeling, thinking etc., in sleep and yet there is the being.

D.: But no. I cannot say that I was in deep sleep.

M.: Do you deny your existence in sleep?

D.: I may be or may not be in sleep. God knows.

M.: When you wake up from sleep, you remember what you did before falling asleep.

D.: I can say that I was before and after sleep, but I cannot say if I was in sleep.

269

M.: Do you now say that you were asleep?

D.: Yes.

M.: How do you know unless you remember the state of sleep?

D.: It does not follow that I existed in sleep. Admission of such existence leads nowhere.

M.: Do you mean to say that a man dies every time that sleep overtakes him and that he resuscitates while waking?

D.: Maybe. God alone knows.

M.: Then let God come and find the solution for these riddles. If one were to die in sleep, one will be afraid of sleep, just as one fears death. On the other hand one courts sleep. Why should sleep be courted unless there is pleasure in it?

D.: There is no positive pleasure in sleep. Sleep is courted only to be rid of physical fatigue.

M.: Well, that is right. "To be free from fatigue." There is one who is free from fatigue.

D.: Yes.

M.: So you are in sleep and you are now too. You were happy in sleep without feeling, thinking etc. The same one continuing now, why are you not happy?

D.: How can it be said that there is happiness?

M.: Everyone says *Sukhamahamasvapsam* (I slept happily or was blissfully asleep).

D.: I do not think that they are right. There is no *sukha* (bliss). It is only absence of sorrow.

M.: Your very being is bliss. Therefore everyone says I was blissfully asleep. That means that one remains in the primal uncontaminated state in sleep. As for sorrow, there is no sorrow. Where is it in order that you might speak of its absence in sleep? The present wrong identification of the Self with the body has given rise to all mistakes.

D.: What I want is realisation. I do not feel my inherent happy nature.

M.: Because the Self is now identified with the non-self. The non-self too is not apart from the Self. However, there is the wrong

270

notion that the body is apart and the Self is confounded with the body. This wrong identity must be ended for happiness to manifest.

D.: I am unable to help myself.

The Engineer suggested surrender to the Master.

D.: Agreed.

M.: Your nature is happiness. You say that is not apparent. See what obstructs you from your true being. It is pointed out to you that the obstruction is the wrong identity. Eliminate the error. The patient must himself take the medicine prescribed by the doctor in order that he may be cured of his illness.

D.: The patient is too weak to help himself and places himself unconditionally in the hands of the doctor.

M.: The doctor must be given a free hand and the patient must only remain quiet without saying anything. Similarly keep quiet. That is effortlessness.

D.: That is the most effective medicine too.

The other questions which he wrote down were:

D.: Convince me of the existence of God.

M.: Realisation of the Self amounts to such conviction.

D.: How is *prarabdha* (past karma) related to *purushakara* (one's own effort here)?

M.: Prarabdha is karma (action). There must be a *karta* (doer) for it. See who the *karta* is. *Purushakara* is effort. See who exerts. There is identity established. The one who seeks to know their relation is himself the link.

D.: What is karma and rebirth?

M.: See the *karta* (doer) and then the karma (action) becomes obvious. If you are born now, rebirth may follow. See if you are born now.

D.: Help me to have *jyotidarsana* (vision of light).

M.: Darsana (sight) implies *drashta* (seer). Find him and *darsana* (sight) is included in him.

Talk 296.

Poovan, a shepherd, says that he knows Sri Bhagavan since thirty years ago, the days of Virupakshi cave. He used at times to supply milk to the visitors in those days.

Some six years ago he had lost a sheep, for which he was searching for three days. The sheep was pregnant and he had lost all hopes of recovering her, because he thought that she had been set upon by wild animals. He was one day passing by the Asramam, when Sri Bhagavan saw him and enquired how he was. The man replied that he was looking out for a lost sheep. Sri Bhagavan kept quiet, as is usual with Him. Then He told the shepherd to help in lifting some stones, which he did with great pleasure. After the work was finished, Sri Bhagavan told him: "Go this way", pointing the footpath towards the town. "You will find the stray sheep on the way". So he did and found the lost sheep with two little lambs.

He now says, "What a Bhagavan is this! Look at the force of his words! He is great! He never forgets even a poor man like me. He remembers my son Manikkam also with kindness. Such are the great ones! I am happy when I do any little work for Him, such as looking to the cows when they are in heat".

18th December, 1936

Talk 297.

Mr. Cohen asked: Meditation is with mind in the *jagrat* (waking) state. There is mind in dream also. Why is there no meditation in dream? Nor is it possible?

M.: Ask it in the dream.

After a short silence Sri Bhagavan continued: You are told to meditate now and find who you are. Instead of doing it you ask "Why is there no meditation in dream or in sleep?" If you find out for whom there is *jagrat* (waking), it will be clear that dream and sleep are also for the same one. You are the witness of *jagrat* (waking), *svapna* (dream) and *sushupti* (sleep) — rather, they pass before you. Because you are out of meditation now, these questions arise. Stick to meditation and see if these questions arise.

272

23rd December, 1936

Talk 298.

A certain visitor formulated a question, saying that meditation is more direct than investigation, because the former holds on to the truth whereas the latter sifts the truth from untruth.

M.: For the beginner meditation on a form is more easy and agreeable. Practice of it leads to *Atmavichara* which consists in sifting the Reality from unreality.

What is the use of holding on to truth when you are filled with antagonistic factors?

Atmavichara directly leads to realisation by removing the obstacles which make you think that the Self is not already realised.

24th December, 1936

Talk 299.

Mr. T. K. S. Iyer asked Sri Bhagavan about the source of sound.

M.: The general opinion is that *para* (sound) comes from the *Muladhara* (the solar plexus) at the bottom of the spine. All sounds beginning from *vaikhar* (thought form) are contained in *para* which proceeds from *Kundalini*; and *Kundalini* is not different from the Heart. In fact the whole *shadadhara* (six-fold centre) is contained in the heart.

The *sushumna* with its source *Kundalini* is included in the Heart.

A visitor asked about *antarena taluke sendrayonih*.

M.: Indrayoni together with the *sushumna nadi* is contained (*leena*) in *para*.

25th December, 1936

Talk 300.

A *brahmachari* youth who has graduated in science has been waiting here for Grace for the last four or five months in order that some job might drop on him like a ripe apple from the tree. He has been making no other efforts to secure a job. His brother yesterday came here to take him away to his parents. But the youth declined to go. An appeal was made to Sri Bhagavan.

273

Sri Bhagavan said: "I do not tell anyone to come nor ask him to go. Everyone pleases himself here. He says he finds peace in the hall and he also wants a job. Evidently the job must be found in the hall itself so that his peace may not be disturbed. Peace is not in the hall. It is in the repose of the Self. It can be gained anywhere."

Some days later the youth threw away his sacred thread and appeared before Sri Bhagavan with his limbs shaking, which the young man later described as his Bliss (*ananda*). Sri Bhagavan told him not to make a habit of sitting in front of Him in the hall and ordered him out. Furthermore He continued: Even a fledgling is protected by the parent birds only till such time it grows its wings. It is not protected for ever. Similarly with devotees. I have shown the way. You must now be able to follow it up and find peace wherever you are.

The young man thinks that Sri Bhagavan gave him *upadesa* in the following words: "The self (*i.e.* ego) must be subdued by oneself."

The man however has refused the offer of a job to him in one of the local schools and thinks that he has been given a mighty job by the Hill or by Sri Bhagavan. "What that job is the world will know later", he says. He had further anticipated all this day's occurrences some months ago and had foretold them to his mother and to his friends. He is further happy at the happenings.

Sri Bhagavan however compared him to another man who is in no way of the right type. And yet the boy thinks that he is Bhagavan in embryo. Later he turned mad and died.

Talk 301.

A gentleman enthusiastically recounted several of his experiences on following Sri Bhagavan's instructions and incidentally mentioned that he and Sri Bhagavan were born on the same day of the week and bore the same name ....

Sri Bhagavan completed it, adding "The same Self is in both."

Talk 302.

A young man from Trichy asked Sri Bhagavan on the mention in *Upadesa Manjari* of *atyanta vairagyam* (total dispassion) as the qualification of a ripe disciple. He continued: "What is *vairagya*? Detachment from worldly pursuits and desire for salvation. Is it not so?"

M.: Who has not got it?

Each one seeks happiness but is misled into thinking pain associated pleasures as happiness. Such happiness is transient. His mistaken activity gives him short-lived pleasure. Pain and pleasure alternate with one another in the world. To discriminate between the pain-producing and pleasure-producing matters and to confine oneself to the happiness-producing pursuit only is *vairagya*. What is it that will not be followed by pain? He seeks it and engages in it. Otherwise, the man has one foot in the world and another foot in the spiritual pursuit (without progressing satisfactorily in either field).

A question was again raised regarding the function of the Guru.

M.: Because the man is not able to help himself, finding himself too weak, he seeks more strength in the shape of a Guru.

Talk 303.

Mr. K. R. V. Iyer sought more light on *nada* (sound).

M.: He who meditates on it feels it. There are ten kinds of *nadas*. After the final thundering *nada* the man gets *laya*. That is his natural and eternal state. *Nada, jyoti,* or enquiry thus take one to the same point. (The former are indirect and the last is direct).

D.: The mind becomes peaceful for a short while and again emerges forth. What is to be done?

M.: The peace often gained must be remembered at other times. That peace is your natural and permanent state. By continuous practice it will become natural. That is called the 'current.' That is your true nature.

Nada, photisms, etc., imply the existence of *triputi* (the triads of cogniser, cognition and the cognised). The current resulting from investigation for the Self is *suddha triputi* or pure *triad* — that is to say, undifferentiated triad.

275

Talk 304.

A Swiss lady described a photism she had to Sri Bhagavan. While she was sitting with her eyes wide open, she saw Sri Bhagavan's face becoming cherub-like and draped in glorious flowers. She was drawn in love towards that child-like face.

M.: The vision is in your mind. Your love is the cause. Paul Brunton saw me as a giant figure; you saw me like a child. Both are visions.

(The lady said: Paul Brunton asked me if I had any spiritual experience here, and I denied it. Now this happens).

M.: Do not be deceived by visions.

D.: If one is miles away in Europe and invokes your aid ....

M.: Where is Europe? It is in you.

D.: I have come here; I would like Maharshi to come there. (Saying it, she laughed gently. Silence for some minutes).

M.: You see the physical body and so you find limitations. Time and space operate on this plane. So long as you think of the gross body there will be differences found as different bodies. On the other hand, knowledge of the real Maharshi will set all doubts at rest.

Are you in India now? Or is India in you? Even now this notion that you are in India must go. India is in you. In order to verify it, look to your sleep. Did you feel that you were in Europe or in India while asleep? You were nevertheless existing then the same as now.

Space is in you. The physical body is in space, but not you.

Paul Brunton had his eyes closed when he saw the vision, whereas you had your eyes open, you say.

D.: Yes. But I have never had vision; whereas he is a psychic.

After a few minutes she asked if it is an advantage or a disadvantage to see visions like this.

M.: It is an advantage.

Sri Bhagavan continued: Probably you had been thinking of a child and that appeared in the vision ......

D.: Yes, only of Siva — of His child-like face ....

M.: That's it.

D.: But Siva is the Destroyer ... (meaning, not a child).

M.: Yes — of sorrows.

After a few minutes Bhagavan continued: You will shortly go to sleep. When you wake up in the morning you will say "I slept well and happily". What happened in sleep is your real nature. That continues now too; otherwise it will not be your real nature. Get the state of sleep even now; it is Siva.

Have we got a form? Find that out before you think of Siva's form. Did you not exist in sleep? Were you aware of any form then? Were you with form in your sleep? You existed all the same. The 'I' which was in sleep is also now present. You were not the body according to your sleep-experience. You are the same now — that is without the body. Being without the body you were happy too in sleep. You are the same now too. That which is enduring must alone be the real nature. There was no body but only experience of happiness in sleep. That endures now too. The Self is bodiless. If you are thus without body how can Siva be with body? If you are with body Siva also is with body. If you are not, He also is not.

D.: Why is He then Siva?

M.: Siva means embodiment of happiness — of auspiciousness.

She was very pleased. After a time she left.

Talk 305.

The visitors were talking among themselves and one of them said: "We, though familiar with our traditional teachings, are unable to follow these teachings (meaning Sri Bhagavan's). How can the foreigners unfamiliar with our ways follow Sri Bhagavan's teachings so easily?"

He seemed to sympathise with their attempts to understand us in spite of their handicaps, and also to pity them for want of proper equipment.

Sri Bhagavan remarked finally: Visions are better than no visions. They get interested in that way. They do not take to foreign ideas; when once they do it, they stick on. So much for their merits.

Sri Bhagavan later referred to Sivaprakasam Pillai's vision. "Visions are not external. They appear only internally. If external

277

they must assert themselves without there being a seer. In that case what is the warranty for their existence? The seer only."

Talk 306.

D.: There is something concrete necessary to meditate upon. How shall we meditate upon 'I'?

M.: We have become rooted in forms and so we require a concrete form for meditating upon. Only that which we contemplate will in the end remain over. When you contemplate the other thoughts disappear. So long as you need to contemplate there are other thoughts, Where are you? You contemplate because you exist. For the contemplator must contemplate. The contemplation can only be where he is. Contemplation wards off all other thoughts. You should merge yourself in the source. At times we merge in the source unconsciously, as in sleep, death, swoon, etc. What is contemplation? It is merging into the source *consciously*. Then the fear of death, of swoon, etc. will disappear, because you are able to merge into the source *consciously*.

Why fear death? Death cannot mean non-being. Why do you love sleep, but not death? Do you not think now? Are you not existing now? Did you not exist in your sleep? Even a child says that it slept well and happily. It admits its existence in sleep, unconsciously though. So, consciousness is our true nature. We cannot remain unconscious. We however say that we were unconscious in our sleep because we refer to qualified consciousness. The world, the body, etc., are so embedded in us that this relative consciousness is taken to be the Self. Does anyone say in his sleep that he is unconscious? He says so now. This is the state of relative consciousness. Therefore he speaks of relative consciousness and not of abstract consciousness. The consciousness is beyond relative consciousness or unconsciousness.

Again reverting to *Tiruvachagam*, Sri Bhagavan said: All the four foremost saints have given out their experiences in the very first stanza. (1) Undifferentiated worship. (2) Never-failing remembrance. (3) Unrisen thought. (4) The ego is not, the Self is. All mean the same.

D.: But this truth is not realised.

M.: It will be realised in due course. Till then there is devotion

278

(*bhakti*): "Even for a trice you do not leave my mind." Does he leave you any moment? It is you who allow your mind to wander away. He remains always steady. When your mind is fixed, you say: "He does not leave my mind even for a trice". How ridiculous!

27th December, 1936

Talk 307.

Mr. Shamanna from Mysore asked Sri Bhagavan: Kindly explain *Aham Sphurana* (the light of 'I-I').

M.: 'I' is not known in sleep. On waking 'I' is perceived associated with the body, the world and non-self in general. Such associated 'I' is *Aham vritti*. When *Aham* represents the Self only it is *Aham Sphurana*. This is natural to the *jnani* and is itself called *jnana* by *jnanis*, or *bhakti* by *bhaktas*. Though ever present, including in sleep, it is not perceived. It cannot be known in sleep all at once. It must first be realised in the waking state, for it is our true nature underlying all the three states. Efforts must be made only in the *jagrat* state and the Self realised here and now. It will afterwards be understood and realised to be continuous Self, uninterrupted by *jagrat, svapna* and *sushupti*. Thus it is *akhandakara vritti* (unbroken experience). *Vritti* is used for lack of a better expression. It should not be understood to be literally a *vritti*. In that case, *vritti* will resemble an 'ocean-like river', which is absurd. *Vritti* is of short duration, it is qualified, directed consciousness; or absolute consciousness broken up by cognition of thoughts, senses, etc. *Vritti* is the function of the mind, whereas the continuous consciousness transcends the mind. This is the natural, primal state of the *jnani* or the liberated being. That is unbroken experience. It asserts itself when relative consciousness subsides. *Aham vritti* ('I-thought') is broken, *Aham sphurana* (the light of 'I-I') is unbroken, continuous. After the thoughts subside, the light shines forth.

31st December, 1936

Talk 308.

A question was asked regarding untouchability.

279

Sri Bhagavan said: The Non-self is untouchable. The social untouchability is man-made, whereas the other untouchability is natural and divine.

D.: Should the untouchables be allowed into our temples?

M.: There are others to decide it.

A question was asked regarding the *avatars* of Vishnu.

M.: Let us know our own *avatara*; the knowledge of the other *avataras* will follow.

Again there was a question on *Isvara*.

M.: Existence of *Isvara* follows from our conception of *Isvara*. Let us first know whose concept He is. The concept will be only according to the one who conceives. Find out who you are and the other problem will solve itself.

1st January, 1937

Talk 309.

D.: What is the difference between *Aham Brahmasmi* (I am Brahman) and *Brahmaivaham* (only Brahman I am).

M.: The former is *Pratyaksha vritti* (direct experience), whereas the latter is *Paroksha jnana* (indirect knowledge). The first begins with the realisation of *Aham* ('I'), whereas the later starts with the hearsay Brahman which cannot be apart from the Self, if the same has been realised.

Talk 310.

Mr. Greenlees: After leaving this Asramam in October I was aware of Bhagavan's peace enfolding me for about ten days. All the time while busy in work there was an undercurrent of that peace of unity; it was almost like the dual consciousness while half asleep in a dull lecture. Then it faded out entirely, and the old stupidities came in instead.

Work leaves no time for separate meditation. Is the constant reminder "I am", trying to feel it while actually at work, enough?

M.: It will become constant when the mind becomes strengthened. Repeated practice strengthens the mind; and such mind is capable of

280

holding on to the current. In that case, engagement in work or no engagement, the current remains unaffected and uninterrupted.

D.: No separate meditation is necessary?

M.: Meditation is your true nature now. You call it meditation, because there are other thoughts distracting you. When these thoughts are dispelled, you remain alone, *i.e.*, in the state of meditation free from thoughts; and that is your real nature which you are now attempting to gain by keeping away other thoughts. Such keeping away of other thoughts is now called meditation. When the practice becomes firm, the real nature shows itself as the true meditation. Other thoughts arise more forcibly when you attempt meditation.

There was immediately a chorus of questions by a few others.

Sri Maharshi continued: Yes, all kinds of thoughts arise in meditation. It is but right. What lies hidden in you is brought out. Unless they rise up how can they be destroyed? They therefore rise up spontaneously in order to be extinguished in due course, thus to strengthen the mind.

A visitor: All are said to be Brahman.

M.: Yes, they are. But so long as you think that they are apart they are to be avoided. If on the other hand they are found to be Self there is no need to say 'all'. For all that exists is only Brahman. There is nothing besides Brahman.

D.: Ribhu Gita speaks of so many objects as unreal, adding at the end that they are all Brahman and thus real.

M.: Yes. When you see them as so many they are *asat, i.e.,* unreal. Whereas when you see them as Brahman they are real, deriving their reality from their substratum, Brahman.

D.: Why then does *Upadesa Sara* speak of the body, etc., as *jada i.e.* insentient?

M.: Inasmuch as you say that they are body, etc., apart from the Self. But when the Self is found this body, etc., are also found to be in it. Afterwards no one will ask the question and no one will say that they are insentient.

D.: Viveka is said to be discrimination between the Self and the non-self. What is the non-self?

M.: There is no non-self, in fact. The non-self also exists in the Self. It is the Self which speaks of the non-self because it has forgotten itself. Having lost hold of itself, it conceives something as non-self, which is after all nothing but itself.

Then the discussion between the protagonists of various theories became warm.

2nd January, 1937

Talk 311.

The 'I' which rises will also subside. That is the individual 'I' or the 'I'-concept. That which does not rise will not subside. It *is* and will be for ever. That is the universal 'I', the perfect 'I', or realisation of the Self.

At 5-30 p.m. the Swiss lady complains to Sri Bhagavan that she gets a headache if meditation be prolonged for some time.

M.: If the meditator and meditation be understood to be the same there will be no headache or similar complaints.

D.: But they are different. How shall we consider them to be the same?

M.: That is due to your outlook. There is only one and there are no differences. On meditation the relative consciousness will vanish. That is not annihilation; for Absolute Consciousness arises. The Bible itself says, "The Kingdom of Heaven is within you" . . . If you consider yourself to be the body there is some difficulty in understanding the statement. On the other hand if you know who you really are, the Kingdom of Heaven and all are included in your true Self. They are concepts arising after the ego has arisen. *Drishtim jnanamayeem krtva pasyet Brahmamayam jagat* (Direct your look within and make it absolute). With that absolute awareness realised, look without and you will realise the universe to be not apart from the realised Absolute.

Because your outlook is externally directed you speak of a *without*. In that state you are advised to look *within*. This *within* is relative to the *without* you are seeking. In fact, the Self is neither without nor within.

282

Speaking of Heaven one thinks of it as above or below, within or without, since one is accustomed to relative knowledge. One seeks only objective knowledge and hence these ideas.

Really speaking there is neither up nor down, neither in nor out. If they were real they must be present in dreamless sleep also. For what is real must be continuous and permanent. Did you feel 'in' or 'out' in sleep? Of course not.

D.: I do not remember.

M.: If there was anything there that could be remembered. But you admit your existence then. The same Self is now speaking. The Self who was undifferentiated in sleep is differentiated in the present state, and sees the diversity. The Real Existence is the only One devoid of objective knowledge. That is absolute consciousness. That is the state of happiness, as admitted by all of us. That state must be brought about even in this waking state. It is called *jagrat sushupti.* That is *mukti.*

D.: The ego is the one which reincarnates.

M.: Yes. But what is reincarnation? The ego remains the same. New bodies appear and hold it. The ego does not change. It does not leave one body, seek and find another. Just see what happens even to your gross body. Suppose you go to London. How do you do it? You take a conveyance, go to the docks, board the steamer and reach London in a few days. What has happened? The conveyances had moved, but not your body. Still you say that you travelled from one part of the globe to the other part. The movements of the conveyances have been superimposed on your body. Similarly also with your ego. The reincarnations are superimpositions. For example, what happens in a dream? Do you go to the dream world or does it occur in you? Surely the latter. Just the same with incarnations. The ego remains changeless all along.

Again, there is no time and space in your sleep. They are concepts which arise after the 'I-thought' has arisen. Before the rise of the 'I-thought' the concepts are absent. Therefore you are beyond time and space. The 'I-thought' is only limited 'I'. The real 'I' is unlimited, universal, beyond time and space. They are absent in sleep. Just on

283

rising up from sleep, and before seeing the objective world, there is a state of awareness which is your pure Self. That must be known.

D.: But I do not realise it.

M.: It is not an object to be realised. You are that. Who is there to realise and what?

Talk 312.

Mr. V. K. Cholkar, of Poona: It is said "Know thyself" or see who the "I" in you is. What is the way to do it? Is it by simply repeating the *mantra* mechanically all along or have you to do it, remembering every moment why you are repeating the *mantra*?

M.: You are always repeating the *mantra* automatically. If you are not aware of the *ajapa* (unspoken chant) which is eternally going on, you should take to *japa*. *Japa* is made with an effort. The effort is meant to ward off other thoughts. Then the *japa* becomes mental and internal. Finally, its *ajapa* and eternal nature will be realised. For it will be found to be going on even without your effort. The effortless state is the state of realisation.

Mr. Cholkar again requested instructions from a practical point of view, *i.e.*, suitable to himself.

M.: It is not external and therefore need not be sought elsewhere. It is internal and also eternal. It is always realised. But you say you are not aware. It requires constant attention to itself. No other effort is necessary. Your effort is only meant not to allow yourself to be distracted by other thoughts.

The person was satisfied.

Talk 313.

Mr. Greenlees: Bhagavan said yesterday that, while one is engaged in search for "God within", outer work would go on automatically. In the life of Sri Chaitanya it is explained that while he sought Krishna (the Self) during his lectures to students, he forgot where his body was and went on talking of Krishna. This rouses doubt whether work can safely be left to itself. Should one keep part-attention on the physical work?

M.: The Self is all. Now I ask you: Are you apart from the Self? Can the work go on apart from the Self? Or is the body apart from the Self? None of them could be apart from the Self. The Self is universal. So all the actions will go on whether you engage in them voluntarily or not. The work will go on automatically. Attending to the Self includes attending to the work.

D.: The work may suffer if I do not attend to it.

M.: Because you identify yourself with the body, you consider that the work is done by you. But the body and its activities, including the work, are not apart from the Self.

What does it matter whether you attend to the work or not? Suppose you walk from one place to another place. You do not attend every single step that you take. After a time, however, you find yourself at your destination. You notice how the work, *i.e.*, walking, goes on without your attention to it. Similarly it is with other kinds of work.

D.: Then it is like sleep-walking.

M.: Quite so. When a child is fast asleep, his mother feeds him in sleep. The child eats the food quite as well as when well awake. But the next morning he says to the mother "Mother! I did not take food last night". The mother and others know that he did. But he says that he did not. He was not aware and yet the action had gone on. Somnambulism is indeed a good analogy for this kind of work.

Take another example: A passenger in a cart has fallen asleep. The bulls move or stand still or are unyoked on the journey. He does not know these occurrences, but finds himself in a different place after he wakes up. He has been blissfully ignorant of the occurrences on the way, but his journey has been finished.

Similarly with the Self of the person. He is asleep in the body. His waking state is the movement of the bulls, his *samadhi* is their standing still (because *samadhi = jagrat sushupti*) *i.e.*, to say, he is aware of but not attached to actions. So the bulls are in harness but do not move. His sleep is the unyoking of the bulls, for there is complete suspension of activities corresponding to the release of the bulls from the yoke.

285

Still another example: Scenes are projected on the screen in a cinema show. But the moving pictures do not affect or alter the screen. The seer pays attention to the pictures and ignores the screen. They cannot remain apart from the screen. Still its existence is ignored. So also the Self is the screen on which the pictures, namely activities, are going on. The man is aware of the latter, ignoring the former. All the same he is not apart from the Self. Whether aware or unaware the actions will continue.

D.: There is an operator in the cinema.

M.: The cinema show is made out of insentient materials. The screen, the pictures, lamp, etc., are insentient and require an operator, a sentient agent. In the case of the Self, it is consciousness itself and therefore self-contained. There cannot be an operator apart.

D.: Protested that he did not confuse the body with the operator as the above answer would imply.

M.: The functions of the body were kept in mind involving the need for the operator. Because there is the body — a *jada* object — an operator, a sentient agent, is necessary.

Because people think that they are *jivas*, Sri Krishna has said that God resides in the Heart as the operator of the *jivas*. In fact there are no *jivas* and no operator. The self comprises all. It is the screen, the pictures, the seer, the actor, the operator, the light and all else. Your confounding it with the body and imagining yourself as the actor amounts to the seer being represented as an actor in a cinema picture. Imagine the actor in the picture asking if he could enact a scene without the screen. Such is the case of the man who thinks of his acting apart from the Self.

D.: It is like asking the spectator to act in the cinema picture. Somnambulism seems to be desirable.

M.: There is the belief that the crow rolls only one iris into either eye to see any object. It has only one iris but two eye sockets. Its sight is manipulated according to its desire.

Or again the elephant has one trunk with which it breathes and does work such as drinking water, etc.

Again serpents are said to use the same apparatus for either seeing or hearing.

286

Similarly the actions and states are according to one's point of view. Sleep waking or waking sleep or dreaming sleep or dreaming wakefulness are about the same.

D.: We have to deal with a physical body in a physical waking world. If we sleep while work is done or work when sleep overtakes us, the work will go wrong.

M.: Sleep is not ignorance; it is your pure state. Wakefulness is not knowledge; it is ignorance. There is full awareness in sleep; there is total ignorance in waking. Your real nature covers both, and extends beyond. The Self is beyond knowledge and ignorance.

Sleep, dream and waking are only modes passing before the Self. They proceed whether you are aware or not. That is the state of the *jnani* in whom pass the states of waking, *samadhi*, deep sleep and dream, like the bulls moving, standing or being unyoked when the passenger is asleep as aforesaid. These questions are from the point of view of the *ajnani*; otherwise these questions do not arise.

D.: Of course they cannot arise for the Self. Who would be there to ask? But unfortunately I have not yet realised the Self.

M.: That is just the obstacle in your way. You must get rid of the idea that you are an *ajnani* yet to realise the Self. You are the Self. Was there ever a time when you were apart from the Self?

D.: So it is an experiment in somnambulism .... or in day-dreaming. Bhagavan laughed.

3rd January, 1937

DROPS OF NECTAR

Talk 314.

In yesterday's answers, Sri Bhagavan said that the Self is pure consciousness in deep slumber, and He also indicated the Self of the transition from sleep to the waking state as the ideal for realisation. He was requested to explain the same.

Sri Bhagavan graciously answered: The Self is pure consciousness in sleep; it evolves as *aham* ('I') without the *idam* ('this') in the transition stage; and manifests as *aham* ('I') and *idam* ('this') in the waking state. The individual's experience is by means of *aham* ('I') only. So he must aim at realisation in the way indicated (*i.e.*, by means of the transitional 'I'). Otherwise the sleep-experience does not matter to him. If the transitional 'I' be realised the substratum is found and that leads to the goal.

Again, sleep is said to be *ajnana* (ignorance). That is only in relation to the wrong *jnana* (knowledge) prevalent in the wakeful state. The waking state is really *ajnana* (ignorance) and the sleep state is *prajnana* (full knowledge). *Prajnana* is Brahman, says the *sruti*. Brahman is eternal. The sleep-experiencer is called *prajna*. He is *prajnanam* in all the three states. Its particular significance in the sleep state is that He is full of knowledge (*prajnanaghana*). What is *ghana*? There are *jnana* and *vijnana*. Both together operate in all perceptions. *Vijnana* in the *jagrat* is *viparita jnana* (wrong knowledge) *i.e.*, *ajnana* (ignorance). It always co-exists with the individual. When this becomes *vispashta jnana* (clear knowledge), It is Brahman. When wrong knowledge is totally absent, as in sleep, He remains pure *prajnana* only. That is *Prajnanaghana*. *Aitareya Upanishad* says *prajnana, vijnana, ajnana, samjnana* are all names of Brahman. Being made up of knowledge alone how is He to be experienced? Experience is always with *vijnana*. Therefore the pure 'I' of the transitional stage must be held for the experience of the *Prajnanaghana*. The 'I' of the waking state is impure and is not useful for such experience. Hence the use of the transitional 'I' or the pure 'I'. How is this pure 'I' to be realised? *Viveka Chudamani* says, *Vijnana kose vilasatyajasram* (He is always shining forth in the intellectual sheath, *vijnana kosa*). *Tripura Rahasya* and other works point out that the interval between two consecutive *sankalpas* (ideas or thoughts) represent the pure *aham* ('I'). Therefore holding on to the pure 'I', one should have the *Prajnanaghana* for aim, and there is the *vritti* present in the attempt. All these have their proper and respective places and at the same time lead to realisation.

Again the pure Self has been described in *Viveka Chudamani* to be beyond *asat*, *i.e.*, different from *asat*. Here *asat* is the contaminated waking 'I'. *Asadvilakshana* means *sat*, *i.e.*, the Self of sleep. He is also described as different from *sat* and *asat*. Both mean the same. He is also *asesha sakshi* (all-seeing witness).

If pure, how is He to be experienced by means of the impure 'I'? A man says "I slept happily". Happiness was his experience. If not, how could he speak of what he had not experienced? How did he experience happiness in sleep, if the Self was pure? Who is it that speaks of that experience now? The speaker is the *vijnanatma* (ignorant self) and he speaks of *prajnanatma* (pure self). How can that hold? Was this *vijnanatma* present in sleep? His present statement of the experience of happiness in sleep makes one infer his existence in sleep. How then did he remain? Surely not as in the waking state. He was there very subtle. Exceedingly subtle *vijnanatma* experiences the happy *prajnanatma* by means of *maya* mode. It is like the rays of the moon seen below the branches, twigs and leaves of a tree.

The subtle *vijnanatma* seems apparently a stranger to the obvious *vijnanatma* of the present moment. Why should we infer his existence in sleep? Should we not deny the experience of happiness and be done with this inference? No. The fact of the experience of happiness cannot be denied, for everyone courts sleep and prepares a nice bed for the enjoyment of sound sleep.

This brings us to the conclusion that the cogniser, cognition and the cognised are present in all the three states, though there are differences in their subtleties. In the transitional state, the *aham* ('I') is *suddha* (pure), because *idam* ('this') is suppressed. *Aham* ('I') predominates.

'Why is not that pure 'I' realised now or even remembered by us? Because of want of acquaintance (*parichaya*) with it. It can be recognised only if it is consciously attained. Therefore make the effort and gain consciously.

Talk 315.

One of the attendants asked: Sri Bhagavan has said: 'Reality and myth are both the same'. How is it so?

M.: The *tantriks* and others of the kind condemn Sri Sankara's philosophy as *maya vada* without understanding him aright. What does

289

he say? He says: (1) Brahman is real; (2) the universe is a myth; (3) Brahman is the universe. He does not stop at the second statement but continues to supplement it with the third. What does it signify? The Universe is conceived to be apart from Brahman and that perception is wrong. The antagonists point to his illustration of *rajju sarpa* (rope snake). This is unconditioned superimposition. After the truth of the rope is known, the illusion of snake is removed once for all.

But they should take the conditioned superimposition also into consideration, *e.g.*, *marumarichika or mrigatrishna* (water of mirage). The mirage does not disappear even after knowing it to be a mirage. The vision is there but the man does not run to it for water. Sri Sankara must be understood in the light of both the illustrations. The world is a myth. Even after knowing it, it continues to appear. It must be known to be Brahman and not apart.

If the world appears, yet to whom does it appear, he asks. What is your reply? You must say the Self. If not, will the world appear in the absence of the cognising Self? Therefore the Self is the reality. That is his conclusion. The phenomena are real as the Self and are myths apart from the Self.

Now, what do the *tantriks*, etc., say? They say that the phenomena are real because they are part of the Reality in which they appear.

Are not these two statements the same? That is what I meant by reality and falsehood being one and the same.

The antagonists continue: With the conditioned as well as the unconditioned illusions considered, the phenomenon of water in mirage is purely illusory because that water cannot be used for any purpose. Whereas the phenomenon of the world is different, for it is purposeful. How then does the latter stand on a par with the former?

A phenomenon cannot be a reality simply because it serves a purpose or purposes. Take a dream for example. The dream creations are purposeful; they serve the dream-purpose. The dream water quenches dream thirst. The dream creation is however contradicted in the waking state. The waking creation is contradicted in the other two states. What is not continuous cannot be real. If real, the thing must ever be real — and not real for a short time and unreal at other times.

So it is with magical creations. They appear real and are yet illusory.

Similarly the universe cannot be real of itself — that is to say, apart from the underlying Reality.

Talk 316.

There is fire on the screen in a cinema show. Does it burn the screen? There is a cascade of water. Does it wet the screen? There are tools. Do they damage the screen?

That is why it is said *achchedyoyam, adahyoyam, akledhyoyam,* etc. Fire, water, etc. are phenomena on the screen of Brahman (*i.e.,* the Self) and they do not affect It.

6th January, 1937

Talk 317.

Mr. Parkhi: Many visitors here tell me that they get visions or thought-currents from you. I am here for the last month and a half and still I have not the slightest experience of any kind. Is it because I am unworthy of your grace? If so, I feel it disgraceful that I being *Vasishtakulotpanna* (of the lineage of Vasishta) should not have your grace, while far-off foreigners should have it. Will you kindly suggest some *prayaschitta* (method of expiation) for removing this disgrace?

M.: Visions and thought-currents are had according to the state of mind. It depends on the individuals and not upon the Universal Presence. Moreover, they are immaterial. What matters is Peace of Mind.

D.: Peace of mind is the result of trance. How is trance got?

M.: Trance is only absence of thoughts. That state prevails in sleep. Do you have enduring peace of mind on that account?

D.: It is said in the journal maintained in the Asramam that trance is necessary.

M.: Trance is not something apart to be got anew. Your natural state is that of trance.

D.: But I do not feel it.

M.: The fact of your contrary belief is the obstruction.

291

D.: Since I have not realised the Self I say that I do not understand my permanent state of trance.

M.: This is only a repetition. That is the obstruction. This arises because you think that the non-self is you. That is the mistake. Do not take the non-self to be the Self. Then the Self will be evident to you.

D.: I understand it theoretically but not practically.

M.: There are no two selves — for the self to speak of the non-realisation of the Self.

D.: It is still theoretical to me. How shall I get the trance?

M.: Trance is only temporary in its effects. There is happiness so long as it lasts. After rising from it the old *vasanas* return. Unless the *vasanas* are destroyed in *sahaja samadhi* (effortless *samadhi*), there is no good of trance.

D.: But trance must precede *sahaja samadhi*?

M.: Trance is the natural state. Although there are activities and phenomena, yet they do not affect the trance. If they are realised to be not apart from the Self, the Self is realised. Where is the use of trance, unless it brings about enduring peace of mind? Know that even now you are in trance whatever happens. That is all.

D.: But how shall I do it?

A scholar remarked: *Yato vacho nivartante aprapya manasa saha* (where words fail to reach, along with the mind).

The questioner retorted: It is also said *manasaiva aptavyam* (to be realised with the mind only).

M.: Yes. The Pure Mind, *i.e.*, the mind free from thoughts is the Self. The pure mind is beyond the impure mind.

D.: Seen with the subtlest of subtle intellect by subtle seers.

M.: What was said of mind applies to this also.

D.: If trance be my natural state, why is it said that trance is necessary to be got before Realisation?

M.: That means that one should be aware of his eternal state of trance. Inattentiveness to it is ignorance. *Pramado vai mrtyuh* (inattention is death itself).

D.: How can I be attentive without getting trance beforehand?

M.: Very well. If you are so anxious for trance any narcotic will bring it about. Drug-habit will be the result and not liberation. There are *vasanas* in the latent state even in trance. The *vasanas* must be destroyed.

Another devotee: Can there be Self-Realisation before the *vasanas* are entirely destroyed?

M.: There are two kinds of *vasanas:* (1) *bandha hetuh,* causing bondage for the ignorant, and (2) *bhoga hetuh,* giving enjoyment for the wise. The latter do not obstruct realisation.

D.: Are the Self-realised persons reborn? *e.g.,* Vamadeva, Jada Bharata, etc.

M.: The Realised ones cannot be reborn. Rebirth is due to *vasanas* which are binding. But they are destroyed in the state of Self-realisation.

D.: Are we to take it that they had gone to the stage of *kevala nirvikalpa* but not to *sahaja nirvikalpa?*

M.: Yes.

D.: If only *vasanas* for enjoyment do not obstruct the state of realisation and if one can look upon the events of the world without his state of bliss being disturbed, it means that attachment alone is bondage. Am I right?

M.: Yes, quite. Attachment is bondage. Attachment disappears with the elimination of the ego.

D.: Realisation is said to be helped by Guru's Grace.

M.: Guru is none other than the Self.

D.: Krishna had Sandipini for his Guru and so Rama had Vasishta.

M.: Guru is said to be external for the seeker. The in-turn of the mind is brought about by the Guru. Since the seeker is out-ward-bent he is advised to learn from a Guru whom he will in due course find to be the Self.

D.: May I have Guru's Grace?

M.: Grace is always there.

D.: But I did not feel the same.

M.: Surrender will make one understand the Grace.

D.: I have surrendered heart and soul. I am the best judge of my heart. Still I do not feel the Grace.

293

M.: If you had surrendered the questions would not arise.

D.: I have surrendered. Still the questions arise.

M.: Grace is constant. Your judgement is the variable. Where else should the fault lie?

D.: I must be enabled to surrender myself.

M.: Thayumanavar has said: "Glory to Thee for enabling me to discuss so much and follow Thy words so far!"

7th January, 1937

Talk 318.

A Hindi gentleman asked how the fear of death could be got over.

M.: Find out if you were born before you think of death. Only he who is born could die. You are as good as dead even in sleep. What fear is there of death?

D.: How are we in sleep?

M.: Ask the question in sleep. You recall the experience of sleep only when you are awake. You recall that state by saying "I slept happily".

D.: What is the instrument by which we experience that state?

M.: We call it *Mayakarana* as opposed to the *antahkarana* to which we are accustomed in our other states. The same instruments are called differently in the different states, even as the *anandatman* of sleep is termed the *vijnanatman* of the wakeful state.

D.: Please furnish me with an illustration for the *mayakarana* experiencing the *ananda*.

M.: How can you say "I slept happily"? The experience is there to prove your happiness. There cannot be the remembrance in the wakeful state in the absence of the experience in the sleep state.

D.: Agreed. But please give me an illustration.

M.: How can it be described? If you dive into water for recovering an article you speak of its recovery only after rising out of the water. You do not say anything while remaining sunk in water.

D.: I do not have fear in sleep whereas I have it now.

M.: Because *dwiteeyadvai bhayam bhavati* — fear is always of a second one. Of what are you afraid?

D.: By reason of the perception of the body, the senses, the world, *Isvara*, doership, enjoyment etc.

M.: Why do you see them if they cause fear?

D.: Because they are inescapable.

M.: But it is you who sees them. For whom is the fear? Is it for them?

D.: No, it is for me.

M.: Because you see them, you fear them. Do not see them and there will be no fear.

D.: What then should I do in the waking state?

M.: Be the Self; there will be no second thing to cause you fear.

D.: Yes. Now I understand. If I see my Self, then the sight is warded off the non-self and there is happiness. Yet there is the fear of death.

M.: Only the one who is born should die. See if you have been born at all in order that death should threaten you.

Talk 319.

Mr. Sridhar, a Hindu from Goa, asked: What is *kousalam* (skill) in *Yogah karmasu kousalam* (yoga is skill in action). How is that gained?

M.: Do actions without caring for the result. Do not think that you are the doer. Dedicate the work to God. That is the skill and also the way to gain it.

D.: Samatvam yoga uchyate (Equanimity is yoga). What is that equanimity?

M.: It is unity in diversity. The universe is now seen to be diverse. See the common factor (*sama*) in all the objects. When that is done equality in the pairs of opposites (*dwandwani*) naturally follows. It is the latter which is however spoken of as equanimity ordinarily.

D.: How is the common factor to be perceived in the diversity?

M.: The seer is only one. They do not appear without the seer. There is no change in the seer, however much the others may change.

Yogah karmasu kousalam = Skill in work is yoga,

Samatvam yoga uchyate = Equanimity is yoga,

Mamekam saranam vraja = Only surrender to Me,

Ekamevadwiteeyam = Only one without a second,

representing Karma, Yoga, *Bhakti* and *Jnana* convey the same meaning. They are only the single Truth presented in different aspects.

Mr. Ekanatha Rao: Is Grace necessary for it?

M.: Yes.

D.: How to gain Divine Grace?

M.: By surrender.

D.: Still I do not feel Grace.

M.: Sincerity is wanting. Surrender should not be verbal nor conditional.

Passages from St. Justinian were read out to illustrate these statements.

Prayer is not verbal. It is from the heart. To merge into the Heart is prayer. That is also Grace.

The Alwar says: "I was all along seeking Thee. But on realising the Self I find you are the Self. The Self is my all, and so you are my All."

D.: Impurities of limitation, ignorance and desire (*anava, mayika,* and *kamya*) place obstacles in the way of meditation. How to conquer them?

M.: Not to be swayed by them.

D.: Grace is necessary.

M.: Yes, Grace is both the beginning and the end. Introversion is due to Grace: Perseverance is Grace; and Realisation is Grace. That is the reason for the statement: *Mamekam saranam vraja* (only surrender to Me). If one has entirely surrendered oneself is there any part left to ask for Grace? He is swallowed up by Grace.

D.: The obstacles are powerful and obstruct meditation.

M.: If a Higher Power is recognised and surrendered to, how will they obstruct you? If you say "They are powerful," the source of their Power must be held so that they do not obstruct you.

Talk 320.

In the course of an informal conversation Sri Bhagavan pointed out that Self-Realisation is possible only for the fit. The *vasanas* must be eliminated before *jnana* dawns. One must be like Janaka for *jnana*

296

to dawn. One must be ready to sacrifice everything for the Truth. Complete renunciation is the index of fitness.

Talk 321.

D.: Miseries appear in *jagrat*. Why should they appear.

M.: If you see your Self they will not appear.

D.: If I turn to look who I am I do not find anything.

M.: How did you remain in your sleep? There was no 'I-thought' there and you were happy. Whereas there are thoughts flowering in the wake of the root-thought 'I' in the *jagrat* and these hide the inherent happiness. Get rid of these thoughts which are the obstacles to happiness. Your natural state is one of happiness as was evident in your sleep.

D.: I do not know anything of my sleep experience.

M.: But you know that it was happiness. Otherwise you would not be saying "I slept happily". When there is no thought, no 'I', and nothing In fact except yourself, you are happy. That is the whole Truth.

This is exactly what is conveyed by the Mahavakya *Tatvamasi* (You are That). Find your Self: and then "That" is known.

D.: How is that Brahman?

M.: Why do you want to know of Brahman apart from yourself? The scripture says "You are That". The Self is intimate to you and you cannot indeed be without the Self. Realise it. That is the Realisation of Brahman also.

D.: But I am unable to do it. I am too weak to realise my Self.

M.: In that case surrender yourself unreservedly and the Higher Power will reveal Itself.

D.: What is unconditional surrender?

M.: If one surrenders oneself there will be no one to ask questions or to be thought of. Either the thoughts are eliminated by holding on to the root-thought 'I' or one surrenders oneself unconditionally to the Higher Power. These are the only two ways for Realisation.

Talk 322.

A cultured lady, daughter of a well-known solicitor of Madras asked: What should one do in order to remain free from thoughts as advised by you? Is it only the enquiry "Who am I?"

M.: Only to remain still. Do it and see.

D.: It is impossible.

M.: Exactly. For the same reason the enquiry "Who am I?" is advised.

D.: Raising the question, no response comes from within.

M.: What kind of response do you expect? Are you not there? What more?

D.: Thoughts rise up more and more.

M.: Then and there raise the same question, "Who am I?"

D.: Should I do so as each thought arises? Well. Is the world our thought only?

M.: Leave this question to the world. Let it ask, "How did I come into being?"

D.: Do you mean that it is not related to me?

M.: Nothing is perceived in deep sleep; all these are seen only after waking; only after thoughts arise the world comes into being; what can it be but thought?

Another visitor asked: What should we do to make the mind still?

M.: First let the mind be caught hold of and brought here: then we shall consider ways and means of stilling it.

D.: I meant to say that it is always changing — even when we do our *japa*.

M.: Japa is meant only for stilling the mind.

D.: What *japa* is good for it?

M.: Anything suitable, such as *Gayatri*.

D.: Will *Gayatri do*?

M.: Can anything excel it? Only those who cannot do it look for others. It contains the whole range of truth in it. Chanting (*japa*) will lead to *dhyana* (meditation) and it is the means for realising the Self.

D.: Will half an hour a day do for it?

M.: It must be done always, or as long as you can.

Talk 323.

While explaining stanza 6 in *Arunachala Ashtaka*, Sri Bhagavan observed as follows:

298

The final word in the previous stanza asks, "Is there one?" The initial words in the present stanza answer, "Yes, there is the One....." It proceeds, "Though it is the only One, yet by its wonderful power it gets reflected on the tiny dot 'I' (the ego) otherwise known as ignorance or the aggregate of latent tendencies; this reflected light is relative knowledge. This, according to one's *prarabdha* (past karma now fructifying), manifests the inner latent tendencies as the outer gross world and withdraws the gross external world as the subtle internal tendencies; such power is called mind in the subtle plane and brain in the physical plane. This mind or brain acts as the magnifier to that Eternal One Being and shows It forth as the expanded universe. In the waking and dream states the mind is out-ward bent and in sleep it is in-ward bent; with the mind as the medium, the one Supreme Being seems diversified in the waking and dream states and remains withdrawn in the sleep state, or swoon, etc. Therefore you are only That and cannot be otherwise. Whatever the changes, the same one Being remains as yourself; there is nothing besides yourself."

The previous stanza says: Once exposed to sunlight, a sensitive plate cannot take on images; similarly, the mind (the sensitive plate), after exposure in Your Light, cannot reflect the world anymore. Moreover, the Sun is of You only. Should his rays be so powerful as to prevent images being formed, how much more so should Your Light be? It is thus said that there is nothing apart from the One Being, Yourself.

In the present stanza the tiny dot = the ego; the tiny dot made up of darkness = the ego consisting of latent tendencies, the seer or the subject or the ego rising, it expands itself as the seen, the object or the *antahkaranas* (the inner organs). The light must be dim in order to enable the ego to rise up. In broad daylight a rope does not look like a snake. The rope itself cannot be seen in thick darkness; so there is no chance of mistaking it for a snake. Only in dim light, in the dusk, in light darkened by shadows or in darkness lighted by dim light does the mistake occur of a rope seeming a snake. Similarly it is for the Pure Radiant Being to rise up as the Ego — it is possible only in Its Light diffused through darkness. This darkness is otherwise known as the Original Ignorance (Original Sin). The Light passing through it is called Reflected Light. The Reflected Light on its own merits is commonly known as the Pure Mind or *Isvara* or God. *Isvara* is well-known to be unified with *Maya:* in other words the Reflected Light is *Isvara*.

The other name — Pure Mind — implies impure mind also. It is the *rajasic* or active mind or the ego; this too can be projected from the former *satvic* mind through another reflection only; thus the ego is the product of the second darkness (*avidya*) Then comes the *tamasic* or the dull mind in the shape of *antahkaranas* (the inner organs); this appears as the world.

From the standpoint of the gross body it may be said to shine forth externally as the world by means of the brain.

But the gross body is of the mind only. The mind may be said to consist of four inner organs, or the principle composed of thoughts, or the sixth sense; or combining intellect with the ego, and *chitta* with the mind (*i.e.* memory-faculty with the thinking faculty), it may be taken to consist of two parts (the ego and the mind). In the latter case the *vijnanatma* (the intellectual Self) or the ego or the seer forms the subject, and the mental sheath or the seen, the object.

The waking, dream and sleep states have their origin in the Original Darkness (*mula avidya*). With the mind outgoing and deriving experiences from its modes in the waking and dream states, and indrawn in sleep, experiencing with modes of *Maya*, a unique power regulates all activities of the individuals and of the universe. All these are only phenomena passing through the Reflected Light on the substratum of the Self-radiant Being.

Just as a rope-snake cannot be seen in broad daylight, nor rope itself in thick darkness, so also the world appears neither in the *samadhi* state of Self-shining pure Being or in deep sleep, swoon, etc. Only in Reflected Light (Light mixed with Darkness or knowledge soiled by Ignorance) can the world, *not independent of its Source*, seem to rise up, flourish and be resolved. Its diversity too cannot be exclusive of the Reality, the original Source. Here a play is going on in which the One Single Being becomes manifold is objectified and then withdrawn. There must be a *Sakti* (Power) to do it, and wonderful too! She cannot also be independent of Her origin. In the Self-shining Pure Being this *Sakti* cannot be seen. Nevertheless, Her actions are only too well-known. How sublime!

From Her sublime original activity (*i.e.*, power vibrating) *satva*-filled reflection results; from it the *rajasic* ego; then *tamasic* thought-forms which are commonly known as knowledge, or the light corresponding to the magnifying lens. Just as the artificial light is projected through a lens on to the screen, so also the Reflected Light passes through thought (the magnifier) before expanding as the world beyond it; furthermore, thought, itself the world in seed form, seems to be the wide external world. Such is the extraordinary Power! In this way *Isvara*, individual and the world are only of the Reflected Light, having the Self-shining Single Being for the substratum.

Now, what is this 'I-thought' (the ego)? Is it the subject or the object, in the scheme of things?

Inasmuch as it witnesses all other objects in the waking and dream states, or at any rate we think that it does so, it must be considered to be the subject. On realising the Pure Self, however, it will be an object only.

Whose is this 'I-thought' (the ego)? This investigation forms the *vichara*.

'I-thought' and 'this'-thought are both emanations from the same light. They are related to *rajoguna* and *tamoguna* respectively. In order to have the Reflected Light (pure *satva*), free from *rajas* and *tamas* it must shine forth as 'I-I', unbroken by 'this'-thought. This pure state momentarily intervenes between sleep and waking. If prolonged it is cosmic consciousness, or even *Isvara*. This is the only passage to the Realisation of the Self-shining Supreme Being.

Again there are two kinds of experiences in deep sleep as recollected after waking, that is, "I slept *happily, unaware* of anything". Happiness and ignorance are the experiences. Thus we see the Power modified as (1) *avarana* (darkness) and (2) *vikshepa* (diversity). The mind is the result of *vikshepa*.

301

SOME REMINISCENCES

Talk 324.

(1) While in Skandasramam, Sri Bhagavan saw a white toad, small and long, at a distance of about 10 feet from Him. Sri Bhagavan stared at it and it stared at Him. Suddenly, it took a long jump and lodged itself precisely on one of the eyes of Sri Bhagavan who quickly closed it and so it was not injured.

(2) There were two peacocks which used to strut with their feathers spread out like a spangled fan. A cobra too used to take part in the pastime and raised its hood and moved about in their midst.

(3) Sri Bhagavan says that the peacock, as soon as it sights a green lizard, goes straight to it and meekly places its neck down before the lizard which bites it off and kills the peacock.

(4) Rangaswami Iyengar was once out on the hill. A leopard was nearby. He threw a stone. It turned towards him. He hurried away for his life. Sri Bhagavan met him on the way and asked what the matter was. Iyengar simply said 'leopard' as he was running. Sri Bhagavan went where the beast was and it moved away soon after. All this happened at the time of the plague. Leopards used to roam freely by the side of the temple, sometimes in twos and threes.

(5) Sri Bhagavan said, "A frog is often compared to a yogi. It remains quiet for a long time, the only sign of life being the rhythmic movement of the under-skin below the neck."

"Again frogs can remain for extraordinary long periods with their animation suspended. They are said to swallow their tongues. Swallowing the tongue is a yogic practice. The animation is suspended. The yogi does not die but the tongue must be drawn out by someone else before life-activity is resumed. It is a wonder how the frog brings out the already swallowed tongue and resumes activity."

11th January, 1937

(6) While reading "Raghuveeran" — *Ramayana* written in easy Malayalam prose — there was a passage relating how Hanuman

302

reached Lanka mentally before he crossed over physically to that island. Sri Bhagavan emphasised the point that the mental approach accomplishes the purpose earlier than physical action.

(7) Sri Bhagavan related the following funny anecdote; Ezhuthachan, a great Malayali saint and author, had a few fish concealed in him when he entered the temple. Some enemy reported it to the worshippers in the temple. The man was searched and taken to the king. The king asked him "Why did you take the fish into the temple"? He replied: "It is not my fault. I had it concealed in my clothes. The others exposed the fish in the temple. The fault lies in exposure. Excreta within the body are not considered filthy; but when excreted, they are considered filthy. So also with this."

12th January, 1937

Talk 325.

Mr. Rama Sastri from Guntur District composed eight slokas on Sri Bhagavan and read them out with feeling.

The Sastri then prayed for guidance. "I am a *samsari* unfit for *jnana marga.* The affairs of the world are distracting me. Please instruct me what I should do."

M.: Think of Bhagavan. How will the affairs of the world distract Him? You and they are in Him.

D.: May I do *nama smarana*? What *nama* shall I take?

M.: You are Rama Sastri. Make that name significant. Be one with Rama.

13th January, 1937

Talk 326.

In answer to a question by a long resident attendant Sri Bhagavan said: "Everybody complains of the restlessness of the mind. Let the mind be found and then they will know. True, when a man sits down to meditate thoughts rush up by dozens. The mind is only a bundle of thoughts. The attempt to push through the barrage of thoughts is unsuccessful. If one can by any means abide in the Self it is good.

For those who are unable to do so, chanting or meditation (*Japa or dhyana*) is prescribed. It is like giving a piece of chain to an elephant to hold in its trunk. The trunk of the elephant is usually restless. It puts it out in all directions when taken out in the streets of the town. If given a chain to carry the restlessness is checked. Similarly with the restless mind. If made to engage in *japa* or *dhyana*, other thoughts are warded off: and the mind concentrates on a single thought. It thus becomes peaceful. It does not mean that peace is gained without a prolonged struggle. The other thoughts must be fought out.

Here is another illustration. Suppose a cow plays rogue and strays into neighbours' fields to graze. She is not easily weaned from her stealthy habit. Think how she can be kept in the stall. If forcibly tethered in the stall she simply bides her time to play the rogue. If she is tempted with fine grass in the stall she takes one mouthful on the first day and again waits for the opportunity to run away. The next day she takes two mouthfuls; so she takes more and more on each succeeding day, until finally she is weaned from her wicked tendencies. When entirely free from bad habits she might be safely left free and she would not stray into neighbours' pasture land. Even when beaten in the stall, she does not afterwards leave the place. Similarly with the mind. It is accustomed to stray outward by the force of the latent *vasanas* manifesting as thoughts. So long as there are *vasanas* contained within they must come out and exhaust themselves. The thoughts comprise the mind. Searching what the mind is, the thoughts will recoil and the seeker will know that they arise from the Self. It is the aggregate of these thoughts that we call 'mind'. If one realises that the thoughts arise from the Self and abide in their source, the mind will disappear. After the mind ceases to exist and bliss of peace has been realised, one will find it then as difficult to bring out a thought, as he now finds it difficult to keep out all thoughts. Here the mind is the cow playing the rogue; the thoughts are the neighbours' pasture; one's own primal being free from thoughts is the stall.

The bliss of peace is too good to be disturbed. A man fast asleep hates to be awakened and ordered to mind his business. The bliss of sleep is too enthralling to be sacrificed to the work born of thoughts. The thought-free state is one's primal state and full of bliss. Is it not miserable to leave such a state for the thought-ridden and unhappy one?

If one wants to abide in the thought-free state, a struggle is inevitable. One must fight one's way through before regaining one's original primal state. If one succeeds in the fight and reaches the goal, the enemy, namely the thoughts, will all subside in the Self and disappear entirely. The thoughts are the enemy. They amount to the creation of the Universe. In their absence there is neither the world nor God the Creator. The Bliss of the Self is the single Being only.

When Prahlada was in *samadhi*, Vishnu thought within Himself: "This *asura* being in *samadhi*, all the *asuras* are in peace. There is no fight, no trial of strength, no search for power, nor the means for gaining power. In the absence of such means for power — *yaga, yajna*, etc., *i.e.*, the gods are not thriving; there is no new creation; nor even is any existence justified. So I will wake him up; then the *asuras* will rise up; their original nature will manifest itself; the gods will challenge them: the *asuras* and others will then seek strength and adopt the means for its acquisition. *Yajnas*, etc., will flourish; the gods will thrive; there will be more and more of creation, more of fight and I shall have enough to do".

So Vishnu awakened Prahlada, blessing him with eternal life and *jivanmukti*. *Deva-asura* fight was resumed and the old order of things was restored so that the universe continues in its eternal nature.

D.: How could God Himself wake up the *asura* element and bring about constant warfare? Is not Pure Goodness the nature of God?

M.: Goodness is only relative. Good always implies bad also; they always co-exist. The one is the obverse of the other.

Talk 327.

The audience in the hall were very attentively listening. One of them, a sincere devotee of Sri Bhagavan, was so impressed by it that he soon lost himself. He later described his experience as follows:

"I was long wondering where the 'current' starts, within the body or elsewhere. Suddenly, my body grew tenuous until it disappeared.

The enquiry 'Who am I?' went on very clearly and forcibly. The sound of 'I-I-I' alone persisted. There was one vast expanse and nothing more. There was a hazy perception of the occurrences in the hall. I knew that people stood up to salute at the end of the Vedic chant. I wanted to stand: the thought soon deserted me. I was again lost in the one expanse. The experience continued until I heard the voice of Sri Bhagavan. That made me collect myself. Then I stood up and saluted. A strange feeling continued for more than half an hour. I cannot forget it. It is still haunting me."

Sri Bhagavan listened to his words and was silent for some minutes. A few observations fell from his lips:

One may seem to go out of the body. But the body itself is not more than our thought. There can be no body in the absence of thought; no outgoing or incoming in absence of body. However, owing to habit, the feeling of going out arises.

A particle of hail falling on the surface of the sea melts away and becomes water, wave, froth, etc., in the sea. Similarly, the subtle intellect, rising up as the tiny dot (ego) from the heart and bulging out, finally enters into and becomes one with the Heart.

Though milk remains as wide as the sea, can you drink it with a mouth as wide as the sea? You can suck it only through the tiny capillaries of the paps.

Nammalvar, the Vaishnavite saint, has said: "Only my Self is you". What does it mean? "Before I realised my Self I was wandering looking out for You; having now realised my Self I see that you are my Self". How will this fit in with qualified monism? It must be explained thus: "Pervading my Self you remain as the *antaryamin* (Immanent Being). Thus I am a part of your body and you are the owner of the body (*sariri*)"

Having given up one's own body as not being oneself why should one become another's (God's) body? If one's body is not the Self other bodies also are non-self. The protagonists of qualified monism think that individuality is necessary to experience the Bliss. Individuality, *i.e.*, 'I-ness' should not be lost. Aha! The Self is not the body but your Self becomes the body of God! Is it not absurd?

306

Or if you make *prapatti* (surrender yourself) to God, you have made yourself over to Him and you are His and no longer yours. If He is in need of a body let Him look out for Himself. You need not say He is the owner of a body.

Talk 328.

A European gentleman began in measured tones and spoke clearly and slowly: "Why should individuals remain caught up in the affairs of this world and reap troubles as a result? Should they not be free? If they are in the spiritual world they will have greater freedom."

M.: The world is only spiritual. Since you are identifying yourself with the physical body you speak of this world as being physical and the other world as spiritual. Whereas, that which is, is only spiritual.

D.: Do the disembodied souls, *i.e.*, the spirits, have a deeper insight and enjoy greater freedom?

M.: Because you identify yourself with this body, you speak of the disembodied souls as being spirits. From these limitations you talk of their limitations and seek to know their capacities. Even the disembodied souls have subtle bodies, otherwise, you would not say "disembodied souls". Disembodiment means "divested of this gross body". Inasmuch as you endow them with individuality they are centred in their subtle bodies. Their limitations will be according to their own state. Just as you feel the burden of your limitations they also feel the burden of their limitations. What I meant by spirit and spiritual world is the absolute spirit and not relative. If you realise yourself as the spirit you will see that this world is only spiritual and not physical.

D.: Are their bodies temporary as our bodies are? Do they reincarnate?

M.: These questions arise because you think yourself the body. This body has birth and death and when this body falls another body arises which is called reincarnation. But are you the body? If you find that you are not this body but the spirit, you will be free from gross or subtle bodies, and then there will be no limitations. Where is

307

the world, physical or spiritual, in the absence of any limitations? How will the question of reincarnation arise?

Again, consider it from another point of view: You create a dream-body for yourself in the dream and act with that dream-body. The same is falsified in the waking state. At present you think that you are this body and not the dream-body. In your dream this body is falsified by the dream-body. So that, you see, neither of these bodies is real. Because each of them is true for a time and false at other times. That which is real must be real for ever. But you say 'I'. This 'I'-consciousness is present all through the three states. There is no change in it. That is alone real. The three states are false. They are only for the mind. It is the mind which obstructs your vision of your true nature. Your true nature is that of infinite spirit. That was the case in your sleep. You note the limitations in the other two states. What is the difference due to? There was no mind in sleep, but it exists in the dream and the waking states. The feeling of limitation is the work of the mind. What is mind? Find it. If you search for it, it will vanish by itself. For it has no real existence. It is comprised of thoughts. It disappears with the cessation of thoughts.

D.: Do I remain then?

M.: What is your experience in sleep? There were no thoughts, no mind, and yet you remained then.

D.: When I try to meditate, I am unable to do so because my mind wanders. What should I do?

M.: Your question furnishes the answer. First, with regard to the first part of the question, you say you concentrate, but do not succeed. 'You' means 'the Self'. On what do you concentrate? Where do you fail? Are there two selves, for the one self to concentrate on the other? Which is the self now complaining of failure? There cannot be two selves. There is only one Self. That need not concentrate.

You ask, "But then, why is there no happiness?" What is it that prevents you from remaining as the spirit which you are in sleep? You yourself admit that it is the wandering mind. Find out the mind. If its 'wandering' stops, it will be found to be the Self — your 'I'-consciousness which is spirit eternal. It is beyond knowledge and ignorance.

D.: I am hard-worked and find little time to practise concentration. Are there any aids for it? Is control of breath a good aid?

M.: Prana and mind arise from the same source. The source can be reached by holding the breath or tracing the mind. If you cannot do the latter the former will no doubt be helpful. Regulation of breath is gained by watching its movements.

If the mind is watched thoughts cease. Peace results and it is your true nature. King Janaka said: "I have now found the robber (namely the mind) who has been robbing me of my 'I'-ness. I will instantly kill this thief." The perturbation owing to thoughts appears to rob the Self of its peace. The perturbation is the mind. When that ceases the mind is said to take flight. The Self remains as the undisturbed substratum.

Another person interposed: The mind must kill the mind.

M.: Yes, if there be the mind. A search for it discloses its non-existence. How can anything that does not exist be killed?

D.: Is not mental *japa* better than oral *japa*?

M.: Oral *japa* consists of sounds. The sounds arise from thoughts. For one must think before one expresses the thoughts in words. The thoughts form the mind. Therefore mental *japa* is better than oral *japa*.

D.: Should we not contemplate the *japa* and repeat it orally also?

M.: When the *japa* becomes mental where is the need for the sounds thereof?

Japa, becoming mental, becomes contemplation. *Dhyana*, contemplation and mental *japa* are the same. When thoughts cease to be promiscuous and one thought persists to the exclusion of all others it is said to be contemplation. The object of *japa* or *dhyana* is the exclusion of several thoughts and confining oneself to one single thought. Then that thought too vanishes into its source — absolute consciousness, *i.e.*, the Self. The mind engages in *japa* and then sinks into its own source.

D.: The mind is said to be from the brain.

M.: Where is the brain? It is in the body. I say that the body itself is a projection of the mind. You speak of the brain when you think of the body. It is the mind which creates the body, the brain in it and also ascertains that the brain is its seat.

309

D.: Sri Bhagavan has said in one of the works that the *japa* must be traced to its source. Is it not the mind that is meant?

M.: All these are only the workings of the mind. *Japa* helps to fix the mind to a single thought. All other thoughts are first subordinated until they disappear. When it becomes mental it is called *dhyana.* *Dhyana* is your true nature. It is however called *dhyana* because it is made with effort. Effort is necessary so long as thoughts are promiscuous. Because you are with other thoughts, you call the continuity of a single thought, meditation or *dhyana.* If that *dhyana* becomes effortless it will be found to be your real nature.

Talk 329.

In the morning Sri Bhagavan read out a short passage from St. Estella in the Tamil *Ramakrishna Vijayam.* Its purport is: "Your enemies are lust, passion, etc. If you feel injured turn within and find out the cause of the injury. It is not external to you. The external causes are mere superimpositions. If you cannot injure yourself, will the all-merciful God injure you in any manner?"

Sri Bhagavan further said that St. Estella was a good saint, whose teachings were quite sound.

Talk 330.

Sri Bhagavan, being asthmatic, is hoarse in throat. Oranges were brought as offerings. Pieces were distributed as usual. Sri Bhagavan was clearing His throat and was obliged to spit out the orange in His mouth. He said that He had to spit it out. A gentleman said: "Probably, it does not suit Sri Bhagavan's health."

M.: Would you say so if you had brought the fruits, instead of the other person?

18th January, 1937

Talk 331.

Mrs. Roorna Jennings, an American lady of the International Peace League, asked Sri Bhagavan about the spread of Peace in the world.

Sri Bhagavan replied that if one gains the Peace of the Self it will spread itself without any effort on the part of the individual.

When one is not oneself peaceful, how can that one spread peace in the world?

The lady asked if it was not true that the East has a scientific approach to the Realisation of the Self.

M.: You are already the Self. No elaborate science is necessary to establish it.

D.: I understand the general truth of it. But there must be a practical method for it which I call 'science'.

M.: The cessation of such thoughts is the realisation of the Self. Illustration: the necklace supposed lost. One does not see the world or one's own body, being away from the Self. Always being the Self, one sees everything else. God and the world are all in the Heart. See the Seer and everything will be found to be the Self. Change your outlook. Look within. Find the Self. Who is the substratum of the subject and the object? Find it and all problems are solved.

The lady was then told of the pamphlet, *Who am I?* She agreed to read it before asking further questions of Sri Bhagavan.

Talk 332.

D.: What are the three voids (*Muppazh*) (முப்பாழ்) in Tamil?

M.: (1) *Tat* = *Isvara turiya.*

(2) *tvam* = *jiva turiya.*

(3) *asi* = *asi turiya.*

Turiya is the substratum of the waking, dream and sleep states.

D.: The first two are all right; what is the third?

M.: All-pervasiveness is said to be the waking;

all-shiningness is said to be the dream;

perfection (*ananta*) is said to be the sleep;

that which underlies these is *asi-turiya.*

D.: It is so strange!

M.: Is that all? There is no limit to polemics. Listen, They say the mahavakya *Tattvamasi* is common; another containing five words *Tat tvam asi ati nijam* is the most secret one taught by Dakshinamurti in Silence; corresponding to the five words they formulate five states. Again look at *Vichara Sagara*; the author distinguishes *adhara* from

311

adhishthana. According to him the rope is always *adhara* both when it looks like a snake and otherwise. The rope is *adhishthana* because it looks different from what it really is: that is common (*samanya adhishthana*). Again its appearance as the snake itself is *visesha adhishthana.* Then the question is raised: the *adhishthana of Jiva* is one; that of *Isvara* is another; how can these two *adhishthanas* become one? He replies, there are the same *adhara* for both the *adhishthanas.* Furthermore he mentions several *khyatis;*

(1) *asat-khyati:* rope being present, there appears the snake which is *not present* there.

(2) *sat-khyati:* rope itself looking like snake.

(3) *atma-khyati:* rope remaining unidentified, the remembrance of snake, formerly seen elsewhere, creates the illusion.

(4) *akhyati:* totally unreal.

(5) *anayatha-khyati:* mental image of snake projected and seen as if it were in front of oneself.

(6) *anirvachaniya-khyati:* inexplicable.

Here he raises the question: Should the world be any one of these, whether illusory or unreal; it must be the result of previous experience. It must have been real at that time: real once, must be real always.

He answers it: the experience need not necessarily be real; not having seen a real snake, but only seeing a picture of it and gaining an impression, one can mistake a rope to be a snake. Thus the world need not be real.

Why waste time in such polemics? Only turn your mind inward and spend the time usefully.

In the union of the individual with the Supreme, the Supreme is hearsay and the individual directly experienced. You can make use only of direct experience; therefore look who you are.

Why is *Isvara* mentioned then?

Because you see the world and want to know how it came into being. They say that it was created by God. If you know that He created you and all else, your mind is a little satisfied and becomes less restless than otherwise. But it is not realisation. It can be only if you realise yourself; this is Perfection or Realisation, etc.

312

To resume polemics — the author of *Vritti Prabhakara* claims to have studied 350,000 books before writing this book. What is the use? Can they bring in Realisation of the Self? *Vichara Sagara* is full of logic and technical terms. Can these ponderous volumes serve any real purpose? However, some people read them and then seek sages only to see if they can meet their questions. To read them, to discover new doubts and to solve them, is a source of pleasure to them. Knowing it to be sheer waste, the sages do not encourage such people. Encourage them once and there will be no end.

Only the enquiry into the Self can be of use.

Those familiar with logic, *Vritti Prabhakara, Vichara Sagara* or *Sutra Bhashya*, or similar large works, cannot relish small works like *Truth Revealed* dealing only with the Self and that pointedly too, because they have accumulated *vasanas*. Only those whose minds are less muddy, or are pure, can relish small and purposeful works.

Talk 333.

Pratyabhijna = Prati + abhijna.

abhijna is direct perception; *prati* is to be reminded of what was already known.

"*This is an elephant*" direct perception

"*This is that elephant*" is *pratyabhijna*

In technical works, *pratyabhijna* is used for realising the ever-present Reality and recognising it.

Sunya (void or blank), *ati sunya* (beyond *sunya*) and *maha sunya* (immense void), all mean the same, *i.e.*, the Real Being only.

20th January, 1937

Talk 334.

Sri Bhagavan said that he felt no sensation in His legs though they were massaged. "If they serve the purpose of walking what does it matter if sensation is lost?" he asked. Then in the course of conversation he related that a ray of light has been found which, when projected, does not reveal the operator but enables him to witness the scene. So it is with *siddhas*. They are only pure light and

313

can see others, whereas, they cannot be seen by others. For example Prabhulinga, while touring in the North, came across Goraknath. The latter displayed his yogic powers *e.g.*, when his arm was cut by a sword, the sword was blunted without inflicting injury on him. This is making the body proof against injury (*kayasiddhi*). Prabhulinga offered himself to be cut. When the sword was thrust, it passed through and through his body as if it was air and there was no injury on the body. Gorak was astonished and offered himself as the disciple of Prabhulinga.

Again, there was a dialogue between Siva and Parvati in Kailas. Siva said that Allama was one who would not be affected by Her blandishments. Parvati wanted to try it and so sent Her *tamasic* quality to incarnate as a king's daughter on the Earth in order that she might entice Allama. She grew up as a highly accomplished girl. She used to sing in the temple. Allama used to go there and play on the drum. She lost herself in the play of the drum. She fell in love with him. They met in her bedroom. When she embraced him he became intangible. She grew lovesick. But a celestial damsel was sent to remind her of her purpose on the Earth. She resolved to overthrow Allama but did not succeed. Finally she went up to Kailas. Then Parvati sent Her *satvic* quality who was born as a Brahman *sanyasini*. When she surrendered to Allama she realised his true greatness.

Sri Bhagavan spoke very appreciatively of Nayana, *i.e.*, Kavyakantha Ganapathi Muni, for about an hour, how he wrote *Uma Sahasram* and *Hara Sahasram*, how he taught his students, how he engaged in dispute with Bhattasri Narayana Sastri, how meek and humble he was though so learned and capable, etc.

Sri Bhagavan related how Nakkirar, a Sanga Pulavar (Poet), faced the wrath of Siva on questioning some composition of Siva in Tamil, how he was taken captive by a spirit and afterwards released.

Nakkirar was doing *tapas* on the bank of a *tirtha*. A leaf fell down from a tree; half the leaf touched the water and the other half was on the ground. Suddenly the water-half became a fish and the land-half became a bird. Each of them was united to the other by the leaf and struggled to go into its own element. Nakkirar was watching it in wonder and suddenly a spirit came down from above and carried him away to a cave where were already 999 captives all of whom were *tapo bhrashta* (those who had fallen away from their austerities).

D.: Was Nakkirar a *tapo bhrashta?*

M.: Yes. While engaged in contemplation why did he fall away from contemplation and take to watching the mysterious happening in front of him?

He continued to say how Nakkirar composed *Tirumuruhatruppadai,* and obtained the release of all the thousand prisoners.

21st January, 1937

Talk 335.

D.: How will the sexual impulse cease to be?

M.: When differentiation ceases.

D.: How can it be effected?

M.: The other sex and its relation are only mental concepts. The Upanishad says that all are dear because the Self is beloved of all. One's happiness is within; the love is of the Self only. It is only within; do not think it to be without: then differentiation ceases to operate.

22nd January, 1937

Talk 336.

A certain Vaisya who seems to have studied the Upanishads and Srimad Bhagavad Gita asked some questions:

D.: How to realise the Self?

M.: The Self is always directly perceived. There is no moment when it is not so. How then is it to be ascertained? Find out the Self. You are that.

D.: But it is said the heart-knots are cut away and all doubts end when the Supreme is found. The word *drishti* is used.

M.: To be the Self is the same as seeing the Self. There are no two selves for the one to see the other.

Later, he continued the same question of investigation of the Self.

D.: How to realise the Self?

M.: It is already realised. One should know this simple fact. That is all.

D.: But I do not know it. How shall I know it?

M.: Do you deny your existence?

D.: No: how can that be done?

M.: Then the truth is admitted.

D.: Yet, I do not see. How shall I realise the Self?

M.: Find out who says 'I'.

D.: Yes. I say 'I'.

M.: Who is this 'I'? Is it the body or some one besides the body?

D.: It is not the body. It is someone besides it

M.: Find it out.

D.: I am unable to do it. How shall I find it?

M.: You are now aware of the body. You were not aware of the body in deep sleep. Still you remained in sleep. After waking up you hold the body and say "I cannot realise the Self". Did you say so in your sleep? Because you were undivided (*akhanda*) then, you did not say so. Now that you are contracted within the limits of the body you say "I have not realised". Why do you limit your Self and then feel miserable? Be of your true nature and happy. You did not say 'I' in sleep. You say so now. Why? Because you hold to the body. Find out wherefrom this 'I' comes. Then the Self is realised.

The body being insentient cannot say 'I'. The Self being infinite cannot say 'I' either. Who then says 'I'?

D.: I do not yet understand. How to find the 'I'?

M.: Find out where from this 'I' arises. Then this 'I' will disappear and the infinite Self will remain. This 'I' is only the knot between the sentient and the insentient. The body is not 'I', the Self is not 'I'. Who, then, is the 'I'? Wherefrom does it arise?

D.: Where from *does* it arise?

M.: Find out.

D.: I do not know. Please enlighten me.

M.: It is not from without. It is from within. Where does it come from? If elsewhere you can be led there. Being within, you must find it out yourself.

D.: From the head?

316

M.: Does the concept of 'head' arise after the 'I' or does 'I' arise from the head? If 'I' be in the head why do you bend it when sleep overpowers you? 'I' is ever constant. So also must its seat be. If the head bends at one time and is erect at another time how can it be the seat of 'I'? Your head is laid flat in sleep. When awake it is raised up. Can it be the 'I'?

D.: Which is it then?

M.: 'I' comes from within. When asleep there is no 'I'. Just before waking there is 'I-thought'.

D.: The heart-knot is said to be between the eyebrows.

M.: Some say "between the eyebrows"; others "at the coccyx", and so on. All these are from the standpoint of the body.

The body comes after the 'I-thought'.

D.: But I cannot divest myself of the body.

M.: So you admit that you are not the body.

D.: If there is pain in this body, I feel it; but not if another body is injured. I cannot get over this body.

M.: This identity is the cause of such feeling. That is the *hrdaya granthi* (heart-knot).

D.: How is this knot to go?

M.: For whom is the knot? Why do you want it to go? Does it ask or do you ask?

D.: It cannot ask; I am asking.

M.: Who is that 'I'? If that is found the knot will not remain.

D.: The knot is concomitant with the body. The body is due to birth. How is rebirth to cease?

M.: Who is born? Is the Self born? Or is it the body?

D.: It is the body.

M.: Then let the body ask how its rebirth may cease.

D.: It will not ask. So I am asking.

M.: Whose is the body? You were without it in your deep sleep. After the 'I-thought' arose the body arose. The first birth is that of 'I-thought'. The body has its birth subsequent to 'I-thought'. So its birth is secondary. Get rid of the primary cause and the secondary one will disappear by itself.

317

D.: How is that 'I-thought' to be checked from rising?

M.: By Self-quest.

D.: I try to understand but without success. Can I find the Self by means of *japa*? If so, please tell me how.

M.: What *japa*? Why should you make artificial *Japa*? You can find out the eternal and natural *japa* always going on within you.

D.: Some *upadesh* will probably help me.

M.: If I say "Do — Rama, Rama" to one who has not struggled through books like you, he will do it and stick to it. If I say so to one like you who have read much and are investigating matters, you will not do it for long, because you will think, "Why should I do it? Above all, who am I that should be repeating the *mantra*? Let me find who I am before I proceed further"; and so you will stop *japa* and begin investigation.

D.: It is said: The senses are out-going (*paranchikhani*); inward turned (is) sight (*avrittachakshuh*). What is *avrittachakshuh* (inward-turned sight)?

M.: It does not mean replacement of the eyeball in the opposite direction. What is *chakshuh*?

D.: The eye.

M.: Does the eye see or is it someone behind the eye that sees? If the eye could see, then does a corpse see? The one who is behind the eye sees through the eye. He is meant by the word *chakshuh*.

D.: *Divya chakshuh* is necessary to see the glory of God. This physical eye is the ordinary *chakshuh*.

M.: Oh! I see. You want to see million-sun-splendour and the rest of it!

D.: Can we not see the glory as million-sun-splendour?

M.: Can you see the single sun? Why do you ask for millions of suns?

D.: It must be possible to do so by divine sight. "Where the sun shines not, etc. That is My Supreme abode". Therefore there is a state where this sun is powerless. That state is that of God.

M.: All right. Find Krishna and the problem is solved.

D.: Krishna is not alive.

M.: Is that what you have learnt from the Gita? Does He not say that He is eternal? Of what are you thinking, His body?

D.: He taught others while alive. Those around Him must have realised. I seek a similar living Guru.

M.: Is Gita then useless after He withdrew His body? Did He speak of His body as Krishna?

Natwewaham jatu nasam ... (Never I was not....)

D.: But I want a living Guru who can say the truth first hand.

M.: The fate of the Guru will be similar to the fate of Krishna.

The questioner retired. Later, Sri Bhagavan said: Divine sight means Self-luminosity. The world *divya* shows it. The full word means the Self. Who is to bestow a divine eye? And who is to see? Again, people read in the books, "hearing, reflection and one-pointedness are necessary". They think that they must pass through *savikalpa samadhi* and *nirvikalpa samadhi* before attaining Realisation. Hence all these questions. Why should they wander in that maze? What do they gain at the end? It is only cessation of the trouble of seeking. They find that the Self is eternal and self-evident. Why should they not get that repose even this moment?

A simple man, not learned, is satisfied with *japa* or worship. A *jnani* is of course satisfied. The whole trouble is for the book-worms. Well, well. They will also get on.

Talk 337.

Mr K. R. V. Iyer: How is the mind to be purified?

M.: The *sastras* say: "By karma, *bhakti* and so on". My attendant asked the same question once before. He was told, "By karma dedicated to God". It is not enough that one thinks of God while doing the karma, but one must continually and unceasingly think of Him. Then alone will the mind become pure.

The attendant applies it to himself and says, "It is not enough that I serve Sri Bhagavan physically. But I must unceasingly remember Him".

To another person, who asked the same question, Bhagavan said: Quest of the Self, meaning, 'I am-the-body' idea must vanish. (*Atma vichara* = disappearance of *dehatma buddhi*)

319

Talk 338.

Mrs. Jennings, an American lady, asked a few questions:

D.: Is not affirmation of God more effective than the quest, "who am I?" Affirmation is positive, whereas the other is negation. Moreover, it indicates separateness.

M.: So long as you seek to know how to realise, this advice is given to find your Self. Your seeking the method denotes your separateness.

D.: Is it not better to say 'I am the Supreme Being' than ask 'Who am I?'

M.: Who affirms? There must be one to do it. Find that one.

D.: Is not meditation better than investigation?

M.: Meditation implies mental imagery, whereas investigation is for the Reality. The former is objective, whereas the latter is subjective.

D.: There must be a scientific approach to this subject.

M.: To eschew unreality and seek the Reality is scientific.

D.: I mean there must be a gradual elimination, first of the mind, then of the intellect, then of the ego.

M.: The Self alone is Real. All others are unreal. The mind and intellect do not remain apart from you.

The Bible says, "Be still and know that I am God". Stillness is the sole requisite for the realisation of the Self as God.

D.: Will the West ever understand this teaching?

M.: There is no question of time and space. Understanding depends on ripeness of mind. What does it matter if one lives in the East or in the West?

Sri Bhagavan referred the lady to a few stanzas in *Truth Revealed* and to *Thayumanavar.* She retired.

Later Sri Bhagavan said the whole Vedanta is contained in the two Biblical statements:

"I am that I AM" and "Be still and know that I am God."

Mr. K. S. N. Iyer, a Railway Officer, said to Sri Bhagavan that the compiler of *Cosmic Consciousness* considers realisation to be possible only within certain limits of age in an individual's life.

M.: Does anyone say "I must come into being before or after some age?" He is here and now. Statements like this are misleading because people come to believe that they cannot realise the Self in this incarnation and must needs take chances in another. It is all absurd.

Talk 339.

With regard to *Siva Visishtadvaita, (i.e., Saiva Siddhanta)*, Sri Bhagavan said: *Garudoham bhavana* 'I am Garuda' — conception does not make a *garuda* of a man. All the same the poisonous effects of snake-bite are cured. Similarly with *Sivoham bhavana* (I-am-Siva) conception also. One is not transformed into Siva, but the ruinous effects of the ego are put an end to. Or the person retains his individuality but remains pure, *i.e.*, fit for constituting a part of the body of Siva. Becoming so he can enjoy the Supreme Bliss. That is liberation — say the *Saiva Siddhantis*. This simply betrays the love of their individuality and is in no way the true experience of liberation.

Talk 340.

Mr. Bose began, "After the return of body-consciousness ..."

M.: What is body-consciousness? Tell us that first. Who are you apart from consciousness? Body is found because there is body-consciousness which arises from 'I'-consciousness which again rises from consciousness.

Consciousness → 'I-consciousness' → body-consciousness → body.

There is always consciousness and nothing but that. What you are now considering to be body-consciousness is due to superimposition. If there is only consciousness and nothing but it, the meaning of the Scripture *Atmanastu kamaya sarvam priyam bhavati* — (All are dear because of the love of the Self) becomes clear.

A question arises, why there should be suicides in that case. Why does one do it? Because he is unhappy and desires to put an end to his unhappiness. He actually does it by ending the association with the body which represents all unhappiness. For there must be a killer to kill the body. He is the survivor after suicide. That is the Self.

Talk 341.

Mrs Jennings: Sri Bhagavan says that the state of Realisation is freedom from the tyranny of thoughts. Have not the thoughts got a place in the scheme of things — maybe on a lower plane?

M.: The thoughts arise from the 'I-thought' which in its turn arises from the Self. Therefore the Self manifests as 'I' and other thoughts. What does it matter if there are thoughts or no thoughts?

D.: Are good thoughts helpful for Realisation? Are they not authentic *via media*, a lower rung of the ladder, to Realisation?

M.: Yes — this way. They keep off bad thoughts. They must themselves disappear before the state of Realisation.

D.: But are not creative thoughts an aspect of Realisation and therefore helpful?

M.: Helpful only in the way said before. They must all disappear in the Self. Thoughts, good or bad, take you farther and not nearer, because the Self is more intimate than thoughts. You are Self, whereas the thoughts are alien to the Self.

D.: So the Self finally absorbs its own creation which had helped its Realisation. Whereas civilisation wrongly worships and so separates and 'short-circuits' its own creations which had helped its advance.

M.: Are you not distinct from thoughts? Do you not exist without them? But can the thoughts exist without you?

D.: Is civilisation generally, slowly but surely, advancing in the right direction towards this Self-Realisation?

M.: Civilisation is in the order of things. It will finally resolve itself — as all others — in the Realisation of the Self.

D.: Is a fine type of primitive man nearer to Realisation than a civilised man governed by intellect and thought?

M.: A realised man may look a savage, but a savage is not a realised man.

D.: Is it right to think that *all* that happens to us are God's ordainment, and therefore only good?

M.: Of course it is. Yet all others and God are not apart from the Self. How can thoughts of them arise when you remain as the Self?

D.: Is 'surrender' accepting all physical annoyances such as ants, mosquitoes, snakes, etc., and, in accepting, willing or ceasing to be really hurt by them?

M.: Whatever it is, is it apart from you, the seer or the thinker?

A Parsi lady from the audience intervened: If they are not apart, do we not feel the sting of the ants?

M.: Whom does the ant sting? It is the body. You are not the body. So long as you identify yourself with the body, you see the ants, plants, etc. If you remain as the Self, there are not others apart from the Self.

D.: The body feels the pain of the sting.

M.: If the body feels it, let it ask. Let the body take care of itself. How does it matter to you?

The American lady again: Does complete surrender mean that all noise and disturbance in our environment, even during meditation, must be accepted? Or should we seek a cave in a mountain for solitude? Did not Bhagavan do this?

M.: There is no going or returning. The Self is said to be unaffected by the elements, infinite, eternal. It cannot move. There is no place to move in for the Self.

D.: But, in the process of finding the Self, is this seeking external help spiritually legitimate?

M.: The error lies in the identification of the Self with the body. If Bhagavan is the body you may ask that body. But understand him whom you address as Bhagavan. He is not the body. He is the Self.

Then she referred to an article in *Harijan* where it is said that everything is God and nothing belongs to the individual, and so on.

M.: Everything, the individual, God and all are only the Self.

Then she read some lines from Shelley and asked if Shelley was not a realised soul.

> Within a cavern of man's trackless spirit
> Is throned an Image so intensely fair
> That the adventurous thoughts that wander near it
> Worship, and as they kneel, tremble and fear
> The splendour of its presence, and the light

Penetrates their dreamlike frame

Till they become charged with the strength of flame.

M.: Yes. The lines are excellent. He must have realised what he wrote.

The lady then thanked Sri Bhagavan and retired.

Talk 342.

At 11 p.m. in the night a group of Andhras came from Guntur, consisting of a middle-aged woman with a sad but firm look, her mother and two men. They requested audience with Sri Bhagavan.

The woman said to Sri Bhagavan:

"When my son was in the womb my husband died. The son was born posthumous. He grew up all right for five years. Then he was attacked by infantile paralysis. When nine he was bedridden. Nevertheless he was bright and cheerful. For two years he was in that condition and now they say that he is dead. I know that he is only sleeping and will awake soon. When they said that he had collapsed I was shocked. I saw in a vision a *sadhu* who appeared to pass his hands over the child's body and the child awoke refreshed. I believe that *sadhu* is yourself. Please come and touch the boy so that he may get up", she prayed.

Sri Bhagavan asked what the doctor said.

She replied, "They say that he is dead. But what do they know? I have brought the boy all the way from Guntur to this place".

Someone asked: "How? Is the corpse brought here?"

She: They said that the corpse would be taken by paying special rates at 1/2 rupee per mile. We have paid Rs. 150 for it, and brought it as luggage.

M.: If your vision be correct the boy will wake up tomorrow.

She: Please touch him. May I bring him into the compound?

The others protested and persuaded them to leave.

They left and the next morning the corpse was reported to have been cremated.

When asked, Sri Bhagavan said: It is said of some saints that they revived the dead. They, too, did not revive all the dead. If that could be done there will be no world, no death, no cemetery, etc.

324

One man asked: The mother's faith was very remarkable. How could she have had such a hopeful vision and still be disappointed? Can it be a superimposition attendant on her child's love?

M.: She and her child not being real, how can the vision alone be a superimposition?

D.: Then how is it to be explained?

No answer.

Talk 343.

D.: Even as the hand is cut off, one must remain unaware of it because Bhagavad Gita declares that the Self is different from the body.

M.: Does *jnana* consist in being unaware of the pain of injury?

D.: Should he not remain unaware of pain?

M.: Major operations are performed under anaesthetics, keeping the patient unaware of the pain. Does the patient gain *jnana* too, at the same time? Insensibility to pain cannot be *jnana*.

D.: Should not a *jnani* (a sage) be insensible to pain?

M.: Physical pain only follows body-consciousness; it cannot be in the absence of body-consciousness. Mind, being unaware of the body, cannot be aware of its pains or pleasures. Read the story of Indra and Ahalya in *Yoga Vasishta*; there death itself is said to be an act of mind.

Pains are dependent on the ego; they cannot be without the 'I', but 'I' can remain without them.

Talk 344

D.: *Vichara Sagara* relates four obstacles to Self-Realisation.

M.: Why only four? Some say they are nine. Sleep is one of them. What is sleep? It is only the obverse of waking. It cannot be independent of waking. Sleep is unalloyed Self. Do not think you are awake: sleep cannot be, nor the three states either. Only forgetting the Self you say you dreamt. Can anything exist in the absence of the Self? Why do you leave it out and hold the non-self?

As the mind tends to go out turn it inwards then and there. It goes out owing to the habit of looking for happiness outside oneself; but the knowledge that the external objects are not the cause of happiness will keep it in check. This is *vairagya* or dispassion. Only after perfect *vairagya* the mind becomes steady.

The mind is only a mixture of knowledge and ignorance or of sleep and waking. It functions in five ways:

Kshipta (active);

Moodha (dull);

Vikshipta (distracted);

Kashaya (latent); and

Ekagrya (one-pointed).

Of these *kashaya* is only the latency of tendencies and not the tendencies themselves such as attachment, repulsion, etc.

Yourself being *ananda* (Bliss), why should you enjoy it saying, "Ah! How blissful!" This is *rasasvada.*

During the marriage ceremonies a virgin feels happy as a bride without experiencing the embrace of man: this is *rasasvada.*

D.: Jivanmukti (liberated while alive) itself being *ananda* . . . .

Sri Bhagavan interrupted: Do not look for *sastras.* What is *jivanmukti?* What is *ananda?* Liberation itself is in doubt. What are all these words? Can they be independent of the Self.

D.: Only we have no experience of all this.

M.: What is not, is always lost; what is, is ever present, here and now. This is the eternal order of things. Example: necklace round the neck.

Talk 345.

Sri Bhagavan continued, after interval: Destroy the power of mind by seeking it. When the mind is examined its activities cease automatically.

Looking for the source of mind is another method. The source may be said to be God or Self or consciousness.

Concentrating on one thought, all other thoughts disappear; finally that thought also disappears. It is necessary to be *aware* while controlling thoughts, otherwise it will lead to sleep.

D.: How to seek the mind?

326

M.: Breath-control may do as an aid but can never lead to the goal itself. While doing it mechanically, take care to be alert in mind and remember the 'I-thought' and seek its source. Then you will find that where breath sinks, there the 'I-thought' arises. They sink and rise together. The 'I-thought' also will sink along with breath. Simultaneously another luminous and infinite "I-I" will manifest and it will be continuous and unbroken. That is the goal. It goes by different names — God, Self, *Kundalini-Sakti*, consciousness etc., etc.

When the attempt is made it will of itself take you to the goal.

Talk 346.

Free will and Destiny last as long as the body lasts. But wisdom transcends both, for the Self is beyond knowledge and ignorance.

Talk 347.

The mind is a bundle of thoughts. The thoughts arise because there is the thinker. The thinker is the ego. The ego, if sought, will automatically vanish. The ego and the mind are the same. The ego is the root-thought from which all other thoughts arise.

Talk 348.

D.: There are times when persons and things take on a vague, almost transparent form, as in a dream. One ceases to observe them as from outside, but is passively conscious of their existence, while not actively conscious of any kind of selfhood. There is a deep quietness in the mind. Is it, at such times, ready to dive into the Self? Or is this condition unhealthy, the result of self-hypnotism? Should it be encouraged as a means of getting temporary peace?

M.: There is consciousness along with quietness in the mind; this is exactly the state to be aimed at. The fact that the question has been framed on this point, without realising that it is the Self, shows that the state is not steady but casual.

The word 'diving' is appropriate to the state of outgoing tendencies when the mind is to be diverted and turned within so as to dive below the surface of externalities. But when deep quietness prevails without obstructing the consciousness, where is the need to dive? If the state be not realised as the Self, the effort to do so may be called 'diving'. The state may in that way be said to be suitable for realisation or 'diving'. Thus the last two questions in the paragraph are unnecessary.

D.: The mind continues to feel partial towards children, possibly because of the form sometimes used to personify the Ideal. How can this preference be outgrown?

M.: Hold the Self. Why think of children and reactions towards them?

D.: This third visit to Tiruvannamalai seems to have intensified the sense of egoism in me and made meditation less easy. Is this an unimportant passing phase or a sign that I should avoid such places hereafter?

M.: It is imaginary. This place or another is within you. Such imaginations must end so that the places have nothing to do with the activities of the mind. Even your surroundings are not of your own accord; they are there as a matter of course. You must rise above them and not get yourself involved.

Talk 349.

SRI SANKARA'S PATH TO SALVATION THROUGH DISCRIMINATION

A NOTE BY SRI MAHARSHI

(In the current issue of *The Vision* is published the following note, being the translation by Mr. S. Krishna, M. A., of Sri Ramana Maharshi's preface to his translation of Sri Sankara's *Viveka Chudamani* or "Crown-gem of Discrimination").

Every being in the world yearns to be always happy, free from the taint of sorrow; and desires to get rid of bodily ailments which are not of his true nature. Further, everyone cherishes the greatest love for himself: and this love is not possible in the absence of happiness. In deep sleep, though devoid of everything, one has the experience of being happy. Yet, due to the ignorance of the real nature of one's own being, which is happiness itself, people flounder in the vast ocean of material existence forsaking the right path that leads to happiness and act under the mistaken belief that the way to be happy consists in obtaining the pleasures of this and the other world.

A SAFE GUIDE: But alas, that happiness which has not the taint of sorrow is not realised. It is precisely for the purpose of pointing out the straight path to happiness that God Siva took on the guise of Sri Sankaracharya, wrote the commentaries on the Triune Institutes (*Prasthana Traya*) of the Vedanta, which extol the excellence of this bliss; and demonstrated it by his own example in life. These commentaries, however, are of little use to those ardent seekers who are intent upon realising the bliss of absolution, but have not the scholarship for studying them.

It is for such as these that Sri Sankara revealed the essence of the commentaries in this short treatise, "The Crown-gem of Discrimination", explaining in detail the points that have to be grasped by those who seek absolution, and thereby directing them to the true and straight path.

LEARNING WON'T DO: Sri Sankara opens the theme by observing that it is hard indeed to attain human birth, and one should (having attained it) strive for the realisation of the bliss of liberation, which is verily the nature of one's being. By *jnana* or Knowledge alone is this bliss realised, and *jnana* is achieved only through *vichara* or steady enquiry. In order to know this method of enquiry, says Sri Sankara, one should seek the favour of a Guru, and proceeds to describe the qualities of the Guru and his *sishya* and how the latter should approach and serve his master. He further emphasises that in order to realise the bliss of liberation one's own individual effort is an essential factor. Mere book-learning never yields this bliss which can be realised only through enquiry or *vichara*, which consists of *sravana* or devoted attention to the precepts of the Guru, *manana* or deep contemplation and *Nididhyasana* or the cultivation of steady poise in the Self.

THE THREE PATHS: The three bodies — physical, subtle and causal — are non-self and are unreal. The Self, or 'I', is quite different from them. It is due to ignorance that the sense of the Self or the 'I' notion is foisted on that which is not Self, and this indeed is bondage. Since from ignorance arises bondage, from Knowledge ensues liberation. To know this from the Guru is *sravana.*

To reject the three bodies consisting of the five sheaths (physical, vital, mental, gnostic and blissful) as not 'I' and to extract through subtle enquiry of "Who am I?" — even as the central blade of grass is delicately drawn out from its whorl — that which is different from all the three bodies and is existent as one and universal in the heart as *Aham* or 'I' and denoted by the words *Tvam* (in the Scriptural dictum — '*Tat-tvam-asi*' — That thou art). This process of subtle enquiry is *manana* or deep contemplation.

THE BEATITUDE: The world of name and form is but an adjunct of *Sat* or Brahman, and being not different from it is rejected as such and is affirmed as nothing else but Brahman. The instruction by the Guru to the disciple of the *Mahavakya, Tat-tvam-asi,* which declares the identity of the Self and the Supreme, is *upadesa.* The disciple is then enjoined to remain in the beatitude of *Aham-Brahman* — 'I' the Absolute. Nevertheless the old tendencies of the mind sprout up thick and strong and form an obstruction (to that state of beatitude). These tendencies are threefold and egoism, which is their root, flourishes in the externalised and differentiating consciousness caused by the forces of *vikshepa* or dissipation (due to *rajas*) and *avarana* or envelopment (due to *tamas*).

CHURNING THE MIND: To install the mind firmly in the heart until these forces are destroyed and to awaken with unswerving, ceaseless vigilance the true and cognate tendency which is characteristic of the Atman and is expressed by the dicta, *Aham Brahmasmi* (I am Brahman), and *Brahmaivaham* (Brahman alone am I) is termed *nididhyasana* or *atmanusandhana, i.e.,* constancy in the Self. This is otherwise called *Bhakti,* Yoga and *Dhyana.*

Atmanusandhana has been likened to churning the curd to draw forth butter, the mind being compared to the churning rod, the heart to the curd and the practice of constancy in the Self to the process of churning. Just as by churning the curd butter is extracted and by friction fire is kindled, even so, by unswerving vigilant constancy in the Self, ceaseless like the unbroken filamentary flow of oil, is generated the natural or changeless trance or *nirvikalpa samadhi*, which readily and spontaneously yields that direct, immediate, unobstructed and universal perception of Brahman, which is at once Knowledge and Experience and which transcends time and space.

LIMITLESS BLISS: This is Self-Realisation; and thereby is cut asunder the *hridaya-granthi* or the Knot of the Heart. The false delusions of ignorance, the vicious and age-long tendencies of the mind, which constitute this knot, are destroyed. All doubts are dispelled and the bondage of Karma is severed.

Thus has Sri Sankara described, in this "Crown-gem of Discrimination," *samadhi* or trance transcendent, which is the limitless bliss of liberation, beyond doubt and duality, and has at the same time indicated the means for its attainments. To realise this state of freedom from duality is the *summum bonum* of life: and he alone that has won it is a *jivanmukta* (the liberated one while yet alive), and not he who has merely a theoretical understanding of what constitutes *purushartha* or the desired end and aim of human endeavour.

FINAL FREEDOM: Thus defining a *jivanmukta*, he is declared to be free from the bonds of threefold Karmas (*sanchita, agami* and *prarabdha*). The disciple who has reached this stage then relates his personal experience. The liberated one is free indeed to act as he pleases, and when he leaves the mortal frame, attains absolution, and returns not to this "birth which is death".

Sri Sankara thus describes Realisation that connotes liberation as twofold, *i.e., jivanmukti* and *videha mukti* referred to above. Moreover, in this short treatise, written in the form of a dialogue between a Guru and his disciple, he has considered many relevant topics.

6th February, 1937

Talk 350.

While speaking to Mr. G. Shanmugham, a very sincere lawyer devotee, Bhagavan observed:

The *sastras* say that one must serve a Guru for 12 years for getting Self-Realisation. What does Guru do? Does he hand it over to the disciple? Is not the Self always realised? What does the common belief mean then? The man is always the Self and yet he does not know it. He confounds it with the non-self, *viz.,* the body etc. Such confusion is due to ignorance. If ignorance be wiped out the confusion will cease to exist and the true knowledge will be unfolded. By remaining in contact with realised sages the man gradually loses the ignorance until its removal is complete. The eternal Self is thus revealed.

This is the meaning conveyed by the story of Ashtavakra and Janaka. The anecdotes differ in different books. We are not concerned with the names and the embellishments. The *tatva, i.e.,* the moral, must not be lost sight of. The disciple surrenders himself to the master. That means there is no vestige of individuality retained by the disciple. If the surrender is complete all sense of individuality is lost and there is thus no cause for misery. The eternal being is only happiness. That is revealed.

Without understanding it aright, people think that the Guru teaches the disciple something like "TATVAMASI" and that the disciple realises "I am Brahman". In their ignorance they conceive of Brahman as something more huge and powerful than anything else. With a limited 'I' the man is so stuck up and wild. What will be the case if the same 'I' grows up enormous? He will be enormously ignorant and foolish! This false 'I' must perish. Its annihilation is the fruit of Guru *seva*. Realisation is eternal and it is not newly brought about by the Guru. He helps in the removal of ignorance. That is all.

7th February, 1937

Talk 351.

Dr. Subramania Iyer, Retired Health Officer of Salem, read out a passage which contained the instructions that one should know that the world is transitory, that worldly enjoyments are useless, that one should therefore turn away in disgust from them, restrain the senses and meditate on the Self to realise it.

Sri Bhagavan observed: How does one know the world to be transitory? Unless something permanent is held, the transitory nature of the world cannot be understood. Because the man is already the

Self, and the Self is the Eternal Reality, his attention is drawn to it; and he is instructed to rivet his attention on the Eternal Reality, the Self.

Talk 352.

THE DIFFERENT CREEDS

The thought rises up as the subject and object. 'I' alone being held, all else disappears. It is enough, but only to the competent few.

The others argue, "Quite so. The world that exists in my sleep has existed before my birth and will exist after my death. Do not others see it? How can the world cease to be if my ego appears not?" The genesis of the world and the different schools of thought are meant to satisfy such people.

D.: Nevertheless, being only products of intellect they cannot turn the mind inward.

M.: Just for this reason the scriptures speak of "in-turned look", "one-pointed look" and so on.

The Self being always the Self, why should only a *dhira* be illumined? Does it mean a man of courage? No; *dhih* = intellect; *rah* = watch; protection. So *dhira* is the one who always keeps the mind inward bent without letting it loose.

8th February, 1937

Talk 353.

D.: What is *turiya*?

M.: There are three states only, the waking, dream and sleep. *Turiya* is not a fourth one; it is what underlies these three. But people do not readily understand it. Therefore it is said that this is the fourth state and the only Reality. In fact it is not apart from anything, for it forms the substratum of all happenings; it is the only Truth; it is your very Being. The three states appear as fleeting phenomena on it and then sink into it alone. Therefore they are unreal.

The pictures in a cinema show are only shadows passing over the screen. They make their appearance; move forward and backward; change from one to another; are therefore unreal whereas the screen all along remains unchanged. Similarly with paintings: the images are unreal and the canvas real. So also with us: the world-phenomena, within or without, are only passing phenomena not independent of our Self. Only the habit of looking on them as being real and located outside ourselves is responsible for hiding our true being and showing forth the others. The ever-present only Reality, the Self, being found, all other unreal things will disappear, leaving behind the knowledge that they are no other than the Self.

Turiya only another name for the Self. Aware of the waking, dream and sleep states, we remain unaware of our own Self. Nevertheless the Self is here and now, it is the only Reality. There is nothing else. So long as identification with the body lasts the world seems to lie outside us. Only realise the Self and they are not.

Talk 354.

An American lady, a theosophist, asked: What is the means by which my approach to my master may be made nearer?

M.: How far away are you now from him?

D.: I am away from him. But I want to get closer to him.

M.: If you first know your Self, you may then find out how far away the other is. Who are you now? Are you the personality?

D.: Yes, I am the personality.

M.: Is the personality independent of the Self?

D.: Sometimes.

M.: At what times?

D.: I mean I have some flashes of the reality and, at other times, I do not have them.

M.: Who is aware of those flashes?

D.: I, I mean my personality.

M.: Is this personality aware as being apart from the Self?

D.: Which Self?

M.: Which do you consider the personality to be?

D.: The lower self.

M.: Then I mean to ask if the lower self is aware independently of the Higher Self?

D.: Yes, at times

M.: Who feels that she is away from the master, just now?

D.: The Higher Self.

M.: Does the Higher Self have a body and say that the master is away from it? Does it speak through your mouth? Are you apart from that?

D.: Can you kindly advise me how I can train myself to be aware of what I do even without the body, as in sleep?

M.: Awareness is your nature. In deep sleep or in waking, it is the same. How can it be gained afresh?

D.: But I do not remember what and how I did in my sleep.

M.: Who says "I do not remember"?

D.: I say now.

M.: You were the same then; why do you not say so in sleep?

D.: I do not remember what I say in sleep.

M.: You say, "I know, I remember", in the wakeful state. This same personality says "I did not know — I did not remember in sleep". Why does not this question arise in sleep?

D.: I do not know what happens in sleep. That is the reason I ask now.

M.: The question affects the sleeping phase and must be raised there. It does not affect the waking phase and there is no apparent reason for this question.

The fact is that you have no limitations in sleep and no question arises. Whereas now you put on limitations, identify yourself with the body and questions of this kind arise.

D.: I understand it, but do not realise it (i.e. unity in variety).

M.: Because you are in variety, you say you understand unity — that you have flashes, etc., remember things, etc.; you consider this variety to be real. On the other hand Unity is the reality, and the variety is false. The variety must go before unity reveals itself — its reality. It is always real. It does not send flashes of its being in this false variety. On the contrary, this variety obstructs the truth.

Then some others pursued the conversation.

M.: Removal of ignorance is the aim of practice, and not acquisition of Realisation. Realisation is ever present, here and now.

335

Were it to be acquired anew, Realisation must be understood to be absent at one time and present at another time. In that case, it is not permanent, and therefore not worth the attempt. But Realisation is permanent and eternal and is here and now.

D.: Grace is necessary for the removal of ignorance.

M.: Certainly. But Grace is all along there. Grace is the Self. It is not something to be acquired. All that is necessary is to know its existence. For example, the sun is brightness only. He does not see darkness. Whereas others speak of darkness fleeing away on the sun approaching. Similarly, ignorance also is a phantom and not real. Because of its unreality, its unreal nature being found, it is said to be removed.

Again, the sun is there and also bright. You are surrounded by sunlight. Still if you would know the sun you must turn your eyes in his direction and look at him. So also Grace is found by practice alone although it is here and now.

D.: By the desire to surrender constantly, increasing Grace is experienced, I hope.

M.: Surrender once for all and be done with the desire. So long as the sense of doership is retained there is the desire; that is also personality. If this goes the Self is found to shine forth pure.

The sense of doership is the bondage and not the actions themselves.

"Be still and know that I am God." Here stillness is total surrender without a vestige of individuality. Stillness will prevail and there will be no agitation of mind. Agitation of mind is the cause of desire, the sense of doership and personality. If that is stopped there is quiet. There 'Knowing' means 'Being'. It is not the relative knowledge involving the triads, knowledge, subject and object.

D.: Is the thought "I am God" or "I am the Supreme Being" helpful?

M.: "I am that I am." "*I am*" is God — not thinking, "I am God". Realise "*I am*" and do not think *I am*. "Know I am God" — it is said, and not "Think I am God."

336

Later Sri Bhagavan continued: It is said "I AM that I AM". That means a person must abide as the 'I'. He is always the 'I' alone. He is nothing else. Yet he asks "Who am I?" A victim of illusion would ask "Who am I?" and not a man fully aware of himself. The wrong identity of the Self with the non-self makes you ask, "Who am I?"

Later still: There are different routes to Tiruvannamalai, but Tiruvannamalai is the same by whichever route it is gained. Similarly the approach to the subject varies according to the personality. Yet the Self is the same. But still, being in Tiruvannamalai, if one asks for the route it is ridiculous. So also, being the Self, if one asks how to realise the Self it looks absurd. You are the Self. Remain as the Self. That is all. The questions arise because of the present wrong identification of the Self with the body. That is ignorance. This must go. On its removal the Self alone *is*.

Talk 355.

D.: Does not education make a sage more useful to the world than illiteracy?

M.: Even a learned man must bow before the illiterate sage.

Illiteracy is ignorance: education is learned ignorance. Both of them are ignorant of their true aim; whereas a sage is not ignorant because there is no aim for him.

Talk 356.

D.: Why should there be sleep in the world?

M.: Owing to sin only.

D.: Can it be destroyed?

M.: Yes.

D.: It ends only after making itself felt, they say.

M.: Why then devotion to God?

D.: How can sleep be destroyed?

M.: Be not aware of its activities and effects.

D.: How can it be done?

M.: Only by enquiry of the Self.

Talk 357.

Sri Bhagavan was recounting some of the incidents of His stay in Tiruvannamalai:

1. He was one day given a small speck of some substance on a leaf, to be licked off. It was said to be a good help for digestion. He licked it. Later He had His meal. After some time, the assembled persons appeared to be surrounded by Light (*tejomaya*). The experience passed away after some time.

2. While He was living in Pavalakunru. He intended to have a bath in one of the rills on the hillside. Palaniswami was informed of it. The news spread, that Jada Padmanabhaswami, who was living on the Hill, had arranged with Palaniswami to take Sri Bhagavan to the hill near his cottage. Palaniswami, without informing Sri Bhagavan, managed to take Him there. A great reception awaited Him. A seat was arranged for Him, milk and fruits were offered and J. P. waited on Him with great kindness.

3. J. P., though represented in the book *Self-Realisation* as having sought to injure Sri Bhagavan, was really kind to Him and his pranks were misunderstood to be acts of malice. His only weakness was that he wanted to make capital out of Sri Bhagavan for raising funds; which, of course, the Maharshi did not like. There was nothing wrong with J. P.

4. Madhavaswami, the attendant, asked if Sri Bhagavan remained without food for months in the underground cellar in the temple.

M.: Um! — Um! — food was forthcoming — Milk, fruits — but whoever thought of food.

5. While staying in the mango-tree cave Sri Bhagavan used to string garlands for the images in the temple, with lotuses, yellow flowers (*sarakonnai*) and green leaves.

6. After the completion of the Kalyanamantapam Sri Bhagavan had stayed there one night in disguise.

7. When He was sitting under a tree in the temple compound He was covered with dirt, for He never used to bathe. In the cold nights

of December He used to fold up the legs, place his head between his legs and remain there without moving. Early in the morning the layer of dirt on His body was soaked with dew and mist and appeared white. After drying up in the sun it appeared dark.

8. When living on the Hill Sri Bhagavan used to help in the *pooja* of J. P., ringing the bell, washing the vessels, etc., all along remaining silent. He also used to read medical works, *e.g.*, *Ashtanga Hridayam* in Malayalam and point out the treatment contained in the book for the patients who sought the other *sadhu's* help. That *sadhu* did not himself know how to read these works.

12th February, 1937

Talk 358.

A SCENE IN THE HALL

It is 8-20 p.m. Sri Bhagavan has returned after supper and stretched Himself on the sofa. The light is dim; there are three men sitting on the floor; one is busy copying something from a journal; another is wrapt in meditation; and the third is looking around, having nothing to do. The hall is silent but for occasional clearing of the throat by Sri Bhagavan.

Madhavaswami, the attendant devotee, slips in noiselessly with a sheaf of betels in hand. He moves to the table. Sri Bhagavan who is reclining on the sofa, sees him and calls out, yet kindly; "Sh, Sh; what are you doing?"

The attendant softly murmurs, "Nothing", leaves the betel there and fumbles hesitatingly.

M.: "I do not want it." (The attendant softly settles down on the floor). Sri Bhagavan: "Kasturi Pill — one after another, every day. The bottle will be empty — and more is ordered. I don't want it." A devotee skilfully blames the *olla podrida* (அவியல்) of the day-meal for the indifferent health of Sri Bhagavan.

M.: "No — no — It was well made. It was good." silence, but for expectoration and eructation. After a few minutes, the attendant slips out and returns with a bottle in hand, goes near Sri Bhagavan and stretches out a pill saying: "Cummin seed-pill". Sri Bhagavan softly

339

murmurs, "It contains lime juice: lime juice is not good for this." One devotee Rangaswamy Iyengar has in the meantime become wide awake from his meditation and looks on. The attendant is still holding out his hand with the pill. Sri Bhagavan continues: "Who is to munch it?"

Rangaswamy Iyengar: "It need not be munched. It may be kept in the mouth and sucked." The attendant hastily agrees. "Yes — yes it is only to be sucked."

M.: "Give it to him" pointing to Rangaswami Iyengar. "Let him munch it or suck it. I do not want it."

The attendant returns disappointed and squats on the floor; again rises up.

M.: "Eh! — Eh! What do you do? I do not want." The attendant moves up to the medicine chest, murmuring "Kasturi pill — it will be effective". Sri Bhagavan: "I shall soon be right even without it. Do not take it out. Eh! — Eh! — keep it there — I won't take it — do what you like." The attendant again settles down and all remain silent before retiring to bed.

13th February, 1937

Talk 359.

At about 7-30 a.m. Sri Bhagavan was climbing up the hill after breakfast. Padananda went and prostrated, stood up and said, "All right, I have had *darsan* ... I shall return."

Sri Bhagavan smilingly, "Whose *darsan*? Why don't you say that you gave *darsan* to me?"

At about 9 a.m. a devotee from Poona (Mr. Parkhi) saluted Sri Bhagavan and read out his *ashtaka* praying to Sri Bhagavan for Grace. The piece finishes with a prayer for quick liberation (*jhatiti mukti*) and the devotee emphasised it.

M.: Mukti, i.e., liberation, is not to be gained hereafter. It is there for ever, here and now.

D.: I agree, but I do not experience it.

M.: The experience is here and now. One cannot deny one's own self.

D.: That means existence and not happiness.

340

M.: Existence = happiness = Being. The word *mukti* (liberation) is so provoking. Why should one seek it? He believes that there is bondage and therefore seeks liberation. But the fact is that there is no bondage but only liberation. Why call it by a name and seek it?

D.: True — but we are ignorant.

M.: Only remove ignorance. That is all there is to be done.

14th February, 1937

Talk 360.

The aristocratic gentleman from Lucknow has written to Mr. Paul Brunton that his wife has since lost that peace of mind which she had gained by her visits to Sri Bhagavan; so he desires that Sri Bhagavan may be pleased to restore the same peace.

When requested, Sri Bhagavan said, "It is due to weakness of mind that peace once gained is later lost."

Talk 361.

Mudaliar Swami, son of the lady who brings *bhiksha* every day to Sri Bhagavan, related the following interesting incident:

During the time Sri Bhagavan was staying in Virupaksha Cave, Sri Bhagavan and Mudaliar Swami were walking together behind the Skandasramam site. There was a huge rock about 15 feet high; it was a cleft, a girl — (a shepherdess) — was standing there crying. Sri Bhagavan asked the reason of her sorrow. She said, "A sheep of mine has slipped into this cleft; so I am crying." Sri Bhagavan descended into the cleft, took the sheep on his shoulders, climbed up to the surface and delivered the sheep to her. Mudaliar Swami says that it was a very remarkable feat for any human being.

Talk 362.

Mr Subbaramiah, a college professor from Nellore, asked about *mukti.*

M.: All questions relating to *mukti* are inadmissible; because *mukti* means release from bondage which implies the present existence of bondage. There is no bondage and therefore no *mukti* either.

D.: The *sastras* speak of it and its grades.

341

M.: The *sastras* are not meant for the wise because they do not need them; the ignorant do not want them. Only the *mumukshus* look up to the *sastras*. That means that the *sastras* are neither for wisdom nor for ignorance.

D.: Vasishta is said to be a *jivanmukta* whereas Janaka was a *videhamukta*.

M.: Why speak of Vasishta or Janaka? What about oneself?

There were many new visitors this day. Two of them were speaking of Ganapati Muni in Sri Bhagavan's presence. Sri Bhagavan put in a few words in their talk:

(1) Some say that *jnana* and *upasana* are the two wings with which to fly to *mukti*. What is *jnana*? What is *upasana*? *Jnana* is ever present. That is the ultimate goal also. When an effort is made the effort is called *upasana*; when it is effortless it is *jnana*, which is the same as *mukti*.

(2) After some discussion among themselves, a visitor said: Some Superior Power must help us to shake off the externalities.

Sri Bhagavan said: Who sees the externalities? Or do they say that they exist? If so let the world say that it exists.

Again, if the world is a projection from the interior it must be recognised that it is projected simultaneously with the 'I-thought'.

Either way the 'I' is the fundamental basis knowing which all else is known.

(3) Another said that Ganapati Muni used to say that he could even go to Indra-loka and say what Indra was doing but he could not go within and find the 'I'.

Sri Bhagavan added that Ganapati Muni used to say that it was easy to move forward but impossible to move backward.

Then Sri Bhagavan remarked: However far one goes there he is. Where is moving backward? The same truth is contained in the *mantra* in Isa-Upanishad.

(4) In reply to a query how Ganapati Muni became an *asu kavi* (inspired poet), Sri Bhagavan said; It is said that while he was making *tapasya* Siva appeared and gave him milk or honey to drink, after which he became *asu kavi*.

342

20th February, 1937

Talk 363.

A European civilian, Mr. Dodwell, Deputy Secretary, Finance, Madras Government, arrived with his wife before 1 p.m. and stayed in the hall till about 3-30 p.m.

The lady asked: The spiritual leaders in the West say that the spiritual centre is in India. Is there any contact among the spiritual leaders in India? Or is contact possible between the leaders of the East and the West?

M.: What do you mean by spiritual centre?

D.: The spiritual centre is the seat of spiritual leaders.

M.: What do you understand by 'spiritual leaders'?

D.: In the West there is a crisis. Scientific knowledge is far advanced. Such knowledge is used for generating destructive forces. There is a movement for making them constructive. When thus diverted it will be for the good of the world. The leaders of this movement are the redeemers.

M.: By 'spiritual leaders' we understand those who are 'spiritual' as opposed to 'physical'. Spirit is unlimited and formless. Such too is the spiritual centre. There is only one such centre. Whether in the West or in the East the centre cannot differ; nor has it any locality. Being unlimited it includes the leaders, the men, the world, the forces of destruction and of construction. There is no differentiation. You speak of contact because you are thinking of the embodied beings as spiritual leaders. The spiritual men are not bodies; they are not aware of their bodies. They are only spirit, limitless and formless. There is always unity among them and all others; nay, they comprise all.

The spirit is the Self. If the Self is realised, these questions cannot arise at all.

Mrs. Jinarajadasa from Adyar: Self Realisation sounds so easy, but yet is so difficult in practice.

M.: What can be easier? The Self is more intimate than anything else. If that cannot be realised, is it easy to realise what is apart and farther away?

343

D.: Self Realisation is so illusory. How can it be made permanent?

M.: The Self can never be illusory. It is the only Reality. That which appears will also disappear and is therefore impermanent. The Self never appears and disappears and is therefore permanent.

D.: Yes — true. You know that, in the Theosophical Society, they meditate to seek the masters to guide them.

M.: The Master is within. Meditation is meant for the removal of ignorance, of the wrong idea that he is without. If he be a stranger whose advent you await he is bound to disappear also. Where is the use of transient being like that?

However, as long as you think that you are an individual or that you are the body, so long the master also is necessary and he will appear with a body. When this wrong identification ceases the master will be found to be the Self.

There is a stanza in *Kaivalya:*

"My Lord! You had remained as my Self within, protecting me in all my past incarnations. Now, by your Grace, you have manifested yourself as my master and revealed yourself as the Self ".

Just see what happens in sleep. There is no ego, no India, no seekers, no master, etc.; and yet you are — and happy too.

The ego, India, seekers, etc., appear now; but they are not apart from nor independent of you.

There was a large group of visitors on account of the election holidays and some of these also joined in the discussion.

One of them asked about reincarnation.

M.: Reincarnation can only be so long as there is ignorance. There is no incarnation either now, nor was there before, nor will be hereafter. This is the truth.

D.: What is the ego-self?

M.: The ego-self appears and disappears and is transitory, whereas the real Self always abides permanent. Though you are actually the true Self yet you wrongly identify the real Self with the ego-self.

D.: How does the mistake come about?

M.: See if it has come about.

D.: One has to sublimate the ego-self into the true Self.

344

M.: The ego-self does not exist at all.

D.: Why does it give us trouble?

M.: To whom is the trouble? The trouble also is imagined. Trouble and pleasure are only for the ego.

D.: Why is the world so wrapped up in ignorance?

M.: Take care of yourself. Let the world take care of itself. See your Self. If you are the body there is the gross world also. If you are spirit all is spirit alone.

D.: It will hold good for the individual, but what of the rest?

M.: Do it first and then see if the question arises afterwards.

D.: Is there *avidya*?

M.: For whom is it?

D.: For the ego-self.

M.: Yes, for the ego. Remove the ego; *avidya* is gone. Look for it, the ego vanishes. The real Self alone remains. The ego professing *avidya* is not to be seen. There is no *avidya* in reality. All *sastras* are meant to disprove the existence of *avidya*.

D.: How did the ego arise?

M.: Ego is not. Otherwise do you admit of two selves? How can there be *avidya* in the absence of the ego? If you begin to enquire, the *avidya* which is already non-existent, will be found not to be or you will say it has fled away.

Ignorance pertains to the ego. Why do you think of the ego and also suffer? What is ignorance again? It is that which is non-existent. However the worldly life requires the hypothesis of *avidya. Avidya* is only our ignorance and nothing more. It is ignorance or forgetfulness of the Self. Can there be darkness before the Sun? Similarly, can there be ignorance before the Self-evident and Self-luminous Self? If you know the Self there will be no darkness, no ignorance and no misery.

It is the mind which feels the trouble, misery, etc. Darkness never comes nor goes. See the Sun and there is no darkness. Similarly, see the Self and *avidya* will be found not to exist.

D.: Sri Ramakrishna and others practised concentration.

M.: Concentration and all other practices are meant for recognising the absence, *i.e.*, non-existence of ignorance. No one can deny his own

345

being. Being is knowledge, *i.e.*, awareness. That awareness implies absence of ignorance. Therefore everyone naturally admits non-existence of ignorance. And yet why should he suffer? Because he thinks he is this or that. That is wrong. "I am" alone is; and not "I am so and so", or "I am such and such". When existence is absolute it is right; when it is particularised it is wrong. That is the whole truth.

See how each one admits that he is. Does he look into a mirror to know his being? His awareness makes him admit his existence or being. But he confuses it with the body, etc. Why should he do so? Is he aware of his body in his sleep? No; yet he himself does not cease to be in sleep. He exists there though without the body. How does he know that he exists in sleep? Does he require a mirror to reveal his own being now? Only be aware, and your being is clear in your awareness.

D.: How is one to know the Self?

M.: "Knowing the Self" means "Being the Self". Can you say that you do not know the Self? Though you cannot see your own eyes and though not provided with a mirror to look in, do you deny the existence of your eyes? Similarly, you are aware of the Self even though the Self is not objectified. Or, do you deny your Self because it is not objectified? When you say "I cannot know the Self" it means absence in terms of relative knowledge, because you have been so accustomed to relative knowledge that you identify yourself with it. Such wrong identity has forged the difficulty of not knowing the obvious Self because it cannot be objectified; and you ask. "How is one to know the Self?" Your difficulty is centred in "How"? Who is to know the Self? Can the body know it?

Let the body answer. Who says that the body is perceived now?

In order to meet this kind of ignorance the *sastras* formulate the theory of God's *leela* or *krida* (*i.e.*, play). God is said to emanate as the mind, the senses and the body and to play. Who are you to say that this play is a trouble to you? Who are you to question the doings of God?

Your duty is *to be:* and not *to be this or that*. "I AM that I AM" sums up the whole truth. The method is summed up in "BE STILL". What does "stillness" mean? It means "destroy yourself". Because

346

any form or shape is the cause of trouble. Give up the notion that "I am so and so". Our *sastras* say: *ahamiti sphurati* (it shines as 'I').

D.: What is *sphurana* (shining)?

M.: (*Aham, aham*) 'I-I' is the Self; (*Aham idam*) "I am this" or "I and that" is the ego. Shining is there always. The ego is transitory; When the 'I' is kept up as 'I' alone it is the Self; when it flies at a tangent and says "this" it is the ego.

D.: Is God apart from the Self?

M.: The Self is God. "I AM" is God. "I am the Self, O Gudakesa!" (*Ahamatma Gudakesa*).

This question arises because you are holding the ego self. This will not arise if you hold the True Self. For the Real Self will not and cannot ask anything. If God be apart from the Self He must be a Self-less God, which is absurd.

D.: What is *namaskara* (prostration)?

M.: Prostration means "subsidence of the ego". What is "subsidence"? To merge into the source of its origin. God cannot be deceived by outward genuflexions, bowings and prostrations. He sees if the individuality is there or not.

Mr. Shamanna: Is there a sixth sense to feel "I AM"?

M.: Do you have it in your sleep? There is only one being functioning through the five senses. Or do you mean that each sense is independent of the Self and there are five selves admitting of a sixth to control them? There is a power working through these five senses. How can you deny the existence of such Power? Do you deny your existence? Do you not remain even in sleep where the body is not perceived? The same 'I' continues to be now; so we admit our existence, whether there is the body or not. The senses work periodically. Their work begins and ends. There must be a substratum on which their activities depend. Where do they appear and merge? There must be a single substratum. Were you to say that the single unit is not perceived, it is an admission of its being single: for you say that there is no second one to know it.

All these discussions are only to get rid of ignorance. When that is done everything will be clear. It is a matter of competence, or ripeness.

D.: Cannot Grace hasten such competence in a seeker?

M.: Leave it to Him. Surrender unreservedly. One of two things must be done. Either surrender because you admit your inability and also require a High Power to help you; or investigate into the cause of misery, go into the source and merge into the Self. Either way you will be free from misery. God never forsakes one who has surrendered. *Mamekam saranam vraja.*

D.: What is the drift of the mind after surrender?

M.: Is the surrendered mind raising the question? (Laughter.)

Talk 364.

The Nellore Professor asked about *visvarupa darsana.*

M.: Visvatma darsana is *visvarupa darsana* i.e., the universal Self of the cosmic Self is the cosmos. Sri Krishna started the discourse in Chapter II, saying, "I have no form". In Chapter XI, He says, "See my form as the Universe". Is it consistent? Again he says, "I transcend the three worlds", but Arjuna sees the three worlds in Him. Sri Krishna says, "I cannot be seen by men, Gods, etc."; yet Arjuna sees himself and the Gods in Him. No one could see and yet Arjuna was endowed with divine sight to see Him. Does it not look a maze of contradictions?

The answer is that the understanding is wrong. *Sthula dristi* on the physical plane is absurd. *Jnana dristi* (subtle understanding) is necessary. That is why Arjuna was given *divya chakshuh* (divine sight). Can such sight be gross? Will such interpretation lead you to a right understanding?

Sri Krishna says *Kalosmi,* 'I am Time'. Does Time have shape?

Again if the universe be His form should it not be one and unchanging? Why does He say to Arjuna, "See in me whatever you desire to see?" That means that His form is according to the desires of the seer. They speak of 'divine sight' and yet paint the scene, each according to his own view. There is the seer also in the seen. What is all this? Even a mesmerist can make you see strange scenes. You call this a trick, whereas the other you call divine. Why this difference? Anything seen cannot be real. That is the truth.

Talk 365.

As Sri Bhagavan was continuing in the same strain, a visitor asked how to overcome the identity of the Self with the body.

M.: What about sleep?

D.: There is ignorance prevailing.

M.: How do you know your ignorance in sleep? Did you exist in sleep, or not?

D.: I do not know.

M.: Do you deny your existence in sleep?

D.: I must admit it by my reasoning.

M.: How do you infer your existence?

D.: By reasoning and experience.

M.: Is reasoning necessary for experience? (Laughter)

D.: Is meditation analytical or synthetic?

M.: Analysis or synthesis are in the region of intellect. The Self transcends the intellect.

Talk 366.

Before leaving at 3-30 p.m., Mrs. Dodwell raised a second question, asking what is meant by *neti-neti*.

M.: There is now wrong identification of the Self with the body, senses, etc. You proceed to discard these, and this is *neti*. This can be done only by holding to the one which cannot be discarded. That is *iti* alone.

21st February, 1937

Talk 367.

A Marathi lady, a casual visitor then taking leave, was almost on the point of bursting into tears; she asked; I know that *mukti* is impossible in one life. Still may I not have peace of mind in this life?

The Master looked at her very kindly and said smiling softly: Life and all else are in Brahman alone. Brahman is here and now. Investigate.

D.: I am practising meditation for a number of years. Yet my mind is not steady and cannot be brought to bear on meditation.

M.: Again looked steadily at her and said: "Do it now and all will be right."

Talk 368.

A young girl of 9 or 10, whose mother is a Research Scholar in Sanskrit in the University of Madras, accompanied by Mr. Maurice Frydman met Sri Bhagavan in Palakothu at about 12 noon. Sri Bhagavan, as usual with Him, kindly smiled on her. She asked Sri Bhagavan: "Why is there misery on earth?"

M.: Due to Karma.

D.: Who makes Karma bear fruits?

M.: God.

D.: God makes us do Karma and gives bad fruits for bad Karma. Is it fair?

Sri Bhagavan almost laughed and was very pleased with her. Later he was coaxing her to read something on returning to the hall. Since then He is watching her.

22nd February, 1937

Talk 369.

A Marathi gentleman and wife, past middle age, are on a visit here. They are quiet and simple. Both of them tearfully took leave and the gentleman even sobbed out a prayer for Sri Bhagavan's Grace. Sri Bhagavan gazed at them, with his lips parted showing the row of white teeth. His eyes also had a tear in them.

Talk 370.

Sri Bhagavan was in the cattle-shed. People were working and he watched their work for a short time. Then someone came and said that a large number of visitors were waiting in the hall. Sri Bhagavan in His calm way said: "Yes — yes, you do your work. Let Me go for Mine. People are waiting for Me. Let Me go." — Then he left the place.

23rd February, 1937

Talk 371.

There was a group of three middle-aged Andhras on a visit to Sri Bhagavan. One of them kneeled and asked: I am performing *hathayoga*, namely *basti, dhauti, neti,* etc. I find a blood vessel hardened in the ankle. Is it a result of Yoga?

M.: The blood-vessel would have hardened under any circumstances. It does not trouble you as much now as it would otherwise. *Hathayoga* is a cleaning process. It also helps peace of mind, after leading you to *pranayama*.

D.: May I do *pranayama*? Is it useful?

M.: Pranayama is an aid for the control of mind. Only you should not stop with *pranayama*. You must proceed further to *pratyahara, dharana, dhyana* and *samadhi*. Full results are reaped finally.

Another of the group asked: How are lust, anger, acquisitiveness, confusion, pride and jealousy overcome?

M.: By *dhyana*.

D.: What is *dhyana*?

M.: Dhyana is holding on to a single thought and putting off all other thoughts.

D.: What is to be meditated upon?

M.: Anything that you prefer.

D.: Siva, Vishnu, and Gayatri are said to be equally efficacious. Which should I meditate upon?

M.: Any one you like best. They are all equal in their effect. But you should stick to one.

D.: How to meditate?

M.: Concentrate on that one whom you like best. If a single thought prevails, all other thoughts are put off and finally eradicated. So long as diversity prevails there are bad thoughts. When the object of love prevails only good thoughts hold the field. Therefore hold on to one thought only. *Dhyana* is the chief practice.

351

A little later Sri Bhagavan continued:

Dhyana means fight. As soon as you begin meditation other thoughts will crowd together, gather force and try to sink the single thought to which you try to hold. The good thought must gradually gain strength by repeated practice. After it has grown strong the other thoughts will be put to flight. This is the battle royal always taking place in meditation.

One wants to rid oneself of misery. It requires peace of mind, which means absence of perturbation owing to all kinds of thoughts. Peace of mind is brought about by *dhyana* alone.

D.: What is the need then for *pranayama*?

M.: Pranayama is meant for one who cannot directly control the thoughts. It serves as a brake to a car. But one should not stop with it, as I said before, but must proceed to *pratyahara, dharana* and *dhyana*. After the fruition of *dhyana*, the mind will come under control even in the absence of *pranayama*. The *asanas* (postures) help *pranayama*, which helps *dhyana* in its turn, and peace of mind results. Here is the purpose of *hatha yoga*.

Later Sri Bhagavan continued:

When *dhyana* is well established it cannot be given up. It will go on automatically even when you are engaged in work, play or enjoyment. It will persist in sleep too. *Dhyana* must become so deep-rooted that it will be natural to one.

D.: What rite or action is necessary for the development of *dhyana*?

M.: Dhyana is itself the action, the rite and the effort. It is the most intense and potent of all. No other effort is necessary.

D.: Is not *japa* necessary?

M.: Is *dhyana* not *vak* (speech)? Why is *japa* necessary for it? If *dhyana* is gained there is no need for anything else.

D.: Is not a vow of silence helpful?

M.: A vow is only a vow. It may help *dhyana* to some extent. But what is the good of keeping the mouth closed and letting the mind run riot? If the mind be engaged in *dhyana*, where is the need for speech?

Nothing is as good as *dhyana*. Should one take to action with a vow of silence, where is the good of the vow?

352

D.: What is *jnana-marga*?

M.: I have been saying it for so long. What is *jnana*? *Jnana* means realisation of the Truth. It is done by *dhyana*. *Dhyana* helps you to hold on to Truth to the exclusion of all thoughts.

D.: Why are there so many Gods mentioned?

M.: The body is only one. Still, how many functions are performed by it? The source of all the functions is only one. It is in the same way with the Gods also.

D.: Why does a man suffer misery?

M.: Misery is due to multifarious thoughts. If the thoughts are unified and centred on a single item there is no misery, but happiness is the result. Then, even the thought, "I do something" is absent; nor will there be an eye on the fruit of action.

Talk 372.

D.: Horripilation, sobbing voice, joyful tears, etc., are mentioned in *Atma Vidya Vilasa* and other works. Are these found in *samadhi*, or before, or after?

M.: All these are the symptoms of exceedingly subtle modes of mind (*vrittis*). Without duality they cannot remain. *Samadhi* is Perfect Peace where these cannot find place. After emerging from *samadhi* the remembrance of the state gives rise to these symptoms. In *bhakti marga* (path of devotion) these are the precursors to *samadhi*.

D.: Are they not so in the path of *jnana*?

M.: May be. There is no definiteness about it. It depends on the nature of the individual. Individuality entirely lost, these cannot find a place. Even the slightest trace of it being present, these symptoms become manifest.

Manickavachagar and other saints have spoken of these symptoms. They say tears rush forth involuntarily and irrepressibly. Though aware of tears they are unable to repress them. I had the same experience when I was staying Virupaksha cave.

D.: Sleep state is said to be the experience of Bliss, yet, on recollecting it the hairs do not stand on end. Why should they do so, if the *samadhi* state is recollected?

M.: Samadhi means sleep in waking state (*jagrat sushupti*). Bliss is overpowering and the experience is very clear, whereas it is different in sleep.

D.: Can we put it that in sleep there is no unhappiness, nor happiness, *i.e.*, the experience is negative not positive.

M.: But the recollection is positive "I slept happily," says the man. So there must be the experience of happiness in sleep.

D.: Does Bliss consist only in the absence of unhappiness, or is it anything positive?

M.: It is positive. Loss of unhappiness and rise of happiness are simultaneous.

D.: Can it be that the recollection of happiness in sleep is not clear and so there is no horripilation, etc.?

M.: The Bliss of *samadhi* is a perfectly clear experience and its recollection also is similar. But the experience of sleep is otherwise.

28th February, 1937

Talk 373.

H. H. The Maharajah of Mysore had a private interview with Sri Bhagavan in the newly built bathroom from 9-15 to 9-30 a.m. His Highness saluted Sri Bhagavan placing his head on Sri Bhagavan's feet and said:

I have read Sri Bhagavan's life and long had a desire to meet Him, but my circumstances are such that intentions of this kind cannot easily be carried into effect. Nor can I stay here as other disciples can, considering all my limitations. While I remain here for about 15 minutes, I shall now pray only for Thy Grace. (On departure H. H. again saluted Sri Bhagavan as before and left after presenting two fine shawls and some money to the office).

13th March, 1937

Talk 374.

H. H. The Maharajah of Travancore had an interview from 4-30 p.m. to 5-15 p.m.

Their Highnesses The Maharajah and the Maharani of Travancore who arrived at Tiruvannamalai by the 8 a.m., train visited the Asramam at 4-15 p.m. The public were excluded from the hall where Bhagavan sat. Even devotees who were daily visiting the hall were by a sad mistake excluded from the interview. The Royal party was introduced to Sri Bhagavan by a retired District Magistrate. Two *aides-de-camp*, the Private Secretary to H. H. The Maharajah, some officials of the Travancore State and an Advocate of Mylapore were present. The discussion started by the District Magistrate went on about *manas*, concentration, Realisation, purpose of creation, etc. Her Highness put some questions expressing her doubts and they were all explained by Sri Bhagavan. H. H. The Maharajah also took part in the discussion. The whole conversation was in Tamil and Malayalam.

During the visit of the Royal Family of Travancore, Her Highness appeared very cultured, vivacious and conversant with Malayalam, Tamil and English. Most of the questions were put by Her Highness. One of the questions was:

D.: What is the purpose of creation?

M.: It is to give rise to this question; investigate the answer to this question, and finally abide in the supreme or rather the primal source of all, including the Self. The investigation will resolve itself into one of quest for the Self and cease only after the non-self is sifted away and the Self realised in its purity and glory.

D.: How is the investigation to start?

M.: The Self is plain to all and the starting also equally plain.

D.: What is the starting point for one in my stage of development.

M.: Each one has some method of *upasana* or *japa*. If that is pursued in all sincerity with due perseverance, it will automatically lead to the investigation of the Self.

[The writer of these notes was not present and the above was gathered from one of the attendants of Sri Maharshi.]

Talk 375.

A middle-aged Kanarese visitor asked about *akarma* (actionless act).

M.: Whatever one does after the ego has vanished is *akarma*.

Talk 376.

A learned Telugu visitor, who had composed a song in praise of Sri Bhagavan, read it out, placed it at His feet and saluted. After a time he asked for *upadesa*.

M.: The *upadesa* is contained in *Upadesa Saram*.

D.: But oral and personal instruction is valuable.

M.: If there be anything new and hitherto unknown *upadesa* will be appropriate. Here it happens to be stilling the mind and remaining free from thoughts.

D.: It looks impossible.

M.: But it is precisely the pristine and eternal state of all.

D.: It is not perceived in our everyday active life.

M.: Everyday life is not divorced from the Eternal State. So long as the daily life is imagined to be different from the spiritual life these difficulties arise. If the spiritual life is rightly understood, the active life will be found to be not different from it.

Can the mind be got at by the mind on looking for it as an object? The source of the mental functions must be sought and gained. That is the Reality.

One does not know the Self owing to the interference of thoughts. The Self is realised when thoughts subside.

D.: "Only one in a million pursues *sadhanas* to completion." (Bh. Gita, VII, 3).

M.: "Whenever the turbulent mind wavers, then and there pull it and bring it under control." (Bh. Gita, VI, 26.) "Seeing the mind with the mind" (*manasa mana alokya*), so proclaim the Upanishads.

D.: Is the mind an *upadhi* (limiting adjunct)?

M.: Yes.

D.: Is the seen (*drisya*) world real (*satya*)?

M.: It is true in the same degree as the seer (*drashta*), subject, object and perception form the triad (*triputi*). There is a reality beyond these three. These appear and disappear, whereas the truth is eternal.

D.: These *triputi sambhava* are only temporal.

M.: Yes, if one recognises the Self even in temporal matters these will be found to be non-existent, rather inseparate from the Self; and they will be going on at the same time.

22nd March, 1937

Talk 377.

A middle-aged Andhra visitor: A man is said to be divine. Why then does he have regrets?

M.: Divinity refers to the essential nature. The regrets are of *Prakriti*.

D.: How is one to overcome regrets?

M.: By realising the Divinity in him.

D.: How?

M.: By practice.

D.: What kind of practice?

M.: Meditation.

D.: Mind is not steady while meditating.

M.: It will be all right by practice.

D.: How is the mind to be steadied?

M.: By strengthening it.

D.: How to strengthen it?

M.: It grows strong by *satsanga* (the company of the wise).

D.: Shall we add prayers, etc.?

M.: Yes.

D.: What of the one who has no regrets?

M.: He is an accomplished Yogi. There is no question about him.

D.: People cite disasters, *e.g.*, earthquakes, famines, etc., to disprove God. How shall we meet their contention?

M.: Wherefrom have they come — those who argue?

D.: They say, "Nature".

M.: Some call it "Nature" — others "God".

D.: Are we to keep anything against a rainy day; or to live a precarious life for spiritual attainments?

M.: God looks after everything.

27th March, 1937

Talk 378.

In the course of a conversation with an Andhra visitor, Sri Bhagavan quoted:

> *Asamsayam mahabaho mano durnigraham chalam*
> *Abhyasena tu kaunteya vairagyena cha grhyate*
> — Bh. Gita, Ch. VI, 35

> Without doubt, O mighty-armed Hero,
> the mind is restless, hard to curb.
> Yet by constant effort, Partha,
> matched with detachment — curbed it *is*.

To explain *vairagya* Sri Bhagavan again quoted:

> *Sankalpaprabhavan kamams tyaktva sarvan aseshatah*
> *Manasaivendriyagramam viniyamya samantatah*
> — (Ch. VI, 24)

> Having cast out without remains
> all longing born of thought for self,
> Having drawn in by mind alone
> his team of senses from all sides -

As for practice (*abhyasa*):

> *Sanaissanairuparamet buddhya dhritigrhitaya*
> *Atmasamstham manah krtva na kinchidapi chintayet*
> — (VI — 25)

> By slow approaches let him come
> to rest, with patient, rock-poised Will;
> His mind at home in Selfhood pure,
> Let him create no *thought* at all.

Again for *jnana*:

> *Yato yato nischarati manas chanchalam asthiram*
> *Tatastato niyamyaitad atmanyeva vasam nayet*
> — (VI — 26)

Though over and over the fickle mind,
    all restlessness, a-wandering goes,
Still over and over let his regain
    control, and poise it back in Self.

2nd April, 1937

Talk 379.

One Tirumalpad of Nilambur, a Malayali gentleman, asked Sri Bhagavan for an explanation of *Atma Vidya*. (Knowledge of the Self.)

M.: Sri Bhagavan explained this short piece of 5 stanzas as follows: Chidambaram is the famous place of pilgrimage associated with Nandanar who sang that *Atma Vidya* is most difficult of attainment. Muruganar (a long-standing devotee of Sri Bhagavan) began however that *Atma Vidya* is the easiest of attainments. *Ayye atisulabham* is the burden of the song. In explanation of this extraordinary statement, he argued that *Atma* being the Self is eternally obvious even to the least of men. The original statement and the subsequent reasoning are incompatible because there need be no *attainment* if the Self is the substratum of all selves and so obvious too. Naturally he could not pursue the theme further and laid the first four lines composed by him before Sri Bhagavan for completion.

Sri Bhagavan admitted the truth of the disciple's statement and pointed out why the Self, though obvious, is yet hidden. It is the wrong identity of the Self with the body, etc.

D.: How did the wrong identity arise?

M.: Due to thoughts. If these thoughts are put an end to, the real Self should shine forth of itself.

D.: How are these thoughts to be ended?

M.: Find out their basis. All of them are strung on the single 'I-thought'. Quell it; all others are quashed. Moreover there is no use knowing all except the Self. If the Self is known all others become known. Hence is Self-Realisation the primary and sole duty of man.

D.: How to quell the 'I-thought'?

M.: If its source is sought it does not arise, and thus it is quelled.

D.: Where and how to find it?

M.: It is in fact the consciousness which enables the individuals to function in different ways. Pure Consciousness is the Self. All that is required to realise the Self is to "Be Still."

D.: What can be easier than that?

M.: So *Atma Vidya* is the easiest of attainment.

Talk 380.

A European gentleman asked: How do you answer the question, "Who are you?"

M.: Ask yourself the question, "Who am I?"

D.: Please tell me how you have found it. I shall not be able to find it myself. (The 'I' is the result of biological forces. It results in silence. I want to know how the Master finds it.)

M.: Is it found only by logic? The scientific analysis is due to intellect.

D.: According to J. C. Bose, nature does not make any difference between a worm and a man.

M.: What is Nature?

D.: It is that which exists.

M.: How do you know the existence?

D.: By my senses.

M.: 'My' implies your existence. But you are speaking of another's existence. You must exist to speak of "my senses". There cannot be 'my' without 'I'.

D.: I am a poor creature. I come to ask you, Great Master that you are, what this existence is. There is no special significance in the word *existence*. He exists, I exist and others exist. What of that?

M.: The existence of anyone posited, shows your own existence. "Existence is your nature."

D.: There is nothing strange in anything existing.

M.: How do you know its existence — rather than your own existence?

D.: What is new in the existence of anything? I take up your book and read there that the one question one should ask oneself is "Who am I"? I want to know "Who are you?" I have my own answer. If another says the same, and so too, millions of others, there is the probability of the Self. I want a positive answer for the question and no playing with words.

M.: In this way you are in the region of probabilities at the best.

D.: Yes. There are no certainties. Even God cannot be proved to be absolute certainty.

M.: Leave God alone for the time being. What of yourself?

D.: I want confirmation of the Self.

M.: You seek the confirmation from others. Each one though addressed as 'you', styles himself 'I'. The confirmation is only from 'I'. There is no 'you' at all. All are comprised in 'I'. The other can be known only when the Self is posited. The others do not exist without the subject.

D.: Again, this is nothing new. When I was with Sir C. V. Raman he told me that the theory of smell could be explained from his theory of light. Smell need no longer be explained in terms of chemistry. Now, there is something new; it is progress. That is what I mean, when I say that there is nothing new in all the statements I hear now.

M.: 'I' is never new. It is eternally the same.

D.: Do you mean to say that there is no progress?

M.: Progress is perceived by the outgoing mind. Everything is still when the mind is introverted and the Self is sought.

D.: The Sciences — what becomes of them?

M.: They all end in the Self. The Self is their finality.

(It was 5 p.m.; Sri Bhagavan left the hall and the gentleman left for the station).

Talk 381.

Mr. Bose, the Bengali Engineer, asked the meaning of the last stanza of *Atma Vidya* (Knowledge of the Self). Sri Bhagavan explained on the following lines:

There is the world perceived, the perception is only apparent; it requires location for existence and light. Such *existence* and *light* are simultaneous with the rise of mind. So the physical existence and illumination are part of mental existence and illumination. The latter is not absolute, for the mind rises and sinks. The mind has its substratum in the Self which is self-evident, *i.e.* its existence and self-luminosity are obvious. That is absolute being, continuous in sleep, waking and dream states also.

The world consists of variety, which is the function of the mind. The mind shines by reflected light — *i.e.* light reflected from the self. Just as the pictures in a cinema show are seen only in diffused, *i.e.* artificial light, but not in a strong glare or in thick darkness, so also the world pictures are perceptible only in diffused, *i.e.* reflected light of the Self through the darkness of *avidya* (ignorance). The world cannot be seen either in pure ignorance as in sleep, or in pure light as in Self-Realisation. *Avidya* is the Cause of variety.

The Engineer said that he understood it only intellectually.

M.: Because intellect holds you at present, *i.e.* you are in the grip of intellect in the waking state when you discuss these matters.

Later it was added that Grace is needed for Realisation.

The Engineer asked how Grace has to be got.

M.: Grace is the Self. It is not manifest because of ignorance prevailing. With *sraddha*, it will become manifest.

Sraddha, Grace, Light, Spirit are all synonymous with the Self.

5th April, 1937

Talk 382.

A Telugu gentleman, quiet in look, but learned in philosophy, asked Sri Bhagavan about *manolaya*.

Sri Bhagavan said that everything is contained in *Upadesa Saram*, a copy of which the man was holding in his hand.

D.: What is mind?

M.: See what it is.

D.: It is *sankalpa vikalpatmaka* (made up of thoughts and their changes).

M.: Whose *sankalpa* (thought)?

D.: Sankalpa is the nature of the mind.

M.: Of what is the *sankalpa*?

362

D.: Of the externalities.

M.: Quite so. Is that your nature?

D.: It is of the mind.

M.: What is your nature?

D.: Suddha Chaitanya (Pure Conscious Light).

M.: Then why do you worry about *sankalpa* and the rest.

D.: The mind is admitted to be changing and unsteady (*chanchala* and *asthira*).

M.: It is also said in the same place that the mind is to be introverted and made to merge into the Self; that the practice must be long because it is slow; and must be continued until it is totally merged in the Self.

D.: I want *prasad, i.e.,* Grace, for it.

M.: It is always with you. All that is required of you is not to confound yourself with the extrovert mind but to abide as the Self. That is *prasad*.

The gentleman saluted and retired.

Talk 383.

Swami Lokesananda, a *sanyasi*, asked Sri Bhagavan: Is there *prarabdha* for a *jivanmukta*?

M.: Who is the questioner? From whom does the question proceed? Is it a *jivanmukta* who is asking?

D.: No, I am not a *mukta* as yet.

M.: Then why not let the *jivanmukta* ask the question for himself?

D.: The doubt is for me.

M.: Quite so. The *ajnani* has doubt but not a *jnani*.

D.: According to the creed that there is no creation (*ajatavada*), the explanations of Sri Bhagavan are faultless; but are they admissible in other schools?

M.: There are three methods of approach in *Advaita vada*.

(1) The *ajatavada* is represented by no loss, no creation, no one bound, no *sadhaka*, no one desirous of liberation, no liberation. This is the Supreme Truth. (*Mandukya Karika*, II — 32).

According to this, there is only One and it admits of no discussion.

(2) *Drishti Srishtivada* is illustrated thus:- Simultaneous creation. There are two friends sleeping side by side. One of them dreams that he goes to Benares with his friend and returns. He tells his friend that both of them have been in Benares. The other denies it. That statement is true from the standpoint of one and the denial from that of the other.

(3) *Srishti Drishtivada* is plain (Gradual creation and knowledge of it).

Karma is posited as past karma, etc., *prarabdha, agami* and *sanchita*. There must be *kartritva* (doership) and *karta* (doer) for it. Karma (action) cannot be for the body because it is insentient. It is only so long as *dehatma buddhi* ('I-am-the-body idea') lasts. After transcending *dehatma buddhi* one becomes a *jnani*. In the absence of that idea (*buddhi*) there cannot be either *kartritva* or *karta*. So a *jnani* has no karma. That is his experience. Otherwise he is not a *jnani*. However an *ajnani* identifies the *jnani* with his body, which the *jnani* does not do. So the *ajnani* finds the *jnani* acting, because his body is active, and therefore he asks if the *jnani* is not affected by *prarabdha*.

The scriptures say that *jnana* is the fire which burns away all karma (*sarvakarmani*). *Sarva* (all) is interpreted in two ways: (1) to include *prarabdha* and (2) to exclude it. In the first way: if a man with three wives dies, it is asked. "can two of them be called widows and the third not?" All are widows. So it is with *prarabdha, agami* and *sanchita*. When there is no *karta* none of them can hold out any longer.

The second explanation is, however, given only to satisfy the enquirer. It is said that all karma is burnt away leaving *prarabdha* alone. The body is said to continue in the functions for which it has taken its birth. That is *prarabdha*. But from the *jnani's* point of view there is only the Self which manifests in such variety. There is no body or karma apart from the Self, so that the actions do not affect him.

D.: Is there no *dehatma buddhi* (I-am-the-body idea) for the *jnani*? If, for instance, Sri Bhagavan be bitten by an insect, is there no sensation?

M.: There is the sensation and there is also the *dehatma buddhi*. The latter is common to both *jnani* and *ajnani* with this difference, that the *ajnani* thinks *dehaiva Atma* (only the body is myself), whereas

364

the *jnani* knows all is of the Self (*Atmamayam sarvam*), or (*sarvam khalvidam Brahma*) all this is Brahma. If there be pain let it be. It is also part of the Self. The Self is *poorna* (perfect).

Now with regard to the actions of the *jnani*, they are only so-called because they are ineffective. Generally the actions get embedded as *samskaras* in the individual. That can be only so long as the mind is fertile, as in the case of the *ajnani*. With a *jnani* the mind is surmised; he has already transcended the mind. Because of his apparent activity the mind has to be inferred in his case, and that mind is not fertile like that of an *ajnani*. Hence it is said that a *jnani's* mind is Brahman. Brahman is certainly no other than the *jnani's* mind. The *vasanas* cannot bear fruit in that soil. His mind is barren, free from *vasanas*, etc.

However, since *prarabdha* was conceded in his case, *vasanas* also must be supposed to exist. If they exist they are only for enjoyment (*bhogahetu*). That is to say, actions bear twofold fruits, the one for enjoyment of their fruits and the other leaving an impress on the mind in the form of *samskaras* for subsequent manifestation in future births. The *jnani's* mind being barren cannot entertain seeds of karma. His *vasanas* simply exhaust themselves by activities ending in enjoyment only (*bhogahetuka karma*). In fact, his karma is seen only from the *ajnani's* standpoint. He remains actionless only. He is not aware of the body as being apart from the Self. How can there be liberation (*mukti*) or bondage (*bandha*) for him? He is beyond both. He is not bound by karma, either now or ever. There is no *jivanmukta* or *videhamukta* according to him.

D.: From all this it looks as if a *jnani* who has scorched all the *vasanas* is the best and that he would remain inactive like a stock or stone.

M.: No, not necessarily. *Vasanas* do not affect him. Is it not itself a *vasana* that one remains like a stock or stone? *Sahaja* is the state.

Talk 384.

The conversation turned on *vasanas*. Sri Bhagavan said that good tendencies and bad ones (*suvasana* and *kuvasana*) are concomitant —

the one cannot exist without the other. Maybe that the one class predominates. Good tendencies (*suvasana*) are cultivated and they must also be finally destroyed by *jnana*.

A young prodigy was mentioned. Sri Bhagavan remarked that latent impressions of previous births (*purva janma samskara*) were strong in him.

D.: How does it manifest as the ability to cite well-known saints? Is it *vasana* in the form of a seed only?

M.: Yes. Predisposition (*samskara*) is acquired knowledge and kept in stock. It manifests under favourable circumstances. One with strong *samskara* understands the thing when presented to him much quicker than another with no *samskara* or weak *samskara*.

D.: Does it hold good with inventors also?

M.: "There is nothing new under the sun." What we call inventions or discoveries are merely rediscoveries by competent men with strong *samskara* in the directions under consideration.

D.: Is it so with Newton, Einstein, etc.?

M.: Yes. Certainly. But the *samskaras*, however strong, will not manifest unless in a calm and still mind. It is within the experience of everyone that his attempts to rake up his memory fail, whereas something flashes in the mind when he is calm and quiet. Mental quiet is necessary even for remembrance of forgotten things. The so-called genius is one who worked hard in his past births and acquired knowledge and kept it in store as *samskaras*. He now concentrates his mind until it merges in the subject. In that stillness the submerged ideas flash out. That requires favourable conditions also.

6th April, 1937

Talk 385.

Mr. Vankata Rao, an Andhra gentleman, in the course of conversation with Sri Bhagavan, was told:

"Until you gain *jnana* you cannot understand the state of a *jnani*. There is no use asking about the work of *Isvara* and the rest. Some ask why Siva went naked in Daruka forest and spoiled the chastity of the *rishi's* wives. The *puranas* which record this incident have also

366

said that Siva had previously saved the *Devas* and the universe by consuming the poison *halahala* at the time of churning the ocean of milk. He, who could save the world from the deadly poison and lead the sages to emancipation, had also wandered nude amongst their women. Their actions are incomprehensible to ordinary intellects. One must be a *jnani* to understand a *jnani* or *Isvara*."

D.: Should we not learn the *jnani's* ways and imitate them?

M.: It is no use. *Vasanas* are of four kinds:

(1) Pure (*Suddha*), (2) Impure (*malina*), (3) Mixed (*madhya*) and (4) Good (*Sat*), according as the *jnanis* are the Supreme (*varishta*), the best (*variya*), better (*vara*), and good (*vit*). Their fruits are reaped in three ways: (1) of our own will (*swechha*), and by others' will (*parechha*) and involuntarily (*anichha*). There have been *jnanis* like Gautama, Vyasa, Suka and Janaka.

D.: Was Vyasa also a *jnani*?

M.: Yes. Certainly.

D.: Why then did the bathing angels don clothes when he appeared before them, but not when Suka passed?

M.: That same Vyasa sent Suka to Janaka for instruction; Suka was tested by Janaka and finally he returned convinced of Vyasa's greatness.

D.: Is *jnana* the same as *arudha*?

M.: So it is.

D.: What is the relation between *bhakti* and *jnana*?

M.: Eternal, unbroken, natural state is *jnana*. Does it not imply love of Self? Is it not *bhakti*?

D.: Idol worship does not seem good. They worship the formless God in Islam.

M.: What is their conception of God?

D.: As Immanence, etc.

M.: Is not God even then endowed with attributes? Form is only one kind of attribute. One cannot worship God without some notions. Any *bhavana* premises a God with attributes (*saguna*). Moreover, where is the use of discussing the form or formlessness of God? Find out if you have a form. You can then understand God.

D.: I admit I have no form.

M.: All right. You have no form in sleep, but in the waking state you identify yourself with a form. See which is your real state. That is understood to be without form on investigation. If you know your Self to be formless by your *jnana,* should you not concede the same amount of *jnana* to God and understand Him to be formless?

D.: But there is the world for God.

M.: How does the world appear? How are we? Knowing this, you know God. You will know if He is Siva, or Vishnu or any other or all put together.

D.: Is *Vaikuntha* in *Paramapada, i.e.,* in the transcendent Self?

M.: Where is *Paramapada* or *Vaikuntha* unless in you?

D.: Vaikuntha, etc., appear involuntarily.

M.: Does this world appear voluntarily?

The questioner returned no answer.

M.: The self-evident 'I', ignoring the Self, goes about seeking to know the non-Self. How absurd!

D.: This is *Samkhya* Yoga. Being the culmination of all kinds of other yogas, how can it be understood to start with? Is not *bhakti* antecedent to it?

M.: Has not Sri Krishna started the Gita with *Sankhya*?

D.: Yes. I understand it now.

Talk 386.

D.: In Sri Ramakrishna's *Life* it is said that an idol, Ramlal was animate. Is it true?

M.: Can you account for the animation of this body? Is the movement of the idol more mysterious than the movement of this body?

D.: Metal does not move itself.

M.: Is not the body a corpse? You will probably consider it a mystery if the corpse moves. Is that so?

Talk 387.

Three persons came on a short visit; the eldest of them asked: There is one process of creation mentioned in the Upanishads and another in Puranas. Which of them is true?

368

M.: They are many, and meant to indicate that the creation has a cause and a creator should be posited so that one might seek the cause. The emphasis is on the purpose of the theory and not on the process of creation. Moreover, the creation is perceived by someone. There are no objects without the subject, *i.e.*, the objects do not come and tell you that they are, but it is you who says that there are the objects. The objects are therefore what the seer makes of them. They have no existence independent of the subject. Find out what you are and then you understand what the world is. That is the object of the theory.

D.: The soul is only a small particle whereas the creation is so huge. How can we surmise it?

M.: The particle speaks of the huge creation; where is the contradiction?

Talk 388.

Later Sri Bhagavan continued:

There are so many theories, scriptural and scientific. Have they reached any finality? They cannot. Brahman is said to be subtler than the subtlest, wider than the widest. *Anu* is an atom, infinitesimal. It ends in subtle perception. The subtlety is of the *sukshma* body, *i.e.*, the mind. Beyond the mind there is the Self. The greatest of things are also conceptions, the conceptions are of the mind; beyond the mind there is the Self. So the Self is subtler than the subtlest.

There may be any number of theories of creation. All of them extend outwardly. There will be no limit to them because time and space are unlimited. They are however only in the mind. See the mind; time and space are transcended and the Self is realised.

Creation is explained scientifically or logically to one's own satisfaction. But is there any finality about it? Such explanations are called *krama srishti* (gradual creation). On the other hand, *drishti srishti* (simultaneous or sudden creation) is *yugapad srishti*. Without the seer there are no objects seen. Find the seer and the creation is comprised in him. Why look outward and go on explaining the phenomena which are endless?

369

Talk 389.

With regard to presents to Sri Bhagavan, He observed: Why do they bring presents? Do I want them? Even if I refuse they thrust presents on me. What for? If I accept them I must yield to their wishes. It is like giving a bait to catch the fish. Is the angler anxious to feed the fish? No, he is anxious to feed on the fish.

Swami Lokesananda, a *sannyasi:* What is meant by *jnana* and *vijnana*?

M.: These words may mean differently according to the context. *Jnana = samanya jnana* or Pure consciousness. *Vijnana = Visesha jnana. Visesha* may be (1) worldly (relative knowledge); and (2) transcendental (Self-Realisation).

Mind is necessary for *visesha*; it modifies the purity of absolute consciousness. So *vijnana* represents intellect and the sheath composing it, *i.e.*, relative knowledge. In that case *jnana* is common (*samanya*) running through *vijnana samjnana, prajnana, ajnana, mati, dhirti* — different modes of knowledge (vide *Aitareyopanishad*, Chapter 3) or *jnana* is *paroksha* (hearsay) and *vijnana* is *aparokska* (direct perception) as in *jnana vijnana triptatma*, one perfectly content with *jnana* and *vijnana*.

D.: What is the relation between Brahman and *Isvara*?

M.: Brahman is called *Isvara* in relation to the world.

D.: Is it possible to speak to *Isvara* as Sri Ramakrishna did?

M.: When we can speak to each other why should we not speak to *Isvara* in the same way?

D.: Then why does it not happen with us?

M.: It requires purity and strength of mind and practice in meditation.

D.: Does God become evident if the above conditions exist?

M.: Such manifestations are as real as your own reality. In other words, when you identify yourself with the body as in *jagrat* you see gross objects; when in subtle body or in mental plane as in *svapna*, you see objects equally subtle; in the absence of identification as in *sushupti* you see nothing. The objects seen bear a relation to the state of the seer. The same applies to visions of God.

By long practice the figure of God, as meditated upon, appears in dream and may later appear in *jagrat* also.

D.: Is that the state of God-realisation?

M.: Listen to what happened once, years ago.

There was a saint by name Namdev. He could see, talk and play with Vithoba as we do with one another. He used to spend most of his time in the temple playing with Vithoba.

On one occasion the saints had assembled together, among whom was one Jnandev of well-established fame and eminence. Jnandev asked Gora Kumbhar (a potter-saint) to use his proficiency in testing the soundness of baked pots and find out which of the assembled saints was properly baked clay. So Gora Kumbhar took his stick and gently struck each one's head in joke as if to test. When he came to Namdev the latter protested in a huff; all laughed and hooted. Namdev was enraged and he sought Vithoba in the temple. Vithoba said that the saints knew best; this unexpected reply upset Namdev all the more.

He said: You are God. I converse and play with you. Can there be anything more to be gained by man?

Vithoba persisted: The saints know.

Namdev: Tell me if there is anything more real than you.

Vithoba: We have been so familiar with each other that my advice will not have the desired effect on you. Seek the beggar-saint in the forest and know the truth.

Accordingly Namdev sought out the particular saint mentioned by Vithoba. Namdev was not impressed with the holiness of the man for he was nude, dirty and was lying on the floor with his feet resting on a *linga*. Namdev wondered how this could be a saint. The saint, on the other hand, smiled on Namdev and asked, "Did Vithoba send you here?" This was a great surprise to Namdev who was now more inclined to believe the man to be great. So Namdev asked him: "You are said to be a saint, why do you desecrate the *linga*?" The saint replied. "Indeed I am too old and weak to do the right thing. Please lift my feet and place them where there is no *linga*." Namdev accordingly lifted the saint's feet and placed them elsewhere.

371

But there was again a *linga* below them. Wherever the feet were placed then and there appeared a *linga* underneath. Namdev finally placed the feet on himself and he turned into a *linga*. Then Namdev understood that God was immanent and learnt the truth and departed. He went home and did not go to the temple for several days. Vithoba now sought him out in his home and asked why Namdev would not go to the temple to see God. Namdev said: "Is there a place where He is not?"

The moral of the story is clear. Visions of God have their place below the plane of Self-Realisation.

Talk 390.

D.: When I read Sri Bhagavan's works I find that investigation is said to be the one method for Realisation.

M.: Yes, that is *vichara*.

D.: How is that to be done?

M.: The questioner must admit the existence of his self. "I AM" is the Realisation. To pursue the clue till Realisation is *vichara*. *Vichara* and Realisation are the same.

D.: It is elusive. What shall I meditate upon?

M.: Meditation requires an object to meditate upon, whereas there is only the subject without the object in *vichara*. Meditation differs from *vichara* in this way.

D.: Is not *dhyana* one of the efficient processes for Realisation?

M.: *Dhyana* is concentration on an object. It fulfils the purpose of keeping away diverse thoughts and fixing the mind on a single thought, which must also disappear before Realisation. But Realisation is nothing new to be acquired. It is already there, but obstructed by a screen of thoughts. All our attempts are directed for lifting this screen and then Realisation is revealed.

If a true seeker is advised to meditate, many may go away satisfied with the advice. But someone among them may turn round and ask, "Who am I to meditate on an object?" Such a one must be told to find the Self. That is the finality. That is *Vichara*.

D.: Will *vichara* alone do in the absence of meditation?

M.: Vichara is the process and the goal also. 'I AM' is the goal and the final Reality. To hold to it with effort is *vichara*. When spontaneous and natural it is Realisation.

Talk 391.

The same *sannyasi* visitor, Swami Lokesananda, asked about *samadhi*.

M.: (1) Holding on to Reality is *samadhi*.

(2) Holding on to Reality with effort is *savikalpa samadhi*.

(3) Merging in Reality and remaining unaware of the world is *nirvikalpa samadhi*.[1]

(4) Merging in Ignorance and remaining unaware of the world is sleep. (Head bends but not in *samadhi*).

(5) Remaining in the primal, pure natural state without effort is *sahaja nirvikalpa samadhi*.

D.: It is said that one remaining in *nirvikalpa samadhi* for 21 days must necessarily give up the physical body.

M.: Samadhi means passing beyond *dehatma buddhi* (I-am-the-body idea) and non-identification of the body with the Self is a foregone conclusion.

There are said to be persons who have been immersed in *nirvikalpa samadhi* for a thousand years or more.

Talk 392.

(Swami Lokesananda continued another series of questions).

D.: They say that *Kundalini* must be roused before Realisation and that its awakening makes the body feel hot. Is that so?

M.: The yogis call it *Kundalini Sakti*. It is the same as *vritti* [2] of the form of God (*Bhagavatakara vritti*) of the *bhaktas* and *vritti* of the form of Brahman (*Brahmakara vritti*) of the *jnanis*. It must be preliminary to Realisation. The sensation produced may be said to be hot.

D.: Kundalini is said to be of the shape of a serpent but *vrittis* cannot be so.

---

[1] See table on page 374
[2] *vritti* = mode of mind

They can be further subdivided thus:

	SAVIKALPA SAMADHI		NIRVIKALPA SAMADHI	
	(Bahya) External	(Antar) Internal	(Bahya) External	(Antar) Internal
	(Drisyanuvidha) The mind jumps from one object to another. Keep it steady, fixed on the Reality behind them.	The mind is afflicted by Kama, Krodha, etc. See wherefrom they arise and how they have their being. Hold on to their source.	Merging in the one Reality underlying all the phenomena and remaining unaware of the transitory manifestations.	Merging in the Inmost Being which is the One Reality giving rise to all thoughts, etc., and remaining unaware of anything else.
	(Sabdanuvidha) There are the external phenomena which are said to have their origin from the Single Reality. Search for It and hold on to it.	There are all manner of thoughts which rise up from the Reality within and manifest themselves. Hold on to that Reality.	This state is compared to the waveless ocean whose waters are still and placid.	This state is compared to a flame unagitated by currents of air, but burning quite steady
	All these four kinds of savikalpa samadhi are attended with effort		When these four kinds of nirvikalpa samadhi are not attended with effort and it is realised that the waveless ocean of external samadhi and the steady flame of internal samadhi are identical, the state is said to be sahaja nirvikalpa samadhi.	

M.: The *Kundalini* of *jnana marga* is said to be the Heart, which is also described in various ways as a network of *nadis*, of the shape of a serpent, of a lotus bud, etc.

D.: Is this Heart the same as the physiological heart?

M.: No, *Sri Ramana Gita* defines it as the origin of the 'I-thought'.

D.: But I read that it is on the right of the chest.

M.: It is all meant to help the *bhavana* (imagery). There are books dealing with six centres (*shadchakra*) and many other *lakshyas* (centres), internal and external. The description of the Heart is one among so many *lakshyas*. But it is not necessary. It is only the source of the 'I-thought'. That is the ultimate truth.

D.: May we take it to be the source of the *antahkaranas*?

M.: The inner organs (*antakaranas*) are classified as five: (1) Knowledge — *Jnana*; (2) Mind — *Manas*; (3) Intellect — *Buddhi*; (4) Memory — *Chitta*; and (5) The ego — *Ahankara*; some say only the latter four; others say only two, namely (1) *Manas*, mind and (2) *Ahankara*, the ego; still others say the *Antahkarana* is only one whose different functions make it appear differently and hence its different names. Heart is thus the source of the *Antahkaranas*.

There is the body which is insentient; there is the Self which is eternal and self-luminous; in between the two there has arisen a phenomenon, namely the ego, which goes under these different names, mind (*manas*), intellect (*buddhi*), memory (*chitta*), the ego (*ahankara*), power (*sakti*), life current (*prana*), etc. Seek your source; the search takes you to the Heart automatically. The *antahkaranas* are only ideas (*kalpana*) to explain the subtle body (*sukshma sarira*). The physical body (*sarira*) is made up of the elements: earth, air, fire, water and ether; it is insentient. The Self is pure and self-luminous and thus self-evident. The relation between the two is sought to be established by positing a subtle body, composed of the subtle aspects of the five elements on the one hand, and the reflected light of the Self on the other. In this way the subtle body which is synonymous with the mind, is both sentient and insentient, *i.e.*, *abhasa*. Again, by the play of the pure quality (*satva guna*) on the elements, their brightness (*satva* aspect) manifests as the mind (*manas*), and the senses (*jnanendriyas*); by the

375

play of *rajas* (active quality), the *raja* (active) aspect manifests as life (*prana*) and limbs (*karmendriyas*); by the play of dullness (*tamas*) the *tama* (dark) aspect manifests as the gross phenomena of the body, etc.

D.: But the mind is reputed to have these three qualities also.

M.: Yes. There is purity (*satva*) in *satva* (in the pure quality); activity in it (*rajas* in *satva*); and dullness also (*tamas* in *satva*); and so on, *Suddha satva* is quite pure; *misra* (mixed *satva*) is a combination of *satva* with other qualities. The quality *satva* implies only its predominance over the other two qualities.

Later Sri Bhagavan continued: The intricate maze of philosophy of different schools is said to clarify matters and reveal the Truth. But in fact they create confusion where no confusion need exist. To understand anything there must be the Self. The Self is obvious. Why not remain as the Self? What need to explain the non-self?

Take the *Vedanta* for instance: They say there are fifteen kinds of *prana*. The student is made to commit the names to memory and also their functions. The air goes up and is called *prana*; goes down and is called *apana*; operates the *indriyas* and is called something. Why all this? Why do you classify, give names and enumerate the functions, and so on? Is it not enough to know that one *prana* does the whole work?

The *antahkarana* thinks, desires, wills, reasons, etc., and each function is attributed to one name such as mind, intellect, etc. Has anyone seen the *pranas* or the *antahkaranas*? Have they any real existence? They are mere conceptions. When and where will such conceptions end?

Consider the following:-

A man sleeps. He says on waking that he slept. The question is asked: 'Why does he not say in his sleep that he is sleeping?' The answer is given that he is sunk in the Self and cannot speak, like a man who has dived in water to bring out something from the bottom. The diver cannot speak under water; when he has actually recovered the articles he comes out and speaks. Well, what is the explanation?

Being in water, water will flow into his mouth if he were to open the mouth for speaking. Is it not simple? But the philosopher is not content with this simple fact. He explains, saying that fire is the deity presiding over speech; that it is inimical to water and therefore cannot function! This is called philosophy and the learners are struggling to learn all this! Is it not a sheer waste of time? Again the Gods are said to preside over the limbs and senses of the individual (*vyashti*). They are the limbs and senses of *Virat* (*samashti*). So they go on explaining *Hiranyagarbha*, etc. Why should confusion be created and then explained away? Ah! Fortunate is the man who does not involve himself in this maze!

I was indeed fortunate that I never took to it. Had I taken to it, I would probably be nowhere — always in confusion. My *purva vasanas* (former tendencies) directly took me to the enquiry "Who am I?" It was indeed fortunate!

11th April, 1937

Talk 393.

D.: There is a short account of the spiritual experiences of St. Theresa, in the March number of the *Prabuddha Bharata*. She was devoted to a figure of the Madonna which became animated to her sight, and she was in bliss. Is it the same as *Saktipata*?

M.: The animated figure indicates depth of meditation (*dhyana bala*). *Saktipata* prepares the mind for introversion. There is a process of concentration of mind on one's own shadow which in due course becomes animated and answers questions put to it. That is due to strength of mind or depth of meditation. Whatever is external is also transitory. Such phenomena may produce joy for the time being. But abiding peace, *i.e.*, *santi*, does not result. This is got only by the removal of *avidya* (ignorance).

Talk 394.

D.: How is the mind to be stilled?

M.: Looking at the mind with the mind, or fixing the mind in the Self, brings the mind under control of the Self.

D.: Is there any yoga, *i.e.*, a process for it?

M.: Vichara (investigation) alone will do.

377

Talk 395.

D.: How is *Poorna* Brahman to be attained? What is the method best suited to a *grihasta*?

M.: You have already said *poorna, i.e.,* perfection. Are you apart from *Poorna*? If apart from it, will it be *poorna*? If not apart how does the question arise? The knowledge that Brahman is *poorna* and that you are not apart from the same is the finality. See it and you will find that you are not a *grihasta* or any limited being.

D.: What are the *tatvas*?

M.: Knowledge of *poorna* Brahman will elucidate the other matters automatically.

12th April, 1937

Talk 396.

A Dutch lady, Mrs. Gongrijp, an ardent theosophist, who had worked long in Java and is now living in Adyar, came here for a short visit. She asked:

Theosophy speaks of *tanha*, meaning thirst for rebirth. What is its cause?

M.: Thirst for rebirth is the desire to be reborn so as to end successive births. The spirit is at present moribund; it must be revived so that rebirth may take place after the present apparent death. Forgetfulness of your real nature is the present death; remembrance of it is the rebirth. It puts an end to successive births. Yours is eternal life.

D.: I take *tanha* to mean 'clinging to life' — the desire for eternal life.

M.: No doubt it is so. How does the desire arise? Because the present state is unbearable. Why? Because it is not your true nature. Had it been your real nature no desire would disturb you. How does the present state differ from your real nature? You are spirit in truth. However that spirit is wrongly identifying itself with the gross body. The body has been projected by the mind; the mind itself has originated from the spirit. If the wrong identification ceases, there will be peace and permanent untellable bliss.

D.: Life is of the body and rebirth is to incarnate in another body.

378

M.: Mere change of body produces no effect. The ego associated with this body is transferred to another body. How can that satisfy anyone?

Moreover, what is life? Life is existence which is your Self. That is life Eternal. Otherwise can you imagine a time when you are not?

That life is now conditioned by the body and you wrongly identify your being with that of the body. You are life unconditioned. These bodies attach themselves to you as mental projections and you are now afflicted by 'I-am-the-body' idea. If this idea ceases you are your Self.

Where or how were you before being born? Were you in sleep? How were you? You exist then too without the body. Then the ego arises, and then the mind which projects the body. 'I-am-the-body' idea is the result. Because the body exists you say that it was born and that it will die, and transfer the idea to the Self saying that you are born and that you will die. In fact you remain without the body in sleep; but now you remain with the body. The Self can remain without the body, but the body cannot exist apart from the Self.

'I-am-the-body' thought is ignorance; that the body is not apart from the Self is knowledge. That is the difference between knowledge and ignorance.

The body is a mental projection, the mind is the ego; and the ego rises from the Self. So the body-thought is distracting and strays away from the Self. For whom is the body or the birth? It is not for the Self, the Spirit. It is for the non-self which imagines itself separate. So long as there is the sense of separation there will be afflicting thoughts. If the original source is regained and the sense of separation is put an end to, there is peace.

Consider what happens when a stone is thrown up. It leaves its source and is projected up, tries to come down and is always in motion until it regains its source, where it is at rest. So also the waters of the ocean evaporate, form clouds which are moved by winds, condense into water, fall as rain and the waters roll down the hill in streams and rivers, until they reach their original source, the ocean, reaching which they are at peace. Thus, you see, wherever there is a sense of separateness from the source there is agitation and movement until the sense of separateness is lost. So it is with yourself. Now that you identify yourself with the body you think that you are separate from the Spirit — the true Self. You must regain your source before the false identity ceases and you are happy.

Gold is not an ornament, but the ornament is nothing but gold. Whatever shape the ornament may assume and however different the ornaments are, there is only one reality, namely gold. So also with the bodies and the Self. The single reality is the Self. To identify oneself with the body and yet to seek happiness is like attempting to cross a river on the back of an alligator. The body identity is due to extroversion and the wandering of the mind. To continue in that state will only keep one in an endless tangle and there will be no peace. Seek your source, merge in the Self and remain all alone.

Rebirth means discontent with the present state, and desire to be born where there will be no discontent. Births, being of the body, cannot affect the Self. The Self remains over even after the body perishes. The discontent is due to the wrong identity of the Eternal Self with the perishable body. The body is a necessary adjunct of the ego. If the ego is killed the eternal Self is revealed in all its glory.

The body is the Cross. Jesus, the son of man, is the ego or 'I am-the-body' idea. When he is crucified, he is resurrected as the Glorious Self — Jesus, the Son of God! — "Give up this life if thou wouldst live"

Talk 397.

D.: Fear is consequent on the possibility of non-existence. It pertains to the body. One is not aware of the body in sleep. One is not afraid of, but courts sleep, whereas one dreads death. Why is this difference between the two outlooks?

M.: Desire of sleep or fear of death are when the mind is active and not in the respective states themselves. The mind knows that the body entity persists and reappears after sleep. Therefore sleep is not attended with fear but the pleasure of non-bodily existence is sought. Whereas the mind is not sure of reappearance after the so-called death and dreads it.

380

14th April, 1937

Talk 398.

Dandapani, a resident devotee now on a North Indian tour, sent an extract from the Modern Psychological Review which stated that the dynamic centre of the Heart is on the right and not on the left whereas the physical organ is on the left.

Conversation followed on that subject.

M.: The yoga *marga* speaks of the six centres each of which must be reached by practice and transcended until one reaches *sahasrara* where nectar is found and thus immortality. The yogis say that one enters into the *paranadi* which starts from the sacral plexus whereas the *jnanis* say that the same *nadi* starts from the heart. Reconciliation between the seeming]y contradictory statements is effected in the secret doctrine which distinctly states the *yogic paranadi* is from *muladhara* and the *jnana paranadi* is from the Heart. The truth is that the *paranadi* should be entered. By yogic practice one goes down, then rises up, wanders all through until the goal is reached; by *jnana abhyas* one settles down directly in the centre.

D.: Is not *para* followed by *pasyanti*, etc.?

M.: You are speaking of *vak* which is divided into (1) *para*, (2) *pasyanti*, (3) *madhyama* and (4) *vaikhari*; *Vak* is *prana sakti* whereas the mind is *tejorupa* or *chit sakti*. The *sakti* is the manifestation of the unmanifest origin.

The Yogis attach the highest importance to going up to *sahasrara* i.e., the brain centre or the thousand-petalled-lotus. Some yogis say that there are other centres higher up with greater involutions *e.g.*, 100,000 (100) petalled or 100,000,000 (108) petalled ones. Let us omit them for the present. They point out the scriptural statement that the life-current enters the body through the fontanelle and argue that, *viyoga* (separation) having come about that way, yoga (union) must also be effected in the reverse way. Therefore we must by yoga practice, gather up the *pranas* and enter the fontanelle for the consummation of yoga. The *jnanis* point out that the yogi assumes

381

the existence of the body, its separateness from the Self, and therefore advises effort for reunion by the practice of yoga.

In fact, the body is in the mind which has the brain for its seat, which again functions by light borrowed from another source as admitted by the yogis themselves in their fontanelle theory. The *jnani* further argues: if the light is borrowed it must come from its native source. Go to the source direct and do not depend on borrowed resources. Just as an iron ball comes into being separate from the mass of iron, gets fiery, in fire, later cools down giving up the fire, but must again be made fiery to reunite with the original mass, so also the cause of separation must also form the factor of reunion.

Again if there is an image reflected there must be a source and also accessories like the Sun and a pot of water for reflection. To do away with the reflection either the surface is covered up corresponding to reaching the fontanelle according to the yogis or the water is drained away which is called *tapas* (*Tapo Brahmeti* — *tapas* is Brahman). That is to say, the thoughts or the brain activities are made to cease. This is *jnana-marga*.

All these are however on the assumption that the *jiva* is separate from the Self or Brahman. But are we separate? "No", says the *jnani*. The ego is simply wrong identity of the Self with the non-self, as in the case of a colourless crystal and its coloured background. The crystal though colourless appears red because of its background. If the background is removed the crystal shines in its original purity. So it is with the Self and the *antahkaranas*.

Still again the illustration is not quite appropriate. For the ego has its source from the Self and is not separate like the background from the crystal. Having its source from the Self, the ego must only be retraced in order that it might merge in its source.

The centre of the ego and its core is called the Heart, the same as the Self.

A gentleman asked if the yogis also reach the *anahata* and thus realise the Heart-centre as is done by the *jnanis* but in a different way.

M.: *Anahata* is not the same as the Heart-centre. If so, why should they wander further on to *Sahasrara*? Moreover, the question arises

382

because of the sense of separateness persisting in us. We are never away from the Heart-centre. Before reaching *anahata* or after passing it, one is only in the centre. Whether one understands it or not, one is not away from the centre. Practice of yoga or *vichara* is done, always remaining in the centre only.

D.: What is to be our *sadhana*?

M.: Sadhana for the *sadhaka* is the *sahaja* of the *siddha*. *Sahaja* is the original state, so that *sadhana* amounts to the removal of the obstacles to the realisation of this abiding truth.

D.: Is concentration of mind one of the *sadhanas*?

M.: Concentration is not thinking one thing. It is, on the other hand, putting off all other thoughts which obstruct the vision of our true nature. All our efforts are only directed to lifting the veil of ignorance. Now it appears difficult to quell the thoughts. In the regenerate state it will be found more difficult to call in thoughts. For are there things to think of? There is only the Self. Thoughts can function only if there are objects. But there are no objects. How can thoughts arise at all?

The habit makes us believe that it is difficult to cease thinking. If the error is found out, one would not be fool enough to exert oneself unnecessarily by way of thinking.

D.: Is not grace more effective than *abhyasa*?

M.: Guru simply helps you in the eradication of ignorance. Does he hand over Realisation to you?

D.: We are ignorant.

M.: Inasmuch as you say you are ignorant, you are wise. Is he a madman who says that he is mad? Guru's Grace is like a hand extended to help you out of water, or it makes your way easier for the removal of ignorance.

D.: Is it not like a medicine to cure the disease of *avidya*?

M.: What is medicine for? It is only to restore the patient to the original state of health. What is this talk of Guru. Grace, God, etc.? Does the Guru hold you by the hand and whisper something in your ear? You imagine him to be like yourself. Because you are with a body you think that he is also a body in order to do something tangible

383

to you. His work lies within. How is Guru gained? God, who is immanent, in his Grace takes pity on the loving devotee and manifests Himself as a being according to the devotee's standard. The devotee thinks that he is a man and expects relationship as between bodies. But the Guru, who is God or Self incarnate, works from within, helps the man to see the error of his ways, guides him in the right path until he realises the Self within.

After such realisation the disciple feels, "I was so worried before. I am after all the Self, the same as before but not affected by anything; where is he who was miserable? He is nowhere to be seen."

What should we do now? Only act up to the words of the master, work within. The Guru is both within and without. So he creates conditions to drive you inward and prepares the interior to drag you to the centre. Thus he gives a push from without and exerts a pull from within so that you may be fixed at the centre.

In sleep you are centred within. Simultaneously with waking your mind rushes out, thinking this, that and all else. This must be checked. It is possible only for the agent who can work both within and without. Can he be identified with a body? We think that the world can be conquered by our efforts. When frustrated externally and driven internally, we feel "Oh! oh! There is a power higher than man." The existence of the higher power must be admitted and recognised. The ego is a very powerful elephant and cannot be brought under control by anyone less than a lion, who is no other than the Guru in this instance; whose very look makes the elephant tremble and die. We will know in due course that our glory lies where we cease to exist. In order to gain that state, one should surrender oneself saying "LORD! Thou art my Refuge!" The master then sees "This man is in a fit state to receive guidance," and so guides him.

D.: What is Self-surrender?

M.: It is the same as self-control; control is effected by removal of *samskaras* which imply the functioning of the ego. The ego submits only when it recognises the Higher Power. Such recognition is surrender or submission, or self-control. Otherwise the ego remains stuck up like the image carved on a tower, making a pretence by its strained look and posture that it is supporting the tower on its shoulders. The ego cannot exist without the Power but thinks that it acts of its own accord.

D.: How can the rebellious mind be brought under control?

M.: Either seek its source so that it may disappear or surrender that it may be struck down.

D.: But the mind slips away from our control.

M.: Be it so. Do not think of it. When you recollect yourself bring it back and turn it inward. That is enough.

No one succeeds without effort. Mind control is not one's birthright. The successful few owe their success to their perseverance.

A passenger in a train keeps his load on the head by his own folly. Let him put it down: he will find the load reaches the destination all the same. Similarly, let us not pose as the doers, but resign ourselves to the guiding Power.

D.: Swami Vivekananda says that a spiritual Guru can transfer spirituality substantially to the disciple.

M.: Is there a substance to be transferred? Transfer means eradication of the sense of being the disciple. The master does it. Not that the man was something at one time and metamorphosed later into another.

D.: Is not Grace the gift of the Guru?

M.: God, Grace and Guru are all synonymous and also eternal and immanent. Is not the Self already within? Is it for the Guru to bestow It by his look? If a Guru thinks so, he does not deserve the name.

The books say that there are so many kinds of *diksha* (initiations — *hasta diksha, sparsa diksha, chakshu diksha, mano diksha*, etc.) They also say that the Guru makes some rites with fire, water, *japa, mantras*, etc., and call such fantastic performances *dikshas*, as if the disciple (*sishya*) becomes ripe only after such processes are gone through by the Guru.

If the individual is sought he is nowhere to be found. Such is the Guru. Such is Dakshinamurti. What did he do? He was silent; the disciples appeared before him. He maintained silence, the doubts of the disciples were dispelled, which means that they lost their

385

individual identities. That is *jnana* and not all the verbiage usually associated with it.

Silence is the most potent form of work. However vast and emphatic the sastras may be, they fail in their effect. The Guru is quiet and peace prevails in all. His silence is more vast and more emphatic than all the sastras put together. These questions arise because of the feeling, that having been here so long, heard so much, exerted so hard, one has not gained anything. The work proceeding within is not apparent. In fact the Guru is always within you.

Thayumanavar says: "Oh Lord! Coming with me all along the births, never abandoning me and finally rescuing me!" Such is the experience of Realisation.

Srimad Bhagavad Gita says the same in a different way, "We two are not only now but have ever been so."

D.: Does not the Guru take a concrete form?

M.: What is meant by *concrete*? Because you identify your being with your body, you raise this question. Find out if you are the body.

The Gita says: *param bhavam ajanantah* (Bh. Gita IX — II) — that those who cannot understand the transcendental nature (of Sri Krishna) are fools, deluded by ignorance.

The master appears to dispel that ignorance. As Thayumanavar puts it, he appears as a man to dispel the ignorance of a man, just as a deer is used as a decoy to capture the wild deer. He has to appear with a body in order to eradicate our ignorant "I-am-the-body" idea.

15th April, 1937

Talk 399.

Mr. Bose, the Bengali Engineer, has since read *Gaudapada Karikas* and Sir S. Radhakrishnan's *Indian Philosophy* and so asked questions as follows:

D.: Is there any genuine difference between dream experience and waking state?

M.: Because you find the dream creations transitory in relation to the waking state there is said to be a difference. The difference is only apparent and not real.

386

D.: Is the waking state independent of existing objects?

M.: Were it so, the objects must exist without the seer; that is to say, the object must tell you that it exists. Does it do so? For example, does a cow moving in front of you say that she is moving? Or do you say of your own accord "There is a cow moving"? The objects exist because of the seer cognising them.

D.: Gaudapada in *Mandukya Karikas* says that there is no difference between the two states from the standpoint of Reality-Absolute.

M.: Of course not.

D.: I believe Bhagavan also says so. Prof. Radhakrishnan in his *Indian Philosophy* says that in his Brahma Sutra Commentary Sri Sankara makes a distinction between the two states. Is it a fact? If so, what is it? How can there be any distinction from the viewpoint of reality? So long as the mind exists in any form there will be distinction. But from the standpoint of *Atman*, non-dual Brahman, can there be any distinction?

M.: The dream is for the one who says that he is awake. In fact, wakefulness and dream are equally unreal from the standpoint of the Absolute.

D.: In pure *Advaita* can evolution, creation or manifestation have any place? What about the theory of *vivarta* according to which Brahman appears as the world without forgetting its essential nature, like the rope appearing as snake?

M.: There are different methods of approach to prove the unreality of the universe. The example of the dream is one among them. *Jagrat, svapna* and *sushupti* are all treated elaborately in the scripture in order that the Reality underlying them might be revealed. It is not meant to accentuate differences among the three states. The purpose must be kept clearly in view.

Now they say that the world is unreal. Of what degree of unreality is it? Is it like that of a son of a barren mother or a flower in the sky, mere words without any reference to facts? Whereas the world is a fact and not a mere word. The answer is that it is a superimposition on the one Reality, like the appearance of a snake on a coiled rope seen in dim light.

But here too the wrong identity ceases as soon as the friend points out that it is a rope. Whereas in the matter of the world it persists even after it is known to be unreal. How is that? Again the appearance of water in a mirage persists even after the knowledge of the mirage is recognised. So it is with the world. Though knowing it to be unreal, it continues to manifest.

But the water of the mirage is not sought to satisfy one's thirst. As soon as one knows that it is a mirage, one gives it up as useless and does not run after it for procuring water.

D.: Not so with the appearance of the world. Even after it is repeatedly declared to be false one cannot avoid satisfying one's wants from the world. How can the world be false?

M.: It is like a man satisfying his dream wants by dream creations. There are objects, there are wants and there is satisfaction. The dream creation is as purposeful as the *jagrat* world and yet it is not considered real.

Thus we see that each of these illustrations serves a distinct purpose in establishing the stages of unreality. The realised sage finally declares that in the regenerate state the *jagrat* world also is found to be as unreal as the dream world is found to be in the *jagrat* state.

Each illustration should be understood in its proper context; it should not be studied as an isolated statement. It is a link in a chain. The purpose of all these is to direct the seeker's mind towards the one Reality underlying them all.

D.: Is there that difference in the philosophy of Sankara and Gaudapada which the learned Professor wants us to believe?

M.: The difference is only in our imagination.

D.: Sir S. Radhakrishnan writes:

"The general idea pervading Gaudapada's work that bondage and liberation, the individual soul and the world are all unreal, makes a caustic critic observe that the theory which has nothing better to say than that an unreal soul is trying to escape from an unreal Supreme Good, may itself be an unreality. It is one thing to say that the unchangeable reality expressing itself in the changing universe without forfeiting its nature is a mystery, and another to dismiss the

388

whole changing universe as a mere mirage. If we have to play the game of life we cannot do so with the conviction that the play is a show and all the prizes in it are mere blanks. No philosophy can consistently hold such a theory and be at rest with itself. The greatest condemnation of such a theory is that we are obliged to occupy ourselves with objects the existence and value of which we are continually denying in theory. It only shows that there is something else which includes and transcends the world but it does not imply the world is a dream."

M.: As was already said, the purpose of the whole philosophy is to indicate the underlying Reality whether of the *jagrat, svapna* and *sushupti* states, or the individual souls, the world and God.

There are three outlooks possible:-

(1) The *Vyavaharika:* The man sees the world in all its variety, surmises the creator and believes in himself as the subject. All these are thus reduced to the three fundamentals, *jagat, jiva* and *Isvara.* He learns the existence of the creator and tries to reach him in order to gain immortality. If one is thus released from bondage, there are all other individuals existing as before who should work out their own salvation. He more or less admits the One Reality underlying all these phenomena. The phenomena are due to the play of *maya.* *Maya* is the *sakti of Isvara* or the activity of Reality. Thus, existence of different souls, objects, etc., do not clash with the *advaitic* point of view.

(2) The *Pratibhasika*: The *jagat, jiva* and *Isvara* are all cognised by the seer only. They do not have any existence independent of him. So there is only one *jiva*, be it the individual or God. All else is simply a myth.

(3) The *Paramarthika*: *i.e., ajatavada* (no-creation doctrine) which admits of no second. There is no reality or absence of it, no seeking or gaining, no bondage or liberation and so on.

The question arises why then do all the *sastras* speak of the Lord as the creator? How can the creature that you are create the creator and argue that the *jagat, jiva* and *Isvara* are mental conceptions only?

The answer is as follows:-

389

You know that your father of this *jagrat* state is dead and that several years have elapsed since his death. However you see him in your dream and recognise him to be your father, of whom you were born and who has left patrimony to you. Here the creator is in the creature. Again, you dream that you are serving a king and that you are a part in the administrative wheel of the kingdom. As soon as you wake up all of them have disappeared leaving you, the single individual, behind. Where were they all? Only in yourself. The same analogy holds good in the other case also.

D.: In the *Vyavaharika*, above mentioned, how does *maya* come in?

M.: Maya is only *Isvara-Sakti* or the activity of Reality.

D.: Why does it become active?

M.: How can this question arise? You are yourself within its fold. Are you standing apart from that universal activity in order to ask this question? The same Power is raising this doubt in order that all doubts may finally cease.

D.: The dream world is not purposeful as the *jagrat* world, because we do not feel that wants are satisfied.

M.: You are not right. There are thirst and hunger in dream also. You might have had your fill and kept over the remaining food for the next day. Nevertheless you feel hungry in dream. This food does not help you. Your dream-hunger can be satisfied only by eating dream-food. Dream-wants are satisfied by dream-creations only.

D.: We recollect our dreams in our *jagrat* but not *vice-versa*.

M.: Not right again. In the dream you identify yourself with the one now speaking.

D.: But we do not know that we are dreaming as apart from waking as we do now.

M.: The dream is the combination of *jagrat* and *sushupti*. It is due to the *samskaras* of the *jagrat* state. Hence we remember dreams at present. *Samskaras* are not formed contrariwise; therefore also we are not aware of the dream and *jagrat* simultaneously. Still everyone will recollect strange perplexities in dream. One wonders if he dreams or is awake. He argues and determines that he is only awake. When really awake, he finds that it was all only a dream.

390

Talk 400.

In the course of another conversation Sri Bhagavan said: Photisms add zest to meditation and nothing more.

16th April, 1937

Talk 401.

Mr. Krishnamurti, an Andhra gentleman, asked as follows:- When we make *tapas*, on what object must we fix our sight? Our mind is fixed on what we utter.

M.: What is *tapas* for?

D.: For Self-Realisation.

M.: Quite so. *Tapas* depends on the competency of the person. One requires a form to contemplate. But it is not enough. For can anyone keep looking at an image always? So the image must be implemented by *japa*. *Japa* helps fixing the mind on the image, in addition to the eyesight. The result of these efforts is concentration of mind, which ends in the goal. He becomes what he thinks. Some are satisfied with the name of the image. Every form must have a name. That name denotes all the qualities of God. Constant *japa* puts off all other thoughts and fixes the mind. That is *tapas*. One-pointedness is the *tapas* wanted.

The question what *tapas* is was asked in order to know what purpose to serve. It will take the form required for the purpose.

D.: Are not physical austerities also *tapas*?

M.: May be one form of it. They are due to *vairagya* (dispassion)

D.: I have seen a man with his arm lifted all his life.

M.: That is *vairagya*.

D.: Why should one afflict his body for the purpose?

M.: You think it is affliction whereas it is a vow and for the other man it is an achievement and a pleasure.

Dhyana may be external or internal or both. *Japa* is more important than external form. It must be done until it becomes natural. It starts with effort and is continued until it proceeds of itself. When natural it is called Realisation.

391

Japa may be done even while engaged in other work. That which is, the One Reality. It may be represented by a form, a *japa, mantra, vichara* or any kind of attempt. All of them finally resolve themselves into that One Single Reality. *Bhakti, vichara, japa* are only different forms of our efforts to keep out the unreality. The unreality is an obsession at present. Reality is our true nature. We are wrongly persisting in unreality, that is, thoughts and worldly activities. Cessation of these will reveal the Truth. Our attempts are directed towards keeping them out. It is done by thinking of the Reality only. Although it is our true nature it looks as if we are thinking of the Reality. What we do really amounts to the removal of obstacles for the revelation of our true Being. Meditation or *vichara* is thus a reversion to our true nature.

D.: Are our attempts sure to succeed?

M.: Realisation is our nature. It is nothing new to be gained. What is new cannot be eternal. Therefore there is no need for doubting if one would lose or gain the Self.

Talk 402.

While speaking of the Brain and the Heart Sri Bhagavan recalled an incident of old days as follows:-

Kavyakantha Ganapati Muni once argued that the brain was the most important centre and Sri Bhagavan maintained that the Heart was even more so. There were others watching the discourse. A few days after Sri Bhagavan received a letter containing a short poem in English on that discourse from a young boy, N. S. Arunachalam, who had not yet matriculated.

That poem is remarkable for its poetic imagination. Sri Bhagavan, Kavyakantha, and the assemblage of other persons are represented as the Heart, the brain and the body respectively, and again as the sun, the moon and the earth also. The light from the sun is reflected on the moon and the earth is illumined. Similarly the brain acts by consciousness derived from the Heart and the body is thus protected. This teaching of Sri Bhagavan is found in *Ramana Gita* also. The Heart is the most important centre from which vitality and light radiate to the brain, thus enabling it to function. The *vasanas* are enclosed in the Heart in their subtlest form, later flowing to the brain which reflects them highly magnified corresponding to a cinema-show at every stage. That is how the world is said to be nothing more than a cinema-show. Sri Bhagavan also added:-

Were the *vasanas* in the brain instead of in the Heart they must be extinguished if the head is cut off so that reincarnations will be at an end. But it is not so. The Self obviously safeguards the *vasanas* in its closest proximity, *i.e.* within itself in the Heart, just as a miser keeps his most valued possessions (treasure) with himself and never out of contact. Hence the place where the *vasanas* are, is the Self, *i.e.*, the Heart, and not the brain (which is only the theatre for the play of the *vasanas* from the greenhouse of the Heart.)

17th April, 1937

Talk 403.

There was some reference to the extract from the *Modern Psychological Review*, wondering if any instruments could be of use in detecting the Heart-centre and if proper subjects were available for recording the experience of the adepts in the spiritual path, and so on. Others were speaking. Sri Bhagavan said: In the incident mentioned in the book *Self-Realization* that I became unconscious and symptoms of death supervened, I was all along aware. I could feel the action of the physical heart stopped and equally the action of the Heart-centre unimpaired. This state lasted about a quarter of an hour.

We asked if it was true that some disciples have had the privilege of feeling Sri Bhagavan's Heart-centre to be on the right by placing their hands on Sri Bhagavan's chest. Sri Bhagavan said, "Yes." (Mr. Viswanatha Iyer, Narayana Reddi and others have said they felt Sri Bhagavan's Heart-centre to be on the right by placing their hands on his chest).

A devotee rightly observed that if hands could feel and locate the Heart-centre, delicate scientific instruments should certainly do it.

D.: The Heart is said to be on the right, on the left or in the centre. With such differences of opinion how are we to meditate on *Hridaya*?

M.: You *are* and it is a fact. *Dhyana* is by you, of you, and in you. It must go on where you are. It cannot be outside you. So you are the centre of *dhyana* and that is the Heart.

A location is however given to it with reference to the body. You know that you *are*. Where are you? You are in the body and not out of it. Yet not the whole body. Though you pervade the whole body still you admit of a centre where from all your thoughts start and wherein they subside. Even when the limbs are amputated you are there but with defective senses. So a centre must be admitted. That is called the Heart. The Heart is not merely the centre but the Self. Heart is only another name for the Self.

Doubts arise only when you identify it with something tangible and physical. The scriptures no doubt describe it as the source of 101 *nadis*, etc. In *Yoga Vasishta* Chudala says that *kundalini* is composed of 101 *nadis*, thus identifying one with the other.

Heart is no conception, no object for meditation. But it is the seat of meditation; the Self remains all alone. You see the body in the Heart, the world in it. There is nothing separate from it. So all kinds of effort are located there only.

18th April, 1937

Talk 404.

A casual visitor asked:

What is *nishta*? How is the look to be directed between the eyebrows?

M.: How do we see these things? There is a light by which these are seen. Your question amounts to asking how that light is seen.

D.: What is the significance of the spot between the eyebrows?

M.: That is mentioned as if to say: "Do not see with your eyes."

D.: What is regulation of breath for?

M.: Only to control the mind.

394

Again after a few minutes Sri Bhagavan continued: The mind functions both as light and as objects. If divested of things the light alone will remain over.

D.: But we must know that there is such light.

M.: Sight or cognition is impossible without such light. How do you cognise anything in sleep? Our cognition pertains to the present state because there is light. Light is the essential requisite for sight. It is plain in our daily life. Among the lights, sunlight is the most important. Hence they speak of the glory of millions of suns.

D.: There is light if we press the eyelids with our fingers.

Another questioner: What is the use of seeing such a light?

M.: It is done lest we forget the goal. The practice helps one not to divert the attention to other pursuits.

The object is seen or the light is recognised because there is the subject to do so. How does it affect the subject whether the objects are seen or not? If the light, *i.e.*, the cogniser or the consciousness is seen, there will be no object to be seen. Pure light, *i.e.*, Consciousness, will alone remain over.

D.: Why then is the regulation of breath necessary?

M.: Control of breath or its regulation is only for controlling the mind so that the mind may not wander away.

D.: Is it for control of mind only?

M.: It is not enough that light is seen; it is also necessary to have the mind engaged in a single activity, *e.g.*, the elephant trunk and the chain.

D.: How long will it take for one to gain *Chintamani* (the celestial gem granting all the wishes of its owner)?

M.: The example of *Chintamani* is found in *Yoga Vasishta*. *Chintamani* signifies the Real nature of the Self. The story is as follows:-

A man was making *tapasya* for gaining *Chintamani*. A gem mysteriously fell into his hands. He thought that it could not be *Chintamani* because his efforts had been too short and too little to gain the gem. He discarded it and continued the *tapas*. Later a *sadhu* placed before him a brilliant pebble with facets cut. The man was taken in by its appearance but found that it could not fulfil his desires as he originally supposed. Similarly, the Self, being inherent, should not be sought for elsewhere.

Again, an elephant used to be often teased by its keeper. He once had an accident and fell down. The elephant could have killed him on the spot but did not do so. Later, however, the keeper dug a big pit in the forest and killed the elephant.

Chudala illustrated Sikhidhvaja's error by this story. He had *vairagya* even while ruling his kingdom and could have realised the Self if only he had pushed his *vairagya* to the point of killing the ego. He did not do it, but came to the forest, had a timetable of *tapas* and yet did not improve even after 18 years of *tapas*. He had made himself a victim of his own creation. Chudala advised him to give up the ego and realise the Self which he did and was liberated.

It is clear from Chudala's story that *vairagya* accompanied by ego is of no value, whereas all possessions in the absence of ego do not matter.

19th April, 1937

Talk 405.

A respectable and orthodox gentleman asked about Sri Chakra.

M.: It has a deep significance. There are 43 corners with sacred syllables in them. Its worship is a method for concentration of mind. The mind is wont to move externally. It must be checked and turned within. Its habit is to dwell on names and forms, for all external objects possess names and forms. Such names and forms are made symbolic mental conceptions in order to divert the mind from external objects and make it dwell within itself. The idols, *mantras, yantras*, are all meant to give food to the mind in its introvert state, so that It may later become capable of being concentrated, after which the superb state is reached automatically.

20th April, 1937

Talk 406.

Mr. Cohen, a resident disciple, has been for some days past thinking about a book called *Nirvana* written by a prominent Theosophist, wherein the author claims to reach *nirvana* every night after going to sleep. He claims to see his own Master and other Masters of the Theosophical Society as bright lights within the ocean of light which is *nirvana*. He asked Sri Bhagavan how it could be possible, considering the *Advaitic* teaching that the *nirvanic* experience is the same as that of the pure consciousness of Being.

M.: Nirvana is Perfection. In the Perfect State there is neither subject nor object; there is nothing to see, nothing to feel, nothing to know. Seeing and knowing are the functions of the mind. In *nirvana* there is nothing but the blissful pure consciousness "I am."

D.: How then can a prominent T. S. leader, who claims clairvoyance of a high order, praise the author for his supposed correct and vivid description of *nirvana*, and why is the T. Society so much obsessed by the idea of 'Service'?

M.: Well, Theosophy and other kindred movements are good inasmuch as they make a man unselfish and prepare him for the highest truth. Service, like prayers, *japas* and even business done in God's name, lead to the highest goal — Self-Realisation.

D.: But after how long? and why should a man who is ready for the Absolute knowledge stick to the knowledge of the Relative?

M.: Everything happens in its own time. The one who is ready for the absolute knowledge will be made somehow to hear of it and follow it up. He will realise that *Atmavidya* is the highest of all virtues and also the end of the journey.

Then, asked about the difference between external and internal *nirvikalpa samadhis*, referring to article 391 above, the Master said:

External *samadhi* is holding on to the Reality while witnessing the world, without reacting to it from within. There is the stillness of a waveless ocean. The internal *samadhi* involves loss of body-consciousness.

D.: Is loss of body-consciousness a perquisite to the attainment of *sahaja samadhi*?

M.: What is body-consciousness? Analyse it. There must be a body and consciousness limited to it which together make up body-consciousness. These must lie in another Consciousness which is absolute and unaffected. Hold it. That is *samadhi*. It exists when there is no body-consciousness because it transcends the latter, it also exists when there is the body-consciousness. So it is always there. What does it matter whether body-consciousness is lost or retained? When lost it is internal *samadhi:* when retained, it is external *samadhi*. That is all.

A person must remain in any of the six *samadhis* so that *sahaja samadhi* may be easy for him.

D.: The mind does not sink into that state even for a second.

M.: A strong conviction is necessary that I am the Self, transcending the mind and the phenomena.

D.: Nevertheless, the mind proves to be a cord against attempts to sink it.

M.: What does it matter if the mind is active? It is so only on the substratum of the Self. Hold the Self even during mental activities.

D.: I cannot go within sufficiently deep.

M.: It is wrong to say so. Where are you now if not in the Self? Where should you go? All that is necessary is the stern belief that you are the Self. Say rather that the other activities throw a veil on you.

D.: Yes, it is so.

M.: That means that the conviction is weak.

D.: I understand that the 'I' is only artificial (*krtrima*), my attempts at realising the real 'I' are unavailing because the artificial 'I' is brought into action for realising the other.

M.: Viveka Chudamani makes it clear that the artificial 'I' of the *vijnana kosa* is a projection and through it one must look to the significance (*vachya*) of 'I', the true principle.

Talk 407.

D.: St. Theresa and others saw the image of Madonna animated. It was external. Others see the images of their devotion in their mental sight. This is internal. Is there any difference in degree in these two cases?

M.: Both indicate that the person has strongly developed meditation. Both are good and progressive. There is no difference in degree.

The one has a conception of divinity and draws mental images and feels them. The other has the conception of divinity in the image and feels it in the image. The feeling is within in both instances.

21st April, 1937

Talk 408.

With reference to the location of the Heart centre on the right side of the human body, Sri Bhagavan said:-

I had been saying all along that the Heart centre was on the right, notwithstanding the refutation by some learned men that physiology taught them otherwise. I speak from experience. I knew it even in my home during my trances. Again during the incident related in the book *Self-Realisation* I had a very clear vision and experience. All of a sudden a light came from one side erasing the world vision in its course until it spread all round when the vision of the world was completely cut out. I felt the muscular organ on the left had stopped work, I could understand that the body was like a corpse, that the circulation of blood had stopped and the body became blue and motionless. Vasudeva Sastri embraced the body, wept over my death, but I could not speak. All the time I was feeling that the Heart centre on the right was working as well as ever. This state continued 15 or 20 minutes. Then suddenly something shot out from the right to the left resembling a rocket bursting in air. The blood circulation was resumed and normal condition restored. I then asked Vasudeva Sastri to move along with me and we reached our residence.

The Upanishads say that 101 *nadis* terminate in the Heart and 72,000 originate from them and traverse the body. The Heart is thus the centre of the body. It can be a centre because we have been accustomed to think that we remain in the body. In fact the body and all else are in that centre only.

REMINISCENCES

Talk 409.

A middle-aged man prostrated himself before Sri Bhagavan, who asked him about his well-being. After a few minutes Sri Bhagavan

399

recalled an incident saying that this was the only person whom Sri Bhagavan had slapped; it happened about 30 years earlier.

Sri Bhagavan was living in Mulaippal Tirtha. There was a Jada Swami living in the neighbourhood (*Mamarathu Guhai*). This man, who was then about 8 years of age, used to play pranks with all, including Sri Bhagavan. One day he went to Maharshi and said that Jada Swami wanted a bucket. Without waiting for permission, he took away the bucket. Palani Swami the attendant, was not there. So Sri Bhagavan followed the boy to Jada Swami's place. Before Bhagavan reached the place the boy had told the other that Brahmanaswami had sent him a bucket. Jada Swami was wondering why! In a few minutes Maharshi reached the place and learnt what had passed. So he raised His hand to give a slap to the boy but the mind would not yield to slapping. But He argued within Himself and determined that the urchin should be slapped and so he did it.

Talk 410.

There is a Tamil stanza by Awai. It is an address of the *prana* to the stomach; its meaning is:

"O stomach! How difficult it is to get on with you! You cannot starve when no food is available, nor can you take more and keep it in reserve when food is plenty! You will take only what you want and when you want; thus you are troublesome to me, allowing me no rest."

Sri Bhagavan altered it thus: Stomach addressing the *prana*: "O *Prana*! How troublesome you are to me! You never allow me to rest but continue loading me with food off and on. It is so difficult to get on with you."

Saying it Sri Bhagavan laughed. Sri Bhagavan often says that He is made to eat more than is good for Him.

21st May, 1937

Talk 411.

Sri Bhagavan, while speaking of the marriage ceremony among the Brahmins, said that the *Kasiyatra* represents the bridegroom to be a *vairagi-purusha*. It is therefore right that he should be given a

400

kanya (virgin) for leading a householder's life. It follows that a *vairagi* can alone be a good householder.

Talk 412.

Once on a cold day Sri Bhagavan was sitting in a cave on the hill with His hands folded on the breast as a protection against the cold. Some Andhra visitor had come; he broke a coconut and poured the cold juice on Sri Bhagavan's head as *abhisheka*; Sri Bhagavan was surprised.

Talk 413.

A visitor asked:

While making *nama-japa* and after continuing it for an hour or more I fall into a state like sleep. On waking up, I recollect that my *japa* has been interrupted. So I proceed again.

M.: "Like sleep." That is right. It is the natural state. Because you are now associated with the ego you consider the natural state to be something which interrupts your work. You must repeat the experience until you realise that it is your natural state. You will then find that *japa*, etc., is extraneous. Still, it will be going on automatically. Your present doubt is due to the false identity.

Japa means clinging to one thought to the exclusion of all other thoughts. That is the purpose of *japa*; it leads to *dhyana* which ends in Self-Realisation.

Talk 414.

Mr. G. V. Subbaramiah, a devotee, has written some short poems, which are interesting. Some of them refer to a child. Sri Bhagavan said God becomes a child, and *vice versa*. That means that the *samskaras* are yet latent in the child and thus its innocence is complete. When they are eradicated even a grown up man becomes a child once again, and thus remains God.

The author said: The child creates the 'home' atmosphere.

Sri Bhagavan: Yes. The children are always in the 'home'. We too are there but are dreaming and imagining that we are outside the home.

Sri Bhagavan added: I have rendered the word 'youth' (*yuva*) in *Dakshinamurti Stotra* by 'child' (*bala*). This seems more appropriate. To be reborn is to become children over again. One must be reborn before gaining *jnana*, *i.e.*, recovering the natural state.

Talk 415.

Sri Bhagavan read out some stanzas on the greatness of the Tamil language from the preface to a Tamil-Tamil Dictionary and explained the references in a very interesting manner. Of the three tests for establishing the superiority of Saivism over Jainism, the first related to Tirujnanasambandar entering the royal presence for curing the Pandya king of his illness. The queen was anxious because of his tender age, *i.e.*, 12 years. Tirujnanasambandar set her doubts at rest by composing a stanza which said that, though tender, he was more than a match to the strong group of innumerable Jains. While reciting the stanza Sri Bhagavan choked and could not proceed with it.

The second test was the fire leaving the cadjan leaf unburnt, and the third the cadjan leaves opposing the current of the river (Tiruvedakam).

Sri Bhagavan also related the story of God Isvara begging food as an old man, taking food as a youth and saving the devotee woman as a babe, all at once.

He again pointed out 'like babe, lunatic, spirit' (*Balonmatta-pisachavat*) describing the states of *jnanis*. There babe (*bala*) is given precedence over others.

Talk 416.

Sri Bhagavan said that *Kamba Ramayana* consists of 12,000 stanzas to Valmiki's 24,000. Kamba's can be understood only by the learned and not by all. Tulasidas had heard *Kamba Ramayana* recited to him in Hindi by a Tamil saint and later wrote his famous Ramayana.

Talk 417.

The Perfect Master is a book on Meher Baba published in 1937.

There is an incident of a ship's officer instructing the reluctant Immigration Officer to let Baba and his party land in New York,

USA. When one of the party went to thank him he was nowhere to be found.

The incident is recorded so as to leave an impression of a miracle happening in favour of Baba. The passage was read out to Sri Bhagavan.

Bhagavan said: Yes, yes, what of that?

D.: Is it a miracle?

M.: Maybe. But did not the Immigration Officer recognise the other to be his superior officer whose orders should be obeyed? There is an end of the matter. If a man of Baba's party could not find him — well, it may be due to several reasons.

Talk 418.

Asked if Sri Bhagavan had read *Kamba Ramayana*, Sri Bhagavan said: No. I have not read anything. All my learning is limited to what I learnt before my 14th year. Since then I have had no inclination to read or learn. People wonder how I speak of Bhagavad Gita, etc. It is due to hearsay. I have not read Gita nor waded through commentaries for its meaning. When I hear a sloka I think that its meaning is clear and I say it. That is all and nothing more. Similarly with my other quotations. They come out naturally. I realise that the Truth is beyond speech and intellect. Why then should I project the mind to read, understand and repeat stanzas, etc.? Their purpose is to know the Truth. The purpose having been gained, there is no use engaging in studies.

Someone remarked: If Sri Bhagavan had been inclined to study there would not be a saint today.

M.: Probably all my studies were finished in past births and I was surfeit. There is therefore no *samskara* operating now in that direction.

Talk 419.

The week before the Mahapuja (3rd June, 1937) has brought many visitors including some relatives of Sri Bhagavan. There is among them an elderly lady — the widow of Subbier in whose house Sri Bhagavan was living when he left home in August 1896.

Old memories revived when Sri Bhagavan saw her.

He remembered how on a festive occasion he was asked to help her in making some *modakas* (delicacies), but he hesitated and finally refused, because he was obliged to change his clothes and he could put on only *koupina* (loin-cloth or codpiece) which made him feel shy. He was reprimanded by his uncle and this lady. The uncle's wife said with humility and gentleness: "Quite. No wonder that one destined for this high state could not do such humble work in those days."

Then Sri Bhagavan remarked, "If I refused to wear *koupina* once, I am now made to pay the penalty by wearing it always."

The lady recalled to her mind how Sri Ramana was suffering from headache for several days together.

Sri Bhagavan said: Yes, yes! It was the month before I left Madura. It was not headache, but an inexpressible anguish which I suppressed at the time; these were however the outward symptoms which, I said, were due to headache. I remember how anxious you grew on account of my headache. You used to rub some ointment on my forehead every day. My anguish continued until I left Madura and reached this place.

4th June, 1937

Talk 420.

A certain lawyer from Cuddalore quoted as follows: "Neither the sun shines there, nor the moon, nor the stars, nor lightning. How can fire shine there? All these luminaries shine in His Light only. With His Light, all these shine forth!" He asked, what does 'with His Light' mean here? Does all else shine on account of Him, or in His Light?

M.: There is only He. He and His Light are the same. There is no individual to perceive other things, because the perceiver and the perceived are only He. The sun, the moon, etc., shine forth. How? Do they come and tell you that they shine forth or does another apart from them say that they shine forth?

D.: Of course I say that they shine forth.

M.: Therefore they shine on account of you. Again consciousness is necessary to know that they shine forth. That consciousness is your

Self or you. So then you or your consciousness is the same as He and His Light by which all else shine forth.

D.: Is that Light like sunlight?

M.: No. The sunlight is *jada* (insentient). You are aware of it. It makes objects perceptible and chases away darkness, whereas consciousness is that Light which makes not only light but also darkness perceptible. Darkness cannot exist before sunlight, but it can remain in the Light of Consciousness. Similarly, this consciousness is pure Knowledge in which both knowledge and ignorance shine.

D.: If God is all why does the individual suffer for his actions? Are not the actions prompted by Him for which the individual is made to suffer?

M.: He who thinks he is the doer is also the sufferer.

D.: But the actions are prompted by God and the individual is only His tool.

M.: This logic is applied only when one suffers, but not when one rejoices. If the conviction prevails always, there will be no suffering either.

D.: When will the suffering cease?

M.: Not until individuality is lost. If both the good and bad actions are His, why should you think that the enjoyment and suffering are alone yours? He who does good or bad, also enjoys pleasure or suffers pain. Leave it there and do not superimpose suffering on yourself.

Talk 421.

A resident devotee, Kunju Swami, related an observation of Sri Maharshi after the robbery in the Asramam in 1923.

Some disciples were asking why the robbers should be allowed to molest even *sadhus* and why the *sadhus* would not protect themselves and their dependents from the robbers.

Sri Bhagavan observed: There were *rishis* like Visvamitra who could duplicate the universe if they wished. They lived during the lifetime of Ravana who caused agony even to Sita and Rama among others. Could not Visvamitra have destroyed Ravana by his occult powers? Though capable he kept still. Why? The occurrences are known to the sages, but pass away without leaving an impression on their minds. Even a deluge will appear a trifle to them; they do not care for anything.

Talk 422.

Dr. Venkata Rao, a visitor from Guntur, asked: A Guru asks his disciple to do things contrary to ethical principles. But the disciple, having accepted the person as the master, desires to please the master but his moral sense obstructs him. What should he do under the circumstances?

M.: (No reply).

D.: I shall make myself clear. The Guru asked his disciple to commit a theft and the disciple did not do it. The master then said, "I wanted to test you to see if you had completely surrendered yourself or retained your individuality. It is now clear what it is." Is the Guru right in ordering the disciple that way?

M.: (Still no reply).

Another person observed: There are persons on whom I refuse to sit in judgement. Still I cannot help feeling if they deserve the appellation of Gurus. They appear bogus men. If they be really worthy they would not order the disciples in that way.

M.: But the person says, "It is for a test."

The questioner continued: Should it be carried out?

M.: Your original statement contains the answer to your question.

Both the questioners jointly asked: The action is disagreeable. Can it be done?

M.: The question might be referred to the person himself, *i.e.*, the Guru. He is responsible for the situation.

Talk 423.

A young man asked: I try to cultivate will-power but do not succeed. How should I do it?

M.: (No answer)

D.: I came here three years ago and Sri Bhagavan said that will-power is necessary for strength of mind. Since then I have been desiring to cultivate it but without success.

M.: (No answer)

D.: During these years I have had 4 or 5 reverses. They upset me considerably. There is always the fear of failure haunting my attempts. This results in want of faith in myself which certainly foredooms my efforts to failure. Nothing in fact succeeds like success; and also nothing foils one's attempts like failure. Hence my question.

M.: (No answer).

D.: Is not will-power necessary for success? It should ensure success and also rule out failure.

M.: (No answer)

D.: I try to gain will-power. After these years I find myself only where I began. There is no progress.

M.: (No answer)

D.: What are the means for gaining will-power?

M.: Your idea of will-power is success insured. Will-power should be understood to be the strength of mind which makes it capable for meeting success or failure with equanimity. It is not synonymous with certain success. Why should one's attempts be always attended with success? Success develops arrogance and the man's spiritual progress is thus arrested. Failure on the other hand is beneficial, inasmuch as it opens the eyes of the man to his limitations and prepares him to surrender himself. Self-surrender is synonymous with eternal happiness. Therefore one should try to gain the equipoise of mind under all circumstances. That is will-power. Again, success and failure are the results of *prarabdha* and not of will-power. A man may be doing only good and noble actions and yet prove a failure. Another may do otherwise and yet be uniformly successful. This does not mean that the will-power is present in the one and not in the other.

D.: Is it not said in the book *Truth Revealed* (*Ulladu Narpadu*) that the world is a product of the mind?

M.: Yes.

407

D.: Does it not follow that the mind grown strong brings the world under control?

M.: The mind in its external activities gives rise to the world. Such activities fritter away the strength of the mind. Its strength lies in being confined to itself with the external activities arrested.

D.: There is an idiot who cannot count up to ten. His mind does not certainly wander as does that of a thinker. Is the former a better man than the latter?

M.: Who says that he is an idiot? Your mind in its wandering says so.

D.: Is will-power gained by divesting oneself of thoughts?

M.: Rather by confining oneself to a single thought. Ultimately this will also disappear, leaving Pure Consciousness behind. Concentration helps one to it.

D.: So then, it is gained by directing the mind and concentrating it. The personality has nothing to do with it.

M.: Personality is the root-cause of external activities. It must sink for gaining the highest good.

Talk 424.

In the course of conversation with a learned man who asked about *Purusha* and *Prakriti*, Sri Bhagavan said:

Purusha and *Prakriti* are only the bifurcation of the one Supreme. They are surmised because the student has the sense of duality deep rooted. The same Gita also says that *Purushottama* lies beyond *Purusha* and *Prakriti*.

D.: What are *para-nadi*, *Sushumna nadi* and the Heart?

M.: But *Sushumna* resolves into the *para* (*Sushumnatu pareleena*). Heart is usually understood to be the muscular organ lying on the left of the chest. The Modern Psychological Review speaks of the physical organ on the left and the Heart centre on the right. The Bible says that a fool's heart is on the left and a wise man's on the right. *Yoga Vasishta* says that there are two hearts; the one is *samvit*; and the other the blood-vessel.

D.: What is *Anahata*?

408

M.: Anahata is the *chakra* lying behind the heart. It is not *samvit*. *Lalita Sahasranama* has it, *Anahata chakrasthayai namo namah* (Salutations to the core situated in *Anahata*) and the next mantra *Hrit* (in the Heart). Thus it is clear that *Anahata* is not the same as *Hrit*.

Talk 425.

Will-power or any other is gained by practice (*abhyasa*).

D.: Is success not dependent on Guru's Grace?

M.: Yes, it is. Is not your practice itself due to such Grace? The fruits are the result of the practice and follow it automatically. There is a stanza in *Kaivalya* which says, "O Guru! You have been always with me watching me through several reincarnations, and ordaining my course until I was liberated." The Self manifests externally as Guru when occasion arises; otherwise He is always within, doing the needful.

12th June, 1937

Talk 426.

Mr. Das, of Allahabad University: Has the food which one usually takes anything to do with increase or decrease of one's spirituality? That is, does it influence spirituality for good or bad?

M.: Yes. *Satvic* food in moderate quantity is helpful to spiritual development.

D.: For a *grihi, i.e.,* a man of the world (householder), what conduct in life will help him *most* spiritually?

M.: Dhyana or *bhakti*, which mean the same thing.

D.: What is meant by taking the name of God? How to reconcile the following two ideas?

The Bible says: "Do not take the name of God in vain."

The Hindu *sastras* enjoin taking the name of God all the time.

M.: One should not use the name of God artificially and superficially without feeling. To use the name of God one must call upon Him and surrender to Him unreservedly. After such surrender the name of God is constantly with the man.

D.: What are the fundamental tests for discovering men of great spirituality, since some are reported to behave like insane people?

M.: The *jnani's* mind is known only to the *jnani*. One must be a *jnani* oneself in order to understand another *jnani*. However the peace of mind which permeates the saint's atmosphere is the only means by which the seeker understands the greatness of the saint.

His words or actions or appearance are no indications of his greatness, for they are ordinarily beyond the comprehension of common people.

D.: Has man any Free-Will or is everything in his life predestined and preordained?

M.: Free-Will holds the field in association with individuality. As long as individuality lasts so long there is Free-Will. All the *sastras* are based on this fact and they advise directing the Free-Will in the right channel.

Find out to whom Free-Will or Destiny matters. Abide in it. Then these two are transcended. That is the only purpose of discussing these questions. To whom do these questions arise? Find out and be at peace.

D.: Are intellect and emotion, like the physical body, growths which come with the birth of man; and do they dissolve or survive after death?

M.: Before considering what happens after death, just consider what happens in your sleep. Sleep is only the interval between two waking states. Do they survive that interval?

D.: Yes, they do.

M.: The same holds good for death also. They represent body-consciousness and nothing more. If you are the body they always hold on to you. If you are not the body they do not affect you. The one who was in sleep is now in waking state just speaking. You were not the body in sleep. Are you the body now? Find it out. Then the whole problem is solved.

Similarly, that which is born must die. Whose is the birth? Were you born? If you say you were, of whose birth are you speaking? It is the body which was born and it is that which will die. How do birth and death affect the eternal Self?

Think and say to whom the questions arise. Then you will know.

Talk 427.

D.: It is said that the Universe consists of light and sound. Are these two constituents like the light and sound in the physical world? Can they be seen and heard with the physical organs — eye and ear? Or are they to be experienced only subjectively?

M.: Light and sound correspond to *bindu* and *nada* in *Tantrik* terminology, and to the mind and life-current in the *Vedantic*. They are gross, subtle and transcendental. The organs can perceive the gross aspect; the other aspects are not so perceptible. The subtle can be inferred and the transcendental is only transcendental.

D.: Hinduism lays down reincarnation of the *jiva*. What happens to the *jiva* during the interval between the death of one body and the birth of the next one?

M.: Solve this question by referring to the state of sleep. What happens to you in sleep?

D.: I do not know.

M.: Yet you exist. Therefore existence beyond knowledge and ignorance is indicated. Although ignorance was prevailing, according to your present idea, yet you did not say so in sleep. You continued to exist all the same. Mere ignorance does not rule out the fact of your existence.

D.: In the practice of meditation are there any signs of the nature of subjective experience or otherwise, which will indicate the aspirant's progress towards Self-Realisation

M.: The degree of freedom from unwanted thoughts and the degree of concentration on a single thought are the measure to gauge the progress.

D.: Is it necessary to take to *sanyasa* for Self-Realisation?

M.: *Sanyasa* is to renounce one's individuality. This is not the same as tonsure and ochre robes. A man may be a *grihi*; yet, if he does not think he is a *grihi*, he is a *sanyasi*. On the contrary a man may wear ochre robes and wander about: yet if he thinks he is a *sanyasi* he is not that. To think of *sanyasa* defeats its own purpose.

Sri Bhagavan remarked:

411

People see the world. The perception implies the existence of a seer and the seen. The objects are alien to the seer. The seer is intimate, being the Self. They do not however turn their attention to finding out the obvious seer but run about analysing the seen. The more the mind expands, the farther it goes and renders Self-Realisation more difficult and complicated. The man must directly see the seer and realise the Self.

D.: So then, it amounts to synthesising phenomena and finding the one Reality behind.

M.: Why do you still consider the phenomena? See who the seer is. Synthesis means engaging the mind in other pursuits. That is not the way to Realisation.

D.: I want to eliminate the non-self so that the Self may be realised. How shall I do it? What are the characteristics of the non-self?

M.: There is one who says that the non-self must be eliminated. Who is he?

D.: I mean this man. When I travel from Calcutta to Madras I must know Madras so that I may not alight at an intermediate station out of ignorance. There are the sign boards and the timetable to guide me in my travel. But what is the guide in my search for the Self?

M.: It is all right for the journey. You know how far away you are from Madras. Can you tell me how far away you are from the Self in order that you should seek it?

D.: I do not know.

M.: Are you ever divorced from the Self? Is it possible to be divorced? Are not all these alien to you and the Self the most intimate? Where should you go to gain the Self?

D.: I am now away from the Self. I must retrace my steps in order to regain it.

M.: How far away? Who says that he is apart? Can there be two selves?

D.: It is said that individuals are modifications of the Self, just as ornaments are of gold.

M.: When a man speaks in terms of ornaments ignoring their substance gold, he is told that they are gold. But here the man is

412

consciousness and speaks of himself as its modification. Do you remain apart from Self that you speak of yourself as Its modification?

D.: Cannot gold be imagined to say that it has become an ornament?

M.: Being insentient, it does not say so. But the individual is sentient and cannot function apart from consciousness. The Self is Pure Consciousness. Yet the man identifies himself with the body which is itself insentient and does not say "I am the body" of its own accord. Someone else says so. The unlimited Self does not. Who else is he that says so? A spurious 'I' arises between the Pure Consciousness and the insentient body and imagines itself limited to the body. Seek this and it will vanish as a phantom. That phantom is the ego, or the mind or the individuality.

All the *sastras* are based on the rise of this phantom, whose elimination is their purpose. The present state is mere illusion. Disillusionment is the goal and nothing more.

D.: The mind is said to be a bundle of thoughts.

M.: Because it functions on account of a single root the 'I-thought'.

मानसंतु किं मार्गणेकृते नैव मानसं मार्ग आर्जवात्

Manasantu kim margane krte naiva manasam marga arjavat.

It has no real existence as a separate entity.

D.: Are not thoughts projections from the mind?

M.: In that case the mind is taken to be synonymous with the 'I-thought' or the ego.

15th December, 1937

Talk 428.

Sri Bhagavan has selected 10 stanzas from the famous work of Sri Sankara — *Sivananda Lahari* — describing devotion (*bhakti*):

(1) What is *bhakti*?

Just as the *ankola* fruit falling from the tree rejoins it or a piece of iron is drawn to magnet, so also thoughts, after rising up, lose themselves in their original source. This is *bhakti*. The original source of thoughts is the feet of the Lord, *Isvara*. Love of His Feet forms *bhakti*. (61)

413

(2) Fruit of *bhakti:*

The thick cloud of *bhakti*, formed in the transcendental sky of the Lord's Feet, pours down a rain of Bliss (*ananda*) and fills the lake of mind to overflowing. Only then the *jiva*, always transmigrating to no useful end, has his real purpose fulfilled. (76)

(3) Where to place *bhakti*?

Devotion to gods, who have themselves their origin and end, can result in fruits similarly with origin and end. In order to be in Bliss everlasting our devotion must be directed to its source, namely the Feet of the ever blissful Lord. (83)

(4) *Bhakti* is a matter only for experience and not for words:

How can Logic or other polemics be of real use? Can the *ghatapatas* (favourite examples of the logicians, meaning the pot and the cloth) save you in a crisis? Why then waste yourself thinking of them and on discussion? Stop exercising the vocal organs and giving them pain. Think of the Feet of the Lord and drink the nectar! (6)

(5) Immortality is the fruit of Devotion:

At the sight of him who in his heart has fixed the Lord's Feet, Death is reminded of his bygone disastrous encounter with Markandeya and flees away.

All other gods worship only Siva, placing their crowned heads at His feet. Such involuntary worship is only natural to Siva.

Goddess Liberation, His consort, always remains part of Him. (65)

(6) If only Devotion be there — the conditions of the *jiva* cannot affect him.

However different the bodies, the mind alone is lost in the Lord's Feet. Bliss overflows! (10)

(7) Devotion always unimpaired:

Wherever or however it be, only let the mind lose itself in the Supreme. It is Yoga! It is Bliss! Or the Yogi or the Bliss incarnate! (12)

(8) Karma Yoga also is *Bhakti*:

To worship God with flowers and other external objects is troublesome. Only lay the single flower, the heart, at the feet of Siva and remain at Peace. Not to know this simple thing and to wander about! How foolish! What misery! (9)

414

(9) This Karma Yoga puts an end to one's *samsara*:

Whatever the order of life (*asrama*) of the devotee, only once thought of, Siva relieves the devotee of his load of *samsara* and takes it on Himself. (11)

(10) Devotion is *Jnana*:

The mind losing itself in Siva's Feet is Devotion. Ignorance lost! Knowledge! Liberation! (91)

16th December, 1937

Talk 429.

A few ladies had come from Bangalore. One among them asked: The world is composed of differences, from our point of view. How shall we able to get over these differences and comprehend the One Essence of all things?

M.: The differences are the result of the sense of doership (*kartritva*). The fruits will be destroyed if the root is destroyed. So relinquish the sense of doership; the differences will vanish and the essential reality will reveal itself.

In order to give up the sense of doership one must seek to find out who the doer is. Enquire within; the sense of doership will vanish. *Vichara* (enquiry) is the method.

22nd December, 1937

Talk 430.

A Marathi gentleman asked: I have read much about Self-Realisation; I do *japa*, *puja*, etc.; nothing seems to satisfy me. Can Sri Bhagavan kindly guide me?

M.: What is that you seek to gain? Everyone seeks happiness. Happiness is one's lot in everyday sleep. Bring about that state of happiness even in the waking state. That is all.

D.: I do not follow. How is it to be done?

M.: *Atma Vichara* is the way.

D.: It seems too difficult to adopt, being so intangible. What shall I do if I feel unfit for this method of enquiry?

M.: Guidance is there. It is for individuals to avail themselves of it.

415

25th December, 1937

Talk 431.

A Telugu gentleman stood up and asked: The mind is said to be pure when all its *vasanas* are wiped out. It is also the finality. When there is something to be gained is it not duality?

M.: Let the mind be first made pure. If the same question arises thereafter the answer may then be sought.

26th December, 1937

Talk 432.

An Andhra visitor asked: What is sleep?

M.: Why, you experience it every day.

D.: I want to know exactly what it is, so that it may be distinguished from *samadhi*.

M.: How can you know sleep when you are awake? The answer is to go to sleep and find out what it is.

D.: But I cannot know it in this way.

M.: This question must be raised in sleep.

D.: But I cannot raise the question then.

M.: So, that is sleep.

Sri Bhagavan went out for a few minutes. On his return the same man asked:

Self-realised *jnanis* are seen to take food and do actions like others. Do they similarly experience the states of dream and of sleep?

M.: Why do you seek to know the state of others, maybe *jnanis*? What do you gain by knowing about others? You must seek to know your own real nature.

Who do you think that you are? Evidently, the body.

D.: Yes.

M.: Similarly, you take the *jnani* to be the visible body whereon the actions are superimposed by you. That makes you put these questions. The *jnani* himself does not ask if he has the dream or sleep state. He has no doubts himself. The doubts are in you. This must convince you of your wrong premises. The *jnani* is not the body. He is the Self of all.

416

The sleep, dream, *samadhi*, etc., are all states of the *ajnanis*. The Self is free from all these. Here is the answer for the former question also.

D.: I sought to know the state of *sthita prajnata* (unshaken knowledge).

M.: The *sastras* are not for the *jnani*. He has no doubts to be cleared. The riddles are for *ajnanis* only. The *sastras* are for them alone.

D.: Sleep is the state of nescience and so it is said of *samadhi* also.

M.: *Jnana* is beyond knowledge and nescience. There can be no question about that state. It is the Self.

Talk 433.

Mr. Thomas, Professor of Sanskrit, University of Oxford, had presided over the Oriental Conference in Trivandrum and on his way to Calcutta he visited Sri Bhagavan. He is an elderly gentleman with a broad forehead and a quiet manner. He speaks softly and slowly. He evinces great interest in oriental literature, especially Sanskrit. He had heard of the richness of Tamil. He desired to know which of the English translations of *Srimad Bhagavad Gita* was the best. The hall was crowded and a few of them mentioned, with each his own opinion, Thibaut's, Mahadeva Sastri's, Telang's, etc. Sri Bhagavan made mention of F. T. Brooks. Mr. Thomas desires one in metrical form because it is the proper vehicle for *rasa* (the essence) contained in it. *Rasa* is also Peace, he said.

M.: Yes, Brahman is only *rasa*.

D.: *Rasa* is also Bliss.

M.: *Rasa, Ananda*, Peace are all names for the same Bliss.

The Professor was shown Mr. Grant Duff's speech in the Philosophical Conference held at Paris. Later the book 'Dharma' by Dr. G. H. Mees was placed in his hands, on seeing which he asked what Sri Bhagavan thought of castes.

M.: The castes relate to bodies and not to Self. The Self is Bliss. To realise Bliss one realises the Self. No need to worry oneself about caste, etc.

D.: The *ahamkar* is also called the Self.

417

M.: Ahamkar is limited, whereas the Self is beyond it.

D.: There is much literature in English relating to Eastern philosophy and religion. There are different exponents. The system of Ramanuja is well presented. Prof. Radhakrishnan expounds the *advaitic* system. He lays more stress on experience than on evidence. Sankara shows a highly developed mind.

A discussion followed on direct perception. The Professor spoke of mental perception also as different from sense perception.

M.: To infer one's existence no other evidence is necessary. The *indriyas* (senses) and the mind arising from the ego cannot serve as evidence relating to the Self. The Self is their basis. They do not exist independently of the Self. One's own existence is self-evident. Bliss is the Self. All become dear only owing to the love of Self.

D.: Love postulates duality. How can the Self be the object of love?

M.: Love is not different from the Self. Love of an object is of an inferior order and cannot endure. Whereas the Self is Love, in other words, God is Love.

D.: It is also the Christian idea.

He also asked Sri Bhagavan which of the methods was the best for the attainment of the goal. Is not Patanjali's the best?

M.: Yogas chitta vritti nirodhah — (Yoga is to check the mind from changing) — which is acceptable to all. That is also the goal of all. The method is chosen according to one's own fitness. The goal for all is the same. Yet different names are given to the goal only to suit the process preliminary to reaching the goal. *Bhakti, Yoga, Jnana* are all the same. *Svasvarupanusandhanam bhaktirity abhidheeyate* (Self contemplation is called *bhakti*).

D.: Does Sri Bhagavan advocate *advaita*?

M.: Dvaita and *advaita* are relative terms. They are based on the sense of duality. The Self is as it is. There is neither *dvaita* nor *advaita*. I AM THAT I AM. Simple Being is the Self.

D.: This is not *mayavada*.

M.: The mind is *maya*. Reality lies beyond the mind. So long as the mind functions there is duality, *maya*, etc. Once it is transcended

418

the Reality shines forth. Although it is said to shine forth Self-effulgence is the Self.

D.: It is *Sat-chit-ananda.*

M.: *Sat-chit-ananda* is said to indicate that the Supreme is not *asat* (different from unreal), not *achit* (different from insentient) and not an *anananda* (different from unhappiness). Because we are in the phenomenal world we speak of the Self as *Sacchidananda.*

D.: *Aham* 'I' applies to the individual and also to Brahman. It is rather unfortunate.

M.: It is *upadhi bheda* (owing to different limiting adjuncts). The bodily limitations pertain to the *aham* ('I') of the *jiva*, whereas the universal limitations pertain to the *aham* ('I') of Brahman. Take off the *upadhi* (limiting adjunct); the 'I' (*Aham*) is pure and single.

D.: Does Bhagavan give *diksha* (initiation)?

M.: *Mowna* (silence) is the best and the most potent *diksha*. That was practised by Sri Dakshinamurti. Touch, look, etc., are all of a lower order. Silence (*mowna diksha*) changes the hearts of all. There is no Guru and no disciple. The *ajnani* confounds his body with the Self and so he takes the other's body for the Guru. But does the Guru think his body to be the Self? He has transcended the body. There are no differences for Him. So the *ajnani* cannot appreciate the standpoint of Guru and of *sishya.*

D.: Is there then no difference between the one and the other?

M.: There are differences from the standpoint of the phenomenal world but not from that of Reality.

The Professor was thankful. He hoped to appreciate Sri Bhagavan's writings better after having seen Him and conversed with Him.

In the course of conversation, Sri Bhagavan said that *upasana* and *dhyana* are possible so long as there is the mind and they must cease with the cessation of the mind. They are mere preliminaries to final eradication of thoughts and the stillness of mind.

D.: *Saiva Siddhanta* postulates three fundamentals as being eternal. Is it opposed to *Vedanta*?

M.: The three entities are *jiva*, God and bondage. Such trinities are common in all religions. They are true so long as the mind is operative. They are mere creations of the mind. One can postulate God only after the mind arises. God is not different from the Self. The Self is objectified as God. So also with Guru.

The Professor returned in the evening and asked something about good actions. He further wondered why Brahman is said to be *sacchidananda*, but not God.

M.: Sat denotes being beyond *sat* and *asat*:

Chit beyond *chit* and *achit*;

Ananda beyond bliss and non-bliss.

What is it then? Even if not *sat* nor *asat*, It must be admitted to be *sat* only. Compare the term *jnana*. It is the state beyond knowledge and ignorance. Yet *jnana* is not ignorance but knowledge. So also with *Sat-chit-ananda*.

D.: It favours the one aspect.

After a word about *Atma-vichara* he took leave saying that he would not trouble Sri Maharshi any further although he had several doubts yet to be cleared and that he wanted to make *nididhyasana* of what he had heard so far.

A judge from Mysore asked: *Upasana* and *dhyana* were said to be due to mental activities. Cessation of activities was also said to be Realisation. Now, how to realise without *upasana* or *dhyana*?

M.: They are preliminaries. Such action will lead to the desired inaction.

D.: The Heart is said to be experienced on the right. Physiologically it is on the left.

M.: Spiritual experience is spoken of.

D.: Is it the psychic heart?

M.: Yes.

D.: How to know that it is on the right?

M.: By experience.

D.: Is there any indication to that effect?

M.: Point out to yourself and see.

420

28th December, 1937

Talk 434.

Being Christmas holidays, there is a great rush of visitors from far and near. A group of them sat down and two among them asked as follows:

D.: Do you know English?

Prompted to ask questions, he continued:

D.: Have you realised your Self?

Sri Bhagavan smiled and said, "Go on, continue."

D.: Have you experienced *nirvikalpa samadhi*?

He was asked to finish his questions.

D.: Can you enter into *nirvikalpa samadhi* at will? Is it not necessary that sages should influence their surroundings?

Another man asked: Can Sri Bhagavan help us to realise the Truth?

M.: Help is always there.

D.: Then there is no need to ask questions. I do not feel the ever-present help.

M.: Surrender and you will find it.

D.: I am always at your feet. Will Bhagavan give us some *upadesha* to follow? Otherwise how can I get the help living 600 miles away?

M.: That *Sadguru* is within.

D.: *Sadguru* is necessary to guide me to understand it.

M.: The *Sadguru* is within.

D.: I want a visible Guru.

M.: That visible Guru says that He is within.

D.: Can I throw myself at the mercy of the *Sadguru*?

M.: Yes. Instructions are necessary only so long as one has not surrendered oneself.

D.: Is no particular time necessary for meditation?

M.: Meditation depends on strength of mind. It must be unceasing, even when one is engaged in work. Particular time is meant for novices.

D.: Will *Sadguru* place His hand on my head to assure me of His help? I will have the consolation that His promise will be fulfilled.

M.: A bond will be the next requisition and a suit will be filed if you imagine no help forthcoming. (Laughter).

D.: May I come near, Sir? (for blessing).

M.: Such doubts should not arise in you. They contradict your statement of surrender. *Sadguru* is always on your head.

D.: Surrender comes after effort.

M.: Yes, it becomes complete in due course.

D.: Is a teacher necessary for instructions?

M.: Yes, if you want to learn anything new. But here you have to unlearn.

D.: Yet a teacher is necessary.

M.: You have already got what you seek elsewhere. So no teacher is necessary.

D.: Is there any use of the man of Realisation for the seeker?

M.: Yes. He helps you to get rid of your delusion that you are not realised.

D.: So, tell me how.

M.: The paths are meant only to de-hypnotise the individual.

D.: De-hypnotise me. Tell me what method to follow.

M.: Where are you now? Where should you go?

D.: I know 'I am'; but I do not know what I am.

M.: Are there two 'I's then?

D.: It is begging the question.

M.: Who says this? Is it the one who is, or is it the other who does not know what he is?

D.: I am, but do not know what or how?

M.: 'I' is always there.

D.: Does the 'I' undergo any transformation, say in death?

M.: Who witnesses the transformation?

D.: You seem to speak *Jnana yoga*. This is *Jnana yoga*.

M.: Yes, it is.

D.: But surrender is *bhakti yoga*.

M.: Both are the same

After some time the man continued: Then I have to conclude that I am Consciousness and that nothing occurs except by my presence.

M.: It is one thing to conclude it by reasoning and another thing to be convinced.

The other man continued: I shall wait three months and see if help is forthcoming. Now, may I have the assurance?

M.: Is this what is asked by one who has surrendered?
Four visitors retired. The same man continued to say "Fulfil your promise." (Laughter).

He also said: God has given me enough for bread and butter and I am happy. In addition I want peace of mind. Hence this request.

29th December, 1937

Talk 435.

Two ladies and two gentlemen from Ceylon.

D.: Have you realised God? If so, in what shape?

M.: Who remains there to see God? The question might well be if one has known oneself.

D.: I have known myself.

M.: Is the 'I' different from the Self that you say you have known the Self?

D.: I know the Self as identical with the body. If the Self be different from the body let Bhagavan tell me how to see the Self separate from the body. He has realised God. He can teach me.

M.: Why should the Self be separated from the body? Let the body remain as it is.

D.: The soul when disembodied can see through all bodies.

M.: Are there others then? Or is there even your own body? Consider your sleep — You do not know your body then. But still you are there all the same. Did you then perceive the world through this or other bodies? Nevertheless, you cannot deny your existence then. There must be a subject to see the world and the subject must also be limited. If unlimited how can there be others beside the unlimited Self?

D.: Does God have any limits?

M.: Leave God alone. What limits were there for your Self in your sleep?

423

D.: Death must then be the highest state.

M.: Yes. We are now living in Death. Those who have limited the unlimited Self have committed suicide by putting on such limitations.

D.: Concentrate on the Self, you say. How to do it?

M.: If that is solved everything else is solved.

D.: Know thyself, you say. How to know the Self?

M.: You now know that you are the body.

D.: *Raja yoga* realises through the body, senses, etc., and Sri Bhagavan advises realisation by thinking. This is *jnana yoga*.

M.: How can you think without the body?

D.: God does not think.

M.: Why then did you start asking, "In what shape did you see God?"

D.: God must be felt through the senses.

M.: Are you not feeling God?

D.: Is everybody feeling God always?

M.: Yes.

D.: Then what is realisation?

M.: Realisation is to get rid of the delusion that you have not realised.

D.: I don't catch the point.

They left, having taken a snapshot.

Talk 436.

D.: What is *visvarupa*?

M.: It is to see the world as the Self of God. In the *Bhagavad Gita* God is said to be various things and beings, and also the whole universe. How to realise it or see it so? Can one see one's Self? Though not seen, can the Self be denied? What is the Truth?

D.: Is it then wrong to say that some have seen it?

M.: It is true in the same degree as you are. The *Gita* begins saying that no one was born; in the fourth chapter it says, "the numerous incarnations, yours and mine, have taken place; I know them but you do not." Of these two statements, which is the truth? The instruction is according to the listener's understanding. If the second chapter contains the whole Truth, why should so many more chapters follow it?

424

In the *Bible* God says "I AM before Abraham." He does not say "I was" but "I AM."

Talk 437.

M.: People have read of Vivekananda having asked Sri Ramakrishna, "Have you seen God?" and imitate him now. They also ask, "Have you realised God?"

I ask what is *realisation.*

Realisation implies perfection. When you are limited, your perception also is limited. Your knowledge is thus imperfect. Of what value is that imperfect knowledge?

In *Visvarupa Darsan*, Arjuna is told to see whatever he desired and not what was presented before him. How can that *darsan* be real?

30th December, 1937

Talk 438.

A visitor asked: For beginners like me which is most suited: either worship of qualified God or contemplation of "I am Brahman"?

M.: The answer is contained in the question. The question itself shows it to be worship of qualified God.

D.: "I" is felt in the waking and dream states but not in deep sleep. Why so?

M.: If so, does it not exist in deep sleep?

D.: Because there are mental modes in these two states and no such mode in the other.

Talks with Sri Ramana Maharshi

Volume III

3rd January, 1938

Talk 439.

D.: Rama asks: "Brahman being Pure, how can *maya* arise from Him and veil Him also? "Vasishta replies: "In pure mind associated with strong dispassion this question will not arise." Of course in *advaita* (non-dualistic) philosophy there can be no place for *jiva, Isvara* and *maya*. Oneself sinking into the Self, the *vasanas* (tendencies) will entirely disappear, leaving no room for such a question.

M.: The answers will be according to the capacity of the seeker. It is said in the second chapter of *Gita* that no one is born or dies: but in the fourth chapter Sri Krishna says that numerous incarnations of His and of Arjuna had taken place, all known to Him but not to Arjuna. Which of these statements is true? Both statements are true, but from different standpoints. Now a question is raised: How can *jiva* rise up from the Self? I must answer. Only know Your Real Being, then you will not raise this question.

Why should a man consider himself separate? How was he before being born or how will he be after death? Why waste time in such discussions? What was your form in deep sleep? Why do you consider yourself as an individual?

D.: My form remains subtle in deep sleep.

M.: As is the effect so is the cause. As is the tree so is its seed. The whole tree is contained in the seed which later manifests as the tree. The expanded tree must have a substratum which we call *maya*. As a matter of truth there is neither seed nor tree. There is only Being.

D.: Vasanakshaya (total end of all predispositions) — *Mano nasa* (annihilation of mind) — *Atma-sakshatkara* (Realisation of the Self). They seem to be interdependent.

M.: The different expressions have only one meaning. They differ according to the individual's stage of progress. Dispassion, Realisation, all mean the same thing; also they say 'practice and dispassion'. Why practice? Because the modes of mind once subside and then rise up; again subside and rise up, and so on.

D.: Beginningless predisposition makes one do wrong. Without *jnana* this predisposition cannot vanish. But *jnana* looks almost impossible. Expiation alone cannot undo all the karma; for how much expiation will be needed! Look where we will! Everything looks difficult, even impossible. Association with the wise seems to be the only cure of all ills.

M.: What is to be done? Reality is One only. How can It be realised? Realisation is thus an illusion. Practice seems to be necessary. Who is to practise? Looking for the doer, the act and the accessories disappear.

Moreover, if Realisation is not present here and now, how can It, newly got, be of any use? What is permanent must be eternally present. Can it be newly got and be permanent also?

Realise what is present here and now. The sages did so before and still do that only. Hence they say that it looks as if newly got. Once veiled by ignorance and later revealed, Reality looks as if newly realised. But it is not new.

D.: Karma, *bhakti, yoga* and *jnana* and their subdivisions only confuse the mind. To follow the elders' words seems to be the only right thing to do. What should I hold? Please tell me. I cannot sift the *srutis* and *smritis*; they are too vast. So please advise me.

(No answer.)

Talk 440.

D.: Without logic, without learned terminology, please instruct me the way to the Bliss of Self. Let it be of Guru's grace only.

M.: Have a clear idea of your requirement. Who seeks to gain what? Then ask the method.

D.: Bliss manifests occasionally but I am unable to describe it. At times there is illumination, but is it the Reality? If so, how to make it permanent? The method must be simple. Please make it clear without logic, learned discussions or mystifying words.

(No answer.)

Another visitor asked: Please tell me which is the most efficacious of all the methods, *e.g.*, prayer to God, Guru *anugraha*, *i.e.*, master's grace, concentration of mind, etc.

M.: The one is the consequence of the other. Each of them leads to the next stage. They form a continuous whole. God, Guru, and the Self are not different. They are one and the same. Therefore the methods offer no choice.

Talk 441.

Mr. Pannalal, I. C. S., a high Government official from Allahabad, with his wife, a highly cultured lady, and Mr. Brijnarayan, a retired judge, were on a visit for a week. The night previous to their departure they wanted to have their doubt cleared. Their doubt was:

We had a great sage for our Guru. He advised us to "take the name of Hari," saying that it is all in all; no effort is necessary for concentrating the mind. Concentration will come of itself if Harinam is persisted in. So we are doing it. The Guru passed away. We felt like a rudderless ship in mid-ocean. In our anxiety to find a safe guide we read and heard of you and so desired to come here. Our desire has been fulfilled after two years' longing. On coming here and hearing Sri Bhagavan we understand that the Master teaches *Atma-vichara* (self-quest). This is the method of knowledge (*jnana marga*), whereas the other master taught us *bhakti marga* (method of devotion). What shall we do now? Are we to give up the other method and take to this new method? If once we change shall we not change many times more according to the masters we meet? What progress can be made by such frequent changes? Pray remove this doubt and bless us.

The Master referred the gentleman to an article in the September number of *Vision*, a monthly journal issued by the Anandasram, Kanhangad.

428

PHILOSOPHY OF THE DIVINE NAME
ACCORDING TO ST. NAMDEV

The name permeates the entire universe densely; who can tell to what depths in the nether regions and to what height in the heaven It extends?

The ignorant fools undergo the eighty-four lakhs of species of births, not knowing the essence of things. The Name is immortal. Forms are innumerable but Name is all that.

The Name itself is form and form itself is Name. There is no distinction between Name and form. God became manifest and assumed Name and form. Hence the Name the Vedas have established. Beware, there is no mantram beyond the Name. Those who say otherwise are ignorant fools. Name is Keshava Himself. This is known only to the loving devotees of the Lord.

The all-pervading nature of the Name can only be understood when one recognises his own 'I'. When one's own name is not recognised, it is impossible to get all-pervading Name. When one knows oneself then one finds the Name everywhere.

None can realise the Name by the practice of knowledge, meditation or austerity. Surrender yourself at first at the feet of the Guru and learn to know who the 'I' in you is. After finding the source of that 'I', merge your individuality in that Oneness — which is Self-existent and devoid of all duality. It is that Name that permeates the three worlds.

The Name is *Paramatman* Itself where there is no action arising out of *dvaita* (duality).

8th January, 1938

Talk 442.

While explaining a stanza of his own Sri Bhagavan observed: The sun illumines the universe, whereas the Sun of Arunachala is so dazzling that the universe is obscured and an unbroken brilliance remains. But it is not realised in the present state and can be realised only if the lotus of the heart blossoms. The ordinary lotus blossoms

429

in the light of the visible sun, whereas the subtle Heart blossoms only before the Sun of Suns. May Arunachala make my heart blossom so that His unbroken brilliance may shine all alone!

Further on, Sri Bhagavan continued: The mirror reflects objects; yet they are not real because they cannot remain apart from the mirror. Similarly, the world is said to be a reflection in the mind as it does not remain in the absence of mind. The question arises: if the universe is a reflection, there must be a real object known as the universe in order that it might be reflected in the mind. This amounts to an admission of the existence of an objective universe. Truly speaking, it is not so.

Therefore the dream illustration is set forth. The dream world has no objective existence. How then is it created? Some mental impressions should be admitted. They are called *vasanas*. How were the *vasanas* in the mind? The answer is: they were subtle. Just as a whole tree is contained potentially in a seed, so the world is in the mind.

Then it is asked: A seed is the product of the tree which must have existed once in order that it may be reproduced. So the world also must have been there some time. The answer is, No! There must have been several incarnations to gather the impressions which are re-manifested in the present form. I must have existed before as I do now. The straight way to find an answer will be to see if the world is there. Admitting the existence of the world I must admit a seer who is no other than myself. Let me find myself so that I may know the relation between the world and the seer. When I seek the Self and abide as the Self there is no world to be seen. What is the Reality then? The seer only and certainly not the world.

Such being the truth the man continues to argue on the basis of the reality of the world. Whoever asked him to accept a brief for the world?

Yoga Vasishta clearly defines Liberation as the abandonment of the false and remaining as Being.

Talk 443.

A visitor asked: The illustration of the mirror relates to the sense of sight only. The world is perceived by the other senses also. Can the unreality be established in relation to the other senses as well?

M.: A figure on the screen in the cinema show appears to watch the whole world. What is the reality behind the subject and the object in the same show? An illusory being watches an illusory world.

D.: But I am the witness of the show.

M.: Certainly you are. You and the world are as real as the cinema figure and the cinema world.

Talk 444.

An advocate visitor: The mind becomes aware of the world through the senses. When the senses are active, one cannot help feeling the existence of the world. How can karma yoga be of any use for pure awareness?

M.: The world is perceived by the mind through the senses. It is of the mind. The seer sees the mind and the senses as within the Self and not apart from it. The agent, remaining unaffected by the actions, gets more purified until he realises the Self.

9th January, 1938

Talk 445.

Explaining a stanza in *Aksharamanamalai* Sri Bhagavan said that *mowna* is the highest form of *upadesa*. It signifies 'silence' as master, disciple and practiser. Three *sanyasins*, who were visiting Sri Bhagavan, began a discussion.

D.: If one remained quiet how is action to go on? Where is the place for karma yoga?

M.: Let us first understand what Karma is, whose Karma it is and who is the doer. Analysing them and enquiring into their truth, one is perforce obliged to remain as the Self in peace. Nevertheless the actions will go on.

D.: How will the actions go on if I do not act?

M.: Who asks this question? Is it the Self or another? Is the Self concerned with actions?

D.: No, not the Self. It is another, different from the Self.

M.: So it is plain that the Self is not concerned with actions and the question does not arise.

D.: I agree.

431

Another asked: What is the state of the realised man? Is he not acting?

M.: The question implies that the realised man is not the questioner. Why should you concern yourself with another? Your duty is to look to yourself and not ask of others.

D.: The scriptures hold him up as the ideal.

M.: Certainly. He is the ideal. You should realise the Self. Even if his state be now described, your understanding of it will be only according to your capacity. You admit that your capacity is limited. The scriptures say that the realised state admits of no limits. So then, the only way to understand his state is to realise the Self and experience the state. If the question arises afterwards the answer will be found.

Another visitor asked: There is differentiation made between the sentient and the insentient (*chit* and *jada*) in the opening verse of *Upadesa Sara*.

M.: The *Upadesa* is from the standpoint of the hearer. There is no truth in the insentient (*jada*). One whole consciousness (*chit*) prevails all alone.

24th January, 1938

Talk 446.

Mr. Grant Duff was in the hall. Sri Bhagavan was mentioning some new publications and *Maha Yoga* among others. He also remarked that Mr. G. D. having read *Sat Darsana Bhashya* would be surprised at the different view of *Maha Yoga*. Both claim to represent Sri Bhagavan's philosophy; but they differ so much that *Maha Yoga* actually condemns the other.

Someone cited the curious claim of *Sat Darsana Bhashya* that individuality is retained even after the loss of ego. Sri Bhagavan remarked:

What is to be done? The Upanishads say: *Brahmavid Brahmaiva bhavati* (Knower of Brahman becomes Brahman). There are more than one *Brahmavid* at a time. "Are all of them the same? Are they not separate?" So ask some persons. They look to the bodies only. They do not look to the realisation. There is no difference in the realisation of the *Brahmavid*. That is the Truth. But when the question is raised from the standpoint of the body the reply is necessarily bound to be "Yes. They are different". This is the cause of the confusion.

Mr. G. Duff: The Buddhists deny the world; the Hindu philosophy admits its existence, but says that it is unreal. Am I right?

M.: The difference of view is according to the difference in the angles of vision.

D.: They say that Sakti creates the world. Is the knowledge of unreality due to the unveiling of *maya*?

M.: All admit Sakti's creation. What is the nature of the Creatrix? It can only be in conformity with the nature of the creation. The Creatrix is of the same nature as Her creation.

D.: Are there degrees of illusion?

M.: Illusion is itself illusory. Illusion must be seen by one beyond it. Can such a seer be subject to illusion? Can he then speak of degrees of illusion?

There are scenes floating on the screen in a cinema show. Fire appears to burn buildings to ashes. Water seems to wreck vessels. But the screen on which the pictures are projected remains unscorched and dry. Why?

Because the pictures are unreal and the screen is real.

Again reflections pass through a mirror; but the mirror is not in any way affected by the quality or quantity of the reflections on it.

So the world is a phenomenon on the single Reality, which is not affected in any manner. Reality is only one.

The discussion about illusion is due to the difference in the angle of vision. Change your angle of vision to one of *jnana* and then find the universe to be only Brahman. Being now in the world, you see the world as such. Get beyond it and this will disappear: the Reality alone will shine.

Talk 447.

Sri Bhagavan said that a saint Namah Sivaya who was formerly living in Arunachala must have undergone considerable difficulties. For he has sung a song saying: "God proves the devotee by means of severe ordeals. A washerman beats the cloth on a slab, not to tear it, but only to remove the dirt."

25th January. 1938

Talk 448.

LITERAL TRANSLATION OF NAMDEV'S "PHILOSOPHY OF THE DIVINE NAME."

I. The Name permeates densely the sky and the lowest regions and the entire universe. Who can tell to what depths in the nether regions and to what height in the heavens It extends? The ignorant undergo the eighty-four lakhs of species of births, not knowing the essence of things. Namdev says the Name is immortal. Forms are innumerable, but the Name is all that.

II. The Name itself is form; and form itself is Name. There is no distinction between Name and form. God became manifest and assumed Name and form. Hence the Name the Vedas have established. Beware, there is no *mantra* beyond the Name. Those who say otherwise are ignorant. Namdev says the Name is Keshava Himself. This is known only to the loving devotees of the Lord.

III. The all-pervading nature of the Name can only be understood when one recognises his 'I'. When one's own name is not recognised, it is impossible to get the all-pervading Name. When one knows oneself, then one finds the Name everywhere. To see the Name as different from the Named creates illusion. Namdev says, "Ask the Saints."

IV. None can realise the Name by practice of knowledge, meditation or austerity. Surrender yourself first at the feet of the Guru and learn to know that 'I' myself is that Name. After finding the source of that 'I', merge your individuality in that one-ness, which is Self-existent and devoid of all duality. That which pervades beyond *dwaita* and *dwaitatita*, that Name has come into the three worlds. The Name is *Para Brahman* itself, where there is no action arising out of duality.

When Sri Bhagavan had read this, a certain musician came into the hall and began to sing Tyagaraja *Kirtanas* in Telugu. One of them

434

says: "Find the source of the sound which is transcendental (*mooladhara sabda*) by diving deep like a pearl-diver diving for pearls." Then again another song was: "For a man who has controlled his mind where is the use of *tapasya*? Give up 'I-am-the-body' idea and realise 'I am not; Thou art all'."

This song was translated to Mr. G. D. who was then in the hall.

Mr. G. D. asked: Is it necessary to control one's breath? What becomes of the man who has not practised breath-control?

M.: Breath-control is only an aid for diving deep. One may as well dive down by control of mind. On the mind being controlled, the breath becomes controlled automatically. One need not attempt breath-control; mind-control is enough. Breath-control is recommended for the man who cannot control his mind straightaway.

Naham — I am not this — corresponds to *rechaka*

Koham — Who am I? (search for the I) — corresponds to *puraka*

Soham — He am I; (The Self alone) — corresponds to *kumbhaka*.

So these are the functions of *pranayama*.

Again the three formulae are:

Na — Aham (Not — I).

Ka — Aham (Who — I).

Sa — Aham (He — I).

Delete the prefixes and hold on to the common factor in all of them. That is *Aham*-'I', that is the gist of the whole matter.

Later on Sri Bhagavan referred to the songs and said: Tyagaraja says well. The mind should be controlled. The question arises "What is mind?" He himself answers in the next couplet, saying that it is the "I-am-the-body" idea. The next question is how the control is effected. He answers again, saying "By complete surrender. Realise that I am not and that all is He." The song is fine and compact. He also mentions the other method, namely, control of breath.

31st January, 1938

Talk 449.

After Mr. G. D. had left, there was some reference to his visit to the Asramam. Sri Bhagavan remarked, "Some *Sakti* draws people

435

from all parts of the globe to this centre." A devotee aptly said, "That *Sakti* is not different from Sri Bhagavan." Sri Bhagavan immediately remarked, "What *Sakti* drew me here originally? The same *Sakti* draws all others as well."

Sri Bhagavan was, happily, in the mood to relate the following stories.

I. There was king with a devoted queen. She was a devotee of Sri Rama and yearned that her husband should similarly be a devotee. One night she found that the king mumbled something in his sleep. She kept her ears close to his lips and heard the word 'Rama' repeated continually as in *japa*. She was delighted and the next day ordered the minister to hold a feast. The king having partaken of the feast asked his wife for an explanation. She related the whole occurrence and said that the feast was in gratitude to God for the fulfilment of her long cherished wish. The king was however annoyed that his devotion should have been found out. Some say that having thus betrayed God he considered himself unworthy of God and so committed suicide. It means that one should not openly display one's piety. We may take it that the king told the queen not to make a fuss over his piety and they then lived happily together.

II. THONDARADIPODI (*Bhaktanghrirenu*) ALWAR: One who delights in the dust of the feet of devotees. A devotee (of this name) was keeping a plot of land in which he grew *tulasi*, the sacred basil, made garlands of it, and supplied the same to the God in the temple. He remained a bachelor and was respected for his life and conduct. One day two sisters, who lived by prostitution, walked near the garden and sat under a tree. One of them said, "How disgusting is my life that I soil my body and mind every day. This man's life is most desirable." The other replied, "How do you know his mind? Maybe he is not as good as he appears to be. The bodily functions may be forcibly controlled and the mind may be revelling in riotous thoughts. One cannot control one's *vasanas* as easily as the physical frame."

The former said, "The actions are only the indices of the mind. His life shows his mind to be pure."

The other said, "Not necessarily. His mind has not been proved as yet."

The first challenged her to prove his mind. She accepted. The second desired to be left alone with only a shred of garment in which to clothe herself. The first sister returned home, leaving the other alone with flimsy clothing. As the latter continued to remain under the tree, she appeared penitent and humble. The saint noticed her and approached her after some time. He asked what had happened to her that she looked so lowly. She pleaded penitence for her past life, desired to lead a purer and nobler life and finished with a prayer to him to accept her humble services in the garden or attendance on himself. He advised her to return home and lead a normal life. But she protested. So he detained her for watering the *tulasi* plants. She accepted the function with delight and began to work in the garden.

One rainy night this woman was found standing under the eaves of the thatched shed in which the saint was. Her clothes were dripping and she was shivering with cold. The master asked why she was in such a pitiable state. She said that her place was exposed to the rains and so she sought shelter under the eaves and that she would retire as soon as the rain ceased. He asked her to move into the hut and later told her to change her wet clothes. She did not have dry cloth to put on. So he offered her one of his own clothes. She wore it, still later she begged permission to massage his feet. He consented. Eventually they embraced.

The next day she returned home, had good food and wore fine clothes. She still continued to work in the garden.

Sometimes she used to remain long in her home. Then this man began to visit her there until he finally lived with her. Nevertheless he did not neglect the garden nor the daily garlands for God. There was public scandal regarding his change of life. God then resolved to restore him to his old ways and so assumed the shape of the saintly devotee himself. He appeared to the *dasi* and secretly offered her a rich present, an anklet of God.

She was very pleased with it and hid it under her pillow. He then disappeared. All these were secretly observed by a maid servant in the house.

The ornament was found missing in the temple. The worshipper reported the loss to the proper authorities. They offered a tempting reward for anyone who would give the clue for the recovery of the lost property. The maid servant afforded the clue and claimed the reward. The police recovered the ornament and arrested the *dasi* who said that the devotee gave her the same. He was then roughly handled. A supernatural voice said. "I did it. Leave him alone."

The king and all others were surprised. They fell prostrate at the man's feet and set him free. He then led a better and nobler life.

III. KADUVELI SIDHAR was famed as a very austere hermit. He lived on the dry leaves fallen from trees. The king of the country heard of him, saw him and offered a reward for the one who would prove this man's worth. A rich *dasi* agreed to do it. She began to live near the recluse and pretended to attend on him. She gently left pieces of *pappadam* along with the dry leaves picked by him. When he had eaten them she began to leave other kinds of tasty food along with the dry leaves. Eventually he took good tasty dishes supplied by her. They became intimate and a child was born to them. She reported the matter to the king.

The king wanted to know if she could prove their mutual relationship to the general public. She agreed and suggested a plan of action. Accordingly the king announced a public dancing performance by that *dasi* and invited the people to it. They gathered there and she also appeared, but not before she had given a dose of physic to the child and left it in charge of the saint at home.

The dance was at its height here; the child was crying at home for the mother. The father took the babe in his arms and went to the dancing performance. She was dancing hilariously. He could not approach her with the child. She noticed the man and the babe. She contrived to kick her legs in the dance so as to unloose one of her anklets just as she approached the place where the saint was. She gently lifted her foot and he tied the anklet. The public shouted and laughed. But he remained unaffected. Yet to prove his worth, he sang a Tamil song meaning:

"For victory, let go my anger! I release my mind when it rushes

438

away. If it is true that I sleep day and night quite aware of my Self, may this stone burst into twain and become the wide expanse!"

Immediately the stone (idol) burst with a loud noise The people were astounded.

Sri Bhagavan continued:

Thus he proved himself an unswerving *jnani*. One should not be deceived by the external appearance of *jnani*. Thus *Vedantachudamani* — V. 181.

Its meaning is as follows:

Although a *jivanmukta* associated with body may, owing to his *prarabdha*, appear to lapse into ignorance or wisdom, yet he is only pure like the ether (*akasa*) which is always itself clear. whether covered by dense clouds or cleared of clouds by currents of air. He always revels in the Self alone, like a loving wife taking pleasure with her husband alone, though she attends on him with things obtained from others (by way of fortune, as determined by her *prarabdha*). Though he remains silent like one devoid of learning, yet his supineness is due to the implicit duality of the *vaikhari vak* (spoken words) of the Vedas; his silence is the highest expression of the realised non-duality which is after all the true content of the Vedas. Though he instructs his disciples, yet he does not pose as a teacher, in the full conviction that the teacher and disciple are mere conventions born of illusion (*maya*), and so he continues to utter words (like *akasvani*); if on the other hand he mutters words incoherently like a lunatic, it is because his experience is inexpressible like the words of lovers in embrace. If his words are many and fluent like those of an orator, they represent the recollection of his experience, since he is the unmoving non-dual One without any desire awaiting fulfilment. Although he may appear grief-stricken like any other man in bereavement, yet he evinces just the right love of and pity for the senses which he earlier controlled before he realised that they were mere instruments and manifestations of the Supreme Being. When he seems keenly interested in the wonders of the world, he is only ridiculing the ignorance born of superimposition. If he appears indulging in sexual pleasures, he must be taken to enjoy the ever-

439

inherent Bliss of the Self, which, divided Itself into the Individual Self and the Universal Self, delights in their reunion to regain Its original Nature. If he appears wrathful he means well to the offenders. All his actions should be taken to be only divine manifestations on the plane of humanity. There should not arise even the least doubt as to his being emancipated while yet alive. He lives only for the good of the world.

Sri Bhagavan now warned the hearers against the mistake of disparaging a *jnani* for his apparent conduct and again cited the story of Parikshit. He was a still-born child. The ladies cried and appealed to Sri Krishna to save the child. The sages round about wondered how Krishna was going to save the child from the effects of the arrows (*apandavastra*) of Asvatthama. Krishna said, "If the child be touched by one eternally celibate (*nityabrahmachari*) the child would be brought to life." Even Suka dared not touch the child. Finding no one among the reputed saints bold enough to touch the child, Krishna went and touched it, saying, "If I am eternally celibate (*nityabrahmachari*) may the child be brought to life." The child began to breathe and later grew up to be Parikshit.

Just consider how Krishna surrounded by 16,000 *gopis* is a *brahmachari*! Such is the mystery of *jivanmukti*! A *jivanmukta* is one who does not see anything separate from the Self.

If however a man consciously attempts to display *siddhis* he will receive only kicks.

3rd February, 1938

Talk 450.

Miss Umadevi, a Polish lady convert to Hinduism, asked Sri Bhagavan: I once before told Sri Bhagavan how I had a vision of Siva at about the time of my conversion to Hinduism. A similar experience recurred to me at Courtallam. These visions are momentary. But they are blissful. I want to know how they might be made permanent and continuous. Without Siva there is no life in what I see around me. I am so happy to think of Him. Please tell me how His vision may be everlasting to me.

440

M.: You speak of a vision of Siva. Vision is always of an object. That implies the existence of a subject. The value of the vision is the same as that of the seer. (That is to say, the nature of the vision is on the same plane as that of the seer.) Appearance implies disappearance also. Whatever appears must also disappear. A vision can never be eternal. But Siva is eternal.

The *pratyaksha* (vision) of Siva to the eye signifies the existence of the eyes to see; the *buddhi* (intellect) lying behind the sight; the seer behind the *buddhi* and the sight; and finally the Consciousness underlying the seer. This *pratyaksha* (vision) is not as real as one imagines it to be, because it is not intimate and inherent; it is not first-hand. It is the result of several successive phases of Consciousness. Of these, Consciousness alone does not vary. It is eternal. It is Siva. It is the Self.

The vision implies the seer. The seer cannot deny the existence of the Self. There is no moment when the Self as Consciousness does not exist; nor can the seer remain apart from Consciousness. This Consciousness is the eternal Being and the only Being. The seer cannot see himself. Does he deny his existence because he cannot see himself with the eyes as *pratyaksha* (in vision)? No! So, *pratyaksha* does not mean seeing, but BE-ing.

"To BE" is to realise — Hence I AM THAT I AM. I AM is Siva. Nothing else can be without Him. Everything has its being in Siva and because of Siva.

Therefore enquire "Who am I?" Sink deep within and abide as the Self. That is Siva as BE-ing. Do not expect to have visions of Him repeated. What is the difference between the objects you see and Siva? He is both the subject and the object. You cannot be without Siva. Siva is always realised here and now. If you think you have not realised Him it is wrong. This is the obstacle for realising Siva. Give up that thought also and realisation is there.

D.: Yes. But how shall I effect it as quickly as possible?

M.: This is the obstacle for realisation. Can there be the individual without Siva? Even now He is you. There is no question of time. If there be a moment of non-realisation, the question of realisation can arise. But as it is you cannot be without Him. He is already realised, ever realised and never non-realised.

Surrender to Him and abide by His will whether he appears or vanishes; await His pleasure. If you ask Him to do as you please, it is not surrender but command to Him. You cannot have Him obey you and yet think that you have surrendered. He knows what is best and when and how to do it. Leave everything entirely to Him. His is the burden: you have no longer any cares. All your cares are His. Such is surrender. This is *bhakti*.

Or, enquire to whom these questions arise. Dive deep in the Heart and remain as the Self. One of these two ways is open to the aspirant.

Sri Bhagavan also added: There is no being who is not conscious and therefore who is not Siva. Not only is he Siva but also all else of which he is aware or not aware. Yet he thinks in sheer ignorance that he sees the universe in diverse forms. But if he sees his Self he is not aware of his separateness from the universe; in fact his individuality and the other entities vanish although they persist in all their forms. Siva is seen as the universe. But the seer does not see the background itself. Think of the man who sees only the cloth and not the cotton of which it is made; or of the man who sees the pictures moving on the screen in a cinema show and not the screen itself as the background; or again the man who sees the letters which he reads but not the paper on which they are written. The objects are thus Consciousness and forms. But the ordinary person sees the objects in the universe but not Siva in these forms. Siva is the Being assuming these forms and the Consciousness seeing them. That is to say, Siva is the background underlying both the subject and the object, and again Siva in Repose and Siva in Action, or Siva and Sakti, or the Lord and the Universe. Whatever it is said to be, it is only Consciousness whether in repose or in action. Who is there that is not conscious? So, who is not realised? How then can questions arise doubting realisation or desiring it? If 'I' am not *pratyaksha* to me, I can then say that Siva is not *pratyaksha*.

These questions arise because you have limited the Self to the body, only then the ideas of within and without, of the subject and the object, arise. The objective visions have no intrinsic value. Even if they are everlasting they cannot satisfy the person. Uma has Siva always with Her. Both together form *Ardhanariswara*. Yet she wanted to know Siva in His true nature. She made *tapas*. In her *dhyana* she saw a bright light. She thought: "This cannot be Siva for it is within the compass of my vision. I am greater than this light." So she resumed her *tapas*. Thoughts disappeared. Stillness prevailed. She then realised that BE-ing is Siva in His true nature.

Muruganar cited Appar's stanza:-

"To remove my darkness and give me light, Thy Grace must work through ME only."

Sri Bhagavan mentioned Manickavachagar's:

"We do *bhajana* and the rest. But we have not seen nor heard of those who had seen Thee." One cannot see God and yet retain individuality. The seer and the seen unite into one Being. There is no cogniser, nor cognition, nor the cognised. All merge into One Supreme Siva only!

4th February, 1938

Talk 451.

Mr. S. S. Suryanarayana Sastri, Reader in Philosophy, Madras University, arrived this night. He had a doubt which he said had been cleared on reading Sarma's commentary on "Knowledge of Self". The doubt was:

How can the world be an imagination or a thought? Thought is a function of the mind. The mind is located in the brain. The brain is within the skull of a human being, who is only an infinitesimal part of the universe. How then can the universe be contained in the cells of the brain?

Sri Bhagavan answered saying: So long as the mind is considered to be an entity of the kind described, the doubt will persist. But what is mind? Let us consider. The world is seen when the man wakes up from sleep. It comes after the 'I-thought'. The head rises up. So the mind has become active. What is the world? It is objects spread out in space. Who comprehends it? The mind. Is not the

443

mind, which comprehends space, itself space (*akasa*)? The space is physical ether (*bhootakasa*). The mind is mental ether (*manakasa*) which is contained in transcendental ether (*chidakasa*). The mind is thus the ether principle, *akasa tattva*. Being the principle of knowledge (*jnana sattva*), it is identified with ether (*akasa*) by metaphysics. Considering it to be ether (*akasa*), there will be no difficulty in reconciling the apparent contradiction in the question. Pure mind (*suddha manas*) is ether (*akasa*). The dynamic and dull (*rajas* and *tamas*) aspects operate as gross objects, etc. Thus the whole universe is only mental.

Again, consider a man who dreams. He goes to sleep in a room with doors closed so that nothing can intrude on him while asleep. He closes his eyes when sleeping so that he does not see any object. Yet when he dreams he sees a whole region in which people live and move about with himself among them. Did this panorama get in through the doors? It was simply unfolded to him by his brain. Is it the sleeper's brain or in the brain of the dream individual? It is in the sleeper's brain. How does it hold this vast country in its tiny cells? This must explain the oft-repeated statement that the whole universe is a mere thought or a series of thoughts.

A Swami asked: I feel toothache. Is it only a thought?

M.: Yes.

D.: Why can I not think that there is no toothache and thus cure myself?

M.: When engrossed in other thoughts one does not feel the toothache. When one sleeps toothache is not felt.

D.: But toothache remains all the same.

M.: Such is the firm conviction of the reality of the world that it is not easily shaken off. The world does not become, for that reason, any more real than the individual himself.

D.: Now there is the Sino-Japanese war. If it is only in imagination, can or will Sri Bhagavan imagine the contrary and put an end to the war?

M.: The Bhagavan of the questioner is as much a thought as the Sino-Japanese war. (Laughter.)

444

Talk 452.

Mr. Dhar, I. C. S., a high Officer and his wife, both young, highly cultured and intelligent, are on a visit here. But they fell ill since they arrived here. She desired to know how meditation could become steady.

M.: What is meditation? It consists in expulsion of thoughts. All the present troubles are due to thoughts and are themselves thoughts. Give up thoughts. That is happiness and also meditation.

D.: How are thoughts given up?

M.: The thoughts are for the thinker. Remain as the Self of the thinker and there is an end of thoughts.

Mr. Dhar asked Sri Bhagavan why Brahma, who is Perfection, creates and puts us to ordeals for regaining Him.

M.: Where is the individual who asks this question? He is in the universe and included in the creation. How does he raise the question when he is bound in the creation? He must go beyond it and see if any question arises then.

8th February, 1938

Talk 453.

Three ladies are on a short visit here, Mrs. Hearst from New Zealand, Mrs. Craig and Mrs. Allison from London.

One asked: What is the best way to work for world peace?

M.: What is world? What is peace, and who is the worker? The world is not in your sleep and forms a projection of your mind in your *jagrat*. It is therefore an idea and nothing else. Peace is absence of disturbance. The disturbance is due to the arising of thoughts in the individual, who is only the ego rising up from Pure Consciousness.

To bring about peace means to be free from thoughts and to abide as Pure Consciousness. If one remains at peace oneself, there is only peace all about.

D.: If it is a question of doing something one considers wrong, and hereby saving someone else from a great wrong, should one do it or refrain?

445

M.: What is right and wrong? There is no standard by which to judge something to be right and another to be wrong. Opinions differ according to the nature of the individual and according to the surroundings. They are again ideas and nothing more. Do not worry about them. But get rid of thoughts. If you always remain in the right, then right will prevail in the world.

D.: What should one think of when meditating?

M.: What is meditation? It is expulsion of thoughts. You are perturbed by thoughts which rush one after another. Hold on to one thought so that others are expelled. Continuous practice gives the necessary strength of mind to engage in meditation.

Meditation differs according to the degree of advancement of the seeker. If one is fit for it one might directly hold the thinker; and the thinker will automatically sink into his source, namely Pure Consciousness.

If one cannot directly hold the thinker one must meditate on God; and in due course the same individual will have become sufficiently pure to hold the thinker and sink into absolute Being.

One of the ladies was not satisfied with this answer and asked for further elucidation.

Sri Bhagavan then pointed out that to see wrong in another is one's own wrong. The discrimination between right and wrong is the origin of the sin. One's own sin is reflected outside and the individual in ignorance superimposes it on another. The best course for one is to reach the state in which such discrimination does not arise. Do you see wrong or right in your sleep? Did you not exist in sleep? Be asleep even in the wakeful state. Abide as the Self and remain uncontaminated by what goes on around.

Moreover, however much you might advise them, your hearers may not rectify themselves. Be in the right yourself and remain silent. Your silence will have more effect than your words or deeds. That is the development of will-power. Then the world becomes the Kingdom of Heaven, which is within you.

D.: If one is to withdraw oneself, why is there the world?

446

M.: Where is the world and where does one go withdrawing oneself? Does one fly in an aeroplane beyond space? Is it withdrawal? The fact is this: the world is only an idea. What do you say: Are you within the world or is the world within you?

D.: I am in the world. I am part of it.

M.: That is the mistake. If the world were to exist apart from you, does it come and tell you that it exists? No, you see it exists. You see it when you are awake and not when asleep. If it exists apart from you, it must tell you so and you must be aware of it even in your sleep.

D.: I became aware of it in my *jagrat.*

M.: Do you become aware of yourself and then of the world? Or do you become aware of the world and then of yourself? Or do you become aware of both simultaneously?

D.: I must say simultaneously.

M.: Were you or were you not, before becoming aware of yourself? Do you admit your continued existence before and when you become aware of the world?

D.: Yes.

M.: If always existing yourself, why are you not aware of the world in sleep if it exists apart from the Self?

D.: I become aware of myself and of the world also.

M.: So you become aware of yourself. Who becomes aware of whom? Are there two selves?

D.: No.

M.: So you see that it is wrong to suppose that awareness has passing phases. The Self is always aware. When the Self identifies itself as the seer it sees objects. The creation of the subject and the object is the creation of the world. Subjects and objects are creations in Pure Consciousness. You see pictures moving on the screen in a cinema show. When you are intent on the pictures you are not aware of the screen. But the pictures cannot be seen without the screen behind. The world stands for the pictures and Consciousness stands for the screen. The Consciousness is pure. It is the same as the Self which is eternal and unchanging. Get rid of the subject and object and Pure Consciousness will alone remain.

D.: But why did Pure Brahman become *Isvara* and manifest the universe if He did not mean it?

M.: Did Brahman or *Isvara* tell you so? You say that Brahman became *Isvara*, and so on. This too you did not say in your sleep. Only in your *jagrat* state you speak of Brahman, *Isvara* and universe. The *jagrat* state is a duality of subject and object — owing to the rise of thoughts. So they are your thought creations.

D.: But the world exists in my sleep even though I am not aware.

M.: What is the proof of its existence?

D.: Others are aware of it.

M.: Do they say so to you when you are in sleep or do you become aware of others who see the world in your sleep?

D.: No, but God is always aware.

M.: Leave God alone. Speak for yourself. You do not know God. He is only what you think of Him. Is he apart from you? He is that Pure Consciousness in which all ideas are formed. You are that Consciousness.

10th February, 1938

Talk 454.

Mrs. Dhar: Sri Bhagavan advises practice of enquiry even when one is engaged in external activities. The finality of such enquiry is the realisation of the Self and consequently breath must stop. If breath should stop, how will work go on or, in other words, how will breath stop when one is working?

M.: There is confusion between the means and the end (*i.e.*, *sadhana* and *sadhya*). Who is the enquirer? The aspirant and not the *siddha*. Enquiry signifies that the enquirer considers himself separate from enquiry.

So long as this duality lasts the enquiry must be continued, *i.e.*, until the individuality disappears and the Self is realised to be only the eternal Be-ing (including enquiry and enquirer).

The Truth is that Self is constant and unintermittent Awareness. The object of enquiry is to find the true nature of the Self as Awareness. Let one practise enquiry so long as separateness is perceived.

If once realisation arises there is no further need for enquiry. The question will also not arise. Can awareness ever think of questioning who is aware? Awareness remains pure and simple.

The enquirer is aware of his own individuality. Enquiry does not stand in the way of his individual awareness; nor does external work interfere with such awareness. If work, seemingly external, does not obstruct the individual awareness, will the work, realised to be not separate from the Self, obstruct the uninterrupted Awareness of the Self, which is One without a second and which is not an individual separate from work?

Talk 455.

Mrs. Dhar: I form part of the creation and so remain dependent. I cannot solve the riddle until I become independent. Yet I ask Sri Bhagavan, should He not answer the question for me?

M.: Yes. It is Bhagavan that says, "Become independent and solve the riddle yourself. It is for you to do it." Again: where are you now that you ask this question? Are you in the world, or is the world within you? You must admit that the world is not perceived in your sleep although you cannot deny your existence then. The world appears when you wake up. So where is it? Clearly the world is your thought. Thoughts are your projections. The 'I' is first created and then the world. The world is created by the 'I' which in its turn rises up from the Self. The riddle of the creation of the world is thus solved if you solve the creation of the 'I'. So I say, find your Self.

Again, does the world come and ask you "Why do 'I' exist? How was 'I' created?" It is you who ask the question. The questioner must establish the relationship between the world and himself. He must admit that the world is his own imagination. Who imagines it? Let him again find the 'I' and then the Self.

Moreover, all the scientific and theological explanations do not harmonise. The diversities in such theories clearly show the uselessness of seeking such explanations. Such explanations are purely mental or intellectual and nothing more. Still, all of them are true according to the standpoint of the individual. There is no creation in the state of realisation. When one sees the world, one does not see oneself. When one sees the Self, the world is not seen. So see the Self and realise that there has been no creation.

The lady being laid up is unable to go to the hall and so feels unhappy that, though near, she cannot go into the hall. This was mentioned to Sri Bhagavan. He said, "Well, thinking like this keeps her always in the Presence. This is better than remaining in the hall and thinking of something else."

11th February, 1938

Talk 456.

CONTACT WITH SAINTS

A DANGER:

"Seek the company of saints by all means; but do not remain indefinitely with them. The adage, familiarity breeds contempt, applies even to their case," writes Swami Ramdas in the course of an article in *The Vision*.

"Spiritual growth is, no doubt, largely dependent on suitable association. Company of saints is, therefore, held to be essential for a seeker after truth. But it must not be understood by the company of saints to mean that the seeker should permanently stick on to them.

"He may, for a brief period, remain in their contact and, thereby drawing inspiration and guidance, get himself thoroughly awakened to the consciousness of the indwelling Reality. It would be well for him to depart from them before the light and inspiration that he has received diminishes or disappears.

MAY TURN SCOFFERS:

"There are many cases known to the writer and many others of which he has heard and read, in which such continued dwelling in the company of saints has not only cooled down the ardour and aspiration of the seekers but also turned them into scoffers and sceptics. The fall of a *sadhak* from faith, purity and aspiration does him incalculable harm.

"A young plant growing beneath the shade of a full-grown giant tree does not develop strength and stature. Its growth will be dwarfed, shrivelled and diseased. Whereas if the same plant were put into the open ground directly exposed to the storms, heat, cold, and other rigours of changing weather, it is bound to grow into a mighty tree drawing sustenance both from above and below.

STIFLED GROWTH:

"This analogy of the plant aptly illustrates the stunted life of a seeker who is attached merely to the outward personality of a saint and spends all his days in close association with him. Here the initiative for a free expression of his unique spiritual possibilities is stifled. He fails to cultivate the fundamental qualities for his advancement — fearlessness, self-dependence and endurance. The one great Guide that should control his mind, speech and body should be the almighty Spirit within him. To surrender to this Spirit and become its very embodiment is his goal. To stand on his own legs, struggle and grow by his own strength and experience and lastly to hand himself over to God by his own endeavour brings true liberation and peace.

"From what has been said above, it must not be construed that reflection is cast upon the greatness and efficacy of the company of God-realised souls. Such a contact is the most effective means for a rapid spiritual evolution of the soul. In fact, the grace of saints is an invaluable aid for *sadhana* and without it the condition of the aspirant is like a bird beating in vain its wings against the bars of the cage for freedom. Saints are the saviours and liberators. The Hindu conception of a saint is that he is the very embodiment of God himself. So honour him, derive the rare benefit of his society, serve him with a frank and pure heart, listen intently to his words of advice, and strive to act up to them and achieve the fullest knowledge of the Truth you are in quest of. But seek not to remain attached to his person and lose the spiritual gifts you obtained from him by first contacts."

This cutting was read out to Sri Bhagavan. He listened and remained silent. He was requested to say if contact with saints could be a danger. Sri Bhagavan then quoted a Tamil stanza which says

451

that contact with Guru should be kept up till *videhamukti* (being disembodied). Again he asked where is the *Satpurusha*? He is within. Then he quoted another stanza meaning:

"O Master, Who has been within me in all my past incarnations and Who manifested as a human being, only to speak the language understood by me and lead me."

12th February, 1938

Talk 457.

Mrs. Rosita Forbes was said to be in India. Sri Bhagavan said: The explorers seek happiness in finding curiosities, discovering new lands and undergoing risks in adventures. They are thrilling. But where is pleasure found? Only within. Pleasure is not to be sought in the external world.

13th February, 1938

Talk 458.

Sri Bhagavan said that non-dual idea is advised, but not *advaita* in action. How will one learn *advaita*, if one does not find a master and receive instructions? Is there not duality then? That is the meaning.

14th February, 1938

Talk 459.

Quoting Alexander Selkirk's soliloquy, Sri Bhagavan said: The happiness of solitude is not found in retreats. It may be had even in busy centres. Happiness is not to be sought in solitude or in busy centres. It is in the Self.

17th February, 1938

Talk 460.

Observing the moon before the rising sun, Sri Bhagavan remarked:
See the moon and also the cloud in the sky. There is no difference in their brilliance. The moon looks only like a speck of cloud. The *jnani's* mind is like this moon before sunlight. It is there but not shining of itself.

452

Talk 461.

As Sri Bhagavan was going through the letters which arrived this day, He read out one of them as follows:

A Brahmin boy working in a household went to sleep as usual. In his sleep he cried out. When he woke up he said that he felt his *prana* going out of the body through the mouth and nostrils. So he cried. Soon after he found himself dead and the soul taken to *Vaikunta* where God Vishnu was surrounded by other gods and devotees with prominent Vaishnavite marks on their foreheads. Vishnu said, "This man should be brought here at 2 o'clock tomorrow. Why has he been brought here now? "The boy then woke up and related his experience. The next day at 2 o'clock he passed away.

Talk 462.

Mrs. Dhar had been anxious to ask some questions and get help from Sri Bhagavan. She approached Him with great hesitation and gently related her troubles: My attempts at concentration are frustrated by sudden palpitations of the heart and accompanying hard, short and quick breaths. Then my thoughts also rush out and the mind becomes uncontrollable. Under healthy conditions I am more successful and my breath comes to a standstill with deep concentration. I had long been anxious to get the benefit of Sri Bhagavan's proximity for the successful culmination of my meditation and so came here after considerable effort. I fell ill here. I could not meditate and so I felt depressed. I made a determined effort to concentrate my mind even though I was troubled by short and quick breaths. Though partly successful it does not satisfy me. The time for my leaving the place is drawing near. I feel more and more depressed as I contemplate leaving the place. Here I find people obtaining peace by meditation in the hall; whereas I am not blessed with such peace. This itself has a depressing effect on me.

M.: This thought, 'I am not able to concentrate,' is itself an obstacle. Why should the thought arise?

D.: Can one remain without thoughts rising all the 24 hours of the day? Should I remain without meditation?

M.: What is 'hours' again? It is a concept. Each question of yours is prompted by a thought.

Your nature is Peace and Happiness. Thoughts are the obstacles to realisation. One's meditation or concentration is meant to get rid of obstacles and not to gain the Self. Does anyone remain apart from the Self? No! The true nature of the Self is declared to be Peace. If the same peace is not found, the non-finding is only a thought which is alien to the Self. One practises meditation only to get rid of these alien fancies. So, then, a thought must be quelled as soon as it rises. Whenever a thought arises, do not be carried away by it. You become aware of the body when you forget the Self. But can you forget the Self? Being the Self how can you forget it? There must be two selves for one to forget the other. It is absurd. So the Self is not depressed; it is not imperfect: it is ever happy. The contrary feeling is a mere thought which has actually no stamina in it. Be rid of thoughts. Why should one attempt meditation? Being the Self one remains always realised, only be free from thoughts.

You think that your health does not permit your meditation. This depression must be traced to its origin. The origin is the wrong identification of the body with the Self. The disease is not of the Self. It is of the body. But the body does not come and tell you that it is possessed by the disease. It is you who say it. Why? Because you have wrongly identified yourself with the body.

The body itself is a thought. Be as you really are. There is no reason to be depressed.

The lady was called away and she retired. The question was however pursued as follows:

D.: Sri Bhagavan's answers do not permit us to put further questions, not because our minds are peaceful but we are unable to argue the point. Our discontent is not at an end. For the physical ailments to go the mental ailments should go. Both go when thoughts go. Thoughts do not go without effort. Effort is not possible with the present weakness of mind. The mind requires grace to gain strength.

454

Grace must manifest only after surrender. So all questions, wittingly or unwittingly, amount to asking for Sri Bhagavan's Grace.

M.: Smiled and said, "Yes."

D.: Surrender is said to be *bhakti*. But Sri Bhagavan is known to favour enquiry for the Self. There is thus confusion in the hearer.

M.: Surrender can take effect only when done with full knowledge. Such knowledge comes after enquiry. It ends in surrender.

D.: The knowledge of the Supreme Being is after transcending the individual self. This is *jnana*. Where is the need for surrender?

M.: Quite so. There is no difference between *jnana* and surrender. (Smile).

D.: How is the questioner satisfied then? The only alternative left is association with the wise or devotion to God (*satsanga* or *Isvara bhakti*).

M.: Smiled and said, "Yes."

21st February, 1938

Talk 463.

In the course of the conversation Sri Bhagavan spoke appreciatingly of the services of Palanisami and Ayyasami — his former attendants.

He said that they raised in the garden two crude platforms which were occupied by Himself and Palanisami; they were most comfortable. They were made of straw and bamboo mats and were even more comfortable than the sofa here. Palanisami used to pass through the footpath between rows of prickly pear to bring begged food every night from Kizhnathoor. Though Sri Bhagavan protested Palanisami persisted in doing so. He was free from greed or attachment of any kind. He had earned some money by service in the Straits Settlements and deposited his small savings with someone in the town from whom he used to draw in his emergencies. He was offered a comfortable living in his native village which he refused and continued to live with Sri Bhagavan till the end.

Ayyasami had worked under a European in South Africa and was clean, active and capable. He could manage even ten asramams at a time. He was also free from any attachment or greed. He was loyal to Palanisami, even fond of him. He was more capable than the other.

Annamalai first visited Maharshi in Virupaksha cave; he later went to Kovilur and studied some Tamil scriptures. He returned to Skandasramam. He died in January, 1922 in his 29th year. In the meantime he had composed 36 stanzas in Tamil full of significance and fervour.

Sri Bhagavan had them read out and briefly explained their meaning.

5th March, 1938

Talk 464.

A passage from *Arunachala Mahatmya* (the Glory of Arunachala) was read out. It related to Pangunni (a lame sage) who had his legs made whole by the grace of Sri Arunachala. Sri Bhagavan then related the story of a man whom Sri Maharshi had seen when He was in Gurumurtham. The man was one Kuppu Iyer. His legs were useless and he could not walk. He was once on his way to Vettavalam, moving on his buttocks. An old man suddenly appeared before him and said "Get up and walk. Why do you move on your buttocks?" Kuppu Iyer was excited and beside himself. Involuntarily he rose up and walked freely. After going a short distance, he looked behind to see the stranger who made him walk. But he could not find anyone. He narrated the incident to all those who were surprised to see him walk. Any old man in the town can bear witness to Kuppu Iyer regaining the use of his legs.

Again a girl from the Girl's School was decoyed and was being robbed of her jewels. Suddenly an old man appeared on the scene, rescued the girl, escorted her to her home and then disappeared.

Often such mysterious happenings occur in Tiruvannamalai.

6th March, 1938

Talk 465.

Sri Bhagavan explained to a retired Judge of the High Court some points in the *Upadesa Saram* as follows:-

(1) Meditation should remain unbroken as a current. If unbroken it is called *samadhi or Kundalini sakti*.

(2) The mind may be latent and merge in the Self; it must necessarily rise up again; after it rises up one finds oneself only as ever before. For in this state the mental predispositions are present there in latent form to remanifest under favourable conditions.

(3) Again the mind activities can be completely destroyed. This differs from the former mind, for here the attachment is lost, never to reappear. Even though the man sees the world after he has been in the *samadhi* state, the world will be taken only at its worth, that is to say it is the phenomenon of the One Reality. The True Being can be realised only in *samadhi*; what was then is also now. Otherwise it cannot be Reality or Ever-present Being. What was in *samadhi* is here and now too. Hold it and it is your natural condition of Being. *Samadhi* practice must lead to it. Otherwise how can *nirvikalpa samadhi* be of any use in which a man remains as a log of wood? He must necessarily rise up from it sometime or other and face the world. But in *sahaja samadhi* he remains unaffected by the world.

So many pictures pass over the cinema screen: fire burns away everything; water drenches all; but the screen remains unaffected. The scenes are only phenomena which pass away leaving the screen as it was. Similarly the world phenomena simply pass on before the *Jnani*, leaving him unaffected.

You may say that people find pain or pleasure in worldly phenomena. It is owing to superimposition. This must not happen. With this end in view practice is made.

Practice lies in one of the two courses: devotion or knowledge. Even these are not the goals. *Samadhi* must be gained; it must be continuously practised until *sahaja samadhi* results. Then there remains nothing more to do.

Talk 466.

Mr. Vaidyalingam, an employee of the National Bank: By meditation manifestation disappears and then *ananda* results. It is short-lived. How is it made ever abiding?

457

M.: By scorching the predispositions.

D.: Is not the Self the witness only (*sakshimatra*)?

M.: 'Witness' is applicable when there is an object to be seen. Then it is duality. The Truth lies beyond both. In the mantra, *sakshi cheta kevalo nirgunascha*, the word *sakshi* must be understood as *sannidhi* (presence), without which there could be nothing. See how the sun is necessary for daily activities. He does not however form part of the world actions; yet they cannot take place without the sun. He is the witness of the activities. So it is with the Self.

7th March, 1938

Talk 467.

Yogi Ramiah: All actions take place owing to *Sakti*. How far does *Sakti* go? Can she effect anything without one's own effort?

M.: The answer to the question depends on what the *Purusha* is understood to be. Is he the ego or the Self?

D.: Purusha is *svarupa*.

M.: But he cannot make any *prayatna* (effort).

D.: Jiva is the one who makes the *prayatna*.

M.: So long as egoity lasts *prayatna* is necessary. When egoity ceases to be, actions become spontaneous. The ego acts in the presence of the Self. He cannot exist without the Self.

The Self makes the universe what it is by His *Sakti*, and yet He does not Himself act. Sri Krishna says in the *Bhagavad Gita*, "I am not the doer and yet actions go on". It is clear from the *Mahabharata* that very wonderful actions were effected by Him. Yet He says that He is not the doer. It is like the sun and the world actions.

D.: He is without *abhimana* (attachment) whereas the *jiva* is with *abhimana*.

M.: Yes. Being attached, he acts and also reaps the fruits. If the fruits are according to his desire he is happy; otherwise he is miserable. Happiness and misery are due to his attachment. If actions were to take place without attachment there would be no expectation of fruit.

D.: Can actions take place spontaneously without individual effort? Should we not cook our food in order to eat it later?

458

M.: Atman acts through the ego. All actions are due to efforts only. A sleeping child is fed by its mother. The child eats food without being wide awake and then denies having taken food in sleep. However the mother knows what happened. Similarly the *jnani* acts unawares. Others see him act, but he does not know it himself. Owing to fear of Him wind blows, etc. That is the order of things. He ordains everything and the universe acts accordingly, yet He does not know. Therefore He is called the great Doer. Every embodied being (*ahankari*) is bound by *niyama*. Even Brahma cannot transgress it. [This devotee later explained the significance of his question. He hears Sri Bhagavan say that the world goes on and the individual needs are met by Divine Will. But he finds that Sri Bhagavan wakes up the Asramites at about 4 a.m. to cut vegetables for the day's curry. He wanted to have the doubt cleared for his own benefit and the question was not meant for discussion].

10th March, 1938

Talk 468.

As Sri Bhagavan was going out, the following Vedic chant was heard from a hut:

Antaraditya manasa jvalantam — Brahmana vindat. Sri Bhagavan drew our attention to it and remarked:-

In the *Taittriya Upanishad* also, He is said to be made of gold, etc. What does it all mean? Although the sun and the other luminaries are said to be self luminous, yet they do not shine forth of themselves but they shine by the light of the Supreme Being. (*na tatra suryo....vibhati*). So long as they are said to be separate from Brahman their 'Self-luminosity' is the luminosity of Brahman. All these *mantras* mentioning the sun, etc., speak only of Brahman.

Talk 469.

Yogi Ramiah asked: A master is approached by an aspirant for enlightenment. The master says that Brahman has no qualities, nor stain, nor movement, etc. Does he not then speak as an individual? How can the aspirant's ignorance be wiped off unless the master speaks thus? Do the words of the master as an individual amount to Truth?

M.: To whom should the master speak? Whom does he instruct? Does he see anyone different from the Self?

D.: But the disciple is asking the master for elucidation.

M.: True, but does the master see him as different? The ignorance of the disciple lies in not knowing that all are Self-realised. Can anyone exist apart from the Self? The master simply points out that the ignorance lies there and therefore does not stand apart as an individual.

What is Realisation? Is it to see God with four hands, bearing conch, wheel, club, etc.? Even if God should appear in that form, how is the disciple's ignorance wiped out? The truth must be eternal realisation. The direct perception is ever-present Experience. God Himself is known as directly perceived. It does not mean that He appears before the devotee as said above. Unless the Realisation be eternal it cannot serve any useful purpose. Can the appearance with four hands be eternal realisation? It is phenomenal and illusory. There must be a seer. The seer alone is real and eternal.

Let God appear as the light of a million suns: Is it *pratyaksha*?

To see it, the eyes, the mind, etc. are necessary. It is indirect knowledge, whereas the seer is direct experience. The seer alone is *pratyaksha*. All other perceptions are only secondary knowledge. The present super-imposition of the body as 'I' is so deep-rooted, that the vision before the eyes is considered *pratyaksha* but not the seer himself. No one wants realisation because there is no one who is not realised. Can anyone say that he is not already realised or that he is apart from the Self? No. Evidently all are realised. What makes him unhappy is the desire to exercise extraordinary powers. He knows that he cannot do so. Therefore he wants God to appear before him, confer all His powers on the devotee, and keep Himself in the background. In short, God should abdicate His powers in favour of the man.

D.: It is all right for *mahatmas* like Sri Bhagavan to speak out so plainly. Because the Truth does not swerve from you, you consider it easy for all others. Nevertheless, the common folk have a real difficulty.

M.: Then does anyone say that he is not the Self?

D.: I meant to say that no one else has the courage to put things straight like Maharshi.

M.: Where is the courage in saying things as they are?

Talk 470.

As a European Countess was leaving for Europe tonight she requested him to bless her and her family.

M.: You do not go anywhere away from the Presence as you imagine. The Presence is everywhere. The body moves from place to place; yet it does not leave the one Presence. So no one can be out of sight of the Supreme Presence. Since you identify one body with Sri Bhagavan and another body with yourself, you find two separate entities and speak of going away from here. Wherever you may be, you cannot leave ME.

To illustrate it: The pictures move on the screen in a cinema show; but does the screen itself move? No. The Presence is the screen: you, I, and others are the pictures. The individuals may move but not the Self.

Talk 471.

D.: The *avatars* are said to be more glorious than the self-realised *jnanis. Maya* does not affect them from birth; divine powers are manifest; new religions are started; and so on.

M.: (1) *"Jnani tvatmaiva me matam."*

(2) *"Sarvam khalvidam brahma."*

How is an *avatar* different from a *jnani*; or how can there be an *avatar* as distinct from the universe?

D.: The eye (*chakshu*) is said to be the repository (*ayatana*) of all forms; so the ear (*srotra*) is of all sounds, etc. The one *Chaitanya* operates as all; no miracles are possible without the aid of the senses (*indriyas*). How can there be miracles at all? If they are said to surpass human understanding so are the creations in dreams. Where then is the miracle?

The distinction between *Avataras* and *Jnanis* is absurd.

"Knower of Brahman becomes Brahman only" is otherwise contradicted.

M.: Quite so.

461

Talk 472.

A large group of Punjabis arrived here in a pilgrim special. They came to the Ramanasramam at about 8-45 a.m. and sat quiet for a long time. At about 9-20 one of them said: "Your reputation has spread in the Punjab. We have travelled a long distance to have your *darsan*. Kindly tell us something by way of instruction." There was no oral reply. Sri Bhagavan smiled and gazed on. After some time the visitor asked: "Which is the best — the yoga, the *bhakti* or the *jnana* path?" Still Sri Bhagavan smiled and gazed as before. Sri Bhagavan left the hall for a few minutes. The visitors began to disperse. Still a sprinkling of them continued to sit in the hall. A long standing disciple told the visitor that Sri Bhagavan had replied to his questions by His Silence which was even more eloquent than words. After Sri Bhagavan returned, the visitor began to speak a little. In the course of his speech, he asked:

D.: It is all right for those who believe in God. Others ask — Is there a God?

M.: Are you there?

D.: Quite so. That is the question. I see before my eyes a battalion of sepoys passing. Therefore I am. The world must have been created by God. How shall I see the Creator?

M.: See yourself, who sees these, and the problem is solved.

D.: Is it to sit silent or to read sacred books or to concentrate the mind? *Bhakti* helps concentration. People fall at the feet of the *bhakta*. If it does not happen he feels disappointed and his *bhakti* fades.

M.: The longing for happiness never fades. That is *bhakti*.

D.: How shall I get it quicker? Suppose I concentrate two hours today. If I try to lengthen the period the next day, I fall asleep because I get tired of the job.

M.: You do not get tired in sleep. The same person is now present here. Why should you be tired now? Because your mind is restless and wanders, it gets tired, and not you.

D.: I am a business man. How shall I get on with business and get peace of mind also?

462

M.: This is also a thought. Give up this thought also and remain as your true Self.

D.: It is said: Do your duty without any expectation of results. How shall I get that frame of mind?

M.: You need not aspire for or get any new state. Get rid of your present thoughts, that is all.

D.: How shall I get the *bhakti* necessary for it?

M.: It is *bhakti* to get rid of thoughts which are only alien to you (*i.e.* the Self).

D.: What is thought-force, mesmerism, etc.? There was a doctor in Paris called Dr. Coue. He was illiterate, but yet was able to cure many incurable diseases by will-force. He used to say: Generate power to cure yourself. The power is within you.

M.: It is through the same will-power that the seat of all diseases, the body, has risen.

D.: So it is said thoughts manifest as objects.

M.: This thought must be for *mukti* (liberation).

D.: God must enable us to get rid of the other thoughts.

M.: This is again a thought. Let that which has incarnated raise the question. You are not that because you are free from thoughts.

Another visitor from Rawalpindi asked: The Atman is formless. How shall I concentrate on it?

M.: Leave alone the Atman which you say is formless or intangible. Mind is tangible to you. Hold the mind and it will do.

D.: Mind itself is very subtle and is also the same as the Atman. How shall we know the nature of the mind? You have said that all supports are useless. What should be our stand then?

M.: Where does your mind stand?

D.: Where does it stand?

M.: Ask the mind itself.

D.: I ask you now. Should we concentrate on mind then?

M.: Um!

D.: But what is the nature of the mind? It is formless. The problem is perplexing.

M.: Why are you perplexed?

463

D.: The *sastras* want us to concentrate and I cannot do so.

M.: Through what *sastras* have we known our existence?

D.: It is a matter of experience. But I want to concentrate.

M.: Be free from thoughts. Do not hold on to anything. They do not hold you. Be yourself.

D.: I do not yet understand as to where I take my stand and concentrate. Can I meditate on my mind?

M.: Whose mind?

D.: My own mind?

M.: Who are you? The question now resolves itself all right.

(All retired for lunch. The visitor returned at 2-30 p.m. and pursued the same question.)

He said: Maharshi advises the seeker to get rid of thoughts. On what should I concentrate the mind after all the thoughts are expelled? I do not see where I stand then and on what I should concentrate.

M.: For whom is the concentration?

D.: For the mind.

M.: Then concentrate the mind.

D.: On what?

M.: Answer the question yourself. What is the mind? Why should you concentrate?

D.: I do not know what the mind is. I ask Maharshi.

M.: Maharshi does not seek to know the mind. The questioner must question the mind itself as to what it is.

D.: Maharshi advises that the mind should be divested of thoughts.

M.: This is itself a thought.

D.: When all thoughts disappear what remains over?

M.: Is the mind different from thoughts?

D.: No. The mind is made up of thoughts. My point is this: When all thoughts are got rid of, how shall I concentrate the mind?

M.: Is not this also a thought?

D.: Yes, but I am advised to concentrate.

M.: Why should you concentrate? Why should you not allow your thoughts free play?

464

D.: The *sastras* say that the thoughts, thus playing free, lead us astray, that is, to unreal and changeful things.

M.: So then, you want not to be led to unreal and changeful things. Your thoughts are unreal and changeful. You want to hold the Reality. That is exactly what I say. The thoughts are unreal. Get rid of them.

D.: I understand now. Yet there is a doubt. "Not a trice can you remain inactive." How shall I be able to rid myself of thoughts?

M.: The same *Gita* says: "Although all actions take place, I am not the doer." It is like the sun towards the world activities. The Self always remains actionless, whereas thoughts arise and subside. The Self is Perfection; it is immutable; the mind is limited and changeful. You need only to cast off your limitations. Your perfection thus stands revealed.

D.: Grace is necessary for it.

M.: Grace is ever present. All that is necessary is that you surrender to It.

D.: I surrender and pray that even if I go wrong I may be forcibly drawn to it.

M.: Is this surrender? Surrender to be complete must be unquestioning.

D.: Yes, I surrender. You say I must dive into the ocean of the Self like a pearl-diver into the sea.

M.: Because you are now thinking that you are out of the ocean of Consciousness.

D.: I practise *pranayama*. It generates heat in the body. What should I do?

M.: The heat will pass away when the mind gains calm

D.: That is true but most difficult.

M.: This is again a thought which is an obstacle.

Talk 473.

Someone remarked: It is said that they get *mukti* unasked who live or die within a radius of 30 miles round Arunachala. It is also admitted that only by *jnana* is liberation obtained. The *purana* also remarks that *Vedanta Vijnana* is difficult to get. So *mukti* is difficult. But life or death round about the Hill bestows *mukti* so easily. How can it be?

M.: Siva says, "By My command." Those who live here need no initiation, *diksha*, etc., but get *mukti*.. Such is the command of Siva.

D.: The *purana* also says that those who are born here are Siva's group of followers, such as ghosts, spirits, disembodied beings, etc.

M.: So it is said of other *kshetras* as well, *e.g.*, Tiruvarur, Chidambaram.

D.: How does mere life or death here confer *mukti*? It is difficult to understand.

M.: Darsanad Abhrasadasi jananat Kamalalaye, Kasyantu maranam muktih smaranad Arunachale.

"To see Chidambaram, to be born in Tiruvarur, to die in Benares, or merely to think of Arunachala, is to be assured of Liberation."

Jananat Kamalalaye means "by being born in *Kamalalaya*". What is it? It is the Heart.

Similarly, *Abhrasadasi* — Seat of Consciousness. Again, *Kasi* is the Light of Realisation. Remembering Arunachala completes the verse. It must also be understood in the same sense.

D.: So *bhakti* is necessary.

M.: Everything depends on the outlook. One sees that all born in Tiruvarur, or visiting Chidambaram, or dying in Banares, or contemplating Arunachala, are *muktas*.

D.: I think of Arunachala, but still I am not a *mukta*.

M.: Change of outlook is all that is necessary. See what such a change did for Arjuna. He had the vision, of the Cosmic Self. Sri Krishna says: "Gods and saints are eager to see my Cosmic Form. I have not fulfilled their desire. Yet I endow divine sight by which you can see that Form." Well, having said so, does He show what He is? No. He asks Arjuna to see in Him all that he desires to see. If that were His real form it must be changeless and known for what it is worth. Instead, Arjuna is commanded to see whatever he desires. So where is the Cosmic Form? It must be in Arjuna.

466

Furthermore, Arjuna finds Gods and saints in that form and they are praising the Lord. If the form be withheld from the Gods and saints as said by Krishna, who are they of Arjuna's vision?

D.: They must be in his imagination.

M.: They are there because of Arjuna's outlook.

D.: Then the outlook must be changed by God's Grace.

M.: Yes. That happens to *bhaktas*.

D.: A man dreams of a tiger, takes fright and wakes up. The dream-tiger appears to the dream ego who is also frightened. When he wakes up how is it that that ego disappears, and the man wakes up as the waking ego?

M.: That establishes that the ego is the same. Dream, wakefulness and sleep are passing phases for the same ego.

D.: It is so difficult to spot the mind. The same difficulty is shared by all.

M.: You can never find the mind through mind. Pass beyond it in order to find it non-existent.

D.: Then one must directly go to seek the ego. Is it so?

M.: That's it.

Mind, ego, intellect are all different names for one single inner organ (*antahkarana*). The mind is only the aggregate of thoughts. Thoughts cannot exist but for the ego. So all thoughts are pervaded by ego (*aham*). Seek wherefrom the 'I' rises and the other thoughts will disappear.

D.: What remains over cannot be 'I', but Pure Consciousness.

M.: Quite so. You start seeking happiness. On analysis you find that misery is caused by thoughts. They are called the mind. While trying to control the mind you seek the 'I' and get fixed in Being-Knowledge-Bliss.

Another devotee: What then is the mind?

M.: Mind is consciousness which has put on limitations. You are originally unlimited and perfect. Later you take on limitations and become the mind.

D.: It is *avarana* (veiling) then. How does this happen?

M.: To whom is the *avarana*? It is the same as *avidya* (ignorance), ego or the mind.

467

D.: Avarana means obscuration. Who is obscured? How does it arise?

M.: The limitation is itself obscuration. No questions will arise if limitations are transcended.

16th March, 1938

Talk 474.

There was some reference to the heart. Sri Bhagavan said: The yoga *sastras* speak of 72,000 *nadis*, of 101 *nadis*, etc. A reconciliation is effected by others that 101 are the main *nadis*, which subdivide into 72,000. These *nadis* are supposed by some to spread out from the brain, by others from the Heart and by some others from the coccyx. They speak of a *paranadi* which is said to rise up from the coccyx through the *Sushumna* to the brain and descends to the heart. Others say that the *Sushumna* ends in *Para*.

A few advise seeking realisation in the head (*Sahasrara*); a few between the eyebrows; a few in the heart; others in the solar plexus. If realisation amounts to gaining the *Paranadi*, one might enter it from the Heart. But the yogi is engaged in cleansing the *nadis*; then *Kundalini* is awakened which is said to rise up from the coccyx to the head. The yogi is later advised to come down to the Heart as the final step.

The Vedas say: "The Heart is like a lotus turned down, or a plantain bud."

"There is a bright spot atom-like, like the end of a grain of paddy."

"That spot is like a flame and in its centre, transcendental Brahman is seated." Which is that Heart? Is it the heart of the physiologists? If so, the physiologists know best.

The Heart of the Upanishads is construed as *Hridayam*, meaning: This (is) the centre. That is, it is where the mind rises and subsides. That is the seat of Realisation. When I say that it is the Self the people imagine that it is within the body. When I ask where the Self remains in one's sleep they seem to think that it is within the body, but unaware of the body and its surroundings like a man confined in a dark room. To such people it is necessary to say that the seat of

468

Realisation is somewhere within the body. The name of the centre is the Heart; but it is confounded with the heart organ.

When a man dreams, he creates himself (*i.e.*, the *ahamkar*, the seer) and the surroundings. All of them are later withdrawn into himself. The one became many, along with the seer. Similarly also, the one becomes many in the waking state. The objective world is really subjective. An astronomer discovers a new star at immeasurable distance and announces that its light takes thousands of light years to reach the earth. Well, where is the star in fact? Is it not in the observer? But people wonder how a huge globe, larger than the Sun, at such a distance can be contained in the brain-cells of a man. The space, the magnitudes and the paradox are all in the mind only. How do they exist there? Inasmuch as you become aware of them, you must admit a light which illumines them. These thoughts are absent in sleep but rise up on waking. So this light is transient, having an origin and an end. The consciousness of 'I' is permanent and continuous. So this cannot be the aforesaid light. It is different but has no independent existence. Therefore it must be *abhasa* (reflected light). The light in the brain is thus reflected knowledge (*abhasa samvit*) or reflected being (*abhasa sat*). The true knowledge (*Samvit*) or Being (*Sat*) is in the centre called Heart (*Hridaya*). When one wakes up from sleep it is reflected in the head, and so the head is no longer lying prone but rises up. From there the consciousness spreads all over the body and so the superimposed 'I' functions as the wakeful entity.

The pure light in the brain is *suddha manas* (the pure mind) which later becomes contaminated and is *malina manas*, the one ordinarily found.

All these are however contained in the Self. The body and its counterparts are in the Self. The Self is not confined in the body, as is commonly supposed.

16th March, 1938

Talk 475.

Sri Maharshi read out a news item from a paper to the following effect: A forest guard armed with a rifle was going in the jungle and noticed two bright spots in a thicket. On closer approach to find out what they were, he was face to face with a huge tiger within a few yards of him. He threw down his gun and assumed a prayerful attitude towards the jungle king. The tiger stood up and slowly moved away without injuring him.

21st March, 1938

Talk 476.

Dr. Stanley Jones, a Christian missionary, visited Maharshi. He writes books and delivers lectures. He has two Asramams under his control in North India. He was accompanied by another gentleman and two ladies. He is at present writing a book *On the Indian Road* and wants to meet the spiritually great men in India so that he may collect material for the book. He desired to know how the Indian sages have proceeded and what they have found as their experience in divinity. So he asked questions. (This is only a short sketch of his interview).

D.: What is your quest? What is the goal? How far have you progressed?

M.: The goal is the same for all. But tell me why you should be in search of a goal? Why are you not content with the present condition?

D.: Is there then no goal?

M.: Not so. What makes you seek a goal? It is a counter-question to be answered by you.

D.: I have my own ideas of these subjects. I want to know what Maharshi has to say.

M.: Maharshi has no doubts to be cleared.

D.: Well, I consider the goal to be the realisation by the lower mind of the higher mind so that the Kingdom of Heaven might endure here on earth. The lower mind is incomplete and it must be made perfect by realisation of the higher mind.

M.: So then you admit a lower mind which is incomplete and which seeks realisation of the higher so that it may become perfect. Is that lower mind apart from the higher mind? Is it independent of the other?

470

D.: The Kingdom of Heaven was brought down on Earth by Jesus Christ. I consider Him to be the Kingdom personified. I want everyone to realise the same. He said: "I am hungry with other men's hunger;" and so on. Mutual partnership in pleasure and pain is the Kingdom of Heaven. If that Kingdom is universalised everyone will feel at one with the rest.

M.: You speak of the differences between the lower and the higher minds, pleasures and pains. What becomes of these differences in your sleep?

D.: But I want to be wide awake.

M.: Is this your wide awakened state? It is not. It is only a dream in your long sleep. All are in sleep, dreaming of the world and things and actions.

D.: This is all Vedantic, I have no use for it. The existing differences are not imaginary. They are positive. However, what is that real waking? Can Maharshi tell us what he has found it to be?

M.: Real waking lies beyond the three states of waking, dream and sleep.

D.: I am really awake and know that I am not in sleep.

M.: Real waking lies beyond the plane of differences.

D.: What is the state of the world then?

M.: Does the world come and tell you "I exist"?

D.: No. But the people in the world tell me that the world needs spiritual, social and moral regeneration.

M.: You see the world and the people in it. They are your thoughts. Can the world be apart from you?

D.: I enter into it with love.

M.: Before entering thus do you stand aloof?

D.: I am identified with it and yet remaining apart. Now I came here to ask Maharshi and hear him. Why does he ask me questions?

M.: Maharshi has replied. His reply amounts to this: Real waking does not involve differences.

D.: Can such realisation be universalised?

M.: Where are differences there? There are no individuals in it.

D.: Have you reached the goal?

471

M.: The goal cannot be anything apart from the Self nor can it be something to be gained afresh. If that were so, such goal cannot be abiding and permanent. What appears anew will also disappear. The goal must be eternal and within. Find it within yourself.

D.: I want to know your experience.

M.: Maharshi does not seek enlightenment. The question is of no use to the questioner. Whether I have realised or not, how does it affect the questioner?

D.: Not so. Each one's experience has a human value in it and can be shared by others.

M.: The problem must be solved by the questioner himself. The question is best directed to oneself.

D.: I know the answer to the question.

M.: Let us have it.

D.: I was shown the Kingdom of Heaven twenty years ago. It was by God's grace only. I made no effort for it. I was happy. I want to universalise, moralise and socialise it. At the same time I want to know Maharshi's experience of the Divine.

Mrs. Jinarajadasa intervened and spoke softly: We all agree that Maharshi has brought the Kingdom of Heaven on Earth. Why do you press him to answer your questions relating to his realisation? It is for you to seek and gain it.

The questioner listened to her, argued slightly and resumed his questions to Maharshi. After one or two light questions, Major Chadwick spoke sternly: "The Kingdom of Heaven is within you," says the *Bible.*

D.: How shall I realise it?

Major Chadwick: Why do you ask Maharshi to realise it for you?

D.: I do not.

Major Chadwick: The Kingdom is within you. You should realise it.

D.: It is *within* only for those who hear it.

Major Chadwick: The *Bible* says *within you,* and adds no qualifications.

The questioner felt his conversation was already too long and so retired after thanking Maharshi and others.

472

Talk 477.

Mrs. Jinarajadasa: How shall we be able to remember the truth experienced in dreams?

M.: Your present waking state, your dreams and your desire to remember are all thoughts. They arise only after the mind has arisen. Were you not existing in the absence of the mind?

D.: Yes, I was.

M.: The fact of your existence is also your realisation

D.: I understand it intellectually. The truth is felt in temporary flashes only. It is not abiding.

M.: Such thoughts smother up the state of your eternal realisation.

D.: The rough and tumble of town life is not congenial to realisation. Jungle retreats afford the necessary quiet and solitude.

M.: One can be free in a town and may yet be bound in jungle retreats. It is all in the mind.

D.: The mind again is *maya*, I suppose.

M.: What is *maya*? The knowledge that the mind is divorced from the Reality is *maya*. The mind is in Reality only and not apart. This knowledge is the elimination of *maya*.

Further conversation led to the question if the mind was identical with the brain. Sri Bhagavan said: The mind is only a force operating on the brain. You are now here and awake. The thoughts of the world and the surroundings are in the brain within the body. When you dream you create another self who sees the world of dream creation and the surroundings just as you do now. The dream visions are in the dream brain which is again in the dream body. That is different from your present body. You remember the dream now. The brains are however different. Yet the visions appear in the mind. The mind therefore is not identical with the brain. Waking, dream and sleep are for the mind only.

D.: The understanding is intellectual.

M.: Intellect. Whose intellect? The problem revolves round that question.

You admit that you exist even in the absence of intellect — say, in sleep. How do you know that you exist if you have not realised your

473

existence? Your very existence is realisation. You cannot imagine a point of time when you do not exist. So there is no period of time when realisation is not.

22nd March, 1938

Talk 478.

A certain man from Madurai asked: How to know the Power of God?

M.: You say 'I AM'. That is it. What else can say I AM?

One's own being is His Power. The trouble arises only when one says, "I am this or that, such and such." Do not do it — Be yourself. That is all.

D.: How to experience Bliss?

M.: To be free from thinking "I am now out of Bliss".

D.: That is to say free from modes of mind.

M.: To be with only one mode of mind to the exclusion of others.

D.: But Bliss must be experienced.

M.: Bliss consists in not forgetting your being. How can you be otherwise than what you really are? It is also to be the Seat of Love. Love is Bliss. Here the Seat is not different from Love.

D.: How shall I be all-pervading?

M.: Give up the thought, "I am not all-pervading now."

D.: How to permeate the separate objects?

M.: Do they exist independently of "I"? Do they say to you "We are"? You see them. You are, and then the objects are also seen. "Without me, these do not exist" — this knowledge is permeation. Owing to the idea "I am the body; there is something in me" the separate objects are seen as if lying outside. Know that they are all within yourself. Is a piece of cloth independent of yarn? Can the objects remain without Me?

Talk 479.

D.: Which is the best of all the religions? What is Sri Bhagavan's method?

M.: All religions and methods are one and the same.

D.: Different methods are taught for liberation.

M.: Why should you be liberated? Why not remain as you are now?

D.: I want to get rid of pain. To be rid of it is said to be liberation.

M.: That is what all religions teach.

D.: But what is the method?

M.: To retrace your way back.

D.: Whence have I come?

M.: That is just what you should know. Did these questions arise in your sleep? Did you not exist then? Are you not the same being now?

D.: Yes, I *was* in sleep; so also the mind; but the senses had merged, so I could not speak.

M.: Are you *jiva*? Are you the mind? Did the mind announce itself to you in sleep?

D.: No. But elders say that the *jiva* is different from *Isvara*.

M.: Leave *Isvara* alone. Speak for yourself.

D.: What about myself? Who am I?

M.: That is just it. Know it, when all will be known; if not, ask then.

D.: On waking I see the world and I am not changed from sleep.

M.: But this is not known in sleep. Now or then, the same you remain. Who has changed now? Is your nature to be changing or remain unchanging?

D.: What is the proof?

M.: Does one's own being require a proof? Only remain aware of your own self, all else will be known.

D.: Why then do the dualists and non-dualists quarrel among themselves?

M.: If each one minds his own business, there will be no quarrel.

Talk 480.

A European lady, Mrs. Gasque, gave a slip of paper on which was written:

We are thankful to Nature and the Infinite Intelligence for your Presence among us. We appreciate that your Wisdom is founded upon pure Truth and the basic principle of Life and Eternity. We are happy that you remind us to "Be still and Know THAT".

475

What do you consider the future of this Earth?

Answer: The answer to this question is contained in the other sheet. *Be still and know that* I AM GOD.

"Stillness" here means "Being free from thoughts".

D.: This does not answer the question. The planet has a future — what is it to be?

M.: Time and space are functions of thoughts. If thoughts do not arise there will be no future or the Earth.

D.: Time and space will remain even if we do not think of them.

M.: Do they come and tell you that they are? Do you feel them in your sleep?

D.: I was not conscious in my sleep.

M.: And yet you were existing in your sleep.

D.: I was not in my body. I had gone out somewhere and jumped in here just before waking up.

M.: Your having been away in sleep and jumping in now are mere ideas. Where were you in sleep? You were only what you are, but with this difference that you were free from thoughts in sleep.

D.: Wars are going on in the world. If we do not think, do the wars cease?

M.: Can you stop the wars? He who made the world will take care of it.

D.: God made the world and He is not responsible for the present condition of the world. It is we who are responsible for the present state.

M.: Can you stop the wars or reform the world?

D.: No.

M.: Then why do you worry yourself about what is not possible for you? Take care of yourself and the world will take care of itself.

D.: We are pacifists. We want to bring about Peace.

M.: Peace is always present. Get rid of the disturbances to Peace. This Peace is the Self.

The thoughts are the disturbances. When free from them, you are Infinite Intelligence, *i.e.*, the Self. There is Perfection and Peace.

476

D.: The world must have a future.

M.: Do you know what it is in the present? The world and all together are the same, now as well as in the future.

D.: The world was made by the operation of Intelligence on ether and atoms.

M.: All of them are reduced to *Isvara* and *Sakti*. You are not now apart from Them. They and you are one and the same Intelligence.

After a few minutes one lady asked: "Do you ever intend to go to America?"

M.: America is just where India is (*i.e.,* in the plane of thought).

Another (Spanish) lady: They say that there is a shrine in the Himalayas entering which one gets some strange vibrations which heal all diseases. Is it possible?

M.: They speak of some shrine in Nepal and also in other parts of the Himalayas where the people are said to become unconscious on entering them.

Talk 481.

Muruganar asked what *prajnana* is.

M.: Prajnana (Absolute Knowledge) is that from which *vijnana* (relative knowledge) proceeds.

D.: In the state of *vijnana* one becomes aware of the *samvit* (cosmic intelligence). But is that *suddha samvit* aware by itself without the aid of *antahkaranas* (inner organs)?

M.: It is so, even logically.

D.: Becoming aware of *samvit* in *jagrat* by *vijnana, prajnana* is not found self-shining. If so, it must be found in sleep.

M.: The awareness is at present through *antahkaranas. Prajnana* is always shining even in sleep. If one is continuously aware in *jagrat* the awareness will continue in sleep also.

Moreover, it is illustrated thus: A king comes into the hall, sits there and then leaves the place.

He did not go into the kitchen. Can one in the kitchen for that reason say, "The king did not come here"? When awareness is found in *jagrat* it must also be in sleep.

477

29th April, 1938

Talk 482.

Dr. Pande of Indore is on a visit here. He asked leave of Bhagavan to ask questions so that his doubts might be cleared. He wanted to be shown a practical way to realise the Self.

M.: A man was blindfolded and left in the woods. He then enquired of the way to Gandhara from each one he met on the way until he finally reached it. So also all the ways lead to Self-Realisation. They are aids to the common goal.

D.: Dhyana will be easy if there is a *pratikam* (symbol). But the enquiry into the Self does not show any *pratikam*.

M.: You admit the existence of the Self. Do you point to the *pratikam* (symbol) and say that it is the Self? Maybe you think the body is the Self. But consider your deep sleep. You do exist then. What is the *pratikam* there? So the Self can be realised without *pratikam*.

D.: Quite true. I see the force of the words. But yet are not *mantras*, etc., helpful?

M.: They are helpful. What is *mantra*? You are thinking of the simple sounds of the *mantra*. Repetition of the same excludes all other thoughts. The single thought of the *mantra japa* remains. That too drops away giving place to the Infinite Self, which is the *mantra* itself.

Mantra, dhyana, bhakti, etc., are all aids and finally lead to *Swarupa*, the Self, which is they themselves.

After a few minutes Maharshi continued:

Everyone is the Self, indeed infinite. Yet each one mistakes the body for the Self. To know anything, illumination is necessary. Such illuminating agency can only be in the form of light which is however lighting the physical light and darkness. So then that other Light lies beyond the apparent light and darkness. It is itself neither light nor darkness but is said to be Light because It illumines both. It is also Infinite and remains as Consciousness. Consciousness is the Self of which everyone is aware. No one is away from the Self. So each one

478

is Self-realised. Yet what a mystery that no one knows this fundamental fact, and desires to realise the Self? This ignorance is due to the mistaking of the body for the Self. Realisation now consists in getting rid of this false idea that one is not realised. Realisation is not anything newly got. It must be already there in order that it may be permanent. Otherwise Realisation is not worth attempting.

After the false notion 'I-am-the-body' or 'I have not realised' is removed, Supreme Consciousness or the Self alone is left over, which is however called Realisation in the present state of knowledge. However, the truth is that Realisation is eternal and already there, here and now.

Finally, Realisation amounts to elimination of ignorance and nothing more or less.

D.: My profession requires my stay in my place. I cannot remain in the vicinity of *sadhus*. Can I have realisation even in the absence of *sat sanga* as necessitated by my circumstances?

M.: Sat is aham pratyaya saram = the Self of selves. The *sadhu* is that Self of selves. He is immanent in all. Can anyone remain without the Self? No. So no one is away from *sat sanga*.

30th April, 1938

Talk 483.

Mr. Sitaramiah, a visitor: What does *samyamana* mean in Patanjali Yoga Sutra?

M.: One-pointedness of mind.

D.: By such *samyamana* in the Heart, *chitta samvit* is said to result. What does it mean?

M.: Chitta samvit is *Atma jnana i.e.,* Knowledge of the Self.

Talk 484.

D.: I think that celibacy and initiation are prerequisites even for a householder in order that he may succeed in self-investigation. Am I right?

Or can a householder observe celibacy and seek initiation from a master on occasions only?

M.: First ascertain who the wife and the husband are. Then these questions will not arise.

D.: Engaged in other pursuits, can the mental activities be checked and the query "Who am I?" pursued? Are they not contrary to each other?

M.: These questions arise only in the absence of strength of mind. As the mental activities diminish its strength increases.

D.: Does the Karma theory mean that the world is the result of action and reaction? If so, action and reaction of what?

M.: Until realisation there will be Karma, *i.e.*, action and reaction; after realisation there will be no Karma, no world.

Talk 485 .

D.: While engaged in *Atma vichara* (the investigation of the Self), I fall asleep. What is the remedy for it?

M.: Do *nama-sankirtana* (sing the name of God).

D.: It is ruled out in sleep.

M.: True. The practice should be continued while awake. Directly you wake up from sleep, you must resume it. The sleeper does not care for *Atma vichara*. So he need not practise anything. The waking self desires it and so he must do it.

In the course of conversation Sri Bhagavan continued: The mind is something mysterious. It consists of *satva, rajas* and *tamas*. The latter two give rise to *vikshepa*. In the *satva* aspect, it remains pure and uncontaminated. So there are no thoughts there and it is identical with the Self. The mind is like *akasa* (ether). Just as there are the objects in the *akasa*, so there are thoughts in the mind. The *akasa* is the counterpart of the mind and objects are of thought. One cannot hope to measure the universe and study the phenomena. It is impossible. For the objects are mental creations. To measure them is similar to trying to stamp with one's foot on the head of the shadow cast by oneself. The farther one moves the farther the shadow does also. So one cannot plant one's foot on the head of the shadow. (Here Sri Bhagavan related several incidents connected with shadows including the pranks of monkeys and a mirror). A child sees his own shadow and tries to hold the head of the shadow. As he bends and puts out his arm the head moves further. The child struggles more and more. The mother, seeing the struggle, pities the young one. So she takes hold of the young hand and keeps it on his own head and tells the child to observe the head of the shadow caught in the hand. Similarly with the ignorant practiser to study the universe. The universe is only an object created by the mind and has its being in the mind. It cannot be measured as an exterior entity. One must reach the Self in order to reach the universe.

Again people often ask how the mind is controlled. I say to them, "Show me the mind and then you will know what to do." The fact is that the mind is only a bundle of thoughts. How can you extinguish it by the thought of doing so or by a desire? Your thoughts and desires are part and parcel of the mind. The mind is simply fattened by new thoughts rising up. Therefore it is foolish to attempt to kill the mind by means of the mind. The only way of doing it is to find its source and hold on to it. The mind will then fade away of its own accord. Yoga teaches *chitta vritti nirodha* (control of the activities of the mind). But I say *Atma vichara* (Self-investigation). This is the practical way. *Chitta vritti nirodha* is brought about in sleep, swoon or by starvation. As soon as the cause is withdrawn there is recrudescence of thoughts. Of what use is it then? In the state of stupor there is peace and no misery. But misery recurs when the stupor is removed. So *nirodha* (control) is useless and cannot be of lasting benefit.

How then can the benefit be made lasting? It is by finding the cause of misery. Misery is due to objects. If they are not there, there will be no contingent thoughts and so misery is wiped off. "How will objects cease to be?" is the next question. The *shrutis* and the sages say that the objects are only mental creations. They have no substantive being. Investigate the matter and ascertain the truth of the statement. The result will be the conclusion that the objective world is in the subjective consciousness. The Self is thus the only Reality which permeates and also envelops the world. Since there is no duality, no thoughts will arise to disturb your peace. This is Realisation of the Self. The Self is eternal and so also its Realisation.

In the course of the discourse Sri Bhagavan also made a few points clearer:

Abhyasa consists in withdrawal within the Self every time you are disturbed by thought. It is not concentration or destruction of the mind but withdrawal into the Self.

Dhyana, bhakti, japa, etc., are aids to keep out the multiplicity of thoughts. A single thought prevails which too eventually dissolves in the Self.

The questioner quoted that the mind starved of ideas amounted to realisation and asked what the experience is in that state. He himself read out a passage from Mr. Brunton that it was indescribable. The answer was there. He again ventured out that it must be like looking through an unsilvered mirror, as contrasted with the present experience corresponding to looking on a silvered mirror.

Sri Bhagavan said it was a mirror facing another clear mirror, *i.e.,* no reflection.

2nd May, 1938

Talk 486.

Mr. Ganapatram: How shall I find out "Who am I"?

M.: Are there two selves for the one self to find the other?

D.: The Self must be only one consisting of two aspects of 'I' and *sankalpa* (*i.e.,* of thinker and thought).

After a time he continued: Please say how I shall realise the 'I'. Am I to make the *japa,* "Who am I?"

M.: No *japa* of the kind is meant.

D.: Am I to think "Who am I"?

M.: You have known that the 'I-thought' springs forth. Hold the 'I-thought' and find its *moola* (source).

D.: May I know the way?

M.: Do as you have now been told and see.

D.: I do not understand what I should do.

M.: If it is anything objective the way can be shown objectively. This is subjective.

D.: But I do not understand.

482

M.: What! Do you not understand that you are?

D.: Please tell me the way.

M.: Is it necessary to show the way in the interior of your own home? This is within you.

D.: What do you advise me to do?

M.: Why should you do anything and what should you do? Only keep quiet. Why not do so? Each one must do according to his own state.

D.: Please tell me what is suitable to me. I want to hear from you. (No answer.)

Talk 487.

An English lady, a young woman, came here dressed in a Muslim sari. She had evidently been in North India and met Dr. G. H. Mees.

Sri Bhagavan read out a stanza "The Black Sun" from the anniversary number of *The Vision*, written by Swami Bharatananda. After a few minutes, Miss J. asked:

One gathers from the stanza that one should keep on meditating until one gets merged in the state of consciousness. Do you think it right?

M.: Yes.

D.: I go further and ask: Is it right that one should, by conscious will, go into that state from which there is no return?

(No answer) — Dinner bell.

Afternoon

D.: What is the object of Self-Realisation?

M.: Self-Realisation is the final goal and it is the end in itself.

D.: I mean, what is the use of Self-Realisation?

M.: Why should you seek Self-Realisation? Why do you not rest content with your present state? It is evident that you are discontented with the present state. The discontent is at an end if you realise the Self.

D.: What is that Self-Realisation which removes the discontent? I am in the world and there are wars in it. Can Self-Realisation put an end to it?

M.: Are you in the world? Or is the world in you?

483

D.: I do not understand. The world is certainly around me.

M.: You speak of the world and happenings in it. They are mere ideas in you. The ideas are in the mind. The mind is within you. And so the world is within you.

D.: I do not follow you. Even if I do not think of the world, the world is still there.

M.: Do you mean to say that the world is apart from the mind and it can exist in the absence of the mind?

D.: Yes.

M.: Does the world exist in your deep sleep?

D.: It does.

M.: Do you see it in your sleep?

D.: No, I don't. But others, who are awake, see it.

M.: Are you so aware in your sleep? Or do you become aware of the other's knowledge now?

D.: In my waking state.

M.: So you speak of waking knowledge and not of sleep-experience. The existence of the world in your waking and dream states is admitted because they are the products of the mind. The mind is withdrawn in sleep and the world is in the condition of a seed. It becomes manifest over again when you wake up. The ego springs forth, identifies itself with the body and sees the world. So the world is a mental creation.

D.: How can it be?

M.: Do you not create a world in your dream? The waking state also is a long drawn out dream. There must be a seer behind the waking and dream experiences. Who is that seer? Is it the body?

D.: It cannot be.

M.: Is it the mind?

D.: It must be so.

M.: But you remain in the absence of the mind.

D.: How?

M.: In deep sleep.

D.: I do not know if I am then.

M.: If you were not how do you recollect yesterday's experiences? Is it possible that there was a break in the continuity of the 'I' during sleep?

D.: It may be.

M.: If so, a Johnson may wake up as a Benson. How will the identity of the individual be established?

D.: I don't know.

M.: If this argument is not clear, follow a different line. You admit "I slept well", "I feel refreshed after a sound sleep". So sleep was your experience. The experiencer now identifies himself with the 'I' in the speaker. So this 'I' must have been in sleep also.

D.: Yes.

M.: So 'I' was in sleep, if the world was then there, did it say that it existed?

D.: No. But the world tells me its existence now. Even if I deny its existence, I may knock myself against a stone and hurt my foot. The injury proves the existence of the stone and so of the world.

M.: Quite so. The stone hurts the foot. Does the foot say that there is the stone?

D.: No. — 'I'.

M.: Who is this 'I'? It cannot be the body nor the mind as we have seen before. This 'I' is the one who experiences the waking, dream and sleep states. The three states are changes which do not affect the individual. The experiences are like pictures passing on a screen in the cinema. The appearance and disappearance of the pictures do not affect the screen. So also, the three states alternate with one another leaving the Self unaffected. The waking and the dream states are creations of the mind. So the Self covers all. To know that the Self remains happy in its perfection is Self-Realisation. Its use lies in the realisation of Perfection and thus of Happiness.

D.: Can it be complete happiness to remain Self-realised if one does not contribute to the happiness of the world? How can one be so happy when there is a war in Spain, a war in China? Is it not selfishness to remain Self-realised without helping the world?

M.: The Self was pointed out to you to cover the universe and also transcend it. The world cannot remain apart from the Self. If the realisation of such Self be called selfishness that selfishness must cover the world also. It is nothing contemptible.

D.: Does not the realised man continue to live just like a non-realised being?

M.: Yes, with this difference that the realised being does not see the world as being apart from the Self, he possesses true knowledge and the internal happiness of being perfect, whereas the other person sees the world apart, feels imperfection and is miserable. Otherwise their physical actions are similar.

D.: The realised being also knows that there are wars being waged in the world, just like the other man.

M.: Yes.

D.: How then can he be happy?

M.: Is the cinema screen affected by a scene of fire burning or sea rising? So it is with the Self.

The idea that I am the body or the mind is so deep that one cannot get over it even if convinced otherwise. One experiences a dream and knows it to be unreal on waking. Waking experience is unreal in other states. So each state contradicts the others. They are therefore mere changes taking place in the seer, or phenomena appearing in the Self, which is unbroken and remains unaffected by them. Just as the waking, dream and sleep states are phenomena, so also birth, growth and death are phenomena in the Self. which continues to be unbroken and unaffected. Birth and death are only ideas. They pertain to the body or the mind. The Self exists before the birth of this body and will remain after the death of this body. So it is with the series of bodies taken up in succession. The Self is immortal. The phenomena are changeful and appear mortal. The fear of death is of the body. It is not true of the Self. Such fear is due to ignorance. Realisation means True Knowledge of the Perfection and Immortality of the Self. Mortality is only an idea and cause of misery. You get rid of it by realising the Immortal nature of the Self.

The same lady continued: If the world is only a dream, how should it be harmonised with the Eternal Reality?

M.: The harmony consists in the realisation of its inseparateness from the Self.

D.: But a dream is fleeting and unreal. It is also contradicted by the waking state.

M.: The waking experiences are similar.

D.: One lives fifty years and finds a continuity in the waking experience which is absent in dreams.

M.: You go to sleep and dream a dream in which the experiences of fifty years are condensed within the short duration of the dream, say five minutes. There is also a continuity in the dream. Which is real now? Is the period covering fifty years of your waking state real or the short duration of five minutes of your dream? The standards of time differ in the two states. That is all. There is no other difference between the experiences.

D.: The spirit remains unaffected by the passing phenomena and by the successive bodies of repeated births. How does each body get the life to set it acting?

M.: The spirit is differentiated from matter and is full of life. The body is animated by it.

D.: The realised being is then the spirit and unaware of the world.

M.: He sees the world but not as separate from the Self.

D.: If the world is full of pain why should he continue the world-idea?

M.: Does the realised being tell you that the world is full of pain? It is the other one who feels the pain and seeks the help of the wise saying that the world is painful. Then the wise one explains from his experience that if one withdraws within the Self there is an end of pain. The pain is felt so long as the object is different from oneself. But when the Self is found to be an undivided whole who and what is there to feel? The realised mind is the Holy Spirit and the other mind is the home of the devil. For the realised being this is the Kingdom of

Heaven. "The Kingdom of Heaven is within you." That Kingdom is *here* and *now*.

Talk 488.

A group of young men asked: "It is said that healthy mind can be only in a healthy body. Should we not attempt to keep the body always strong and healthy?"

M.: In that way there will be no end of attention to the health of the body.

D.: The present experiences are the result of past Karma. If we know the mistakes committed in the past, we can rectify them.

M.: If one mistake is rectified there yet remains the whole *sanchita* which is going to give you innumerable births. So that is not the procedure. The more you prune a plant, the more vigorously it grows. The more you rectify your Karma, the more it accumulates. Find the root of Karma and cut it off.

4th May, 1938

Talk 489.

Another group of visitors was asking the method of Realisation. In the course of a reply Sri Bhagavan said: "Holding the mind and investigating it is advised for a beginner. But what is mind after all? It is a projection of the Self. See for whom it appears and from where it rises. The 'I-thought' will be found to be the root-cause. Go deeper; the 'I-thought' disappears and there is an infinitely expanded 'I-consciousness'. That is otherwise called *Hiranyagarbha*. When it puts on limitations it appears as individuals."

Talk 490.

The English lady desired to have a private talk with Sri Bhagavan. She began, "I am returning to England. I leave this place this evening. I want to have the happiness of Self-Realisation in my home. Of course it is not easy in the West. But I shall strive for it. What is the way to do it?"

M.: If Realisation be something outside you a way can be shown consistent with the safety of the individual, his capacity. etc. Then the questions if it is realisable and, if so, in what time — will also arise. But here, Realisation is of the Self. You cannot remain without the Self. The Self is always realised. But only you do not recognise the fact. The Realisation is now obscured by the present world-idea. The world is now seen outside you and the idea associated with it obscures your real nature. All that is needed is to overcome this ignorance and then the Self stands revealed. No special effort is necessary to realise the Self. All efforts are for eliminating the present obscuration of the Truth.

A lady is wearing a necklace round her neck. She forgets it, imagines it to be lost and impulsively looks for it here, there and everywhere. Not finding it, she asks her friends if they have found it anywhere, until one kind friend points to her neck and tells her to feel the necklace round the neck. The seeker does so and feels happy that the necklace is found. Again, when she meets her other friends, they ask her if her lost necklace was found. She says 'yes' to them, as if it were lost and later recovered. Her happiness on re-discovering it round her neck is the same as if some lost property was recovered. In fact she never lost it nor recovered it. And yet she was once miserable and now she is happy. So also with the realisation of the Self. The Self is always realised. The Realisation is now obscured. When the veil is removed the person feels happy at rediscovering the ever-realised Self. The ever-present Realisation appears to be a new Realisation.

Now, what should one do to overcome the present ignorance. Be eager to have the true knowledge. As this eagerness grows the wrong knowledge diminishes in strength until it finally disappears.

D.: The other day you were saying that there is no awareness in deep sleep. But I have on rare occasions become aware of sleep even in that state.

M.: Now, of these three factors, the awareness, sleep and knowledge of it, the first one is changeless. That awareness, which cognised sleep as a state, now sees the world also in the waking state. The negation of the world is the state of sleep. The world may appear or disappear — that is to say, one may be awake or asleep — the

489

awareness is unaffected. It is one continuous whole over which the three states of waking, dream and sleep pass. Be that awareness even now. That is the Self — that is Realisation — there is Peace — there is Happiness. The lady thanked Maharshi and retired.

7th May. 1938

Talk 491.

Mr. Kishorelal Mashruwala, President, Gandhi Seva Sangh, asked: "How is *Brahmacharya* to be practised in order that it may be successfully lived up to?"

M.: It is a matter of will-power. *Satvic* food, prayers, etc., are useful aids to it.

D.: Young men have fallen into bad habits. They desire to get over them and seek our advice.

M.: Mental reform is needed.

D.: Can we prescribe any special food, exercise, etc., to them?

M.: There are some medicines. Yogic *asanas* and *satvic* food are also useful.

D.: Some young persons have taken a vow of *brahmacharya*. They repent of the vow after the lapse of ten or twelve years. Under these circumstances should we encourage young persons to take the vow of *brahmacharya*?

M.: This question will not arise in the case of true *brahmacharya*.

D.: Some young men take the vow of *brahmacharya* without knowing its full implications. When they find it difficult to carry it out in practice, they seek our advice.

M.: They need not take a vow but they may try it without the vow.

D.: Is *naishthika brahmacharya* (life-long celibacy) essential as a *sadhana* for Self-Realisation?

M.: Realisation itself is *naishthika brahmacharya*. The vow is not *brahmacharya*. Life in Brahman is *brahmacharya* and it is not a forcible attempt at it.

D.: It is said that *kama* (desire), *krodha* (anger), etc.. vanish in the presence of the Sadguru. Is it so?

490

M.: It is correct. *Kama* and *krodha* must vanish before Self-Realisation.

D.: But all the disciples of a guru are not of the same degree of advancement. There are found lapses in a few cases. Who is responsible for such lapses?

M.: There is no connection between Self-Realisation and individual predispositions (*samskara*). It is not always possible to live up to the ideal of the Guru.

D.: Do not passions affect Realisation?

M.: The attempt to cleanse oneself will be automatic.

D.: Is it not necessary to wash off all impurities before Realisation?

M.: *Jnana* will wash them clean.

D.: Gandhiji is often perplexed finding his intimate disciples going wrong. He wonders how it could happen and thinks that it is due to his own defects. Is it so?

M.: (Sri Bhagavan smiled and answered after a few minutes) Gandhiji has struggled so long to perfect himself. All others will be right in due course.

D.: Is the Hindu view of reincarnation correct?

M.: No definite answer is possible for this question. There are pros and cons for the view. Even the present birth is denied *natvevaham jatu nasam* etc., (*Bhagavad Gita*). We were never born, etc.

D.: Is not individuality *anadi* (without beginning)?

M.: Investigate and see if there is any individuality at all. Ask this question after solving this problem. Nammalvar says: "In ignorance I took the ego to be myself; however, with right knowledge, the ego is nowhere and only you remain as the SELF." Both monists and dualists are agreed on the necessity of Self-Realisation. Let us do it first and then discuss the side-issues. *Advaita* or *dvaita* cannot be decided on theoretical considerations alone. If the Self is realised the question will not arise at all. Even Suka had no confidence in his *brahmacharya* whereas Sri Krishna was sure of his *brahmacharya*. Self-Realisation is designated by so many different names, *satya, brahmacharya*, etc. What is natural to the state of Self-Realisation forms the disciplinary course in the other state. "I-am-the-body" idea will become extinct only on Self-Realisation. With its extinction the *vasanas* become extinct and all virtues will remain ever.

D.: Samskaras are said to persist even in a *jnani*.

M.: Yes. They are *bhoga hetu* (leading to enjoyment only) and not *bandha hetu*.

D.: This fact is often abused by fakes who pretend to be *sadhus* but lead vicious lives. They say it is *prarabdha* (remnant of past Karma). How shall we mark off the fakes from the genuine *sadhus*?

M.: The one who has given up the idea of being the doer cannot repeat, "This is my *prarabdha*". "The *jnanis* lead different lives" is said for the benefit of others. The *jnanis* cannot make use of this in explanation of their lives and conduct.

(After a few minutes, Sri Bhagavan remarked about Mr. Kishorelal's weak body).

Mr. Kishorelal: I am asthmatic. I have never been strong. Even as a baby I was not fed on my mother's milk.

M.: Here the mind is strong and the body is weak.

D.: I wanted to practise Raja Yoga. I could not do it because of my physical unfitness. The mind also began to wander with the movement of the body.

M.: If the mind be kept immovable let the body change as much as it likes.

D.: Is it not a handicap to the beginner?

M.: Attempts must be made in spite of handicaps.

D.: Of course. But they will be momentary.

M.: The idea of 'momentary' is one among so many other ideas. So long as thoughts persist this idea also will recur. Concentration is our own nature (*i.e.* BE-ing). There is the effort now: but it ceases after Self-Realisation.

D.: It is said to be the interval between flights of mind

M.: This too is due to the activity of the mind.

The Devotee submitted that whenever he had thought that he had found something original, he later discovered that he was already forestalled.

492

Sri Bhagavan pointed out that everything remains already in the germinal form and so there can be nothing new.

8th May, 1938

Talk 492.

In a suit by the temple against the Government regarding the ownership of the Hill Sri Bhagavan was cited as a witness. He was examined by a commission. In the course of the examination-in-chief Sri Bhagavan said that Siva always remains in three forms: (1) as *Parabrahman* (2) as *Linga* (here as the Hill) and (3) as *Siddha*. (*Brahma Rupa; Linga Rupa; Siddha Rupa*).

There are some *tirthas* on the Hill, *e.g.*, *Mulaipal Tirtha* and *Pada Tirtha*, said to have been originated for or by Virupakshi Devar and Guha Namassivayar. There is also *Rshabha Tirtha*. All of them are in good condition.

Siva originally appeared as a column of Light. On being prayed to, the Light disappeared into the Hill and manifested as Linga. Both are Siva.

Maharshi said: The buildings or asramams grow around me. I do not wish for them. I do not ask for them nor prevent their formation. I have known that actions are done even though I did not want them to be done. So I conclude that they *must* happen and I therefore do not say 'no'.

Question: Is the present Sarvadhikari to be your successor?

M.: Yes. Only management.

(*i.e.*, succession here means simple supervision).

Question: Is the work now being carried out by him?

M.: He simply supervises the work. The work is being done by others as well.

18th May, 1938

Talk 493.

An Andhra visitor: What will aid me to fix my attention always at Thy Holy Feet?

M.: The thought 'Am I ever away from the feet?'

493

D.: How is this thought to be fixed?

M.: By driving away other thoughts which counteract this.

Talk 494.

Sri Bhagavan had gone through "Turn Eastwards" — the whole book of Mademoiselle Pascaline Maillert — and spoke for about an hour on that book. He said that the writing is full of feeling and the writer is sincere. The book is written in simple style and finishes off with remembrance of Himself. A few errors here and there might be pointed out to be corrected in subsequent editions. Nandanar Charitra has been repeated twice under the mistaken notion that the incident was on two different occasions. *Prithvi, Ap,* etc., *lingas* are wrongly located. Sri Bhagavan thinks the book well-written. He interprets "Turn Eastwards" as "Turn to the Source of Light". This book is a good supplement to Mr. Brunton's book.

29th May, 1938

Talk 495.

A Cochin Brahmin, Professor in the Ernakulam College, had an interesting conversation with Sri Bhagavan. Sri Bhagavan advised surrender to God. The visitor gave a glimpse of an ICS Officer. The gentleman while a student was an atheist or an agnostic. He is very pious now and the change has surprised everyone who had known him before.

In further conversation, the following points were noteworthy —

The visitor said: "One must become satiate with the fulfilment of desires before they are renounced." Sri Bhagavan smiled and cut in: "Fire might as well be put out by pouring spirit over the flames. (All laugh). The more the desires are fulfilled, the deeper grows the *samskara.* They must become weaker before they cease to assert themselves. That weakness is brought about by restraining oneself and not by losing oneself in desires.

D.: How can they be rendered weaker?

M.: By knowledge. You know that you are not the mind. The desires are in the mind. Such knowledge helps one to control them.

D.: But they are not controlled in our practical lives.

M.: Every time you attempt satisfaction of a desire the knowledge comes that it is better to desist. Repeated reminders of this kind will in due course weaken the desires. What is your true nature? How can you ever forget it? Waking, dream and sleep are mere phases of the mind. They are not of the Self. You are the witness of these states. Your true nature is found in sleep.

D.: But we are advised not to fall into sleep during meditation.

M.: That is stupor you must guard against. That sleep which alternates with waking is not true sleep. That waking which alternates with sleep is not true waking. Are you now awake? You are not. You are required to wake up to your real state. You should not fall into false sleep nor keep falsely awake. Hence:

Laye sambodhayeccittam vikshiptam samayet punah.

What does it mean? It means that you should not fall into any one of these states but remain amidst them in your true unsullied nature.

D.: The states are of our mind only.

M.: Whose mind? Hold it and see.

D.: The mind cannot be held. It is that which creates all these. It is known only by its effects and not in its true nature.

M.: Quite so. You see the colours of the spectrum. Together they form the white light. But seven colours are seen through the prism. Similarly, the one Self resolves itself into so many phases, mind, world, body, etc. The Self is seen as the mind, the body or the world. That is to say, it becomes whatever you perceive it to be.

D.: These are difficult to follow in practice. I will hold on to God and surrender.

M.: That is the best.

D.: How can I do my duties without attachment? There is my wife, there are my children. I must do my duty towards them. Affection is necessary. Am I right?

M.: How do you do your work in the College?

D.: (laughing) For wages.

M.: Not because you are attached, simply as doing your duty.

D.: But my pupils expect me to love them.

M.: "Detachment in the interior and attachment in appearance," says *Yoga Vasishta*.

9th June, 1938

Talk 496.

A *Swami* belonging to Sri Ramakrishna Mission had a very interesting conversation with Sri Bhagavan in the course of which Sri Bhagavan observed:

M.: Avidya (ignorance) is the obstacle for knowing your true nature even at the present moment.

D.: How is one to get over *Avidya*?

M.: Ya na vidyate sa avidya (What is not, is *avidya*). So it is itself a myth. If it really be, how can it perish? Its being is false and so it disappears.

D.: Although I understand it intellectually, I cannot realise the Self.

M.: Why should this thought disturb your present state of realisation.

D.: The Self is One, but yet I do not find myself free from the present trouble.

M.: Who says this? Is it the Self which is only one? The question contradicts itself.

D.: Grace is necessary for realisation.

M.: Inasmuch as you, being a man, now understand that there is a higher power guiding you, it is due to Grace. Grace is within you. *Isvaro gururatmeti* (*Isvara*, Guru and the Self are synonymous).

D.: I pray for that Grace.

M.: Yes, yes.

10th June, 1938

Talk 497.

In the course of a different conversation. Sri Bhagavan said:
Satva is the light,
Rajas is the subject, and
Tamas is the object.

496

Even the *satva* light is only reflected light. Were it pure, original Light, there would be no modification in it. The *manokasa* (mind-ether) is reflected as *bhootakasa* (element-ether) and objects are seen as being separate from the subject.

Samadhi is present even in *vyavaharadasa* (practical life). Our activities (*vyavahara*) have no existence apart from *samadhi*. The screen is there when the pictures move past on it and also when they are not projected. Similarly, the Self is always there in *vyavahara* (activity) or in *shanti* (peace).

Talk 498.

People often say that a *mukta purusha* should go out and preach his message to the people. They argue, how can anyone be a *mukta* so long as there is misery by his side? True. But who is a *mukta*? Does he see misery beside him? They want to determine the state of a *mukta* without themselves realising the state. From the standpoint of the *mukta* their contention amounts to this: a man dreams a dream in which he finds several persons. On waking up, he asks, "Have the dream individuals also wakened?" It is ridiculous.

Again, a good man says, "It does not matter even if I do not get *mukti*. Or let me be the last man to get it so that I shall help all others to be *muktas* before I am one." It is all very good. Imagine a dreamer saying, "May all these wake up before I do". The dreamer is no more absurd than the amiable philosopher aforesaid.

Talk 499.

The *Swami* of Sri Ramakrishna Mission had more questions to ask:

Swamiji, I went up the hill to see the *asramas* in which you lived in your youth. I have also read your life. May I know if you did not then feel that there is God to whom you should pray or that you should practise something in order to reach this state?

M.: Read the life and you will understand. *Jnana* and *ajnana* are of the same degree of truth; that is, both are imagined by the ignorant; that is not true from the standpoint of the *jnani*.

D.: Is a *jnani* capable or likely to commit sins?

M.: An *ajnani* sees someone as a *jnani* and identifies him with the body. Because he does not know the Self and, mistakes his body for the Self, he extends the same mistake to the state of the *jnani*. The *jnani* is therefore considered to be the physical frame.

Again since the *ajnani*, though he is not the doer, yet imagines himself to be the doer and considers the actions of the body his own, he thinks the *jnani* to be similarly acting when the body is active. But the *jnani* himself knows the Truth and is not confounded. The state of a *jnani* cannot be determined by the *ajnani* and therefore the question troubles only the *ajnani* and never does it arise for the *jnani*. If he is a doer he must determine the nature of the actions. The Self cannot be the doer. Find out who is the doer and the Self is revealed.

D.: There could be no *advaita* in actions. That is how the questions arose.

M.: But the stanza says there should be. This 'do' is applicable only to the practiser and not the accomplished ones.

D.: Yes. I quite see it. Moreover, *advaita* cannot be practised in one's dealings with the Guru. For, consistently with it, he cannot receive instructions.

M.: Yes, the Guru is within and not without. A Tamil saint has said, "O Guru! always abiding within me, but manifesting now in human form only to guide and protect me!" What is within as the Self manifests in due course as Guru in human shape.

D.: So it amounts to this. To see a *jnani* is not to understand him. You see the *jnani's* body and not his *jnanam*. One must therefore be a *jnani* to know a *jnani*.

M.: The *jnani* sees no one as an *ajnani*. All are only *jnanis* in his sight. In the ignorant state one superimposes his ignorance on a *jnani* and mistakes him for a doer. In the state of *jnana*, the *jnani* sees nothing separate from the Self. The Self is all shining and only pure *jnana*. So there is no *ajnana* in his sight. There is an illustration for this kind of allusion or super-imposition. Two friends went to sleep side by side. One of them dreamt that both of them had gone on a long journey and had strange experiences. On waking up he recapitulated them and asked his friend if it was not so. The other

498

one simply ridiculed him saying that it was only his dream and could not affect the other.

So it is with the *ajnani* who superimposes his illusive ideas on others.

Regarding *ajnana* in early youth and *jnana* at the present time, Sri Bhagavan said:

There is no *jnana* as it is commonly understood. The ordinary ideas of *jnana* and *ajnana* are only relative and false. They are not real and therefore not abiding. The true state is the non-dual Self. It is eternal and abides whether one is aware or not. It is like *kanthabharana* or the tenth man.

D.: Someone else points it out.

M.: That one is not external. You mistake the body for the Guru. But the Guru does not think himself so. He is the formless Self. That is within you; he appears without only to guide you.

Talk 500.

D.: When all the thoughts are banished and the mind is still or enters into a state of nothingness or emptiness, what is the nature of effort needed on the part of the 'seeker' to have a *pratyakshabhava* of the 'sought' (*e.g.*, seeing a mango as a mango)?

M.: Who sees nothingness or emptiness? What is *pratyaksha*? Do you call perception of mango *pratyaksha*? It involves the play of *karma, karta,* and *karya* (action, doer and deed). So it is relative and not absolute. Because you see a thing now you say there is nothing afterwards (*i.e.*, when you no longer see it). Both are functions of the mind. What lies behind both these assertions is *pratyaksha*. There is *indriya pratyaksha* (directly perceived by senses), *manasa pratyaksha* (directly perceived by the mind) and *sakshat pratyaksha* (realised as the very Being). The last alone is true. The others are relative and untrue.

D.: If no effort is needed, can the perpetuated state of emptiness of mind be called the state of realisation?

M.: Effort is needed so long as there is mind. The state of emptiness has been the bone of contention in all philosophies.

499

D.: Is there anything like *pratyakshabhava* in the state of realisation or is realisation merely felt or experienced as the very Being or *Sthiti* of the soul?

M.: Pratyaksha is very being and it is not feeling, etc.

D.: Until the seeker realizes that he is the sought, the above questions arise for him (the former).

M.: True. See if you are the seeker. The Self is often mistaken for the knower. Is there not the Self in deep sleep, *i.e.,* nescience? Therefore the Self is beyond knower and knowledge. These doubts are in the realm of mind. To speak from this point of view, the advice is to keep the mind clear, and when *rajas* and *tamas* are wiped off, then the *satva* mind alone exists. So the 'I' vanishes in the *satva* (*oonadhal kan*).

Jnana chakshus does not mean that it is an organ of perception like the other sense-organs. *Jnanameva chakshuh.* Television, etc., are not functions of *jnana chakshus*. So long as there is a subject and also an object it is only relative knowledge. *Jnana* lies beyond relative knowledge. It is absolute.

The Self is the source of subject and object. Now ignorance prevailing, the subject is taken to be the source. The subject is the knower and forms one of the triads whose components cannot exist independent of one another. So the subject or the knower cannot be the ultimate Reality. Reality lies beyond subject and object. When realised there will be no room for doubt.

> *"Bhidyate hridayagranthih*
> *chhidyante sarvasamsayah."*

The heart knot is snapped; doubts are set at rest. That is called *pratyaksha* and not what you are thinking of. *Avidya nasa* is alone Self-Realisation. Self-Realisation is only *owpacharika.* Self-Realisation is only a euphemism for elimination of ignorance.

12th July, 1938

Talk 501.

A young Mysorean asked:

D.: How did I get this body?

500

M.: You speak of 'I' and the 'body'. There is the relationship between the two. You are not therefore the body. The question does not occur to the body because it is inert. There is an occasion when you are not aware of the body — namely, in deep sleep. The question does not arise then. Nevertheless you are there in sleep. To whom does the question arise now?

D.: The ego.

M.: Yes. The body and the ego rise up together and sink together. There is an occasion when you are not associated with the ego in deep sleep. Now you are associated with the ego. Of these two states which is your real state? You are present in sleep and the same "You" is present now too. Why should the doubt arise now and not then? You are right in saying that it is for the ego. You are not the ego. The ego is intermediate between the Self and the body. You are the Self. Find out the origin of the ego and see if the doubt persists.

Sri Bhagavan added after a few minutes:

The answer, according to *sastras*, will be that the body is due to *karma*. The question will be how did *karma* arise? We must say "from a previous body" and so on without end. The direct method of attack is not to depend on invisible hypotheses but to ask "Whose *Karma* is it? Or whose body?" Hence I answered in this manner. This is more purposeful.

14th August, 1938

Talk 502.

Sjt. Rajendra Prasad and Sjt. Jamnalal Bajaj with others are on a visit to Sri Maharshi.

16th August — Sjt. J. B. asked questions:

D.: How is the mind to be steadily kept right?

M.: All living beings are aware of their surroundings and therefore intellect must be surmised in all of them. At the same time, there is a difference between the intellect of man and that of other animals, because man not only sees the world as it is and acts accordingly, but also seeks fulfilment of desires and is not satisfied with the existing state of affairs. In his attempt to fulfil his desires he extends his vision far and wide and yet he turns away dissatisfied. He now begins to think and reason.

The desire for permanency of happiness and of peace bespeaks such permanency in his own nature. Therefore he seeks to find and regain his own nature, *i.e.*, his Self. That found, all is found.

Such inward seeking is the path to be gained by man's intellect. The intellect itself realises after continuous practice that it is enabled by some Higher Power to function. It cannot itself reach that Power. So it ceases to function after a certain stage. When it thus ceases to function the Supreme Power is still left there all alone. That is Realisation; that is the finality; that is the goal.

It is thus plain that the purpose of the intellect is to realise its own dependence upon the Higher Power and its inability to reach the same. So it must annihilate itself before the goal is gained.

D.: A sloka is quoted which means: "I do not desire kingdoms, etc. Only let me serve Thee for ever and there lies my highest pleasure." Is that right?

M.: Yes. There is room for *kama* (desire) so long as there is an object apart from the subject (*i.e.*, duality). There can be no desire if there is no object. The state of no-desire is *moksha*. There is no duality in sleep and also no desire. Whereas there is duality in the waking state and desire also is there. Because of duality a desire arises for the acquisition of the object. That is the outgoing mind, which is the basis of duality and of desire. If one knows that Bliss is none other than the Self the mind becomes inward turned. If the Self is gained all the desires are fulfilled. That is the *apta kamah atma kamah akamascha* (fulfilment of desire) of the *Brihadaranyaka Upanishad*. That is *moksha*.

Here J. B. tried to make himself clear by saying that what he meant by *sadbuddhi* was not the same as *buddhi*. It means that which holds fast to the good, the right and the chosen path. He wanted to know how such steadfastness could be gained.

M.: What is wanted for gaining the highest goal is loss of individuality. The intellect is co-extensive with individuality. Loss of individuality can only be after the disappearance of *buddhi*, good or bad. The question therefore does not arise.

D.: But yet one must know the right thing, choose the right path, practise the right *dharma* and hold fast to it. Otherwise he is lost.

M.: True strength accrues by keeping in the right direction without swerving from it.

D.: Difficulties are met with. How is one to get the strength necessary to overcome the obstacles which beset one's path?

M.: By means of devotion and company of the sages.

D.: Loss of individuality was just before mentioned as a prerequisite to *moksha*. Now devotion and association with the wise are advised as the methods. Is there not individuality implied in them *e.g.*, in "I am a *bhakta*", "I am a *satsangi*"?

M.: The method is pointed out to the seeker. The seeker has certainly not lost his individuality so far. Otherwise the question would not have arisen. The way is shown to effect the loss of individuality of the seeker. It is thus appropriate.

D.: Is the desire for *swaraj* right?

M.: Such desire no doubt begins with self-interest. Yet practical work for the goal gradually widens the outlook so that the individual becomes merged in the country. Such merging of the individuality is desirable and the related *karma* is *nishkama* (unselfish) .

D.: If *swaraj* is gained after a long struggle and terrible sacrifices, is not the person justified in being pleased with the result and elated by it?

M.: He must have in the course of his work surrendered himself to the Higher Power whose Might must be kept in mind and never lost sight of. How then can he be elated? He should not even care for the result of his actions. Then alone the *karma* becomes unselfish.

D.: How can unerring rectitude be ensured for the worker?

M.: If he has surrendered himself to God or to Guru the Power to which he had surrendered will take him on the right course. The worker need no longer concern himself about the rectitude or otherwise of the course. The doubt will arise only if he fails to obey the Master in all details.

D.: Is there not any Power on earth which can bestow Grace on Its devotees so that they may grow strong to work for the country and gain *swaraj*? (Sri Maharshi remained silent. This, He later said, signified that such was the case).

D.: Is not the *tapasya* of the ancient *mahatmas* of the land available for the benefit of its present-day inheritors?

M.: It is, but the fact must not be overlooked that no one can claim to be the sole beneficiary. The benefits are shared by all alike. (After a pause) Is it without such saving Grace that the present awakening has come into being? (Here Sri Bhagavan said that before His arrival in Tiruvannamalai in 1896, there was not any clear political thought in India. Only Dadabhai Nauroji had become an M. P.).

After a short pause, J. B. said: Sri Rajendra Prasad is such a noble and selfless worker for the country that he has sacrificed a very lucrative career for this work. The country needs him. And yet he is not in good health, and is always weak and ailing. Why should there be such cruelty to such a noble son of the country?

(Sri Maharshi simply smiled a benign smile).

17th August, 1938

Talk 503.

An American gentleman, Mr. J. M. Lorey, has been staying in the Asramam for about two months. He asked:

I am leaving tonight. It gives me pain to tear myself away from this place. But I must go to America. I ask for a message from the Master. The Master understands me even better than I do myself. So I pray for a message to keep me up when I am away from the Master.

M.: The Master is not outside you as you seem to imagine. He is within, is in fact the Self. Recognise this truth. Seek within you and find Him there. Then you will have constant communion with Him. The message is always there; it is never silent; it can never forsake you: nor can you ever move away from the Master.

Your mind is outgoing. Because of that tendency it sees objects as being outside and the Master among them. But the Truth is different. The Master is the Self. Turn the mind within and you will find the objects within. You will also realise that it is the Master who is your very Self and there is nothing but Him.

Because you identify yourself with the body you have accepted objects as being outside you. But are you the body? You are not. You are the Self. *There* are all the objects and the whole universe. Nothing can escape the Self. How then can you move away from the Master who is your very Self? Suppose your body moves from place to place; does it ever move away from your Self? Similarly, you can never be without the Master.

Mr. Lorey was struck by the answer although he was already familiar with the Master's ways. He was even visibly moved. He prayed that the Grace of the Master might abide with him.

Sri Bhagavan: The Master being the Self. Grace is inseparable from the Self.

Mr. L. Saluted Sri Maharshi with intense fervour, saying: that he might be enabled to realise the Truth.

M.: Is there any moment when you have not realised the Self? Can you ever be apart from the Self? You are always That.

D.: You are the great Master shedding joy and bliss on the world. Your love is indeed unlimited that you choose to abide in the world in human shape! But I wish to know if one should necessarily realise one's Self before being of help to the country and a leader of men.

M.: Realise the Self first and the rest will follow.

D.: America is now the foremost country in industrial matters, mechanical engineering, scientific advance and other worldly affairs. Will she come up to the same level in spiritual life also?

M.: Certainly, she is bound to.

D.: Thank God that it will be so! I am a partner in an Engineering firm. But it is not of vital concern to me. I try to bring spiritual ideals into the work-a-day life of the firm.

M.: That is good. If you surrender yourself to the Higher Power all is well. That Power sees your affairs through. Only so long as you think that you are the worker you are obliged to reap the fruits of your actions. If on the other hand, you surrender yourself and recognise your individual self as only a tool of the Higher Power,

505

that Power will take over your affairs along with the fruits of actions. You are no longer affected by them and the work goes on unhampered. Whether you recognise the Power or not the scheme of things does not alter. Only there is a change of outlook. Why should you bear your load on the head when you are travelling on a train? It carries you and your load whether the load is on your head or on the floor of the train. You are not lessening the burden of the train by keeping it on your head but only straining yourself unnecessarily. Similar is the sense of doership in the world by the individuals.

D.: I have been interesting myself in metaphysics for over twenty years. But I have not gained any novel experience as so many others claim to do. I have no powers of clairvoyance, clairaudience, etc. I feel myself locked up in this body and nothing more.

M.: It is right. Reality is only one and that is the self. All the rest are mere Phenomena in it, of it and by it. The seer, the objects and the sight, all are the self only. Can anyone see or hear, leaving the self aside? What difference does it make to see or hear anyone in close proximity or over enormous distance? The organs of sight and hearing are needed in both cases; so also the mind is required. None of them can be dispensed with in either case. There is dependence one way or another. Why then should there be a glamour about clairvoyance or clairaudience?

Moreover, what is acquired will also be lost in due course. They can never be permanent.

The only permanent thing is Reality; and *that* is the Self. You say "I am", "I am going", "I am speaking", "I am working", etc. Hyphenate "I am" in all of them. Thus I — AM. *That* is the abiding and fundamental Reality. This truth was taught by God to Moses: "I AM that I-AM". "Be still and know that I-AM God." so "I-AM" is God.

· You know that you are. You cannot deny your existence at any moment of time. For you must be there in order to deny it. This (Pure Existence) is understood by stilling your mind. The mind is the outgoing faculty of the individual. If that is turned within, it becomes still in course of time and that "I-AM" alone prevails. "I-AM" is the whole Truth.

506

D.: I appreciate the whole answer.

M.: Who is there to appreciate what?

A question about Heart. Sri Bhagavan said: Leave alone the idea of *right* and *left*. They pertain to the body. The Heart is the Self. Realise it and then you will see for yourself. (Mr. Lorey thanked Sri Bhagavan and saluted him before retiring.)

18th August, 1938

Talk 504.

A visitor asked Sri Bhagavan about the 'over-mind', and 'super-mind', the 'Psychic', the 'Divine' of Sri Aurobindo's terminology.

M.: Realise the Self or the Divine. All these differences will disappear.

Talk 505.

Babu Rajendra Prasad said: I have come here with Mahatma Gandhiji's permission and I must return to him soon. Can Sri Bhagavan give me any message for him?

M.: Adhyatma sakti is working within him and leading him on. That is enough. What more is necessary?

19th August, 1938

Talk 506.

Explaining the opening stanza of *Sad Vidya*, Sri Bhagavan said: *Sat* (Being) is *Chit* (Knowledge Absolute); also *Chit* is *Sat*; what is, is only one. Otherwise the knowledge of the world and of one's own being will be impossible. It denotes both being and knowledge. However, both of them are one and the same. On the other hand, be it *Sat* only and not *Chit* also, such *Sat* will only be insentient (*jada*). In order to know it another *Chit* will be needed; such *Chit* being other than *Sat* cannot be. But it must be. Now taking *Chit* to be *Sat*, since *Sat* is *Jada*, *Chit* also becomes *jada* which is absurd. Again to know it another *Chit* is required, which is also absurd.

Therefore *Sat* and *Chit* are only one and the same.

507

Talk 507.

An Arya Samajist from Bangalore with a companion visited Sri Maharshi. He asked: What is the use of yoga-practice? Is it for personal use or universal benefit?

M.: Yoga means union of two entities. What are they? Enquire. Use or benefit is in relation to some centre. What is it? Enquire.

D.: Should there be distinction of castes?

M.: Who is it that sees such distinction? Find it out.

D.: I find that it is observed in this Asramam. Probably without the approval of Sri Bhagavan others observe it here.

M.: Who are you that speak of others, etc.? Did you notice others, etc., in your *sushupti*?

D.: I am the individuality here. I may not see others in my sleep but I see them now.

M.: No doubt you do. But the one who sees now and the one who did not see in sleep are you only — the same individual. Why should you notice differences now and be troubled? Be as you were in sleep.

D.: That cannot be. I see it now whereas I do not see it in my sleep. That does not alter the existing state of affairs.

M.: Do the objects exist in the absence of the subject?

D.: Their existence is independent of the subject.

M.: Do you say that they exist, or do they come and announce their existence to you?

D.: I know that they exist.

M.: So it is your knowledge of them only. Their existence is not absolute.

D.: Even if I did not know they will continue to exist.

M.: Do you claim their existence in the absence of your knowledge of them? (Laughter).

D.: Brahman is equal to all. There cannot be any distinction there. Caste-distinction is against the highest principle.

M.: Why do you drag in Brahman? He has no grievances. Let him who has grievances pursue the matter.

D.: You are a Mahatma. You cannot admit castes. But how do the people here enforce such distinctions?

M.: Did I tell you that I am a *jnani* or a *mahatma*? You are saying it yourself. Nor did I make a grievance of this caste affair.

D.: Paramatma is the same in all.

M.: Why do you bring in all these names? They can take care of themselves. They do not require your help.

D.: Mahatma Gandhi also admits equality...

M.: Gandhi is not here.

D.: Aurobindo does not approve of castes. Do you approve of them?

M.: As for Aurobindo, you ask him. As for my opinion, how does it matter to you? How will it be of use to you? Have you got any opinion on the matter? That alone will affect you, not the opinion of others.

D.: I do not approve of the caste system. Mahatma's opinion is valuable as a guidance. I want your blessings in my attempts.

M.: Mahatma has told you to seek and find your Self. You will not do it but require his blessings.

D.: I am trying to follow the instructions. But caste-distinction is painful. It must go.

M.: To whom does it cause pain?

D.: The members of the society...

M.: It is you who say it. There are countries where there are no such distinctions of caste. Are they free from trouble? There are wars, internecine struggle, etc. Why do you not remedy the evils there?

D.: There are troubles here also.

M.: Differences are always there. There are not only human beings, but also animals, plants, etc. The state of affairs cannot be helped.

D.: We do not mind the animals, etc., at present.

M.: Why not? If they could speak they would claim equality with you and dispute your claims no less vigorously than human beings.

D.: But we cannot help it. It is God's work.

M.: If that is God's work then the other part is your work, is that so?

D.: It is man-made distinction.

M.: You need not notice these distinctions. There is diversity in the world. A unity runs through the diversity. The Self is the same in all. There is no difference in spirit. All the differences are external and superficial. You find out the Unity and be happy.

The pain of diversity is overcome by the joy of the perception of unity. Moreover, a king may disguise himself as a servant. That makes no difference in the person.

D.: I do not object to differences. But the claims of superiority are wrong.

M.: There are differences in the limbs of one's body. When the hand touches the foot the hand is not defiled. Each limb performs its function. Why do you object to differences?

D.: The people feel the injustice of caste distinction. It must be rooted out.

M.: You can individually arrive at the state where such distinctions are not perceived and be happy. How can you hope to reform the world? Even if you try you cannot succeed. Kavyakantha Ganapati Sastri offered to initiate Harijans with *mantras* and make Brahmins of them. But the Harijans did not come forward to accept the offer. That shows they are themselves afflicted by an inferiority complex. Remove that complex first before you try to reform others.

Moreover, why do you go to places where such distinctions are observed and cause pain to yourself? Why should you not seek places where they are not observed and be happy there?

Gandhiji also tries to bring about equality. He is also up against the barrier of inferiority complex afflicting the lower orders. He cannot enforce his views on others. He observes non-violence. So matters stand as they are.

D.: We must work to obliterate caste-distinctions.

M.: Then do it. If you have succeeded in the world, then see if the distinctions persist in this place.

D.: This must be the first place where I want to effect the reform.

M.: Why do you exert yourself so much to effect reforms? Go to sleep and see if there are differences. There you obliterate differences without any effort. (Laughter).

510

24th August, 1938

Talk 508.

An Indian I. C. S. Officer was in the hall for a few hours. He asked: "Can *ahimsa* put an end to wars in the world?" Sri Bhagavan did not answer and it was time to go out for the evening walk. The next day when someone else repeated the question, Sri Bhagavan said that the question contained its answer. It is patent that in a state of perfect *ahimsa* there can be no war.

26th August, 1938

Talk 509.

Mr. MacIver had an interview with Sri Bhagavan and spoke about *diksha*.

Sri Bhagavan asked: What is this *diksha*? After a pause, He continued, "*Diksha* is of various kinds, by word, by sight, by touch and so forth."

D.: Bhagavan's is *mowna diksha*, is it not?

M.: Yes, this the highest form of *diksha*.

D.: Is it applicable to the *vichara marga* only?

M.: All the *margas* are included in the *vichara marga*.

D.: Yes, but if one wished to take them separately, it would not be applicable. Would it?

M.: No.

D.: Supposing one feels the need for aids to Realisation these are to be regarded as belonging to accessory *margas*. Are they not?

M.: Yes.

D.: And for these then other *dikshas* would be necessary.

M.: Yes.

D.: From this another question arises: So long as I am at Bhagavan's feet, I cannot be regarded as a faithful Christian.

Sri Bhagavan interrupted saying that this was the essence of Christianity.

D.: Yes, but not in the eyes of the present representatives of the Church. Accordingly I can no longer look to the side of the Church for aid. Have I Bhagavan's leave to look elsewhere?

511

M.: That is left to you.

After a pause Sri Bhagavan spoke to the effect that people who come here are brought by some mysterious Power which will look to their needs. The conversation practically ended with this.

7th September, 1938

Talk 510.

Mr. T. K. S. Iyer read out a passage from a book which admitted of five different divisions of *antahkaranas* as follows: (1) *Ullam*, (2) mind, (3) intellect, (4) *chittam*, (5) ego.

Sri Bhagavan said: Four divisions are usual. The fifth item *ullam* has been brought in to correspond to five *tattvas* thus:

(1) *Ullam* (consciousness) is *akasa* (ether) *tattva* from the cranium to the brows.

(2) *Manas* (thinking faculty) is *vayu* (air) *tattva* from the brows to the throat.

(3) *Buddhi* (intellect) is *agni* (light) *tattva* from the throat to the heart.

(4) *Chitta* (memory) is *jala* (water) *tattva* from the heart to the navel, and,

(5) *Ahankar* (ego) is *prithvi* (earth) *tattva* from the navel to the coccyx.

Ullam is thus the pure mind or the mind in its pure being, *i.e.,* mind divested of all thoughts. It is the ether of mind corresponding to the expanse of mind without being crowded by thoughts. When a person wakes up from sleep the head is raised and there is the light of awareness. This light was already there in the heart which is later reflected on the brain and appears as consciousness. But this is not particularised until *ahankar* steps in. In the undifferentiated state it is cosmic (cosmic mind or cosmic consciousness). This state lasts usually for a minute interval and passes off unnoticed. It becomes particularised or differentiated by the intrusion of the ego and the person says 'I'. This is always associated with an entity (here, the body). So the body is identified as 'I' and all else follows.

Because *ullam* is only the reflected light, it is said to be the moon. The original light is in the heart which is said to be the sun.

9th September, 1938

Talk 511.

Major Chadwick had translated *Na karmana na prajaya* ... into English. Sri Bhagavan was explaining its meaning. *Brahmaloka* may be interpreted subjectively or objectively. The latter meaning requires faith in the *sastras* which speak of such *lokas*, whereas the former meaning is purely of experience and requires no external authority. *Brahmaloka* would mean *Brahma jnana* (Knowledge of Brahman) or Self-Realisation (*Atma-Sakshatkara*). *Parantakala* as opposed to *aparantakala*. In the latter the *jivas* pass into oblivion to take other births. Their oblivion is enveloped in ignorance (*avidya*). *Para* is beyond the body. *Parantakala* is transcendence over the body, etc., *i.e., jnana* (knowledge). *Paramritat prakriteh* = beyond *prakriti*. *Sarve* implies that all are qualified for knowledge and liberation (*moksha*). *yatayah* = *yama niyama sametah sat purushah* = good men well disciplined. The whole passage implies passing into the real beyond the unreal.

> *na karmana na prajaya dhanena tyagenaike amritatvamanasuh*
> *parena nakam nihitam guhayam, vibhrajate yadyatayo visanti*
> *vedanta vijnana sunishchitarthah sanyasayogadyatayah shuddha*
> *satvah*
>
> *te brahmaloke tu parantakale paramritat parimuchyanti sarve*
> *dahram vipapam paravesmabhutum yat pundarikam puramadhya*
> *samstham*
>
> *tatrapi dahram gaganam visokastasmin yadantastadupasitavyam*
> *yo vedadau svarah prokto vedante cha pratishtitah tasya*
> *prakritilinasya yah parah sa Mahesvarah*

[Deathlessness is not obtained through action or begetting offspring or wealth. Some attain that state through renunciation.

The Sages (that have conquered the senses) attain that *Sat* which is more supreme than Heaven and shining all alone in the Heart.

The adepts who by renunciation and one-pointedness are pure in heart and have known the certainty of Truth by the special knowledge

513

proclaimed by Vedanta, get fully released in the *Brahmaloka* from the causal *Maya* at the dissolution of the body.

That alone which shines as the tiny *Akasa* void of sorrow, in the lotus heart, the tiny seat of the spotless Supreme in the (inner) core of the body is worthy of worship.

He alone is the Supreme Lord, who is beyond the Primal Word which is the beginning and end of the Veda and in which merges the creative Cause].

Mr. T. K. S. Iyer later asked something about *muktaloka* (region of liberated souls). Śri Bhagavan said that it meant the same as *Brahmaloka*.

D.: Asked if some *sukshma tanu* (subtle body) such as *pranava tanu* or *suddha tanu* (*tanu* = body; *suddha* = pure) was required to gain such *loka*.

M.: Pranava means *real japa*. It is however interpreted to be *A, U, M, Nada* and *Bindu*. Of these, the first three are interpreted as *Visva, Taijasa, Prajna* and *Virat, Hiranyagarbha, Isvara, Nada* and *Bindu* correspond to *prana* and *manas* (mind).

The Mandukya Upanishad speaks of the three *matras* and *turiya matra*. The final meaning is that it represents the real state.

To a further question, Bhagavan answered: There are said to be *Panchapada Mahavakyani* (*mahavakyas* with five words) *e.g., Tattvamasi atinijam* ('you are that' is the great truth). The first three words have their *lakshya artha* (significance) all of which signify only the one Truth. So many efforts and so much discipline are said to be necessary for eradicating the non-existing *avidya*!

11th September, 1938

Talk 512.

Sri Bhagavan said: All mistake the mind-consciousness for Self-Consciousness. There is no mind in deep sleep; but no one denies his being in sleep. Even a child says on waking, "I slept well," and does not deny its existence. The 'I' rises up, the mind turns outward through the five senses and perceives objects, this they call direct perception. Asked if 'I' is not directly perceived, they get confused, because 'I'

514

does not announce itself as an object in front and only the perception with the senses can be recognised by them as knowledge: this habit is so strong with them. A stanza in *Thevaram* says: "O sages, eager to get over all misery, worry not about inferences and examples! Our Light is ever shining forth from within! With mind clear, live in God!"

This is direct perception. Will the common people admit it? They want God to appear in front of them as a bright Being mounted on a bull. Such a vision once originated must also end. It is therefore transient. *Thevaram* speaks of the Eternal and Ever-experienced Being. This *Thevaram* takes one directly to the Reality.

16th September, 1938

Talk 513.

Major Chadwick again gave his versified translation of the *mantra* for Sri Bhagavan to read. Sri Bhagavan softly spoke of the interpretation of the *Bhashyakara* and further explained the same. To consider the *Brahmaloka* as a region is also admissible. That is what the *pouraniks* say and many other schools also imply it by expounding *kramamukti* (liberation by degrees). But the Upanishads speak of *sadyomukti* (immediate liberation) as in *Na tasya prana utkramanti; ihaiva praleeyante* — the *pranas* do not rise up; they lose themselves here. So *Brahmaloka* will be Realisation of Brahman (*Brahmasakshatkara*). It is a state and not a region. In the latter case, *paramritat* must be properly understood. It is *para* inasmuch as *avyakrita* is the causal Energy transcending the universe, *amrita* because it persists until the Self is realised. So that *paramritat* will mean *avyakrita*. The *kramamukti* (liberation by degrees) school say that the *upasaka* goes to the region of his *Ishta Devata* which is *Brahmaloka* to him. The souls passing to all other *lokas* return to be reborn. But those who have gained the *Brahmaloka* do not. Moreover those desirous of a particular *loka* can by proper methods gain the same. Whereas *Brahmaloka* cannot be gained so long as there is any desire left in the person. Desirelessness alone will confer the *loka* on him. His desirelessness signifies the absence of the incentive for rebirth.

515

The age of Brahma is practically immeasurable. The presiding deity of the *loka* is said to have a definite period of life. When he passes away his *loka* also is dissolved. The inmates are emancipated at the same time, irrespective of the different nature of individual consciousness in them prior to Self-realisation.

The *kramamukti* school objects to the idea of *sadyomukti* (immediate liberation) because the *jnani* is supposed to lose body-consciousness at the same time that ignorance is dispelled but he continues to live in the body. They ask, "How does the body function without the mind?" The answer is somewhat elaborate:

Knowledge (*jnana*) is not incompatible with ignorance (*ajnana*) because the Self in purity is found to remain along with ignorance-seed (*ajnana beeja*) in sleep. But the incompatibility arises only in the waking and dream states. *Ajnana* has two aspects: *avarana* (veiling) and *vikshepa* (multiplicity). Of these, *avarana* (veiling) denotes the veil hiding the Truth. That prevails in sleep. Multiplicity (*vikshepa*) is activity in different times. This gives rise to diversity and prevails in waking and dream states (*jagrat* and *svapna*). If the veil, *i.e.*, *avarana* is lifted, the Truth is perceived. It is lifted for a *jnani* and so his *karana sarira* (causal body) ceases to exist. *Vikshepa* alone continues for him. Even so, it is not the same for a *jnani* as it is for an *ajnani*. The *ajnani* has all kinds of *vasanas*, *i.e.*, *kartrtva* (doership) and *bhoktrtva* (enjoyership), whereas the *jnani* has ceased to be doer (*karta*). Thus only one kind of *vasana* obtains for him. That too is very weak and does not overpower him, because he is always aware of the *Sat-Chit-Ananda* nature of the Self. The tenuous *bhoktrtva vasana* is the only remnant of the mind left in the *jnani* and he therefore appears to be living in the body.

This explanation when applied to the *mantra* amounts to this: A *jnani* has his *karana sarira* destroyed; the *sthula sarira* (gross body) has no effect on him and is for all practical purposes destroyed too. The *sukshma sarira* (subtle body) alone remains. It is otherwise called *ativahika sarira*. It is this which is held by all persons after the physical body is given up. And with this they traverse to other *lokas* until another suitable physical body is taken. The *jnani* is supposed to

516

move in *Brahmaloka* with this *sukshma sarira*. Then that is also dissolved and he passes to final Liberation.

The whole explanation is meant only for the onlooker. The *jnani* himself will never raise such questions. He knows by his experience that he is not bound by any kind of limitations.

D.: What is the 'final emancipation' according to the foregoing explanation?

M.: The *ativahika* or the *sukshma sarira* corresponds to the pure light which one experiences just after sleep and before the rise of the ego. It is Cosmic Consciousness. That is only the Light reflected from the Heart. When the reflection ceases and abides as the Original Light in the Heart it is final emancipation.

D.: But *Yoga Vasishtha* says that the *chitta* (mind) of a *jivanmukta* is *achala* (unchanging).

M.: So it is. *Achala chitta* (unchanging mind) is the same as *suddha manas* (pure mind). The *jnani's manas* is said to be *suddha manas*. The *Yoga Vasishtha* also says that *Brahman* is no other than the *jnani's* mind. So *Brahman* is *suddha manas* only.

D.: Will the description of *Brahman* as *Sat-Chit-Ananda* suit this *suddha manas*? For this too will be destroyed in the final emancipation.

M.: If *suddha manas* is admitted, the Bliss (*Ananda*) experienced by the *jnani* must also be admitted to be reflected. This reflection must finally merge into the Original. Therefore the *jivanmukti* state is compared to the reflection of a spotless mirror in another similar mirror. What will be found in such a reflection? Pure *Akasa* (Ether). Similarly, the *jnani's* reflected Bliss (*Ananda*) represents only the true Bliss.

These are all only words. It is enough that a person becomes *antarmukhi* (inward-bent). The *sastras* are not needed for an inward turned mind. They are meant for the rest.

Talk 514.

Mr. MacIver, a resident devotee, asked Sri Bhagavan if he might go to Switzerland where a Guru was inviting him. Sri Bhagavan said:

Some Force brought him here and the same is taking him to Europe. Let him always remember that the world is only a projection of the mind, and the mind is in the Self. Wherever the body may move the mind must be kept under control. The body moves, but not the Self. The world is within the Self, that is all.

17th September, 1938

Talk 515.

D.: In the explanation given yesterday, it is said that the removal of *avarana* results in the annihilation of the *karana sarira*. That is clear. But how is the gross body considered to fall off too?

M.: The *vasanas* are of two kinds: *bandha hetu* (causing bondage) and *bhoga hetu* (only giving enjoyment). The *jnani* has transcended the ego and therefore all the causes of bondage are inoperative. *Bandha hetu* is thus at an end and *prarabdha* (past *karma*) remains as *bhoga vasana* (to give enjoyment) only. Therefore it was said that the *sukshma sarira* alone survives *jnana*. *Kaivalya* says that *sanchita* Karma (stored Karma) is at an end simultaneously with the rise of *jnana*; that *agami* (Karma now collecting) is no longer operative owing to the absence of the sense of bondage, and that *prarabdha* will be exhausted by enjoyment (*bhoga*) only. Thus the last one will end in course of time and then the gross body also falls away with it.

Sarira traya (the three bodies) and Karma *traya* (the three Karmas) are mere phrases meant for the delectation of debaters. A *jnani* is not affected by any of them.

An aspirant is instructed to find who he is. If he does so, he will take no interest in discussing such matters as the above. Find the Self and rest in Peace.

22nd September, 1938

Talk 516.

A question arose if the world is real or unreal, since it is claimed to be both by the *advaitins* themselves. Sri Bhagavan said that it is unreal if viewed as apart from the Self and real if viewed as the Self.

518

25th September, 1938

Talk 517.

There was some reference of two *slokas* in *Yoga Vasishtha* where spiritism in *mlechcha desa* is mentioned. Mr. MacIver said that black magic is more prevalent in the West than is ordinarily known to the observer. The writer then remembered how Mr. Paul Brunton had once said that he actually feared a woman for her association with black magic.

Sri Bhagavan asked if the gentleman had read *Devikalottaram*. He then said that *abhichara prayoga* (black magic) is condemned there. He also added that by such practices one compasses one's own ruin. *Avidya* (ignorance) is itself bad and makes one commit suicide. Why should black magic be also added to it?

D.: What is the *pratikriya* (remedy) open to the victim of black magic?

M.: Bhakti (devotion to God).

D.: Non-resistance seems to be the only remedy for all kinds of evil such as slander.

M.: Quite so. If one abuses another or injures him the remedy does not lie in retort or resistance. Simply keep quiet. This quiet will bring peace to the injured but make the offender restless until he is driven to admit his error to the injured party.

This black magic is said to have been used even against the greatest saints in India since time immemorial. The *tapasvis* of Daruka forest used it against Siva Himself.

Then the conversation turned on *Brahmaloka*.

Sri Bhagavan said *Brahmaloka* is the same as *Atmaloka*. Again *Brahmaiva lokah* = *Brahmalokah* (Brahma is Himself the region) and *Brahma* is *Atma*. So *Brahmaloka* is only the Self.

Loka, aloka are both synonymous. It is the same as *andamillakkan* in *Ulladu Narpadu*. *Lokyate iti lokah* (That which is seen is *loka*).

27th September, 1938

Talk 518.

Mr. V. Gupta, a Telugu Pandit, is on a visit here. Sri Bhagavan said in the course of conversation: *Ahamkriti* (the ego) is not the same as *aham*. The latter is the Supreme Reality whereas the former is the ego. It is to be overcome before the Truth is realised. The Supreme Being is unmanifest and the first sign of manifestation is *Aham Sphurana* (light of 'I'). The Brihadaranyaka Upanishad says *Aham nama abhavat* (He became 'I' named). That is the original name of the Reality.

The Pandit asked about the operation of Grace. Is it the mind of the Guru acting on the mind of the disciple or anything different?

M.: The Highest Form of Grace is Silence (*mowna*). It is also the highest *upadesa*.

D.: Vivekananda has also said that silence is the loudest form of prayer.

M.: It is so, for the seeker's silence Guru's silence is the loudest *upadesa*. It is also Grace in its highest form. All other *dikshas* (initiations), *e.g., sparsa, chakshus* are derived from *mowna* (silence). They are therefore secondary. *Mowna* is the primary form. If the Guru is silent the seeker's mind gets purified by itself.

D.: Is it proper that one prays to God or Guru when one is afflicted by worldly ills?

M.: Undoubtedly.

Talk 519.

M.: The *mahavakyas* and their interpretation lead to interminable discussions and keep the minds of the seekers engaged externally. To turn the mind inward the man must directly settle down in the 'I'. Then there is an end of external activities and perfect Peace prevails.

Later, a passage from the *Yoga Vasishtha* was read out before Sri Bhagavan, indicating initiation by look and initiation by touch.

Sri Bhagavan observed: Dakshinamurti observed silence when the disciples approached Him. That is the highest form of initiation.

It includes the other forms. There must be subject-object relationship established in the other *dikshas*. First the subject must emanate and then the object. Unless these two are there how is the one to look at the other or touch him? *Mowna diksha* is the most perfect; it comprises looking, touching and teaching. It will purify the individual in every way and establish him in the Reality.

Talk 520.

An Australian gentleman (Mr. Lowman) is on a visit here. He seems to be studying the Hindu system of Philosophy. He started saying that he believed in unity, the *jiva* is yet in illusion and so on.

M.: What is the unity you believe in? How can the *jiva* find a place in it?

D.: The Unity is the Absolute.

M.: The *jiva* cannot find a place in Unity.

D.: But the *jiva* has not realised the Absolute and imagines itself separate.

M.: Jiva is separate because it must exist in order to imagine something.

D.: But it is unreal.

M.: Any unreal thing cannot produce effects. It is like saying that you killed some animal with the horn of a hare. A hare does not grow horns.

D.: I see the absurdity. But I speak from the physical plane.

M.: You say, 'I'. Who is that 'I'? If that is found you can later say whose is the illusion.

A little later Sri Bhagavan asked:

You say you are in the physical plane now. In which plane are you in dreamless sleep?

D.: I think in the physical plane again.

M.: You say, "I think". That means that you are saying it now when you are awake. Anyway you admit that you exist in deep sleep. Don't you?

D.: Yes, but I did not function then.

M.: So then, you existed in deep sleep. You are the same one who continues to exist? Are you not?

521

D.: Yes.

M.: With this difference — that you did not function in your sleep. Rather you are associated with the thinking faculty in your waking state and you are dissociated from it in sleep. Is it not so?

D.: Yes.

M.: Which is then your real nature? Is it to be associated with thinking or to be dissociated?

D.: I see it now. But I was not aware of my being in sleep.

M.: You say so now. You do not say so in your sleep. Or do you deny your being (very existence in sleep)?

D.: No.

M.: It amounts to this that you exist in both states. The Absolute Existence is the Self. You are also conscious of the Existence. That Existence is also consciousness (*Sat* and *Chit*). That is your real nature.

D.: But thinking is necessary even for realisation.

M.: That thinking is aimed at the elimination of all thinking.

D.: Owing to my ignorance, I do not realise the Absolute Existence-Consciousness.

M.: Who is the 'I'? Whose is the ignorance! Answers to these questions will alone suffice to prove that you are already realised. Is there anyone who denies his own existence? Or can anyone say that he did not exist in his sleep? Pure Existence is thus admitted. The admission also implies consciousness. Thus all men are realised. There is no ignorant man at all.

D.: Yes, I understand. But I have a small question to ask. The state of Realisation is one of desirelessness. If a human being is desireless he ceases to be human.

M.: You admit your existence in sleep. You did not function then. You were not aware of any gross body. You did not limit yourself to this body. So you could not find anything separate from your Self.

Now in your waking state you continue to be the same Existence with the limitations of the body added. These limitations make you see other objects. Hence arises desire. But the state of desirelessness in sleep made you no less happy than now. You did not feel any want. You did not make yourself miserable by not entertaining

522

desires. But now you entertain desires because you are limited to this human frame. Why do you wish to retain these limitations and continue to entertain desires?

Sri Bhagavan continued:

Does the body tell you that it is there? It is certainly something apart from the body that remains aware. What is it?

Do you say that it is the 'I', meaning the ego which arises simultaneously with the waking of the individual from sleep? Be it so. The body is not sentient. The Absolute does not speak. The ego does. One does not aspire for liberation in sleep. The aspiration arises only in the waking state. The functions of the waking state are those of the ego which is synonymous with the 'I'. Find out who this 'I' is. On doing so and abiding as 'I', all these doubts will be cleared up.

28th September, 1938

Talk 521.

Some Congressmen handed over the following questions to Maharshi:

1. How long is India destined to suffer bondage?

2. Have not the sons of India made enough sacrifice for her liberation?

3. Will India get freedom during Mahatma Gandhi's lifetime?

The above questions were not answered categorically. Sri Bhagavan simply remarked:

Gandhiji has surrendered himself to the Divine and works accordingly with no self-interest. He does not concern himself with the results but accepts them as they turn up. That must be the attitude of national workers.

Q.: Will the work be crowned with success?

M.: This question arises because the questioner has not surrendered himself.

Q.: Should we not then think of and work for the welfare of the country?

M.: First take care of yourself and the rest will naturally follow.

Q.: I am not speaking individually but for the country.

523

M.: First surrender and see. The doubts arise because of the absence of surrender. Acquire strength by surrender and then your surroundings will be found to have improved to the degree of strength acquired by you.

Q.: Should we not know if our actions will be worthwhile?

M.: Follow the example of Gandhiji in the work for the national cause. 'Surrender' is the word.

The following slip was also handed over to Sri Bhagavan:

"Four of us have come from Coorg and we had gone to Delhi to wait as a deputation on the Working Committee of the Indian National Congress and we are now going back. We are sent from the Coorg Congress Committee and so kindly give us some message to the Coorg District Congress Committee and the people of Coorg in general."

When this slip was handed over, Sri Bhagavan said that the same answer holds good here too. The message is contained in the word 'Surrender'.

29th September, 1938

Talk 522.

A visitor asked Sri Bhagavan:

I want knowledge.

M.: Who wants knowledge?

D.: I want it.

M.: Who is that 'I'? Find the 'I' and see later what further knowledge is required.

2nd October, 1938

Talk 523.

A Pilgrims' special train brought several visitors from Bengal. One of them said that he had read Mr. Paul Brunton's book and since then he was anxious to see Sri Bhagavan. He also asked: How shall I overcome my passions?

M.: Find their root and then it will be easy. (Later) What are the passions? *Kama* (lust), *krodha* (anger), etc. Why do they arise?

Because of likes and dislikes towards the objects seen. How do the objects project themselves in your view? Because of your *avidya, i.e.,* ignorance. Ignorance of what? Of the Self. Thus, if you find the Self and abide therein there will be no trouble owing to the passions.

(Later) Again, what is the cause of the passions? Desire to be happy or enjoy pleasure. Why does the desire for happiness arise? Because your nature is happiness itself and it is natural that you come into your own. This happiness is not found anywhere besides the Self. Do not look for it elsewhere. But seek the Self and abide therein.

Still again, that happiness which is natural is simply re-discovered, so it cannot be lost. Whereas the happiness arising from other objects are external and thus liable to be lost. Therefore it cannot be permanent and so it is not worth seeking.

Moreover craving for pleasures should not be encouraged. One cannot put out burning fire by pouring petrol over it. An attempt to satisfy your craving for the time being, so that the passion may later be suppressed, is simply foolish.

There are, no doubt, other methods for the suppression of passion. They are (1) regulated food, (2) fasting, (3) yoga practice, (4) medicines. But their effects are transitory. The passions reappear with greater force as soon as the check is removed. The only way to overcome them is to eradicate them. That is done by finding their source as stated above.

Talk 524.

Another pilgrim asked: I am a man with a family. Is it possible for those in a family to get release, and if so how?

M.: Now what is family? Whose family is it? If the answers to these questions are found the other questions solve themselves.

Tell me: Are you in the family, or is the family in you?

The visitor did not answer. Then Sri Bhagavan's answer was continued: Who are you? You include three aspects of life, namely, the waking, the dream and the sleep states. You were not aware of the family and their ties in your sleep and so these questions did not

525

arise then. But now you are aware of the family and their ties and therefore you seek release. But you are the same person throughout.

D.: Because I now feel that I am in the family it is right that I should seek release.

M.: You are right. But consider and say: Are you in the family or is the family in you?

Another visitor interposed: What is family?

M.: That's it. It must be known.

D.: There is my wife and there are also my children. They are dependent on me. That is the family.

M.: Do the members of the family bind your mind? Or do you bind yourself to them? Do they come and say to you "We form your family. Be with us"? Or do you consider them as your family and that you are bound to them?

D.: I consider them as my family and feel bound to them.

M.: Quite so. Because you think that so-and-so is your wife and so-and-so are your children you also think that you are bound to them. These thoughts are yours. They owe their very existence to you. You can entertain these thoughts or relinquish them. The former is bondage and the latter is release.

D.: It is not quite clear to me.

M.: You must exist in order that you may think. You may think these thoughts or other thoughts. The thoughts change but not you. Let go the passing thoughts and hold on to the unchanging Self. The thoughts form your bondage. If they are given up, there is release. The bondage is not external. So no external remedy need be sought for release. It is within your competence to think and thus to get bound or to cease thinking and thus be free.

D.: But it is not easy to remain without thinking.

M.: You need not cease thinking. Only think of the root of the thoughts; seek it and find it. The Self shines by itself. When that is found the thoughts cease of their own accord. That is freedom from bondage.

D.: Yes. I understand it now. I have learnt it now. Is a Guru necessary?

526

M.: So long as you consider yourself as an individual, a Guru is necessary to show to you that you are not bound by limitations and that your nature is to be free from limitations.

Talk 525.

Another visitor asked: Actions are bondage. One cannot remain without some kind of activity. So bondage goes on increasing. What is one to do under the circumstances?

M.: One should act in such a manner that the bondage is not strengthened but gets weakened. That is selfless action.

3rd October, 1938

Talk 526.

A visitor asked Sri Bhagavan: People give some names to God and say that the name is sacred and repetitions of the name bestow merit on the individual. Can it be true?

M.: Why not? You bear a name to which you answer. But your body was not born with that name written on it, nor did it say to anyone that it bore such and such a name. And yet a name is given to you and you answer to that name, because you have identified yourself with the name. Therefore the name signifies something and it is not a mere fiction. Similarly, God's name is effective. Repetition of the name is remembrance of what it signifies. Hence its merit.

But the man did not look satisfied. Finally he wanted to retire and prayed for Sri Bhagavan's Grace.

Sri Bhagavan now asked how mere sounds assuring him of Grace would satisfy him unless he had faith.

Both laughed and the visitor retired.

4th October, 1938

Talk 527.

A group of respectable Coorg ladies was in the hall.

One of them asked: I have received a *mantra*. People frighten me saying that it may have unforeseen results if repeated. It is only *Pranava*. So I seek advice. May I repeat it? I have considerable faith in it.

M.: Certainly, it should be repeated with faith.

D.: Will it do by itself? Or can you kindly give me any further instructions?

M.: The object of *mantra japa* is to realise that the same *japa* is already going on in oneself even without effort. The oral *japa* becomes mental and the mental *japa* finally reveals itself as being eternal. That *mantra* is the person's real nature. That is also the state of realisation.

D.: Can the bliss of *samadhi* be gained thus?

M.: The *japa* becomes mental and finally reveals itself as the Self. That is *samadhi*.

D.: Please show Grace to me and strengthen me in my efforts!

13th October, 1938

Talk 528.

A middle-aged Andhra man asked: "Is thought of God necessary for fixing one's sight (or making the mind one-pointed)?"

M.: What is the practice?

D.: To fix the look.

M.: What for?

D.: To gain concentration.

M.: The practice gives work for the eye right enough; but where is the work for the mind in the process?

D.: What should I do for it?

M.: Thought of God, certainly.

D.: Does the practice make one ill?

M.: Maybe. But all will be rightly adjusted of its own accord.

D.: I practised *dhyana* for four hours a day and fixation of sight for two hours. I became ill. Then others said that it was owing to my practice. So I gave up *dhyana*.

M.: Matters will adjust themselves.

D.: Is it not better that the gaze of the eye becomes fixed naturally?

M.: What do you mean?

D.: Is practice necessary to fix the gaze or is it better to leave it to happen of its own accord?

528

M.: What is practice if it is not an attempt to make something natural? It will become natural after long practice.

D.: Is *pranayama* necessary?

M.: Yes. It is useful.

D.: I did not practise it. But should I undertake it?

M.: Everything will be all right with sufficient strength of mind.

D.: How shall I get the strength of mind?

M.: By *pranayama*.

D.: Is food-regulation also necessary?

M.: It is certainly useful.

D.: Should my contemplation be on the Infinite or the limited being?

M.: What do you mean?

D.: May I contemplate on Sri Krishna or Sri Rama alternately?

M.: Bhavana implies *khanda i.e.*, division.

15th October, 1938

Talk 529.

In the course of conversation Sri Bhagavan said that Thirujnanasambandar had sung in praise of Sri Arunachala. He also mentioned the story briefly as follows:

Jnanasambandar was born in an orthodox family about 1,500 years ago. When he was three years old his father took him to the temple in Shiyali. He left the boy on the bank of the sacred tank and went in to bathe. As he dipped in the water the boy, not finding his father, began to cry out. Immediately Siva and Parvati appeared in a *vimana*. Siva told Parvati to feed the boy with her milk. So she drew out milk in a cup and handed it to the boy. He drank it and was happy.

The father as he came out of the water saw the boy smiling and with streaks of milk round his lips. So he asked the boy what happened to him. The boy did not answer. He was threatened and the boy sang songs. They were hymns in praise of Siva who appeared before him. He sang, "The One with ear-rings... the Robber, who robbed me of my mind...."

He thus became one of the most famous *bhaktas* and was much sought after. He led a vigorous and active life; went on pilgrimage to several places in South India. He got married in his sixteenth year. The bride and the bridegroom went to have *darsan* of God in the local temple soon after the marriage ceremonies were over. A large party went with them. When they reached the temple the place was a blaze of light and the temple was not visible. There was however a passage visible in the blaze of light. Jnanasambandar told the people to enter the passage. They did so. He himself went round the light with his young wife, came to the passage and entered it as the others had done earlier. The Light vanished leaving no trace of those who entered it. The temple again came into view as usual. Such was the brief but very eventful life of the sage.

In one of his tours he had come to Ariyanainallur or Tirukkoilur, eighteen miles from Tiruvannamalai. The place is famous for its Siva temple. (It was here that Sri Bhagavan had that vision of Light on his way to Tiruvannamalai in his seventeenth year. Sri Bhagavan did not then know that the place was sanctified by the feet of Tirujnanasambandar some fifteen centuries ago.)

When the ancient sage was staying in Ariyanainallur an old man who carried a flower-basket came to him. The young sage asked the old man who he was. The latter replied that he was a servitor of Sri Arunachala the God residing as the Hill here.

Sage: How far is it from here?

The old man: I walk every day from there to here collecting flowers for daily worship. So it is only near.

Sage: Then I shall go with you to that place.

The old man: A rare pleasure, indeed, for me!

They went together, with a large crowd following the Sage. After walking some distance the Sage wanted to ask how much further the place was. But the old man had disappeared in the meantime. Soon after, a gang of dacoits waylaid the pilgrims who surrendered all that they had with them. They plodded their way and reached their destination. The young Sage fell into contemplation. God appeared and said that the dacoits were only His followers and that his needs would be met. Accordingly, the group of pilgrims found all their wants. The Sage had sung hymns in praise of Sri Arunachala. In one of the stanzas, he says:

"You are a dense mass of *jnana*, capable of removing the 'I-am-the-body' idea from Your devotees! Herds of gazelles, of boars and of bears come down Your slopes in the night to search for food on the plains. Herds of elephants go from the plains to Your slopes where they may rest. So different herds of animals meet on Your slopes."

Sri Bhagavan continued: So this Hill must have been a dense forest 1,500 years ago. It has since been denuded of the forests by the wood-cutters, etc., through these several centuries.

The account of Sri Arunachala given by the mysterious old man to Jnanasambandar is contained in 300 *slokas* in Upamanyu's *Bhakta Charita*. One of the Archakas of the temple had it with him and showed it to Sri Bhagavan on the occasion of the temple suit within the last few months. Sri Bhagavan copied the slokas.

Talk 530.

The following is taken from the diary of Annamalai Swami, a good devotee of Sri Bhagavan and resident of Sri Ramanasramam:

The Teachings of Sri Ramana Bhagavan.

(1) That man who is active in the world and yet remains desireless, without losing sight of his own essential nature, is alone a true man.

This was in answer to the Swami who wanted to retire into a cave for practising meditation.

(2) He asked about *sannyas*. Should not a man renounce everything in order that he might get Liberation?

M.: Even better than the man who thinks "I have renounced everything" is the one who does his duty but does not think "I do this" or "I am the doer". Even a *sannyasi* who thinks "I am a *sannyasi*" cannot be a true *sannyasi*, whereas a householder who does not think "I am a householder" is truly a *sannyasi*.

Talk 531.

D.: One person says one thing one way. Another says the same thing in a different way. How is the truth to be ascertained?

M.: Each one sees his own Self only, always and everywhere. He finds the world and God according to what he is.

A Nayanar went to Kalahasti for the *darsan* of God. He saw all the people there as Siva and Sakti because he himself was so. Again, Dharmaputra considered that the whole world was composed of people having some merit or other and that each of them was even better than he himself for some reason or other. Whereas Duryodhana could not find even a single good person in the world. Each reflects his own nature.

Talk 532.

D.: Is there no way of escape from the miseries of the world?

M.: There is only one way and that consists in not losing sight of one's Self under any circumstances.

To enquire "Who am I?" is the only remedy for all the ills of the world. It is also perfect bliss.

Talk 533.

Soon after the announcement in the newspapers that Gandhiji was going to fast twenty-one days in Yerwada jail, two young men came to Sri Bhagavan; they were very excited. They said "Mahatma is now fasting for twenty-one days. We want permission from Sri Bhagavan to run up to Yerwada so that we may also fast as long as he does. Please permit us. We are in a haste to go." Saying so they made ready to rush out. Sri Bhagavan smiled and said, "It is a good sign that you have such feelings. But what can you do now? Get the strength which Gandhiji has already got by his *tapasya*. You will afterwards succeed."

Talk 534.

Sri Bhagavan often used to say, "*Mowna* is the utmost eloquence. Peace is utmost activity. How? Because the person remains in his essential nature and so he permeates all the recesses of the Self. Thus he can call up any power into play and whenever or wherever it is necessary. That is the highest *siddhi*."

Annamalai asked: Namadev, Tukaram, Tulsidas and others are said to have seen Maha Vishnu. How did they see Him?

M.: In what manner? Just in the same manner as you see me now and I see you here. They would also have seen Vishnu in this way only.

(He records that, on hearing it, his hairs stood on end and an intense joy overpowered him.)

Talk 535.

Once 'A' asked: How can one be worshipful while engaged in daily work?

Sri Bhagavan did not reply. Ten minutes passed. A few girls came for *darsan* of Sri Bhagavan. They began to sing and dance. Their song was to the effect: "We will churn the milk without losing thought of Krishna."

Sri Bhagavan turned to the Swami and said that there was the reply to his question. This state is called *Bhakti*, Yoga and Karma.

Talk 536.

The person soaked in the "I-am-the-body" idea is the greatest sinner and he is a suicide. The experience of "I-am-the-Self" is the highest virtue. Even a moment's *dhyana* to that effect is enough to destroy all the *sanchita* Karma. It works like the sun before whom darkness is dispelled. If one remains always in *dhyana*, can any sin, however heinous it be, survive his *dhyana*?

Talk 537.

Once Sri Bhagavan said, "Desire constitutes *maya*, and desirelessness is God."

Talk 538.

'A' asked: What is the exact difference between worldly activity and *dhyana*?

M.: There is no difference. It is like naming one and the same thing by two different words in two different languages. The crow has two eyes but only one iris which is rolled into either eye as it pleases. The trunk of an elephant is used for breathing and for drinking water. The snake sees and hears with the same organ.

Talk 539.

When Sri Bhagavan was going up the hill, the Swami asked: Does the closing or the opening of the eyes make any difference during *dhyana*?

M.: If you strike on a wall with a rubber-ball and you stand at a distance, the ball rebounds and runs back to you. If you stand near the wall, the ball rebounds and runs away from you. Even if the eyes are closed, the mind follows thoughts.

Talk 540.

Once 'A' asked: There is more pleasure in *dhyana* than in sensual enjoyments. Yet the mind runs after the latter and does not seek the former. Why is it so?

M.: Pleasure or pain are aspects of the mind only. Our essential nature is happiness. But we have forgotten the Self and imagine that the body or the mind is the Self. It is that wrong identity that gives rise to misery. What is to be done? This *vasana* is very ancient and has continued for innumerable past births. Hence it has grown strong. That must go before the essential nature, viz., happiness, asserts itself.

Talk 541.

A certain visitor asked Sri Bhagavan:

There is so much misery in the world because wicked men abound in the world. How can one find happiness here?

M.: All are gurus to us. The wicked say by their evil deeds, "Do not come near me". The good are always good. So then, all persons are like gurus to us.

Talk 542.

'A' asked: I often desire to live in solitude where I can find all I want with ease, so that I may devote all my time to meditation only. Is such a desire good or bad?

M.: Such thoughts will bestow a *janma* (reincarnation) for their fulfilment. What does it matter where and how you are placed? The essential point is that the mind must always remain in its source. There is nothing external which is not also internal. The mind is all.

If the mind is active even solitude becomes like a market place. There is no use closing your eyes. Close the mental eye and all will be right. The world is not external to you. The good persons will not care to make plans previous to their actions. Why so? For God who has sent us into the world has His own plan and that will certainly work itself out.

Talk 543.

Many visitors came on one occasion and they all saluted Sri Bhagavan with the single prayer, "Make me a *bhakta*. Give me *moksha*." After they left Sri Bhagavan said, thinking aloud: All of them want *bhakti* and *moksha*. If I say to them, 'Give yourself to me' they will not. How then can they get what they want?

Talk 544.

On one occasion a few devotees were discussing among themselves the relative merits of some famous *bhaktas*. They did not agree among themselves and referred the matter to Sri Bhagavan. He remained silent. The discussion grew hot.

Finally Sri Bhagavan said: One cannot know about another nor can confer bondage or release on another. Each one desires to become famous in the world. It is natural for man. But that desire alone does not bring about the end in view. He who is not accepted by God is certainly humiliated. He who has surrendered himself, body and mind, to God becomes famous all over the world.

Talk 545.

'A' was once badly distracted by sexual thoughts.

He fought against them. He fasted three days and prayed to God so that he might be free from such thoughts. Finally, he decided to ask Sri Bhagavan about it.

Sri Bhagavan listened to him and remained silent for about two minutes. Then He said: Well, the thoughts distracted you and you fought against them. That is good. Why do you continue to think of them now? Whenever such thoughts arise, consider to whom they arise and they will flee away from you.

535

Talk 546.

'A' asked: A person does something good but he sometimes suffers pain even in his right activities. Another does something wicked but is also happy. Why should it be so?

M.: Pain or pleasure is the result of past Karma and not of the present Karma. Pain and pleasure alternate with each other. One must suffer or enjoy them patiently without being carried away by them. One must always try to hold on to the Self. When one is active one should not care for the results and must not be swayed by the pain or pleasure met with occasionally. He who is indifferent to pain or pleasure can alone be happy.

Talk 547.

D.: What is the significance of Guru's Grace in the attainment of liberation?

M.: Liberation is not anywhere outside you. It is only within. If a man is anxious for Deliverance, the Guru within pulls him in and the Guru without pushes him into the Self. This is the Grace of the Guru.

Talk 548.

A visitor asked Sri Bhagavan (in writing) the following questions: (1) Were the differences in the world simultaneous, with creation? Or are they of later growth? (2) Is the Creator impartial? Then why is one born lame, another blind, and so on? (3) Are the eight Dikpalas, thirty-three crores of gods and the seven *rishis* existent even today?

M.: Refer these questions to yourself and the answer will be found.

After a pause, Sri Bhagavan continued: if we first know our Self then all other matters will be plain to us. Let us know our Self and then enquire concerning the Creator and creation. Without first knowing the Self, to seek knowledge of God, etc., is ignorance. A man suffering from jaundice sees everything yellow. If he tells others that all things are yellow who will accept his statement?

The creation is said to have an origin. How? Like a tree and the seed from which it has grown. How was the seed produced? From a similar tree. Where is the end to the series of questions? Therefore one must know one's Self before the world is known.

Talk 549.

Sri Bhagavan often speaks of *namaskar* (prostration) in the following strain: "This *namaskar* was originally meant by the ancient sages to serve as a means of surrender to God. The act still prevails but not the spirit behind it. The doer of *namaskar* intends to deceive the object of worship by his act. It is mostly insincere and deceitful. It is meant to cover up innumerable sins. Can God be deceived? The man thinks that God accepts his *namaskar* and that he himself is free to continue his old life. They need not come to me. I am not pleased with these *namaskars*. The people should keep their minds clean; instead of that they bend themselves or lie prostrate before me. I am not deceived by such acts."

Talk 550.

Somerset Maugham, a well-known English author, was on a visit to Sri Bhagavan. He also went to see Maj. Chadwick in his room and there he suddenly became unconscious. Maj. Chadwick requested Sri Bhagavan to see him. Sri Bhagavan went into the room, took a seat and gazed on Mr. Maugham. He regained his senses and saluted Sri Bhagavan. They remained silent and sat facing each other for nearly an hour. The author attempted to ask questions but did not speak. Maj. Chadwick encouraged him to ask. Sri Bhagavan said, "All finished. Heart-talk is all talk. All talk must end in silence only." They smiled and Sri Bhagavan left the room.

Talk 551.

A man asked Sri Bhagavan: "How is it that *Atma vidya* is said to be the easiest?"

M.: Any other *vidya* requires a knower, knowledge and the object to be known, whereas this does not require any of them. It is the Self. Can anything be so obvious as that? Hence it is the easiest. All that you need do is to enquire, "Who am I?"

A man's true name is *mukti* (liberation)

Talk 552.

There are some buildings in the Asramam. They used to have some plan which somehow could not be followed in entirety.

Therefore 'A' and the Sarvadhikari did not agree on many details and there used to be trouble between them. 'A' was once highly disgusted with the state of affairs. He asked Sri Bhagavan what could be done under the circumstances.

Sri Bhagavan said: "Which of the buildings was according to a plan made by these people here? God has His own plans and all these go on according to that. No one need worry as to what happens."

Talk 553.

The Asramites once asked Sri Bhagavan, "How were we all in our previous births? Why do we not know our own past?"

M.: God in His mercy has withheld this knowledge from people. If they knew that they were virtuous, they will grow proud; contrariwise they will be depressed. Both are bad. It is enough that one knows the Self.

Talk 554.

M.: Just as a river does not continue its flow after its discharge into the ocean, so also a person loses all movements after he merges in the Self.

Talk 555.

Sri Bhagavan once recounted how Kavyakantha Ganapathi Muni asked Him: My own opinion is that a man can live on Rs. 3 a month. What is Sri Bhagavan's opinion in the matter?

M.: A man can live happily only if he knows that he requires nothing wherewith to live.

Talk 556.

Maj. Chadwick asked Sri Bhagavan one night: The world is said to become manifest after the mind becomes manifest. There is no mind when I sleep. Is the world not existent to others at that time? Does it not show that the world is the product of a universal mind? How then shall we say that the world is not material but only dream-like?

M.: The world does not tell you that it is of the individual mind or of the universal mind. It is only the individual mind that sees the world. When this mind disappears the world also disappears.

There was a man who saw in his dream his father who had died thirty years earlier. Furthermore he dreamt that he had four more brothers and that his father divided his property among them. A quarrel ensued, the brothers assaulted the man and he woke up in a fright. Then he remembered that he was all alone, he had no brothers and the father was dead long ago. His fright gave place to contentment. So you see — when we see our Self there is no world, and when we lose sight of the Self we get ourselves bound in the world.

Talk 557.

A visitor asked: "We are advised to concentrate on the spot in the forehead between the eyebrows. Is it right?"

M.: Everyone is aware, 'I am'. Leaving aside that awareness one goes about in search of God. What is the use of fixing one's attention between the eyebrows? It is mere folly to say that God is between the eyebrows. The aim of such advice is to help the mind to concentrate. It is one of the forcible methods to check the mind and prevent its dissipation. It is forcibly directed into one channel. It is a help to concentration.

But the best means of realisation is the enquiry "Who am I?" The present trouble is to the mind and it must be removed by the mind only.

D.: Are there restrictions to be observed in food?

M.: Sattva food taken in moderation.

D.: There are several *asanas* mentioned. Which of them is the best?

M.: Nididhyasana (one-pointedness of the mind) is the best.

Talk 558.

A visitor asked: "Sri Bhagavan! When I heard of you, a strong desire arose in me to see you. Why should it be so?"

M.: The desire arose in the same way as the body arises to the Self.

D.: What is the purpose of life?

M.: To seek to know the significance of life is itself the result of good karma in past births. Those who do not seek such knowledge are simply wasting their lives.

Talk 559.

A man asked Sri Bhagavan: "Sri Bhagavan can know when I shall become a *jnani*. Please tell me when it will be."

M.: If I am Bhagavan then there is no one apart from me to whom *jnana* should arise or to whom I should speak. If I am an ordinary man like others then I am as ignorant as the rest. Either way your question cannot be answered.

Talk 560.

When Sri Bhagavan was taking His bath a few *bhaktas* were around Him, speaking to themselves. Then they asked Him about the use of *ganja* (hashish). Sri Bhagavan had finished His bath by that time. He said: "Oh *ganja*! The users feel immensely happy when they are under its influence. How shall I describe their happiness! They simply shout *ananda! ananda...*" Saying so, He walked as if tipsy. The *bhaktas* laughed. He appeared as if He stumbled, placed His hands round 'A' and cried "*ananda! ananda!*"

'A' records that his very being was transformed from that time. He had remained an inmate for the past eight years. He further says that his mind now remains at peace.

Talk 561.

D.: What is *svarupa* (form) and *arupa* (formless) of the mind?

M.: When you wake up from sleep a light appears, that is the light of the Self passing through *Mahat tattva*. It is called cosmic consciousness. That is *arupa*. The light falls on the ego and is reflected therefrom. Then the body and the world are seen. This mind is *svarupa*. The objects appear in the light of this reflected consciousness. This light is called *jyoti*.

21st October, 1938

Talk 562.

There is a statement in the book *Vichara Sangraha* that though a person realises the Self once, he cannot, for that simple reason alone, become a *mukta*. He continues to remain a victim of *vasanas* (latencies). Sri Bhagavan was asked whether the realisation referred to was the same as the *jnani's*, and if so why there should be a difference in their effects.

M.: The experience is the same. Every person experiences the Self consciously or unconsciously. The *ajnani's* experience is clouded by his latencies whereas the *jnani's* is not so. The *jnani's* experience of the Self is therefore distinct and permanent.

A practiser may by long practice gain a glimpse of the Reality. This experience may be vivid for the time being. And yet he will be distracted by the old *vasanas* and so his experience will not avail him. Such a man must continue his *manana* and *nididhyasana* so that all the obstacles may be destroyed. He will then be able to remain permanently in the Real State.

D.: What is the difference between a man who makes no attempts and remains an *ajnani*, and another who gains a glimpse and returns to *ajnana*?

M.: In the latter case a stimulus is always present to goad him on to further efforts until the realisation is perfect.

D.: The *Srutis* say: *Sakrit vibhatoyam brahmaloka* (This knowledge of Brahman shines forth once and forever).

M.: They refer to the permanent realisation and not to the glimpse.

D.: How is it possible that a man forgets his very experience and falls back into ignorance?

Sri Bhagavan illustrated it with the following story:

There was a king who treated his subjects well. One of his ministers gained his confidence and misused the influence. All the other ministers and officers were adversely affected and they hit upon a plan to get rid of him. They instructed the guards not to let the man enter the palace. The king noted his absence and enquired after him. He was informed that the man was taken ill and could not therefore come to the palace. The king deputed his physician to attend on the minister. False reports were conveyed to the king that the minister was sometimes improving and at other times collapsing. The king desired to see the patient. But the pandits said that such an action was against *dharma*. Later the minister was reported to have died. The king was very sorry when he heard the news.

The arrogant minister was kept informed of all the happenings by spies of his own. He tried to foil the other ministers. He waited for the king to come out of the palace so that he might report himself to the king. On one occasion he climbed up a tree, hid himself among the branches and awaited the king. The king came out that night in the palanquin and the man in hiding jumped down in front of the palanquin and shouted his identity. The companion of the king was equally resourceful. He at once took out a handful of sacred ashes (*vibhuti*) from his pocket and scattered it in the air so that the king was obliged to close his eyes. The companion shouted victory (*'jai'*) to the king and ordered the band to play so that the other man's shout was drowned in the noise. He also ordered the palanquin-bearers to move fast and he himself sang incantations to keep off evil spirits. The king was thus left under the impression that the dead man's ghost was playing pranks with him.

The disappointed man became desperate and retired into the forest for *tapasya* (austerities). After a long time the king happened to go hunting. He came across the former minister seated in deep contemplation. But he hastened away from the spot lest the ghost should molest him.

The moral of the story is that even though the man was seen in flesh and blood, yet the wrong notion that he was a ghost prevented right values being taken. So it is with a forced realisation of the Self.

22nd October, 1938

Talk 563.

A group of people came on a visit to Sri Bhagavan. One of them asked: "How can I keep my mind aright?"

M.: A refractory bull is lured to the stall by means of grass. Similarly the mind must be lured by good thoughts.

D.: But it does not remain steady.

M.: The bull accustomed to stray takes delight in going astray. However he must be lured with luscious grass to the stall. Even so he will continue to trespass into the neighbour's fields. He must gradually be made to realise that the same kind of good grass can be had in his own place. After a time he will remain in the stall without straying. Later a time will come when, even if driven out of the stall, he will return to the stall without going into the neighbouring fields. So also the mind must be trained to take to right ways. It will gradually grow accustomed to good ways and will not return to wrong ways.

D.: What are the good ways to be shown to the mind?

M.: Thought of God.

23rd to 26th October, 1938

Talk 564.

Pandit Bala Kak Dhar, a jagirdar from Kashmir, had come all the way from Srinagar to have *darshan* of Sri Bhagavan on Deepavali Day. He gave a bundle of papers to Sri Bhagavan containing an account of his life and position. His talks with Sri Bhagavan were all of them personal.

One of his questions was: "Now that I have had the *darshan* of Sri Bhagavan and it is enough for me, may I throw away all the charms, *tantras* and *pujas* into the river?"

M.: Daily *puja* as prescribed in the *Dharma sastras* is always good. It is for the purification of the mind. Even if one feels oneself too advanced to need such *puja*, still it must be performed for the sake of others. Such action will be an example to one's children and other dependents.

Talk 565.

A gentleman from Mysore asked: How is the mind to be kept in the right way?

M.: By practice. Give it good thoughts. The mind must be trained in good ways.

D.: But it is not steady.

M.: The Bhagavad Gita says: *Sanaissanairuparamet* (The mind must gradually be brought to a standstill); *Atma samstham manah krtva* (making the mind inhere in the Self); *Abhyasa-vairagyabhyam* (by practice and dispassion).

Practice is necessary. Progress will be slow.

D.: What is the Self referred to in *Atma samstham* (fixing it in the Self)?

M.: Do you not know your Self? You certainly exist. Or do you deny your existence? The question may arise "Who is this Self", only if you do not exist, but you cannot ask anything unless you exist at the same time. Your question shows that you exist. Find out who you are. That is all.

D.: I have read many books. But my mind does not turn to the Self.

M.: Because the Self is not in the books; but it is in you. Reading books makes one learned. That is its purpose and it is fulfilled.

D.: What is Atma *sakshatkara* (Self-Realisation)?

M.: You are the Atma (Self) and that *sakshat* (here and now) also. Where is the place for *kara* (accomplishment) in it? This question shows that you think you are the non-Self. Or you think that there are two selves, the one to realise the other. It is absurd.

That you identify yourself with the gross body lies at the root of this question. Well, this question arises now. Did it arise in your sleep? Did you not exist then? Certainly you did exist in sleep. What is the difference between these two states that the question should arise now but not in sleep? Now you think that you are the body. You see things around you and you want to see the Self in a similar manner. Such is the force of habit. The senses are mere instruments of perception. *You* are the seer. Remain as the seer only. What else is there to see? Such is the state in deep sleep. Therefore this question does not arise then.

Atma *sakshatkara* (Self-Realisation) is thus only *anatma nirasana* (giving up the non-Self).

D.: Is there only one Self or are there more selves?

M.: This is again due to confusion; you identify the body with the Self. You think: "Here I am; here he is, there is another; and so on". You find many bodies and think they are so many selves. But did you ask in your sleep "I am sleeping here, how many are there who are awake?" Does any question arise, for the matter of that? Why does it not arise? Because you are only one and there are not many.

D.: What is my *tattva* (truth)?

544

M.: You are yourself the *tattva*. Is there a different one to know the *tattva* of another? How can you exist apart from the *tattva*? The very fact of your existence makes you ask this question. Your very existence is the *tattva*. Give up the habiliments of the *tattva* and remain in your essential nature. All the Scriptures tell you only not to waste your efforts in non-truth — non-*tattva*. Give up the non-*tattva*. Then *tattva* remains always shining pure and single.

D.: I want to know my *tattva* and my duties.

M.: Know your *tattva* first and then you may ask what your duties are. You must exist in order to know and do your duty. Realise your existence and then enquire of your duties.

26th October, 1938

Talk 566.

There is a Tamil paper *Arya Dharmam*. An article on *Vairagyam* appeared in it. Sri Bhagavan read it out in answer to a question. The article was briefly as follows:

vairagya = *vi* + *raga* = *vigataraga* (non-attachment).

Vairagya is possible only for the wise. However, it is often misapplied by the common folk. For instance, a man often says "I have determined not to go to cinema shows." He calls it *vairagya*. Such wrong interpretation of the words and old sayings are not uncommon. Again we often hear, "Dog seen, stone is not seen; stone seen, dog is not seen." It is ordinarily understood to mean that one cannot find a brickbat to throw at a stray dog. But this popular saying has a much deeper significance. It is based on a story: A certain wealthy man's house was closely guarded. It had also a ferocious dog chained to a pillar at the gate. The dog and the chain were however very skilful pieces of art. They were sculptured in stone but appeared life-like. A pedestrian on the road once took fright at the sight of the ferocious animal and hurt himself in his attempt to dodge it. A kindly neighbour took pity on him and showed him that it was not a living dog. When the man passed by it the next time he admired the skill of the sculptor and forgot his old experience. Thus when he found it to be a dog, he could not see the stone of which it was made; and again when he found it a piece of sculpture he did not see any dog to hurt him. Hence the proverb. Compare it with 'The elephant hides the wood and the wood hides the elephant.' Here it is a wooden elephant.

Atma is always *Sat-Chit-Ananda*. Of these, the first two are experienced in all the states, whereas the last one is said to be experienced in sleep only. The question arises how the true nature of the Self can be lost in the waking and dream states. It is, really speaking, not lost. In sleep there is no mind and the Self shines as Itself, whereas in the other two states what shines forth is the reflected light of the Self. *Ananda* is felt after the cessation of thoughts in sleep. It is also manifest on other occasions as love, joy, etc., *priya, moda* and *pramoda*. But they are all *chitta vrittis* (modes of mind).

When a man is walking in the street his mind is full of fleeting thoughts. Suppose he passes a bazaar where some fine mangoes are for sale. He likes the mangoes and purchases them. He is next anxious to taste them. So he hastens home and eats them and feels happy. When the fleeting thoughts give way to the pleasure at the sight of mangoes, it is *priya*, when he gets them as his own, the pleasure is *moda*; lastly, when he eats them, the pleasure is *pramoda*. All the three kinds of pleasure are owing to the disappearance of other thoughts.

3rd to 6th November, 1938

Talk 567.

Sri Bhagavan explained to Mr. MacIver the first few stanzas of *Sad Vidya* as follows:

1. The first stanza is the auspicious beginning. Why should the subject-matter of the piece be brought in here? Can knowledge be other than Being? Being is the core — the Heart. How then is the Supreme Being to be contemplated and glorified? Only to remain as the Pure Self is the auspicious beginning. This speaks of attributeless Brahman according to the *jnana marga* (method of knowledge).

2. The second stanza is in praise of God with attributes. In the foregoing, to be as one Self is mentioned; in the present one, surrender to the Lord of all.

546

Furthermore the second indicates (1) the fit reader (2) the subject-matter (3) the relationship and (4) the fruit. The fit reader is the one who is competent for it. Competence consists in non-attachment to the world and desire to be liberated.

All know that they must die some time or other; but they do not think deeply of the matter. All have a fear of death: such fear is momentary. Why fear death? Because of the 'I-am-the-body' idea. All are fully aware of the death of the body and its cremation. That the body is lost in death is well-known. Owing to the I-am-the-body notion, death is feared as being the loss of Oneself. Birth and death pertain to the body only; but they are superimposed on the Self, giving rise to the delusion that birth and death relate to the Self.

In the effort to overcome birth and death man looks up to the Supreme Being to save him. Thus are born faith and devotion to the Lord. How to worship Him? The creature is powerless and the Creator is All-powerful. How to approach Him? To entrust oneself to His care is the only thing left for him; total surrender is the only way. Therefore he surrenders himself to God. Surrender consists in giving up oneself and one's possessions to the Lord of Mercy. Then what is left over for the man? Nothing — neither himself nor his possessions. The body liable to be born and to die having been made over to the Lord, the man need no longer worry about it. Then birth and death cannot strike terror. The cause of fear was the body; it is no longer his; why should he fear now? Or where is the identity of the individual to be frightened?

Thus the Self is realised and Bliss results. This is then the subject-matter: freedom from misery and gain of Happiness. This is the highest good to be gained. Surrender is synonymous with Bliss itself. This is the relationship.

Fruit is to reflect on the subject-matter and gain Knowledge which is ever-present, here and now. The stanza ends with "the immortal ones."

3. The five senses mean the subtle functions (*tanmatras*), namely, hearing, touch, seeing, taste and smell. Variations of these form the whole universe; they vary according to the three *gunas* as follows:

by *tamas* (dullness) the gross elements;

by *rajas* (activity) the instruments for knowing objects;

by *sattva* (clearness) the different kinds of knowledge of the senses; also

by *tamas* — the gross objects *i.e.*, the world;

by *rajas* — the vital airs and the *karmendriyas*

by *sattva* — the sense organs of perception (*jnanendriyas*).

Karmendriyas are organs of holding, walking, speech, evacuation and reproduction.

Now consider the ringing of the bell; the sound is related to hearing; the bell is the object, the modification of *tamoguna*. The *rajasic tanmatras*, changing as the vibrations of sound, extend round the bell, then as ether get connected with the ear in order to be felt as sound. The knowledge recognising it as sound is the *sattva tanmatra*.

So also the other senses: Touch (*vayu*) — air *tanmatra*; form (*rupa*) — *tejas tanmatra*; taste (*ap*) — water *tanmatra*; smell (*prithvi*) — earth *tanmatra*.

To understand the *tanmatras* as the subtlest particles of matter is not right, for it is incomplete. They are only the subtle forms of sound, touch, sight, taste and smell, which form the whole components of the universe. Such is the creation of the world.

For want of proper terminology these ideas cannot be rightly expressed in foreign languages.

4. This stanza says that all are agreed on one point. What is it? The state beyond duality and non-duality, beyond subject and object, beyond *jiva* and God, in short, beyond all differences. It is free from ego. "How to reach it?" is the question. By giving up the world, it says. Here "the world" stands for thoughts relating to it. If such thoughts do not arise, the ego does not rise up. There will be no subject nor object. Such is the state.

Talk 568.

Mr. V. G. Sastri showed a cutting to Sri Bhagavan. It contained some prophecy of Sri Rama Tirtha that India would reach the full height of her former glory before 1950 AD

Sri Bhagavan said: Why should we think that India is not already in the height of her glory? The glory is in your thought.

7th November, 1938

Talk 569.

In reply to Sri K. L. Sarma, Sri Bhagavan spoke about *Dakshinamurti stotra* as follows:

I originally intended to write a commentary on it. Mr. Ranganatha Iyer took away my Tamil version of the *stotra* and printed it along with *Appalapattu*. He later asked me to enlarge it. I had the introduction ready. He saw it and took it away for printing. I did not proceed with the work. As for the *stotra:*

Brahma, the creator, created four sons from his mind. They were Sanaka, Sanandana, Sanathkumara and Sanatsujata. They asked their creator why they were brought into existence. Brahma said: "I must create the universe. But I want to go to do *tapas* for realising the Self. You are brought forth in order that you may create the universe. That will be by multiplying yourselves." They did not like the idea. They wondered why they should take the trouble on themselves. It is natural for one to seek the source. They therefore wanted to regain their source and be happy. So they did not obey the commands of Brahma but left him. They desired guidance for realisation of the Self. They were the best equipped individuals for Self-Realisation. Guidance should be only from the best of Masters. Who could it be but Siva — the *yogiraja*. Siva appeared before them sitting under the sacred banyan tree. Being *yogiraja* should He practise yoga? He went into *samadhi* as He sat; He was in Perfect Repose. Silence prevailed. They saw Him. The effect was immediate. They fell into *samadhi* and their doubts were at an end.

Silence is the true *upadesa*. It is the perfect *upadesa*. It is suited only for the most advanced seeker. The others are unable to draw full inspiration from it. Therefore they require words to explain the Truth. But Truth is beyond words. It does not admit of explanation. All that is possible to do is only to indicate It. How is that to be done?

549

The people are under an illusion. If the spell is removed they will realise the Truth. They must be told to realise the falsity of the illusion. Then they will try to escape its snares. *Vairagya* will result. They will enquire into the Truth, *i.e.*, seek the Self. That will make them abide as the Self. Sri Sankara, being the *avatar* of Siva, was full of compassion for fallen beings. He wanted all of them to realise their blissful Self. He could not reach them all with His Silence. So he composed the *Dakshinamurti stotra* in the form of a hymn so that people might read it and understand the Truth.

What is the nature of the illusion? All are in the grip of enjoyment, *i.e.*, *bhokta, bhogyam, bhoga*. This is due to the wrong notion that *bhogya vastu* (the objects) are real. The ego, the world and the creator are the fundamentals underlying the illusion. If they are known to be not apart from the Self there will be no more illusion.

The first four stanzas deal with the world. It is shown to be the same as the Master whose Self is that of the seeker also, or the Master to whom the seeker surrenders himself. The second four stanzas deal with the individual whose Self is shown to be the Self of the Master. The ninth stanza deals with Isvara and the tenth with the *siddhi* or Realisation.

Such is the scheme of the *stotra*.

Which is the *darpana* (mirror) here? A mirror, as we know it, is an insentient object which reflects light. What corresponds to a mirror in an individual? The light of the Self-luminous Self is reflected on the *Mahatattva*. The reflected light is the mind-ether or the pure mind. This illumines the *vasanas* (latencies) of the individual and hence the sense of 'I' and 'this' arises.

Again, a superficial reading of the *slokas* makes one believe that the bondage, liberation, etc., are all related to the Master *i.e.*, Sri Dakshinamurti. It is absurd. Surrender to Him is meant.

Talk 570.

A visitor: Nirguna upasana is said to be difficult and risky. He quoted the verse from Sri Bhagavad Gita, *avyaktahi* etc. (the manifest, etc.)

550

M.: What is manifest is considered to be unmanifest and doubt is created. Can anything be more immediate and intimate than the Self? Can anything be more plain?

D.: Saguna upasana seems easier.

M.: Do what is easy for you.

Talk 571.

Multiplicity of individuals is a moot point with most persons. A *jiva* is only the light reflected on the ego. The person identifies himself with the ego and argues that there must be more like him. He is not easily convinced of the absurdity of his position. Does a man who sees many individuals in his dream persist in believing them to be real and enquire after them when he wakes up?

This argument does not convince the disputant.

Again, there is the moon. Let anyone look at her from any place at any time; she is the same moon. Everyone knows it. Now suppose that there are several receptacles of water reflecting the moon. The images are all different from one another and from the moon herself. If one of the receptacles falls to pieces, that reflection disappears. Its disappearance does not affect the real moon or the other reflections. It is similar with an individual attaining Liberation. He alone is liberated.

The sectarian of multiplicity makes this his argument against non-duality. "If the Self is single, if one man is liberated, that means that all souls are liberated. In practice it is not so. Therefore *Advaita* is not correct."

The weakness in the argument is that the reflected light of the Self is mistaken for the original Light of the Self. The ego, the world and the individuals are all due to the person's *vasanas*. When they perish, that person's hallucinations disappear, that is to say one pitcher is broken and the relative reflection is at an end.

The fact is that the Self is never bound. There can therefore be no Release for It. All the troubles are for the ego only.

10th November, 1938

A question was asked why it was wrong to say that there is a multiplicity of *jivas*. *Jivas* are certainly many. For a *jiva* is only the ego and forms the reflected light of the Self. Multiplicity of selves may be wrong but not of *jivas*.

M.: *Jiva* is called so because he sees the world. A dreamer sees many *jivas* in a dream but all of them are not real. The dreamer alone exists and he sees all. So it is with the individual and the world. There is the creed of only one Self which is also called the creed of only one *jiva*. It says that the *jiva* is only one who sees the whole world and the *jivas* therein.

D.: Then *jiva* means the Self here.

M.: So it is. But the Self is not a seer. But here he is said to see the world. So he is differentiated as the *Jiva*.

Talk 572.

D.: Of what use is the fear of death which is common to all?

M.: True, it is common to all. Such fear serves no useful purpose because being overpowered by the latent tendencies of the mind the man dies a natural death. It does not lead him to non-attachment and he cannot investigate the matter.

D.: How then are you giving the same instruction without distinction to visitors?

M.: What do I say? The ego in each one must die. Let him reflect on it. Is there this ego or is there not? By repeated reflection one becomes more and more fit.

11th November, 1938

Talk 573.

Mr. Ranganatha Ayyar, a devotee of fourteen years' standing, is on a visit here. He asked: How long is the interval between one's death and reincarnation?

M.: It may be long or short. But a *jnani* does not have any such changes; he merges into the universal Being, so says the *Brihadaranyaka Upanishad*. Some say that those who after death pass into the path of light are not reborn, whereas those who after death take the path of darkness are reborn after they have enjoyed the fruits of karma in their subtle bodies.

If one's merits and demerits are equal, they are directly reborn here. Merits outweighing demerits, the subtle bodies go to heavens and are then reborn here; demerits outweighing merits, they go to hells and are afterwards reborn here.

A *yogabrashta* is said to fare in the same manner. All these are described in the *sastras*. But in fact, there is neither birth nor death. One remains only as what one really is. This is the only Truth.

Talk 574.

D.: What are *asanas* (postures or seats)? Are they necessary?

M.: Many *asanas* with their effects are mentioned in the Yoga *sastras*. The seats are the tiger-skin, grass, etc.; the postures are the 'lotus posture', the 'easy posture' and so on Why all these — only to know oneself? "I am the body; the body requires a seat; it is the earth," thinking thus, he seeks seats. But in sleep did he think of the support or the bed: the bed on the cot and the cot on the earth? Did he not exist in sleep too? How was he then?

The truth is — Being the Self, the ego rising up, confusing himself with the body, mistaking the world to be real, differentiating the objects, covered by the ignorance of the 'I'-conceit, he thinks wildly and also looks for seats. He does not understand that he himself is the Centre of all and thus forms the basis for all.

If questioned he talks of the effects of seats and footwear in terms of gravitation, magnetism and so on. Without them he imagines that the power of his austerities will dwindle away.

Wherefrom do they all derive their power? He looks to the effects, seeks their causes and imagines them to be the power of seats and of footwear. A stone thrown up falls back to the ground. Why? Owing to the gravitation, says he. Well — are all these different from his thoughts? Think and say if the stone, the earth and gravity are different from his thoughts. They are all in his mind only. He is the Power and the wielder of it. He is the Centre of all and their support. He is also the Seat.

The seat is meant to make him sit firm. Where and how can he remain firm except in his own real state? This is the Seat.

Talk 575.

D.: How to conquer desire, anger, etc.?

M.: Desire or lust, anger, etc., give you pain. Why? Because of the 'I'-conceit; this 'I'-conceit is from ignorance; ignorance from differentiation; differentiation from the notion of the reality of the world and this again from 'I-am-the-body' idea. The last can be only after the rise of the ego. The ego not arising, the whole chain of mishaps disappears. Therefore prevent the rise of the ego. This can be done by remaining in your own real nature; then lust, anger, etc., are conquered.

D.: So then all these have their root in ignorance.

M.: Quite so. Ignorance gives rise to error, error to conceit, etc. What is ignorance? Can it be of Pure Brahman which is only the Self or Pure Knowledge? Only let the questioner know his own Self, *i.e.*, be the Knowledge; this question will not arise. Because of ignorance he raises the question. Such ignorance is of the questioner and not of the Self. The sun seen, no darkness persists.

There is hoarded wealth in an iron safe. The man says it is his own; the safe does not say so. It is the ownership-conceit that is responsible for the claim.

Nothing is independent of the Self, not even ignorance; for ignorance is only the power of the Self, remaining there without affecting It. However it affects the 'I'-conceit, *i.e.*, the *jiva*. Therefore ignorance is of the *jiva*.

How? The man says, "I do not know myself." Are there then two selves — one the subject and the other the object? He cannot admit it. Is then ignorance at an end for him? No. The rise of the ego is itself the ignorance and nothing more.

Talk 576.

Sutra Bhashya:—

The *sutras* are meant to elucidate and establish the meanings of the texts. The commentaries try to do so by bringing in the opponent's views, refuting them and arriving at conclusions after long discussions; there are also differences of opinion in the same school of thought; again protagonists and antagonists. Also different schools of thought interpret the same text in different ways and arrive at different conclusions, contrary to each other.

How then is the purpose of the *sutras* served?

15th November, 1938

Talk 577.

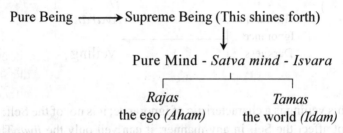

Pure Being ⟶ Supreme Being (This shines forth)

↓

Pure Mind - *Satva mind* - *Isvara*

Rajas　　　　　　*Tamas*
the ego *(Aham)*　　the world *(Idam)*

All these are Vedantic terminology

Talk 578.

Coming here, some people do not ask about themselves. They ask: "Does the sage, liberated while alive (*Jivanmukta*), see the world? Is he affected by Karma? What is liberation after being disembodied? Is one liberated only after being disembodied or even while alive in the body? Should the body of the sage resolve itself in light or disappear from view in any other manner? Can he be liberated though the body is left behind as a corpse?"

Their questions are endless. Why worry oneself in so many ways? Does liberation consist in knowing these?

Therefore I say to them, "Leave liberation alone. Is there bondage? Know this. See yourself first and foremost."

Talk 579.

Avarana (veiling) does not hide the *jiva* in entirety; he knows that he is; only he does not know who he is. He sees the world; but not that it is only Brahman. It is light in darkness (or knowledge in ignorance).

555

In a cinema show the room is first darkened, artificial light is introduced; only in this light are the pictures projected.

For differentiation a reflected light is thus necessary. A sleeper dreams, he is not out of sleep: only in the darkness or ignorance of sleep can he see the unreal dream objects.

Similarly the darkness of ignorance gives rise to the knowledge of the perceptions of the world.

This veiling is a characteristic of ignorance; it is not of the Self: it cannot affect the Self in any manner; it can veil only the *jiva*. The ego is insentient: united with the light from the Self, it is called *jiva*. But the ego and the light cannot be seen distinct from each other; they are always united together. The mixed product is the *jiva*, the root of all differentiation. All these are spoken of to satisfy the questioners.

Sahasrara
(cranium)

Sahasrara
(cranium) } Ether = *Jnana*

Kantham
(throat) } Air = Mind

Hridaya
(Heart) } Light = Intellect

Nabhi
(navel) } Water = Memory

Mula
(Solar plexus) } Earth = The Ego

Such is the representation of the subtle body. The senses and other organs act separately, whereas the inner organs and the vital airs can work only in unison. Therefore the former are *vyashti* (individualistic) and the latter are *samashti* (collective).

Avarana (veiling) gives rise to two kinds of veiling.

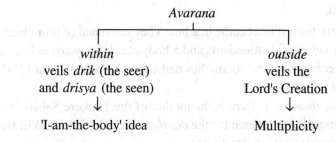

Jiva is not independent of *Isvara*; nor ignorance of *maya*. Only on waking up from sleep, the man perceives the body and the world, but not in sleep. On the strength of the present knowledge he understands that he remained in deep sleep also. Therefore in sleep *jiva* must be concluded to be in pure state in which the body and the world are not perceived.

D.: Is not *jiva* the reflected light, the 'I-thought'?

M.: He is also a *jiva*; before it also he is *jiva*; the one of them is related to the other as cause and effect. The sleeper *jiva* cannot be independent of *Isvara*. On waking he says "I am the body". If all the worlds together form *virat*, the body is a tiny dot in it. Thus the body is in and of *virat*. What belongs to the *jiva* then? Only the conceit makes him claim the body as himself but not the others. He cannot be independent of *virat*. Similarly,

(1) *Isvara*

    (Causal Cosmic Being) → *Prajna* (individual being in deep sleep)

(2) *Hiranyagarbha*

    (Causal Subtle Being) → *Taijasa* (individual subtle being)

(3) *Virat*

    (Causal gross Being) → *Visva* (individual gross being)

(4) *Maya*

    (Causal Ignorance adjunct to *Isvara*) → Ignorance adjunct to *Jiva*

(5) *Brahman*

    (Cause) → *Jiva* (Effect)

They say that all these five groups should be unified. This they call the unity of the Five. All these are only polemics!

Talk 580.

A party from Rajkot came in a bus. They consisted of four chiefs and four ladies with attendants and a bodyguard. They arrived at 11 a.m. After lunch in their room, they had a short conversation at 12-45 p.m. and left at 1-5 p.m.

One of them said: Here is the mother of the Thakore Saheb. We have come a long distance for the *darshan* of Sri Maharshi. Will He kindly give us some instructions?

Sri Bhagavan smiled and answered: Good that they have come such a long distance for the sake of *darshan*. It is enough that they have said it. What is there for me to say?

(Lunch bell).

At 12-45 p.m.

O.: Is a *jnani* different from a *yogi*? What is the difference?

M.: Srimad Bhagavad Gita says that a *jnani* is the true yogi and also a true *bhakta*. Yoga is only a *sadhana* and *jnana* is the *siddhi*.

D.: Is yoga necessary?

M.: It is a *sadhana*. It will not be necessary after *jnana* is attained. All the *sadhanas* are called yogas, *e.g.*, Karma yoga; *Bhakti* yoga; *Jnana* yoga; *Ashtanga* yoga. What is yoga? Yoga means 'union'. Yoga is possible only when there is *'viyoga'* (separation). The person is now under the delusion of *viyoga*. This delusion must be removed. The method of removing it is called yoga.

D.: Which method is the best?

M.: It depends upon the temperament of the individual. Every person is born with the *samskaras* of past lives. One of the methods will be found easy for one person and another method for another. There is no definiteness about it.

D.: How is one to meditate?

M.: What is meditation? It is commonly understood to be concentration on a single thought. Other thoughts are kept out at that time. The single thought also must vanish at the right time. Thought-free consciousness is the goal.

D.: How is the ego to be got rid of?

M.: The ego must be held in order to get rid of it. Hold it first and the rest will be easy.

D.: How is that to be held?

M.: Do you mean to say that there is one ego to hold another ego or to eliminate the other? Are there two egos?

D.: How shall I pray to God?

M.: There-must be 'I' who prays to God. 'I' is certainly immediate and intimate, whereas God is not thought so. Find out that which is more intimate and then the other may be ascertained and prayed to if necessary.

19th November, 1938

Talk 581.

When a child held something to be offered to Sri Bhagavan by the parents, they cajoled the child to offer it to Sri Bhagavan. The child did so gladly. Sri Bhagavan remarked: Look at this! When the child can give a thing away to *Jeja* it is *tyaga*. (*Jeja* — God). See what influence *Jeja* has on children also! Every gift implies unselfishness. That is the whole content of *nishkama* Karma (unselfish action). It means true renunciation. If the giving nature is developed it becomes *tyaga*. If anything is willingly given away it is a delight to the giver and to the receiver. If the same is stolen it is misery to both. *Dana, dharma, nishkama* Karma are all *tyaga* only. When 'mine' is given up it is *chitta suddhi* (purified mind). When 'I' is given up it is *jnana*. When the nature to give away is developed it results in *jnana*.

Again a little later, a young boy came all alone, unescorted by his parents. He had come from Chengam in a bus. Sri Bhagavan remarked, "The boy has left his parents to come here. This is also an instance of *tyaga*."

21st. 22nd November, 1938

Talk 582.

To an Andhra gentleman Sri Bhagavan said: If one goes on wanting, one's wants cannot be fulfilled. Whereas if one remains desireless anything will be forthcoming. We are not in the wife, children, profession, etc.; but they are in us; they appear and disappear according to one's *prarabdha*.

The mind remaining still is *samadhi*, no matter whether the world is perceived or not.

Environment, time and objects are all in me. How can they be independent of me? They may change, but I remain unchanging, always the same. The objects can be differentiated by means of their names and forms, whereas each one's name is only one and that is 'I'. Ask anyone, he says 'I' and speaks of himself as 'I', even if He is *Isvara*. His name too is 'I' only.

So also of a locality. As long as I am identified with the body so long a locality is distinguishable; otherwise not. Am I the body? Does the body announce itself as 'I'?

Clearly all these are in me. All these wiped out entirely, the residual Peace is 'I'. This is *samadhi*, this is 'I'.

Talk 583.

Mr. V. Ganapati Sastri showed Sri Bhagavan a letter from a Spanish lady, Mercedes De Acorta, saying she would be coming here the next day. Sri Bhagavan remarked: "See the trouble to so many because I am here."

23rd November, 1938
REMINISCENCE

Talk 584.

A certain visitor began to pull the *pankah*. Sri Bhagavan said: "Because it is cold, they have placed fire by my side. Why should the *pankah* be pulled?"

Then he continued: "On a cold morning, when I was in Virupaksha cave, I was sitting in the open. I was feeling cold. People used to come, see me and go back. A group of Andhra visitors had come. I did not notice what they were doing. They were behind me. Suddenly a noise '*tak*' — and water over my head! I shivered with cold. I looked back. They had broken a coconut and poured the water on me. They thought that it was worship. They took me for a stone image."

Talk 585.

Sri Bhagavan said that this town is peculiar in that there are nine roads leading to it, not counting the railroad; *navadware pure dehe* (in the body — the city of nine gates).

Talk 586.

An Andhra visitor asked: How is one to be quiet? It is so difficult to be so. Should we practise *yoga* for it? Or is there any other means for it?

M.: What is not difficult looks difficult. A man is prone to wander about. He is told to stay quiet at home, but finds it difficult to do so because he wants to wander about.

D.: Is there any particular *upasana* which is more efficacious than others?

M.: All *upasanas* are equally efficacious. But each one takes easily to one kind of *upasana* which suits his previous *vasanas*.

24th November, 1938

Talk 587.

The Spanish lady and her lady friend have come.

They asked: You say the Heart is on the right. Can you explain how it is so?

Sri Bhagavan handed over the extract from the *Psychological Review* of Philadelphia for her to read. He also added. The Heart is the place wherefrom the 'I-thought' arises.

D.: So you mean the spiritual Heart as distinguished from the physical heart?

M.: Yes. It is explained in Ch. V of *Sri Ramana Gita*.

D.: Is there any stage when one might feel the Heart?

M.: It is within the experience of everyone. Everyone touches the right side of his chest when he says 'I'.

Both the ladies kneeled before Sri Bhagavan one after another and asked for blessings. Then they left for Pondicherry on their way to Colombo.

Talk 588.

To an Andhra seeker, Sri Bhagavan said: *Sannyasa* is mentioned for one who is fit. It consists in renunciation not of material objects but of attachment to them. *Sannyasa* can be practised by anyone even at home. Only one must be fit for it. Again.

A *Kutichaka* is one who takes *sannyasa* and lives in a hermitage;

A *Bahudaka* is one who takes *sannyasa* and goes to places of pilgrimage;

A *Hamsa* is an *upasaka sannyasi*;

A *Paramahamsa* is a realised *sannyasi*.

27th November, 1938

Talk 589.

Somasundara Swami, a long standing devotee, asked: There is *akasa* in a mirror and it reflects images. How are these contained in the mirror?

M.: Objects remain in space. Objects and space are together reflected in the mirror. Just as the things are found in space, so they are in the reflection also. The mirror is itself thin. How can these objects be contained in its compass?

D.: How does the *akasa* in a pot illustrate this point?

M.: There is no reflection in the *akasa* of the pot. The reflection is only in the water in it. Keeping several pots filled with water in a tank, the *akasa* is reflected equally in the water in each of the pots and in the water of the tank. Similarly the whole universe is reflected in each individual.

D.: The mouths of the pots must be above the surface of the water in the tank.

M.: Yes, it must be so. Otherwise can the pots be recognised if sunk in the tank?

D.: How does the reflection take place there?

M.: Pure ether cannot take reflections; only the ether of water can do so. Glass cannot reflect objects; only a plate of glass with an opaque lining on its back can reflect the objects in front of it. Similarly Pure

Knowledge does not contain objects in it nor reflect objects. Only with the limiting adjunct, the mind it reflects the world.

Neither in *samadhi* nor in deep sleep does the world remain. There cannot be illusion either in bright light or in total darkness. Only in dim light a rope seems a snake. Similarly Pure Consciousness remains light only; it is pure knowledge. The mind rising from it is deluded that the objects remain apart.

D.: So then the mind is the mirror.

M.: Mind — mind what is it? It is a mixture of *Chit* (intelligence) and *sankalpas* (thoughts). Therefore it forms all these — the mirror, light, darkness and the reflections.

D.: But I do not see it.

M.: *Chidakasa* (chit-ether) is Pure Knowledge only, It is the source of mind. Just at the moment of rising up, the mind is only light; only afterwards the thought "I am this" rises up; this 'I-thought' forms the *jiva* and the world.

The first light is the pure mind, the mind ether or *Isvara*. Its modes manifest as objects. Because it contains all these objects within itself it is called the mind-ether. Why ether? Like ether containing objects it contains the thoughts, therefore it is the mind-ether.

Again, just as the physical ether though accommodating all the gross objects (the whole universe) is itself the content of the mind-ether, so also the latter is itself the content of *Chit*-ether. The last one is *Chit* Itself. There are no things contained in it. It remains as Pure Knowledge only.

D.: Why call it ether? Physical ether is not sentient.

M.: Ether denotes not only the insentient physical ether but also Pure Knowledge. Knowledge does not consist in knowing objects: this is relative knowledge. But Knowledge in its purity remains all alone, One, unique, transcendent Light!

D.: Well — should we be imagining it in our meditation?

M.: Why imagine? We can think of another only if we are independent of it, whereas here we cannot remain independent of this Pure Knowledge. Rather, only IT is! How can It be imagined to be so and so or such and such?

D.: How are we to proceed?

M.: Only get rid of the non-self.

D.: It looks all right now; but later it is all forgotten.

M.: Your forgetfulness implies knowledge, for you know you forgot; otherwise how can you speak of forgetting it? So forgetfulness also is *Chit-akasa* (Chit-ether) only.

D.: How then is it not clear to me?

M.: *Chit* is knowledge pure and simple. The mind proceeds from it; the mind is made up of thoughts. Darkness or ignorance interposing. Pure Knowledge seems different from what It really is; the same is seen as 'I' and the 'world' which are full of desire, attachment, hatred, etc. Therefore desire, etc., are said to veil the Reality.

D.: How to be rid of thoughts? Is it as said in the *Atma-Vidya* — the eye of the mental eye, etc.?

M.: There the mind stands for ether, Being (*sat*); and the eye for knowledge (*chit*); both *sat* and *chit* together form the universe.

D.: How to realise the same?

M.: As pointed out in the *Atma Vidya* "being the eye of the mental eye, the ether of the mental ether.....", meaning, the Knowledge behind the relative knowledge, the *Chit*-Ether containing the mental ether, remains as the Only One always shining bright.

D.: Still I do not understand. How shall I realise it?

M.: It is also said, "Remain free from thoughts," and "It is realised only in the mind drawn within." Therefore, the mind made free from thoughts, and merged in the Heart, is *Chit* Itself.

D.: Is the aforesaid mental ether *Isvara* or *Hiranyagarbha*?

M.: Can the latter remain independent of the former? The same is *Isvara* and *Hiranyagarbha*.

D.: How do they differ from each other?

M.: The Immanent Being is called *Isvara*.

D.: Is not the Immanent Being *Chit-akasa* only?

M.: Immanence can only be with *Maya*. It is the Knowledge of Being along with *Maya*; from this subtle conceit *Hiranyagarbha*; from the latter the gross conceit *virat*. *Chit-atma* is Pure Being only.

13th December, 1938

Talk 590.

Two ladies, one Swiss and the other French, visited Maharshi. The younger of the ladies asked several questions, of which the most important was: "Brahman is the same as *jiva*. If the *jiva* be under illusion it amounts to saying that Brahman is under illusion. How is that possible?"

M.: If Brahman be under illusion and wants disillusionment let Him raise the question.

14th December, 1938

Talk 591.

D.: Seekers who are in immediate proximity of the Master can get grace by *darsana, sparsana*, etc. (look, touch, etc.). But how does one get the same grace when the person is at a distance?

M.: By yoga *drishti* (yogic look).

Mr. Chopra, a Punjabi employed in Singapore, is on a visit here and raised a few questions.

D.: What is the efficacy of the name?

Sri Bhagavan read out the extract from the *Vision*. It was a translation of Namdev's stanzas.

D.: How does the name help Realisation?

M.: The original name is always going on spontaneously without any effort on the part of the individual. That name is *aham* — 'I'. But when it becomes manifest it manifests as *ahamkara* — the ego. The oral repetition of *nama* leads one to mental repetition which finally resolves itself into the eternal vibration.

D.: But these are all mental or physical.

M.: The mind or the mouth cannot act without the Self. Tukaram, the great Maharashtra Saint, used to remain in *samadhi* in the day and sing and dance at night with large crowds of people. He always used to utter the name of Sri Rama. Once he was answering calls of nature and also saying "Ram, Ram". An orthodox priest was shocked at the unholy mention of the sacred name and so reprimanded him

565

and ordered him to be silent when he answered calls of nature. Tukaram said, "All right!" and remained mute. But at once there arose the name of Rama from every pore of Tukaram and the priest was horrified by the din. He then prayed to Tukaram "Restrictions are only for the common people and not for saints like you."

D.: It is said that Sri Ramakrishna saw life in the image of Kali which he worshipped. Can it be true?

M.: The life was perceptible to Sri Ramakrishna and not to all. The vital force was due to himself. It was his own vital force which manifested as if it were outside and drew him in. Were the image full of life it must have been found so by all. But everything is full of life. That is the fact. Many devotees have had experiences similar to those of Sri Ramakrishna.

D.: How can there be life in stone? It is unconscious.

M.: The whole universe is full of life. You say the stone is unconscious. It is your self-consciousness which now speaks of unconsciousness. When a person wants to see if there is an article in a dark room he takes a lamp to look for it. The light is useful for detecting the presence and the absence of the thing. Consciousness is necessary for discovering if a thing is conscious or not. If a man remains in a dark room one need not take a lamp to find him. If called, he answers. He does not require a lamp to announce his presence. Consciousness is thus self-shining.

Now you say you were unconscious in sleep and self-conscious in the wakeful state. Which is the Reality? The Reality must be continuous and eternal. Neither the unconsciousness nor the self-consciousness of the present is the Reality. But you admit your existence all through. The pure Being is the reality. The others are mere associations. The pure Being cannot be otherwise than consciousness. Otherwise you cannot say that you exist. Therefore consciousness is the reality. When that consciousness is associated with *upadhis* you speak of self-consciousness, unconsciousness, sub-consciousness, super-consciousness, human-consciousness, dog-consciousness, tree-consciousness and so on. The unaltering common factor in all of them is consciousness.

Therefore the stone is as much unconscious as you are in sleep. Is that totally devoid of consciousness?

D.: But a dog-consciousness is different from my consciousness. I cannot read the Bible to the dog. The tree again does not move whereas I move and act.

M.: Call the tree a standing man; and call the man a moving tree.

An American gentleman who also took part in the conversation would not allow Sri Bhagavan to explain and so it stopped here.

Talk 592.

The Punjabi gentleman referred to the popular belief of a worm being metamorphosed to a wasp (*bhramarakita nyaya*) which Sri Bhagavan had mentioned to the ladies in the course of conversation yesterday. Sri Bhagavan recalled some interesting reminiscences:

1. "I had previously heard of this *bhramarakita nyaya*. After I came to Tiruvannamalai, when I was staying in Gurumoortham, I noticed a red wasp construct a hive in which it placed five or six grubs and then flew away. My curiosity was roused and I wanted to test the truth of the oft-quoted *nyaya*. I waited some days, maybe ten days. I then tapped the hive. It broke and there I found that all the five or six grubs had united together and taken the shape of a wasp, but it was white.

2. Later when I was in Virupaksha Cave, I saw a red wasp construct five or six hives in each of which it placed five or six grubs and flew away. After about ten days, a black beetle, smaller than the wasp, buzzed round the hives and closed each of then, with a little black mud and flew away. I was wondering at the intrusion of the beetle on the hive of the wasp. I waited a few days and then gently opened one of the hives. Five or six black bodies came out and each of them was a black beetle. I thought it strange.

3. Again when I was in Pachyamman Temple, I saw a red wasp constructing five or six hives on a pillar in the temple. It placed five or six grubs in each of them and buzzed away. I watched it for several days. The wasp did not return. There was no black beetle also. After about fifteen days, I opened one of the hives. All the grubs had united

567

into a white mass of wasp-like form. It dropped down and was stunned by the fall. After a few minutes, it began to crawl. Its colour was gradually changing. In a short time, there were two little specks on its sides which grew into wings as I watched and the full-grown wasp flew away from the ground.

4. When I was in the Mango-Tree Cave I noticed a caterpillar-like worm crawl up a wall. It stopped in one place and fixed two spots which it later connected up with a thin filament from its body. It held the filament with its mouth and rested its tail end on the wall. It remained so several days. I was watching it. It shrivelled up in course of time. I wondered if there was life in it. So I gently tickled it with a thin stalk. There was no life within. I left it there. But in a few days more I found that there was only a thin dry skin left behind and the inner thing had flown away.

5. I had also seen the flies carrying tiny grubs on their legs which they deposited on offal. The grubs later flew away as flies."

D.: They may be eggs laid by the flies.

M.: But they move and struggle and then shape themselves as flies.

Talk 593.

Sri Bhagavan mentioned another interesting reminiscence. "When I was a boy I had seen the fishermen divert water from its main course and keep a pot through which the diverted water flowed. The artificial way was spread with tobacco stems. Strangely enough the larger fishes always took the new way and fell into the pot. The fishermen who were simply sitting quiet used to take the fish out from the pot and throw them into their baskets. I thought at the time it was strange. Later, when I was staying here I heard some man recite a piece from Thayumanavar which mentioned the same trick of the fishermen."

15th December, 1938

Talk 594.

The Spanish lady, Madam Mercedes De Acorta, has written a letter to Mr. Hague, the American mining engineer who is here as a temporary resident for the last two months. She has raised a few questions there: "If the individual Self merges into the universal Self, how can one pray to God for the uplift of humanity?" The question seems to be common among the thinkers of the West.

Sri Bhagavan said: They pray to God and finish with "Thy Will be done!" If His Will be done why do they pray at all? It is true that the Divine Will prevails at all times and under all circumstances. The individuals cannot act of their own accord. Recognise the force of the Divine Will and keep quiet. Each one is looked after by God. He has created all. You are one among 2,000 millions. When He looks after so many will He omit you? Even common sense dictates that one should abide by His Will.

Again there is no need to let Him know your needs. He knows them Himself and will look after them.

Still more, why do you pray? Because you are helpless yourself and you want the Higher Power to help you. Well, does not your Creator and Protector know your weakness? Should you parade your weakness in order to make Him know it?

D.: But God helps those who help themselves.

M.: Certainly. Help yourself and that is itself according to God's Will. Every action is prompted by Him only. As for prayer for the sake of others, it looks so unselfish on the surface of it. But analyse the feeling and you will detect selfishness there also. You desire others' happiness so that you may be happy. Or you want the credit for having interceded on others' behalf. God does not require an intermediary. Mind your business and all will be well.

D.: Does not God work His Will through some chosen person?

M.: God is in all and works through all. But His presence is better recognised in purified minds. The pure ones reflect God's actions more clearly than the impure minds. Therefore people say that they are the chosen ones. But the 'chosen' man does not himself say so. If he thinks that he is the intermediary then it is clear that he retains his individuality and that there is no complete surrender.

D.: Are not the Brahmins considered to be the priests or intermediaries between God and others?

569

M.: Yes. But who is a Brahmin? A Brahmin is one who has realised Brahman. Such a one has no sense of individuality in him. He cannot think that he acts as an intermediary.

Again, as for prayer, a realised man does not see others as different from oneself. How can he pray at all, and to whom and for what? His very presence is the consummation of happiness for all. So long as you think that there are others different from you, you pray for them. But the sense of separateness is ignorance. This ignorance is again the cause of feeling helplessness. You know that you are weak and helpless. How then can you help others? If you say, "By prayer to God", God knows His business and does not require your intercession for others.

Help yourself so that you may become strong. That is done by complete surrender. That means you offer yourself to Him. So you cannot retain your individuality after surrender. You then abide by His Will. Thus Silence is the Highest of all achievements.

Silence is the ocean in which all the rivers of all the religions discharge themselves. So says Thayumanavar. He also adds that the Vedic religion is the only one which combines both philosophy and religion.

16th December, 1938

Talk 595.

The two lady visitors returned in the morning and the younger one asked:

"Is the experience of the Highest State the same to all? Or is there any difference?"

M.: The Highest State is the same and the experience is also the same.

D.: But I find some difference in the interpretations put on the Highest Truth.

M.: The interpretations are made with the mind. The minds are different and so the interpretations are different.

D.: I mean to ask if the seers express themselves differently?

M.: The expressions may differ according to the nature of the seekers. They are meant to guide the seekers.

One seer speaks in the terms of Christianity, another in those of Islam, a third of Buddhism, etc. Is that due to their upbringing?

M.: Whatever may be their upbringing, their experience is the same. But the modes of expression differ according to circumstances.

Talk 596.

A visitor asked: Sri Bhagavan said last night that God is guiding us. Then why should we make an effort to do anything?

M.: Who asks you to do so? If there was that faith in the guidance of God this question would not have arisen.

D.: The fact is that God guides us. Then what is the use of these instructions to people?

M.: They are for those who seek instructions. If you are firm in your belief in the guidance of God, stick to it, and do not concern yourself with what happens around you. Furthermore, there may be happiness or misery. Be equally indifferent to both and abide in the faith of God. That will be so only when one's faith is strong that God looks after all of us.

Mr. Chopra asked: "How shall I secure that firm faith?"

M.: Exactly. It is for such as these who want instructions. There are persons who seek freedom from misery. They are told that God guides all and so there need not be any concern about what happens. If they are of the best type they at once believe it and firmly abide by faith in God.

But there are others who are not so easily convinced of the truth of the bare statement. They ask: "Who is God? What is His nature? Where is He? How can He be realised?" and so on. In order to satisfy them intellectual discussion is found necessary. Statements are made, their pros and cons are argued, and the truth is thus made clear to the intellect.

When the matter is understood intellectually the earnest seeker begins to apply it practically. He argues at every moment, "For whom are these thoughts? Who am I?" and so forth, until he is well-established in the conviction that a Higher Power guides us. That is firmness of faith. Then all his doubts are cleared and he needs no further instructions.

D.: We also have faith in God.

M.: If it had been firm no questions would have arisen. The person will remain perfectly happy in his Faith in the Omnipotent.

D.: Is the enquiry into the Self the same as the above mentioned faith?

M.: The enquiry into the Self is inclusive of all, faith, devotion, *jnana*, yoga and all.

D.: A man sometimes finds that the physical body does not permit steady meditation. Should he practise yoga for training the body for the purpose?

M.: It is according to one's *samskaras* (predispositions). One man will practise *hatha yoga* for curing his bodily ills; another man will trust to God to cure them; a third man will use his will-power for it and a fourth man may be totally indifferent to them. But all of them will persist in meditation. The quest for the Self is the essential factor and all the rest are mere accessories.

A man may have mastered the *Vedanta* philosophy and yet remain unable to control his thoughts. He may have a predisposition (*purva samskara*) which takes him to practise *hatha* yoga. He will believe that the mind can be controlled only by yoga and so he will practise it.

D.: What is most suitable for gaining facilities for steady *dhyana*?

M.: It depends on one's *samskara*. One may find *hatha* yoga suitable and another man *nama japa*, and so on. The essential point is the *atma-vichara* — enquiry into the Self.

D.: Is it enough if I spend some time in the mornings and some time in the evenings for this *atma-vichara*? Or should I do it always — say, even when I am writing or walking?

M.: Now what is your real nature? Is it writing, walking, or being? The one unalterable reality is *Being*. Until you realise that state of pure being you should pursue the enquiry. If once you are established in it there will be no further worry.

No one will enquire into the source of thoughts unless thoughts arise. So long as you think "I am walking," "I am writing," enquire who does it.

These actions will however go on when one is firmly established in the Self. Does a man always say, "I am a man, I am a man, I am a man," every moment of his life? He does not say so and yet all his actions are going on.

D.: Is an intellectual understanding of the Truth necessary?

M.: Yes. Otherwise why does not the person realise God or the Self at once, *i.e.*, as soon as he is told that God is all or the Self is all? That shows some wavering on his part. He must argue with himself and gradually convince himself of the Truth before his faith becomes firm.

20th December, 1938

Talk 597.

A Swiss lady, Mrs. J. C. S. Hick-Riddingh, asked: "Does Self-Realisation imply occult powers also?"

M.: The Self is the most intimate and eternal Being whereas the *siddhis* are foreign. The one requires effort to acquire and the other does not.

The powers are sought by the mind which must be kept alert whereas the Self is realised when the mind is destroyed. The powers manifest only when there is the ego. The ego makes you aware of others and in its absence there are no others to be seen. The Self is beyond the ego and is realised after the ego is eliminated. The elimination of the ego makes one unaware of others. How can the question of others arise and where is the use of occult powers for a Self-Realised Being?

Self-Realisation may be accompanied by occult powers or it may not be. If the person had sought such powers before Realisation, he may get the powers after Realisation. There are others who had not sought such powers and had attempted only Self-Realisation. They do not manifest such powers.

These powers may also be sought and gained even after Self-Realisation. But then they are used for a definite purpose, *i.e.* the benefit of others as in the case of Chudala.

Sikhidhvaja was a pious king. His spouse was Chudala. They received instructions from a sage. The king, being busy with the

573

administration of his kingdom, could not put the instructions into practice, whereas Chudala put them into practice and gained Self-Realisation. Consequently she appeared more charming than before. The king was struck by her growing charm and asked her about it. She said that all charm was due to the Self and he was only noting the charm of Self-Realisation in her. He said that she was silly. There were great *tapasvis* who could not realise the Self even after long periods of *tapas* and what about a silly woman who was all along in the family and in the worldly life? However, Chudala was not offended because she was firm in the Self and only wished that her husband should realise the Self and be happy. She then thought that unless she could prove her worth by manifesting some extraordinary powers he could not be convinced and she began to seek occult powers and gained them. But she did not betray them just then. Constant association with her made the king dispassionate. He began to dislike the worldly life and desired to retire into the forest for performing *tapasya*. So he told his wife that he wanted to leave the world for the forest. She was delighted at the development, but pretended to be very much concerned with his unkind decision. He hesitated out of consideration for her. In the meantime, his dispassion gained in force and he decided to leave home even without her consent.

When the queen was sleeping one night he suddenly left the palace by stealth and retired into the forest. He was seeking some solitary spot where he could perform his *tapas*. When the queen woke up she did not find her husband and immediately found out by her occult powers what had really happened. She rejoiced in her husband's determination. She called the ministers and said that the king had gone on some important business and that the administration should be carried on as efficiently as ever. She herself administered the state in the absence of the king.

Eighteen years passed. She then knew that the king was fit for Self-Realisation. So she appeared to him disguised as Kumbha and so on. He then realised the Self and returned to rule the kingdom with the queen.

The point is that occult powers are sought and gained for the benefit of others by Self-Realised persons also. But the sages are not deluded by the possession of such powers.

D.: Does the sage use occult powers for making others realise the Self or is the mere fact of his Self-Realisation enough for it?

M.: The force of his Self-Realisation is far more powerful than the use of all other powers.

Inasmuch as there is no ego in him, there are not others for him. What is the highest benefit that can be conferred on others? It is happiness. Happiness is born of Peace. Peace can reign only when there is no disturbance. Disturbance is due to thoughts which arise in the mind. When the mind itself is absent there will be perfect Peace. Unless a person had annihilated his mind he cannot gain peace and be happy. Unless he himself is happy he cannot bestow happiness on others.

When there is no mind he cannot be aware of others. So the mere fact of his Self-Realisation is itself enough to make all others happy.

D.: Can *samadhi* come and go?

M.: What is *samadhi*? *Samadhi* is one's essential nature. How then can it come or go?

If you do not realise your essential nature, your sight remains obstructed. What is the obstruction? Find it and remove it. So one's efforts are meant only for the removal of obstructions which hide the true vision. The real nature remains the same. When once it is realised it is permanent.

D.: But Mr. Brunton says that he had one hour's *samadhi*. Therefore I asked the question.

M.: A practiser gains peace of mind and is happy. That peace is the result of his efforts. But the real state must be effortless. The effortless *samadhi* is the true one and the perfect state. It is permanent. The efforts are spasmodic and so also their results.

When the real, effortless, permanent, happy nature is realised it will be found to be not inconsistent with the ordinary activities of life. The *samadhi* reached after efforts looks like abstraction from the external activities. A person might be so abstracted or live freely

575

among people without detriment to his Peace and Happiness because
that is his true nature or the Self.

21st December, 1938

Talk 598.

Sri Bhagavan shows great humour at times: He read *Upamanya
Bhakta Vilas* which contains a passage where Arunachalesvara is said
to have robbed Tirujnanasambandar and his group of followers of all
their possessions by His *bhutaganas* disguised as dacoits. Sri
Bhagavan remarked: "Siva Himself was waylaid in *Tiruvudal Utsava*
and He practised the same trick on His devotees. Can it be so?"

Talk 599.

A saying of Laotze from *Tao Teh Ch'ing* was read out in the hall:
"By his non-action the sage governs all."

Sri Bhagavan remarked: Non-action is unceasing activity. The sage
is characterised by eternal and intense activity. His stillness is like
the apparent stillness of a fast rotating top (gyroscope). Its very speed
cannot be followed by the eye and so it appears to be still. Yet it is
rotating. So is the apparent inaction of the sage. This must be explained
because the people generally mistake stillness to be inertness. It is
not so.

24th December, 1938

Talk 600.

A young man asked in broken Tamil:

How long will it be before Self-Realisation?

M.: First know what Self means and also what Realisation means:
then you will know all.

D.: The mind must realise in the Heart.

M.: Be it so. What is mind?

D.: Mind, Heart are all *avatars* of Perumal (Vaishnavite term for
incarnate God).

M.: If so no need to worry ourselves.

D.: On this basis how can we realise?

M.: Surrender the mind to Perumal (God). His *avatar* cannot remain independent of Him. Render unto Him what is His and be happy.

D.: How to do so?

M.: How is the mind known to us? Owing to its activities, namely, thoughts. Whenever thoughts arise remember they are all modes of Perumal and they cannot be otherwise, this is enough; this is the surrender of the mind. Can anything exist independent of Perumal? All is Perumal alone. He acts through all. Why worry ourselves?

27th December, 1938

Talk 601.

G. V. Subbaramiah, an Andhra devotee, mentioned something about *time*.

M.: What is *time*? It posits a state, one's recognition of it, and also the changes which affect it. The interval between two states is called *time*. A state cannot come into being unless the mind calls it into existence. The mind must be held by the Self. If the mind is not made use of there is no concept of time. Time and space are in the mind but one's true state lies beyond the mind. The question of time does not arise at all to the one established in one's true nature.

Mr. Narayana Iyer: Sri Bhagavan's words are so pleasing to hear but their import is beyond our comprehension. That seems to be far too much for us even to hope to realise.

G. V. S.: Our grasp is only intellectual. If Sri Bhagavan be pleased to direct us with a few instructions we shall be highly benefited.

M.: He who instructs an ardent seeker to do this or that is not a true master. The seeker is already afflicted by his activities and wants Peace and Rest. In other words he wants cessation of his activities. Instead of that he is told to do something in addition to, or in place of, his other activities. Can that be a help to the seeker?

Activity is creation; activity is the destruction of one's inherent happiness. If activity be advocated the adviser is not a master but the killer. Either the Creator (*Brahma*) or Death (*Yama*) may be said to have come in the guise of such a master. He cannot liberate the aspirant but strengthens his fetters.

D.: When we attempt to cease from activity the very attempt is action. So activity seems to be inevitable.

M.: True. Thayumanavar has also alluded to it. A doctor advises a patient to take the prescribed medicine with only one condition. That condition is not to think of a monkey when he takes the medicine. Can the patient ever take the medicine? Will he not think of the monkey whenever he tries not to do so?

So also, when people try to give up thoughts their object is frustrated by their very attempt.

D.: How then is the state to be attained?

M.: What is there to attain? A thing remains to be attained if it is not already attained. But here one's very being is *That*.

Someone: Why do we not then know it?

Annamalaiswami: I should always try to think *I am That*.

M.: Why should one think "I am That"? He is That only. Does a man go on thinking that he is a man?

Mr. Anantachari: The belief 'I am a man' is so deep that we cannot help thinking so.

M.: Why should you think "I am a man"? If you are challenged you may say 'I am a man'. Therefore the thought — 'I am a man' — is called up when another thought, say 'I am an animal', protrudes itself. Similarly, the thought *I am That* is necessary only so long as the other thought *I am a man* persists.

D.: The thought 'I am a man' is so firm that it cannot he got rid of.

M.: Be your true Self. Why should you think 'I am a man'?

D.: The thought 'I am a man' is so natural.

M.: Not so. On the other hand 'I am' is natural. Why do you qualify it with 'a man'?

D.: 'I am a man' is so obvious whereas 'I am That' is not understood by us.

M.: You are neither *That* nor *This*. The truth is 'I am'. "I AM that I AM" according to the Bible also. Mere Being is alone natural. To limit it to 'being a man' is uncalled for.

D.: (Humorously) If votes be taken the majority will be on my side. (Laughter)

M.: I cast my vote also on your side (Laughter). I say also 'I am a man': but I am not limited to the body. It is IN ME. That is the difference.

Someone: The limitation (*upadhi*) of being a man cannot be got rid of.

M.: How were you in deep sleep? There was no thought of being a man.

Another: So, the state of sleep must be brought about even when one is awake.

M.: Yes. It is *jagrat-sushupti*.

Sri Bhagavan continued: Some people even say that while they sleep they are enclosed somewhere in the body. They forget that such an idea did not persist in sleep but rises up only on waking. They bring their waking-state to bear upon their sleep.

The lights went down and all retired.

1st January, 1939

Talk 602.

Dr. Emile Gatheir, S. J., Professor of Philosophy at the Sacred Heart College, Shembaganur, Kodaikanal, asked: "Can you kindly give me a summary of your teachings?"

M.: They are found in small booklets, particularly *Who am I?*

D.: I shall read them. But may I have the central point of your teachings from your lips?

M.: The central point is the thing.

D.: It is not clear.

M.: Find the Centre.

D.: I am from God. Is not God distinct from me?

M.: Who asks this question? God does not ask it. You ask it. So find who you are and then you may find if God is distinct from you.

D.: But God is Perfect and I am imperfect. How can I ever know Him fully?

M.: God does not say so. The question is for you. After finding who you are you may see what God is.

D.: But you have fou... our Self. Please let us know if God is distinct from you.

M.: It is a matter of experience. Each one must experience it himself.

D.: Oh! I see. But God is Infinite and I am finite. I have a personality which can never merge into God. Is it not so?

M.: Infinity and Perfection do not admit of parts. If a finite being comes out of infinity the perfection of infinity is marred. Thus your statement is a contradiction in terms.

D.: No. I see both God and creation.

M.: How are you aware of your personality?

D.: I have a soul. I know it by its activities.

M.: Did you know it in deep sleep?

D.: The activities are suspended in deep sleep.

M.: But you exist in sleep. So do you now too. Which of these two is your real state?

D.: Sleep and waking are mere accidents. I am the substance behind the accidents.

(He looked up at the clock and said that it was time for him to catch the train. He left after thanking Sri Bhagavan. So the conversation ended abruptly).

8th January, 1939

Talk 603.

Lady Bateman came here with her daughter to visit Sri Bhagavan. She brought a letter from Pascaline Maillert, Versailles, which reads as follows:

"Two years have come and gone since last I crossed the threshold of Thy Ashram and yet in spirit I have ever remained there.

"Though illusion still often veils the vision of Reality revealed in the blessed Silence of Thy Presence.

"Though the Silver Thread of Self-awareness be often lost midst changing light and shadows, still the inner urge to realise the Self remains and stronger grows and more insistent as Grace and search go hand in hand.

580

"At times, yet rare, with no apparent cause, spontaneous awareness of the 'I' springs up and bliss fills the heart with glowing warmth. Effortless concentration goes with this state while all desires do come to rest fulfilled in utmost peace, till once more the veil is drawn and illusion seeks to blur the vision of the Real.

"Yet what the soul has experienced and knows repeatedly as Truth, can neither be denied nor ever forgotten and 'That which is' gives constant strength to persevere.

"I pray to Thee as to my Self for light and guidance that I know are ever there and at Thy feet lay offerings of unchanging love."

(Sd.) Pascaline, 11, Rue des Reservous.

Versailles, 21st November, 1938.

10th January, 1939

Talk 604.

A certain lady was singing a devotional song. It said among other things:

"Thou art my father,

Thou art my mother,

Thou art my relations,

My possessions and all," and so on.

Sri Bhagavan remarked with a smile, "Yes, Yes, Thou art this, that and everything except 'I'. Why not say 'I am Thou' and finish it?"

Talk 605.

A certain Andhra visitor gave Sri Bhagavan a slip of paper containing several questions which he desired to be answered. Sri Bhagavan took it in His hands, went through the questions and said:

M.: "All these questions arise so long as there is one who can ask questions. If the questioner is sought and found, the questions will end of their own accord."

The man said in reply: Several people raise these points and I do not know how to meet them. Hence I desire to know the fact (*vishaya* was the word used).

M.: If the *vishayi* (*i.e.*, the basis of the facts) be understood, the *vishayas* (*i.e.*, the facts) become clear.

Talk 606.

Mr. Venkatakrishnayya, a lawyer-devotee, visited Sri Bhagavan ten years before and asked Him what he should do to improve himself. Sri Bhagavan told him to perform *Gayatri Japa*. The young man went away satisfied. When he returned after some years, he asked:

D.: If I meditate on the meaning of the *Gayatri mantra*, my mind again wanders. What is to be done?

M.: Were you told to meditate on the *mantra* or its meaning? You must think of the one who repeats the *mantra*.

Again, the same man had seen another reputed Mahatma who told him to say *Om Namah* instead of "OM" because pure "OM" is meant for *sannyasis* whereas others can repeat *Om Namah*. When he came here he asked Sri Bhagavan about it. Sri Bhagavan replied casually:

Should not others besides the *sannyasis* enquire into the Self and realise it?

17th January, 1939

Talk 607.

Sri Bhagavan said to Lady Bateman: There is a fixed state; sleep, dream and waking states are mere movements in it. They are like pictures moving on the screen in a cinema show.

Everyone sees the screen as well as the pictures but ignores the screen and takes in the pictures alone. The *Jnani* however considers only the screen and not the pictures. The pictures certainly move on the screen yet do not affect it. The screen itself does not move but remains stationary.

Similarly, a person travels in a train and thinks that he moves. Really speaking he sits and reposes in his seat, and it is the train which is steaming fast. He however superimposes the motion of the train on himself because he has identified himself with the body. He says, "I have passed one station — now another — yet another —

and so on". A little consideration will show that he sits unmoved and the stations run past him. But that does not prevent him from saying that he has travelled all the way as if he exerted himself to move every foot of the way.

The *jnani* is fully aware that the true state of Being remains fixed and stationary and that all actions go on around him. His nature does not change and his state is not affected in the least. He looks on everything with unconcern and remains blissful himself.

His is the true state and also the primal and natural state of being. When once the man reaches it he gets fixed there. Fixed once, fixed ever he will be. Therefore that state which prevailed in the days of Pathala Linga Cellar continues uninterrupted, with only this difference that the body remained there immobile but is now active.

There is no difference between a *jnani* and an *ajnani* in their conduct. The difference lies only in their angles of vision. The ignorant man identifies himself with the ego and mistakes its activities for those of the Self, whereas the ego of the *jnani* has been lost and he does not limit himself to this body or that, this event or that, and so on.

There is action in seeming inaction, and also inaction in seeming action as in the following instances:

1. A child is fed while asleep. On waking up the next morning, he denies having been fed. It is a case of inaction in seeming action. For although the mother saw him take his food the child himself is not aware.

2. The cartman sleeps in the cart when it jogs along the way in the night and yet he reaches the destination and claims to have driven the cart. This is a case of action in seeming inaction.

3. A man appearing to listen to a story nods his head to the speaker but yet his mind is otherwise active and he does not really follow the story.

4. Two friends sleep side by side. One of them dreams that both of them travel round the globe and have varied experiences. On waking the dreamer tells the other that both of them have been round the earth. The other treats the story with contempt.

The lady protested that dream and sleep do not make any appeal to her. She was asked why then she should be careful about her bed unless she courted sleep.

She said that it was for relaxation of the exhausted limbs, rather a state of auto-intoxication. "The sleep state is really dull, whereas the waking state is full of beautiful and interesting things."

M.: What you consider to be filled with beautiful and interesting things is indeed the dull and ignorant state of sleep, according to the *Jnani: Ya nisha sarva bhootanam tasyam jagrati samyami.*

The wise one is wide awake just where darkness rules for others. You must certainly wake up from the sleep which is holding you at present.

18th January, 1939

Talk 608.

Mrs. Hick Riddingh wrote two questions on a slip of paper and asked Sri Bhagavan if her interpretations were correct.

M.: The Self is beyond ignorance and knowledge. It is Absolute. These doubts do not arise to the Self for it is Pure Consciousness and cannot admit of dark ignorance.

D.: From our point of view they arise.

M.: See to whom they arise. Go to their root. See if they arise after you reach their source and hold on to it.

D.: But at the present moment -

M.: Such discussions are theoretical and there will be no end to them. One must be practical and try to solve the problems for oneself by the method suggested. The method has been pointed out already. Find out to whom the questions arise. They resolve themselves immediately.

Talk 609.

Lady Bateman and others came to the hall at about 3-30 p.m. In a few minutes she asked in writing if one is nearer to Pure Consciousness in deep sleep than in the waking state.

M.: The sleep, dream and waking states are mere phenomena appearing on the Self which is itself stationary and also a state of

584

simple awareness. Can anyone remain away from the Self at any moment? This question can arise only if that were possible.

D.: Is it not often said that one is nearer Pure Consciousness in deep slumber than in the waking state?

M.: The question may as well be: Am I nearer to myself in my sleep than in my waking state?

For the Self is Pure Consciousness. No one can ever be away from the Self. The question is possible only if there is duality. But there is no duality in the state of Pure Consciousness.

The same person sleeps, dreams and wakes up. The waking state is considered to be full of beautiful and interesting things. The absence of such experiences makes one say that the sleep state is dull. Before we proceed further let us make this point clear. Do you not admit that you exist in your sleep?

D.: Yes, I do.

M.: You are the same person that is now awake. Is it not so?

D.: Yes.

M.: So there is a continuity in the sleep and the waking states. What is that continuity? It is only the state of Pure Being.

There is a difference in the two states. What is that difference? The incidents, namely, the body, the world and the objects appear in the waking state but they disappear in sleep.

D.: But I am not aware in my sleep.

M.: True, there is no awareness of the body or of the world. But you must exist in your sleep in order to say now "I was not aware in my sleep". Who says so now? It is the wakeful person. The sleeper cannot say so. That is to say, the individual who is now identifying the Self with the body says that such awareness did not exist in sleep.

Because you identify yourself with the body, you see the world around you and say that the waking state is filled with beautiful and interesting things. The sleep state appears dull because you were not there as an individual and therefore these things were not. But what is the fact? There is the continuity of Being in all the three states, but no continuity of the individual and the objects.

D.: Yes.

M.: That which is continuous is also enduring, *i.e.* permanent. That which is discontinuous is transitory.

D.: Yes.

M.: Therefore the state of Being is permanent and the body and the world are not. They are fleeting phenomena passing on the screen of Being-Consciousness which is eternal and stationary.

D.: Relatively speaking, is not the sleep state nearer to Pure Consciousness than the waking state?

M.: Yes, in this sense: When passing from sleep to waking the 'I' thought must start; the mind comes into play; thoughts arise; and then the functions of the body come into operation; all these together make us say that we are awake. The absence of all this evolution is the characteristic of sleep and therefore it is nearer to Pure Consciousness than the waking state.

But one should not therefore desire to be always in sleep. In the first place it is impossible, for it will necessarily alternate with the other states. Secondly it cannot be the state of bliss in which the *jnani* is, for his state is permanent and not alternating. Moreover, the sleep state is not recognised to be one of awareness by people, but the sage is always aware. Thus the sleep state differs from the state in which the sage is established.

Still more, the sleep state is free from thoughts and their impression to the individual. It cannot be altered by one's will because effort is impossible in that condition. Although nearer to Pure Consciousness, it is not fit for efforts to realise the Self.

The incentive to realise can arise only in the waking state and efforts can also be made only when one is awake. We learn that the thoughts in the waking state form the obstacle to gaining the stillness of sleep. "Be still and know that I AM God". So stillness is the aim of the seeker. Even a single effort to still at least a single thought even for a trice goes a long way to reach the state of quiescence. Effort is required and it is possible in the waking state only. There is the effort here: there is awareness also; the thoughts are stilled; so there is the peace of sleep gained. That is the state of the *jnani*. It is neither sleep nor waking but intermediate between the two. There is the awareness of the waking state and the stillness of sleep. It is called *jagrat-sushupti*. Call it wakeful sleep or sleeping wakefulness or sleepless waking or wakeless sleep. It is not the same as sleep or waking separately. It is *atijagrat*[1] (beyond wakefulness) or *atisushupti*[2] (beyond sleep). It is the state of perfect awareness and of perfect stillness combined. It lies between sleep and waking; it is also the interval between two successive thoughts. It is the source from which thoughts spring; we see that when we wake up from sleep. In other words thoughts have their origin in the stillness of sleep. The thoughts make all the difference between the stillness of sleep and the turmoil of waking. Go to the root of the thoughts and you reach the stillness of sleep. But you reach it in the full vigour of search, that is, with perfect awareness.

That is again *jagrat-sushupti* spoken of before. It is not dullness; but it is Bliss. It is not transitory but it is eternal. From that the thoughts proceed. What are all our experiences but thoughts? Pleasure and pain are mere thoughts. They are within ourselves. If you are free from thoughts and yet aware, you are That Perfect Being.

Lady Bateman appreciated the discourse and thanked Sri Bhagavan. Later, she said that she would be leaving the next day.

Sri Bhagavan smiled and said: You do not leave one place for another. You are always stationary. The scenes go past you. Even from the ordinary point of view you sit in your cabin and the ship sails but you do not move. We see a picture of a man running several miles and rushing towards us but the screen does not move. It is the picture that moves on and away.

D.: I see, but I can understand it only after I realise the Self.

M.: The Self is always realised. Were Realisation something to be gained hereafter there is an equal chance of its being lost. It will thus be only transitory. Transitory bliss brings pain in its train. It cannot be liberation which is eternal.

Were it true that you realise it later it means that you are not realised now. Absence of Realisation of the present moment may be repeated

---

[1] *Jagrat of jagrat.*

[2] 'Sleep of sleep'. It is beyond *jagrat* and sleep as well as in them.

at any moment in the future, for Time is infinite. So too, such realisation is impermanent. But that is not true. It is wrong to consider Realisation to be impermanent. It is the True Eternal State which cannot change.

D.: Yes, I shall understand it in course of time.

M.: You are already That. Time and space cannot affect the Self. They are in you; so also all that you see around you are in you. There is a story to illustrate this point: A lady had a precious necklace round her neck. Once in her excitement she forgot it and thought that the necklace was lost. She became anxious and looked for it in her home but could not find it. She asked her friends and neighbours if they knew anything about the necklace. They did not. At last a kind friend of hers told her to feel the necklace round the neck. She found that it had all along been round her neck and she was happy! When others asked her later if she found the necklace which was lost, she said, "Yes, I have found it." She still felt that she had recovered a lost jewel.

Now did she lose it at all? It was all along round her neck. But judge her feelings. She is happy as if she had recovered a lost jewel. Similarly with us, we imagine that we would realise that Self some time, whereas we are never anything but the Self.

D.: I feel that I am transplanted into some other land than the earth.

Sri Bhagavan, while looking into some correspondence, heard it, smiled and said: This is the Kingdom of Heaven. The Kingdom of Heaven mentioned in the Bible and this world are not two different regions. "The Kingdom is within you," says the Bible. So it is. The realised being sees this as the Kingdom of Heaven whereas the others see it as 'this world'. The difference lies only in the angles of vision.

D.: How can we deny the world and the people therein? I hear some music. It is sweet and grand. I recognise it to be Wagner's music. I cannot claim it to be mine.

M.: Does Wagner or his music exist apart from you? Unless you are there to say that it is Wagner's music, can you be aware of it? Without being aware of it, can it be said to exist? To make it more clear, do you recognise Wagner's music in your deep sleep? And yet you admit that you exist in sleep. So it is clear that Wagner and music are only your thoughts. They are in you and not out of you.

D.: It is beautiful.

[*Compiler's remarks:* Everyone is apt to be confused from time to time. Although the truth is heard and understood, at times it is forgotten, and mistakes are committed when facts face the person. Knowledge gives place to ignorance and confusion is the result. But the sage alone can give the right turn to our thoughts from time to time. That is the necessity for *Satsanga i.e.,* association with the Wise.]

Talk 610.

A devotee came with these questions.

1. Since individual souls and the Brahman are one, what is the cause of this creation?

2. Is the Brahma-*jnani* liable to bodily pains and rebirth? Can he extend his span of life or curtail it?

M.: The object of creation is to remove the confusion of your individuality. The question shows that you have identified yourself with the body and therefore see yourself and the world around. You think that you are the body. Your mind and intellect are the factors of your wrong identity.

Do you exist in your sleep?

D.: I do.

M.: The same being is now awake and asks these questions. Is it not so?

D.: Yes.

M.: These questions did not arise in your sleep. Did they?

D.: No.

M.: Why not? Because you did not see your body and no thoughts arose. You did not identify yourself with the body then. Therefore these questions did not arise.

They arise now because of your identity with the body. Is it not so?

D.: Yes.

M.: Now see which is your real nature. Is it that which is free from thoughts or that which is full of thoughts?

589

Being is continuous. The thoughts are discontinuous. So which is permanent?

D.: Being.

M.: That is it. Realise it. That is your true nature. Your nature is simple Being, free from thoughts.

Because you identify yourself with the body you want to know about creation. The world and the objects including your body appear in the waking state but disappear in the state of sleep. You exist all through these states. What is it then that persists through all these states? Find it out. That is your Self.

D.: Supposing it is found, what then?

M.: Find it out and see. There is no use asking hypothetical questions.

D.: Am I then one with Brahman?

M.: Leave Brahman alone. Find who you are. Brahman can take care of Himself.

If you cease to identify yourself with the body no questions regarding creation, birth, death, etc., will arise. They did not arise in your sleep. Similarly they will not arise in the true state of the Self.

The object of creation is thus clear, that you should proceed from where you find yourself and realise your true Being

You could not raise the question in your sleep because there is no creation there. You raise the question now because your thoughts appear and there is creation. Creation is thus found to be only your thoughts.

Take care of yourself and the Brahma-*jnani* will take care of Himself. If you know your true nature, you will understand the state of Brahma-*jnana*. It is futile to explain it now. Because you think that you see a *jnani* before you and you identify him with a body just as you have identified yourself with yours, you also think that he feels pains and pleasures like yourself.

D.: But I must know if he is a *jnani* for I must be inspired by him.

M.: Yes, he tells you; he inspires. Do as he tells you. You want to learn and not test him.

Jnana lakshanas are stated in the *sastras* to be an incentive to a seeker to get rid of misery and seek happiness. The methods are given.

If they are followed the result will be *jnana* having those *lakshanas*. They are not meant for testing others.

Talk 611.

D.: I think that the soul is the light within. If after death it becomes one with Brahman how can there be transmigration of soul?

M.: Within whom? Who dies?

D.: I shall then frame my question in a different way.

M.: Dialectics are not wanted. Consider the answer and see.

D.: How?

M.: Now that you identify yourself with the body you say that the soul is the light within. You mean that there is light within the body.

Think a little and say if the body can raise any questions. It is insentient and cannot say 'I'. Something else says 'I'. What is it? Can it be the Self? The Self is pure and is not aware of any other so as to be able to say 'I'. Who then says 'I'? It is the link between the pure *Chit* (the Self) and the *jada* (the body). That is the ego. Who are you now? What is it that is born? The Self is eternal and cannot be born. The body appears and disappears and your identity with it makes you speak of birth and death. See if the true significance of 'I' can ever take birth. For whom is transmigration?

D.: Sir, we are here to have our doubts cleared.

M.: Certainly.

D.: Our doubts can be cleared only when we ask questions.

M.: Yes. No one objects to questions being asked.

D.: It is said *pariprasnena sevaya* (by questioning again and again and by service). So we should ask questions and the Master should kindly remove our doubts.

M.: Continue your quotation *upadekshyanti tattvam* (They give instructions in Truth).

D.: Yes. But our doubts must be cleared.

M.: So it was with Arjuna. For he says in the end *nashto mohah smritirlabdha* (lost is my ignorance; memory restored).

D.: It was in the end. Before then he asked so many questions.

M.: The Truth was revealed even at the start. For the very first sloka of Sri Krishna's *upadesa* starts: "No birth and no death, no change, etc."

D.: Sri Krishna also says, "We have had many rebirths. I am aware of them; but you are not."

M.: That was only because the question arose how Sri Krishna could claim to have taught the eternal Truth to Aditya. The Truth was stated even at the start. Arjuna did not understand it. The *jnani's* state was later described and also the means of attainment. Incidentally Sri Krishna said that the Truth was eternal and that He had originally taught the same to Aditya. Arjuna was all along identifying himself with the body and therefore thought that Sri Krishna also was the body in front of him. He therefore asked, "How can it be? You (Sri Krishna) were born of Devaki some years before. Aditya was among those who started creation. How could you have taught this Truth to Aditya?"

Sri Krishna continues to answer Arjuna's questions in that strain: "Many rebirths we have had. I know them all; but you do not," and so on.

D.: We must also know the Truth.

M.: You are taught the Truth. Instructions have been given. See who you are. That is the whole instruction.

19th January, 1939

Talk 612.

Mrs. Hick Riddingh asked Sri Bhagavan in writing:

When Bhagavan writes about the help given towards attaining Self-Realisation by the gracious glance of the Master or looking upon the Master, how exactly is this to be understood?"

M.: Who is the Master? Who is the seeker?

D.: The Self.

M.: If the Self be the Master and also the seeker, how can the questions arise at all?

D.: That is just my difficulty. I must seek the Self within myself. What is then the significance of the writing above referred to? It seems contradictory.

M.: It is not. The statement has not been rightly understood.

If the seeker knows the Master to be the Self he sees no duality in other respects either and is therefore happy, so that no questions arise for him.

But the seeker does not bring the truth of the statement to bear in practice. It is because of his ignorance. This ignorance is however unreal. The Master is required to wake up the seeker from the slumber of ignorance and he therefore uses these words in order to make Reality clear to others.

The only thing that matters is that you see the Self. This can be done wherever you remain. The Self must be sought within. The search must be steadfast. If that is gained there is no need to stay near the Master as a physical being.

The 'statement' is meant for those who cannot find the Self remaining where they are.

Mr. Ward Jackson: The lady's difficulty is real and I sympathise with her. She asks, "If we could see the Self within ourselves, why should we have come all the way to see Him? We had been thinking of Him so long and it is only right that we came here. Is it then unnecessary to do so?"

M.: You have done well in having come. *"Isvaro gururatmeti"* (The Self is the God and Guru). A person seeks happiness and learns that God alone can make one happy. He prays to God and worships Him. God hears his prayers, and responds by appearing in human shape as a Master in order to speak the language of the devotee and make him understand the Reality. The Master is thus God manifest as human being. He gives out His experience so that the seeker might also gain it. His experience is to abide as the Self. The Self is within. God, Master and the Self are therefore seeming stages in the Realisation of the Truth. You have doubts on reading books. You have come here to have them cleared. That is only right.

Mrs. H. R.: I understand the Self to be the Master and must be sought within. So I can do it where I live.

M.: The understanding has been theoretical. When it is put into practice difficulties and doubts arise. If you can feel the presence of the Master where you are, your doubts are readily overcome, for the Master's part consists in removing the doubts of the seeker.

The purpose of your visit is fulfilled if the doubts do not arise hereafter, and you apply yourself steadily in the search for the Self.

D.: I understand it all along.

M.: Good. The objection is not to your conclusion but it is to your doubts.

Mr. W. J.: When we read about it we read it intellectually. But it is all too remote. When we see you in body we are brought nearer to Reality and it gives us courage to bring our knowledge into our everyday life.

If one realised the Self and acted up to it in the West, one would be locked up in a lunatic asylum. (Laughter.)

M.: You will be locking yourself in. Because the world is mad, considers you mad. Where is the lunatic asylum if it is not within. You will not be in it, but it will be in you. (Laughter).

Uncertainties, doubts and fears are natural to everyone until the Self is realised. They are inseparable from the ego, rather they are the ego.

D.: How are they to disappear?

M.: They are the ego. If the ego goes they go with it. The ego is itself unreal. What is the ego? Enquire. The body is insentient and cannot say 'I' . The Self is pure consciousness and non-dual. It cannot say 'I' . No one says, 'I' in sleep. What is the ego then? It is something intermediate between the inert body and the Self. It has no *locus standi*. If sought for it vanishes like a ghost. You see, a man imagines that there is something by his side in darkness; it may be some dark object. If he looks closely the ghost is not to be seen, but some dark object which he could identify as a tree or a post, etc. If he does not look closely the ghost strikes terror in the person. All that is required is only to look closely and the ghost vanishes. The ghost was never there. So also with the ego. It is an intangible link between the body and Pure Consciousness. It is not real. So long as one does not look closely it continues to give trouble. But when one looks for it, it is found not to exist.

594

Again, in a Hindu marriage function, the feasts continue five or six days. A stranger was mistaken for the best man by the bride's party and they therefore treated him with special regard. Seeing him treated with special regard by the bride's party, the bridegroom's party considered him to be some man of importance related to the bride's party and therefore they too showed him special respect. The stranger had altogether a happy time of it. He was also all along aware of the real situation. On one occasion the groom's party wanted to refer to him on some point. They asked for him. He scented trouble and made himself scarce. So it is with the ego. If looked for, it disappears. If not, it continues to give trouble.

How it is to be looked for is learnt from those who have already done so. That is the reason why the Master is approached.

D.: If the search has to be made within, is it necessary to be in the physical proximity of the Master?

M.: It is necessary to do so until all doubts are at an end.

D.: If the ego is unreal and troublesome why did we take so much pains to develop it?

M.: Its growth and the trouble consequent on such growth make you look for the cause of it all. Its development is for its own destruction.

D.: Is it not said that one must be like a child before one advances spiritually?

M.: Yes, because the ego is not developed in the child.

D.: I mean exactly the same. We could have remained like the child instead of having developed the ego.

M.: The state of the child is meant. No one can take lessons from the child for the Realisation of the Self. The Master's state is like the state of the child. There is a difference between the two. The ego is potential in the child, whereas it is totally destroyed in the saint.

D.: Yes, I see, I understand it now.

M.: The Reality is alone and eternal. To understand it is good enough. But the old ignorance should not return. A good watch must be kept lest the present understanding of the Truth suffers later on.

A disciple served a master a long time and realised the Self. He was in Bliss and wanted to express his gratitude to the master. He was in tears of joy and his voice choked when he spoke. He said, "What a wonder that I did not know my very Self all these years? I suffered long and you so graciously helped me to realise the Self. How shall I repay your Grace? It is not in my power to do it!" The master replied: "Well, well. Your repayment consists in not lapsing into ignorance over again but in continuing in the state of your real Self."

[*Compiler's remarks:* The Self is the Master and all else. The Realisation of the Self means Self-surrender or merging into the Master. What more can anyone do? That is the highest form of gratitude to the Master].

21st January, 1939

Talk 613.

A young man asked: "Are thoughts mere matter?"

M.: What do you mean? Do you mean 'matter' like the things you see around you?

D.: Yes — gross.

M.: Who asks this question? Who is the thinker?

D.: The thinker is spirit.

M.: Do you then mean that spirit generates matter?

D.: I want to know.

M.: How do you distinguish between matter and spirit?

D.: Spirit is consciousness and the other not.

M.: Can consciousness generate non-consciousness, or light darkness?

24th January, 1939

Talk 614.

There were a few respectable men in the hall. Sri Bhagavan spoke to them some time after their arrival. Where is the use of trying to remember the past or discover the future? That which matters is only the present. Take care of it and the other things will take care of themselves.

D.: Is it bad to desire something?

M.: One should not be elated on having his desire fulfilled or disappointed on being frustrated. To be elated on the fulfilment of desire is so deceitful. A gain will certainly be lost ultimately. Therefore elation must end in pain at a future date. One should not give place to feelings of pleasure or pain, come what may. How do the events affect the person? You do not grow by acquiring something nor wither away by losing it. You remain what you always are.

D.: We worldly men cannot resist desire.

M.: You may desire but be prepared for any eventuality. Make effort, but do not be lost in the result. Accept with equanimity whatever happens. For pleasure and pain are mere mental modes. They have no relation to the objective realities.

D.: How?

M.: There were two young friends in a village in South India. They were learned and wanted to earn something with which they might afford relief to their respective families. They took leave of their parents and went to Benares on a pilgrimage. On the way one of them died. The other was left alone. He wandered for a time, and in the course of a few months he made a good name and earned some money. He wanted to earn more before he returned to his home. In the meantime he met a pilgrim who was going south and would pass through the native village of the young pandit. He requested the new acquaintance to tell his parents that he would return after a few months with some funds and also that his companion had died on the way. The man came to the village and found the parents. He gave them the news, but changed the names of the two men. Consequently the parents of the living man bemoaned his supposed loss and the parents of the dead man were happy expecting the return of their son bringing rich funds as well.

You see therefore that pleasure and pain have no relation to the actualities but are mere mental modes.

Talk 615.

Another from the group asked: How is the ego to be destroyed?

M.: Hold the ego first and then ask how it is to be destroyed. Who asks this question? It is the ego. Can the ego ever agree to kill itself? This question is a sure way to cherish the ego and not to kill it. If you seek the ego you will find it does not exist. That is the way to destroy it.

In this connection I am often reminded of a funny incident which took place when I was living in the West Chitrai Street in Madura. A neighbour in an adjoining house anticipated the visit of a thief to his house. He took precautions to catch him. He posted policemen in mufti to guard the two ends of the lane, the entrance and the back-door to his own house. The thief came as expected and the men rushed to catch him. He took in the situation at a glance and shouted "Hold him, hold him. There — he runs — there — there." Saying so he made good his escape.

So it is with the ego. Look for it and it will not be found. That is the way to get rid of it.

23rd to 28th January, 1939

Talk 616.

D.: Is the *Jivanadi* an entity or a figment of the imagination?

M.: The *yogis* say that there is a *nadi* called the *jivanadi, atmanadi* or *paranadi*. The Upanishads speak of a centre from which thousands of *nadis* branch off. Some locate such a centre in the brain and others in other centres. The *Garbhopanishad* traces the formation of the foetus and the growth of the child in the womb. The *jiva* is considered to enter the child through the fontanelle in the seventh month of its growth. In evidence thereof it is pointed out that the fontanelle is tender in a baby and is also seen to pulsate. It takes some months for it to ossify. Thus the *jiva* comes from above, enters through the fontanelle and works through the thousands of the *nadis* which are spread over the whole body. Therefore the seeker of Truth must concentrate on the *sahasrara*, that is the brain, in order to regain his source. *Pranayama* is said to help the *yogi* to rouse the *Kundalini Sakti* which lies coiled in the solar plexus. The *sakti* rises through a nerve called the *Sushumna*, which is imbedded in the core of the spinal cord and extends to the brain.

If one concentrates on the *Sahasrara* there is no doubt that the ecstasy of *samadhi* ensues. The *vasanas*, that is the latencies, are not however destroyed. The *yogi* is therefore bound to wake up from the *samadhi*, because release from bondage has not yet been accomplished. He must still try to eradicate the *vasanas* in order that the latencies yet inherent in him may not disturb the peace of his *samadhi*. So he passes down from the *sahasrara* to the heart through what is called the *jivanadi*, which is only a continuation of the *Sushumna*. The *Sushumna* is thus a curve. It starts from the solar plexus, rises through the spinal cord to the brain and from there bends down and ends in the heart. When the *yogi* has reached the heart, the *samadhi* becomes permanent. Thus we see that the heart is the final centre.

Some Upanishads also speak of 101 nadis which spread from the heart, one of them being the vital *nadi*. If the *jiva* comes down from above and gets reflected in the brain, as the *yogis* say, there must be a reflecting surface in action. That must also be capable of limiting the Infinite Consciousness to the limits of the body. In short the Universal Being becomes limited as a *jiva*. Such reflecting medium is furnished by the aggregate of the *vasanas* of the individual. It acts like the water in a pot which reflects the image of an object. If the pot be drained of its water there will be no reflection. The object will remain without being reflected. The object here is the Universal Being-Consciousness which is all-pervading and therefore immanent in all. It need not be cognised by reflection alone; it is self-resplendent. Therefore the seeker's aim must be to drain away the *vasanas* from the heart and let no reflection obstruct the Light of Eternal Consciousness. This is achieved by the search for the origin of the ego and by diving into the heart. This is the direct method for Self-Realisation. One who adopts it need not worry about *nadis*, the brain, the *Sushumna*, the *Paranadi*, the *Kundalini, pranayama* or the six centres.

The Self does not come from anywhere else and enter the body through the crown of the head. It is as it is, ever sparkling, ever steady, unmoving and unchanging. The changes which are noticed are not inherent in the Self which abides in the Heart and is self-luminous like the Sun. The changes are seen in Its Light. The relation between the Self and the body or the mind may be compared to that of a clear crystal and its background. If the crystal is placed against a red flower, it shines red; if placed against a green leaf it shines green, and so on. The individual confines himself to the limits of the changeful body or of the mind which derives its existence from the unchanging Self. All that is necessary is to give up this mistaken identity, and that done, the ever-shining Self will be seen to be the single non-dual Reality.

The reflection of Consciousness is said to be in the subtle body (*sukshma sarira*), which appears to be composed of the brain and the nerves radiating from it to all parts of the trunk, chiefly through the spinal column and the solar plexus.

When I was on the Hill, Nayana (Kavyakantha Ganapathi Muni) once argued that the brain was the seat of the *vasanas*, because it consisted of innumerable cells in which the *vasanas* were contained and illuminated by the light of the Self which projected from the heart. Only this set a person working or thinking.

But I said, "How can it be so? The *vasanas* must be with one's Self and can never remain away from the Self. If, as you say, the *vasanas* be contained in the brain and the Heart is the seat of the Self, a person who is decapitated must be rid of his *vasanas* and should not be reborn. You agree that it is absurd. Now can you say that the Self is in the brain with the *vasanas*? If so, why should the head bend down when one falls asleep? Moreover a person does not touch his head and say 'I'. Therefore it follows that the Self is in the Heart and the *vasanas* are also there in an exceedingly subtle form.

"When the *vasanas* are projected from the Heart they are associated with the Light of the Self and the person is said to think. The *vasanas* which lie imbedded in an atomic condition grow in size in their passage from the heart to the brain. The brain is the screen on which the images of the *vasanas* are thrown and it is also the place of their functional distribution. The brain is the seat of the mind, and the mind works through it."

So then this is what happens. When a *vasana* is released and it comes into play, it is associated with the light of the Self. It passes from the heart to the brain and on its way it grows more and more until it holds the field all alone and all the *vasanas* are thus kept in

600

abeyance for the time being. When the thought is reflected in the brain it appears as an image on a screen. The person is then said to have a clear perception of things. He is a great thinker or discoverer. Neither the thought that is extolled as being original, nor the thing, nor the country which is claimed to be a new discovery, is really original or new. It could not manifest unless it was already in the mind. It was of course very subtle and remained imperceptible, because it lay repressed by the more urgent or insistent thoughts or *vasanas*. When they have spent themselves this thought arises and by concentration the Light of the Self makes it clear, so that it appears magnificent, original and revolutionary. In fact it was only within all along.

This concentration is called *samyamana* in the Yoga *Sastras*. One's desires can be fulfilled by this process and it is said to be a *siddhi*. It is how the so-called new discoveries are made. Even worlds can be created in this manner. *Samyamana* leads to all *siddhis*. But they do not manifest so long as the ego lasts. Concentration according to yoga ends in the destruction of the experiencer (ego), experience and the world, and then the quondam desires get fulfilled in due course. This concentration bestows on individuals even the powers of creating new worlds. It is illustrated in the *Aindava Upakhyana* in the *Yoga Vasishta* and in the *Ganda Saila Loka* in the *Tripura Rahasya*.

Although the powers appear to be wonderful to those who do not possess them, yet they are only transient. It is useless to aspire for that which is transient. All these wonders are contained in the one changeless Self. The world is thus within and not without. This meaning is contained in verses 11 and 12 — Chapter V of *Sri Ramana Gita* "The entire Universe is condensed in the body, and the entire body in the Heart. Thus the Heart is the nucleus of the whole Universe." Therefore *Samyamana* relates to concentration on different parts of the body for the different *siddhis*. Also the *Visva* or the *Virat* is said to contain the cosmos within the limits of the body. Again, "The world is not other than the mind, the mind is not other than the Heart; that is the whole truth." So the Heart comprises all. This is what is taught to Svetaketu by the illustration of the seed of a fig tree.

The source is a point without any dimensions. It expands as the cosmos on the one hand and as Infinite Bliss on the other. That point is the pivot. From it a single *vasana* starts, multiplies as the experiencer 'I', experience, and the world. The experiencer and the source are referred to in the *mantra*. Two birds, exactly alike, arise simultaneously.

When I was staying in the Skandasramam I sometimes used to go out and sit on a rock. On one such occasion there were two or three others with me including Rangaswami Iyengar. Suddenly we noticed some small moth-like insect shooting up like a rocket into the air from a crevice in the rock. Within the twinkling of an eye it had multiplied itself into millions of moths which formed a cloud and hid the sky from view. We wondered at it and examined the place from which it shot up. We found that it was only a pinhole and knew that so many insects could not have issued from it in such a short time.

That is how *ahankara* (ego) shoots up like a rocket and instantaneously spreads out as the Universe.

The Heart is therefore the centre. A person can never be away from it. If he is he is already dead. Although the Upanishads say that the *jiva* functions through other centres on different occasions, yet he does not relinquish the Heart. The centres are simply places of business (vide *Vedanta Chudamani*). The Self is bound to the Heart, like a cow tethered to a peg. The movements are controlled by the length of the rope. All its wanderings centre around the peg.

A caterpillar crawls on a blade of grass and when it has come to the end, it seeks another support. While doing so it holds on with its hind-legs to the blade of grass, lifts the body and sways to and fro before it can hold another. Similarly it is with the Self. It stays in the Heart and holds other centres also according to circumstances. But its activities always centre round the Heart.

Talk 617.

There are five states for the individual. They are: (1) *Jagrat*, (2) *Swapna*, (3) *Sushupti*, (4) *Turiya*, (5) *Turyatita*. Of these the *jagrat* is the waking state.

In it the *jiva* in the *Visva* aspect and the Lord in the *Virat* aspect, abiding together in the eight petals of the Heart lotus, function through the eyes and enjoy novel pleasures from various objects by means of all the senses, organs, etc. The five gross elements which are widespread, the ten senses, the five vital airs, the four inner faculties, the twenty-four fundamentals — all these together form the gross body. The *jagrat* state is characterised by *satva guna* denoted by the letter *A* and presided over by the deity Vishnu. The *swapna* is the dream state in which the *jiva* in the *Taijasa* aspect and the Lord in the *Hiranyagarbha* aspect, abiding together in the corolla of the Heart-Lotus, function in the neck and experience through the mind the results of the impressions collected in the waking state. All the principles, the five gross elements, the will and the intellect, seventeen in all, together form the subtle body of the dream which is characterised by the *rajo guna* denoted by the letter *U* and presided over by the deity Brahma, so say the wise.

The *sushupti* is the state of deep sleep in which the *jiva* in the *Prajna* aspect and the Lord in the *Isvara* aspect, abiding together in the stamen of the Heart-Lotus, experience the bliss of the Supreme by means of the subtle *avidya* (nescience). Just as a hen after roaming about in the day calls the chicks to her, enfolds them under her wings and goes to rest for the night, so also the subtle individual being, after finishing the experiences of the *jagrat* and *swapna* for the time being, enters with the impressions gathered during those states into the causal body which is made up of nescience, characterised by *tamo guna*, denoted by the letter *M* and presided over by the deity Rudra.

Deep sleep is nothing but the experience of pure *being*. The three states go by different names, such as the three regions, the three forts, the three deities, etc. The being always abides in the Heart, as stated above. If in the *jagrat* state the Heart is not relinquished, the mental activities are stilled and Brahman alone is contemplated, the state is called the *Turiya*. Again when the individual being merges in the Supreme it is called the *turyatita*. The vegetable kingdom is always in *sushupti*; the animals have both *swapna* and *sushupti*; the gods (celestials) are always in *jagrat*; man has all the three states; but the

603

clear-sighted yogi abides only in *turiya*, and the highest yogi remains in *turyatita* alone.

The three states alternate involuntarily for the average man. The last two (*turiya* and *turyatita*) are however the results of practice and form clear aids to liberation. Of the other three states (*Jagrat, swapna* and *sushupti*) each one is exclusive of the other two and limited by the conditions of time and space. They are therefore unreal.

Our very experience of the *jagrat* and the *swapna* states proves that the Consciousness as the Self underlies all the five states, remains perfect all along and witnesses all of them. But with regard to similar consciousness in the deep sleep, every person is known to say "I was not aware of anything; I slept soundly and happily". Two facts emerge from the statement (unawareness of anything and the happiness of sound sleep). Unless these existed and were experienced in sleep they could not find expression by the same person in the waking state. Inference also leads to the same conclusion. Just as the eye sees the darkness which remains enveloping all objects, so also the Self sees the darkness of nescience which remained covering the phenomenal world.

This darkness was experienced when it (the Self) emerged in dots of supreme bliss, shone a trice and fleeted away in such fine subtlety as the rays of the moon which peer through the waving foliage. The experience was however not through any media (such as the senses of the mind), but bears out the fact that consciousness does exist in deep sleep. The unawareness is owing to the absence of relative knowledge, and the happiness to the absence of (seething) thoughts.

If the experience of bliss in deep sleep is a fact, how is it that no one among all the human beings recollects it? A diver who has found the desired thing under water cannot make his discovery known to the expectant persons on the shore until he emerges from the water. Similarly the sleeper cannot express his experience because he cannot contact the organs of expression until he is awakened by his *vasanas* in due course. Therefore it follows that the Self is the light of *Sat, Chit, Ananda.*

Visva, Taijasa and *Prajna* are the denominations of the experiencer in the waking, dream and deep sleep states respectively. The same individual underlies all of them. They do not therefore represent the True Self which is pure *Sat, Chit, Ananda*. The experience in deep sleep was said to be the bliss of Brahman. It is only the negative aspect of such bliss, as it is the result of the absence of thoughts. Moreover it is transitory. Such a bliss is only the *abhasa*, the counterfeit of Supreme Bliss. It is not different from the blissful feeling of sensual pleasures. In deep sleep the *Prajna* is said to be united with the Self. So the individuality is potential in sleep.

The Self is the basis of all the experiences. It remains as the witness and the support of them all. The Reality is thus different from the three states, the waking, the dream and the deep sleep.

1st February, 1939

Talk 618.

A gentleman from Hardwar: When I go on analysing myself I go beyond the intellect, and then there is no happiness.

M.: Intellect is only an instrument of the Self. It cannot help you to know what is beyond itself.

D.: I understand it. But there is no happiness beyond it.

M.: The intellect is the instrument wherewith to know unknown things. But you are already known, being the Self which is itself knowledge; so you do not become the object of knowledge. The intellect makes you see things outside, and not that which is its own source.

D.: The question is repeated.

M.: The intellect is useful thus far, it helps you to analyse yourself, and no further. It must then be merged into the ego, and the source of the ego must be sought. If that be done the ego disappears. Remain as that source and then the ego does not arise

D.: There is no happiness in that state.

M.: 'There is no happiness' is only a thought. The Self is bliss, pure and simple. You are the Self. So you cannot but be bliss; being so, you cannot say here is no happiness. That which says so cannot

605

be the Self; it is the non-Self and must be got rid of in order to realise the bliss of the Self.

D.: How is that to be done?

M.: See wherefrom the thought arises. It is the mind. See for whom the mind or intellect functions. For the ego. Merge the intellect in the ego and seek the source of the ego. The ego disappears. 'I know' and 'I do not know' imply a subject and an object. They are due to duality. The Self is pure and absolute, One and alone. There are no two selves so that one may know the other. What is duality then? It cannot be the Self which is One and alone. It must be non-Self. Duality is the characteristic of the ego. When thoughts arise duality is present; know it to be the ego, and seek its source.

The degree of the absence of thoughts is the measure of your progress towards Self-Realisation. But Self-Realisation itself does not admit of progress; it is ever the same. The Self remains always in realisation. The obstacles are thoughts. Progress is measured by the degree of removal of the obstacles to understanding that the Self is always realised. So thoughts must be checked by seeking to whom they arise. So you go to their Source, where they do not arise.

D.: Doubts are always arising. Hence my question.

M.: A doubt arises and is cleared; another arises and that is cleared, making way for another, and so it goes on. So there is no possibility of clearing away all doubts. See to *whom* the doubts arise. Go to their source and abide in it. Then they cease to arise. That is how doubts are to be cleared. *Atma samstham manah krtva na kinchidapi chintayet.*

D.: Grace alone can help me to it.

M.: Grace is not exterior. In fact your very desire for grace is due to grace that is already in you.

Talk 619.

An Andhra gentleman read out a verse from the *Viveka Chudamani* setting forth the sense of the *Maitreyi Brahmana* of the *Brihadaranyaka Upanishad* and asked the meaning of *atma* which occurred there.

M.: The Self.

D.: Is not *prema* (love) for something else?

M.: The desire for happiness (*sukha prema*) is a proof of the ever-existing happiness of the Self. Otherwise how can desire for it arise in you? If headache was natural to human beings no one would try to get rid of it. But everyone that has a headache tries to get rid of it, because he has known a time when he had no headache. He desires only that which is natural to him. So too he desires happiness because happiness is natural to him. Being natural, it is not acquired. Man's attempts can only be to get rid of misery. If that be done the ever-present bliss is felt. The primal bliss is obscured by the non-self which is synonymous with non-bliss or misery. *Duhkha nasam = sukha prapti.* (Loss of unhappiness amounts to gain of happiness.) Happiness mixed with misery is only misery. When misery is eliminated then the ever-present bliss is said to be gained. Pleasure which ends in pain is misery. Man wants to eschew such pleasure. Pleasures are *priya, moda* and *pra-moda.* When a desired object is near at hand there arises *priya*: when it is taken possession of *moda* arises; when it is being enjoyed *pra-moda* prevails. The reason for the pleasureableness of these states is that *one thought excludes all others, and then this single thought also merges into the Self.* These states are enjoyed in the *Anandamaya kosa* only. As a rule *Vijnanamaya kosa* prevails on waking. In deep sleep all thoughts disappear and the state of obscuration is one of bliss; there the prevailing body is the *Anandamaya.* These are sheaths and not the core, which is interior to all these. It lies beyond waking, dream and deep sleep. That is the Reality and consists of true bliss (*nijananda*).

D.: Is not *hatha* yoga necessary for the inquiry into the Self?

M.: Each one finds some one method suitable to himself, because of latent tendencies (*purva samskara*).

D.: Can *hatha* yoga be accomplished at my age?

M.: Why do you think of all that? Because you think it exterior to yourself you desire it and try for it. But do you not exist all along? Why do you leave yourself and go after something external?

D.: It is said in *Aparoksha-anubhuti* that *hatha* yoga is a necessary aid for inquiry into the Self.

M.: The *hatha* yogis claim to keep the body fit so that the enquiry may be effected without obstacles. They also say that life must be prolonged so that the enquiry may be carried to a successful end. Furthermore there are those who use some medicines (*kayakalpa*) with that end in view. Their favourite example is: the screen must be perfect before the painting is begun. Yes, but *which is the screen and which the painting*? According to them the body is the screen and the inquiry into the Self is the painting. But is not the body itself a picture on the screen, the Self?

D.: But *hatha* yoga is so much spoken of as an aid.

M.: Yes. Even great pandits well versed in the Vedanta continue the practice of it. Otherwise their minds will not subside. So you may say it is useful for those who cannot otherwise still the mind.

D.: Saguna upasana (worship of the personal God) is said to be imperfect. It is also said that *nirguna upasana* (devotion to the impersonal) is hard and risky. I am fit for the former only. What is to be done?

M.: The *Saguna* merges into the *nirguna* in the long run. The *saguna* purifies the mind and takes one to the final goal. The afflicted one, the seeker of knowledge, and the seeker of gains are all dear to God. *But the jnani is the Self of God.*

Talk 620.

D.: "Not this — not this". That is the teaching to the seeker. He is told that the Self is Supreme. How is it to be found?

M.: The Self is said to be the hearer, thinker, knower, etc. But that is not all. It is also described as the ear of ear, the mind of mind, etc.; and by what means to know the knower?

D.: But this does not say what the Self is.

M.: "Not this — not this".

D.: It only negates.

M.: (Silence).

The devotee complains that the Self is not pointed out.

M.: A man wants to know what he is. He sees animals and objects around him. He is told: 'You are not a cow, not a horse, not a tree, not

608

this, not that, and so on'. If again the man asks saying 'You have not said what I am,' the answer will be, 'It is not said you are not a man'. He must find out for himself that he is a man. So you must find out for yourself what you are.

You are told, 'You are not this body, nor the mind, nor the intellect, nor the ego, nor anything you can think of; find out what truly you are'. Silence denotes that the questioner is himself the Self that is to be found. In a *svayamvara* the maiden goes on saying 'no' to each one until she faces her choice and then she looks downwards and remains silent.

Talk 621.

Mr. Raj Krishna found Sri Bhagavan alone on the Hill at about 5-30 p.m. and prayed: I have been desiring since my tenth year to have a glimpse of the Reality. I firmly believe that I can be helped in this only by a sage like Sri Bhagavan. So I pray for Thy help.

Sri Bhagavan looked at him for a few minutes. The devotee interrupted, saying: "Even if I cannot realise in my life let me at least not forget it on my death bed: let me have a glimpse at least at the moment of death so that it may stand me in good stead in the future."

M.: It is said in the Bhagavad Gita, Ch. VIII, that whatever may be the last thought at death, it determines the later birth of the person. It is necessary to experience the Reality now in life in order that it may be experienced at death. See if this moment be different from the last one, and try to be in that desired state.

D.: I have limitations. I am unable to rise to the occasion. Grace can achieve for me what I cannot achieve myself.

M.: True, but unless there is grace this desire will not arise.

They were walking slowly, conversing at the same time. The devotee said: "There is a girl of eleven in Lahore. She is very remarkable. She says she can call upon Krishna twice and remain conscious, but if she calls the third time she becomes unconscious and remains in trance for ten hours continuously."

M.: So long as you think that Krishna is different from you, you call upon Him. Falling into trance denotes the transitoriness of the *samadhi*. You are always in *samadhi; that is what should be realised.*

609

D.: God-vision is glorious.

M.: God-vision is only vision of the Self objectified as the God of one's own faith. Know the Self.

Talk 622.

Sri Bhagavan has a bandage on his finger. Someone asked, "What is that?" Bhagavan replied: "The finger came upon a knife". (The Knife is inert, and relative to it the finger is a conscious agent).

Talk 623.

Sri Bhagavan said to another devotee that there are five states:

(1) Sleep, (2) Before waking, a state free from thoughts, (3) Sense of happiness of that freedom from thoughts (*rasasvada*), (4) The internal movement of the *vasanas* (*kashaya*) and (5) Complete waking with (distraction) *vikshepa*. The second of those should be made permanent.

4th February, 1939

Talk 624.

A devotee asked Sri Bhagavan: With every thought the subject and the object appear and disappear. Does not the 'I' disappear when the subject disappears thus? If that be so how can the quest of the 'I' proceed?

M.: The subject (knower) is only a mode of mind. Though the mode (*vritti*) passes, the reality behind it does not cease. The background of the mode is the 'I' in which the mind modes arise and sink.

D.: After describing the Self as *srota* (hearer), *manta* (thinker), *vijnata* (knower), etc., it is again described as *asrota, amanta, avijnata,* non-hearer, non-thinker, non-knower, Is it so?

M.: Just so. The common man is aware of himself only when modifications arise in the intellect (*vijnanamaya kosa*); these modifications are transient; they arise and set. Hence the *vijnanamaya* (intellect) is called a *kosa* or sheath. When pure awareness is left over it is itself the *Chit* (Self) or the Supreme. To be in one's natural state on the subsidence of thoughts is bliss; if that bliss be transient —

arising and setting — then it is only the *sheath* of bliss (*Anandamaya kosa*), not the pure Self. What is needed is to fix the attention on the pure 'I' after the subsidence of all thoughts and not to lose hold of it. This has to be described as an extremely subtle thought; else it cannot be spoken of at all, since it is no other than the Real Self. Who is to speak of it, to whom and how?

This is well explained in the *Kaivalyam* and the *Viveka Chudamani*. Thus though in sleep the awareness of the Self is not lost, the ignorance of the *jiva* is not affected by it. For this ignorance to be destroyed this subtle state of mind (*vrittijnanam*) is necessary; in the sunshine cotton does not burn; but if the cotton be placed under a lens it catches fire and is consumed by the rays of the Sun passing through the lens. So too, though the awareness of the Self is present at all times, it is not inimical to ignorance. If by meditation the subtle state of thought is won, then ignorance is destroyed. Also in *Viveka Chudamani: ativa sukshmam paramatma tattvam na sthoola drishtya* (the exceedingly subtle Supreme Self cannot be seen by the gross eye) and *esha svayam jyotirasesha sakshi* (this is Self-shining and witnesses all).

This subtle mental state is not a modification of mind called *vritti*. Because the mental states are of two kinds. One is the *natural state* and the other is a transformation into forms of objects. The first is the truth, and the other is according to the doer (*kartru-tantra*). When the latter perishes, *jale kataka renuvat* (like the clearing nut paste in water) the former will remain over.

The means for this end is meditation. Though this is with the triad of distinction (*triputi*) it will finally end in pure awareness (*jnanam*) Meditation needs effort: *jnanam* is effortless. Meditation can be done, or not done, or wrongly done, *jnanam* is not so. Meditation is described as *kartru-tantra* (as doer's own), *jnanam* as *vastu-tantra* (the Supreme's own).

7th February, 1939

Talk 625.

Miss Merston, an English lady visitor: I have read *Who am I?* While inquiring who the 'I' is, I cannot hold it for any length of time.

Secondly, I have no interest in the environment, but yet I have hopes that I shall find some interest in life.

M.: If there are no interests it is good. (The interpreter points out that the questioner hopes to find some interest in life).

M.: That means there are those *vasanas*. A dreamer dreams a dream. He sees the dream world with pleasures, pains. etc. But he wakes up and then loses all interest in the dream world. So it is with the waking world also. Just as the dream-world, being only a part of yourself and not different from you, ceases to interest you, so also the present world would cease to interest you if you awake from this waking dream (*samsara*) and realise that it is a part of your Self, and not an objective reality. Because you think that you are apart from the objects around you, you desire a thing. But if you understand that the thing was only a thought-form you would no longer desire it.

All things are like bubbles on water. You are the water and the objects are the bubbles. They cannot exist apart from the water, but they are not quite the same as the water.

D.: I feel I am like froth.

M.: Cease that identification with the unreal and know your real identity. Then you will be firm and no doubts can arise.

D.: But I *am* the froth.

M.: Because you think that way there is worry. It is a wrong imagination. Accept your true identity with the Real. Be the water and not the froth. That is done by diving in.

D.: If I dive in, I shall find........

M.: But even without diving in, *you are That*. The ideas of exterior and interior exist only so long as you do not accept your real identity.

D.: But I took the idea from you that you want me to dive in.

M.: Yes, quite right. It was said because you are identifying yourself with the froth and not the water. Because of this confusion the answer was meant to draw your attention to this confusion and bring it home to you. All that is meant is that the Self is infinite inclusive of all that you see. There is nothing beyond It nor apart from It. Knowing this, you will not desire anything; not desiring, you will be content.

612

The Self is always realised. There is no seeking to realise what is already — always — realised. For you cannot deny your own existence. That existence is consciousness — the Self.

Unless you exist you cannot ask questions. So you must admit your own existence. That existence is the Self. It is already realised. Therefore the effort to realise results only in your realising your present mistake — that you have not realised your Self. There is no fresh realisation. The Self becomes revealed.

D.: That will take some years.

M.: Why years? The idea of time is only in your mind. It is not in the Self. There is no time for the Self. Time arises as an idea after the ego arises. But you are the Self beyond time and space; you exist even in the absence of time and space.

9th February, 1939

Talk 626.

Another devotee: Is it not that the 'I' exists only in relation to a 'this' (*aham — idam*)?

M.: 'I', 'this' appear together now. But 'this' is contained (*vyaptam*) in the 'I' — they are not apart. 'This' has to merge into and become one with 'I'. The 'I' that remains over is the true 'I'.

Talk 627.

D.: What is staying with the Guru?

M.: It means studying the sacred lore.

D.: But there is the special virtue of the Guru's presence.

M.: Yes. That purifies the mind.

D.: That is the effect or reward. I asked about how the disciple ought to behave.

M.: That differs according to the type of disciple — student, householder, what are his own ingrained mental tendencies and so on.

D.: If so, will it naturally come out right?

M.: Yes. In former times the Rishis sent their sons to others for education.

D.: Why?

613

M.: Because affection stood in the way.

D.: That cannot be for the *jnanis*. Was it in respect of the disciples?

M.: Yes.

D.: If so would not this obstacle get removed along with all the others, through the Master's grace?

M.: There will be delay. Owing to the disciple's want of reverence, grace may become effective only after a long time.

It is said that awaking from ignorance is like awaking from a fearful dream of a beast. It is thus. There are two taints of mind, namely veiling and restlessness (*avarana* and *vikshepa*). Of the two, the former is evil, the latter is not so. So long as the veiling effect of sleep persists there is the frightful dream; on awaking the veiling ceases; and there is no more fear. Restlessness is not a bar to happiness. To get rid of the restlessness caused by the world, one seeks the restlessness (activity) of being with the Guru, studying the sacred books and worshipping God with forms, and by these awakening is attained.

What happens in the end? Karna was ever the son of Kunti. The tenth man was such all along. Rama was Vishnu all the time. Such is *jnanam*. It is being aware of That which always is.

13th February, 1939

Talk 628.

After his return from Europe, Mr. D. had a private interview with Sri Bhagavan for a few minutes. He said that his former visit had had some effect but not as much as he wanted. He could concentrate on his work. Is not concentration indispensable for spiritual progress? Karma appealed to him because that helped towards concentration.

Sri Bhagavan: There is no karma without a *karta* (doer). On seeking for the doer he disappears. Where is Karma then?

Mr. D. sought practical instruction.

M.: Seek the *karta*. That is the practice.

Mrs. D. said there were breaks in her awareness and desired to know how the awareness might be made continuous.

M.: Breaks are due to thoughts. You cannot be aware of breaks unless you think so. It is only a thought. Repeat the old practice, "To

614

whom do thoughts arise?" Keep up the practice until there are no breaks. Practice alone will bring about continuity of awareness.

17th February, 1939

Talk 629.

This is Sivaratri day. Sri Bhagavan was beaming with Grace in the evening. A *Sadhaka* raised the following question:

D.: Enquiry into the Self seems to take one into the subtle body (*ativahika sariram* or *puriashtakam* or *jivatma*). Am I right?

M.: They are different names for the same state, but they are used according to the different points of view. After some time *puriashtakam* (the eight fold subtle body) will disappear and there will be the '*Eka*' (one) only.

Vritti jnana alone can destroy '*ajnana*' (ignorance). Absolute *jnana* is not inimical to *ajnana*.

There are two kinds of *vrittis* (modes of mind). (1) *vishaya vritti* (objective) and (2) *atma vritti* (subjective). The first must give place to the second. That is the aim of *abhyasa* (practice), which takes one first to the *puriashtaka* and then to the One Self.

Talk 630.

In the course of conversation a devotee said in passing: Sivaprakasam Pillai, who is such a good man, such an ardent devotee and a longstanding disciple, has written a poem saying that Sri Bhagavan's instructions could not be carried out by him effectively in practice. What can be the lot of others then?

M.: Sri Acharya also says similar things when he composes songs in praise of any deity. How else can they praise God?
Saying this Sri Bhagavan smiled.

Talk 631.

The *Sadhaka* repeated his question in a different way:

D.: The enquiry into the Self seems to lead to the *ativahika*, the *puriashtaka* or the *jivatma*. Is it right?

M.: Yes. It is called '*sarira*' (body or abode, city or individual, *puri* or *jiva* according to the outlook). They are the same.

Vritti-jnanam is usually associated with objective phenomena. When these cease there remains the *atma-vritti* or the subjective *vritti* that is the same as *jnanam*. Without it *ajnanam* will not cease. The *puriashtaka* also will not be found associated with anything outside, and the Self will shine forth uniform and harmonious.

18th February, 1939

Talk 632.

Mr. Satyanarayana Rao, a teacher in Vellore Mahant School, is a well-known devotee of Sri Maharshi. He has been ailing from a cancer of the gullet and the doctors have no hopes for him. He has been given a room in the Asramam and the Sarvadhikari is very kind to him. It is now about two months and the patient is very weak.

At about 9 a.m., Sri Bhagavan was reading the *tapals*. The brother of the patient appeared in the hall with an anxious look to ask Sri Bhagavan about the patient, who was gasping. The Sarvadhikari also came to the hall on behalf of the sufferer. Sri Bhagavan continued to read the *tapals*. In a few minutes another devotee also came there for the same purpose. Sri Bhagavan asked: Did you call the doctor?

D.: Yes, but he is too busy in the hospital.

M.: What can I do? (After a short time) They will be pleased if I go there.

Soon Bhagavan left the hall and went to the patient's side, massaged him gently and placed His hand on the heart and the other on his head. The patient, whose tongue was protruding, mouth open and eyes fixed, showed signs of relief and in about twenty minutes gently murmured, "Oh Help of the helpless, how I have troubled Thee! What return can I make for this kindness?" The people felt relieved. Sri Bhagavan returned to the hall. Someone offered soap and water to Sri Bhagavan to wash his hands. *But he declined them and rubbed His hands over His body*. However the patient passed away a few days later.

A well-known devotee remarked: "Sri Bhagavan appears so unconcerned under all circumstances. But He is all along so loving and gracious."

23rd February, 1939

Talk 633.

A visitor from Dindigul said: I suffer in both mind and body. From the day of my birth I never had happiness. My mother too suffered from the time she conceived me, I hear. Why do I suffer thus? I have not sinned in this life. Is all this due to the sins of past lives?

M.: If there should be unrelieved suffering all the time, who would seek happiness? That is, if suffering be the natural state, how can the desire to be happy arise at all? However the desire does arise. So to be happy is natural; all else is unnatural. Suffering is not desired, only because it comes and goes.

The questioner repeated his complaint.

M.: You say the mind and body suffer. But do they ask the questions? *Who is the questioner*? Is it not the one that is beyond both mind and body?

You say the body suffers in *this* life; the cause of this is the previous life: its cause is the one before it, and so on. So, like the case of the *seed and the sprout*, there is no end to the causal series. It has to be said that all the lives have their first cause in ignorance. That same ignorance is present even now, framing this question. That ignorance must be removed by *jnanam*.

"Why and to whom did this suffering come?" If you question thus you will find that the 'I' is separate from the mind and body, that the Self is the only eternal being, and that It is eternal bliss. That is *jnanam*.

D.: But why should there be suffering now?

M.: If there were no suffering how could the desire to be happy arise? If that desire did not arise how would the Quest of the Self be successful?

D.: Then is all suffering good?

M.: Quite so. What is happiness? Is it a healthy and handsome body, timely meals, and the like? Even an emperor has troubles without end though he may be healthy. So all suffering is due to the false notion "I am the body". Getting rid of it is *jnanam*.

Talk 634.

An Andhra gentleman, retired from Government Service, asked: "I have been doing *omkara upasana* for long. In the left ear I am always hearing a sound. It is like the piping of a *nadasvaram* (pipe). Even now I hear it. Some luminous visions are also seen. I do not know what I should do."

M.: There must be one to hear sounds or see visions. That one is the 'I'. If you seek it, asking "Who am I?" the subject and objects would coalesce. After that there is no quest. Till then thought will arise, things will appear and disappear; you ask yourself what has happened, and what will happen. If the subject be known then the objects will merge in the subject. If without that knowledge, one applies the mind to objects, because these objects appear and disappear, and one does not know that one's true nature is that which remains over as the Self. On the vanishing of objects, fear arises. That is, the mind being bound to objects there is suffering when the objects are absent. But they are transient and the Self is eternal. If the eternal Self be known subject and object merge into one, and the One without a second will shine.

D.: Is there the merger of the *Omkara*?

M.: Om is the eternal truth. That which remains over after the disappearance of objects is *Om*. It does not merge in anything. It is the State of which it is said: "Where one sees none other, hears none other, knows none other, that is Perfection." *Yatra nanyat pasyati, nanyat srunoti, nanyat vijanati sa bhuma*? All the *upasanas* are ways to winning it. One must not get stuck in the *upasanas*, but must query "Who am I?" and find the Self.

D.: I have no pleasure in the house. There remains nothing for me to do in the family. I have finished doing what I had to do. Now there are grandsons and granddaughters. May I remain in the house, or should I leave it and go away?

M.: You should stay just where you are now. But where are you now? Are you in the house, or is the house in you? Is there any house apart from you? If you get fixed in your own place, you will see all things have merged into you, and there will be no cause for such questions as these.

D.: Yes. Then it seems as if I may remain at home.

M.: You must remain in your real state.

Talk 635.

An Andhra gentleman of Hospet has returned from pilgrimage to Kailas, Amarnath, etc. He described how fine those places are and how difficult the journey was. He finally asked for something to remind him of Maharshi, meaning some instruction.

M.: You have been to Kailas etc. Have you been to Muktinath?

D.: No. It was too difficult a journey for me. I have however been in Nepal. Have you been to those places?

M.: No, no. I mentioned Muktinath casually.

Then Sri Bhagavan remarked: "To go to Kailas and return is just a new birth. For there the body-idea drops off."

Talk 636.

Mrs. Kelly Hack asked if the waking and the dream states might be imagined to be excursions from the natural state of the Self.

M.: There must be a place for excursions. The place must also lie outside oneself. It is not possible in the true nature of the Self.

D.: But I meant that it might be imagined to be so.

M.: One might as well imagine the true nature of the Self

D.: The illustration of the screen is very beautiful.

M.: The cinema screen is not sentient and so requires a seer, whereas the screen of the Self includes the seer and the seen — rather, it is full of light.

The pictures of the cinema-show cannot be seen without the help of darkness, for you cannot have a show in broad daylight. Similarly, the mind thinks thoughts and sees objects owing to an underlying ignorance (*avidya*). The Self is pure knowledge, pure light where there is no duality. Duality implies ignorance. The Knowledge of the Self is beyond relative knowledge and ignorance, the Light of the Self is beyond the ordinary light and darkness. The Self is all alone.

Talk 637.

There was some question about progress.

Sri Bhagavan said that progress is for the mind and not for the Self. The Self is ever perfect.

2nd March, 1939

Talk 638.

For the last few days a rule is in force by which the visitors are not allowed to enter the hall between 12 noon and 2-30 p.m. A few Muslim visitors came to the Asramam in the interval today. The attendant promptly told them that they should not disturb Sri Bhagavan's rest at this hour. Sri Bhagavan quietly got down from the sofa and came out of the hall; He sat on the stone pavement adjoining the wall and asked the visitors also to sit close to Him. He went on reading a newspaper and also laid Himself on the stone. He was finally requested to go in.

Talk 639.

While speaking to Mr. K. L. Sarma of Pudukotah, Sri Bhagavan said: Leaving out what is intimate and immediate, why should one seek the rest? The scriptures say "That Thou art". In this statement 'Thou' is directly experienced; but leaving it out they go on seeking 'That'!

D.: In order to find the oneness of 'That' and of 'Thou'.

M.: 'Thou' is the Inner Self immanent in all; in order to find the same, he leaves himself out and sees the world objectively. What is the world? What is Immanent in it? It is 'That'. All such ideas arise only on forgetting one's own Self. I never bothered myself with such matters. Only after a time it occurred to me that men had investigated such matters.

3rd March, 1939

Talk 640.

At about 4 p.m. Sri Bhagavan, who was writing something intently, turned His eyes slowly towards the window to the north; He closed the fountain pen with the cap and put it in its case: He closed the notebook and put it aside; He removed the spectacles, folded them in the case and left them aside. He leaned back a little, looked up overhead, turned His face this way and that; and looked here and there. He passed His hand over His face and looked contemplative. Then He turned to someone in the hall and said softly:

M.: The pair of sparrows just came here and complained to me that their nest had been removed. I looked up and found their nest missing." Then He called for the attendant, Madhava Swami, and asked: "Madhava, did anyone remove the sparrows' nest?

The attendant, who walked in leisurely, answered with an air of unconcern: "I removed the nests as often as they were built. I removed the last one this very afternoon."

M.: That's it. That is why the sparrows complained. The poor little ones! How they take the pieces of straw and shreds in their tiny beaks and struggle to build their nests!

Attendant: But, why should they build here, over our heads?

M.: Well — well. Let us see who succeeds in the end (After a short time Sri Bhagavan went out).

Talk 641.

Explaining the opening stanza of the *Sad Vidya*, Sri Bhagavan observed: The world is always apparent to everyone. All must know "I and this world exist". On enquiry "do these always exist?" and "if indeed real, they must remain even unrelated to time, space and differentiation; are they so?" It is evident that only in the waking and dream states these are perceived but not in deep sleep. Therefore 'I' and the world appear sometimes and disappear also. They are created, have their being and later vanish. Whence do they arise? Wherein do they remain? Where do they go on vanishing from view? Can such phenomena be admitted to be real?

Furthermore, I and the world, objects of creation, sustenance and destruction, are perceived in the waking and dream states only and not in deep sleep. How does deep sleep differ from the other two states? In sleep there are no thoughts whereas in the other two states there are. There the thoughts must be the origin of the 'I' and the world.

Now what about thoughts? They cannot be natural; otherwise they cannot appear at one moment and disappear at another. Wherefrom do they arise? Their source, ever-present and not subject to variations, must be admitted to be. It must be the eternal state as said in the *upadesa mantra* — That from which all beings come forth, that in which they remain and that into which they resolve.

This stanza is not in praise or adoration but only an expression of the Reality.

Talk 642.

Mr. K. L. Sarma asked:
Svasvarupanusandhanam bhaktirityabhidhiyate.
Again — *Svatmatattvanusadhanam bhaktirityapare joguh.*
What is the difference between the two?

M.: The former is *vichara* — Who am I? (*Koham?*) It represents *jnana*.

The latter is *dhyana* — Whence am I? (*Kutoham?*) This admits a *jivatma* which seeks the *Paramatma*.

Talk 643.

An elderly, learned Andhra asked: "Are the two methods Karma *marga* and *jnana marga* separate and independent of each other? Or is the Karma *marga* only a preliminary which after successful practice should be followed by *jnana marga* for the consummation of the aim? The Karma advocates non-attachment to action and yet an active life, whereas the *jnana* means renunciation. What is the true meaning of renunciation? Subjugation of lust, passion, greed, etc., is common to all and forms the essential preliminary step for any course. Does not freedom from passions indicate renunciation? Or is renunciation different, meaning cessation of the active life? These questions are troubling me and I beg lights to be thrown on those doubts."

Bhagavan smiled and said: "You have said all. Your question contains the answer also. Freedom from passions is the essential requisite. When that is accomplished all else is accomplished."

D.: Sri Sankara emphasises the *jnana marga* and renunciation as preliminary to it. But there are clearly two methods *dwividha* mentioned in the Gita. They are Karma and *Jnana* (*Lokesmin dwividha nishtha...*).

M.: Sri Acharya has commented on the Gita and on that passage also.

D.: The Gita seems to emphasise Karma. For Arjuna is persuaded to fight; Sri Krishna Himself set the example by an active life of great exploits.

M.: The Gita starts saying that you are not the body, that you are not therefore the *karta*.

D.: What is the significance?

M.: That one should act without thinking that oneself is the actor. The actions go on despite his egolessness. The person has come into manifestation for a certain purpose. That purpose will be accomplished whether he considers himself the actor or not.

D.: What is Karma yoga? Is it non-attachment to Karma or its fruit?

M.: Karma yoga is that yoga in which the person does not arrogate to himself the function of being the actor. The actions go on automatically.

D.: Is it the non-attachment to the fruits of actions?

M.: The question arises only if there is the actor. It is being all along said that you should not consider yourself the actor.

D.: So Karma yoga is *kartrtva buddhi rahita karma* — action without the sense of doership.

M.: Yes. Quite so.

D.: The Gita teaches active life from beginning to end.

M.: Yes, the actor-less action.

D.: Is it then necessary to leave the home and lead a life of renunciation?

M.: Is the home in you? Or are you in the home?

D.: It is in my mind.

M.: Then what becomes of you when you leave the physical environment?

D.: Now I see. Renunciation is only action without the sense of being the *karta*.

Is there not action for a *jivanmukta*?

M.: Who raises the question? Is he a *jivanmukta* or another?

D.: Not a *jivanmukta*.

M.: Let the question be raised after *jivanmukti* is gained if it is found necessary. *Mukti* is admitted to be freedom from the mental activities also. Can a *mukta* think of action?

D.: Even if he gives up the action, the action will not leave him. Is it not so?

M.: With what is he identified in order that this question might apply?

D.: Yes, I see all right. My doubts are now cleared.

Talk 644.

A District Official, a Muslim: What is the necessity for reincarnation?

M.: Let us first see if there is incarnation before we speak of reincarnation.

D.: How?

M.: Are you now incarnated that you speak of reincarnation?

D.: Yes. Certainly. An amoeba developed into higher organisms until the human being has been evolved. This is now the perfection in development. Why should there be further reincarnation?

M.: Who is to set limits to this theory of evolution?

D.: Physically it is perfect. But for the soul, further development may be required which will happen after the death of the man.

M.: Who is the man? Is he the body or the soul?

D.: Both put together.

M.: Do you not exist in the absence of the body?

D.: How do you mean? It is impossible.

M.: What was your state in deep sleep?

D.: Sleep is temporary death. I was unconscious and therefore I cannot say what the state was.

M.: But you existed in sleep. Did you not?

D.: In sleep the soul leaves the body and goes out somewhere. Then it returns to the body before waking. It is therefore temporary death.

M.: A man who is dead never returns to say that he died, whereas the man who had slept says that he slept.

D.: Because this is temporary death.

M.: If death is temporary and life is temporary, what is it that is real?

D.: What is meant by the question?

M.: If life and death be temporary, there must be something which is not temporary. Reality is that which is not temporary.

D.: There is nothing real. Everything is temporary. Everything is *maya*.

M.: On what does *maya* appear?

D.: Now I see you; it is all *maya*.

M.: If everything is *maya*, how does any question arise?

D.: Why should there be reincarnation?

M.: For whom?

D.: For the perfect human being.

M.: If you are perfect, why do you fear to be reborn? It indicates imperfection.

D.: Not that I fear. But you say that I must be reborn.

M.: Who says it? You are asking the question.

D.: What I mean is this. You are a Perfect Being; I am a sinner. You tell me that I being a sinner must be reborn in order to perfect myself?

M.: No, I do not say so. On the other hand I say that you have no birth and therefore no death.

D.: Do you mean to say that I was not born?

M.: Yes, you are now thinking that you are the body and therefore confuse yourself with its birth and death. But you are not the body and you have no birth and death.

D.: Do you not uphold the theory of rebirth?

M.: No. On the other hand, I want to remove your confusion that you will be reborn. It is you who think that you will be reborn.

See for whom this question arises. Unless the questioner is found, the questions can never be set at rest.

D.: This is no answer to my question.

M.: On the other hand, this is the answer to elucidate the point and all other doubts as well.

D.: This will not satisfy all others.

M.: Leave others alone. If you take care of yourself others can take care of themselves.

Silence followed. He left in a few minutes apparently dissatisfied with the discourse.

Sri Bhagavan said after a few minutes: This will work in him. The discourse will have its effect.

He does not admit any Reality. Well — who is it that has determined everything to be unreal? Otherwise the determination also becomes unreal.

The theory of evolution is enlarged upon by the person in this state. Where is it, if not in his mind?

To say that the soul must be perfected after death, the soul must be admitted to exist. Therefore the body is not the person. It is the soul.

To explain evolution Sri Bhagavan continued:

One sees an edifice in his dream. It rises up all of a sudden. Then he begins to think how it should have been already built brick by brick by so many labourers during such a long time. Yet he does not see the builders working. So also with the theory of evolution. Because he finds himself a man he thinks that he has developed to that stage from the primal state of the amoeba.

Another devotee: It is an illustration of the saying that he sees the universe full of cause and effect *Visram pasyati karyakaranataya.*

M.: Yes. The man always traces an effect to a cause, there must be a cause for the cause, the argument becomes interminable. Relating the effect to a cause makes the man think. He is finally driven to consider who he is himself. When he knows the Self there is Perfect Peace. It is for that consummation that man is evolved.

Later in the evening, another devotee said to Sri Bhagavan that the Muslim official continued to speak of the same topic to the Municipal Commissioner.

Then Sri Bhagavan said: He says that body and soul together

626

form the man. But I ask what is the state of the man in deep sleep. The body is not aware whereas the man is there all along.

D.: But he says that sleep is temporary death.

M.: Yes, so he says. But he qualifies the word death by the word temporary, so that the man returns to the body. How does he find the body to re-enter it? Moreover, he is sure to return. That means that he must exist to return to the body or to claim the body for himself.

The scriptures however say that the *prana* protects the body in sleep. For when the body lies on the floor, a wolf or a tiger may feed on it. The animal sniffs and feels that there is life within and therefore does not feed on it as on a corpse. That again shows that there is someone in the body to protect it in deep sleep.

General remarks by Sri Bhagavan:

All knowledge is meant only to lead the person to the realisation of the Self. The scriptures or religions are well-known to be for that purpose. What do they all mean? Leave alone what they say of the past or of the future; for it is only speculative. But the present existence is within the experience of all. Realise the pure Being. There is an end to all discourses and disputes.

But the intellect of man does not easily take to this course. It is only rarely that a man becomes introverted. The intellect delights in investigating the past and the future but does not look to the present.

D.: Because it must lose itself if it sank within in search of the Self. But the other investigation gives it not only a lease of life but also food for growth.

M.: Yes. Quite so. Why is intellect developed? It has a purpose. The purpose is that it should show the way to realise the Self. It must be put to that use.

12th March, 1939

Talk 645.

A man of about 30, of good appearance came to the hall with a few companions. The man abruptly began: "To say 'I-I' cannot help anyone to reach the goal. How can 'I' be pointed out?"

627

M.: It must be found within. It is not an object so that it may be shown by one to another.

D.: When the instruction to find the 'I' is given, the instruction must be made complete by showing what it is.

M.: The instruction here amounts to direction only. It depends on the seeker to use the direction.

D.: The seeker is ignorant and seeks instruction.

M.: He is therefore guided to find the Truth.

D.: But it is not enough. The 'I' must be pointed out specifically.

The man assumed an aggressive attitude and did not listen. Sri Bhagavan tried to explain, but he would not allow Sri Bhagavan to do so.

Finally Sri Bhagavan said: This is not the attitude of the seeker. When someone teaches humility to the seeker, he will reach the way and not till then.

The chanting of the Vedas began.

The conversation was casually referred to by a devotee present.

Sri Bhagavan again said: The seeker must listen and try to understand. If on the other hand he wants to prove me, let him do so by all means. I do not argue.

The man again began: "My attitude was not properly understood. I want to know the 'I'. It must be pointed out to me."

But he displayed considerable malice. The others did not like it and so tried to bring him round. He became worse. Sri Bhagavan finally said: "Go back the way you came. Do it externally or internally, as it suits you."

The man grew excited and others also were equally excited. He was finally led out of the hall and sent away.

Later it was learnt that the man was an adherent of yoga and that he used to abuse all other methods. He used to vilify *jnana* and the *jnanis*.

At night, after supper, Sri Bhagavan spoke of one Govinda Yogi, a Malayali Brahmin pandit of some repute, who used to extol yoga and vilify the other methods. He always cited the Gita, the Upanishads, etc., to support his statements. Others, *e.g.*, Sri Narayana Guru, used to refute him on the same grounds.

628

Later Sri Bhagavan spoke appreciating the amiability of Amritanatha. He is a great *tapasvi*, who had made considerable *japa*. He had fed the poor on many occasions in many places. He could easily gain the goodwill of others including great men like Sir P. Ramanathan and Pandit Malaviya.

13th March, 1939

Talk 646.

Sri Bhagavan referred to the following passage of Gandhiji in the *Harijan* of the 11th instant:

"How mysterious are the ways of God! This journey to Rajkot is a wonder even to me. Why am I going, whither am I going? What for? I have thought nothing about these things. And if God guides me, what should I think, why should I think? Even thought may be an obstacle in the way of His guidance.

"The fact is, it takes no effort to stop thinking. The thoughts do *not* come. Indeed there is no vacuum — but I mean to say that there is no thought about the mission."

Sri Bhagavan remarked how true the words were and emphasised each statement in the extract. Then He cited Thayumanavar in support of the state which is free from thoughts:

"Although I had often heard that all the *Srutis* declare the state of stillness to be one of Bliss, all Bliss — yet I continued to be ignorant. Again I did not follow the advice of my Lord — the Silent Master — because of my folly. I wandered in the forest of illusion: alas! it was my fate."

"Bliss will reveal itself if one is still. Why then is this illusory yoga practice? Can it (*i.e.*, Bliss) be revealed by directing the intellect in a particular way? Do not say so, you who are given to the practice and are therefore an innocent babe."

"The eternal Being is that state where you have disappeared. Are you not in it too? You, who cannot speak of it, do not be perplexed. Although you do not manifest, yet you are not lost. For you are eternal and also still. Do not be in pain. Here is Bliss — come on!"

629

15th March, 1939

Talk 647.

D.: Is not what Gandhiji describes, the state in which thoughts themselves become foreign?

M.: Yes, It is only after the rise of the 'I' thought that all other thoughts arise. The world is seen after you have felt "I am". The 'I-thought' and all other thoughts had vanished for him.

D.: Then the body-sense must be absent in that state.

M.: The body-sense also is a thought whereas he describes the state in which "thoughts do not come".

D.: He also says, "It takes no effort to stop thinking".

M.: Of course no effort is necessary to stop thoughts whereas one is necessary for bringing about thoughts.

D.: We are trying to stop thoughts. Gandhiji also says that thought is an obstacle to God's guidance. So it is the natural state. Though natural, yet how difficult to realise. They say that *sadhanas* are necessary and also that they are obstacles. We get confused.

M.: Sadhanas are needed so long as one has not realised it. They are for putting an end to obstacles. Finally there comes a stage when a person feels helpless notwithstanding the *sadhanas*. He is unable to pursue the much-cherished *sadhana* also. It is then that God's Power is realised. The Self reveals itself.

D.: If the state is natural, why does it not overcome the unnatural phases and assert itself over the rest?

M.: Is there anything besides that? Does anyone see anything besides the Self? One is always aware of the Self. So It is always Itself.

D.: It is said, because It shines forth, It is directly perceived. I understand from it that It becomes *pratyaksha* (directly perceived), because It is *pradeepta* (shining). Since it is not realised by us, I take it to be not shining. It is only *pradeepta* (shining), and hence admits of obstacles and goes under them. If the *atma* becomes *prakarshena deepta*, (very shining) it will shine over the rest. So it seems to be necessary to make it shine more.

M.: How can it be so? The Atma cannot be dull at one moment and blazing at another. It is unchanging and uniform.

630

D.: But Chudala says to Sikhidhvaja that she simply helped to trim the wick.

M.: That refers to *nididhyasana.*

By *sravana*, Knowledge dawns. That is the flame.

By *manana*, the Knowledge is not allowed to vanish. Just as the flame is protected by a wind-screen, so the other thoughts are not allowed to overwhelm the right knowledge.

By *nididhyasana*, the flame is kept up to burn bright by trimming the wick. Whenever other thoughts arise, the mind is turned inward to the light of true knowledge.

When this becomes natural, it is *samadhi*.

The enquiry "Who am I?" is the *sravana*.

The ascertainment of the true import of 'I' is the *manana*. The practical application on each occasion is *nididhyasana*.

Being as 'I' is *samadhi*.

D.: Although we have heard it so often and so constantly yet we are unable to put the teaching into practise successfully. It must be due to weakness of mind. Is it possible that one's age is a bar?

M.: The mind is commonly said to be strong if it can think furiously. But here the mind is strong if it is free from thoughts. The yogis say that realisation can be had only before the age of thirty, but not the *jnanis*. For *jnana* does not cease to exist with age.

It is true that in the *Yoga Vasishta*, Vasishta says to Rama in the *Vairagya Prakarana* "You have this dispassion in your youth. It is admirable." But he did not say that *jnana* cannot be had in old age. There is nothing to prevent it in old age.

The *sadhak* must remain as the Self. If he cannot do so, he must ascertain the true meaning of the 'I' and constantly revert to it whenever other thoughts arise. That is the practice.

Some say that one must know the '*tat*' because the idea of the world constantly arises to deflect the mind. If the Reality behind it is first ascertained it will be found to be Brahman. The '*tvam*' is understood later. It is the *jiva*. Finally there will be *jivabrahmaikya* (union of the two).

631

But why all this? Can the world exist apart from the Self? The 'I' is always Brahman. Its identity need not be established by logic and practice. It is enough that one realises the Self. It is always the Brahman.

According to the other school, *nididhyasana* will be the thought *Aham Brahmasmi* (I am Brahman). That is diversion of thought to Brahman. No diversion should be allowed. Know the Self and there is an end of it.

No long process is necessary to know the Self. Is it to be pointed out by another? Does not everyone know that he exists? Even in utter darkness when he cannot see his hand, he answers a call and says "I am here".

D.: But that 'I' is the ego or the 'I-thought' and it is not the Absolute Self that answers the call or is otherwise aware of oneself.

M.: Even the ego can become aware of itself in the absence of light, sight, etc. Much more so should be the Pure Light of the Self.

I am saying that the Self is self-evident. One need not discuss the *tattvas* to find the Self. Some say there are twenty-four *tattvas*, others more and so on. Should we know the *tattvas*, before we admit the existence of the Self? The *sastras* dilate upon them in order to point out that the Self is untouched by them. But for the seeker he can straightaway admit the Self and try to be That, without having recourse to the study of the *tattvas*.

D.: Gandhiji adhered to *satya* (Truth) so long and won realisation of the Self.

M.: What is *satya* except the Self? *Satya* is that which is made up of *sat*. Again *sat* is nothing but the Self. So Gandhiji's *satya* is only the Self.

Each one knows the Self but is yet ignorant. The person is enabled to realise only after hearing the *mahavakya*. Hence the Upanishadic text is the eternal Truth to which everyone who has realised owes his experience. After hearing the Self to be the Brahman the person finds the true import of the Self and reverts to it whenever he is diverted from it. Here is the whole process of Realisation.

17th March, 1939

Talk 648.

Sri Bhagavan said that Tatva Rayar was the first to pour forth Advaita philosophy in Tamil.

He had said that the Earth was his bed, his hands were his plates for taking food, the loin cloth was his clothing and thus there was no want for him.

In *Maharaja Turavu*[*](the renunciation of the king) he says: He was seated on the bare ground, the earth was his seat, the mind was the *chamara*; the sky was the canopy; and renunciation was his spouse:

Then Sri Bhagavan continued: I had no cloth spread on the floor in earlier days. I used to sit on the floor and lie on the ground. That is freedom. The sofa is a bondage. It is a gaol for me. I am not allowed to sit where and how I please. Is it not bondage? One must be free to do as one pleases, and should not be served by others.

'No want' is the greatest bliss. It can be realised only by experience. Even an emperor is no match for a man with no want. The emperor has got vassals under him. But the other man is not aware of anyone beside the Self. Which is better?

18th March, 1939

Talk 649.

Mr. Thompson, a very quiet young gentleman who is staying in India for some years and studying Hindu Philosophy as an earnest student, asked:

Srimad Bhagavad Gita says: "I am the prop for Brahman." In another place, it says: "I am in the heart of each one." Thus the different aspects of the Ultimate Principle are revealed. I take it that there are three aspects, namely (1) the transcendental (2) the immanent and (3) the cosmic. Is Realisation to be in any one of these or in all of them? Coming to the transcendental from the cosmic, the Vedanta discards the names and forms as being *maya*. But I cannot readily appreciate it because a tree means the trunk, branches, leaves, etc. I cannot dismiss the leaves as *maya*. Again the Vedanta also says that

---

*Author, Kumaradevar   633

the whole is Brahman as illustrated by gold and ornaments of gold. How are we to understand the Truth?

M.: The *Gita* says: *Brahmano hi pratishtaham.* If that '*aham*' is known, the whole is known.

D.: It is the immanent aspect only.

M.: You now think that you are an individual, there is the universe and that God is beyond the cosmos. So there is the idea of separateness. This idea must go. For God is not separate from you or the cosmos. The *Gita* also says:

The Self am I, O Lord of Sleep,
In every creature's heart enshrined.
The rise and noon of every form,
I am its final doom as well.

B. G., X. 20.

Thus God is not only in the heart of all, He is the prop of all, He is the source of all, their abiding place and their end. All proceed from Him, have their stay in Him, and finally resolve into Him. Therefore He is not separate.

D.: How are we to understand this passage in the *Gita*: "This whole cosmos forms a particle of Me."

M.: It does not mean that a small particle of God separates from Him and forms the Universe. His *Sakti* is acting; as a result of one phase of such activity the cosmos has become manifest. Similarly, the statement in *Purusha Sukta*, "All the beings form His one foot (*Padosya viswa bhutani*) does not mean that Brahman is in four parts.

D.: I understand it. Brahman is certainly not divisible.

M.: So the fact is that Brahman is all and remains indivisible. He is ever realised. The man does not however know it. He must know it. Knowledge means the overcoming of obstacles which obstruct the revelation of the Eternal Truth that the Self is the same as Brahman. The obstacles form altogether your idea of separateness as an individual. Therefore the present attempt will result in the truth being revealed that the Self is not separate from Brahman.

Talk 650.

An Andhra gentleman of middle age asked Sri Bhagavan how he should make his *japa*.

M.: The *japa* contains the word *namah*. It means that state in which the mind does not manifest apart from the Self. When the state is accomplished there will be an end of the *japa*. For the doer disappears and so also the action. The Eternal Being is alone left. *Japa* should be made until that state is reached. There is no escape from the Self. The doer will be automatically drawn into it. When once it is done the man cannot do anything else but remain merged in the Self.

D.: Will *bhakti* lead to *mukti*?

M.: *Bhakti* is not different from *mukti*. *Bhakti* is being as the Self (*Swarupa*). One is always that. He realises it by the means he adopts. What is *bhakti*? To think of God. That means: only one thought prevails to the exclusion of all other thoughts. That thought is of God which is the Self or it is the Self surrendered unto God. When He has taken you up nothing will assail you. The absence of thoughts is *bhakti*. It is also *mukti*.

The *jnana* method is said to be *vichara* (enquiry). That is nothing but 'supreme devotion' (*parabhakti*). The difference is in words only.

You think that *bhakti* is meditation on the Supreme Being. So long as there is *vibhakti* (the sense of separateness), *bhakti* (reunion) is sought. The process will lead to the ultimate goal as is said in *Srimad Bhagavad Gita*:

> *arto jignasuh artharthi jnani cha Bharatarshabha*
> *tesham jnani nityayukta ekabhaktir visishyate*

— Ch. VII (16, 17).

Any kind of meditation is good. But if the sense of separateness is lost and the object of meditation or the subject who meditates is alone left behind without anything else to know, it is *jnana*. *Jnana* is said to be *ekabhakti* (single-minded devotion). The *jnani* is the finality because he has become the Self and there is nothing more to do. He is also perfect and so fearless, *dwitiyat vai bhayam bhavati* — only the existence of a second gives rise to fear. This is *mukti*. It is also *bhakti*.

23rd March, 1939

Talk 651.

A. W. Chadwick is copying the English translation of the Tamil *Kaivalya Navaneeta*. When he came across some technical terms in it and felt some difficulty in understanding them, he asked Sri Bhagavan about them. Sri Bhagavan said: "Those portions deal with theories of creation. They are not material because the *Srutis* do not mean to set forth such theories. They mention the theories casually so that the enquirer may please himself if he be so inclined. The truth is that the world appears as a passing shadow in a flood of light. Light is necessary to see that shadow also. The shadow does not deserve any special notice, analysis or discussion. The book deals with the Self and that is its purpose. The discussions on creation may be omitted for the present."

Later, Sri Bhagavan continued: "The Vedanta says that the cosmos springs into view simultaneously with the seer. There is no detailed process of creation. This is said to be *yugapat srshti* (instantaneous creation). It is quite similar to the creations in dream where the experiencer springs up simultaneously with the objects of experience. When this is told, some people are not satisfied for they are so rooted in objective knowledge. They seek to find out how there can be sudden creation. They argue that an effect must be preceded by a cause. In short, they desire an explanation for the existence of the world which they see around them. Then the *Srutis* try to satisfy their curiosity by such theories of creation. This method of dealing with the subject of creation is called *krama srshti* (gradual creation). But the true seeker can be content with *yugapat srshti* — instantaneous creation."

24th March, 1939

Talk 652.

A certain person had composed verses in praise of Sri Bhagavan. Therein the word *Avartapuri* occurs. Sri Bhagavan said that it means

Tiruchuzhi, the birth place of Sri Bhagavan. The place goes by different names. *Avarta chuzhi* an eddy. There had been several deluges. God Siva had saved this place from three of them. On one occasion when the whole land surface was immersed in the waters, Siva planted His spear in that place. All the waters, which would have otherwise flooded it, were drawn into that hole. Then an eddy was formed. Hence the name. Again in another deluge, He held the place aloft on the top of the spear. Hence, *Soolapuri.*

Mother Earth was carried away by Hiranyaksha into the waters. When recovered by Vishnu she felt that she had *papasparsa* by that Rakshasa. As an expiation of that impure touch she worshipped Siva in that place. Hence, *Bhuminathesvara Kshetra.*

Gautama is prominent in Arunachala as well as in Tiruchuzhi. Shiva showed Himself to the saint in the dancing posture and also re-enacted the wedding of Gauri Sankar.

Kaundinya was another *rishi* for whose sake the sacred river began to flow there. It goes by the name of the *rishi i.e.,* Kaundinya river which in Tamil was corrupted into Kundaru. It is otherwise called Papahari *i.e.,* the destroyer of sins. There lies a story behind it: A King's daughter was hysterical (*i.e.,* possessed). She was taken on a pilgrimage to various sacred places and *tirthas.* On one occasion the party heard the name of Papahari as a *tirtha* in a *sankalpa* before bathing. They enquired where the *tirtha* was and went to Tiruchuzhi. The girl was bathed in that water and thus made free from the spirit.

The Pandya king also got free from *brahmahatya* in this place. It happens to be the centre of the Pandya Kingdom, which comprised the Madura, Ramnad and Tirunelveli Districts.

The village had a sacred tank in front of the temple, which was the spot of the eddy created by the spear of Siva. Even now the waters in the tank rise at the rate of about a foot every day for ten consecutive days preceding the full moon in the Tamil month Masi (*Maghasuddha Pournami*) and then gradually fall during the succeeding ten days. This phenomenon can be observed every year. It is noted with wonder by the young ones of the village. Pilgrims gather to bathe in those waters on that occasion. That water is sulphurous for the silver jewels of the bathers become dark after bathing in it. Sri Bhagavan said he had noted it when He was a boy.

The village has the river on one side and a huge lake on the other side. The bund of the lake is clayey and runs about three miles in all. The lake is strangely enough twenty feet over the level of the village. Even when it is over-full, the waters escape in other directions leaving the village unaffected.

1st April, 1939

Talk 653.

Some teachers who attended the Teachers' Guild meeting in the town came on a visit to the hall. One of them asked Sri Bhagavan: "I seem to be wandering in a forest because I do not find the way."

M.: This idea of being in a forest must go. It is such ideas which are at the root of the trouble.

D.: But I do not find the way.

M.: Where is the forest and where is the way unless they are in you? You are as you are and yet you speak of a forest and ways.

D.: But I am obliged to move in society.

M.: Society is also an idea similar to that of the forest.

D.: I leave my home and go and mix in society.

M.: Who does it?

D.: The body moves and does all.

M.: Quite so. Now that you identify yourself with the body you feel the trouble. The trouble is in your mind. You think that you are the body or that you are the mind. But there are occasions when you are free from both. For example in deep slumber, you create a body and a world in your dream. That represents your mental activities. In your waking state you think that you are the body and then the idea of forest and the rest arise.

Now, consider the situation. You are an unchanging and continuous being who remains in all these states which are constantly changing and therefore transient. But you are always there. It follows that these fleeting objects are mere phenomena which appear on your being like pictures which move across a screen. The screen does not move when the picture moves. Similarly, you do not move from where you are even when the body leaves the home and mixes in society.

Your body, the society, the forest and the ways are all in you; you are not in them. You are the body also but not this body only. If you remain as your pure Self, the body and its movements need not affect you.

D.: This can be realised only by the Grace of the master. I was reading *Sri Bhagavata*; it says that Bliss can be had only by the dust of the Master's feet. I pray for Grace.

M.: What is Bliss but your own being? You are not apart from Being which is the same as Bliss. You are now thinking that you are the mind or the body which are both changing and transient. But you are unchanging and eternal. That is what you should know.

D.: It is darkness and I am ignorant.

M.: This ignorance must go. Again, who says 'I am ignorant'? He must be the witness of ignorance. That is what you are. Socrates said, "I know that I do not know." Can it be ignorance? It is wisdom.

D.: Why then do I feel unhappy when I am in Vellore and feel peace in Your Presence?

M.: Can this feeling in this place be Bliss? When you leave the place you say you are unhappy. Therefore this peace is not permanent, nay it is mixed with unhappiness which is felt in another place. Therefore you cannot find Bliss in places and in periods of time. It must be permanent in order that it may be useful. Such permanent being is yourself. Be the Self and that is Bliss. You are always That.

You say that you left Vellore, travelled in the train, arrived in Tiruvannamalai, entered the hall and found happiness. When you go back you are not happy in Vellore. Now, do you really move from place to place? Even considering you to be the body, the body sits in a cart at the gate of the home, the cart moves on to the railway station. Then it gets into a railway carriage which speeds on from Vellore to Tiruvannamalai. There it gets into another cart which brings the body here. Yet when you are asked, you say that you travelled all the way from Vellore. Your body remains where it was and all the places went past it.

639

Such ideas are due to the false identity which is so deep-rooted.

Another asked: Should we understand the world as transient (*anitya*)?

M.: Why so? Because you are now considering it to be permanent (*nitya*) the Scriptures tell you that it is not so in order to wean you from wrong ideas. This should be done by knowing yourself to be eternal (*nitya*) and not by branding the world as transitory (*anitya*).

D.: We are told to practise indifference (*udasina*) which is possible only if the world is unreal.

M.: Yes. *Oudasinyam abhipsitam.* Indifference is advised. But what is it? It is absence of love and hatred. When you realise the Self on which these phenomena pass, will you love or hate them? That is the meaning of indifference.

D.: That will lead to want of interest in our work. Should we do our duty or not?

M.: Yes — certainly. Even if you try not to do your duty you will be perforce obliged to do it. Let the body complete the task for which it came into being.

Sri Krishna also says in the Gita, whether Arjuna liked it or not he would be forced to fight. When there is work to be done by you, you cannot keep away; nor can you continue to do a thing when you are not required to do it, that is to say, when the work allotted to you has been done. In short, the work will go on and you must take your share in it — the share which is allotted to you.

D.: How is it to be done?

M.: Like an actor playing his part in a drama — free from love or hatred.

OM TAT SAT

640

CLASSIFIED INDEX

Teachings of Bhagavan

G

I

S

Other Scriptures, Books and Magazines
Referred to or Quoted

Ancient Saints, Sages and Puranic Characters

Other Personalities

Bhagavan's Reminiscences
and Observations on Incidents and Devotees

Incidents about Bhagavan Narrated by Others

Incidents during the Period
"Talks" was Recorded

Names of Devotees and Visitors

Similies

Ball struck on wall and illustration 539
Bartered grain 37
Beads on a thread 290
Bird beating its wings in vain 456
Boring well to obtain water 240
Brake to a car 371
Brahma and Yama,
    Guru who prescribes activity 601
Bubble and ocean 92, 146, 163, 164, 625
Bucket in water 187
Bull, mind like stray 220, 563
Burning camphor 152
Burnt rope 286

Caterpillar, ego is like 286, 616
Central blade of grass
    drawn from whorl 349
Chaff and substance 186
Child and lullaby 148
Child and sage 9, 414
Churning curd to draw butter 349
Cinema show 13, 62, 65, 177, 199, 244,
    313, 316, 323, 353, 381, 402, 443, 446, 450, 453, 465, 470, 487, 497,
    579, 607, 609, 616, 636, 653
Clearing nut paste in water 624
Cloth and yarn 478
Cloudy night 286
Coal, charcoal and gun powder,
    igniting 155
Cork in water 406
Cotton and cloth 450
Cow tethered to peg 616
Cow in shed 213, 326, 563
Crow's eye 313, 538

701

Places Connected with Visitors
and Other Places Mentioned

Stories and Parables

709

Works of Bhagavan

Organisations referred to

Details of Titles found in "Talks"

713

Places Connected with Bhagavan

714

Works on Bhagavan and His Teaching

Talk No.

BIBLIOGRAPHY

Of books in English on the Life and Teachings of Sri Ramana Maharshi

TRANSLATION OF THE ORIGINAL TAMIL WORKS OF SRI BHAGAVAN

Five Hymns to Sri Arunachala: An English translation of *Sri Arunachala Stuti Panchakam,* the devotional hymns sung by Sri Bhagavan.

The Collected Works of Ramana Maharshi edited by Arthur Osborne: A collection of English translations of all Sri Bhagavan's Tamil works, including both His original works and works which He translated from other languages.

The Poems of Sri Ramana Maharshi: Versified English translations by Sadhu Arunachala (A.W. Chadwick) of Sri Bhagavan's philosophical poems and stray verses.

Revelation (**Sri Ramana Hridayam**): A Sanskrit verse-rendering of Sri Bhagavan's *Ulladu Narpadu* (The Forty Verses on Reality) and *Anubandham* (The Supplement to the Forty Verses) with an English translation, both by 'WHO' (K. Lakshmana Sarma).

Truth Revealed (**Sad-Vidya**): An English translation of Sri Bhagavan's *Ulladu Narpadu* and *Anubandham.*

Words of Grace: An English translation of the essay version of *Nan Yar?* (Who am I?), the essay version of *Vichara Sangraham* (Self-Enquiry) and *Upadesa Manjari* (Spiritual Instruction), three prose works which record the teachings of Sri Bhagavan.

Homage to the Presence of Sri Ramana: The English version of 473 verses by Sri Muruganar in praise of Sri Bhagavan.

The Quintessence of Wisdom: Translation into English of Sri Bhagavan's 'Thirty Verses' of spiritual instruction with a short commentary on each.

RECORDS OF DIALOGUES WITH SRI BHAGAVAN

Day by Day with Bhagavan: A diary by Devaraja Mudaliar recording conversations and events in Sri Bhagavan's Hall during the years 1945 to 1947. Interesting insights into the Maharshi's life, his relations with devotees and many unique dialogues are recorded in a charming manner.

Letters from Sri Ramanasramam: A translation of 241 letters Suri Nagamma wrote to her brother. The author, a beloved devotee of the Sage wonderfully captures the unique personality of the Sage and the happenings in the Old Hall.

Maharshi's Gospel: A collection of answers by Sri Bhagavan to questions covering. a range of spiritual topics, arranged and edited subject-wise into thirteen chapters, forming a brief but comprehensive record of His oral teachings.

Self-Enquiry: An English translation by Dr.T.M.P. Mahadevan of the question and answer version of *Vichara Sangraham,* a compilation by Sri Natanananda of answers given by Sri Bhagavan to 40 questions asked by Gambhiram Seshayyar between 1900 and 1902, most of which are questions regarding the two paths of *raja yoga* and *jnana yoga.*

Spiritual Instruction: An English translation by Dr. T.M.P. Mahadevan of *Upadesa Manjari,* a Tamil work containing 70 questions and answers recorded by Sri Natanananda. Sri Bhagavan answers in a simple and easy manner questions regarding difficulties on the path.

Sri Ramana Gita: Sanskrit text of 300 verses by Kavyakantha Ganapati Muni some of which record questions by devotees and answers by Sri Bhagavan, and some of which are verses in praise of Him, with an English translation by Sri Viswanatha Swami and Prof. K. Swaminathan.

Who am I?: About 1902, Sivaprakasam Pillai put several questions to the Maharshi and got answers to them in writing. These answers form the quintessence of Sri Bhagavan's teachings. The English translation is by Dr T.M.P. Mahadevan.

Conscious Immortality: A collection of dialogues with the Maharshi written down by Paul Brunton and Munagala Venkataramiah.

717

COMPILATIONS AND EXPOSITIONS OF
SRI BHAGAVAN'S TEACHINGS

Gems from Bhagavan: An extremely useful collection of Sri Bhagavan's teachings, compiled and edited subject-wise by Devaraja Mudaliar. Incorporates the salient teachings of the Sage.

Guru Ramana Vachana Mala: This book by 'Who' (K. Lakshmana Sharma) contains an English rendering of 350 Sanskrit verses embodying the teachings of Sri Bhagavan. About 300 of the verses are from Sri Muruganar's *Guru Vachaka Kovai* (The Garland of the Guru's Sayings).

Maha Yoga (or The *Upanishadic* Lore in the Light of the Teachings of Bhagavan Sri Ramana) by 'WHO': A profound exposition which elucidates many important and subtle points in Sri Bhagavan's teachings, thereby providing a firm theoretical foundation on which to understand the practical side of His teachings.

Reflections on Talks with Sri Ramana Maharshi by S.S. Cohen: Detailed notes on selected passages from *Talks with Sri Ramana Maharshi,* arranged subject-wise into fourteen chapters.

The Teachings of Bhagavan Sri Ramana Maharshi in His Own Words edited by Arthur Osborne: Selected passages from the works of Sri Bhagavan and from *Talks, Day by Day* and other books, with brief explanatory notes.

COMMENTARIES ON SRI BHAGAVAN'S WORKS

Arunachala Siva by Dr.T.M.P. Mahadevan: A commentary on *Sri Arunachala Aksharamanamalai* (The Bridal Garland of Letters) and *Sri Arunachala Pancharatnam* (The Five Gems in Praise of Arunachala), two of the Five Hymns sung by Sri Bhagavan.

Ramana Maharshi and His Philosophy of Existence by Dr. T.M. P. Mahadevan: A learned and scholarly commentary upon Sri Bhagavan's *Ulladu Narpadu* (The Forty Verses on Reality) and *Anubandham* (The Supplement), and some reflections upon His life and teachings.

Sat-Darshana Bhashya by Kapali Sastri: A commentary upon *Sat-Darshanam* (a free Sanskrit verse-rendering by Kavyakantha

Ganapati Muni of Sri Bhagavan's Tamil work *Ulladu Narpadu*), preceded by a record of some dialogues with Sri Bhagavan.

The Cardinal Teaching of the Maharshi by Kapali Sastri: An English translation of a Sanskrit commentary on *Sri Arunachala Pancharatnam* (The Five Gems in Praise of Arunachala), one of the Five Hymns sung by Sri Bhagavan.

BIOGRAPHIES OF SRI BHAGAVAN

Bhagavan Ramana by Dr. T.M.P. Mahadevan: A sketch of Sri Bhagavan's life, reprinted from the introduction to *Ramana Maharshi and His Philosophy of Existence.*

Bhagavan Sri Ramana - A Pictorial Biography: Compiled and designed by Joan and Matthew Greenblatt: an aesthetically presented biography, profusely illustrated in colour and black and white, with many quotations from Sri Bhagavan and old devotees.

Ramana Maharshi by Prof K. Swaminathan: A biography which depicts Sri Bhagavan both as a man and as a master, giving an account of His life and His works.

Ramana Maharshi and the Path of Self-Knowledge by Arthur Osborne: A popular biography which has done much to spread knowledge of Sri Bhagavan both in India and abroad.

Self-Realization by B.V. Narasimhaswami: The earliest major biography of Sri Bhagavan, first published in 1931, and now containing an epilogue by S.S. Cohen.

Sri Maharshi - A Short Life-Sketch by M.S. Kamath: A profusely illustrated biography written in a simple style.

The Last Days and Maha Nirvana of Bhagavan Sri Ramana: A small booklet that paints a moving picture of the final days of the Maharshi. Also contains photographs taken during the period.

REMINISCENCES ABOUT SRI BHAGAVAN

A Sadhu's Reminiscences of Ramana Maharshi by Sadhu Arunachala (A.W.Chadwick): Reminiscences of an unassuming English devotee, who came to Sri Bhagavan in 1935 and who remained in Tiruvannamalai almost permanently till his passing away in 1962. Contains moving passages that transport the reader directly into the presence of Sri Bhagavan.

At the Feet of Bhagavan by T. K. Sundaresa Aiyer: Leaves from the diary of a humble devotee who lived most of his life with Sri Bhagavan.

Crumbs from His Table by Ramanananda Swarnagiri (K. S. Narayanaswami Aiyer): Reminiscences of a devotee who visited Sri Bhagavan several times during the years 1934 to 1936, and who noted down instructive conversations and illustrative stories told by Sri Bhagavan.

Glimpses of the Life and Teachings of Bhagavan Sri Ramana Maharshi by Frank Humphreys: An account of several meetings with Sri Bhagavan in the year 1911, and of the teachings received from Him, related by His earliest European devotee.

Guru Ramana by S.S.Cohen: Reminiscences about Sri Bhagavan and a record of many conversations with Him, concluding with a diary narrating the events of the last two years of His bodily life.

Letters and Recollections of Sri Ramanasramam by Suri Nagamma: 31 letters which were not included in the English version of *Letters from Sri Ramanasramam,* together with some other reminiscences.

My Life at Sri Ramanasramam by Suri Nagamma: Further reminiscences by the author of *Letters from Sri Ramanasramam.*

My Recollections of Bhagavan Sri Ramana by Devaraja Mudaliar: Reminiscences told in a charming and unassuming style by the author *of Day by Day with Bhagavan.*

My Reminiscences by N. Balarama Reddy: The author records his experiences with Sri Bhagavan.

Reminiscences by Kunju Swami: This staunch devotee records many rare incidents and about little known devotees of Sri Bhagavan.

Residual Reminiscences of Ramana by S.S. Cohen: A supplement to *Guru Ramana* by the author.

Sri Ramana Reminiscences by G.V. Subbaramayya: A personal account of the author's moving experiences with Sri Bhagavan between the years 1933 and 1950.

Sri Ramana the Self Supreme by Prof K. Swaminathan: The author's talks and articles, describing the impact made on him by Sri Bhagavan, are presented here.

The Bloom of Inner Glory by N.N. Rajan: The author writes on Sri Bhagavan and explains His teachings in a clear manner.

The Guiding Presence of Sri Ramana by K.K. Nambiar: This devotee, who moved closely with Sri Bhagavan, recounts his profound experiences here.

MISCELLANEOUS BOOKS ON SRI BHAGAVAN

Arunachala: Holy Hill by R. Henninger: History of the Arunachala Hill. Also a useful guide book containing maps and descriptions of various sites around Arunachala.

Be Still, it is the Wind that Sings by Arthur Osborne: An anthology of inspiring essays and beautiful poems gathered from *The Mountain Path.*

Bhagavan and Nayana by S. Shankaranarayanan: An account of the relationship between Sri Bhagavan and His famous devotee Nayana (Kavyakantha Ganapati Muni). Also contains many of Nayana's works.

Buddhism and Christianity in the Light of Hinduism by Arthur Osborne: The author explains concepts of *Advaita* with clear illustrations of views and comparisions from Buddhism and Christianity.

For Those with Little Dust by Arthur Osborne: Editorials, articles and poems on Sri Bhagavan and his teachings, selected from *The Mountain Path.*

Forty Verses in Praise of Sri Ramana: An English translation of *Sri Ramana Chatvarimsat,* a Sanskrit hymn composed by Kavya-kantha Ganapathi Muni in praise of Sri Bhagavan. This hymn is chanted daily before the *Samadhi* of Sri Bhagavan.

The Garland of the Guru's Sayings (Guru Vachaka Kovai): Translation by Prof K. Swaminathan of Sri Muruganar's Tamil work. This work in poetry embodies a precise, systematic and authoritative exposition of the Maharshi's teachings.

Hunting the I according to Sri Ramana Maharshi by Lucy Cornelssen: A collection of essays on various aspects of the life and teachings of Sri Bhagavan.

Ramana-Arunachala by Arthur Osborne: A collection of essays on the life and teachings of Sri Bhagavan.

Ramana's Arunachala by Devotees of Sri Bhagavan: A compendium on Arunachala — the Hill, the temple, its history and legends — all lucidly explained with map and descriptions. Also an insight into Sri Bhagavan's life and His relationship with Arunachala. A guide for the tourist and seeker alike.

Sri Ramana Stuti Panchakam: An English translation of five Tamil songs composed by Satyamangalam Venkataramaiyer in praise of Sri Bhagavan.

Spiritual Stories as told by Sri Bhagavan: Sri Bhagavan was a consummate storyteller. This is a collection of stories of great devotees of the Lord as narrated by Sri Bhagavan.

The Cow Lakshmi by Devaraja Mudaliar: An account of the famous cow which attained liberation by the Grace of Sri Bhagavan.

The Glory of Arunachala by M.C. Subramanian: An adaptation from the Tamil translation of the original Sanskrit.

The Maharshi by Kapali Sastri: A collection of the author's diary selections, articles and translations from Sanskrit compositions. Kapali Sastri was a devotee of Sri Bhagavan and disciple of Kavyakantha Ganapati Muni.

The Maharshi and His Message by Paul Brunton: A reprint of three chapters from *A Search in Secret India,* the book which first made Sri Bhagavan widely known outside India.

Thus Spake Ramana edited by Swami Rajeswarananda: A pocket-size book containing 125 passages selected from Sri Bhagavan's teachings.

SOME ANCIENT SCRIPTURES REFERRED TO BY SRI BHAGAVAN

Advaita Bodha Deepika **(The Lamp of Non-Dual Knowledge):** An English translation by Munagala Venkataramiah (the recorder of *Talks with Sri Ramana Maharshi*) of a Sanskrit work by Sri Karapatra Swami.

Jewel Garland of Enquiry: An English translation of *Vichara Mani Malai;* a compilation by Sri Bhagavan of salient points from the Tamil version of *Vichara Sagara* (The Ocean of Enquiry), a voluminous work originally written in Hindi by Mahatma Nischaldas.

Kaivalya Navaneeta **(The Cream of Emancipation):** An English translation by Munagala Venkataramiah of a classical Tamil work on *Advaita* philosophy.

The Song Celestial: 42 verses from the *Bhagavad Gita,* selected and reset by Sri Bhagavan, with an English translation and explanatory notes.

Tripura Rahasya **(or The Mystery beyond the Trinity):** An English translation by Munagala Venkataramiah of an ancient Sanskrit work on *Advaita* philosophy.

Yoga Vasishta Sara: An English translation of 230 verses from the *Yoga Vasishta.*

SOUVENIR AND JOURNAL

Advent Centenary Souvenir: A collection of articles by devotees on Sri Bhagavan. Released on the occasion of the centenary celebrations of Sri Bhagavan's Advent at Arunachala in 1996.

Golden Jubilee Souvenir: A collection of articles by veteran devotees and scholars released on the occasion of Sri Bhagavan's completion of 50 years at Arunachala in 1946.

Ramana Smrti: A souvenir published in 1980 to commemorate the birth centenary of Sri Bhagavan, consisting of more than 60 articles by devotees both old and new, many of which contain previously unpublished reminiscences.

Mountain Path: A journal dedicated to Sri Bhagavan, the aim of which is to set forth the traditional wisdom of all religions and all ages, especially as testified to by their saints and mystics, and to clarify the paths available to seekers in the conditions of our modern world.

723

These books are all published and available in India from
Sri Ramanasramam. For current prices,
please contact:

Sri Ramanasramam Book-Depot,
Sri Ramanasramam P.O.,
Tiruvannamalai 606 603.
South India.
e-mail: ashram@sriramanamaharshi.org
website: http://www.sriramanamaharshi.org